Collins
World Atlas

D0306826

Settlements

Population	National capital	Administrative capital	Other city or town
over 10 million	BEIJING ✸	Karachi ◉	New York ◉
5 million to 10 million	JAKARTA ✸	Tianjin ◉	Nova Iguaçu ◉
1 million to 5 million	KĀBUL ✸	Sydney ◉	Kaohsiung ◉
500 000 to 1 million	BANGUI ✸	Trujillo ◉	Jeddah ◉
100 000 to 500 000	WELLINGTON ✿	Mansa ◎	Apucarana ◎
50 000 to 100 000	PORT OF SPAIN ✿	Potenza ○	Arecibo ○
10 000 to 50 000	MALABO ✿	Chinhoyi ○	Ceres ○
under 10 000	VALLETTA ✿	Ati ○	Venta ○

▨ Built-up area

Boundaries

——————	International boundary
—·—·—·—	Disputed international boundary or alignment unconfirmed
————	Administrative boundary
········	Ceasefire line

Miscellaneous

---------	National park
············	Reserve or Regional park
✦	Site of specific interest
▭▭▭▭	Wall

Land and sea features

⠂⠂⠂	Desert
⌄	Oasis
▦	Lava field
1234 △	Volcano height in metres
⁑⁑	Marsh
▧	Ice cap or Glacier
⌐⌐⌐	Escarpment
	Coral reef
⌐*1234*	Pass height in metres

Lakes and rivers

⬡	Lake
⬡	Impermanent lake
⬡	Salt lake or lagoon
⬡	Impermanent salt lake
⬡	Dry salt lake or salt pan
⬡ *123*	Lake height surface height above sea level, in metres
————	River
- - - -	Impermanent river or watercourse
‖	Waterfall
		Dam
		Barrage

Relief

Contour intervals and layer colours

Height

metres		feet
5000		16404
3000		9843
2000		6562
1000		3281
500		1640
200		656
0		0
below sea level		
0		0
200		656
2000		6562
4000		13124
6000		19686

Depth

1234 ▲	Summit height in metres
-123 ·	Spot height height in metres
123 ·	Ocean deep depth in metres

Transport

⇥ - - - -	Motorway (tunnel; under construction)
⇥ - - - -	Main road (tunnel; under construction)
⇥ - - - -	Secondary road (tunnel; under construction)
·········	Track
▬▬▬ - - -	Main railway (tunnel; under construction)
▬▬▬ - - -	Secondary railway (tunnel; under construction)
———— - - -	Other railway (tunnel; under construction)
————	Canal
✈	Main airport
✈	Regional airport

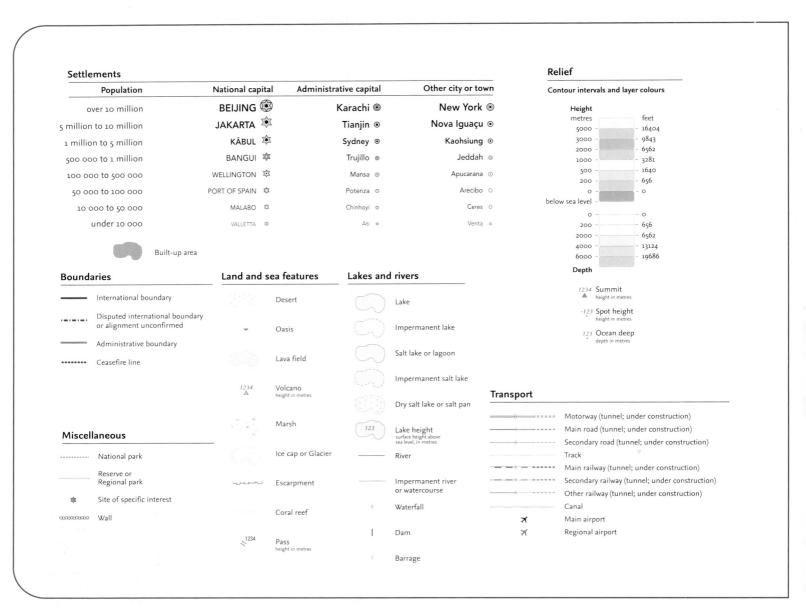

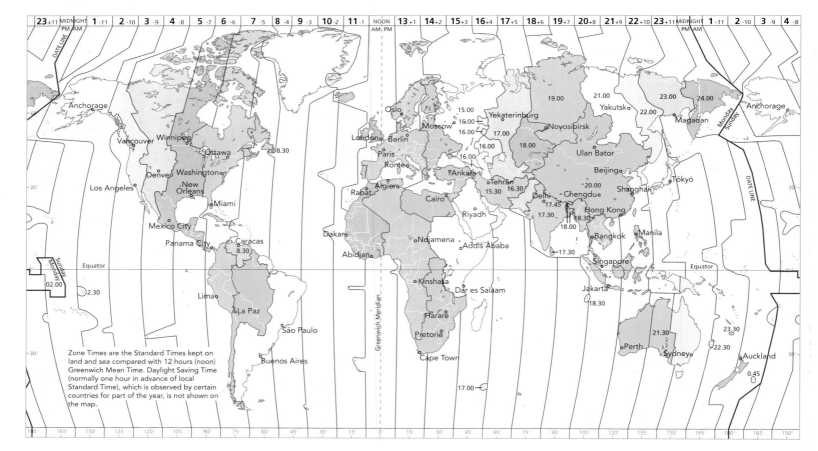

Zone Times are the Standard Times kept on land and sea compared with 12 hours (noon) Greenwich Mean Time. Daylight Saving Time (normally one hour in advance of local Standard Time), which is observed by certain countries for part of the year, is not shown on the map.

Map Symbols and Time Zones

Europe

Europe		Area sq km	Area sq miles	Population	Capital	Languages	Religions	Currency	Internet link
ALBANIA		28 748	11 100	3 190 000	Tirana	Albanian, Greek	Sunni Muslim, Albanian Orthodox, Roman Catholic	Lek	www.km.gov.al
ANDORRA		465	180	75 000	Andorra la Vella	Spanish, Catalan, French	Roman Catholic	Euro	www.andorra.ad
AUSTRIA		83 855	32 377	8 361 000	Vienna	German, Croatian, Turkish	Roman Catholic, Protestant	Euro	www.oesterreich.at
BELARUS		207 600	80 155	9 689 000	Minsk	Belorussian, Russian	Belorussian Orthodox, Roman Catholic	Belarus rouble	www.government.by
BELGIUM		30 520	11 784	10 457 000	Brussels	Dutch (Flemish), French (Walloon), German	Roman Catholic, Protestant	Euro	www.belgium.be
BOSNIA-HERZEGOVINA		51 130	19 741	3 935 000	Sarajevo	Bosnian, Serbian, Croatian	Sunni Muslim, Serbian Orthodox, Roman Catholic, Protestant	Marka	www.fbihvlada.gov.ba
BULGARIA		110 994	42 855	7 639 000	Sofia	Bulgarian, Turkish, Romany, Macedonian	Bulgarian Orthodox, Sunni Muslim	Lev	www.government.bg
CROATIA		56 538	21 829	4 555 000	Zagreb	Croatian, Serbian	Roman Catholic, Serbian Orthodox, Sunni Muslim	Kuna	www.vlada.hr
CZECH REPUBLIC		78 864	30 450	10 186 000	Prague	Czech, Moravian, Slovak	Roman Catholic, Protestant	Czech koruna	www.czechcentrum.cz
DENMARK		43 075	16 631	5 442 000	Copenhagen	Danish	Protestant	Danish krone	www.denmark.dk
ESTONIA		45 200	17 452	1 335 000	Tallinn	Estonian, Russian	Protestant, Estonian and Russian Orthodox	Kroon	www.valitsus.ee
FINLAND		338 145	130 559	5 277 000	Helsinki	Finnish, Swedish	Protestant, Greek Orthodox	Euro	www.valtioneuvosto.fi
FRANCE		543 965	210 026	61 647 000	Paris	French, Arabic	Roman Catholic, Protestant, Sunni Muslim	Euro	www.premier-ministre.gouv.fr
GERMANY		357 022	137 849	82 599 000	Berlin	German, Turkish	Protestant, Roman Catholic	Euro	www.bundesregierung.de
GREECE		131 957	50 949	11 147 000	Athens	Greek	Greek Orthodox, Sunni Muslim	Euro	www.greece.gov.gr
HUNGARY		93 030	35 919	10 030 000	Budapest	Hungarian	Roman Catholic, Protestant	Forint	www.magyarorszag.hu
ICELAND		102 820	39 699	301 000	Reykjavík	Icelandic	Protestant	Icelandic króna	www.iceland.is
IRELAND		70 282	27 136	4 301 000	Dublin	English, Irish	Roman Catholic, Protestant	Euro	www.irlgov.ie
ITALY		301 245	116 311	58 877 000	Rome	Italian	Roman Catholic	Euro	www.governo.it
KOSOVO		10 908	4 212	2 070 000	Prishtinë	Albanian, Serbian	Sunni Muslim, Serbian Orthodox	Euro	www.ks-gov.net
LATVIA		63 700	24 595	2 277 000	Rīga	Latvian, Russian	Protestant, Roman Catholic, Russian Orthodox	Lats	www.saeima.lv
LIECHTENSTEIN		160	62	35 000	Vaduz	German	Roman Catholic, Protestant	Swiss franc	www.liechtenstein.li
LITHUANIA		65 200	25 174	3 390 000	Vilnius	Lithuanian, Russian, Polish	Roman Catholic, Protestant, Russian Orthodox	Litas	www.lrv.lt
LUXEMBOURG		2 586	998	467 000	Luxembourg	Letzeburgish, German, French	Roman Catholic	Euro	www.gouvernement.lu
MACEDONIA (F.Y.R.O.M.)		25 713	9 928	2 038 000	Skopje	Macedonian, Albanian, Turkish	Macedonian Orthodox, Sunni Muslim	Macedonian denar	www.vlada.mk
MALTA		316	122	407 000	Valletta	Maltese, English	Roman Catholic	Euro	www.gov.mt
MOLDOVA		33 700	13 012	3 794 000	Chişinău	Romanian, Ukrainian, Gagauz, Russian	Romanian Orthodox, Russian Orthodox	Moldovan leu	www.moldova.md
MONACO		2	1	33 000	Monaco-Ville	French, Monegasque, Italian	Roman Catholic	Euro	www.visitmonaco.com
MONTENEGRO		13 812	5 333	598 000	Podgorica	Serbian (Montenegrin), Albanian	Montenegrin Orthodox, Sunni Muslim	Euro	www.montenegro.yu
NETHERLANDS		41 526	16 033	16 419 000	Amsterdam/The Hague	Dutch, Frisian	Roman Catholic, Protestant, Sunni Muslim	Euro	www.overheid.nl
NORWAY		323 878	125 050	4 698 000	Oslo	Norwegian	Protestant, Roman Catholic	Norwegian krone	www.norway.no
POLAND		312 683	120 728	38 082 000	Warsaw	Polish, German	Roman Catholic, Polish Orthodox	Złoty	www.poland.gov.pl
PORTUGAL		88 940	34 340	10 623 000	Lisbon	Portuguese	Roman Catholic, Protestant	Euro	www.portugal.gov.pt
ROMANIA		237 500	91 699	21 438 000	Bucharest	Romanian, Hungarian	Romanian Orthodox, Protestant, Roman Catholic	Romanian leu	www.guv.ro
RUSSIAN FEDERATION		17 075 400	6 592 849	142 499 000	Moscow	Russian, Tatar, Ukrainian, local languages	Russian Orthodox, Sunni Muslim, Protestant	Russian rouble	www.gov.ru
SAN MARINO		61	24	31 000	San Marino	Italian	Roman Catholic	Euro	www.consigliograndeegenerale.sm
SERBIA		77 453	29 904	7 778 000	Belgrade	Serbian, Hungarian	Serbian Orthodox, Roman Catholic, Sunni Muslim	Serbian dinar,	www.srbija.sr.gov.yu
SLOVAKIA		49 035	18 933	5 390 000	Bratislava	Slovak, Hungarian, Czech	Roman Catholic, Protestant, Orthodox	Euro	www.government.gov.sk
SLOVENIA		20 251	7 819	2 002 000	Ljubljana	Slovene, Croatian, Serbian	Roman Catholic, Protestant	Euro	www.sigov.si
SPAIN		504 782	194 897	44 279 000	Madrid	Castilian, Catalan, Galician, Basque	Roman Catholic	Euro	www.la-moncloa.es
SWEDEN		449 964	173 732	9 119 000	Stockholm	Swedish	Protestant, Roman Catholic	Swedish krona	www.sweden.se
SWITZERLAND		41 293	15 943	7 484 000	Bern	German, French, Italian, Romansch	Roman Catholic, Protestant	Swiss franc	www.admin.ch
UKRAINE		603 700	233 090	46 205 000	Kiev	Ukrainian, Russian	Ukrainian Orthodox, Ukrainian Catholic, Roman Catholic	Hryvnia	www.kmu.gov.ua
UNITED KINGDOM		243 609	94 058	60 769 000	London	English, Welsh, Gaelic	Protestant, Roman Catholic, Muslim	Pound sterling	www.direct.gov.uk
VATICAN CITY		0.5	0.2	557	Vatican City	Italian	Roman Catholic	Euro	www.vatican.va

Asia

Asia		Area sq km	Area sq miles	Population	Capital	Languages	Religions	Currency	Internet link
AFGHANISTAN		652 225	251 825	27 145 000	Kābul	Dari, Pushtu, Uzbek, Turkmen	Sunni Muslim, Shi'a Muslim	Afghani	www.afghanistan-mfa.net
ARMENIA		29 800	11 506	3 002 000	Yerevan	Armenian, Azeri	Armenian Orthodox	Dram	www.gov.am
AZERBAIJAN		86 600	33 436	8 467 000	Baku	Azeri, Armenian, Russian, Lezgian	Shi'a Muslim, Sunni Muslim, Russian and Armenian Orthodox	Azerbaijani manat	www.president.az
BAHRAIN		691	267	753 000	Manama	Arabic, English	Shi'a Muslim, Sunni Muslim, Christian	Bahrain dinar	www.bahrain.gov.bh
BANGLADESH		143 998	55 598	158 665 000	Dhaka	Bengali, English	Sunni Muslim, Hindu	Taka	www.bangladesh.gov.bd
BHUTAN		46 620	18 000	658 000	Thimphu	Dzongkha, Nepali, Assamese	Buddhist, Hindu	Ngultrum, Indian rupee	www.bhutan.gov.bt
BRUNEI		5 765	2 226	390 000	Bandar Seri Begawan	Malay, English, Chinese	Sunni Muslim, Buddhist, Christian	Brunei dollar	www.brunei.gov.bn
CAMBODIA		181 035	69 884	14 444 000	Phnom Penh	Khmer, Vietnamese	Buddhist, Roman Catholic, Sunni Muslim	Riel	www.cambodia.gov.kh
CHINA		9 584 492	3 700 593	1 313 437 000	Beijing	Mandarin, Wu, Cantonese, Hsiang, regional languages	Confucian, Taoist, Buddhist, Christian, Sunni Muslim	Yuan, HK dollar*, Macau pataca	www.china.org.cn
CYPRUS		9 251	3 572	855 000	Nicosia	Greek, Turkish, English	Greek Orthodox, Sunni Muslim	Euro	www.cyprus.gov.cy
EAST TIMOR		14 874	5 743	1 155 000	Dili	Portuguese, Tetun, English	Roman Catholic	United States dollar	www.timor-leste.gov.tl
GEORGIA		69 700	26 911	4 395 000	T'bilisi	Georgian, Russian, Armenian, Azeri, Ossetian, Abkhaz	Georgian Orthodox, Russian Orthodox, Sunni Muslim	Lari	www.parliament.ge
INDIA		3 064 898	1 183 364	1 169 016 000	New Delhi	Hindi, English, many regional languages	Hindu, Sunni Muslim, Shi'a Muslim, Sikh, Christian	Indian rupee	www.india.gov.in
INDONESIA		1 919 445	741 102	231 627 000	Jakarta	Indonesian, local languages	Sunni Muslim, Protestant, Roman Catholic, Hindu, Buddhist	Rupiah	www.indonesia.go.id
IRAN		1 648 000	636 296	71 208 000	Tehrān	Farsi, Azeri, Kurdish, regional languages	Shi'a Muslim, Sunni Muslim	Iranian rial	www.president.ir
IRAQ		438 317	169 235	28 993 000	Baghdād	Arabic, Kurdish, Turkmen	Shi'a Muslim, Sunni Muslim, Christian	Iraqi dinar	www.iraqigovernment.org
ISRAEL		20 770	8 019	6 928 000	Jerusalem (Yerushalayim) (El Quds)**	Hebrew, Arabic	Jewish, Sunni Muslim, Christian, Druze	Shekel	www.gov.il
JAPAN		377 727	145 841	127 967 000	Tōkyō	Japanese	Shintoist, Buddhist, Christian	Yen	web-japan.org
JORDAN		89 206	34 443	5 924 000	'Ammān	Arabic	Sunni Muslim, Christian	Jordanian dinar	www.jordan.jo
KAZAKHSTAN		2 717 300	1 049 155	15 422 000	Astana	Kazakh, Russian, Ukrainian, German, Uzbek, Tatar	Sunni Muslim, Russian Orthodox, Protestant	Tenge	www.government.kz
KUWAIT		17 818	6 880	2 851 000	Kuwait	Arabic	Sunni Muslim, Shi'a Muslim, Christian, Hindu	Kuwaiti dinar	www.e-gov.kw
KYRGYZSTAN		198 500	76 641	5 317 000	Bishkek	Kyrgyz, Russian, Uzbek	Sunni Muslim, Russian Orthodox	Kyrgyz som	www.gov.kg
LAOS		236 800	91 429	5 859 000	Vientiane	Lao, local languages	Buddhist, traditional beliefs	Kip	www.un.int/lao
LEBANON		10 452	4 036	4 099 000	Beirut	Arabic, Armenian, French	Shi'a Muslim, Sunni Muslim, Christian	Lebanese pound	www.presidency.gov.lb
MALAYSIA		332 965	128 559	26 572 000	Kuala Lumpur/Putrajaya	Malay, English, Chinese, Tamil, local languages	Sunni Muslim, Buddhist, Hindu, Christian, traditional beliefs	Ringgit	www.gov.my

**De facto capital. Disputed   *Hong Kong dollar

		Area sq km	Area sq miles	Population	Capital	Languages	Religions	Currency	Internet link
MALDIVES		298	115	306 000	Male	Divehi (Maldivian)	Sunni Muslim	Rufiyaa	www.maldivesinfo.gov.mv
MONGOLIA		1 565 000	604 250	2 629 000	Ulan Bator	Khalka (Mongolian), Kazakh, local languages	Buddhist, Sunni Muslim	Tugrik (tögrög)	www.pmis.gov.mn
MYANMAR (BURMA)		676 577	261 228	48 798 000	Nay Pyi Taw/Rangoon	Burmese, Shan, Karen, local languages	Buddhist, Christian, Sunni Muslim	Kyat	www.myanmar.com
NEPAL		147 181	56 827	28 196 000	Kathmandu	Nepali, Maithili, Bhojpuri, English, local languages	Hindu, Buddhist, Sunni Muslim	Nepalese rupee	www.nepalhmg.gov.np
NORTH KOREA		120 538	46 540	23 790 000	P'yŏngyang	Korean	Traditional beliefs, Chondoist, Buddhist	North Korean won	www.korea-dpr.com
OMAN		309 500	119 499	2 595 000	Muscat	Arabic, Baluchi, Indian languages	Ibadhi Muslim, Sunni Muslim	Omani riyal	www.omanet.om
PAKISTAN		803 940	310 403	163 902 000	Islamabad	Urdu, Punjabi, Sindhi, Pushtu, English	Sunni Muslim, Shi'a Muslim, Christian, Hindu	Pakistani rupee	www.infopak.gov.pk
PALAU		497	192	20 000	Melekeok	Palauan, English	Roman Catholic, Protestant, traditional beliefs	United States dollar	www.palauembassy.com
PHILIPPINES		300 000	115 831	87 960 000	Manila	English, Filipino, Tagalog, Cebuano, local languages	Roman Catholic, Protestant, Sunni Muslim, Aglipayan	Philippine peso	www.gov.ph
QATAR		11 437	4 416	841 000	Doha	Arabic	Sunni Muslim	Qatari riyal	www.mofa.gov.qa
RUSSIAN FEDERATION		17 075 400	6 592 849	142 499 000	Moscow	Russian, Tatar, Ukrainian, local languages	Russian Orthodox, Sunni Muslim, Protestant	Russian rouble	www.gov.ru
SAUDI ARABIA		2 200 000	849 425	24 735 000	Riyadh	Arabic	Sunni Muslim, Shi'a Muslim	Saudi Arabian riyal	www.saudinf.com
SINGAPORE		639	247	4 436 000	Singapore	Chinese, English, Malay, Tamil	Buddhist, Taoist, Sunni Muslim, Christian, Hindu	Singapore dollar	www.gov.sg
SOUTH KOREA		99 274	38 330	48 224 000	Seoul	Korean	Buddhist, Protestant, Roman Catholic	South Korean won	www.korea.net
SRI LANKA		65 610	25 332	19 299 000	Sri Jayewardenepura Kotte	Sinhalese, Tamil, English	Buddhist, Hindu, Sunni Muslim, Roman Catholic	Sri Lankan rupee	www.priu.gov.lk
SYRIA		185 180	71 498	19 929 000	Damascus	Arabic, Kurdish, Armenian	Sunni Muslim, Shi'a Muslim, Christian	Syrian pound	www.moi-syria.com
TAIWAN		36 179	13 969	22 880 000	T'aipei	Mandarin, Min, Hakka, local languages	Buddhist, Taoist, Confucian, Christian	Taiwan dollar	www.gov.tw
TAJIKISTAN		143 100	55 251	6 736 000	Dushanbe	Tajik, Uzbek, Russian	Sunni Muslim	Somoni	www.tjus.org
THAILAND		513 115	198 115	63 884 000	Bangkok	Thai, Lao, Chinese, Malay, Mon-Khmer languages	Buddhist, Sunni Muslim	Baht	www.thaigov.go.th
TURKEY		779 452	300 948	74 877 000	Ankara	Turkish, Kurdish	Sunni Muslim, Shi'a Muslim	Lira	www.mfa.gov.tr
TURKMENISTAN		488 100	188 456	4 965 000	Aşgabat	Turkmen, Uzbek, Russian	Sunni Muslim, Russian Orthodox	Turkmen manat	www.turkmenistanembassy.org
UNITED ARAB EMIRATES		77 700	30 000	4 380 000	Abu Dhabi	Arabic, English	Sunni Muslim, Shi'a Muslim	United Arab Emirates dirham	www.uae.gov.ae
UZBEKISTAN		447 400	172 742	27 372 000	Toshkent	Uzbek, Russian, Tajik, Kazakh	Sunni Muslim, Russian Orthodox	Uzbek som	www.gov.uz
VIETNAM		329 565	127 246	87 375 000	Ha Nôi	Vietnamese, Thai, Khmer, Chinese, local languages	Buddhist, Taoist, Roman Catholic, Cao Dai, Hoa Hao	Dong	www.na.gov.vn
YEMEN		527 968	203 850	22 389 000	Şan'ā'	Arabic	Sunni Muslim, Shi'a Muslim	Yemeni rial	www.nic.gov.ye

Africa

		Area sq km	Area sq miles	Population	Capital	Languages	Religions	Currency	Internet link
ALGERIA		2 381 741	919 595	33 858 000	Algiers	Arabic, French, Berber	Sunni Muslim	Algerian dinar	www.el-mouradia.dz
ANGOLA		1 246 700	481 354	17 024 000	Luanda	Portuguese, Bantu, local languages	Roman Catholic, Protestant, traditional beliefs	Kwanza	www.angola.org
BENIN		112 620	43 483	9 033 000	Porto-Novo	French, Fon, Yoruba, Adja, local languages	Traditional beliefs, Roman Catholic, Sunni Muslim	CFA franc*	www.gouv.bj/en/index.php
BOTSWANA		581 370	224 468	1 882 000	Gaborone	English, Setswana, Shona, local languages	Traditional beliefs, Protestant, Roman Catholic	Pula	www.gov.bw
BURKINA		274 200	105 869	14 784 000	Ouagadougou	French, Moore (Mossi), Fulani, local languages	Sunni Muslim, traditional beliefs, Roman Catholic	CFA franc*	www.primature.gov.bf
BURUNDI		27 835	10 747	8 508 000	Bujumbura	Kirundi (Hutu, Tutsi), French	Roman Catholic, traditional beliefs, Protestant	Burundian franc	www.burundi.gov.bi
CAMEROON		475 442	183 569	18 549 000	Yaoundé	French, English, Fang, Bamileke, local languages	Roman Catholic, traditional beliefs, Sunni Muslim, Protestant	CFA franc*	www.spm.gov.cm
CAPE VERDE		4 033	1 557	530 000	Praia	Portuguese, creole	Roman Catholic, Protestant	Cape Verde escudo	www.governo.cv
CENTRAL AFRICAN REPUBLIC		622 436	240 324	4 343 000	Bangui	French, Sango, Banda, Baya, local languages	Protestant, Roman Catholic, traditional beliefs, Sunni Muslim	CFA franc*	www.rca-gouv.org
CHAD		1 284 000	495 755	10 781 000	Ndjamena	Arabic, French, Sara, local languages	Sunni Muslim, Roman Catholic, Protestant, traditional beliefs	CFA franc*	www.primature-tchad.org
COMOROS		1 862	719	839 000	Moroni	Comorian, French, Arabic	Sunni Muslim, Roman Catholic	Comoros franc	www.beit-salam.km
CONGO		342 000	132 047	3 768 000	Brazzaville	French, Kongo, Monokutuba, local languages	Roman Catholic, Protestant, traditional beliefs, Sunni Muslim	CFA franc*	www.congo-site.com
CONGO, DEM. REP. OF THE		2 345 410	905 568	62 636 000	Kinshasa	French, Lingala, Swahili, Kongo, local languages	Christian, Sunni Muslim	Congolese franc	www.un.int/drcongo
CÔTE D'IVOIRE (IVORY COAST)		322 463	124 504	19 262 000	Yamoussoukro	French, creole, Akan, local languages	Sunni Muslim, Roman Catholic, traditional beliefs, Protestant	CFA franc*	www.presidence.ci
DJIBOUTI		23 200	8 958	833 000	Djibouti	Somali, Afar, French, Arabic	Sunni Muslim, Christian	Djibouti franc	www.presidence.dj
EGYPT		1 000 250	386 199	75 498 000	Cairo	Arabic	Sunni Muslim, Coptic Christian	Egyptian pound	www.sis.gov.eg
EQUATORIAL GUINEA		28 051	10 831	507 000	Malabo	Spanish, French, Fang	Roman Catholic, traditional beliefs	CFA franc*	www.ceiba-equatorial-guinea.org
ERITREA		117 400	45 328	4 851 000	Asmara	Tigrinya, Tigre	Sunni Muslim, Coptic Christian	Nakfa	www.shabait.com
ETHIOPIA		1 133 880	437 794	83 099 000	Addis Ababa	Oromo, Amharic, Tigrinya, local languages	Ethiopian Orthodox, Sunni Muslim, traditional beliefs	Birr	www.ethiopar.net
GABON		267 667	103 347	1 331 000	Libreville	French, Fang, local languages	Roman Catholic, Protestant, traditional beliefs	CFA franc*	www.legabon.org
THE GAMBIA		11 295	4 361	1 709 000	Banjul	English, Malinke, Fulani, Wolof	Sunni Muslim, Protestant	Dalasi	www.statehouse.gm
GHANA		238 537	92 100	23 478 000	Accra	English, Hausa, Akan, local languages	Christian, Sunni Muslim, traditional beliefs	Cedi	www.ghana.gov.gh
GUINEA		245 857	94 926	9 370 000	Conakry	French, Fulani, Malinke, local languages	Sunni Muslim, traditional beliefs, Christian	Guinea franc	www.guinee.gov.gn
GUINEA-BISSAU		36 125	13 948	1 695 000	Bissau	Portuguese, crioulo, local languages	Traditional beliefs, Sunni Muslim, Christian	CFA franc*	www.republica-da-guine-bissau.org
KENYA		582 646	224 961	37 538 000	Nairobi	Swahili, English, local languages	Christian, traditional beliefs	Kenyan shilling	www.kenya.go.ke
LESOTHO		30 355	11 720	2 008 000	Maseru	Sesotho, English, Zulu	Christian, traditional beliefs	Loti, S. African rand	www.lesotho.gov.ls
LIBERIA		111 369	43 000	3 750 000	Monrovia	English, creole, local languages	Traditional beliefs, Christian, Sunni Muslim	Liberian dollar	www.micat.gov.lr
LIBYA		1 759 540	679 362	6 160 000	Tripoli	Arabic, Berber	Sunni Muslim	Libyan dinar	
MADAGASCAR		587 041	226 658	19 683 000	Antananarivo	Malagasy, French	Traditional beliefs, Christian, Sunni Muslim	Malagasy Ariary, Malagasy franc	www.madagascar.gov.mg
MALAWI		118 484	45 747	13 925 000	Lilongwe	Chichewa, English, local languages	Christian, traditional beliefs, Sunni Muslim	Malawian kwacha	www.malawi.gov.mw
MALI		1 240 140	478 821	12 337 000	Bamako	French, Bambara, local languages	Sunni Muslim, traditional beliefs, Christian	CFA franc*	www.maliensdelexterieur.gov.ml
MAURITANIA		1 030 700	397 955	3 124 000	Nouakchott	Arabic, French, local languages	Sunni Muslim	Ouguiya	www.mauritania.mr
MAURITIUS		2 040	788	1 262 000	Port Louis	English, creole, Hindi, Bhojpurī, French	Hindu, Roman Catholic, Sunni Muslim	Mauritius rupee	www.gov.mu
MOROCCO		446 550	172 414	31 224 000	Rabat	Arabic, Berber, French	Sunni Muslim	Moroccan dirham	www.maroc.ma
MOZAMBIQUE		799 380	308 642	21 397 000	Maputo	Portuguese, Makua, Tsonga, local languages	Traditional beliefs, Roman Catholic, Sunni Muslim	Metical	www.mozambique.mz
NAMIBIA		824 292	318 261	2 074 000	Windhoek	English, Afrikaans, German, Ovambo, local languages	Protestant, Roman Catholic	Namibian dollar	www.grnnet.gov.na
NIGER		1 267 000	489 191	14 226 000	Niamey	French, Hausa, Fulani, local languages	Sunni Muslim, traditional beliefs	CFA franc*	www.delgi.ne/presidence
NIGERIA		923 768	356 669	148 093 000	Abuja	English, Hausa, Yoruba, Ibo, Fulani, local languages	Sunni Muslim, Christian, traditional beliefs	Naira	www.nigeria.gov.ng
RWANDA		26 338	10 169	9 725 000	Kigali	Kinyarwanda, French, English	Roman Catholic, traditional beliefs, Protestant	Rwandan franc	www.gov.rw
SÃO TOMÉ AND PRÍNCIPE		964	372	158 000	São Tomé	Portuguese, creole	Roman Catholic, Protestant	Dobra	www.parlamento.st
SENEGAL		196 720	75 954	12 379 000	Dakar	French, Wolof, Fulani, local languages	Sunni Muslim, Roman Catholic, traditional beliefs	CFA franc*	www.gouv.sn

*Communauté Financière Africaine franc

Africa continued

		Area sq km	Area sq miles	Population	Capital	Languages	Religions	Currency	Internet link
SEYCHELLES		455	176	87 000	Victoria	English, French, creole	Roman Catholic, Protestant	Seychelles rupee	www.virtualseychelles.sc
SIERRA LEONE		71 740	27 699	5 866 000	Freetown	English, creole, Mende, Temne, local languages	Sunni Muslim, traditional beliefs	Leone	www.statehouse-sl.org
SOMALIA		637 657	246 201	8 699 000	Mogadishu	Somali, Arabic	Sunni Muslim	Somali shilling	www.somali-gov.info
SOUTH AFRICA, REPUBLIC OF		1 219 090	470 693	48 577 000	Pretoria/Cape Town	Afrikaans, English, nine official local languages	Protestant, Roman Catholic, Sunni Muslim, Hindu	Rand	www.gov.za
SUDAN		2 505 813	967 500	38 560 000	Khartoum	Arabic, Dinka, Nubian, Beja, Nuer, local languages	Sunni Muslim, traditional beliefs, Christian	Sudanese pound (Sudani)	www.sudan.gov.sd
SWAZILAND		17 364	6 704	1 141 000	Mbabane	Swazi, English	Christian, traditional beliefs	Emalangeni, South African rand	www.gov.sz
TANZANIA		945 087	364 900	40 454 000	Dodoma	Swahili, English, Nyamwezi, local languages	Shi'a Muslim, Sunni Muslim, traditional beliefs, Christian	Tanzanian shilling	www.tanzania.go.tz
TOGO		56 785	21 925	6 585 000	Lomé	French, Ewe, Kabre, local languages	Traditional beliefs, Christian, Sunni Muslim	CFA franc*	www.republicoftogo.com
TUNISIA		164 150	63 379	10 327 000	Tunis	Arabic, French	Sunni Muslim	Tunisian dinar	www.tunisiaonline.com
UGANDA		241 038	93 065	30 884 000	Kampala	English, Swahili, Luganda, local languages	Roman Catholic, Protestant, Sunni Muslim, traditional beliefs	Ugandan shilling	www.mofa.go.ug
ZAMBIA		752 614	290 586	11 922 000	Lusaka	English, Bemba, Nyanja, Tonga, local languages	Christian, traditional beliefs	Zambian kwacha	www.statehouse.gov.zm
ZIMBABWE		390 759	150 873	13 349 000	Harare	English, Shona, Ndebele	Christian, traditional beliefs	Zimbabwean dollar	www.zim.gov.zw

*Communauté Financière Africaine franc

Oceania

		Area sq km	Area sq miles	Population	Capital	Languages	Religions	Currency	Internet link
AUSTRALIA		7 692 024	2 969 907	20 743 000	Canberra	English, Italian, Greek	Protestant, Roman Catholic, Orthodox	Australian dollar	www.gov.au
FIJI		18 330	7 077	839 000	Suva	English, Fijian, Hindi	Christian, Hindu, Sunni Muslim	Fiji dollar	www.fiji.gov.fj
KIRIBATI		717	277	95 000	Bairiki	Gilbertese, English	Roman Catholic, Protestant	Australian dollar	
MARSHALL ISLANDS		181	70	59 000	Delap-Uliga-Djarrit	English, Marshallese	Protestant, Roman Catholic	United States dollar	www.rmiembassyus.org
MICRONESIA, FEDERATED STATES OF		701	271	111 000	Palikir	English, Chuukese, Pohnpeian, local languages	Roman Catholic, Protestant	United States dollar	www.fsmgov.org
NAURU		21	8	10 000	Yaren	Nauruan, English	Protestant, Roman Catholic	Australian dollar	www.un.int/nauru
NEW ZEALAND		270 534	104 454	4 179 000	Wellington	English, Maori	Protestant, Roman Catholic	New Zealand dollar	www.govt.nz
PAPUA NEW GUINEA		462 840	178 704	6 331 000	Port Moresby	English, Tok Pisin (creole), local languages	Protestant, Roman Catholic, traditional beliefs	Kina	www.pngonline.gov.pg
SAMOA		2 831	1 093	187 000	Apia	Samoan, English	Protestant, Roman Catholic	Tala	www.govt.ws
SOLOMON ISLANDS		28 370	10 954	496 000	Honiara	English, creole, local languages	Protestant, Roman Catholic	Solomon Islands dollar	www.commerce.gov.sb
TONGA		748	289	100 000	Nuku'alofa	Tongan, English	Protestant, Roman Catholic	Pa'anga	www.pmo.gov.to
TUVALU		25	10	11 000	Vaiaku	Tuvaluan, English	Protestant	Australian dollar	
VANUATU		12 190	4 707	226 000	Port Vila	English, Bislama (creole), French	Protestant, Roman Catholic, traditional beliefs	Vatu	www.vanuatugovernment.gov.vu

North America

		Area sq km	Area sq miles	Population	Capital	Languages	Religions	Currency	Internet link
ANTIGUA AND BARBUDA		442	171	85 000	St John's	English, creole	Protestant, Roman Catholic	East Caribbean dollar	www.ab.gov.ag
THE BAHAMAS		13 939	5 382	331 000	Nassau	English, creole	Protestant, Roman Catholic	Bahamian dollar	www.bahamas.gov.bs
BARBADOS		430	166	294 000	Bridgetown	English, creole	Protestant, Roman Catholic	Barbados dollar	www.barbados.gov.bb
BELIZE		22 965	8 867	288 000	Belmopan	English, Spanish, Mayan, creole	Roman Catholic, Protestant	Belize dollar	www.belize.gov.bz
CANADA		9 984 670	3 855 103	32 876 000	Ottawa	English, French, local languages	Roman Catholic, Protestant, Eastern Orthodox, Jewish	Canadian dollar	canada.gc.ca
COSTA RICA		51 100	19 730	4 468 000	San José	Spanish	Roman Catholic, Protestant	Costa Rican colón	www.casapres.go.cr
CUBA		110 860	42 803	11 268 000	Havana	Spanish	Roman Catholic, Protestant	Cuban peso	www.cubagob.gov.cu
DOMINICA		750	290	67 000	Roseau	English, creole	Roman Catholic, Protestant	East Caribbean dollar	www.ndcdominica.dm
DOMINICAN REPUBLIC		48 442	18 704	9 760 000	Santo Domingo	Spanish, creole	Roman Catholic, Protestant	Dominican peso	www.cig.gov.do
EL SALVADOR		21 041	8 124	6 857 000	San Salvador	Spanish	Roman Catholic, Protestant	El Salvador colón, United States dollar	www.casapres.gob.sv
GRENADA		378	146	106 000	St George's	English, creole	Roman Catholic, Protestant	East Caribbean dollar	www.gov.gd
GUATEMALA		108 890	42 043	13 354 000	Guatemala City	Spanish, Mayan languages	Roman Catholic, Protestant	Quetzal, United States dollar	www.congreso.gob.gt
HAITI		27 750	10 714	9 598 000	Port-au-Prince	French, creole	Roman Catholic, Protestant, Voodoo	Gourde	www.haiti.org
HONDURAS		112 088	43 277	7 106 000	Tegucigalpa	Spanish, Amerindian languages	Roman Catholic, Protestant	Lempira	www.congreso.gob.hn
JAMAICA		10 991	4 244	2 714 000	Kingston	English, creole	Protestant, Roman Catholic	Jamaican dollar	www.jis.gov.jm
MEXICO		1 972 545	761 604	106 535 000	Mexico City	Spanish, Amerindian languages	Roman Catholic, Protestant	Mexican peso	www.gob.mx
NICARAGUA		130 000	50 193	5 603 000	Managua	Spanish, Amerindian languages	Roman Catholic, Protestant	Córdoba	www.asamblea.gob.ni
PANAMA		77 082	29 762	3 343 000	Panama City	Spanish, English, Amerindian languages	Roman Catholic, Protestant, Sunni Muslim	Balboa	www.pa
ST KITTS AND NEVIS		261	101	50 000	Basseterre	English, creole	Protestant, Roman Catholic	East Caribbean dollar	www.gov.kn
ST LUCIA		616	238	165 000	Castries	English, creole	Roman Catholic, Protestant	East Caribbean dollar	www.stlucia.gov.lc
ST VINCENT AND THE GRENADINES		389	150	120 000	Kingstown	English, creole	Protestant, Roman Catholic	East Caribbean dollar	
TRINIDAD AND TOBAGO		5 130	1 981	1 333 000	Port of Spain	English, creole, Hindi	Roman Catholic, Hindu, Protestant, Sunni Muslim	Trinidad and Tobago dollar	www.gov.tt
UNITED STATES OF AMERICA		9 826 635	3 794 085	305 826 000	Washington D.C.	English, Spanish	Protestant, Roman Catholic, Sunni Muslim, Jewish	United States dollar	www.firstgov.gov

South America

		Area sq km	Area sq miles	Population	Capital	Languages	Religions	Currency	Internet link
ARGENTINA		2 766 889	1 068 302	39 531 000	Buenos Aires	Spanish, Italian, Amerindian languages	Roman Catholic, Protestant	Argentinian peso	www.info.gov.ar
BOLIVIA		1 098 581	424 164	9 525 000	La Paz/Sucre	Spanish, Quechua, Aymara	Roman Catholic, Protestant, Baha'i	Boliviano	www.bolivia.gov.bo
BRAZIL		8 514 879	3 287 613	191 791 000	Brasília	Portuguese	Roman Catholic, Protestant	Real	www.brazil.gov.br
CHILE		756 945	292 258	16 635 000	Santiago	Spanish, Amerindian languages	Roman Catholic, Protestant	Chilean peso	www.gobiernodechile.cl
COLOMBIA		1 141 748	440 831	46 156 000	Bogotá	Spanish, Amerindian languages	Roman Catholic, Protestant	Colombian peso	www.gobiernoenlinea.gov.co
ECUADOR		272 045	105 037	13 341 000	Quito	Spanish, Quechua, other Amerindian languages	Roman Catholic	US dollar	www.ec-gov.net
GUYANA		214 969	83 000	738 000	Georgetown	English, creole, Amerindian languages	Protestant, Hindu, Roman Catholic, Sunni Muslim	Guyana dollar	www.gina.gov.gy
PARAGUAY		406 752	157 048	6 127 000	Asunción	Spanish, Guaraní	Roman Catholic, Protestant	Guaraní	www.presidencia.gov.py
PERU		1 285 216	496 225	27 903 000	Lima	Spanish, Quechua, Aymara	Roman Catholic, Protestant	Sol	www.peru.gob.pe
SURINAME		163 820	63 251	458 000	Paramaribo	Dutch, Surinamese, English, Hindi	Hindu, Roman Catholic, Protestant, Sunni Muslim	Suriname guilder	www.kabinet.sr.org
URUGUAY		176 215	68 037	3 340 000	Montevideo	Spanish	Roman Catholic, Protestant, Jewish	Uruguayan peso	www.presidencia.gub.uy
VENEZUELA		912 050	352 144	27 657 000	Caracas	Spanish, Amerindian languages	Roman Catholic, Protestant	Bolívar fuerte	www.gobiernoenlinea.ve

World
Countries

The current pattern of the world's countries and territories is a result of a long history of exploration, colonialism, conflict and politics. The fact that there are currently 195 independent countries in the world – the most recent, Kosovo, only being created in February 2008 – illustrates the significant political changes which have occurred since 1950 when there were only eighty-two. There has been a steady progression away from colonial influences over the last fifty years, although many dependent overseas territories remain.

The shapes of countries and the pattern of international boundaries reflect both physical and political processes. Some borders follow natural features – rivers, mountain ranges, etc – others are defined according to political agreement or as a result of war. Some are still subject to dispute between two or more countries, and many remain undefined on the ground.

Facts

- The longest single continuous land border stretches for 6 416 kilometres between Canada and the USA

- Both China and the Russian Federation have land borders with 14 different countries

- Vatican City, the smallest independent country, was created in 1929 as an enclave within Rome, the capital of Italy

- All countries of the world are members of the United Nations except Kosovo, Taiwan and Vatican City

Internet Links

United Nations	www.un.org
Foreign and Commonwealth Office	www.fco.gov.uk
International Boundaries Research Unit	www.dur.ac.uk/ibru
Permanent Committee on Geographical Names	www.pcgn.org.uk
U.S. Board on Geographic Names	geonames.usgs.gov

Abbreviation Key

A.	ANDORRA	HUN.	HUNGARY	R.F.	RUSSIAN FEDERATION
AL.	ALBANIA	ISR.	ISRAEL	ROM.	ROMANIA
ARM.	ARMENIA	JOR.	JORDAN	S.	SERBIA
AUST.	AUSTRIA	K.	KOSOVO	SL.	SLOVENIA
AZER.	AZERBAIJAN	L.	LUXEMBOURG	SLA.	SLOVAKIA
B.	BURUNDI	LAT.	LATVIA	SUR.	SURINAME
BE.	BENIN	LEB.	LEBANON	SW.	SWITZERLAND
BEL.	BELGIUM	LITH.	LITHUANIA	T.	TOGO
B.H.	BOSNIA-HERZEGOVINA	M.	MONTENEGRO	TAJIK.	TAJIKISTAN
BULG.	BULGARIA	MA.	MACEDONIA	TURKM.	TURKMENISTAN
CR.	CROATIA	MOL.	MOLDOVA	U.A.E.	UNITED ARAB EMIRATES
CZ.R.	CZECH REPUBLIC	NETH.	NETHERLANDS	U.K.	UNITED KINGDOM
EST.	ESTONIA	N.Z.	NEW ZEALAND	U.S.A.	UNITED STATES OF AMERICA
GEOR.	GEORGIA	R.	RWANDA	UZBEK.	UZBEKISTAN

High-resolution satellite image of **Vatican City**, the world's smallest country by both population and area.

World extremes

Countries			
Largest country (area)	**Russian Federation**	17 075 400 sq km	6 592 849 sq miles
Smallest country (area)	**Vatican City**	0.5 sq km	0.2 sq miles
Largest country (population)	**China**	1 313 437 000	
Smallest country (population)	**Vatican City**	557	
Most densely populated country	**Monaco**	17 500 per sq km	35 000 per sq mile
Least densely populated country	**Mongolia**	1.7 per sq km	4.4 per sq mile
Capitals			
Largest national capital (population)	**Tōkyō, Japan**	35 676 000	
Smallest national capital (population)	**Melekeok, Palau**	391	
Most northerly national capital	**Reykjavík, Iceland**	64° 08'N	
Most southerly national capital	**Wellington, New Zealand**	41° 18'S	
Highest national capital	**La Paz, Bolivia**	3 636 m	11 910 ft

World
Landscapes

The earth's physical features, both on land and on the sea bed, closely reflect its geological structure. The current shapes of the continents and oceans have evolved over millions of years. Movements of the tectonic plates which make up the earth's crust have created some of the best-known and most spectacular features. The processes which have shaped the earth continue today with earthquakes, volcanoes, erosion, climatic variations and man's activities all affecting the earth's landscapes.

The total topographic range of the earth's surface is nearly 20 000 metres, from the highest point Mount Everest, to the lowest point in the Mariana Trench. Major mountain ranges include the Himalaya, the Andes and the Rocky Mountains, each of which give rise to some of the world's greatest rivers. In contrast, the deserts of the Sahara, Australia, the Arabian Peninsula and the Gobi cover vast areas and each provide unique landscapes.

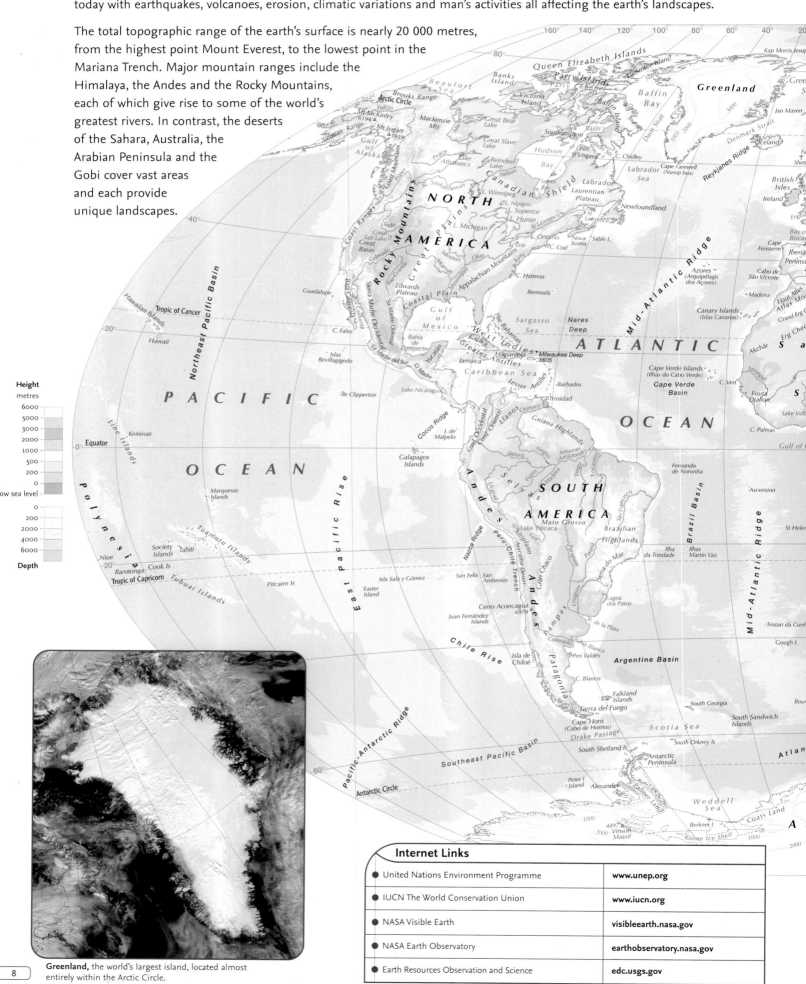

Height
metres
6000
5000
3000
2000
1000
500
200
0
below sea level

0
200
2000
4000
6000

Depth

Greenland, the world's largest island, located almost entirely within the Arctic Circle.

Internet Links	
● United Nations Environment Programme	**www.unep.org**
● IUCN The World Conservation Union	**www.iucn.org**
● NASA Visible Earth	**visibleearth.nasa.gov**
● NASA Earth Observatory	**earthobservatory.nasa.gov**
● Earth Resources Observation and Science	**edc.usgs.gov**

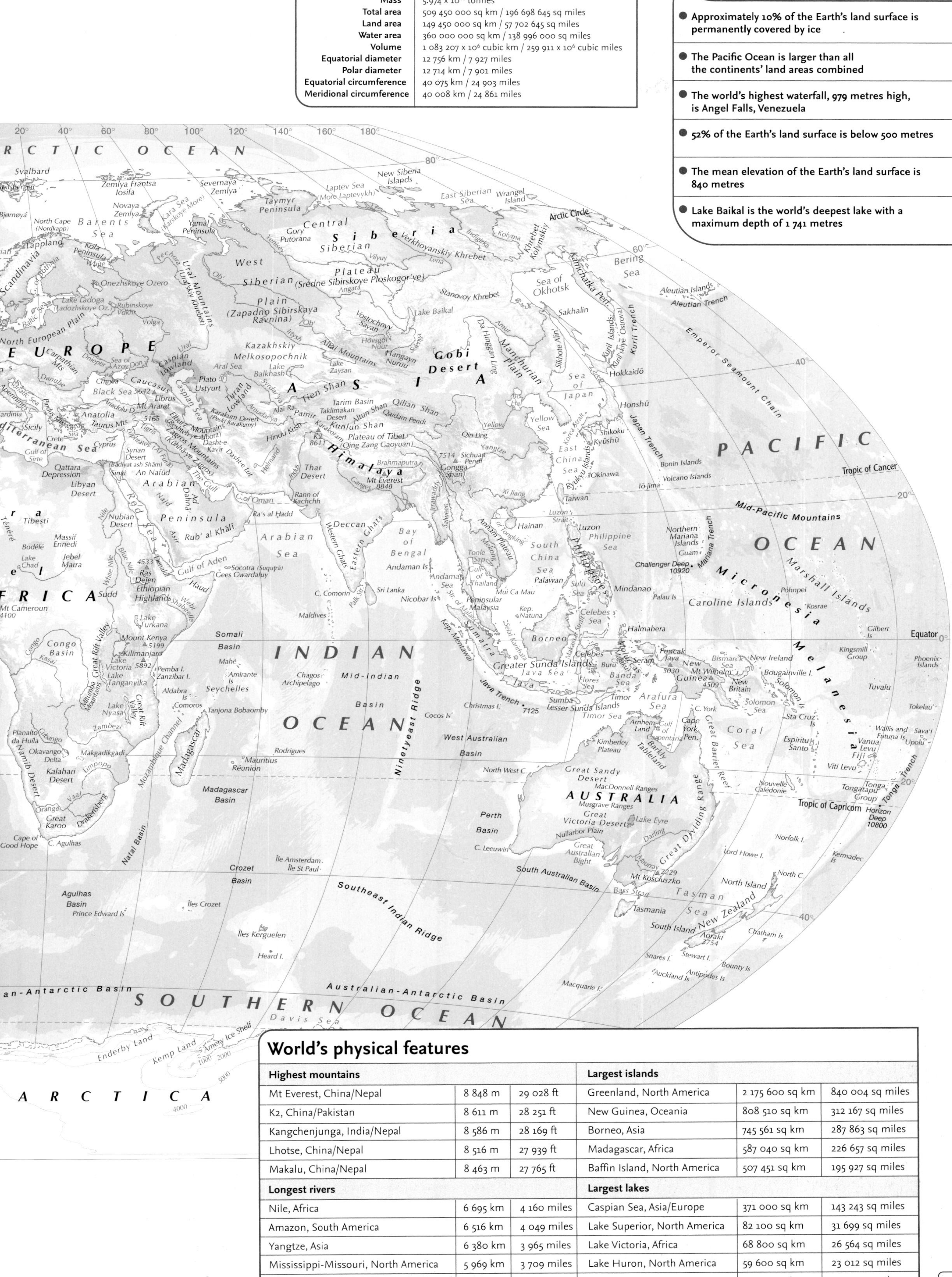

Earth's dimensions

Mass	5.974 x 10²¹ tonnes
Total area	509 450 000 sq km / 196 698 645 sq miles
Land area	149 450 000 sq km / 57 702 645 sq miles
Water area	360 000 000 sq km / 138 996 000 sq miles
Volume	1 083 207 x 10⁶ cubic km / 259 911 x 10⁶ cubic miles
Equatorial diameter	12 756 km / 7 927 miles
Polar diameter	12 714 km / 7 901 miles
Equatorial circumference	40 075 km / 24 903 miles
Meridional circumference	40 008 km / 24 861 miles

Facts

- Approximately 10% of the Earth's land surface is permanently covered by ice
- The Pacific Ocean is larger than all the continents' land areas combined
- The world's highest waterfall, 979 metres high, is Angel Falls, Venezuela
- 52% of the Earth's land surface is below 500 metres
- The mean elevation of the Earth's land surface is 840 metres
- Lake Baikal is the world's deepest lake with a maximum depth of 1 741 metres

World's physical features

Highest mountains			Largest islands		
Mt Everest, China/Nepal	8 848 m	29 028 ft	Greenland, North America	2 175 600 sq km	840 004 sq miles
K2, China/Pakistan	8 611 m	28 251 ft	New Guinea, Oceania	808 510 sq km	312 167 sq miles
Kangchenjunga, India/Nepal	8 586 m	28 169 ft	Borneo, Asia	745 561 sq km	287 863 sq miles
Lhotse, China/Nepal	8 516 m	27 939 ft	Madagascar, Africa	587 040 sq km	226 657 sq miles
Makalu, China/Nepal	8 463 m	27 765 ft	Baffin Island, North America	507 451 sq km	195 927 sq miles
Longest rivers			**Largest lakes**		
Nile, Africa	6 695 km	4 160 miles	Caspian Sea, Asia/Europe	371 000 sq km	143 243 sq miles
Amazon, South America	6 516 km	4 049 miles	Lake Superior, North America	82 100 sq km	31 699 sq miles
Yangtze, Asia	6 380 km	3 965 miles	Lake Victoria, Africa	68 800 sq km	26 564 sq miles
Mississippi-Missouri, North America	5 969 km	3 709 miles	Lake Huron, North America	59 600 sq km	23 012 sq miles
Ob'-Irtysh, Asia	5 568 km	3 460 miles	Lake Michigan, North America	57 800 sq km	22 317 sq miles

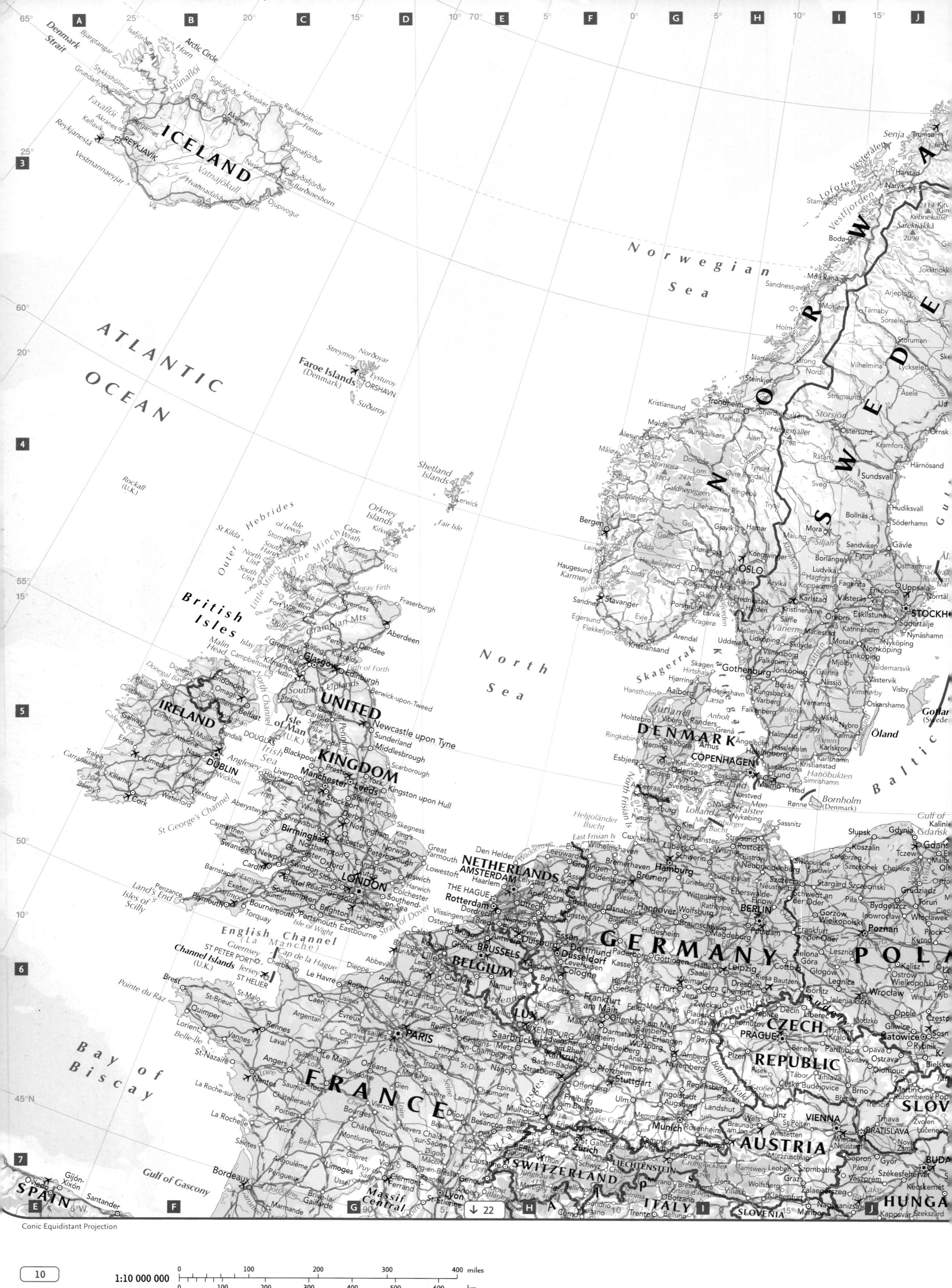

Conic Equidistant Projection

1:10 000 000

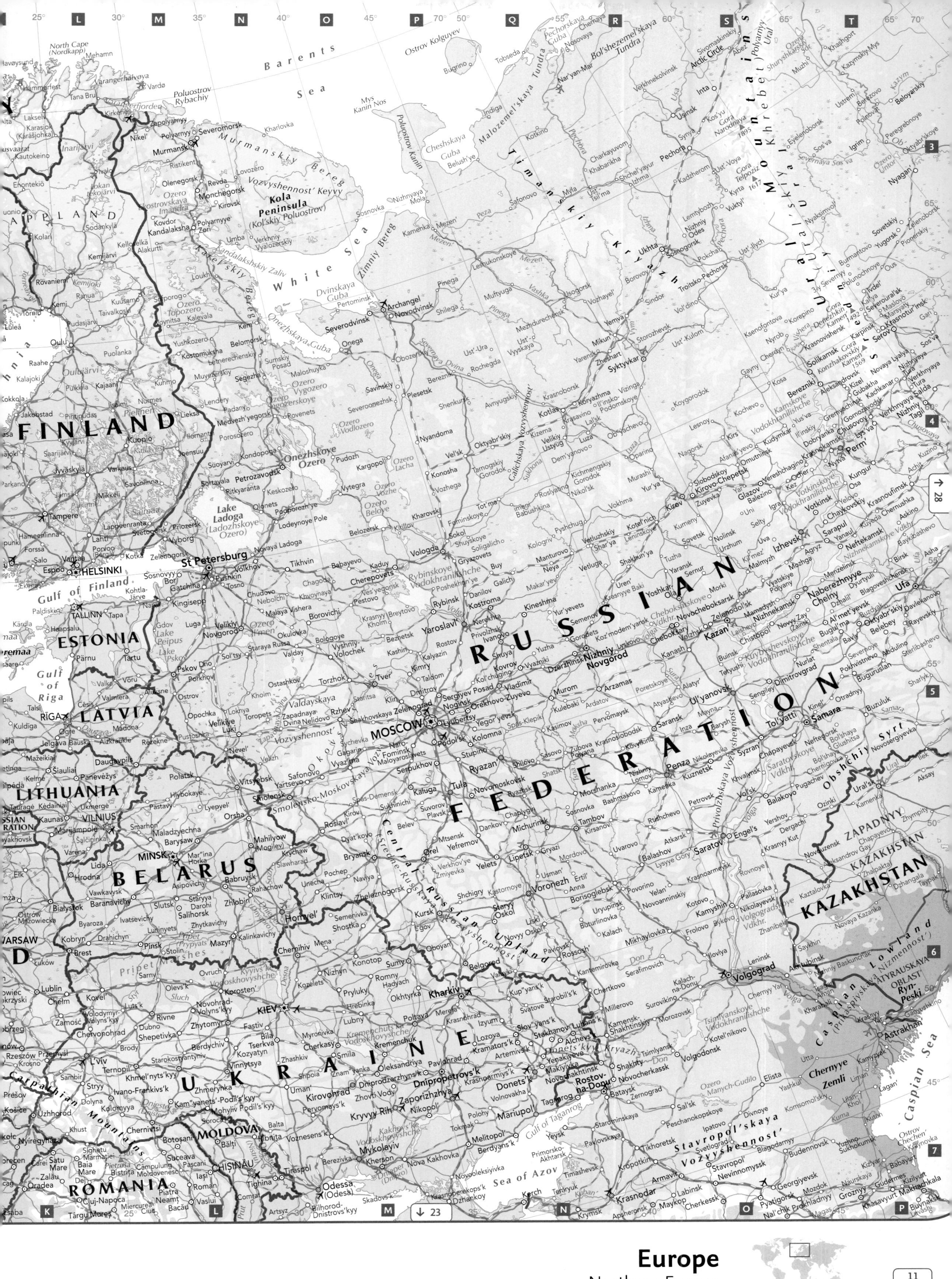

Europe
Northern Europe

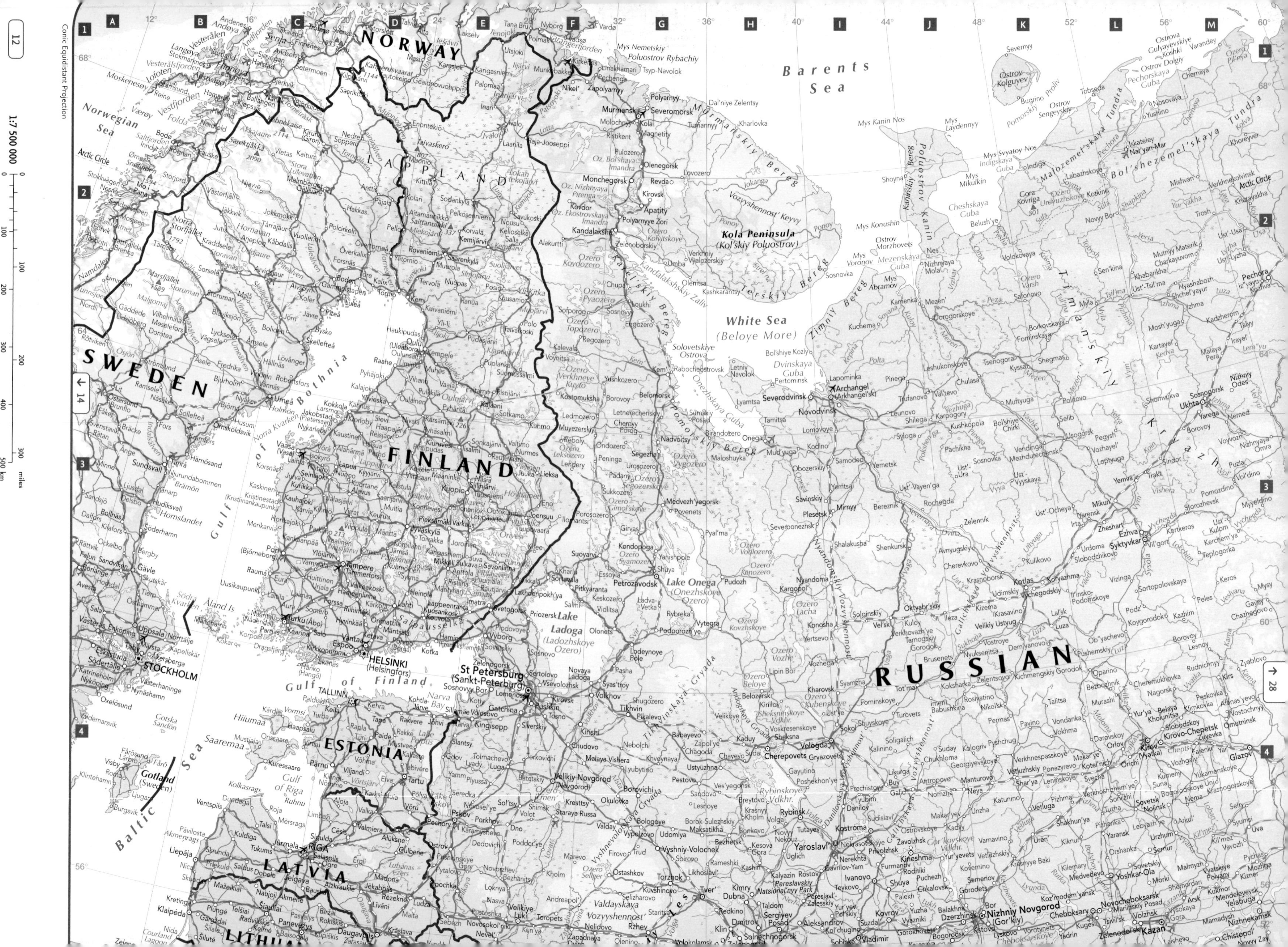

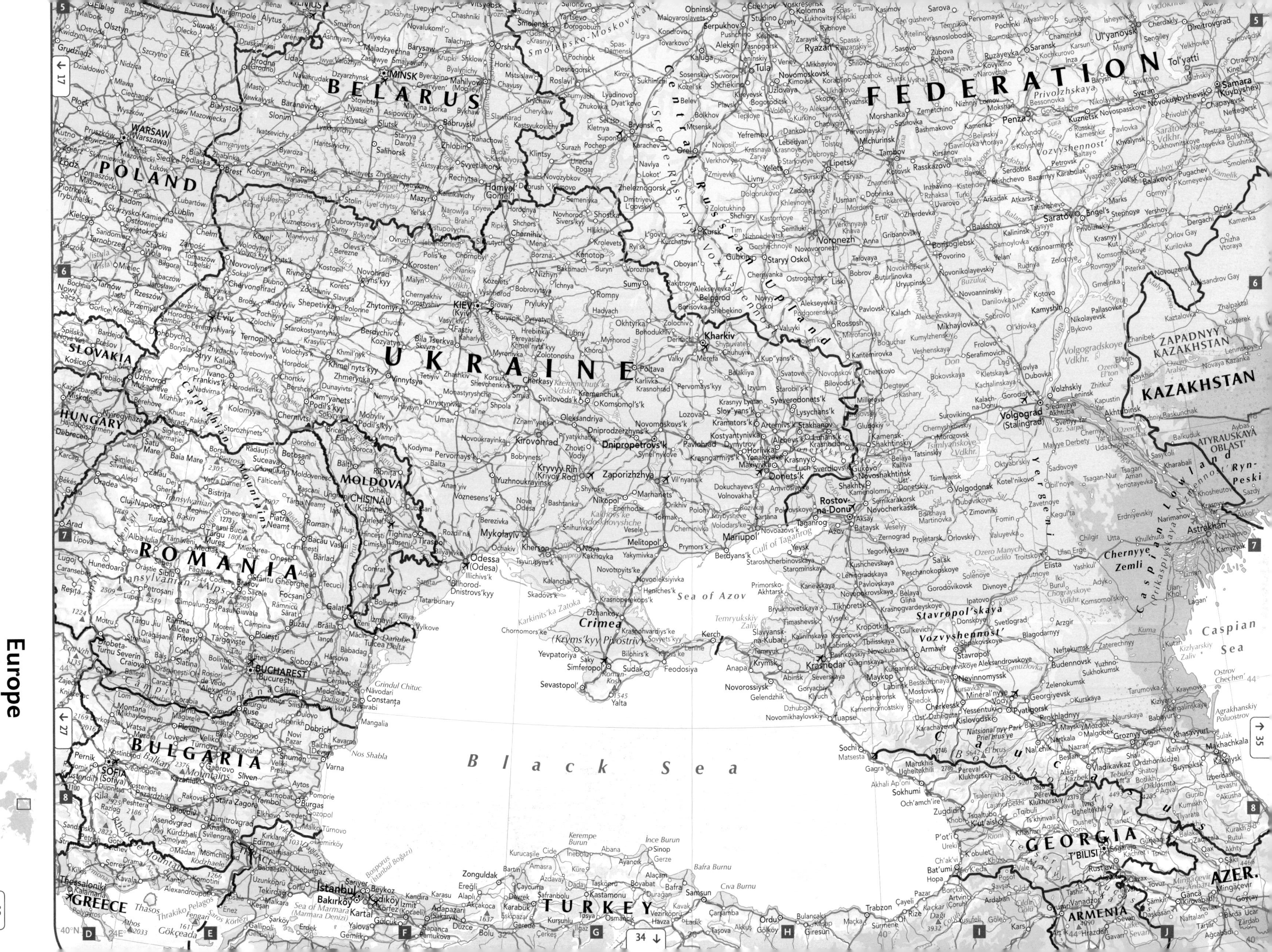

Europe
Western Russian Federation

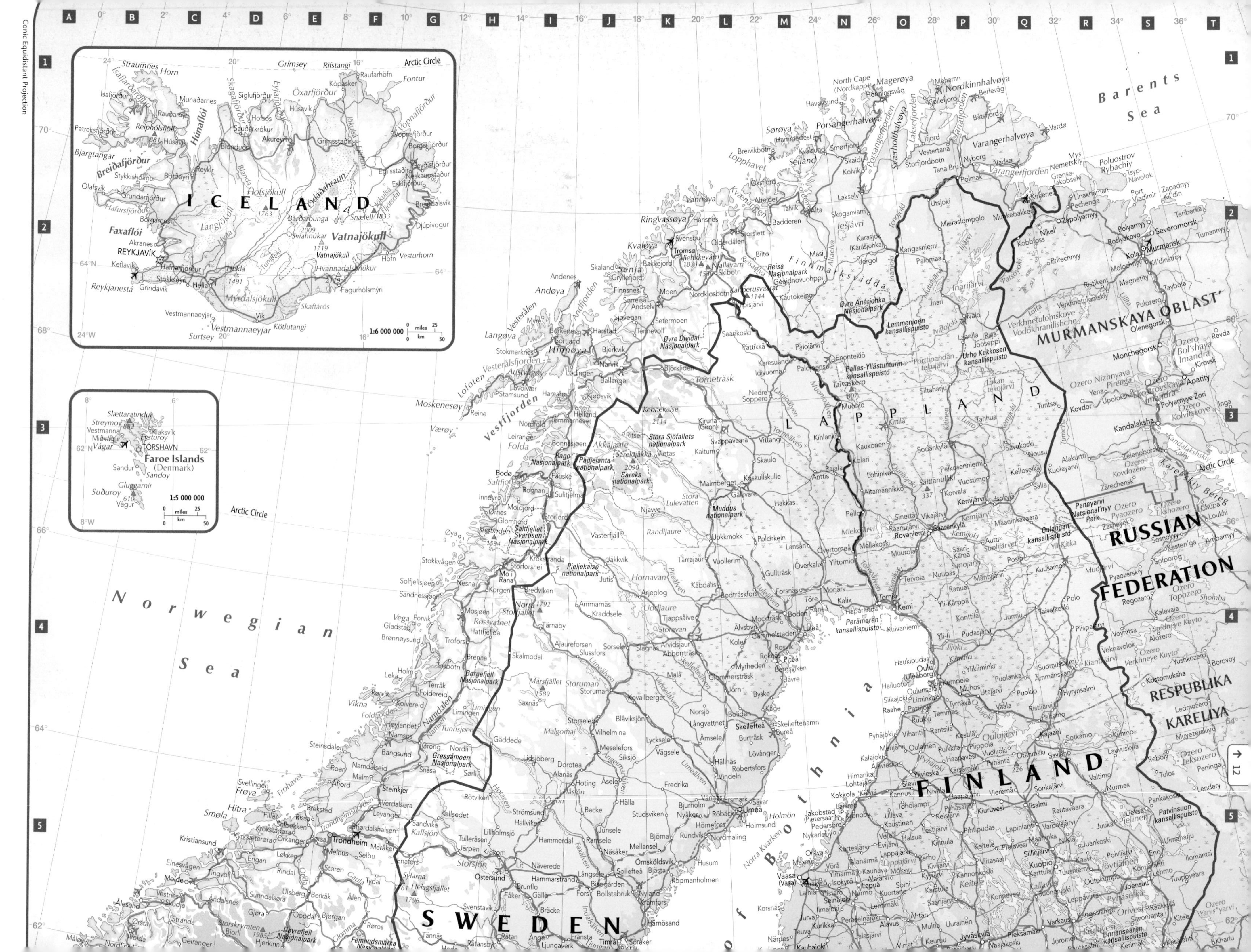

1:5 000 000

Conic Equidistant Projection

Europe

Scandinavia and the Baltic States

17 →

NORWAY
SWEDEN
FINLAND
RUSSIAN FEDERATION
ESTONIA
LATVIA
LITHUANIA
BELARUS
POLAND
GERMANY
DENMARK
LENINGRADSKAYA OBLAST'
PSKOVSKAYA OBLAST'
RUSSIAN FEDERATION
OSLO
STOCKHOLM
HELSINKI (Helsingfors)
TALLINN
RIGA
VILNIUS
MINSK
WARSAW (Warszawa)
BERLIN
COPENHAGEN (København)
St Petersburg (Sankt-Peterburg)
Gothenburg (Göteborg)
Hamburg
Gdańsk
Kaliningrad
Baltic Sea
Gulf of Finland
Gulf of Riga
Gulf of Gdańsk
Skagerrak
Kattegat
Åland Islands
Gotland (Sweden)
Öland
Saaremaa
Hiiumaa
Bornholm (Denmark)
Zealand
Jutland
Rügen
Lake Peipus
Lake Ladoga
Vänern
Vättern
North Frisian Islands
East Frisian Islands
German Bight
Pomeranian Bay
Hanöbukten
→ 13

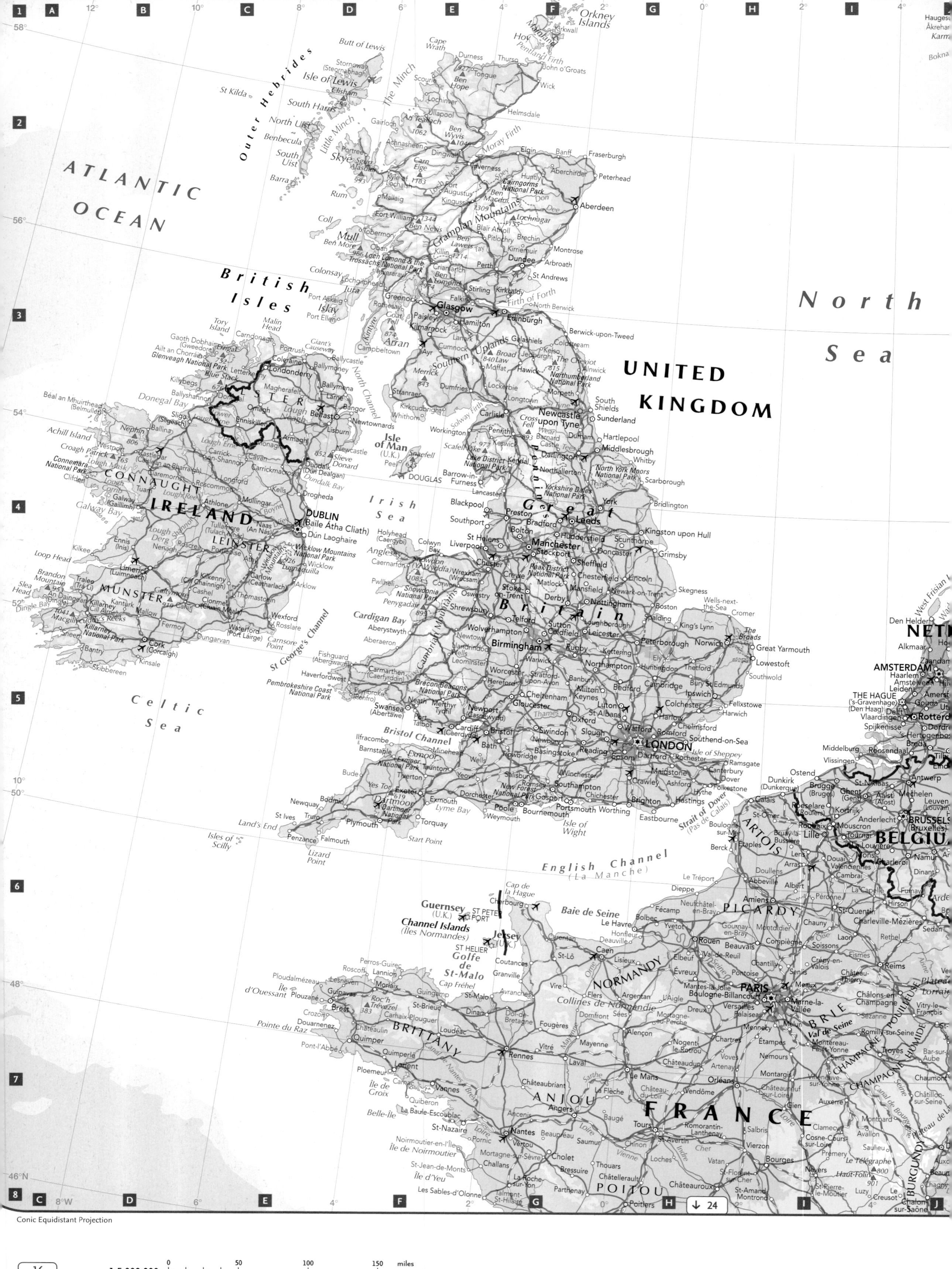

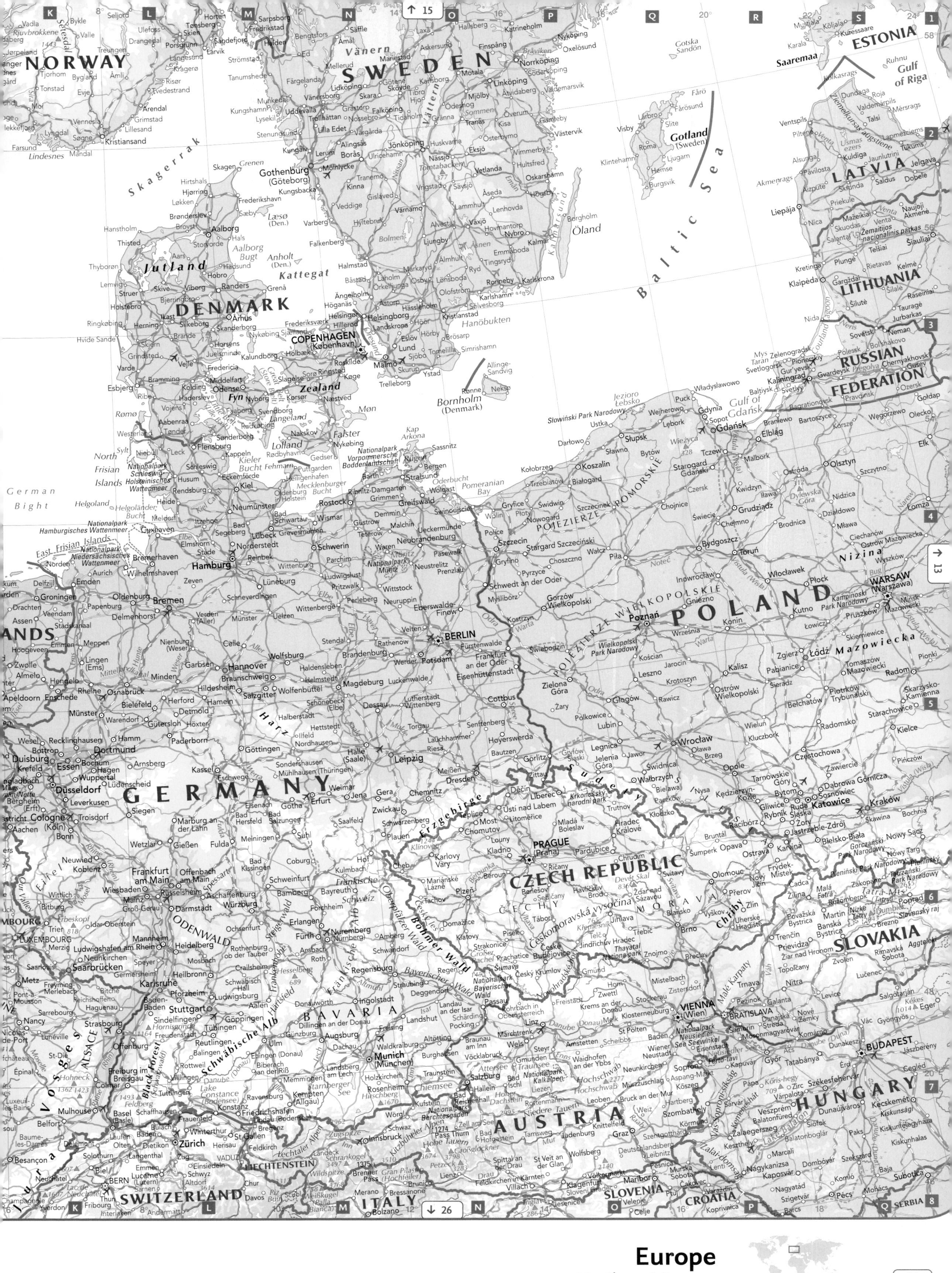

Europe
Northwest Europe

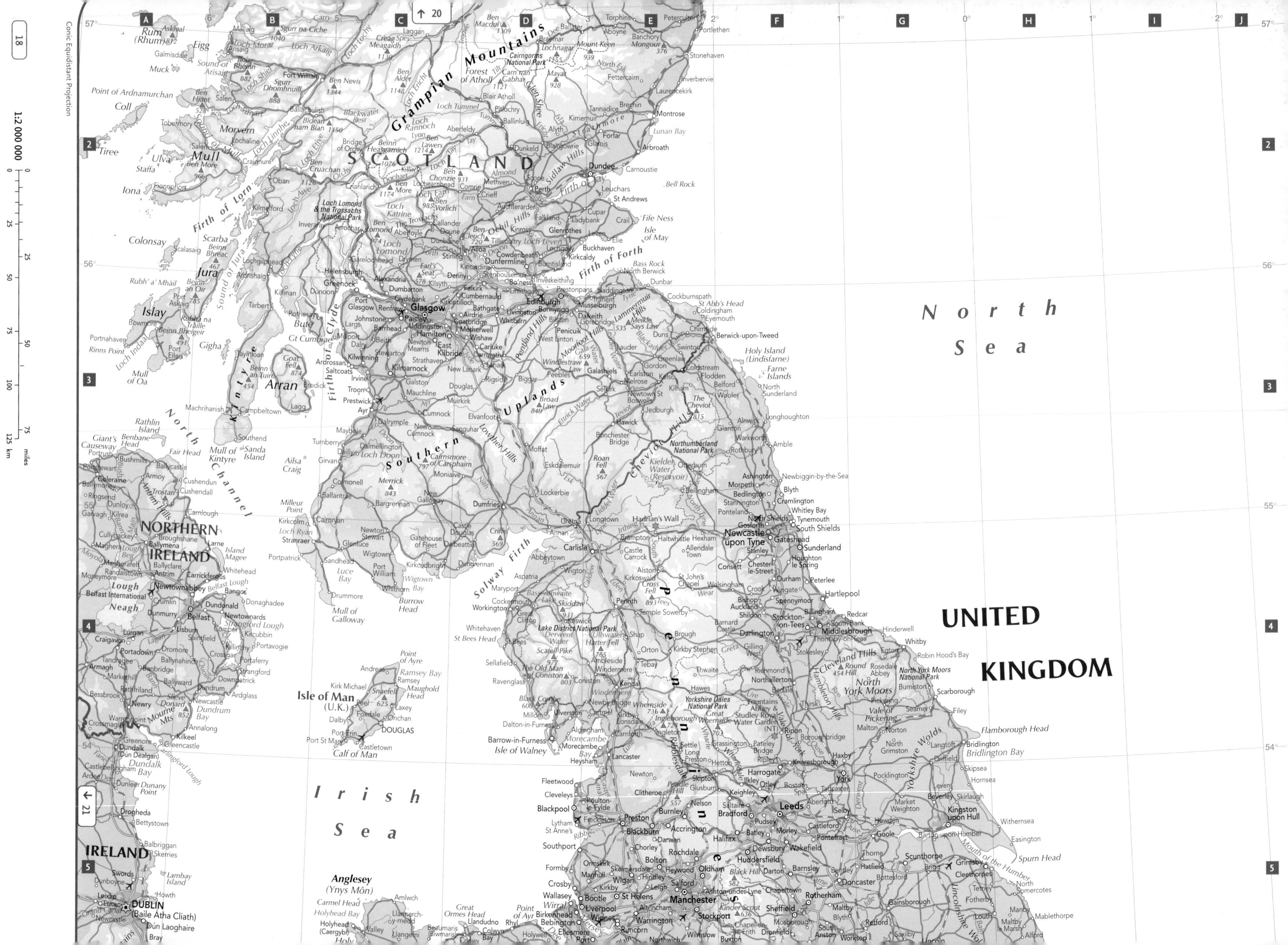

Conic Equidistant Projection

1:2 000 000

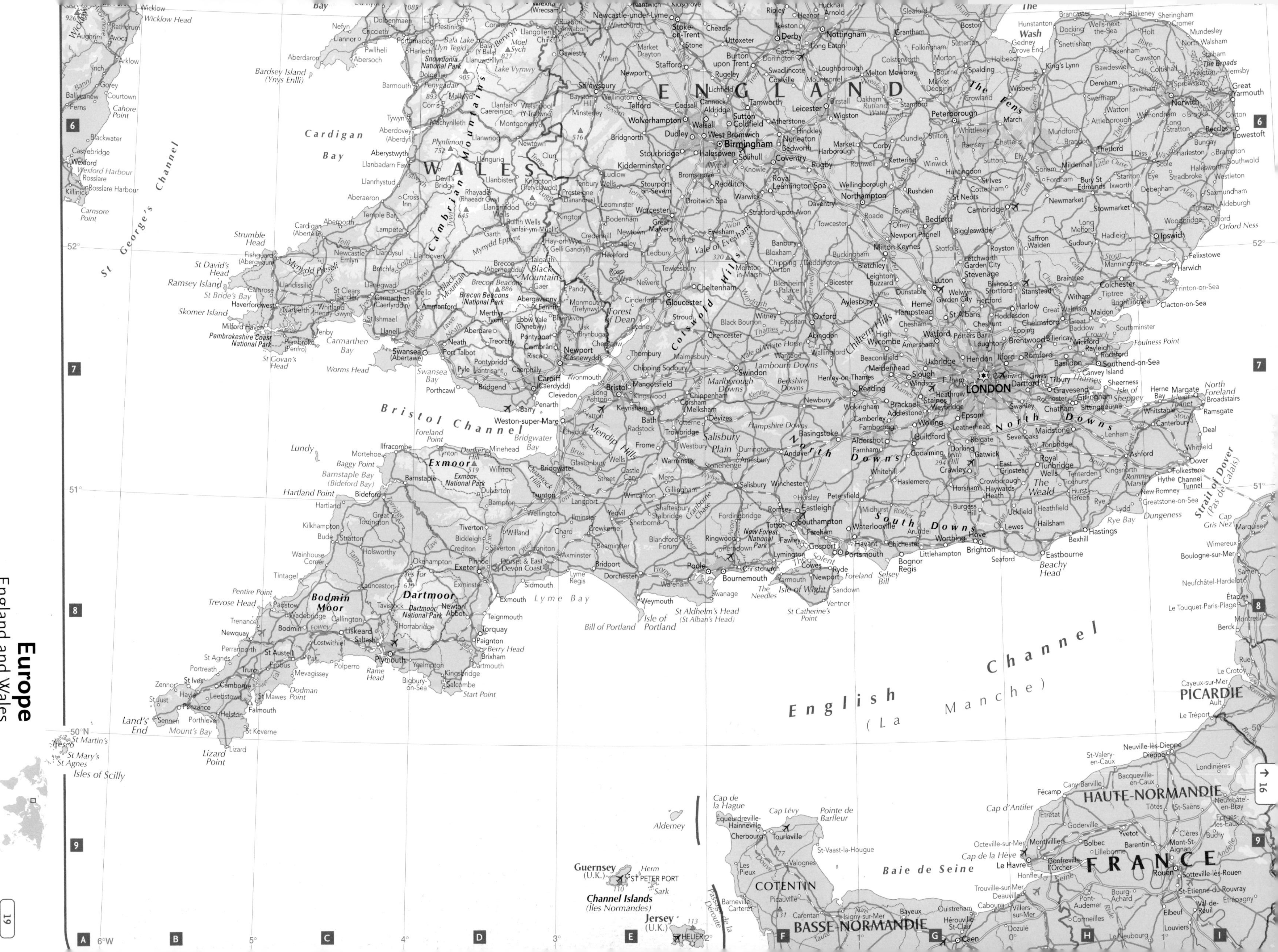

Europe
England and Wales

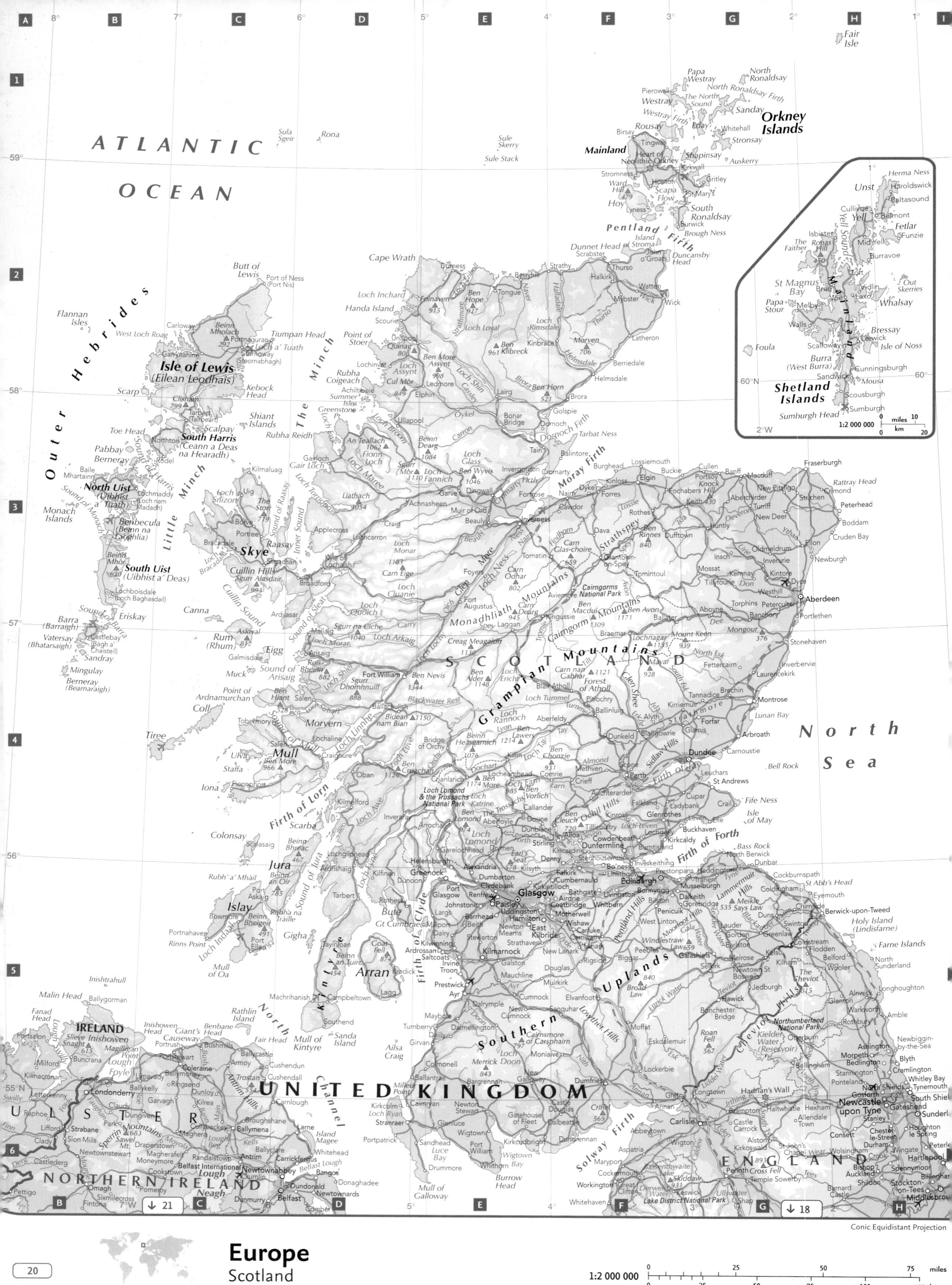

Europe
Scotland

Conic Equidistant Projection

1:2 000 000

Conic Equidistant Projection

1:2 000 000

Conic Equidistant Projection

1:10 000 000

| 0 | 100 | 200 | 300 | 400 miles |

| 0 | 100 | 200 | 300 | 400 | 500 | 600 km |

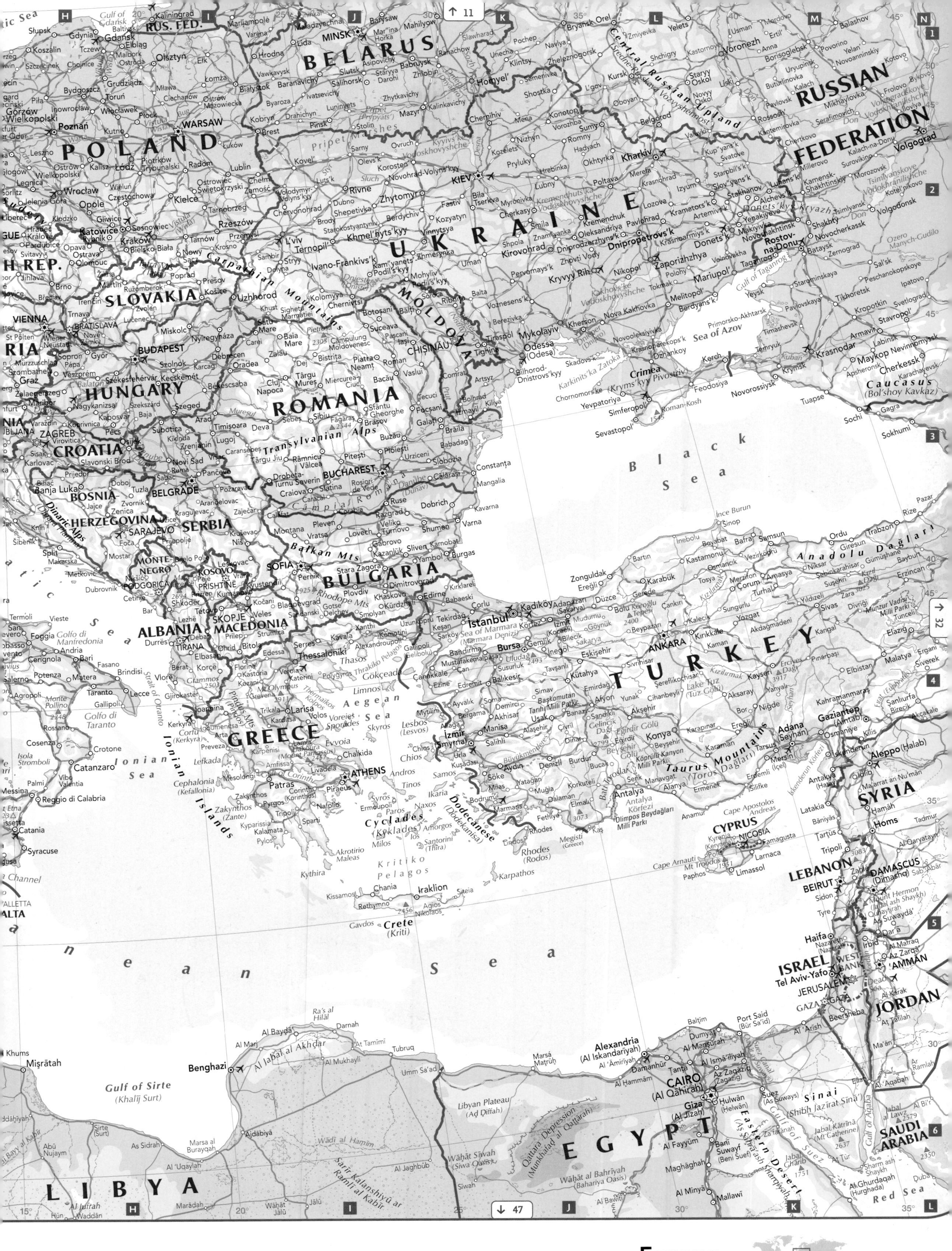

Europe
Southern Europe and the Mediterranean

Conic Equidistant Projection

Europe
France

1:5 000 000

| 0 | | 50 | | 100 | | 150 | miles |

| 0 | 50 | 100 | 150 | 200 | 250 km |

Conic Equidistant Projection

1:5 000 000

Europe
Spain and Portugal

Conic Equidistant Projection

1:5 000 000

| 0 | 50 | 100 | 150 | miles |

| 0 | 50 | 100 | 150 | 200 | 250 | km |

Europe
Italy and the Balkans

↑ 13
UKRAINE
MOLDOVA
CHIȘINĂU (Kishinev)
Odessa (Odesa)
Crimea (Krymskyy Pivostriv)
ROMANIA
BUCHAREST (București)
Transylvanian Alps
Carpathian Mountains
Transylvanian Basin
Danube Delta
DOBRUJA
Black Sea
SERBIA
BELGRADE (Beograd)
VOJVODINA
BULGARIA
SOFIA
Balkan Mountains (Stara Planina)
Sredna Gora
Rhodope Mountains
LUDOGORIE
THRACE
KOSOVO
PRISHTINË (Priština)
MACEDONIA (F.Y.R.O.M.)
SKOPJE
ALBANIA
TIRANA (Tiranë)
GREECE
ATHENS (Athina)
Thessaloniki
Peloponnese
Pindus Mountains
Aegean Sea
Cyclades (Kyklades)
Dodecanese (Dodekanisa)
Crete (Kriti)
Rhodes (Rodos)
Lesbos (Lesvos)
Chios
Evvoia
Kritiko Pelagos
Mirtoo Pelagos
Thrakiko Pelagos
Ionian Islands
Sea
Corfu (Kerkyra)
Cephalonia (Kefallonia)
Zakynthos (Zante)
TURKEY
İstanbul
İzmir (Smyrna)
Bursa
Sea of Marmara (Marmara Denizi)
Bosporus (İstanbul Boğazı)
MYSIA
LYDIA
BITHYNIA
LYCIA
PAMPHYLIA
Köroğlu Dağları
Toros Dağları
→ 34

Northern Asia: Russian Federation, Central Asia and surrounding regions map (page 28)

Conic Equidistant Projection

1:20 000 000

0 200 400 600 miles
0 200 400 600 800 1000 km

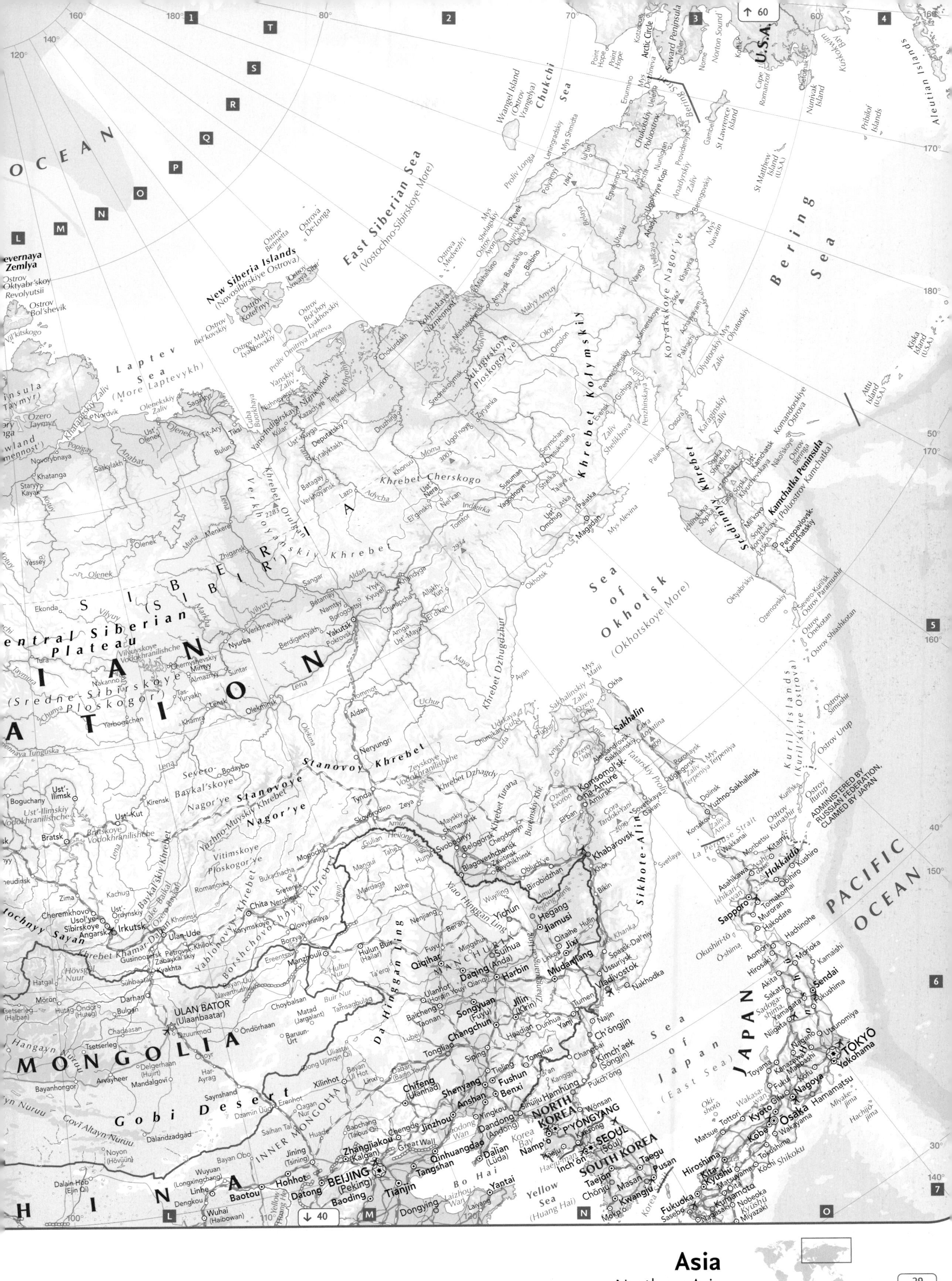

Asia

Northern Asia

A B C D E F

Albers Conic Equal Area Projection

1:20 000 000

| 0 | 200 | 400 | 600 miles |
| 0 | 200 | 400 | 600 | 800 | 1000 km |

Asia

Central and Southern Asia

↑ 29
→ 40
→ 41
↓ 73
RUSSIAN FEDERATION
MONGOLIA
CHINA
INNER MONGOLIA
XINJIANG
TIBET
KYRGYZSTAN
JAMMU AND KASHMIR
AKSAI CHIN CLAIMED BY INDIA, UNDER CHINESE ADMIN.
INDIA
NEPAL
BHUTAN
BANGLADESH
MYANMAR (BURMA)
LAOS
VIETNAM
THAILAND
CAMBODIA
MALAYSIA
INDONESIA
SRI LANKA
MALDIVES
SINGAPORE
ULAN BATOR (Ulaanbaatar)
BEIJING (Peking)
NEW DELHI
KATHMANDU
THIMPHU
DHAKA (Dacca)
NAY PYI TAW
VIENTIANE (Viangchan)
HA NOI
BANGKOK (Krung Thep)
PHNOM PENH
KUALA LUMPUR
PUTRAJAYA
SRI JAYEWARDENEPURA KOTTE
BISHKEK (Frunze)
ASTANA (Akmola)
ISLAMABAD
Gobi Desert
Tarim Basin (Tarim Pendi)
Taklimakan Desert (Taklimakan Shamo)
Plateau of Tibet (Qingzang Gaoyuan)
Qaidam Pendi
Altai Mountains
Tien Shan
Kunlun Shan
Altun Shan
Qilian Shan
Tanggula Shan
Himalaya
Kazakhskiy Melkosopochnik
Hangayn Nuruu
Gichgeniyn Nuruu
Govĭ Altayn Nuruu
Deccan
Western Ghats
Eastern Ghats
Thar Desert
Bay of Bengal
Andaman Sea
South China Sea
Gulf of Thailand
Gulf of Tongking
Gulf of Mannar
Strait of Malacca
Bo Hai
Coromandel Coast
Malabar Coast
Mouths of the Ganges
Mouths of the Irrawaddy
Mouths of the Mekong
Andaman Islands (India)
Nicobar Islands (India)
Ten Degree Channel
Nine Degree Channel
Eight Degree Channel
Tropic of Cancer
Omsk
Novosibirsk
Barnaul
Novokuznetsk
Kemerovo
Irkutsk
Ulan-Ude
Almaty (Alma-Ata)
Ürümqi
Lanzhou
Xi'an
Chengdu
Chongqing
Kunming
Wuhan
Zhengzhou
Taiyuan
Tianjin
Baotou
Hohhot
Xining
Lhasa
Guiyang
Nanning
Guangzhou
Hong Kong
Macao
Lahore
Amritsar
Delhi
Agra
Lucknow
Kanpur
Varanasi
Patna
Kolkata (Calcutta)
Mumbai (Bombay)
Pune (Poona)
Ahmadabad
Hyderabad
Nagpur
Bangalore
Chennai (Madras)
Madurai
Colombo
Chittagong
Mandalay
Rangoon (Yangon)
Chiang Mai
Ho Chi Minh City (Saigon)
Da Nang
Hainan
Medan
Penang

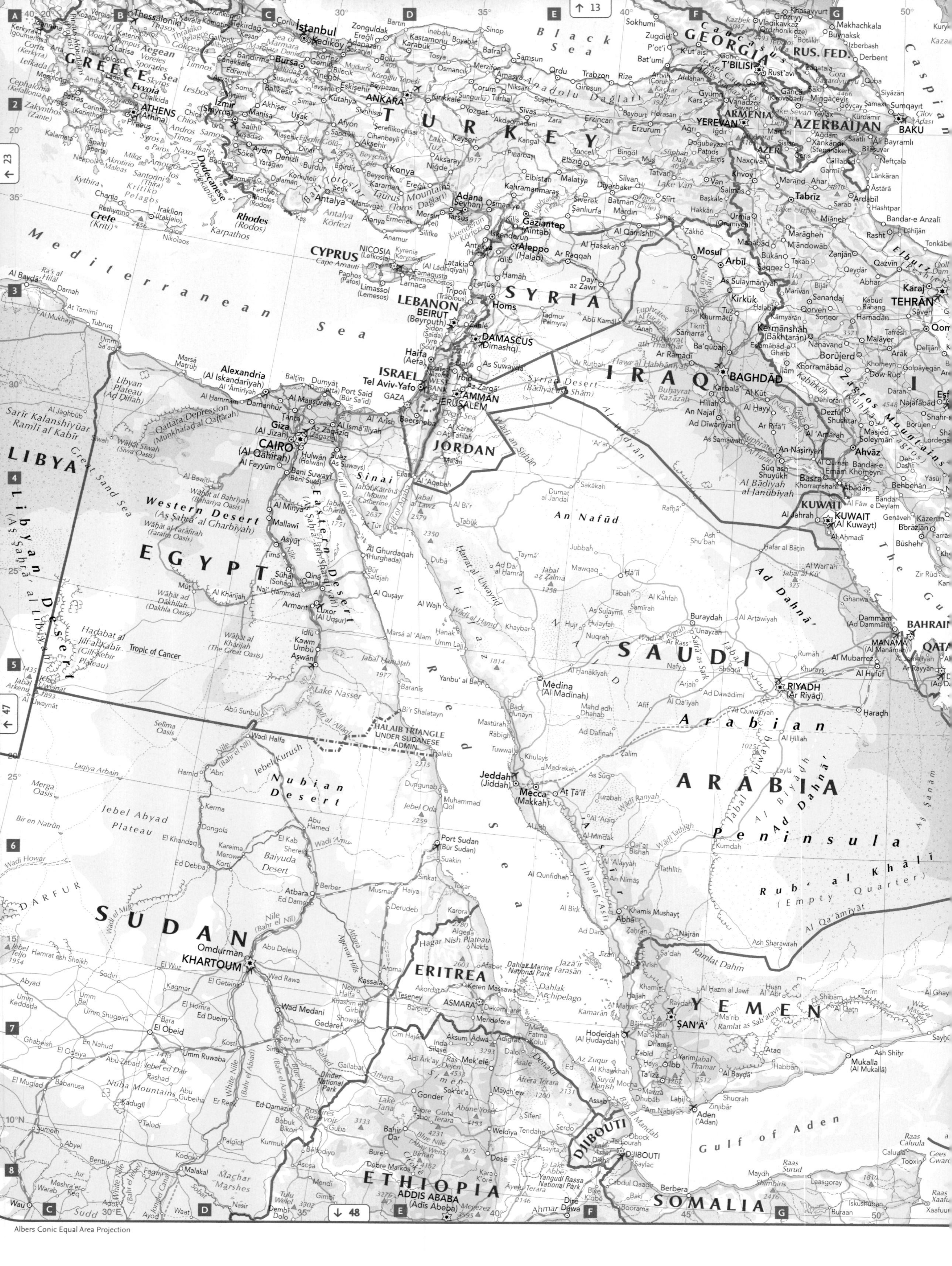

Albers Conic Equal Area Projection

1:13 000 000

| | 100 | 200 | 300 | 400 | 500 miles |
| 0 | 100 | 200 | 300 | 400 | 500 | 600 | 700 | 800 km |

Asia

Southwest Asia

KAZAKHSTAN
KYRGYZSTAN
UZBEKISTAN
TURKMENISTAN
TAJIKISTAN
AFGHANISTAN
PAKISTAN
INDIA
CHINA
NEPAL
OMAN
XINJIANG UYGUR ZIZHIQU
(SINKIANG)
XIZANG ZIZHIQU
(TIBET)
JAMMU
AND KASHMIR
AKSAI
CHIN
LINE OF CONTROL
Taklimakan Desert
Tarim Basin
Karakum Desert
Hindu Kush
Kunlun Shan
Himalaya
Arabian Sea
Gulf of Oman
Strait of Hormuz
Gulf of Kachchh
Gulf of Khambhat
Thar Desert
Deccan
Western Ghats
Malabar Coast
Laccadive Islands
(India)
Nine Degree Channel
Socotra
(Suquṭrá)
(Yemen)
ASGABAT
(Ashkhabad)
TOSHKENT
(Tashkent)
DUSHANBE
KĀBUL
ISLAMABAD
MUSCAT
(Masqaṭ)
NEW DELHI
Delhi
Karachi
Mumbai
(Bombay)
Lahore
Hyderabad
Bangalore
Ahmadabad
Mashhad
Herāt
Kandahār
Quetta
Peshawar
Rawalpindi
Multan
Faisalabad
Amritsar
Jaipur
Agra
Lucknow
Kanpur
Nagpur
Pune
(Poona)
Surat
Vodadara
(Baroda)
Dubai
(Dubayy)
Cochin
(Kochi)
Trivandrum
(Thiruvananthapuram)
Coimbatore
Calicut
(Kozhikode)
Mangalore
↑ 30
→ 42
→ 31

Administrative divisions in Russian Federation numbered on the map:

1. RESPUBLIKA KALMYKIYA – KHALM'G-TANGCH (G1)
2. RESPUBLIKA DAGESTAN (G2)
3. CHECHENSKAYA RESPUBLIKA (G2)
4. RESPUBLIKA INGUSHETIYA (G2)
5. RESPUBLIKA SEVERNAYA OSETIYA - ALANIYA (G2)
6. KABARDINO-BALKARSKAYA RESPUBLIKA (F2)
7. KARACHAYEVO-CHERKESSKAYA RESPUBLIKA (F2)
8. RESPUBLIKA ADYGEYA (F1)

Conic Equidistant Projection

1:7 000 000

0   100   200   miles

0   100   200   300   400   km

RUSSIAN FEDERATION
STAVROPOL'SKIY KRAY
GEORGIA
T'BILISI
ARMENIA
YEREVAN
AZERBAIJAN
BAKU
KAZAKHSTAN
MANGISTAUSKAYA OBLAST'
UZBEKISTAN
TURKMENISTAN
IRAN
TEHRĀN
IRAQ
BAGHDĀD
KUWAIT
KUWAIT (Al Kuwayt)
ARABIA
MESOPOTAMIA
Caspian Sea
The Gulf
Ustyurt Plateau
Elburz Mountains
Zagros Mountains
Dasht-e Kavīr
Garabogazköl Aylagy
Lake Urmia (Daryācheh-ye Orūmīyeh)
Lake Van (Van Gölü)
Toros Dağlar
Widyān
An Nafūd
Stavropol'
Makhachkala
Derbent
Groznyy
Vladikavkaz
Sokhumi
Bat'umi
Trabzon
Erzurum
Gyumri
Gäncä
Sumqayıt
Aktau (Shevchenko)
Türkmenbaşy
Tabrīz
Rasht
Qazvīn
Karaj
Qom
Hamadān
Kermānshāh (Bākhtarān)
Eşfahān (Işfahān)
Shīrāz
Ahvāz
Abādān
Bandar-e Būshehr
Mosul
Arbīl
Kirkūk
As Sulaymānīyah
Al Hillah
Karbalā'
An Najaf
An Nāşirīyah
Al 'Amārah
Basra
Dayr az Zawr
Al Qāmishlī
↑ 28
→ 33
↓ 32

Administrative divisions in India
numbered on the map:

1. DADRA AND NAGAR HAVELI (C5)
2. DAMAN AND DIU (B5, C5)

Conic Equidistant Projection

1:7 000 000

| 0 | 100 | 200 | miles |

| 0 | 100 | 200 | 300 | 400 | km |

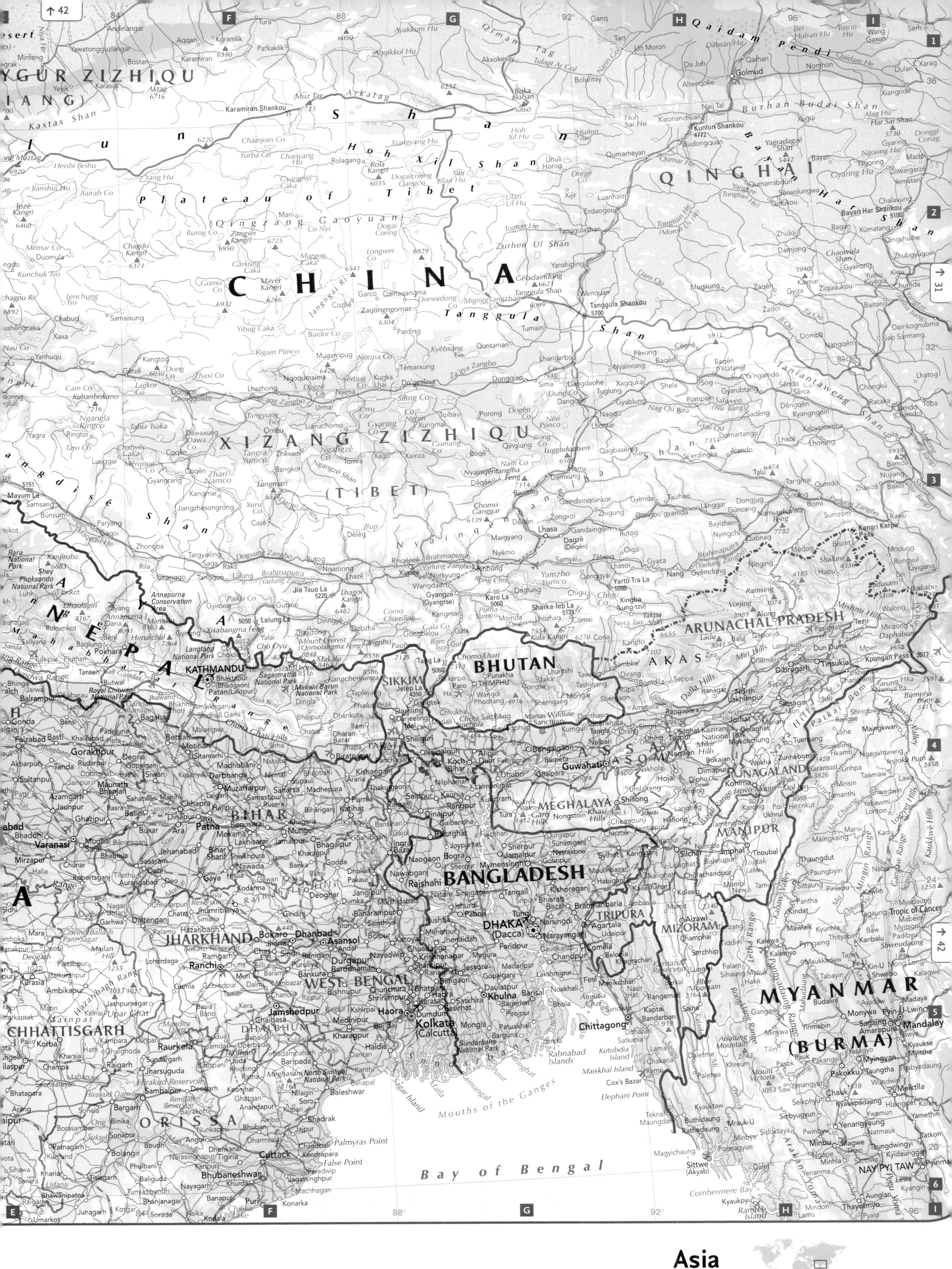

Asia

Northern India, Nepal, Bhutan and Bangladesh

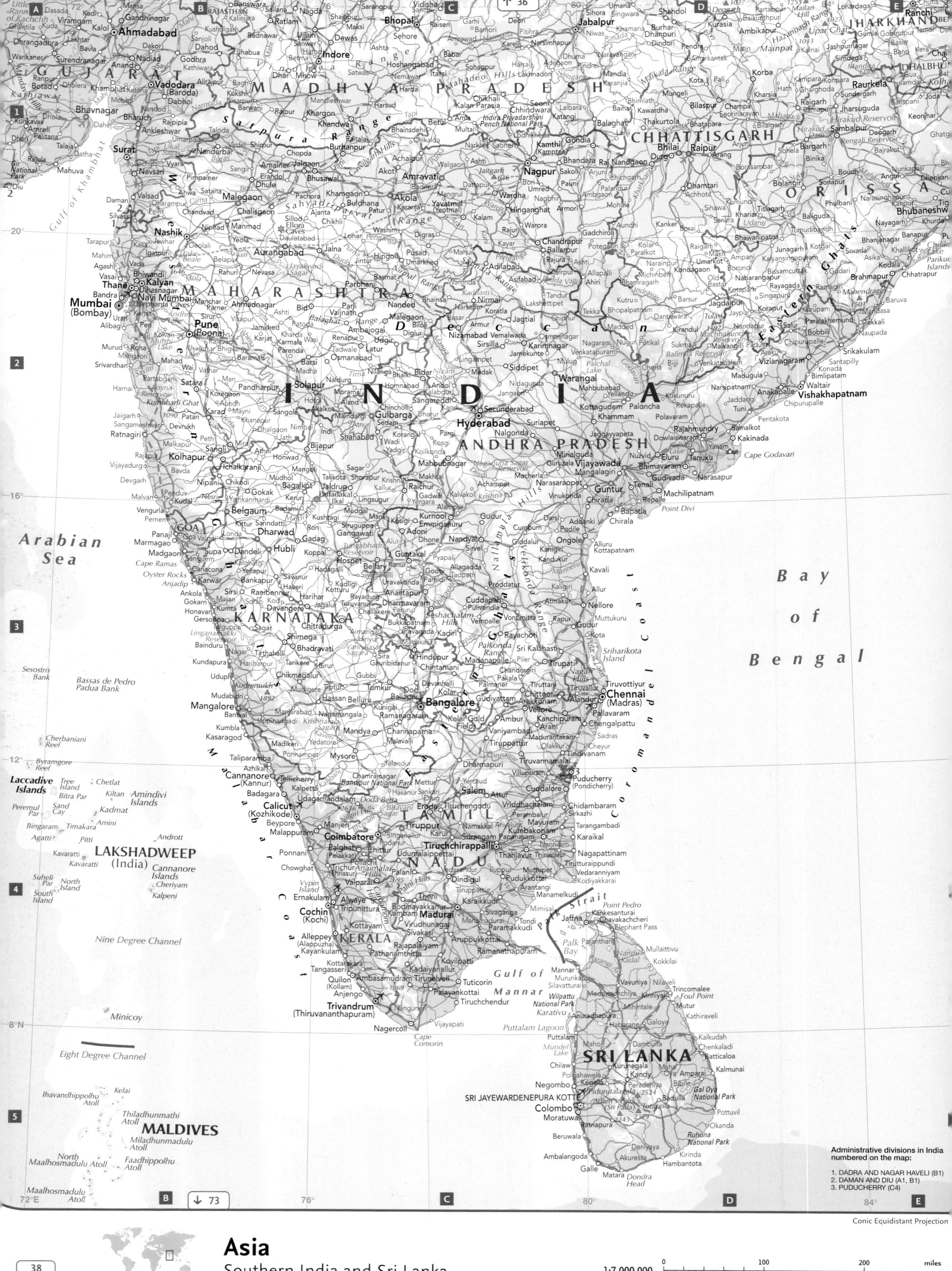

Asia
Southern India and Sri Lanka

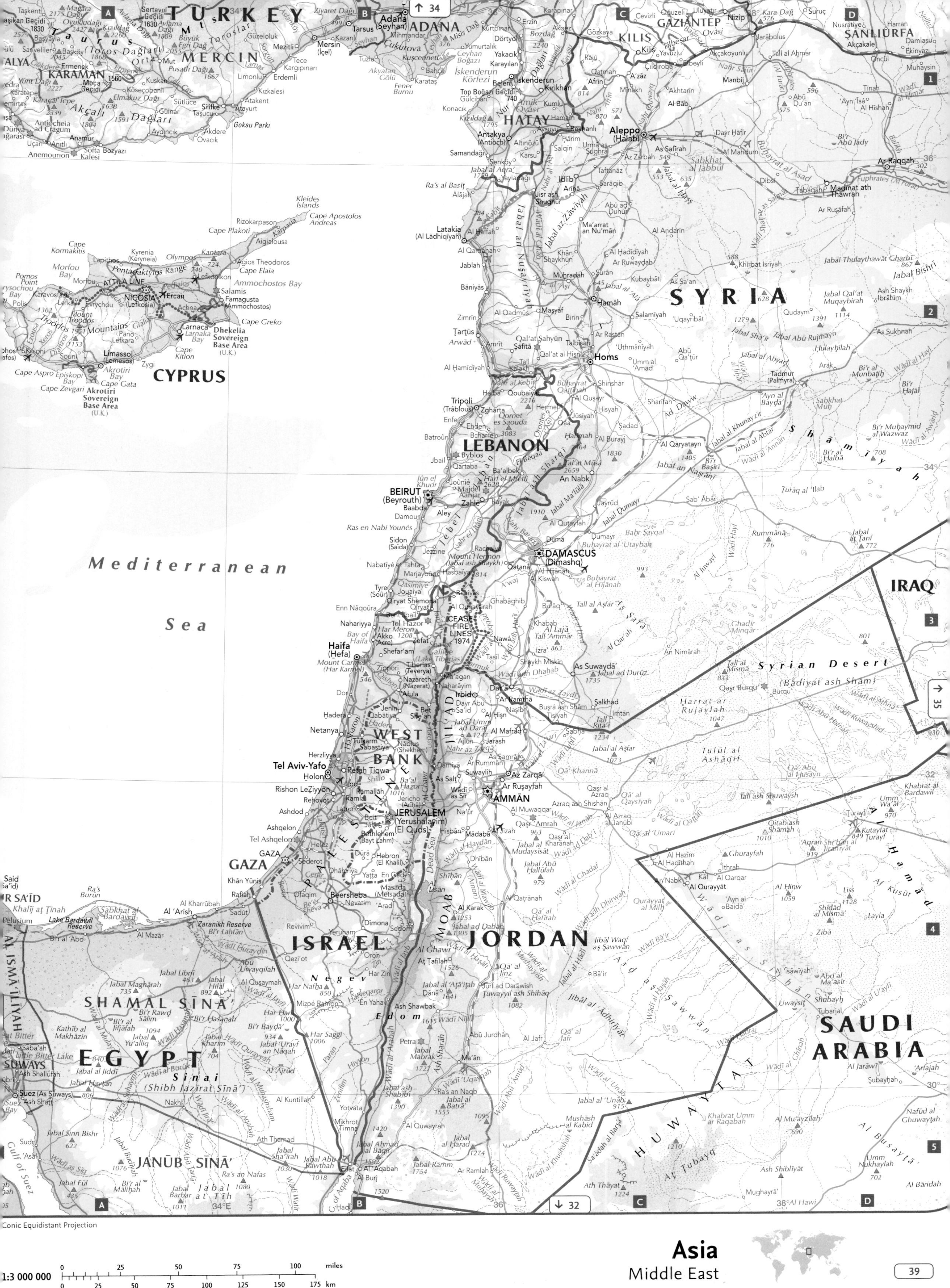

Asia
Middle East

Conic Equidistant Projection

1:3 000 000

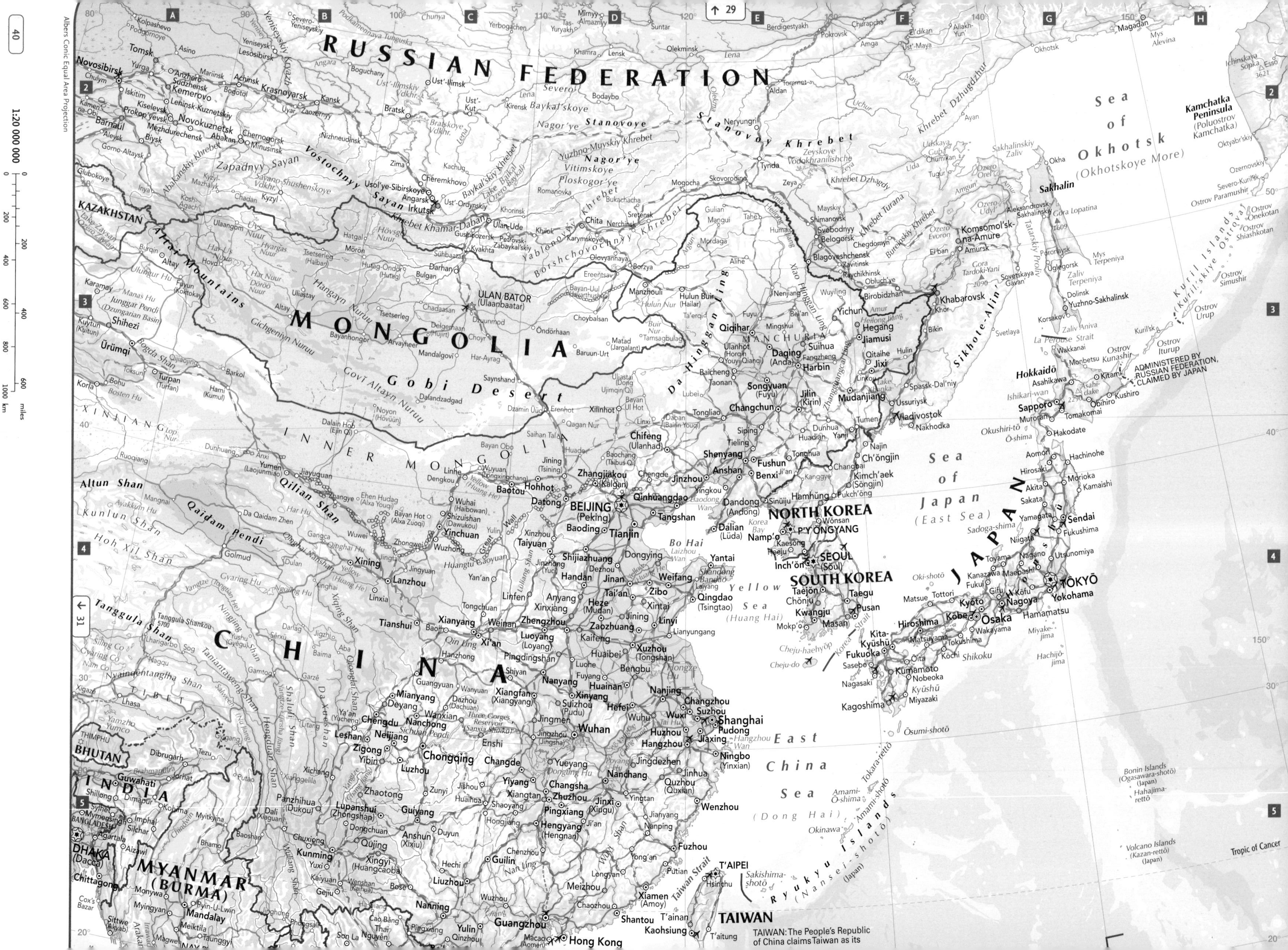

Albers Conic Equal Area Projection

1:20 000 000

Asia

Eastern and Southeast Asia

PACIFIC OCEAN
INDIAN OCEAN
South China Sea
Philippine Sea
Celebes Sea
Sulu Sea
Timor Sea
Arafura Sea
Andaman Sea
Gulf of Thailand
Gulf of Carpentaria
Laut Jawa (Java Sea)
Laut Banda (Banda Sea)
Laut Maluku (Molucca Sea)
PHILIPPINES
MALAYSIA
INDONESIA
VIETNAM
CAMBODIA
THAILAND
BRUNEI
SINGAPORE
EAST TIMOR
PALAU
PAPUA NEW GUINEA
FEDERATED STATES OF MICRONESIA
AUSTRALIA
WESTERN AUSTRALIA
NORTHERN TERRITORY
QUEENSLAND
Northern Mariana Islands (U.S.A.)
Guam (U.S.A.)
Christmas Island (Australia)
Cocos Islands (Australia)
Ashmore and Cartier Islands (Australia)
Borneo
Sumatra (Sumatera)
Java (Jawa)
Celebes (Sulawesi)
New Guinea
Luzon
Mindanao
Palawan
Hainan
Moluccas (Maluku)
MANILA
KUALA LUMPUR
JAKARTA
BANGKOK (Krung Thep)
PHNOM PENH
VIENTIANE (Viangchan)
RANGOON (Yangon)
BANDAR SERI BEGAWAN
DILI
Ho Chi Minh City (Saigon)
Equator
Tropic of Capricorn
Great Sandy Desert
Tanami Desert
↑ 52
↓ 52

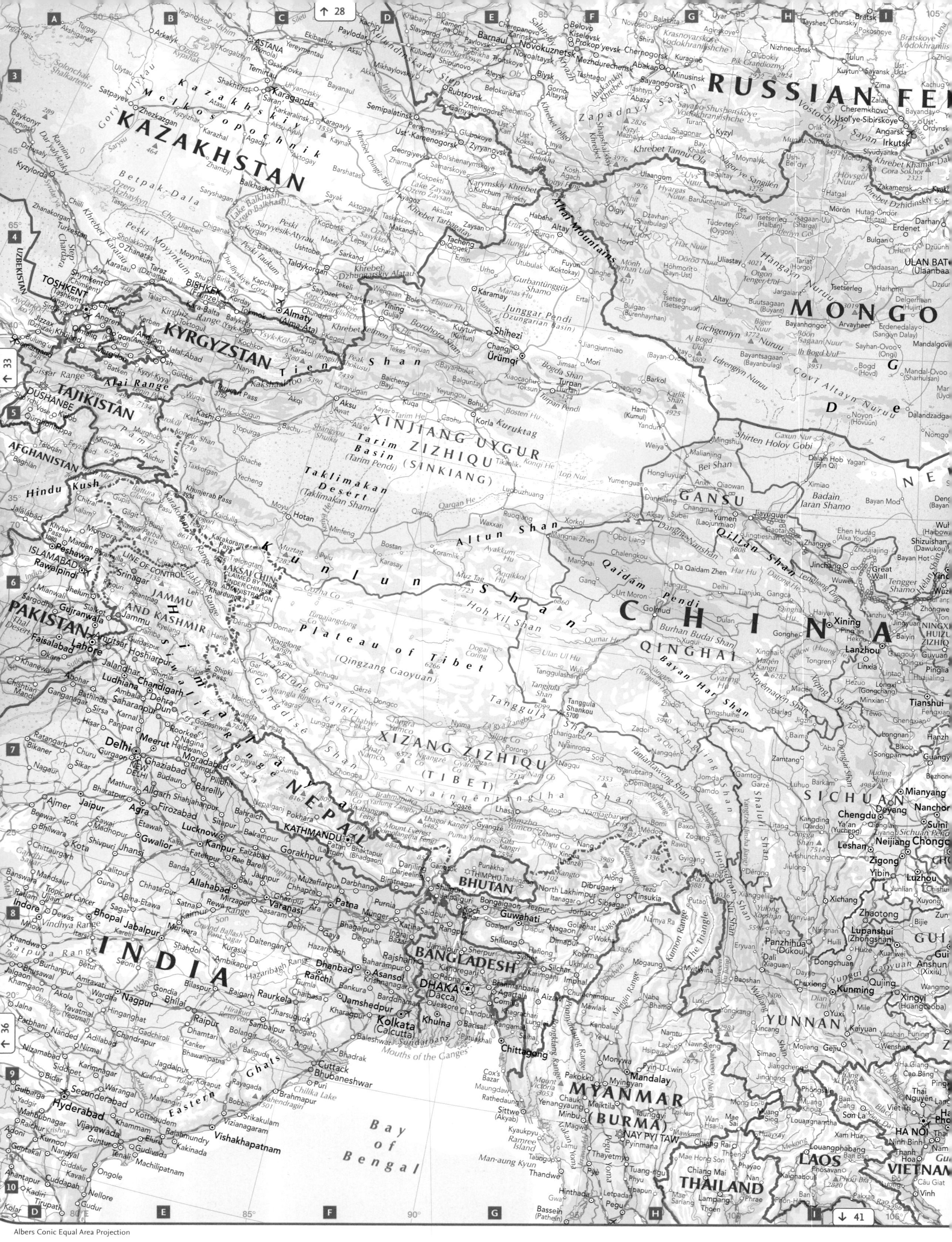

Albers Conic Equal Area Projection

1:15 000 000

Asia
Eastern Asia

RATION
NORTH KOREA
SOUTH KOREA
JAPAN
TAIWAN
PHILIPPINES
PACIFIC OCEAN
Sea of Japan (East Sea)
Sea of Okhotsk (Okhotskoye More)
Yellow Sea (Huang Hai)
East China Sea (Dong Hai)
South China Sea
Bo Hai
Korea Bay
Korea Strait
Taiwan Strait
Bashi Channel
Luzon Strait
Babuyan Channel
La Pérouse Strait
Tatarskiy Proliv
Sakhalin
Hokkaidō
Honshū
Shikoku
Kyūshū
Ryukyu Islands (Nansei-shotō) (Japan)
Kuril Islands (Kuril'skiye Ostrova)
Bonin Islands (Ogasawara-shotō) (Japan)
Volcano Islands (Kazan-rettō) (Japan)
Tropic of Cancer
ADMINISTERED BY RUSSIAN FEDERATION, CLAIMED BY JAPAN
TAIWAN: The People's Republic of China claims Taiwan as its 23rd province
HEILONGJIANG
JILIN
LIAONING
HEBEI
SHANXI
SHANDONG
HENAN
JIANGSU
ANHUI
SHANGHAI
HUBEI
HUNAN
JIANGXI
ZHEJIANG
FUJIAN
GUANGDONG
HAINAN
MANCHURIA
NEI MONGOL ZIZHIQU (INNER MONGOLIA)
BEIJING (Peking)
Tianjin
Shanghai
Nanjing
Wuhan
Hong Kong
Guangzhou
Shenzhen (Bao'an)
T'AIPEI
P'YŎNGYANG
SEOUL (Sŏul)
Pusan
TŌKYŌ
Yokohama
Ōsaka
Nagoya
Kyōto
Sapporo
Sendai
Hiroshima
Fukuoka
Vladivostok
Khabarovsk
Harbin
Shenyang
Dalian (Lüda)
Qingdao (Tsingtao)
Kaohsiung
Xiamen (Amoy)
Komsomol'sk-na-Amure
Yuzhno-Sakhalinsk
↑ 29
↓ 41

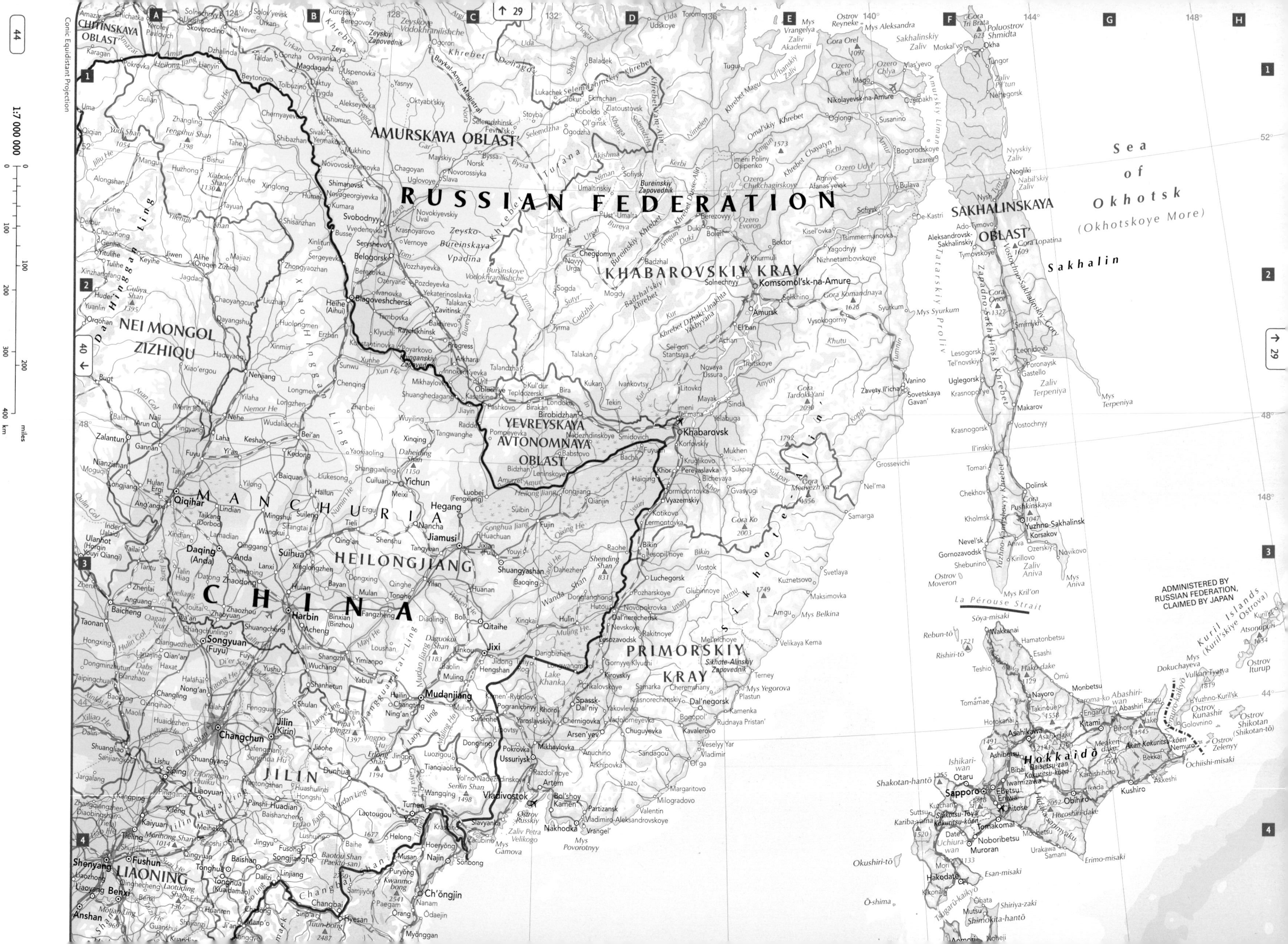

Conic Equidistant Projection

1:7 000 000

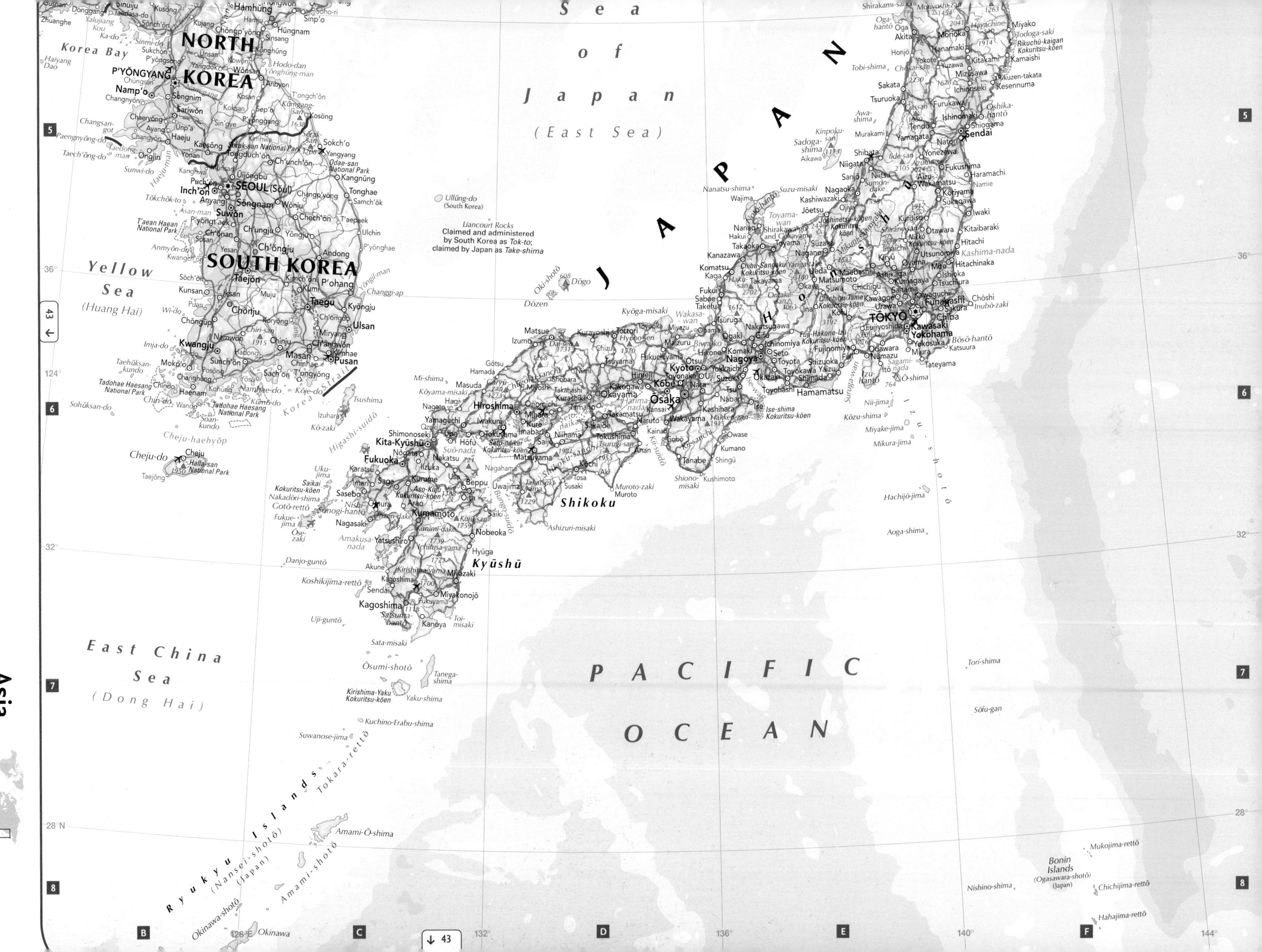

Asia
Japan, North Korea and South Korea

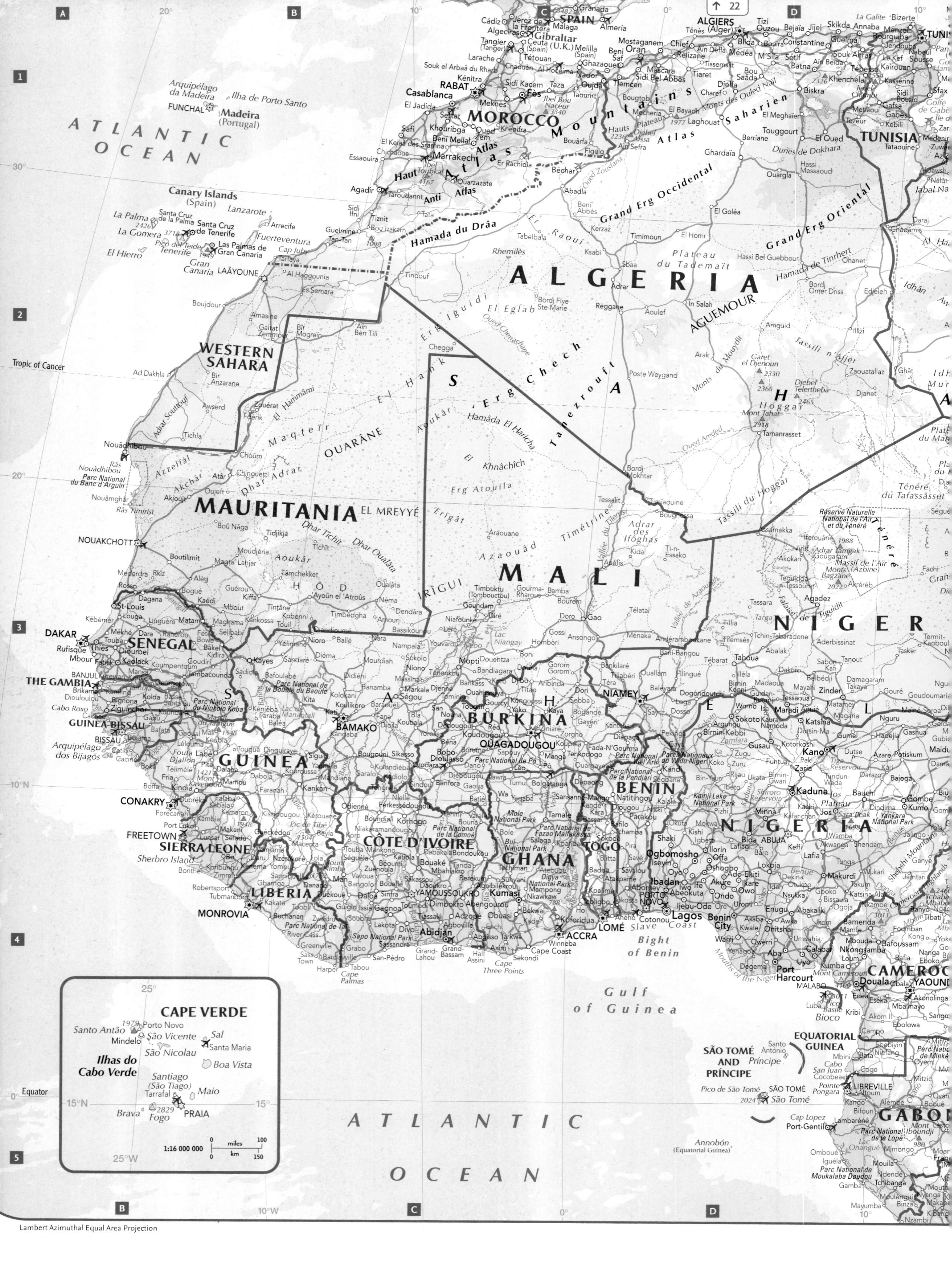

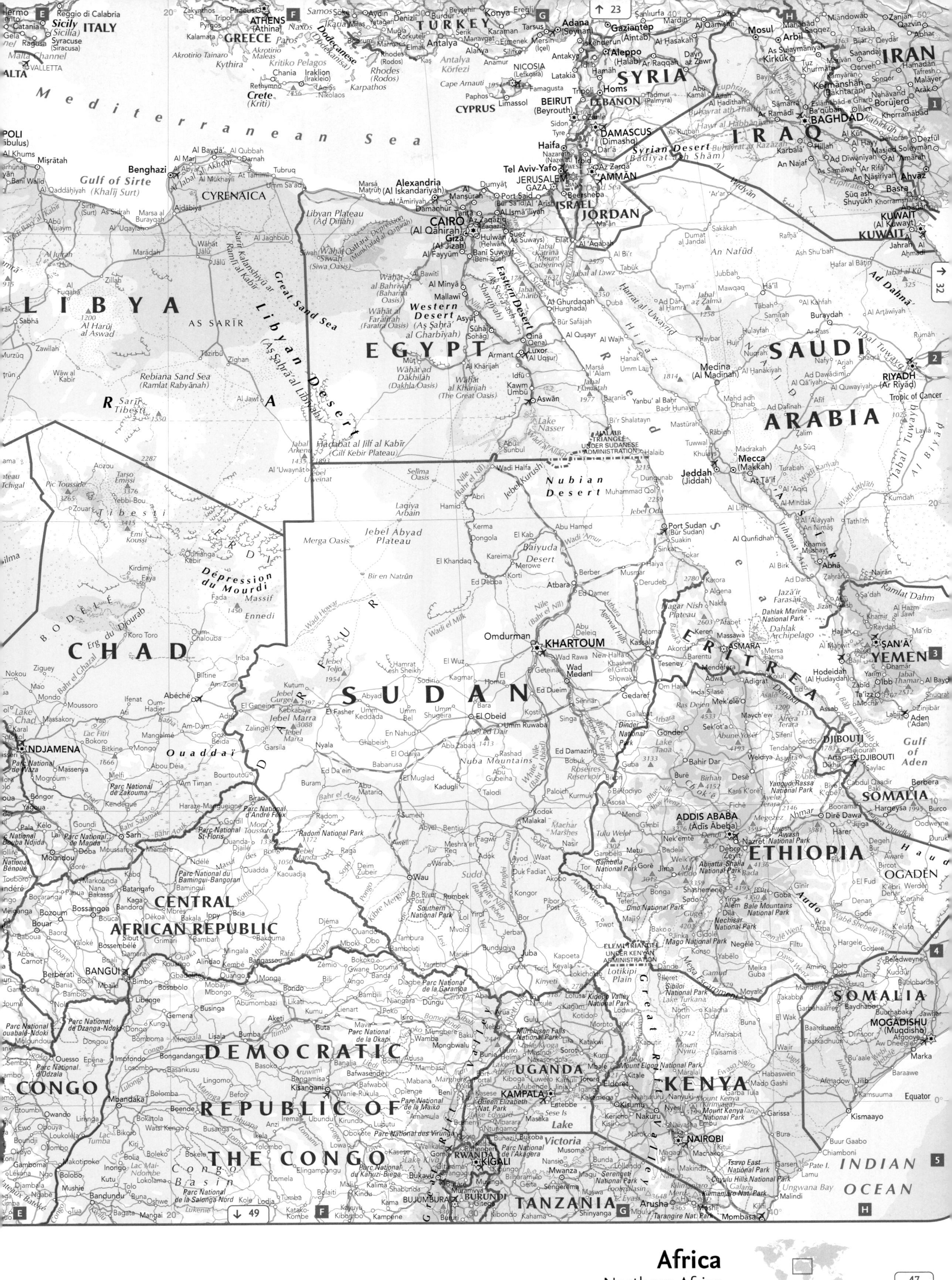

Africa
Northern Africa

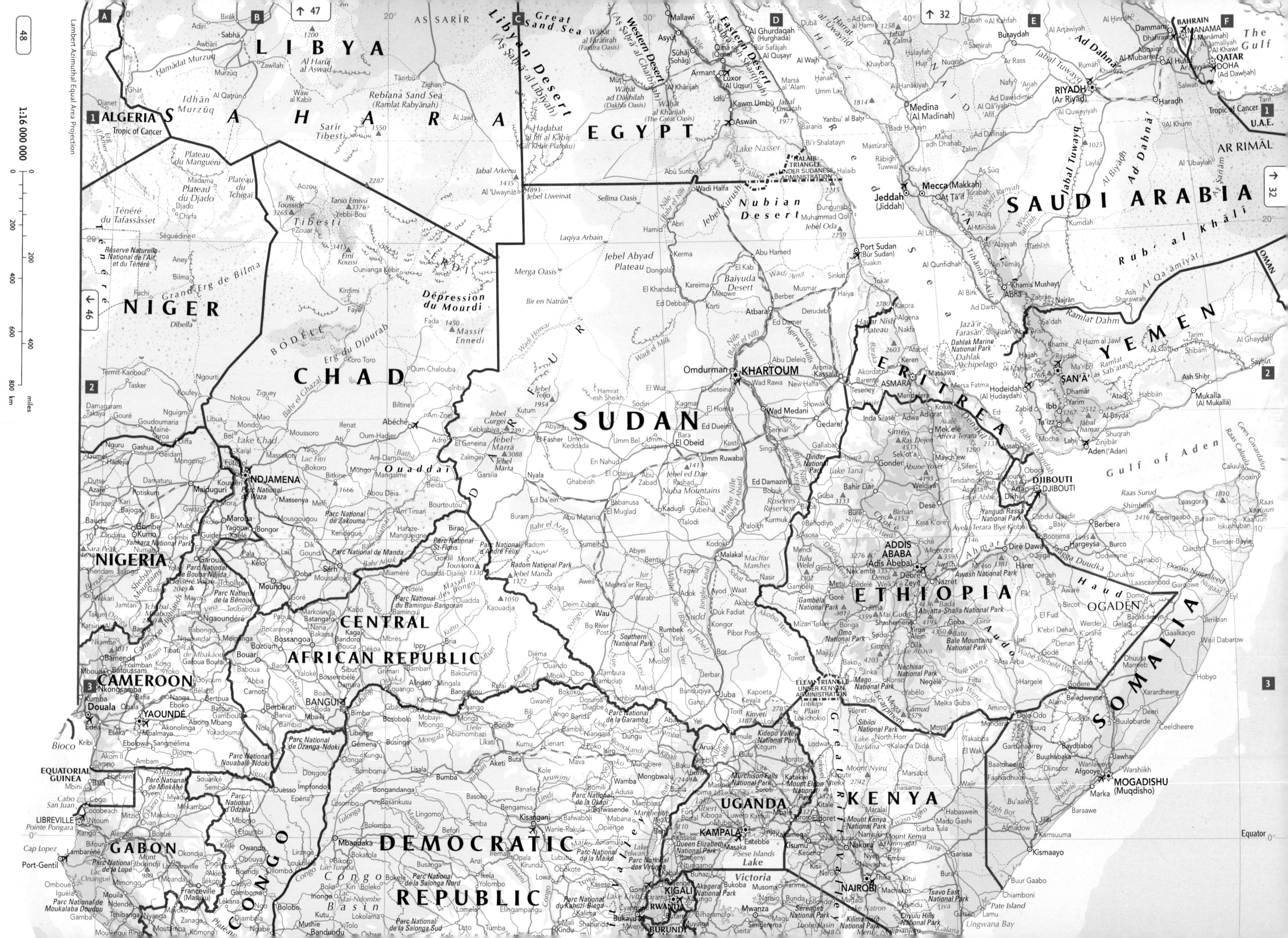

Lambert Azimuthal Equal Area Projection

1:16 000 000

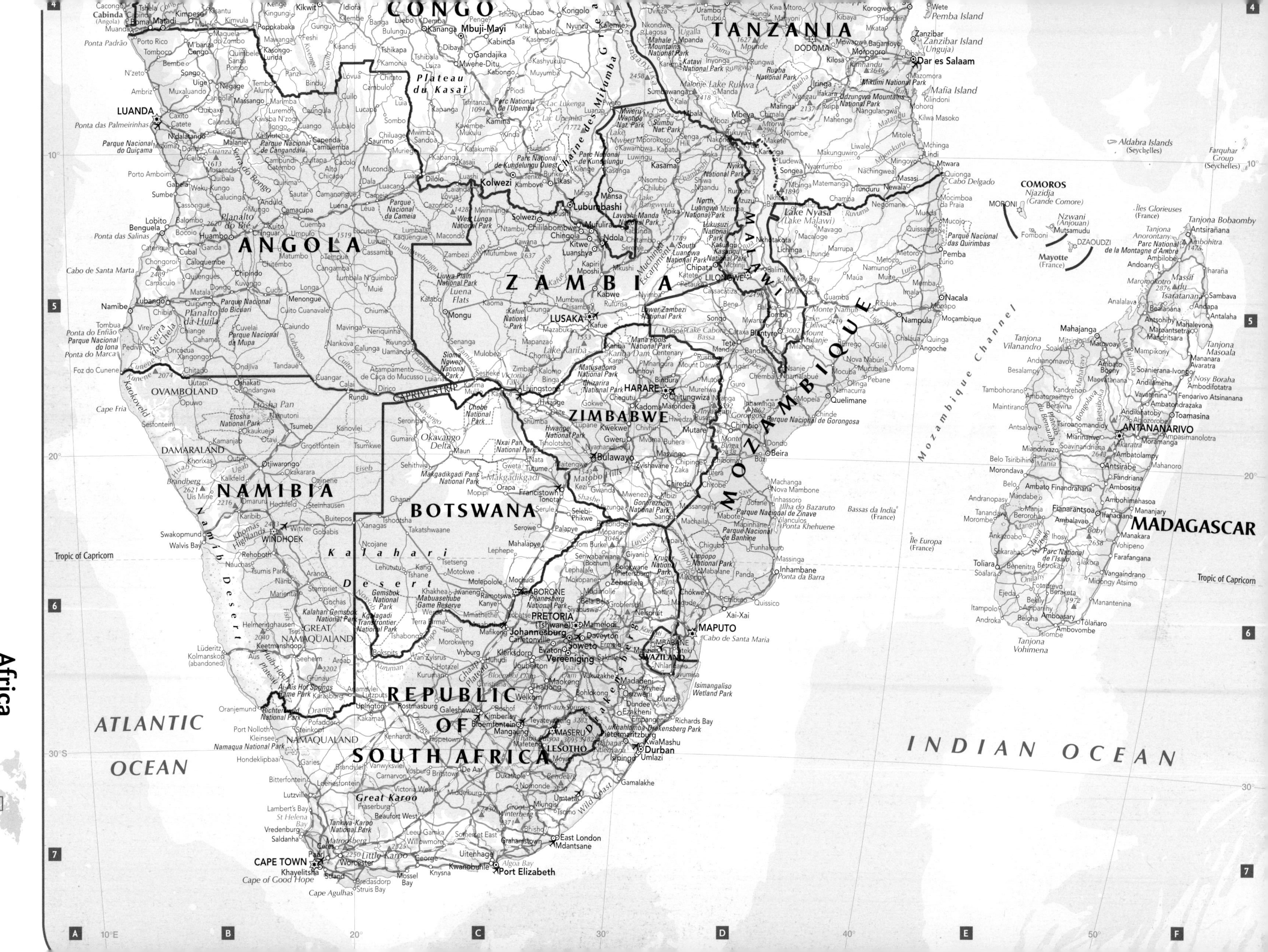

Africa
Central and Southern Africa

ATLANTIC

OCEAN

GHANZI

BOTSWANA
Central Kalahari Game Reserve

ERONGO

KHOMAS

OMAHEKE

NAMIBIA

KALAHARI

KGALAGADI

Desert

Gemsbok
National Park

Kalahari
Gemsbok
National
Park

Kgalagadi
Transfrontier
Park

KWENE

SOUTHE

HARDAP

GREAT NAMAQUALAND

KARAS

REPUBLI

NORTHERN

OF

CAPE

SOUTH AF

NORT

GRIQUALAND WEST

NAMAQUALAND

Great Karoo

WESTERN CAPE

Little Karoo

CAPE TOWN

Lambert Azimuthal Equal Area Projection

1:5 000 000

Africa
Republic of South Africa

ZIMBABWE
MOZAMBIQUE
CENTRAL
LIMPOPO
GAZA
INHAMBANE
MPUMALANGA
GAUTENG
MAPUTO
SWAZILAND
KWAZULU-NATAL
FREE STATE
LESOTHO
EASTERN CAPE
INDIAN
OCEAN
Drakensberg
Tropic of Capricorn
PRETORIA (Tshwane)
Johannesburg
Soweto
Vereeniging
Bloemfontein
MASERU
Pietermaritzburg
Durban
Richards Bay
East London
Port Elizabeth
Polokwane (Pietersburg)
Nelspruit
Kruger National Park
Parque Nacional de Banhine
Limpopo National Park
Great Limpopo Transfrontier Park
GABORONE
Mafikeng
Welkom
Kroonstad
Newcastle
Ladysmith
Port Shepstone
Port Edward
Queenstown
Mdantsane
Grahamstown
Cape Recife
Great Fish Point
Cape Hermes
Wild Coast
Lake St Lucia
Kosi Bay
Bala de Maputo
Inhambane
Xai-Xai
Chókwè
Lagoa Poelela
Lake Sibayi
Isimangaliso Wetland Park
Hluhluwe-Umfolozi Park
Royal Natal National Park
uKhahlamba-Drakensberg Park
Golden Gate Highlands National Park
Addo Elephant National Park
Mapungubwe National Park
MATABELELAND SOUTH
MASVINGO
GRIQUALAND EAST
EASTERN CAPE
Steenkampsberge
Soutpansberg
Maluti Mountains
22°
24°
26°
28°
30°
32°
34°
36°
J
K
M
1
2
3
4
5
6
7
8

INDIAN
OCEAN

A U S T R A L I A

WESTERN

AUSTRALIA

NORTHERN

TERRITORY

QUEENSLAND

SOUTH

AUSTRALIA

NEW SOUTH WALES

VICTORIA

TASMANIA

INDONESIA

PAPUA

NEW GUINEA

Lambert Azimuthal Equal Area Projection

1:20 000 000

| 0 | 200 | 400 | 600 | miles |

| 0 | 200 | 400 | 600 | 800 | 1000 | km |

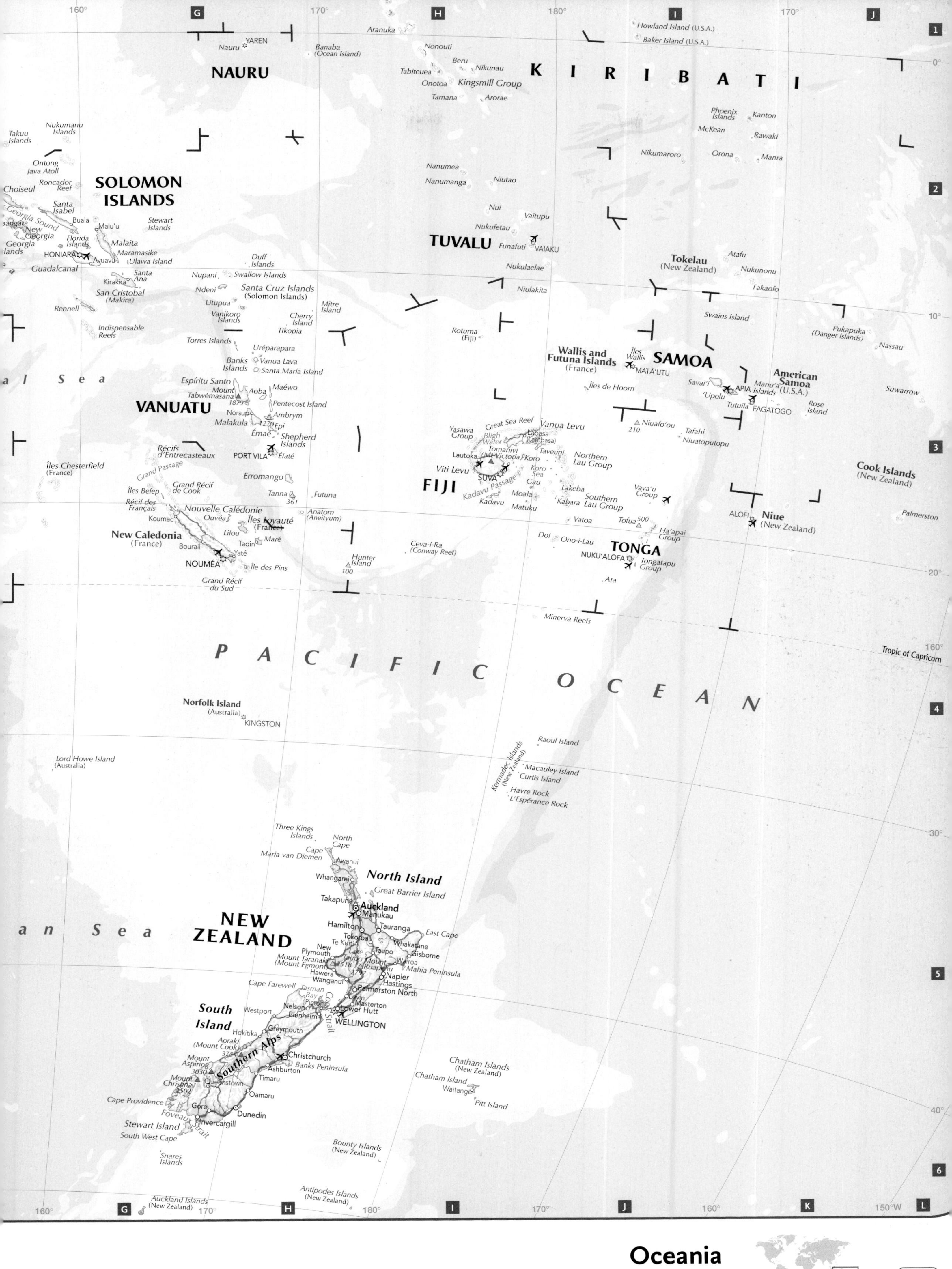

Oceania
Australia, New Zealand and Southwest Pacific

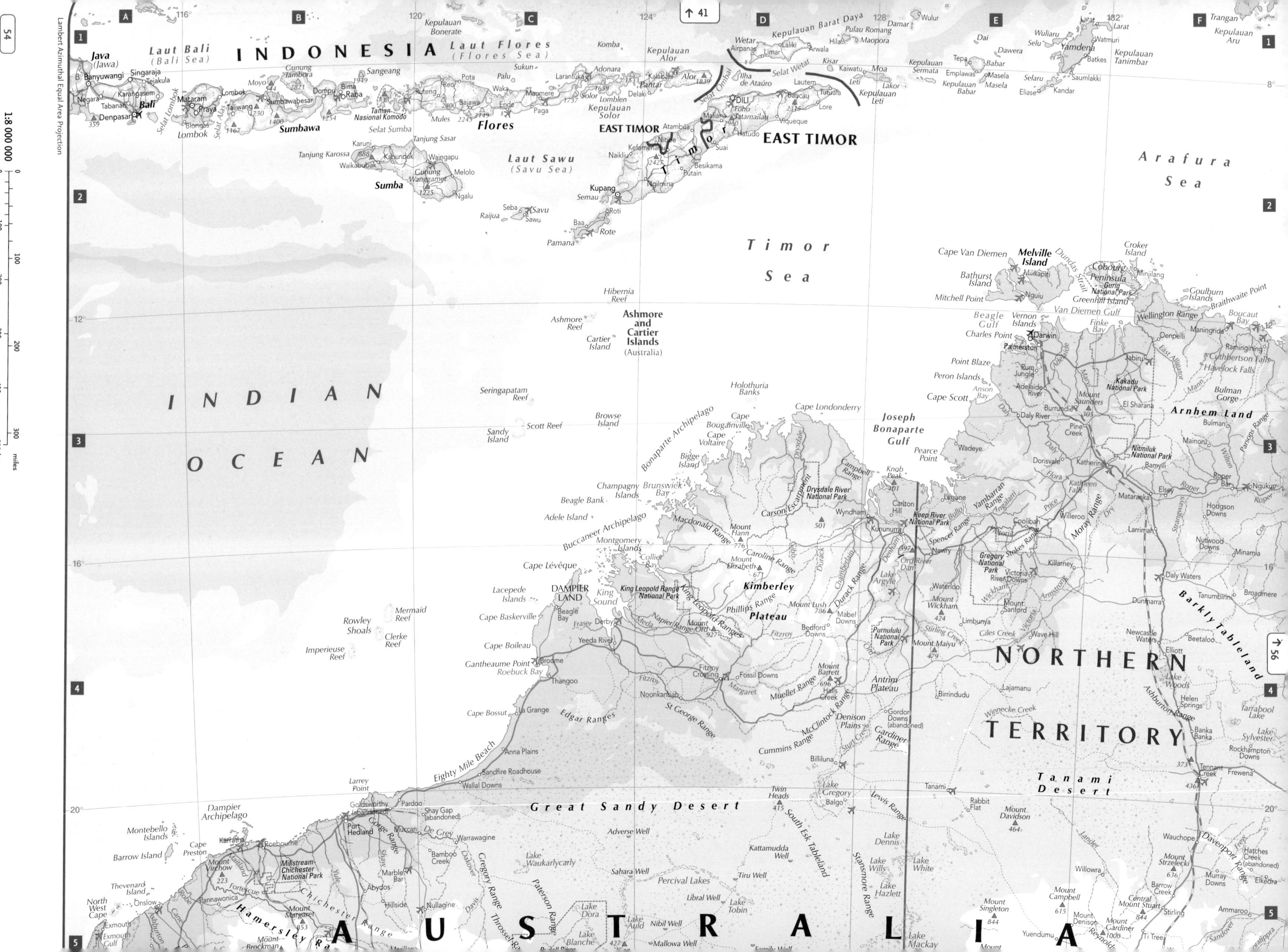

Lambert Azimuthal Equal Area Projection

1:8 000 000

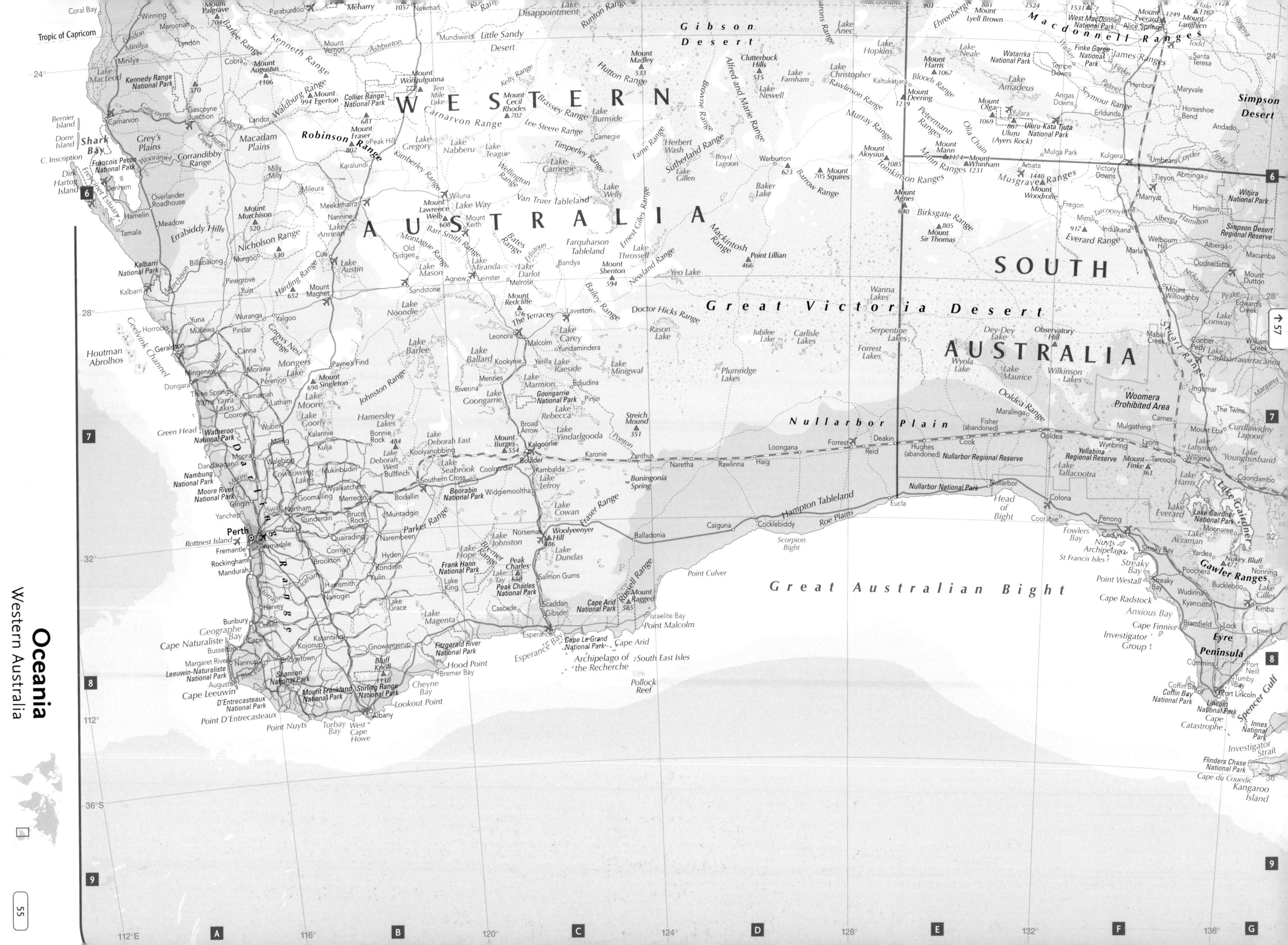

Oceania
Western Australia

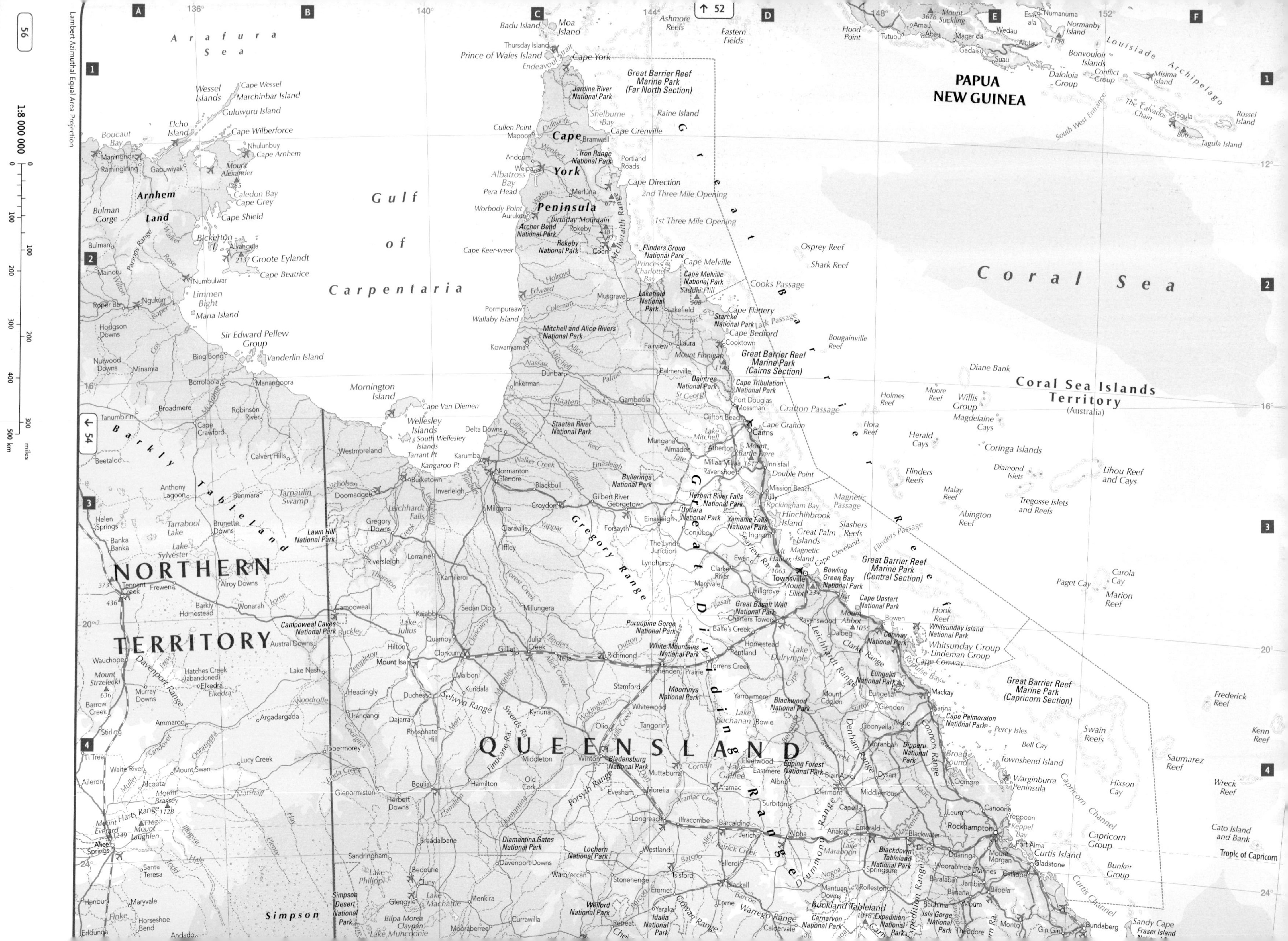

Lambert Azimuthal Equal Area Projection

1:8 000 000

| 0 | 100 | 200 | 300 | miles |
| 0 | 100 | 200 | 300 | 400 | 500 | km |

PAPUA
NEW GUINEA

Coral Sea

Coral Sea Islands
Territory
(Australia)

Gulf
of
Carpentaria

Arafura
Sea

Arnhem
Land

Cape
York
Peninsula

Great Barrier Reef
Marine Park
(Far North Section)

Great Barrier Reef
Marine Park
(Cairns Section)

Great Barrier Reef
Marine Park
(Central Section)

Great Barrier Reef
Marine Park
(Capricorn Section)

Great Dividing Range

QUEENSLAND

NORTHERN

TERRITORY

Barkly Tableland

Simpson

Tropic of Capricorn

Oceania

Eastern Australia

SOUTH AUSTRALIA
NEW SOUTH WALES
VICTORIA
TASMANIA
AUSTRALIAN CAPITAL TERRITORY
JERVIS BAY TERRITORY
Tasman Sea
Bass Strait
Spencer Gulf
Gulf St Vincent
Kangaroo Island
Eyre Peninsula
Yorke Peninsula
Great Dividing Range
Darling Downs
Sturt Stony Desert
Strzelecki Desert
Simpson Desert Regional Reserve
Lake Eyre (North)
Lake Eyre (South)
Lake Torrens
Lake Gairdner
Flinders Ranges
Gawler Ranges
Grey Range
Stuart Range
Barrier Range
Flinders Island
King Island
Brisbane
Sydney
Canberra
Melbourne
Adelaide
Hobart
Newcastle
Wollongong
Gold Coast
Launceston
Geelong
Broken Hill
Mildura
Bendigo
Ballarat
Toowoomba
Port Augusta
Port Lincoln
Dubbo
Wagga Wagga
Albury
Mount Gambier
Cape Howe
Wilson's Promontory
1:8 000 000
← 55

Oceania
Southeast Australia

1:5 000 000

Lambert Azimuthal Equal Area Projection

Oceania
New Zealand

1:5 250 000

0 50 100 150 miles
0 50 100 150 200 250 km

onic Equidistant Projection

Tasman Sea

NEW ZEALAND

North Island

South Island

PACIFIC OCEAN

Three Kings Islands
Cape Maria van Diemen
North Cape
Te Paki
Ninety Mile Beach
Cape Karikari
Doubtless Bay
Ahipara Bay
Tauroa Point
Awanui
Kaitaia
Kerikeri
Broadwood
Bay of Islands
Cape Brett
Russell
Kawakawa
Poor Knights Islands
Donnellys Crossing
Whangarei
Dargaville
Bream Bay
Mokohinau Islands
Maungaturoto
Little Barrier
Port Fitzroy
Great Barrier Island
North Head
Kaipara Harbour
Wellsford
Leigh
Kawau Island
Colville Channel
Hauraki Gulf
Orewa
East Coast Bays
Takapuna
Auckland
Waiheke Island
Colville
Mercury Islands
Manukau Harbour
Manukau
Whitianga
Coromandel Peninsula
The Aldermen Islands
Papakura
Pukekohe
Waiuku
Thames
Port Waikato
Whangamata
Mayor Island
Huntly
Matakana Island
Whakaari
Cape Runaway
Hamilton
Tauranga
Motiti Island
Bay of Plenty
Hicks Bay
Te Araroa
East Cape
Kawhia Harbour
Te Awamutu
Cambridge
Whakatane
Otorohanga
Rotorua
Te Kuiti
Piopio
Mangakino
Tokoroa
Mount Tarawera
Opotiki
Hikurangi
Ruatoria
Raukumara Range
Tokomaru Bay
Awakino
Mokau
Urewera National Park
Tolaga Bay
North Taranaki Bight
Taupo
Lake Taupo
New Plymouth
Mount Taranaki (Mount Egmont)
Tongariro National Park
Gisborne
Poverty Bay
Cape Egmont
Egmont National Park
Whanganui National Park
Mount Ruapehu
Kaimanawa Mountains
Opunake
Hawera
South Taranaki Bight
Patea
Waiouru
Taihape
Wairoa
Nuhaka
Table Cape
Hawke Bay
Mahia Peninsula
Bay View
Napier
Hastings
Cape Kidnappers
Havelock North
Waimarama
Wanganui
Marton
Feilding
Palmerston North
Dannevirke
Waipukurau
Porangahau
Cape Turnagain
Levin
Eketahuna
Pongaroa
Kapiti Island
Paraparaumu
Masterton
Castlepoint
Upper Hutt
Porirua
Lower Hutt
Featherston
WELLINGTON
Martinborough
Palliser Bay
Cape Palliser
Cook Strait
Cape Farewell
Farewell Spit
Collingwood
Golden Bay
Cape Stephens
D'Urville Island
Kahurangi Point
Abel Tasman National Park
Tasman Bay
Tasman Mountains
Karamea
Kahurangi National Park
Karamea Bight
Motueka
Nelson
Richmond
Havelock
Picton
Blenheim
Seddonville
Hope Saddle
Westport
Waimangaroa
Charleston
Seddon
Cape Campbell
Paparoa National Park
Reefton
Inland Kaikoura Range
Tapuaenuku
Clarence
Greymouth
Springs Junction
Lewis Pass
Nelson Lakes Nat. Park
Kaikoura
Hokitika
Ross
Arthur's Pass National Park
Culverden
Cheviot
Abut Head
Southern Alps
Westland National Park
Franz Josef Glacier
Fox Glacier
Mount Arrowsmith
Aoraki (Mount Cook)
Aoraki/Mount Cook National Park
Lake Pukaki
Lake Tekapo
Oxford
Pegasus Bay
Rangiora
Kaiapoi
Christchurch
Sumner
Lyttelton
Banks Peninsula
Akaroa
Canterbury Plains
Lake Ellesmere
Ashburton
Canterbury Bight
Jackson Head
Cascade Point
Awarua Point
Mount Aspiring National Park
Mount Aspiring
Timaru
Temuka
Geraldine
Fairlie
Twizel
Milford Sound
George Sound
Lake Wanaka
Wanaka
Lake Hawea
Omarama
Kurow
Studholme Junction
Waimate
Oamaru
Pukeuri Junction
Cape Wanbrow
Fiordland
Secretary Island
Doubtful Sound
Lake Te Anau
Te Anau
Fiordland National Park
Lake Manapouri
Breaksea Sound
Resolution Island
Queenstown
Alexandra
Ranfurly
Hyde
Middlemarch
Moeraki Point
Shag Point
Palmerston
Waikouaiti
Port Chalmers
Otago Peninsula
Dunedin
Lumsden
Roxburgh
Beaumont
Milton
Balclutha
Kaitangata
Nugget Point
Gore
Mataura
Owaka
Caroline Peak
Winton
Edendale
Invercargill
Riverton
Te Waewae Bay
Cape Providence
Puysegur Point
Solander Island
Foveaux Strait
Bluff
Fortrose
Long Point
Chaslands Mistake
Codfish Island
Mason Bay
Ruapuke Island
Stewart Island
Halfmoon Bay
Shelter Point
Titi Islands (Muttonbird Islands)
South West Cape
North Trap

Lambert Conformal Conic Projection

↓ 62

1:16 000 000

0   200   400   miles
0   200   400   600   800 km

Greenland
(Kalaallit Nunaat)
(Denmark)
Nationalparken i
Nord- og Østgrønland
ICELAND
REYKJAVÍK
Arctic Circle
Denmark Strait
Baffin Bay
Davis Strait
Labrador Sea
Hudson Bay
James Bay
Hudson Strait
Foxe Basin
Foxe Channel
Baffin Island
Queen Elizabeth Islands
Parry Islands
Ellesmere Island
Axel Heiberg Island
Devon Island
Lancaster Sound
Somerset Island
Prince of Wales Island
Boothia Peninsula
Gulf of Boothia
Melville Peninsula
Southampton Island
Coats Island
Mansel Island
Belcher Islands
Péninsule d'Ungava
Cumberland Peninsula
Hall Peninsula
Meta Incognita Peninsula
Resolution Island
Cape Chidley
North Geomagnetic Pole (2008)
NUNAVUT
CANADA
MANITOBA
ONTARIO
QUÉBEC
NEWFOUNDLAND AND LABRADOR
Labrador
Newfoundland
NEW BRUNSWICK
NOVA SCOTIA
PRINCE EDWARD I.
Gulf of St Lawrence
Île d'Anticosti
Cabot Strait
St-Pierre and Miquelon (France)
Sable Island
ATLANTIC OCEAN
Gulf of Maine
Lake Superior
Lake Michigan
Lake Huron
Lake Erie
Lake Winnipeg
OTTAWA
Montréal
Québec
Toronto
Winnipeg
Chicago
Detroit
Boston
New York
MINNESOTA
WISCONSIN
MICHIGAN
IOWA
PENNSYLVANIA
NEW YORK
MAINE
AMERICA
Wapusk National Park
Ukkusiksalik National Park
Auyuittuq Nat. Park
Sirmilik Nat. Park
↓ 63
States in the U.S.A. numbered on the map:
1. CONNECTICUT (K5)
2. MASSACHUSETTS (K5)
3. NEW HAMPSHIRE (K5)
4. RHODE ISLAND (K5)
5. VERMONT (K5)

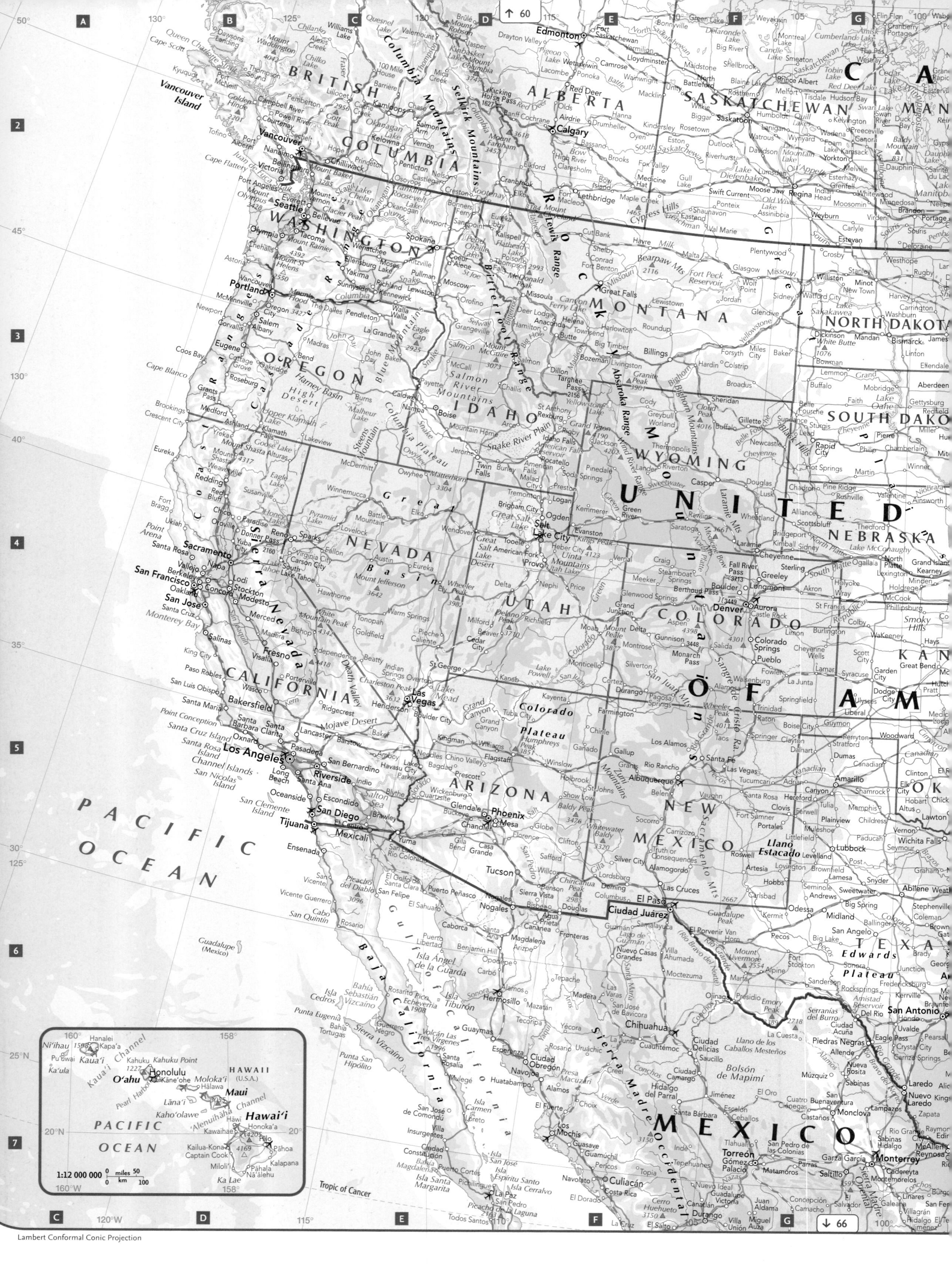

Lambert Conformal Conic Projection

62   1:12 000 000

↑ 61
↓ 67
CANADA
UNITED STATES OF AMERICA
ONTARIO
QUÉBEC
NEW BRUNSWICK
NOVA SCOTIA
PRINCE EDWARD ISLAND
MINNESOTA
WISCONSIN
MICHIGAN
IOWA
ILLINOIS
INDIANA
OHIO
PENNSYLVANIA
NEW YORK
VERMONT
NEW HAMPSHIRE
MAINE
MASSACHUSETTS
CONNECTICUT
RHODE ISLAND
NEW JERSEY
DELAWARE
MARYLAND
WEST VIRGINIA
VIRGINIA
KENTUCKY
MISSOURI
TENNESSEE
NORTH CAROLINA
SOUTH CAROLINA
GEORGIA
ALABAMA
MISSISSIPPI
ARKANSAS
LOUISIANA
FLORIDA
THE BAHAMAS
CUBA
ATLANTIC OCEAN
Gulf of Mexico
Gulf of Maine
Gulf of St Lawrence
James Bay
Lake Superior
Lake Michigan
Lake Huron
Lake Erie
Lake Ontario
Appalachian Mountains
Allegheny Mountains
Cumberland Plateau
Ozark Plateau
Coastal Plain
Straits of Florida
Great Bahama Bank
Tropic of Cancer
OTTAWA
WASHINGTON D.C.
NASSAU
New York
Chicago
Philadelphia
Boston
Toronto
Montréal
Detroit
Cleveland
Pittsburgh
Baltimore
Atlanta
Charlotte
Memphis
Nashville
St Louis
Indianapolis
Columbus
Cincinnati
Louisville
Milwaukee
Minneapolis
Buffalo
Jacksonville
Orlando
Tampa
Miami
New Orleans
Houston
Dallas
Virginia Beach
Providence
Québec
Birmingham

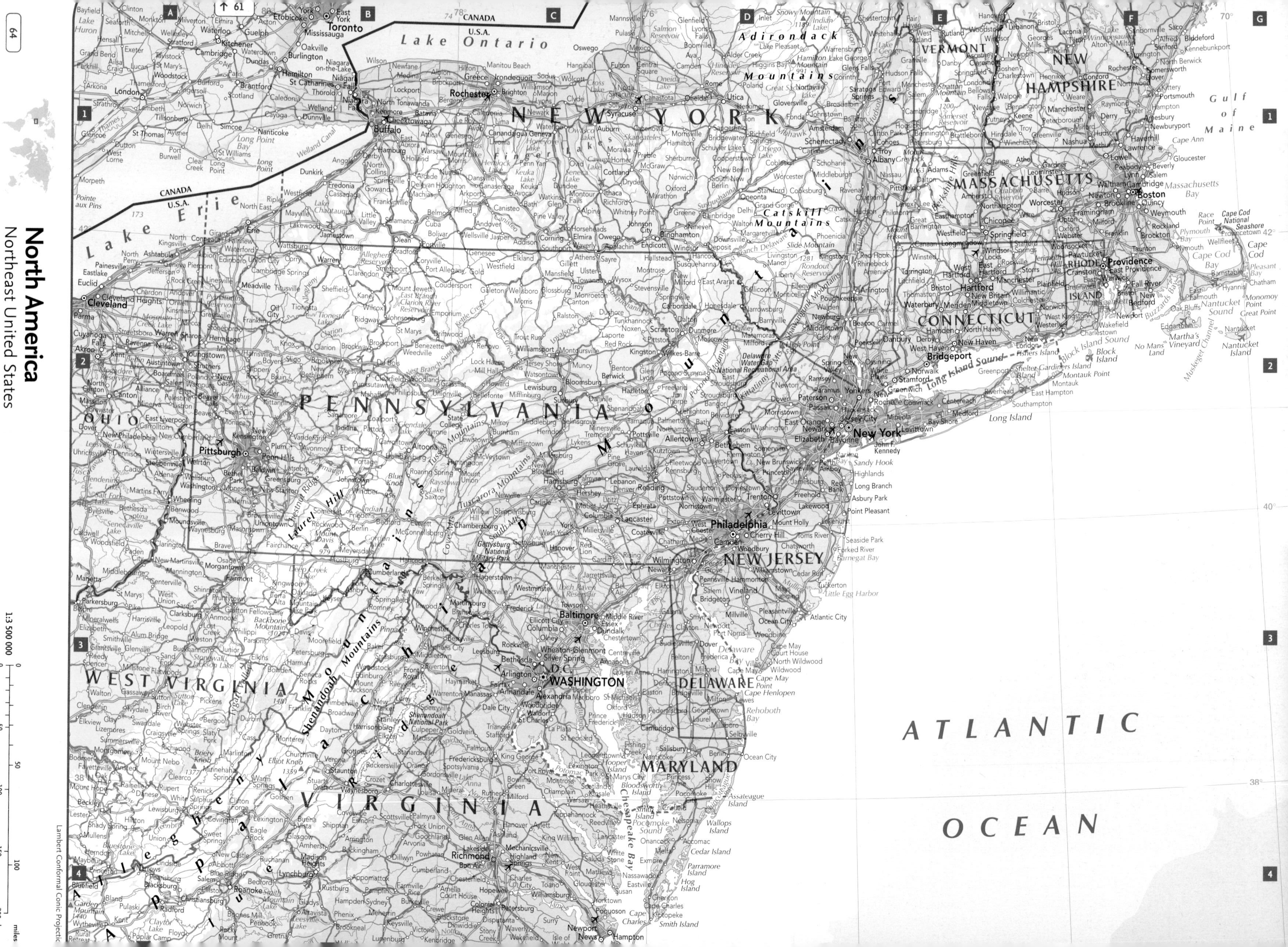

North America
Northeast United States

Lambert Conformal Conic Projection

1:3 500 000

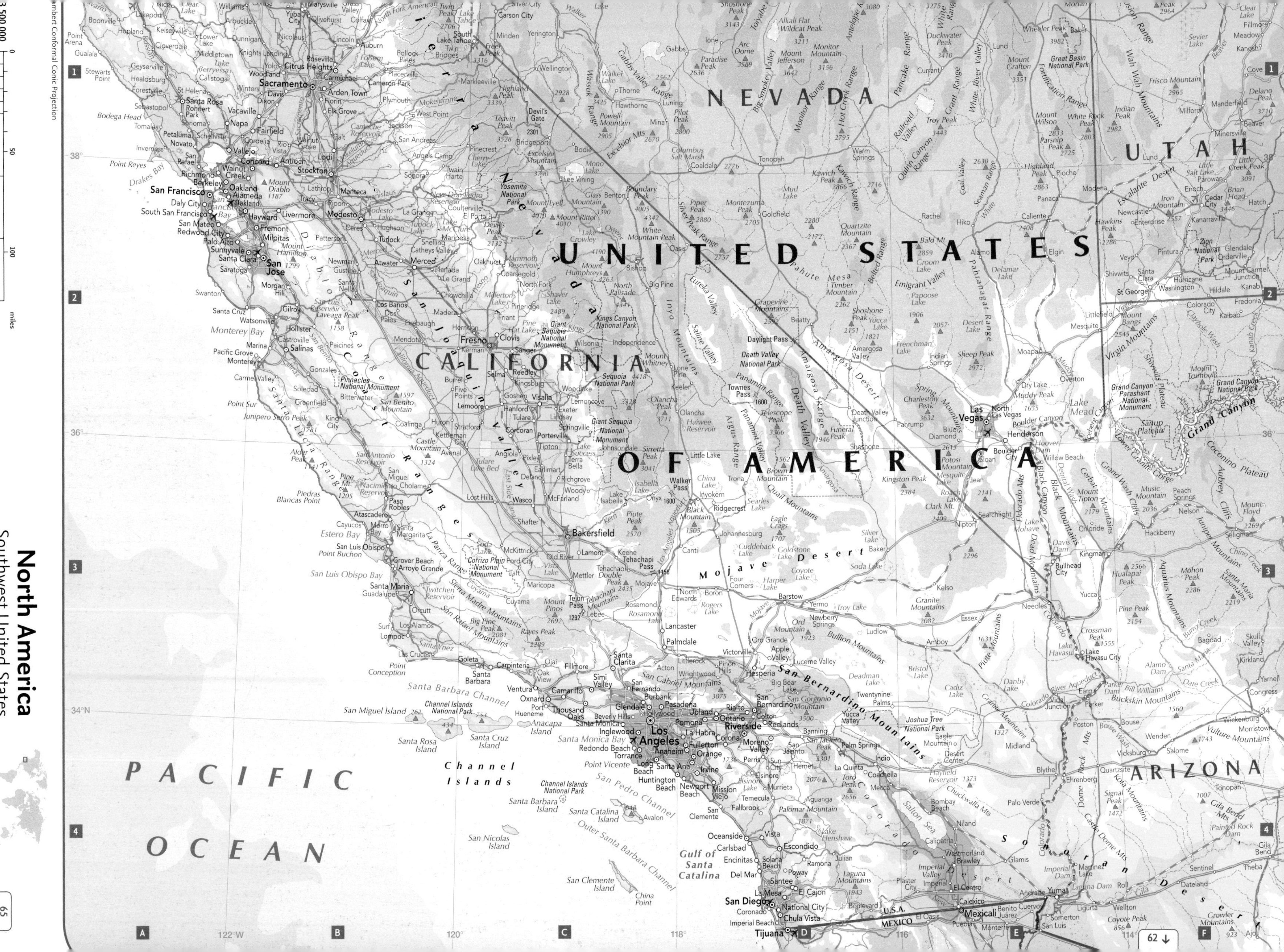

North America

Southwest United States

1

A Death Valley B C D E F

Wasco
Bakersfield
CALIFORNIA 35
Santa Clarita
Oxnard
Long Los
Beach Angeles
Pasadena
San Bernardino
Riverside
Channel Is
Oceanside
Escondido
San El Centro
Diego Tijuana Mexicali
Ensenada

Charleston
Peak 3615
Henderson Las Vegas
Baker
Kingman
Needles
Parker
Blythe
Chino Valley
Prescott Bagdad
Wickenburg
Buckeye Glendale Phoenix
Mesa Chandler
Gila Bend
Casa
Grande
Yuma Nogales Tucson
Santa
Ana Sierra Vista
Nogales
Agua Prieta

Lake
Mead Grand
Canyon Colorado
Plateau Tuba City Kayenta
Humphreys Chinle
3851 Flagstaff
Ganado
Holbrook Gallup
Show
Low St Johns
3476 Whitewater
Baldy
Clifton
Safford Silver
City
Lordsburg Deming
Benson Sierra Vista
Douglas 2985

Durango Alamosa 105
COLORADO Trinidad
Farmington Wheeler Peak
4011 Raton
Los Alamos Taos Springer
Santa Fe
Albuquerque Las Vegas
Belen Santa Rosa
Vaughn
Socorro Fort Sumner
Truth or
Consequences Carrizozo Portales
Alamogordo Roswell
Las Cruces Artesia
El Paso Carlsbad
Ciudad
Juárez

PACIFIC
OCEAN

Lambert Conformal Conic Projection

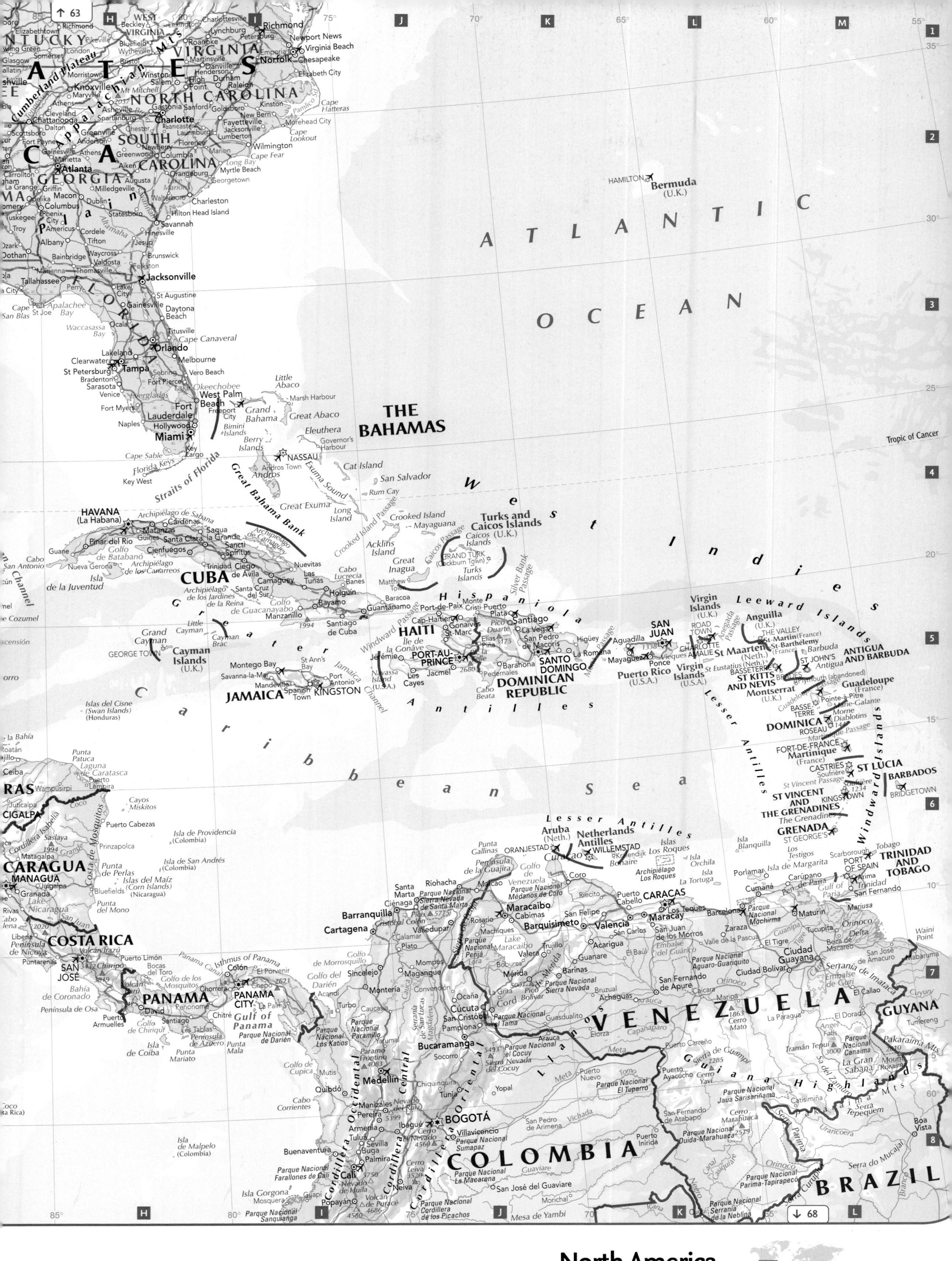

North America
Central America and the Caribbean

PACIFIC

OCEAN

NICARAGUA

MANAGUA

COSTA RICA

SAN JOSE

PANAMA

PANAMA CITY

Gulf of
Panama

COLOMBIA

BOGOTÁ

Medellín

Cali

QUITO

ECUADOR

Guayaquil

Galapagos Islands
(Islas Galápagos)
(Ecuador)

Equator

1:14 000 000

VENEZUELA

CARACAS

Maracaibo

Maracay

Valencia

Barquisimeto

GRENADA

ST GEORGE

Netherlands
Antilles

ORANJESTAD

WILLEMSTAD

Aruba

PORT OF
SPAIN

TRINIDAD
AND
TOBAGO

PERU

LIMA

Callao

Cusco
(Cuzco)

Arequipa

BOLIVIA

LA PAZ

SUCRE

Santa
Cruz

Lake Titicaca

CHILE

ARGENTINA

Tropic of Capricorn

Lambert Azimuthal Equal Area Projection

1:14 000 000

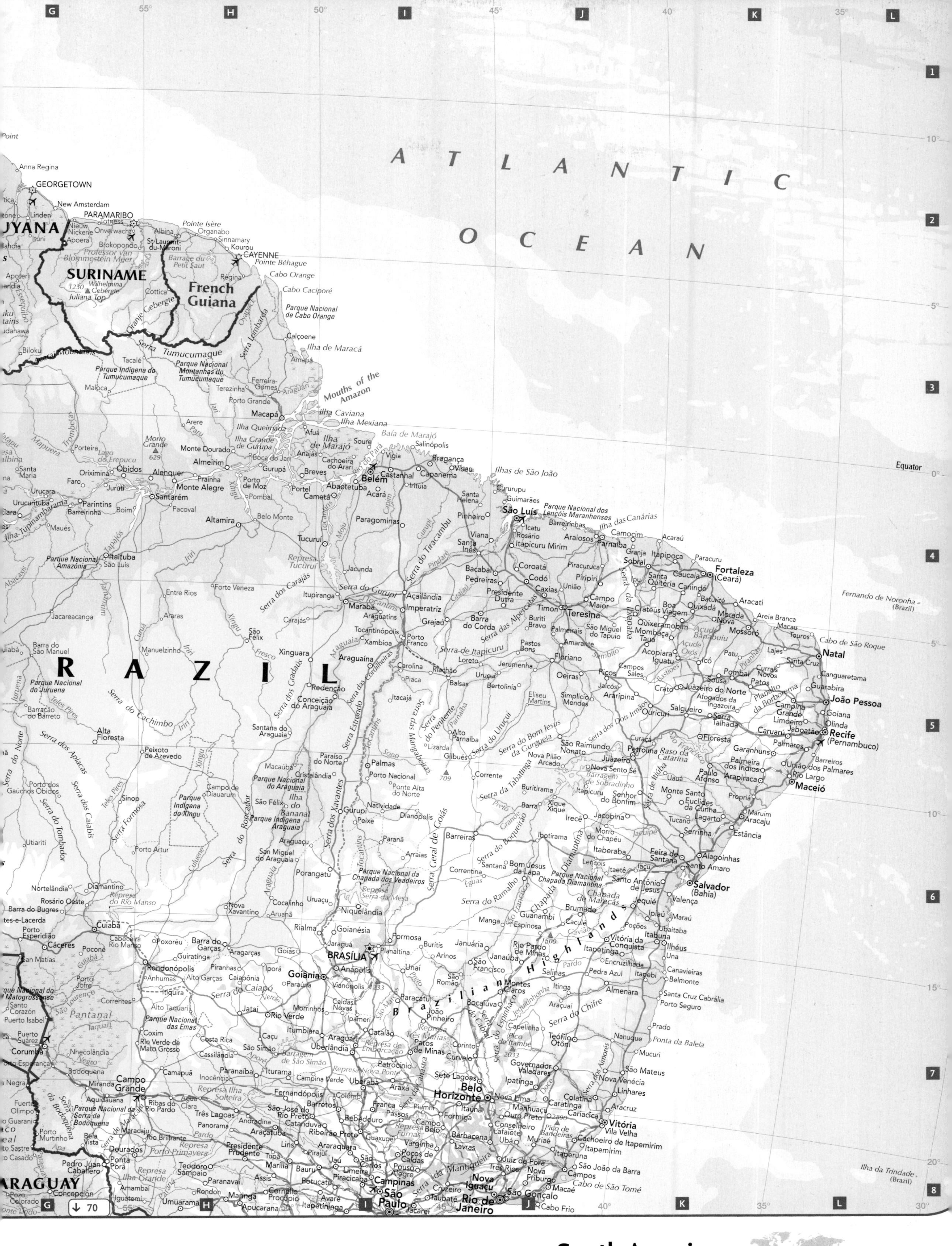

ATLANTIC OCEAN

South America
Northern South America

South America
Southern South America

Lambert Azimuthal Equal Area Projection

1:14 000 000

South America
Southeast Brazil

1:7 000 000

Lambert Azimuthal Equal Area Projection

Lambert Azimuthal Equal Area Projection

72

1:50 000 000

0   500   1000   1500 miles

0   500   1000   1500   2000   2500 km

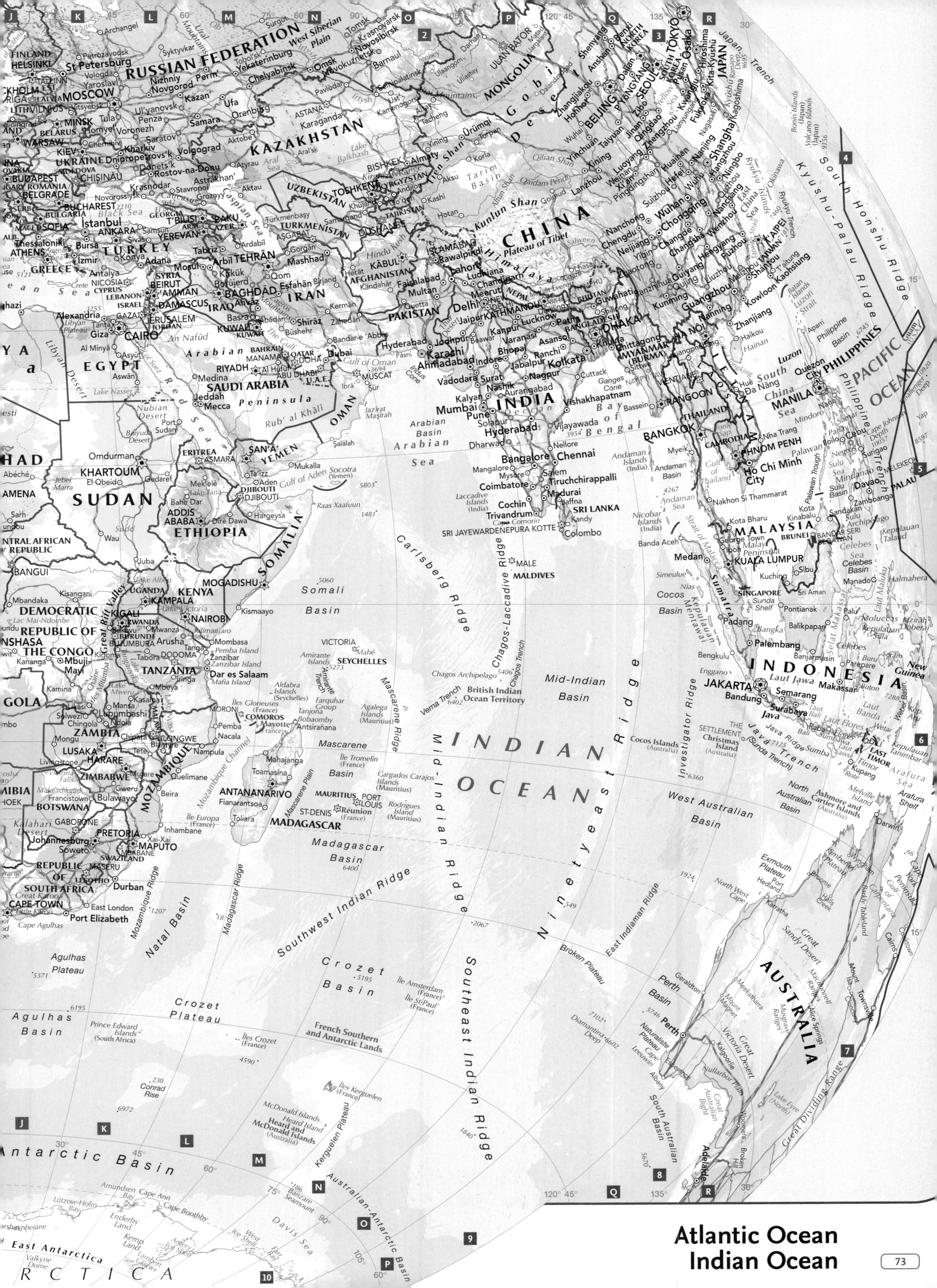

Atlantic Ocean
Indian Ocean

73

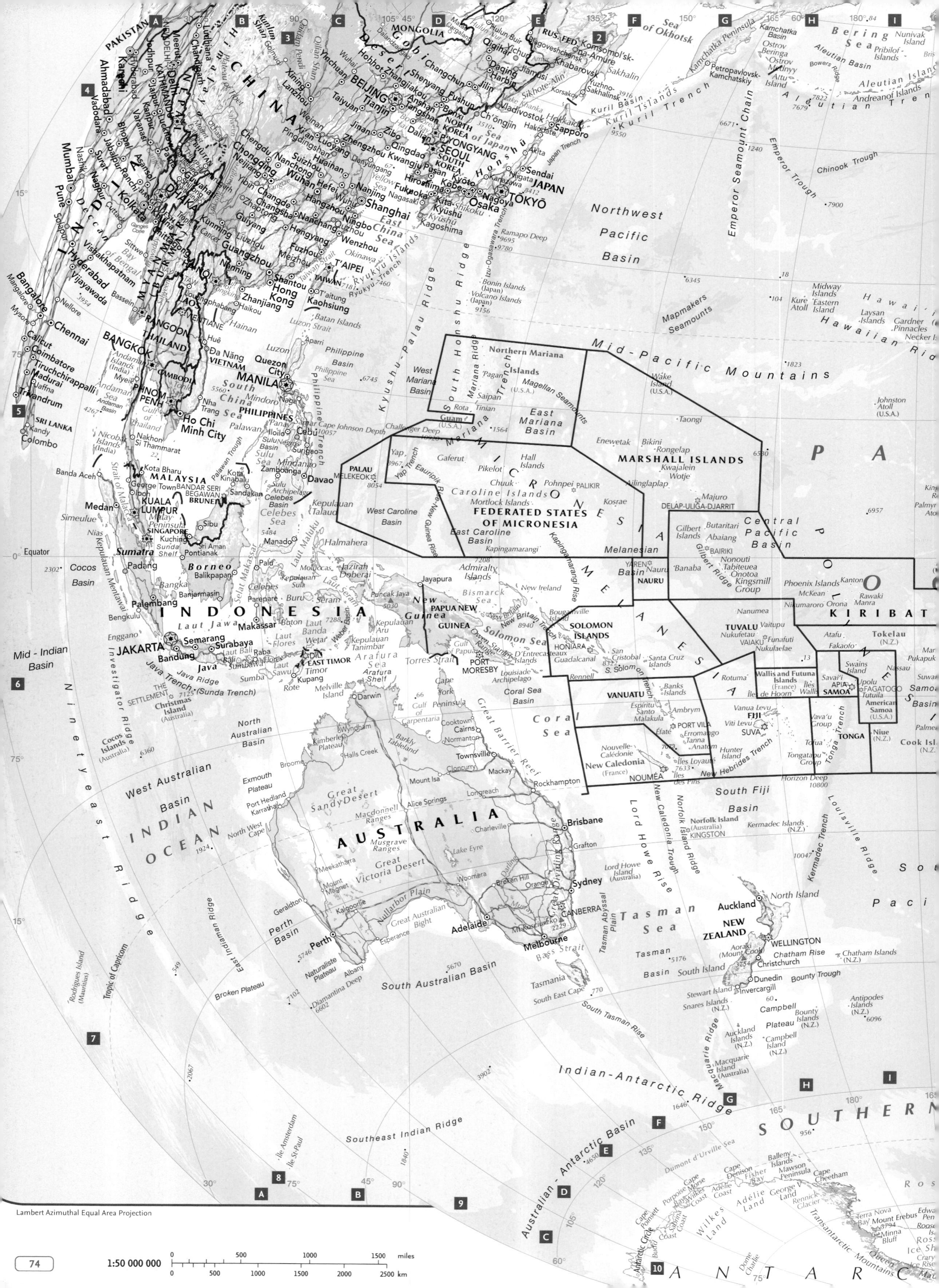

A
B
C
D
E
F
G
H
I
1
2
3
4
5
6
7
8
9
10
PAKISTAN
CHINA
MONGOLIA
Gobi Desert
RUS. FED.
Sea of Okhotsk
Kamchatka Peninsula
Bering Sea
Aleutian Basin
Aleutian Islands
Komsomol'sk-na-Amure
Khabarovsk
Sakhalin
Petropavlovsk-Kamchatskiy
Hulun Buir
Qiqihar
Daqing
Harbin
Jilin
Changchun
Shenyang
Fushun
BEIJING
Tianjin
Hohhot
Taiyuan
Yinchuan
Lanzhou
Xining
Xi'an
Luoyang
Zhengzhou
Jinan
Zibo
Qingdao
Dalian
NORTH KOREA
P'YONGYANG
SEOUL
SOUTH KOREA
Kwangju
Pusan
Sea of Japan
Vladivostok
Ch'ŏngjin
Sapporo
Hakodate
Honshū
Sendai
Niigata
JAPAN
TŌKYŌ
Nagoya
Ōsaka
Kyōto
Kōbe
Hiroshima
Kita-Kyūshū
Fukuoka
Nagasaki
Kagoshima
Kyūshū
Shikoku
Kuril Islands
Kuril Trench
Kuril Basin
Japan Trench
Izu-Ogasawara Trench
Ramapo Deep
Emperor Seamount Chain
Emperor Trough
Chinook Trough
Northwest Pacific Basin
Chengdu
Chongqing
Neijiang
Yibin
Nanchong
Suizhou
Wuhan
Hefei
Huainan
Nanjing
Wuhu
Shanghai
Hangzhou
Ningbo
Wenzhou
Nanchang
Changsha
Changde
Hengyang
Guiyang
Kunming
Liuzhou
Guangzhou
Nanning
Fuzhou
Meizhou
Shantou
Hong Kong
Zhanjiang
Haikou
Hainan
East China Sea
Yellow Sea
Okinawa
Ryukyu Islands
Ryukyu Trench
T'AIPEI
TAIWAN
Kaohsiung
T'aitung
Taiwan Strait
Luzon Strait
Batan Islands
INDIA
NEPAL
KATHMANDU
DELHI
NEW DELHI
Meerut
Chandigarh
Ludhiana
Hyderabad
Karachi
Ahmadabad
Vadodara
Jodhpur
Jaipur
Agra
Kanpur
Lucknow
Varanasi
Patna
Bhopal
Jabalpur
Nagpur
Ranchi
Asansol
Kolkata
DHAKA
BHUTAN
Guwahati
Mumbai
Nashik
Surat
Pune
Solapur
Deccan
Cuttack
Visakhapatnam
Vijayawada
Hyderabad
Bay of Bengal
Bangalore
Mangalore
Mysore
Nellore
Chennai
Calicut
Coimbatore
Tiruchchirappalli
Madurai
Jaffna
Trivandrum
SRI LANKA
Kandy
Colombo
MYANMAR
Sittwe
Chittagong
Bassein
RANGOON
LAOS
VIENTIANE
Loungphabang
HANOI
THAILAND
BANGKOK
Huê
Đa Năng
VIETNAM
CAMBODIA
PHNOM PENH
Ho Chi Minh City
Nha Trang
Gulf of Thailand
Andaman Islands (India)
Andaman Sea
Andaman Basin
Nicobar Islands (India)
Nakhon Si Thammarat
South China Sea
Luzon
Quezon City
MANILA
PHILIPPINES
Philippine Sea
Philippine Basin
Philippine Trench
Mindoro
Palawan
Panay
Iloilo
Cebu
Surigao
Samar
Cape Johnson Depth
Sulu Basin
Sulu Sea
Mindanao
Zamboanga
Davao
Palawan Trough
Kota Bharu
MALAYSIA
BANDAR SERI BEGAWAN
BRUNEI
Kota Kinabalu
Sandakan
Sulu Archipelago
Celebes Basin
Celebes Sea
George Town
Ipoh
KUALA LUMPUR
Malay Peninsula
SINGAPORE
Kuching
Sibu
Medan
Banda Aceh
Strait of Malacca
Simeulue
Nias
Sumatra
Padang
Sunda Shelf
Pontianak
Equator
Borneo
Balikpapan
Palu
Manado
Halmahera
Kepulauan Talaud
Kepulauan Sula
Moluccas
Laut Maluku
Celebes
Jazirah Doberai
Jayapura
Buru
Seram
Laut Seram
Banda
Laut Banda
Puncak Jaya
New Guinea
PAPUA NEW GUINEA
Bismarck Sea
New Britain
New Ireland
Admiralty Islands
Bougainville Island
SOLOMON ISLANDS
HONIARA
Guadalcanal
San Cristobal
Santa Cruz Islands
Solomon Sea
PORT MORESBY
Gulf of Papua
Owen Stanley Range
D'Entrecasteaux Islands
Louisiade Archipelago
Torres Strait
Arafura Sea
Arafura Shelf
Kepulauan Aru
Kepulauan Tanimbar
Weber Basin
Timor
DILI
EAST TIMOR
Kupang
Rote
Sawu
Sumba
Flores
Laut Flores
Bali
Lombok
Sumbawa
Raba
Laut Bali
Java
Java Sea
Laut Jawa
Makassar
Selat Makassar
Banjarmasin
INDONESIA
Bangka
Palembang
Bengkulu
Enggano
JAKARTA
Bandung
Semarang
Surabaya
Java Ridge
Java Trench (Sunda Trench)
Kepulauan Mentawai
Cocos Basin
Mid - Indian Basin
Investigator Ridge
Ninetyeast Ridge
THE SETTLEMENT
Christmas Island (Australia)
Cocos Islands (Australia)
North Australian Basin
West Australian Basin
INDIAN OCEAN
Kyushu-Palau Ridge
South Honshu Ridge
West Mariana Basin
Mariana Trench
Mariana Ridge
Northern Mariana Islands
Pagan
Saipan
Tinian
Rota
Guam (U.S.A.)
Magellan Seamounts
East Mariana Basin
Bonin Islands (Japan)
Volcano Islands (Japan)
Challenger Deep
Yap
Yap Trench
PALAU
MELEKEOK
Gaferut
Pikelot
Hall Islands
Chuuk
Caroline Islands
Mortlock Islands
Pohnpei
PALIKIR
Kosrae
FEDERATED STATES OF MICRONESIA
West Caroline Basin
East Caroline Basin
Kapingamarangi
Eauripik-New Guinea Rise
MICRONESIA
MELANESIA
Kapingamarangi Rise
Mid-Pacific Mountains
Wake Island (U.S.A.)
Taongi
Enewetak
Bikini
Rongelap
MARSHALL ISLANDS
Kwajalein
Wotje
Ailinglaplap
Majuro
DELAP-ULIGA-DJARRIT
Mapmakers Seamounts
Central Pacific Basin
Gilbert Islands
Butaritari
Abaiang
BAIRIKI
Nonouti
Tabiteuea
Onotoa
Kingsmill Group
Gilbert Ridge
Banaba
Nauru Basin
YAREN
NAURU
Phoenix Islands
Kanton
McKean
Nikumaroro
Orona
Rawaki
Manra
KIRIBATI
Nanumea
TUVALU
Nukufetau
Vaitupu
VAIAKU
Funafuti
Nukulaelae
Atafu
Fakaofo
Tokelau (N.Z.)
Swains Island
Wallis and Futuna Islands (France)
Îles Wallis
Île de Hoorn
Rotuma
Savai'i
APIA
SAMOA
Upolu
FAGATOGO
Tutuila
American Samoa (U.S.A.)
Nassau
Pukapuka
Vanua Levu
FIJI
Viti Levu
SUVA
Vava'u Group
Tofua
Tonga Trench
TONGA
Tongatapu Group
Niue (N.Z.)
Cook Islands (N.Z.)
Horizon Deep
VANUATU
Banks Islands
Espiritu Santo
Malakula
Ambrym
Éfaté
PORT VILA
Erromango
Tanna
Anatom
Hunter Island
New Hebrides Trench
Îles Loyauté
Nouvelle-Calédonie
New Caledonia (France)
NOUMÉA
Île des Pins
Coral Sea
Coral Sea Basin
Great Barrier Reef
Hawaiian Islands
Hawaiian Ridge
Midway Islands
Kure Atoll
Eastern Island
Laysan Island
Gardner Pinnacles
Necker Island
Johnston Atoll (U.S.A.)
PACIFIC
POLYNESIA
Darwin
Melville Island
Gulf of Carpentaria
Cape York Peninsula
Cooktown
Cairns
Normanton
Townsville
Mackay
Rockhampton
Cloncurry
Mount Isa
Barkly Tableland
Wyndham
Kimberley Plateau
Halls Creek
Broome
Exmouth Plateau
Port Hedland
Karratha
North West Cape
Great Sandy Desert
Macdonnell Ranges
Alice Springs
Longreach
AUSTRALIA
Musgrave Ranges
Charleville
Lake Eyre
Great Victoria Desert
Meekatharra
Mount Magnet
Geraldton
Kalgoorlie
Nullarbor Plain
Great Australian Bight
Perth
Perth Basin
Esperance
Albany
Naturaliste Plateau
Adelaide
Woomera
Broken Hill
Darling
Murray
Orange
Great Dividing Range
Brisbane
Grafton
Sydney
CANBERRA
Mt Kosciuszko
Melbourne
Bass Strait
Tasmania
South East Cape
Lord Howe Rise
Lord Howe Island (Australia)
New Caledonia Trough
Norfolk Island Ridge
Norfolk Island (Australia)
KINGSTON
South Fiji Basin
Kermadec Islands (N.Z.)
Kermadec Trench
Louisville Ridge
Tasman Sea
Tasman Abyssal Plain
Tasman Basin
NEW ZEALAND
North Island
Auckland
WELLINGTON
Aoraki (Mount Cook)
South Island
Christchurch
Dunedin
Invercargill
Stewart Island
Snares Islands (N.Z.)
Chatham Rise
Chatham Islands (N.Z.)
Bounty Trough
Campbell Plateau
Bounty Islands (N.Z.)
Antipodes Islands (N.Z.)
Campbell Island (N.Z.)
Auckland Islands (N.Z.)
Macquarie Island (Australia)
Macquarie Ridge
South Tasman Rise
South Australian Basin
Diamantina Deep
Broken Plateau
East Indiaman Ridge
Tropic of Capricorn
Rodrigues Island (Mauritius)
Île Amsterdam
Île St-Paul
Southeast Indian Ridge
Australian - Antarctic Basin
Indian-Antarctic Ridge
SOUTHERN
Dumont d'Urville Sea
Cape Poinsett
Budd Coast
Sabrina Coast
Porpoise Bay
Cape Morse
Wilkes Land
Adélie Coast
Adélie Land
Cape Denison
Fisher Bay
Balleny Islands
Mawson Peninsula
George V Land
Cape Cheetham
Rennick Glacier
Transantarctic Mountains
Terra Nova Bay
Mount Erebus
Minna Bluff
Antarctic Circle
Dome Charlie
ANTARCTICA
Lambert Azimuthal Equal Area Projection
1:50 000 000
0 500 1000 1500 miles
0 500 1000 1500 2000 2500 km

CANADA
Gulf of Alaska
Alexander Archipelago
Kodiak Island
Coast Mountains
Rocky Mountains
Edmonton
Calgary
Saskatoon
Regina
Winnipeg
Vancouver
Seattle
Victoria
Olympia
Portland
Salem
Eugene
Boise
Prince Rupert
Prince George
Queen Charlotte Sound
Tufts Abyssal Plain
Thunder Bay
Timmins
Quebec
Montreal
OTTAWA
Toronto
Detroit
Buffalo
Boston
Providence
New York
Philadelphia
Baltimore
WASHINGTON D.C.
Richmond
Minneapolis
St Paul
Milwaukee
Chicago
Des Moines
Omaha
Lincoln
Cleveland
Pittsburgh
Columbus
Indianapolis
Charleston
St Louis
Nashville
Raleigh
Charlotte
Columbia
Atlanta
Memphis
Huntsville
Macon
Savannah
Jacksonville
Montgomery
Mobile
Tallahassee
Grand Forks
Bismarck
Billings
Rapid City
Sioux Falls
Casper
Cheyenne
Denver
Topeka
Salt Lake City
UNITED STATES OF AMERICA
Great Basin
Colorado Plateau
Oklahoma City
Tulsa
Amarillo
Little Rock
Lubbock
Dallas
Fort Worth
Shreveport
Jackson
Baton Rouge
New Orleans
Houston
Austin
San Antonio
Corpus Christi
Sacramento
San Francisco
San Jose
Las Vegas
Albuquerque
Phoenix
Los Angeles
San Diego
Ensenada
Mexicali
Tucson
El Paso
Ciudad Juárez
Hermosillo
Chihuahua
Los Mochis
Matamoros
Monterrey
Orlando
Tampa
Miami
NASSAU
THE BAHAMAS
Great Abaco
Andros
ATLANTIC OCEAN
New England Seamounts
Corner Seamounts
Bermuda Rise
Bermuda (UK)
Hatteras Abyssal Plain
Sargasso Sea
Nares Deep
Nares Abyssal Plain
Mid-Atlantic Ridge
Tropic of Cancer
Gulf of Mexico
Sigsbee Deep
Guadalupe (Mexico)
Villa Insurgentes
La Paz
Gulf of California
Mazatlán
Durango
MEXICO
San Luis Potosí
Tampico
León
Guadalajara
Morelia
MEXICO CITY
Puebla
Veracruz
Poza Rica
Mérida
Bahía de Campeche
Villahermosa
Oaxaca
Acapulco
Islas Revillagigedo (Mexico)
HAVANA
CUBA
Yucatan Channel
Cayman Islands
Holguín
PORT-AU-PRINCE
HAITI
DOMINICAN REPUBLIC
SANTO DOMINGO
Puerto Rico Trench
SAN JUAN
Puerto Rico (U.S.A.)
ANTIGUA AND BARBUDA
Guadeloupe (France)
ST KITTS AND NEVIS
DOMINICA
Martinique (France)
ST LUCIA
BARBADOS
ST VINCENT AND THE GRENADINES
GRENADA
PORT OF SPAIN
TRINIDAD AND TOBAGO
JAMAICA
KINGSTON
Caribbean Sea
Venezuelan Basin
Colombian Basin
Demerara Abyssal Plain
BELIZE
BELMOPAN
GUATEMALA
GUATEMALA CITY
HONDURAS
TEGUCIGALPA
SAN SALVADOR
EL SALVADOR
NICARAGUA
MANAGUA
SAN JOSÉ
COSTA RICA
PANAMA
PANAMA CITY
Gulf of Panama
Middle America Trench
Barranquilla
Cartagena
Maracaibo
Barquisimeto
CARACAS
Cumaná
Ciudad Bolívar
GEORGETOWN
PARAMARIBO
CAYENNE
GUYANA
SURINAME
French Guiana
VENEZUELA
San Cristóbal
Puerto Ayacucho
Boa Vista
Medellín
Tunja
BOGOTA
COLOMBIA
Ibagué
Cali
Neiva
Pasto
Esmeraldas
QUITO
ECUADOR
Guayaquil
Isla de Coco (Costa Rica)
Isla de Malpelo (Colombia)
Cocos Ridge
Galapagos Islands (Ecuador)
Galapagos Rise
Île Clipperton (France)
Equator
Belém
São Luís
Santarém
Manaus
Iquitos
Sullana
Chiclayo
Trujillo
Tarapoto
Pucallpa
PERU
LIMA
Huancayo
Cusco
Ica
Arequipa
Juliaca
Peru Basin
Nazca Ridge (Southwest Peru Ridge)
Peru-Chile Trench
BRAZIL
Selvas
Cruzeiro do Sul
Rio Branco
Porto Velho
Teresina
LA PAZ
BOLIVIA
SUCRE
Santa Cruz
Potosí
Arica
Iquique
Antofagasta
Cuiabá
Salvador
BRASILIA
Goiânia
Campo Grande
Uberaba
Belo Horizonte
Teófilo Otôni
Abrolhos Bank
Vitória
PARAGUAY
ASUNCIÓN
Campinas
São Paulo
Rio de Janeiro
Curitiba
Florianópolis
Santos Plateau
Tropic of Capricorn
Vitória Seamount
Islas de los Desventurados (Chile)
Chile Basin
Archipiélago Juan Fernández (Chile)
Valparaíso
SANTIAGO
Talca
Concepción
Chillán
Córdoba
Rosario
BUENOS AIRES
URUGUAY
MONTEVIDEO
Porto Alegre
Rio Grande
Santa Fe
Corrientes
Valdivia
Puerto Montt
Isla de Chiloé
Archipiélago de los Chonos
Neuquén
Bahía Blanca
Mar del Plata
Argentine Rise
ARGENTINA
ANDES
Viedma
Trelew
Golfo San Matías
Comodoro Rivadavia
Golfo San Jorge
Argentine Basin
Argentine Abyssal Plain
Falkland Plateau
Falkland Islands (U.K.)
STANLEY
Bahía Grande
Río Gallegos
Punta Arenas
Puerto Natales
Ushuaia
Isla Grande de Tierra del Fuego
Isla de los Estados
Cape Horn
Drake Passage
Yaghan Basin
Scotia Sea
Scotia Ridge
Mornington Abyssal Plain
PACIFIC OCEAN
Northeast Pacific Basin
East Pacific Rise
Gallego Rise
Honolulu
Maui
Hawai'i
Kiritimati
Malden Island
Vostok Island
Caroline Island (Millennium Island)
Flint Island
Marquesas Islands (Îles Marquises)
Nuku Hiva
Hiva Oa
Îles du Désappointement
Îles du Roi-Georges
Tuamotu Islands (Archipel des Tuamotu)
French Polynesia
PAPEETE
Tahiti
Raiatea
Society Islands (Archipel de la Société)
Manuae
Palliser
Raroia
Anaa
Hao
Héréhérétué
Moruroa
Groupe Actéon
Îles du Duc de Gloucester
Îles Gambier
Maria
Tubuai
Raivavae
Tubuai Islands (Îles Australes)
Rapa
Tiki Basin
Pitcairn Islands (U.K.)
Pitcairn Island
Henderson Island
Ducie Island
ADAMSTOWN
Isla Sala y Gómez (Chile)
Easter Island (Isla de Pascua) (Chile)
Roggeveen Basin
Southwest Basin
Challenger Fracture Zone
Pacific-Antarctic Ridge
Southeast Pacific Basin
Amundsen Abyssal Plain
Amundsen Ridge
Amundsen Sea
Antarctic Circle
Siple Island
Grant Island
Carney Island
Burke Island
Thurston Island
Peter I Island
Driscoll Island
Marie Byrd Land
Rockefeller Plateau
Whitmore Mountains
West Antarctica
Walgreen Coast
Hudson Mountains
Bellingshausen Sea
Alexander Island
Antarctic Peninsula
Palmer Land
Livingston Island
Ronne Entrance
Equator

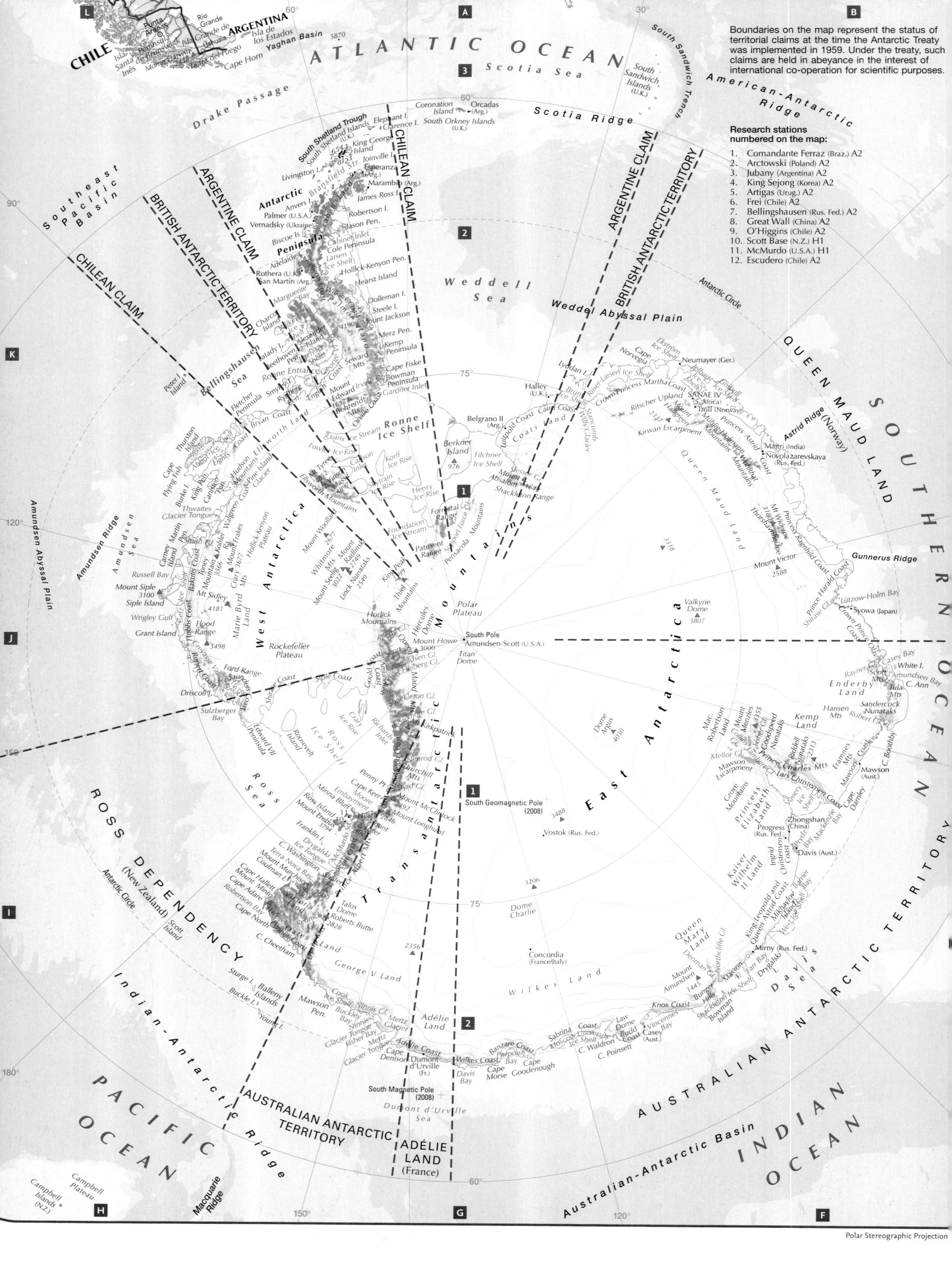

Research stations
numbered on the map:

1. Comandante Ferraz (Braz.) A2
2. Arctowski (Poland) A2
3. Jubany (Argentina) A2
4. King Sejong (Korea) A2
5. Artigas (Urug.) A2
6. Frei (Chile) A2
7. Bellingshausen (Rus. Fed.) A2
8. Great Wall (China) A2
9. O'Higgins (Chile) A2
10. Scott Base (N.Z.) H1
11. McMurdo (U.S.A.) H1
12. Escudero (Chile) A2

Antarctica

1:26 000 000

0   200   400   600   800   1000 miles
0   200 400 600 800 1000 1200 1400 1600 km

Polar Stereographic Projection

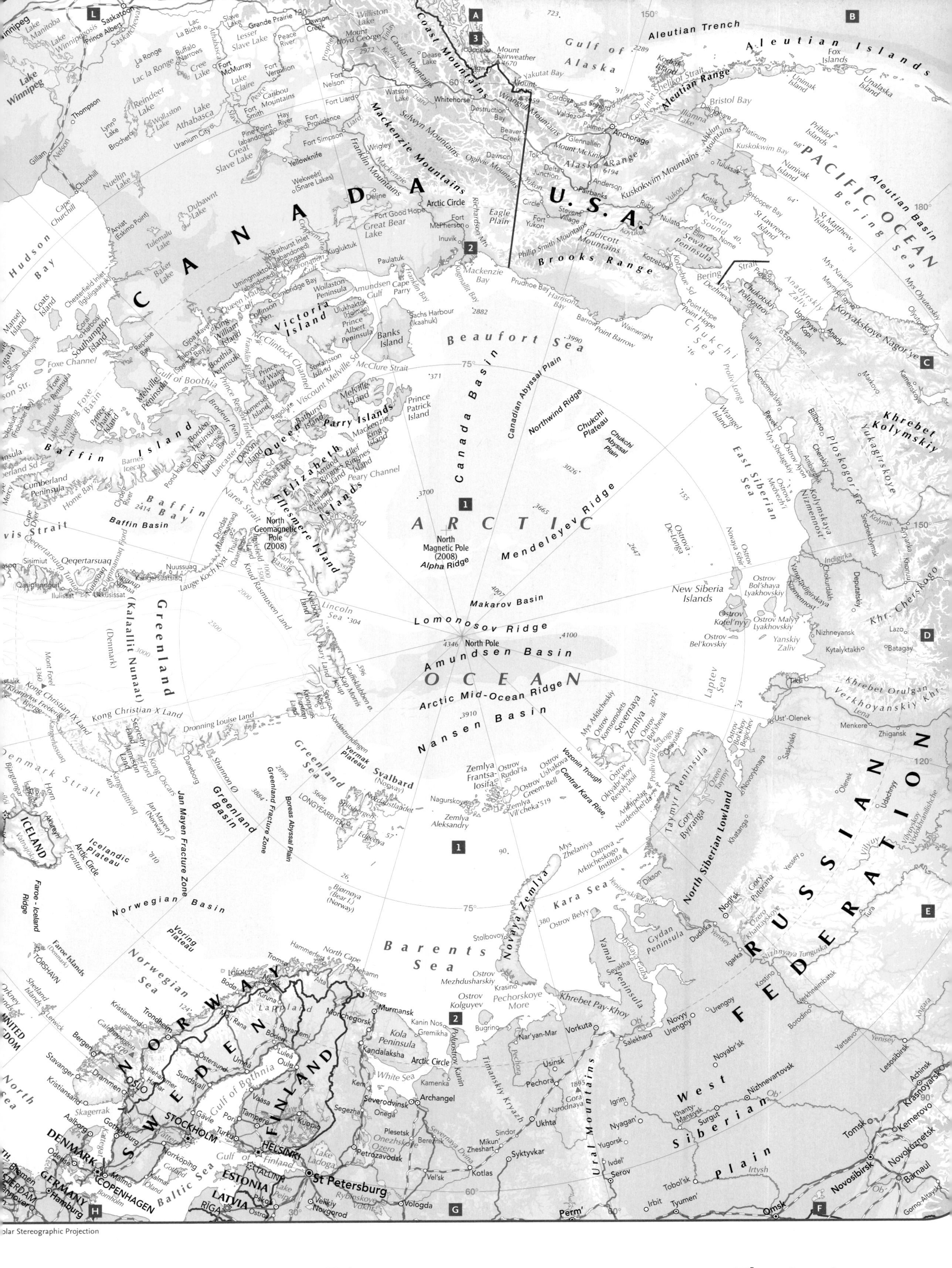

The Arctic

1:26 000 000

0 200 400 600 800 1000 miles

0 200 400 600 800 1000 1200 1400 1600 km

Polar Stereographic Projection

Index

Introduction to the index

The index includes all names shown on the reference maps in the atlas. Each entry includes the country or geographical area in which the feature is located, a page number and an alphanumeric reference. Additional entry details and aspects of the index are explained below.

Name forms

The names policy in this atlas is generally to use local name forms which are officially recognized by the governments of the countries concerned. Rules established by the Permanent Committee on Geographical Names for British Official Use (PCGN) are applied to the conversion of non-roman alphabet names, for example in the Russian Federation, into the roman alphabet used in English.

However, English conventional name forms are used for the most well-known places for which such a form is in common use. In these cases, the local form is included in brackets on the map and appears as a cross-reference in the index. Other alternative names, such as well-known historical names or those in other languages, may also be included in brackets on the map and as cross-references in the index. All country names and those for international physical features appear in their English forms. Names appear in full in the index, although they may appear in abbreviated form on the maps.

Referencing

Names are referenced by page number and by grid reference. The grid reference relates to the alphanumeric values which appear on the edges of each map. These reflect the graticule on the map – the letter relates to longitude divisions, the number to latitude divisions.

Names are generally referenced to the largest scale map page on which they appear. For large geographical features, including countries, the reference is to the largest scale map on which the feature appears in its entirety, or on which the majority of it appears.

Rivers are referenced to their lowest downstream point – either their mouth or their confluence with another river. The river name will generally be positioned as close to this point as possible.

Alternative names

Alternative names appear as cross-references and refer the user to the index entry for the form of the name used on the map.

For rivers with multiple names - for example those which flow through several countries - all alternative name forms are included within the main index entries, with details of the countries in which each form applies.

Administrative qualifiers

Administrative divisions are included in entries to differentiate duplicate names - entries of exactly the same name and feature type within the one country - where these division names are shown on the maps. In such cases, duplicate names are alphabetized in the order of the administrative division names.

Additional qualifiers are included for names within selected geographical areas, to indicate more clearly their location.

Descriptors

Entries, other than those for towns and cities, include a descriptor indicating the type of geographical feature. Descriptors are not included where the type of feature is implicit in the name itself, unless there is a town or city of exactly the same name.

Insets

Where relevant, the index clearly indicates [inset] if a feature appears on an inset map.

Alphabetical order

The Icelandic characters Þ and þ are transliterated and alphabetized as 'Th' and 'th'. The German character ß is alphabetized as 'ss'. Names beginning with Mac or Mc are alphabetized exactly as they appear. The terms Saint, Sainte, etc, are abbreviated to St, Ste, etc, but alphabetized as if in the full form.

Numerical entries

Entries beginning with numerals appear at the beginning of the index, in numerical order. Elsewhere, numerals are alphabetized before 'a'.

Permuted terms

Names beginning with generic geographical terms are permuted - the descriptive term is placed after, and the index alphabetized by, the main part of the name. For example, Mount Everest is indexed as Everest, Mount; Lake Superior as Superior, Lake. This policy is applied to all languages. Permuting has not been applied to names of towns, cities or administrative divisions beginning with such geographical terms. These remain in their full form, for example, Lake Isabella, USA.

Abbreviations

admin. dist.	administrative district	IL	Illinois	plat.	plateau
admin. div.	administrative division	imp. l.	impermanent lake	P.N.G.	Papua New Guinea
admin. reg.	administrative region	IN	Indiana	Port.	Portugal
Afgh.	Afghanistan	Indon.	Indonesia	pref.	prefecture
AK	Alaska	Kazakh.	Kazakhstan	prov.	province
AL	Alabama	KS	Kansas	pt	point
Alg.	Algeria	KY	Kentucky	Qld	Queensland
AR	Arkansas	Kyrg.	Kyrgyzstan	Que.	Québec
Arg.	Argentina	l.	lake	r.	river
aut. comm.	autonomous community	LA	Louisiana	reg.	region
aut. reg.	autonomous region	lag.	lagoon	res.	reserve
aut. rep.	autonomous republic	Lith.	Lithuania	resr	reservoir
AZ	Arizona	Lux.	Luxembourg	RI	Rhode Island
Azer.	Azerbaijan	MA	Massachusetts	Rus. Fed.	Russian Federation
b.	bay	Madag.	Madagascar	S.	South, Southern
Bangl.	Bangladesh	Man.	Manitoba	S.A.	South Australia
B.C.	British Columbia	MD	Maryland	salt l.	salt lake
Bol.	Bolivia	ME	Maine	Sask.	Saskatchewan
Bos.-Herz.	Bosnia-Herzegovina	Mex.	Mexico	SC	South Carolina
Bulg.	Bulgaria	MI	Michigan	SD	South Dakota
c.	cape	MN	Minnesota	sea chan.	sea channel
CA	California	MO	Missouri	Sing.	Singapore
Cent. Afr. Rep.	Central African Republic	Moz.	Mozambique	Switz.	Switzerland
CO	Colorado	MS	Mississippi	Tajik.	Tajikistan
Col.	Colombia	MT	Montana	Tanz.	Tanzania
CT	Connecticut	mt.	mountain	Tas.	Tasmania
Czech Rep.	Czech Republic	mts	mountains	terr.	territory
DC	District of Columbia	N.	North, Northern	Thai.	Thailand
DE	Delaware	nat. park	national park	TN	Tennessee
Dem. Rep. Congo	Democratic Republic of the Congo	N.B.	New Brunswick	Trin. and Tob.	Trinidad and Tobago
depr.	depression	NC	North Carolina	Turkm.	Turkmenistan
des.	desert	ND	North Dakota	TX	Texas
Dom. Rep.	Dominican Republic	NE	Nebraska	U.A.E.	United Arab Emirates
E.	East, Eastern	Neth.	Netherlands	U.K.	United Kingdom
Equat. Guinea	Equatorial Guinea	NH	New Hampshire	Ukr.	Ukraine
esc.	escarpment	NJ	New Jersey	U.S.A.	United States of America
est.	estuary	NM	New Mexico	UT	Utah
Eth.	Ethiopia	N.S.	Nova Scotia	Uzbek.	Uzbekistan
Fin.	Finland	N.S.W.	New South Wales	VA	Virginia
FL	Florida	N.T.	Northern Territory	Venez.	Venezuela
for.	forest	NV	Nevada	Vic.	Victoria
Fr. Guiana	French Guiana	N.W.T.	Northwest Territories	vol.	volcano
F.Y.R.O.M.	Former Yugoslav Republic of Macedonia	NY	New York	vol. crater	volcanic crater
g.	gulf	N.Z.	New Zealand	VT	Vermont
GA	Georgia	OH	Ohio	W.	West, Western
Guat.	Guatemala	OK	Oklahoma	WA	Washington
HI	Hawaii	OR	Oregon	W.A.	Western Australia
H.K.	Hong Kong	PA	Pennsylvania	WI	Wisconsin
Hond.	Honduras	Para.	Paraguay	WV	West Virginia
i.	island	P.E.I.	Prince Edward Island	WY	Wyoming
IA	Iowa	pen.	peninsula	Y.T.	Yukon Territory
ID	Idaho	Phil.	Philippines		

y Severnyy Rus. Fed. 11 S3
de Outubro Angola see Xá-Muteba
de Julio Arg. 70 D5
de Mayo Buenos Aires Arg. 70 D5
de Mayo La Pampa Arg. 70 C5
0 Mile House Canada 62 C1

aenraa Denmark 15 F9
chen Germany 17 K5
lborg Denmark 15 G8
lborg Bugt b. Denmark 15 G8
len Germany 17 M6
lesund Norway see Ålesund
ley Belgium 17 I5
ley Lebanon see Aley
naar Fin. see Inari
rhus Denmark see Århus
rhus Bugt b. Denmark 15 F8
a China 42 I6
a Dem. Rep. Congo 48 D3
a Nigeria 46 D4
acaxis r. Brazil 69 G4
ädän Iran 35 H5
adan Turkm. 33 I2
ädeh Iran 35 I8
ädeh Tashk Iran 35 I5
adla Alg. 22 D5
aeté Brazil 71 B2
aetetuba Brazil 69 I4
agnar Qi China see Xilinhot
aiang atoll Kiribati 74 H5
akaliki Nigeria 46 D4
akan Rus. Fed. 42 G2
ak Niger 46 D3
ancay Peru 68 D6
ariringa atoll Kiribati see Kanton
arkūh, Kavīr-e des. Iran 35 I5
arqū Iran 35 I5
ashrashar Iran see Neyshābūr
ashiri Japan 44 G3
ashiri-wan b. Japan 44 G3
au P.N.G. 56 I
aya, Lake Eth. 48 D3
aya Wenz r. Eth./Sudan see Blue Nile
ay Wenz r. Eth./Sudan 48 D3 see Blue Nile
aza Rus. Fed. 42 G2
ba Cent. Afr. Rep. 48 B3
bāsābād Iran 35 I4
basanta Sardegna Italy 26 C4
batis Villa France see Abbeville
be, Lake Djibouti/Eth. 32 F7
beville France 24 E4
beville LA U.S.A. 63 I6
beyfeale Ireland 21 C5
beytown U.K. 18 D4
borrträsk Sweden 14 K4
bot, Mount Australia 56 D4
bot Ice Shelf Antarctica 76 K2
bott VA U.S.A. 64 E4
bottabad Pak. 33 L3
bod al 'Azīz Iran Syria 35 F3
bod al Kūrī i. Yemen 32 H7
bod Allah, Khawr sea chan. Iraq/Kuwait 35 H5
bod al Ma'asir well Saudi Arabia 39 D4
bdānān Iran 35 H4
bdollāhābād Iran 35 I4
bdulino Rus. Fed. 11 Q5
béché Chad 47 F3
bellinum Italy see Avellino
bel Tasman National Park N.Z. 59 D5
bengourou Côte d'Ivoire 46 C4
benrá Denmark see Aabenraa
beokuta Nigeria 46 D4
beraeron U.K. 19 C6
bercorn Zambia see Mbala
bercrombie r. Australia 58 D4
berdare U.K. 19 D7
berdaron U.K. 19 C6
berdeen Australia 58 E4
berdeen S. Africa 50 G7
berdeen U.K. 20 G3
berdeen MD U.S.A. 64 D3
berdeen NY U.S.A. 64 C1
berdovey U.K. 19 C6
berfeldy U.K. 20 F4
berford U.K. 18 F5
berfoyle U.K. 20 E4
bergavenny U.K. 19 D7
bergwaun U.K. see Fishguard
berhonddu U.K. see Brecon
bermaw U.K. see Barmouth
berporth U.K. 19 C6
bersoch U.K. 19 C6
bertawe U.K. see Swansea
berteifi U.K. see Cardigan
berystwyth U.K. 19 C6
beshr Chad see Abéché
bez' Rus. Fed. 11 S2
bhā Saudi Arabia 32 F6
bhar Iran 35 H5
biad, Bahr el r. Sudan/Uganda 32 D6 see White Nile
bidjan Côte d'Ivoire 46 C4
bijatta-Shalla National Park Eth. 48 D3
bilene TX U.S.A. 62 H5
bingdon U.K. 19 F7
bington Reef Australia 56 E3
binsk Rus. Fed. 34 L1
bominga Australia 55 F6
bo Fin. see Turku
bohar India 36 C3
boisso Côte d'Ivoire 46 C4
bomey Benin 46 D4
bong Mbang Cameroon 46 E4
bou Déia Chad 47 E3
bovyan Armenia 35 G2
boyne U.K. 20 G3
bqaiq Saudi Arabia 35 H5
bramov, Mys pt Rus. Fed. 12 I2
bra Pampa Arg. 70 C2
bri Sudan 32 D5
brolhos Bank sea feature S. Atlantic Ocean 72 F7
bruzzo, Parco Nazionale d' nat. park Italy 26 E4
bsalom, Mount Antarctica 76 B1
bsaroka Range mts U.S.A. 62 E3
btar, Jabal al hills Syria 39 C2
bū al Husayn, Qā' imp. l. Jordan 39 D3

Abū 'Alī i. Saudi Arabia 35 H6
Abū 'Āmūd, Wādī watercourse Jordan 39 C4
Abū 'Arīsh Saudi Arabia 32 F6
Abū 'Aweigîla well Egypt see Abū 'Uwayqilah
Abu Deleiq Sudan 32 D6
Abu Dhabi U.A.E. 33 H5
Abū Du'ān Syria 39 D1
Abu Gubeiha Sudan 32 D7
Abū Hafnah, Wādī watercourse Jordan 39 C3
Abu Haggag Egypt see Ra's al Hikmah
Abū Hallūfah, Jabal h. Jordan 39 C4
Abu Hamed Sudan 32 D6
Abuja Nigeria 46 D4
Abū Jurdhān Jordan 39 B4
Abū Kamāl Syria 35 F4
Abumombazi Dem. Rep. Congo 48 C3
Abunã r. Bol. 68 E5
Abunã Brazil 68 E5
Abune Yosēf mt. Eth. 32 E7
Abū Nujaym Libya 47 E1
Abū Qa'tūr Syria 39 C2
Abū Rawthah, Jabal mt. Egypt 39 B5
Aburo mt. Dem. Rep. Congo 48 D3
Abu Road India 31 G4
Abū Rujmayn, Jabal mts Syria 39 D2
Abū Rûtha, Gebel mt. Egypt see Abū Rawthah, Jabal
Abu Simbil Egypt see Abū Sunbul
Abū Sunbul Egypt 32 D5
Abū Ţarfā', Wādī watercourse Egypt 39 A5
Abut Head hd N.Z. 59 C6
Abū 'Uwayqilah well Egypt 39 B4
Abu Zabad Sudan 32 C7
Abū Zabī U.A.E. see Abu Dhabi
Abū Zanimah Egypt 34 D5
Abu Zenîma Egypt see Abū Zanimah
Abyad Sudan 32 C7
Abyad, Jabal al mts Syria 39 C2
Abyār al Hakīm well Libya 34 A5
Abyei Sudan 32 C8
Abydos Australia 54 B5
Abyssinia country Africa see Ethiopia
Academician Vernadskiy research stn Antarctica see Vernadsky
Academy Bay Rus. Fed. see Akademii, Zaliv
Acadia prov. Canada see Nova Scotia
Açailândia Brazil 69 I5
Acamarachi mt. Chile see Pili, Cerro
Acampamento de Caça do Mucusso Angola 49 C5
Acandí Col. 68 C2
A Cañiza Spain 25 B2
Acaponeta Mex. 66 C4
Acapulco Mex. 66 E5
Acapulco de Juárez Mex. see Acapulco
Acará Brazil 69 I4
Acaraú Brazil 69 J4
Acaray, Represa de resr Para. 70 E3
Acarigua Venez. 68 E2
Acatlán Mex. 66 E5
Accho Israel see 'Akko
Accomac VA U.S.A. 64 D4
Accra Ghana 46 C4
Accrington U.K. 18 E5
Achacachi Bol. 68 E7
Achaguas Venez. 68 E2
Achalpur India 36 D5
Achampet India 38 C2
Achan Rus. Fed. 44 D2
Achayvayam Rus. Fed. 29 S3
Acheng China 44 B3
Achhota India 38 D1
Achill Ireland 21 C4
Achillbeg Island Ireland 21 C4
Achill Island Ireland 21 B4
Achiltibuie U.K. 20 D2
Achinsk Rus. Fed. 28 K4
Achit Nuur l. Mongolia 42 G3
Achit Rus. Fed. 11 R4
Achkhoy-Martan Rus. Fed. 35 G2
Achna Cyprus 39 A2
Achnasheen U.K. 20 D3
Acıgöl l. Turkey 27 M6
Acıpayam Turkey 27 M6
Acireale Sicilia Italy 26 F6
Acklins Island Bahamas 67 J4
Acle U.K. 19 I6
Aconcagua, Cerro mt. Arg. 70 B4
Acopiara Brazil 69 K5
Açores terr. N. Atlantic Ocean see Azores
Açores, Arquipélago dos terr. N. Atlantic Ocean see Azores
A Coruña Spain 25 B2
Acqui Terme Italy 26 C2
Acragas Sicilia Italy see Agrigento
Acraman, Lake imp. l. Australia 57 A7
Acre r. Brazil 68 E5
Acre Israel see 'Akko
Acre, Bay of Israel see Haifa, Bay of
Acri Italy 26 G5
Ács Hungary 17 Q7
Actaeon Group is Fr. Polynesia see Actéon, Groupe
Actéon, Groupe is Fr. Polynesia 75 K7
Acton Ont. Canada 64 A1
Acton CA U.S.A. 65 C3
Acungui Brazil 71 A4
Acunum Acusio France see Montélimar
Ada OK U.S.A. 63 D5
Adaja r. Spain 25 D3
Adalia Turkey see Antalya
Adam Oman 33 I5
Adam, Mount h. Falkland Is 70 E8
Adamantina Brazil 71 A3
Adams MA U.S.A. 64 E1
Adam's Peak Sri Lanka 38 D5
Adamstown Pitcairn Is 75 L7
'Adan Yemen see Aden
Adana Turkey 39 B1
Adana prov. Turkey 39 B1
Adana Yemen see Aden
Adapazarı Turkey 27 N4
Adare Ireland 21 D5
Adare, Cape Antarctica 76 H2
Adavale Australia 57 D5
Ad Dabbah Sudan see Ed Debba
Ad Dafinah Saudi Arabia 32 F5
Ad Dahnā' des. Saudi Arabia 32 G5
Ad Dakhla W. Sahara 46 B2
Ad Damir Sudan see Ed Damer
Ad Dammām Saudi Arabia see Dammam
Addanki India 38 C3
Ad Dār al Hamrā' Saudi Arabia 32 E4
Ad Darb Saudi Arabia 32 F6
Ad Dawādimī Saudi Arabia 32 F5
Ad Dawhah Qatar see Doha
Ad Dawr Iraq 35 F4
Ad Dayy plain Syria 39 C2
Ad Dayr Iraq 35 G5
Ad Dibdibah plain Saudi Arabia 35 G6
Ad Diffah plat. Egypt see Libyan Plateau
Addis Ababa Eth. 48 D3
Addison NY U.S.A. 64 C1
Ad Dīwānīyah Iraq 35 G5
Addlestone U.K. 19 G7

Addo Elephant National Park S. Africa 51 G7
Ad Duwayd well Saudi Arabia 35 F5
Ad Duwaym Sudan see Ed Dueim
Adegaon India 36 D5
Adelaide Australia 57 B7
Adelaide r. Australia 54 E3
Adelaide Island Antarctica 76 L2
Adelaide River Australia 54 E3
Adele Island Australia 54 C3
Adélie Coast Antarctica 76 G2
Adélie Land Antarctica 76 G2
Adelong Australia 58 D5
Aden Yemen 32 F7
Aden, Gulf of Somalia/Yemen 32 G7
Adena OH U.S.A. 64 A2
Aderbissinat Niger 46 D3
Aderno Sicilia Italy see Adrano
Adesar India 36 B5
Adh Dhāyūf well Saudi Arabia 35 G6
'Adhfā' well Saudi Arabia 35 F5
'Adhiriyāt, Jibāl al mts Jordan 39 C4
Adi i. Indon. 41 I8
Ādī Ārk'ay Eth. 32 E7
Adige r. Italy 26 E2
Ādigrat Eth. 48 D2
Adilabad India 38 C2
Adilcevaz Turkey 35 F3
Adīrī Libya 47 E2
Adirondack Mountains NY U.S.A. 64 D1
Ādīs Ābeba Eth. see Addis Ababa
Adi Ugri Eritrea see Mendefera
Adıyaman Turkey 34 E3
Adjud Romania 27 L1
Admiralty Island Canada 61 K1
Admiralty Island National Monument-Kootznoowoo Wilderness nat. park U.S.A. 60 E4
Admiralty Islands P.N.G. 52 E2
Ado-Ekiti Nigeria 46 D4
Adok Sudan 32 D8
Adonara i. Indon. 54 C2
Adoni India 38 C3
Ado-Tymovo Rus. Fed. 44 F2
Adour r. France 24 D5
Adra Spain 25 E5
Adramyttium Turkey see Edremit
Adramyttium, Gulf of Turkey see Edremit Körfezi
Adrano Sicilia Italy 26 F6
Adrar Alg. 46 C2
Adrar hills Mali see Ifôghas, Adrar des
Adré Chad 47 F3
Adrian TX U.S.A. 62 G4
Adrian MI U.S.A. 64 C2
Adrianople Turkey see Edirne
Adrianopolis Turkey see Edirne
Adriatic Sea Europe 26 E2
Adua Eth. see Ādwa
Adunara i. Indon. see Adonara
Adusa Dem. Rep. Congo 48 C3
Aduwa Eth. see Ādwa
Adverse Well Australia 54 C5
Ādwa Eth. 48 D2
Adycha r. Rus. Fed. 29 O3
Adyk Rus. Fed. 13 J7
Adzopé Côte d'Ivoire 46 C4
Aegean Sea Greece/Turkey 27 K5
Aegina i. Greece see Aigina
Aegyptus country Africa see Egypt
Aela Jordan see Al 'Aqabah
Aelana Jordan see Al 'Aqabah
Ailt an Chorráin Ireland 21 D3
Aelia Capitolina Israel/West Bank see Jerusalem
Aelönlaplap atoll Marshall Is see Ailinglaplap
Aenus Turkey see Enez
Aeserina Italy see Isernia
A Estrada Spain 25 B2
Afabet Eritrea 32 E6
Afanas'yevo Rus. Fed. 12 L4
Afghânestân country Asia see Afghanistan
Afghanistan country Asia 33 K3
Afgooye Somalia 48 E3
'Afif Saudi Arabia 32 F5
Afiun Karahissar Turkey see Afyon
Åfjord Norway 14 G5
Aflou Alg. 22 E5
Afmadow Somalia 48 E3
Afogados da Ingazoira Brazil 69 K5
A Fonsagrada Spain 25 C2
Afonso Cláudio Brazil 71 C3
Āfrēra Terara vol. Eth. 32 F7
Africa Nova country Africa see Tunisia
'Afrîn Syria 39 C1
'Afrîn, Nahr r. Syria/Turkey 39 C1
Afşin Turkey 34 E3
Afuá Brazil 69 H4
'Afula Israel 39 B3
Afyon Turkey 27 N5
Afyonkarahisar Turkey see Afyon
Agadès Niger see Agadez
Agadez Niger 46 D3
Agadir Morocco 46 C1
Agadyr' Kazakh. 42 C3
Agalega Islands Mauritius 73 L6
Agara Georgia 35 F2
Agartala India 37 G5
Agashi India 38 B2
Agate r. Georgia 35 F2
Agatha France see Agde
Agathonisi i. Greece 27 L6
Agatti i. India 38 B4
Agboville Côte d'Ivoire 46 C4
Ağcabädi Azer. 35 G2
Agdam Azer. 35 G3
Ağdaş Azer. see Ağdaş
Agde France 24 F5
Agdzhabedi Azer. see Ağcabädi
Agedabia Libya see Ajdabiyā
Agen France 24 E4
Aggeneys S. Africa 50 D5
Aggtelek nat. park Hungary 17 R6
Aghil Pass China 36 D1
Ağın Turkey 35 F3
Aginskoye Rus. Fed. 42 G1
Aginum France see Agen
a-Jiddet des. Oman see Harāsīs, Jiddat al
Agios Dimitrios Greece 27 J5
Agios Efstratios i. Greece 27 K5
Agios Georgios i. Greece 27 J6
Agios Nikolaos Greece 27 K7
Agiou Orous, Kolpos b. Greece 27 J4
Agioi Theodoros Cyprus 39 B2
Agiou Greece see Aigio
Agnes, Mount h. Australia 55 B6
Agnew Australia 55 C6
Agnibilékrou Côte d'Ivoire 46 C4
Agnita Romania 27 K2
Agniye-Afanas'yevsk Rus. Fed. 44 E2
Agra India 36 D4
Agrakhanskiy Poluostrov pen. Rus. Fed. 35 G2
Agram Croatia see Zagreb
Ağrı Turkey 35 F3
Agri r. Italy 26 G4
Agria Gramvousa i. Greece 27 J7
Agrigento Sicilia Italy 26 E6
Agrigentum Sicilia Italy see Agrigento
Agrinio Greece 27 I5
Agropoli Italy 26 F4
Agryz Rus. Fed. 11 Q4

Ağsu Azer. 35 H2
Agua, Volcán de vol. Guat. 66 F6
Agua Clara Brazil 70 F2
Aguadilla Puerto Rico 67 K5
Agua Escondida Arg. 70 C5
Aguanga CA U.S.A. 65 D4
Aguapeí r. Brazil 71 A3
Agua Prieta Mex. 66 C3
Aguaro-Guariquito, Parque Nacional nat. park Venez. 68 E2
Aguascalientes Mex. 66 D4
Agudos Brazil 71 A3
Águeda r. Port. 25 B3
Aguelhok Mali 46 D3
Aguemour reg. Alg. 46 D2
Aguié Niger 46 D3
Aguilar de Campóo Spain 25 D2
Aguilas Spain 25 F5
Agulhas, Cape S. Africa 50 E8
Agulhas Basin sea feature Southern Ocean 73 J9
Agulhas Plateau sea feature Southern Ocean 73 J8
Agulhas Ridge sea feature S. Atlantic Ocean 72 I8
Agva Turkey 27 M4
Agvali Rus. Fed. 35 G2
Ahaggar plat. Alg. see Hoggar
Ahar Iran 35 G3
Ahaura N.Z. 59 C6
Ahipara Bay N.Z. 59 D2
Ahiri India 38 D2
Ahklun Mountains U.S.A. 60 B4
Ahmadabad India 36 C5
Ahmad al Bāqir, Jabal mt. Jordan 39 B5
Ahmadnagar India 38 B2
Ahmadpur East Pak. 33 L4
Ahmar mts Eth. 48 E3
Ahmar Mountains Eth. see Ahmar
Ahmedabad India see Ahmadabad
Ahmednagar India see Ahmadnagar
Ahram Iran 35 H5
Āhtäri Fin. 14 N5
Ahtme Estonia 15 O7
Āhū Iran 35 H5
Ahun France 24 F3
Ahvāz Iran 35 H4
Ahwa India 36 C5
Ahwāz Iran see Ahvāz
Ai-Ais Namibia 50 C4
Ai-Ais Hot Springs Game Park nature res. Namibia 50 C4
Aichwara India 36 D4
Aigialousa Cyprus 39 B2
Aigina i. Greece 27 J6
Aigio Greece 27 J5
Aigle de Chambeyron mt. France 24 H4
Aigües Tortes i Estany de Sant Maurici, Parc Nacional d' nat. park Spain 25 G2
Ai He r. China 44 B4
Aihui China see Heihe
Aijal India see Aizawl
Aikawa Japan 45 E5
Aiken S.C. U.S.A. 63 D5
Aileron Australia 54 F5
Ailinglabelab atoll Marshall Is see Ailinglaplap
Ailinglaplap atoll Marshall Is 74 H5
Ailsa Craig Ont. Canada 64 A1
Ailsa Craig i. U.K. 20 D5
Ain r. France 24 G3
Aïn Ben Tili Mauritania 46 C2
'Aïn Dâlla spring Egypt see 'Ayn Dāllah
Aïn Defla Alg. 25 H5
Aïn Deheb Alg. 25 G6
Aïn el Hadjel Alg. 25 H5
'Aïn el Maqfi spring Egypt see 'Ayn al Maqfi
Aïn el Melh Alg. 25 I6
Aïn Mdila well Alg. 26 B7
Aïn-M'Lila Alg. 22 F4
Aïn Oussera Alg. 25 H5
Aïn Salah Alg. see In Salah
Aïn Sefra Alg. 22 D5
Ainsworth U.S.A. 62 H3
Aïn Taya Alg. 25 H5
Aïn Témouchent Alg. 25 F6
'Aïn Tibaghbagh spring Egypt see 'Ayn Tumayrah
'Aïn Timeira spring Egypt see 'Ayn Tumayrah
'Aïn Zeitûn Egypt see 'Ayn Zaytün
Aiquile Bol. 68 E7
Airdrie Canada 62 E1
Airdrie U.K. 20 F5
Aire-sur-l'Adour France 24 D5
Air Force Island Canada 61 K3
Airpanas Indon. 54 D1
Aisatung Mountain Myanmar 37 H5
Aisne r. France 24 F2
Aïssa, Djebel mt. Alg. 22 D5
Aitamännikkö Fin. 14 N3
Aitana mt. Spain 25 F4
Aitape P.N.G. 41 K7
Aït Benhaddou tourist site Morocco 22 C5
Aiud Romania 27 J1
Aix France see Aix-en-Provence
Aix-en-Provence France 24 G5
Aix-la-Chapelle Germany see Aachen
Aix-les-Bains France 24 G4
Aíyina i. Greece see Aigina
Aíyion Greece see Aigio
Aizawl India 37 H5
Aizkraukle Latvia 15 N8
Aizpute Latvia 15 L8
Aizu-Wakamatsu Japan 45 E5
Ajaccio Corse France 24 I6
Ajanta India 38 B1
Ajanta Range hills India see Sahyadriparvat Range
Ajaureforsen Sweden 14 I4
Ajax Ont. Canada 64 F2
Aj Bogd Uul mt. Mongolia 42 H4
Ajdabiyā Libya 47 F1
Ajigasawa Japan 44 F4
Ajka Hungary 17 P7
'Ajlūn Jordan 39 B3
Ajmer India 36 C4
Ajmer-Merwara India see Ajmer
Ajnala India 36 C3
Ajo AZ U.S.A. 65 F4
Ajyyap Turkm. 35 I2
Akabli Alg. 46 D2
Akaki r. Georgia 35 F2
Akalkot India 38 C2
Akal Kul salt l. Kazakh. see Alakol', Ozero
Akamagaseki Japan see Shimonoseki
Akan Kokuritsu-kōen nat. park Japan 44 G4
Akaroa N.Z. 59 D6
Akāshat Iraq 35 F4
Akbarabād Iran 35 I5
Akbarpur Uttar Prad. India 36 E4
Akbarpur Uttar Prad. India 37 E4
Akbez Turkey 39 C1
Akçadağ Turkey 34 E3
Akçakale Turkey 35 F3
Akçakoca Turkey 27 N4
Akçakoyunlu Turkey 39 C1

Akçalı Dağları mts Turkey 39 A1
Akchâr reg. Mauritania 46 B3
Akdağ mt. Turkey 27 M6
Akdağmadeni Turkey 34 D3
Akdere Turkey 39 A1
Åkersberga Sweden 15 K7
Aketi Dem. Rep. Congo 48 C3
Akgyr Erezi hills Turkm. 35 I2
Akhali-Afoni Georgia see Akhali Ap'oni
Akhali Ap'oni Georgia 35 F2
Akhdar, Al Jabal al mts Libya 47 F1
Akhdar, Jabal mts Oman 33 I5
Akhisar Turkey 27 L5
Akhmîm Egypt 32 D4
Akhnoor India 36 C2
Akhsu Azer. see Ağsu
Akhta Armenia see Hrazdan
Akhtarîn Syria 39 C1
Akhtubinsk Rus. Fed. 13 J6
Akhty Rus. Fed. 35 G2
Akhtyrka Ukr. see Okhtyrka
Aki Japan 45 D6
Akiéni Gabon 48 B4
Akimiski Island Canada 63 K1
Akishma r. Rus. Fed. 44 D1
Akjoujt Mauritania 46 B3
Akkajaure l. Sweden 14 J3
Akkerman Ukr. see Bilhorod-Dnistrovs'kyy
Akkeshi Japan 44 G4
'Akko Israel 39 B3
Akkol' Akmolinskaya Oblast' Kazakh. 28 I4
Akkol' Atyrauskaya Oblast' Kazakh. 13 K7
Akku Kazakh. 42 D2
Akkul' Kazakh. see Akkol'
Akkuş Turkey 34 E2
Akkyr, Gory hills Turkm. see Akgyr Erezi
Aklavik Canada 60 E3
Aklera India 36 D4
Ak-Mechet Kazakh. see Kyzylorda
Akmenrags pt Latvia 15 L8
Akmeqit China 36 D1
Akmolinsk Kazakh. see Astana
Akobo Sudan 47 G4
Akobo Wenz r. Eth./Sudan 48 D3
Akokan Niger 46 D3
Akola India 38 C1
Akom II Cameroon 46 E4
Akonolinga Cameroon 46 E4
Akordat Eritrea 32 E6
Akören Turkey 39 A1
Akot India 36 D5
Akpatok Island Canada 61 L3
Akqi China 42 D4
Akra, Jabal h. Syria/Turkey see Aqra', Jabal al
Akranes Iceland 14 [inset]
Åkrehamn Norway 15 D7
Akréréb Niger 46 D3
Akron CO U.S.A. 62 G3
Akron OH U.S.A. 64 A2
Akron NY U.S.A. 64 E1
Akrotiri Bay Cyprus 39 A2
Akrotirion, Kolpos b. Cyprus see Akrotiri Bay
Akrotiri Sovereign Base Area military base Cyprus 39 A2
Aksai Chin terr. Asia 36 D2
Aksaray Turkey 34 D3
Aksay China 42 G5
Aksay Kazakh. 11 Q5
Ak-Say r. Kyrg. 31 N1
Aksay Rus. Fed. 13 H7
Akşehir Turkey 27 N5
Akşehir Gölü l. Turkey 27 N5
Akseki Turkey 34 C3
Aksha Rus. Fed. 43 K2
Akshiganak Kazakh. 42 A3
Akshukur Kazakh. 35 H3
Aksu China 42 D4
Aksu r. Turkey 27 N6
Aksuat Kazakh. 42 E2
Aksu-Ayuly Kazakh. 42 D2
Aksubayevo Rus. Fed. 13 K5
Aksum Eth. 32 E7
Aktag mt. China 37 F1
Aktas Dağı mt. Turkey 35 G3
Aktau Kazakh. 30 E2
Aktobe Kazakh. 30 E1
Aktogay Karagandinskaya Oblast' Kazakh. 42 D3
Aktogay Vostochnyy Kazakhstan Kazakh. 42 D3
Aktsyabrski Belarus 13 F5
Aktyubinsk Kazakh. see Aktobe
Akulivik Canada 61 K3
Akune Japan 45 C6
Akure Nigeria 46 D4
Akuressa Sri Lanka 38 D5
Akureyri Iceland 14 [inset]
Akusha Rus. Fed. 13 J8
Akwanga Nigeria 46 D4
Akxokesay China 37 G1
Akyab Myanmar see Sittwe
Akyatan Gölü salt l. Turkey 39 B1
Akyazı Turkey 27 N4
Akzhaykyn, Ozero salt l. Kazakh. 42 B4
Ål Norway 15 F6
'Alā, Jabal al mts Syria 39 C2
Alabama r. U.S.A. 63 J5
Alabama state U.S.A. 63 J5
Al 'Abṭīyah well Iraq 35 G5
Alacahan Turkey 34 E3
Alaçam Turkey 34 D2
Alaçam Dağları mts Turkey 27 M5
Alacant Valencia Spain see Alicante
Alaçatı Turkey 27 L5
Aladağ Turkey 39 C1
Ala Dağ mts Turkey 35 F3
Ala Dağları mts Turkey 34 D3
Al 'Adam Libya 34 A5
Ala'er China see Alar
Alag Hu l. China 37 I2
Alagir Rus. Fed. 35 G2
Alagoinhas Brazil 71 D1
Alahärrä Fin. 14 M5
Al Ahmadī Kuwait 35 H5
Alajah Syria 35 H4
Alajärvi Fin. 14 M5
Alakanuk U.S.A. 60 B3
Alakol', Ozero salt l. Kazakh. 42 E3
Ala Kul salt l. Kazakh. see Alakol', Ozero
Alakurtti Rus. Fed. 14 Q3
Al 'Alamayn Egypt 34 C6
Al 'Alayyah Saudi Arabia 32 F6
Alama Somalia 48 E3
Al 'Amādīyah Iraq 35 F3
Al 'Amārah Iraq 35 G5
'Alam ar Rūm, Ra's pt Egypt 34 B5
'Alāmarvdasht watercourse Iran 35 I5
'Alam el Rûm, Râs pt Egypt see 'Alam ar Rūm, Ra's
Al Amghar waterhole Iraq 35 G5
Al 'Āmirīyah Egypt 34 C6

Alamo Dam AZ U.S.A. 65 F3
Alamogordo U.S.A. 62 F5
Alamos Sonora Mex. 66 B3
Alamos Sonora Mex. 66 C3
Alamos r. Mex. 62 G2
Alamosa U.S.A. 62 F4
Alampur India 38 C3
Alan Myanmar see Aunglan
Alanäs Sweden 14 I4
Åland is Fin. see Åland Islands
Alando China 37 H3
Alandur India 38 D3
Alanya Turkey 34 D3
Alaplı Turkey 27 N4
Alappuzha India see Alleppey
Alapuzha India see Alleppey
Alarcón, Embalse de resr Spain 25 E4
'Al 'Arīsh Egypt 39 A4
Al Arṭāwīyah Saudi Arabia 32 G4
Alas, Selat sea chan. Indon. 54 C3
Alaşehir Turkey 27 M5
Alaska country Asia see Cyprus
Al Ashmūnayn Egypt 34 C6
Alaska state U.S.A. 60 D3
Alaska, Gulf of U.S.A. 60 D4
Alaska Peninsula U.S.A. 60 C4
Alaska Range mts U.S.A. 60 D3
Älät Azer. 35 H3
Al Atwā' well Saudi Arabia 35 H5
Alatyr' Rus. Fed. 13 J5
Alatyr' r. Rus. Fed. 13 J5
Alausí Ecuador 68 C4
Alaverdi Armenia 35 G2
'Alavī Iran 35 H4
Alavieska Fin. 14 N4
Alavus Fin. 14 M5
Alawoona Australia 57 C7
Alay Kyrka Toosu mts Asia see Alai Range
Alayskiy Khrebet mts Asia see Alai Range
Al 'Azīzīyah Iraq 35 G4
Al 'Azīzīyah Libya 23 G5
Al Azraq al Janūbī Jordan 39 C4
Alba Italy 26 C2
Al Bāb Syria 39 C1
Albacete Spain 25 F4
Al Bādiyah al Janūbīyah des. Iraq 35 G5
Al Bahrayn country Asia see Bahrain
Alba Iulia Romania 27 J1
Albājī Iran 35 H5
Albania country Europe 27 H4
Albany r. Canada 63 K1
Albany GA U.S.A. 63 K5
Albany NY U.S.A. 64 E1
Albany OR U.S.A. 62 C3
Albany Downs Australia 58 D1
Albardão do João Maria coastal area Brazil 70 F4
Al Bardī Libya 34 B5
Al Bāridah hills Saudi Arabia 39 D5
Al Başrah Iraq see Basra
Al Batha' marsh Iraq 35 G5
Albatross Bay Australia 56 C2
Albatross Island Australia 57 [inset]
Al Bawītī Egypt 34 C5
Al Baydā' Libya 32 B3
Al Baydā' Yemen 32 G7
Albemarle Island Galápagos Ecuador see Isabela, Isla
Albenga Italy 26 C2
Alberche r. Spain 25 D4
Alberga Australia 57 A5
Alberga watercourse Australia 57 A5
Albergaria-a-Velha Port. 25 B3
Albert France 24 E2
Albert, Lake Dem. Rep. Congo/Uganda 48 D3
Albert, Parc National nat. park Dem. Rep. Congo see Virunga, Parc National des
Alberta prov. Canada 62 E1
Alberta VA U.S.A. 64 C4
Albert Lea U.S.A. 63 I3
Albert Nile r. Sudan/Uganda 47 F4
Alberto de Agostini, Parque Nacional nat. park Chile 70 B8
Alberton S. Africa 51 I4
Albertville Dem. Rep. Congo see Kalemie
Albertville France 24 H4
Albi France 24 F5
Albina Suriname 69 H2
Albino Italy 26 C2
Albion NY U.S.A. 64 B1
Albion PA U.S.A. 64 A2
Al Biqā' val. Lebanon see El Béqaa
Al Bi'r Saudi Arabia 34 D5
Al Birk Saudi Arabia 32 F6
Al Biyādh reg. Saudi Arabia 32 G5
Alborán, Isla de i. Spain 25 E6
Ålborg Denmark see Aalborg
Ålborg Bugt b. Denmark see Aalborg Bugt
Albro Australia 56 D4
Albufeira Port. 25 B5
Al Buhayrat al Murrah lakes Egypt see Bitter Lakes
Albuquerque U.S.A. 62 F4
Al Buraij Syria 39 C2
Al Buraymī Oman 33 I5
Al Burj Jordan 39 B5
Alburquerque Spain 25 C4
Albury Australia 58 C6
Al Buşayrah Syria 35 F4
Al Buşayyah Iraq 35 G5
Al Bushūk well Saudi Arabia 35 G5
Alcácer do Sal Port. 25 B4
Alcalá de Henares Spain 25 E3
Alcalá la Real Spain 25 E5
Alcamo Sicilia Italy 26 E6
Alcañiz Spain 25 F3
Alcántara Spain 25 C4
Alcaraz Spain 25 E4
Alcázar de San Juan Spain 25 E4
Alcazarquivir Morocco see Ksar el Kebir
Alchevs'k Ukr. 13 H6
Alcobaça Brazil 71 D2
Alcoi Spain see Alcoy-Alcoi
Alcoota Australia 54 F5
Alcoy Spain see Alcoy-Alcoi
Alcoy-Alcoi Spain 25 F4
Alcúdia Spain 25 H4
Aldabra Islands Seychelles 49 K6
Aldan Rus. Fed. 29 N4
Aldan r. Rus. Fed. 29 N3
Alde r. U.K. 19 I6
Aldeburgh U.K. 19 I6
Alder Creek NY U.S.A. 64 D1
Alderney i. Channel Is 19 E9
Alder Peak CA U.S.A. 65 B3
Aldershot U.K. 19 G7
Aldingham U.K. 18 D4
Aldridge U.K. 19 F6
Alegre Espírito Santo Brazil 71 C3

Alegre Minas Gerais Brazil 71 B2
Alegrete Brazil 70 E3
Aleksandra, Mys hd Rus. Fed. 44 E1
Aleksandriya Ukr. see Oleksandriya
Aleksandro-Nevskiy Rus. Fed. 13 I5
Aleksandropol Armenia see Gyumri
Aleksandrov Rus. Fed. 12 H4
Aleksandrov Gay Rus. Fed. 13 K6
Aleksandrovsk Rus. Fed. 11 R4
Aleksandrovsk Ukr. see Zaporizhzhya
Aleksandrovskiy Rus. Fed. see Aleksandrovsk
Aleksandrovskoye Rus. Fed. 35 F1
Aleksandrovsk-Sakhalinskiy Rus. Fed. 44 F2
Aleksandry, Zemlya i. Rus. Fed. 28 F1
Alekseyevka Akmolinskaya Oblast' Kazakh. see Akkol'
Alekseyevka Vostochnyy Kazakhstan Kazakh. see Terekty
Alekseyevka Amurskaya Oblast' Rus. Fed. 44 B1
Alekseyevka Belgorodskaya Oblast' Rus. Fed. 13 H6
Alekseyevka Belgorodskaya Oblast' Rus. Fed. 13 H6
Alekseyevskaya Rus. Fed. 13 I6
Alekseyevskoye Rus. Fed. 12 K5
Aleksin Rus. Fed. 13 H5
Aleksinac Serbia 27 I3
Alèmbé Gabon 48 B4
Ålen Norway 14 G5
Alençon France 24 E2
Alenquer Brazil 69 H4
Alep Syria see Aleppo
Aleppo Syria 39 C1
Alert Canada 61 M1
Alerta Peru 68 D6
Alès France 24 G4
Aleşd Romania 27 J1
Aleshki Ukr. see Tsyurupyns'k
Aleşkirt Turkey see Eleşkirt
Alessandria Italy 26 C2
Alessio Albania see Lezhë
Ålesund Norway 14 E5
Aleutian Basin sea feature Bering Sea 74 H2
Aleutian Islands U.S.A. 60 A4
Aleutian Range mts U.S.A. 60 C4
Aleutian Trench sea feature N. Pacific Ocean 74 I2
Alevina, Mys c. Rus. Fed. 29 Q4
Alevişik Turkey see Samandağı
Alexander, Kap c. Greenland see Ullersuaq
Alexander, Mount h. Australia 56 D2
Alexander Archipelago is U.S.A. 60 E4
Alexander Bay b. Namibia/S. Africa 50 C5
Alexander Bay S. Africa 50 C5
Alexander Island Antarctica 76 L2
Alexandra Australia 58 B6
Alexandra N.Z. 59 B7
Alexandra, Cape S. Georgia 70 I8
Alexandra Land i. Rus. Fed. see Aleksandry, Zemlya
Alexandreia Greece 27 J4
Alexandretta Turkey see İskenderun
Alexandria Afgh. see Ghaznī
Alexandria Egypt 34 C5
Alexandria Romania 27 K3
Alexandria S. Africa 51 H7
Alexandria Turkm. see Mary
Alexandria U.K. 20 E5
Alexandria LA U.S.A. 63 I5
Alexandria VA U.S.A. 64 C3
Alexandria Arachoton Afgh. see Kandahār
Alexandria Areion Afgh. see Herāt
Alexandria Prophthasia Afgh. see Farāh
Alexandrina, Lake Australia 57 B7
Alexandroupoli Greece 27 K4
Alexis Creek Canada 62 C1
Aley Lebanon 39 B3
Aleysk Rus. Fed. 42 E2
Al Farwānīyah Kuwait 35 G5
Al Fas Morocco see Fès
Al Fatḥah Iraq 35 F4
Al Fāw Iraq 35 H5
Al Fayyūm Egypt 34 C5
Alfenas Brazil 71 B3
Alford U.K. 18 H5
Alfred ME U.S.A. 64 F1
Alfred NY U.S.A. 64 C1
Alfred and Marie Range hills Australia 55 D6
Al Fujayrah U.A.E. see Fujairah
Al Fuqahā' Libya 47 E2
Al Furāt r. Asia see Euphrates
Al Furāt r. Asia 39 D2 see Euphrates
Ålgård Norway 15 D7
Algarrobo del Aguilla Arg. 70 C5
Algarve reg. Port. 25 B5
Algeciras Spain 25 D5
Algemesí Spain 25 F4
Algena Eritrea 32 E6
Alger Alg. see Algiers
Algeria country Africa 46 C2
Algérie country Africa see Algeria
Al Ghammās Iraq 35 G5
Al Ghardaqah Egypt see Al Ghurdaqah
Al Ghawr plain Jordan/West Bank 39 B4
Al Ghaydah Yemen 32 H6
Alghero Sardegna Italy 26 C4
Al Ghurdaqah Egypt 32 D4
Algiers Alg. 25 H5
Algoa Bay S. Africa 51 G7
Algona U.S.A. 63 I3
Algorta Spain 25 E2
Algueirao Moz. see Hacufera
Al Habakah well Saudi Arabia 35 F5
Al Ḥabbānīyah Iraq 35 F4
Al Ḥadaqah well Saudi Arabia 35 G5
Al Hadhālīl plat. Saudi Arabia 35 F5
Al Ḥadīdīyah Syria 39 C2
Al Ḥadīthah Iraq 35 F4
Al Hadīthah Saudi Arabia 39 C4
Al Ḥaḍr Iraq see Hatra
Al Ḥafar well Saudi Arabia 35 F5
Al Ḥaffah Syria 39 C2
Al Haggounia W. Sahara 46 B2
Al Ḥajar al Gharbī mts Oman 33 I5
Al Ḥamād plain Asia 34 E5
Al Ḥamādah al Ḥamrā' plat. Libya 46 E2
Alhama de Murcia Spain 25 F5
Al Ḥamīdīyah Syria 39 B2
Al Ḥammām Egypt 34 C5
Al Ḥanākīyah Saudi Arabia 32 F5
Al Haniyah esc. Iraq 35 G5
Al Ḥarrah Egypt 34 C5
Al Harūj al Aswad hills Libya 47 E2
Al Ḥasakah Syria 35 F3
Al Hawi salt pan Saudi Arabia 39 D5
Al Ḥawjā' Saudi Arabia 34 E5
Al Ḥayy Iraq 35 G4
Al Ḥayz Egypt 34 C5
Al Ḥazīm Jordan 39 C4
Al Ḥazm Saudi Arabia 34 E5
Al Ḥazm al Jawf Yemen 32 F6
Al Ḥibāk des. Saudi Arabia 33 H6
Al Hījānah Syria 39 C3
Al Ḥillah Iraq see Hillah
Al Ḥillah Saudi Arabia 32 G5
Al Ḥinnāh Saudi Arabia 48 E1
Al Ḥinw mt. Saudi Arabia 39 D4
Al Hīshah Syria 39 D1
Al Ḥismā plain Saudi Arabia 34 D5
Al Ḥiṣn Jordan 39 B3
Al Hoceima Morocco 25 E6
Al Ḥudaydah Yemen see Hodeidah
Al Ḥufrah reg. Saudi Arabia 34 E5
Al Hūj hills Saudi Arabia 34 E5
Ali China 36 D2
'Alīābād Golestān Iran 35 I3
'Alīābād Hormozgān Iran 33 I4
'Alīābād Kordestān Iran 35 G3
'Alīābād, Kūh-e mt. Iran 35 H4
Aliağa Turkey 27 L5
Aliakmonas r. Greece 27 J4
Alibag India 38 B2
Äli Bayramlı Azer. 35 H3
Alicante Spain 25 F4
Alice r. Australia 56 C2
Alice watercourse Australia 56 D5
Alice U.S.A. 62 H6
Alice, Punta pt Italy 26 G5
Alice Springs Australia 55 F5
Alichur Tajik. 33 L2
Alick Creek r. Australia 56 C4
Aliganj India 36 D4
Aligarh Rajasthan India 36 D4
Aligarh Uttar Prad. India 36 D4
Alīgūdarz Iran 35 H4
Alihe China 44 A2
Alījūq, Kūh-e mt. Iran 35 H5
'Alī Kheyl Afgh. 36 B2
Al Imārāt al 'Arabīyah at Muttaḥidah country Asia see United Arab Emirates
Alimia i. Greece 27 L6
Alindao Cent. Afr. Rep. 48 C3
Alingsås Sweden 15 H8
Aliova r. Turkey 27 M5
Alipura India 36 D4
Alipur Duar India 37 G4
Aliquippa PA U.S.A. 64 A2
Alirajpur India 36 C5
Al 'Irāq country Asia see Iraq
Al 'Īsāwīyah Saudi Arabia 39 C4
Al Iskandarīyah Egypt see Alexandria
Al Iskandarīyah Iraq 35 G4
Al Ismā'īlīyah Egypt 34 D5
Al Ismā'īlīyah governorate Egypt 39 A4
Aliveri Greece 27 K5
Aliwal North S. Africa 51 H6
Al Jafr Jordan 39 C4
Al Jaghbūb Libya 34 B5
Al Jahrah Kuwait 35 G5
Al Jamalīyah Qatar 32 H4
Al Jarāwī well Saudi Arabia 39 D4
Al Jauf Saudi Arabia see Dumat al Jandal
Al Jawf Libya 47 F2
Al Jawsh Libya 46 E1
Al Jaza'ir country Africa see Algeria
Al Jaza'ir Alg. see Algiers
Aljezur Port. 25 B5
Al Jil well Iraq 35 F5
Al Jithāmīyah Saudi Arabia 35 F6
Al Jīzah Egypt see Giza
Al Jīzah Jordan 39 B4
Al Jufrah Libya 47 E2
Al Julayqah well Saudi Arabia 35 H6
Aljustrel Port. 25 B5
Al Juwayf depr. Syria 39 C3
Al Kahfah Al Qaṣīm Saudi Arabia 32 F4
Al Kahfah Ash Sharqīyah Saudi Arabia 35 H6
Al Karak Jordan 39 B4
Al Khalīl West Bank see Hebron
Al Khāliṣ Iraq 35 G4
Al Khārijah Egypt 32 D4
Al Kharrūbah Egypt 39 A4
Al Khaṣab Oman 33 I4
Al Khawkhah Yemen 32 F7
Al Khawr Qatar 32 H4
Al Khums Libya 47 E1
Al Khunfah des. Saudi Arabia 34 E5
Al Khunn Saudi Arabia 48 E1
Al Kifl Iraq 35 G4
Al Kiswah Syria 39 C3
Alkmaar Neth. 16 J4
Al Kūbrī Egypt 39 A4
Al Kumayt Iraq 35 G4
Al Kuntillah Egypt 39 B5
Al Kusūr hills Saudi Arabia 39 D4
Al Kūt Iraq 35 G4
Al Kuwayt country Asia see Kuwait
Al Kuwayt Kuwait see Kuwait
Al Labbah plain Saudi Arabia 35 F5
Al Lādhiqīyah Syria see Latakia
Allagadda India 38 C3
Allahabad India 37 E4
Al Lajā lava field Syria 39 C3
Allakaket U.S.A. 60 C3
Allakh-Yun' Rus. Fed. 29 O3
Allanmyo Myanmar see Aunglan
Allanridge S. Africa 51 H4
Allapalli India 38 D2
'Allāqī, Wādī al watercourse Egypt 32 D5
'Allâqi, Wâdi el watercourse Egypt see 'Allāqī, Wādī al
Alldays S. Africa 51 I2
Allegheny r. PA U.S.A. 64 B2
Allegheny Mountains U.S.A. 64 A4
Allegheny Reservoir PA U.S.A. 64 B2
Allen, Lough l. Ireland 21 D3
Allendale Town U.K. 18 E4
Allende Coahuila Mex. 62 G6
Allenstein Poland see Olsztyn
Allentown PA U.S.A. 64 D2
Alleppey India 38 C4
Aller r. Germany 17 L4
Alliance NE U.S.A. 62 G3
Alliance OH U.S.A. 64 A2
Al Lībīyah country Africa see Libya
Allier r. France 24 F3
Al Lihābah well Saudi Arabia 35 G6
Allinge-Sandvig Denmark 15 I9
Al Lişāfah well Saudi Arabia 35 G6
Al Lisān pen. Jordan 39 B4
Al Līth Saudi Arabia 32 F5
Alloa U.K. 20 F4
Allora Australia 58 F2
Allur India 38 D3
Alluru Kottapatnam India 38 D3
Al Lussuf well Iraq 35 F5
Alma Canada 63 M2
Al Ma'ānīyah Iraq 35 F5
Alma-Ata Kazakh. see Almaty
Almada Port. 25 B4
Al Madāfi' plat. Saudi Arabia 34 E5
Al Ma'danīyāt well Iraq 35 G5
Almaden Australia 56 D3
Almadén Spain 25 D4
Al Madīnah Saudi Arabia see Medina
Al Mafraq Jordan 39 C3
Al Maghrib country Africa see Morocco
Al Mahdum Syria 39 C1
Al Maḥiā depr. Saudi Arabia 34 E6
Al Maḥwīt Yemen 32 F6
Al Manāmah Bahrain see Manama
Almansa Spain 25 F4
Al Manṣūrah Egypt 34 C5
Almanzor mt. Spain 25 D3
Al Mariyyah U.A.E. 33 H5
Al Marj Libya 47 F1
Almas, Rio das r. Brazil 71 A1
Al Maṭarīyah Egypt 34 D5
Almaty Kazakh. 42 D4
Al Mawṣil Iraq see Mosul
Al Mayādīn Syria 35 F4
Al Mazār Egypt 39 A4
Almaznyy Rus. Fed. 29 M3
Almeirim Brazil 69 H4
Almeirim Port. 25 B4
Almelo Neth. 17 K4
Almenara Brazil 71 C2
Almendra, Embalse de resr Spain 25 C3
Almendralejo Spain 25 C4
Almería Spain 25 E5
Almería, Golfo de b. Spain 25 E5
Al'metievsk Rus. Fed. see Al'met'yevsk
Al'met'yevsk Rus. Fed. 11 Q5
Älmhult Sweden 15 I8
Almina, Punta pt Spain 25 D6
Al Mindak Saudi Arabia 32 F5
Al Minyā Egypt 34 C5
Almirós Greece see Almyros
Al Mish'āb Saudi Arabia 35 H5
Almodôvar Port. 25 B5
Almond r. U.K. 20 F4
Almonte Spain 25 C5
Almora India 36 D3
Al Mu'ayzīlah h. Saudi Arabia 39 D5
Al Mubarrez Saudi Arabia 32 G4
Al Muḍaibī Oman 33 I5
Al Mukallā Yemen see Mukalla
Al Mukhā Yemen see Mocha
Al Mukhaylī Libya 32 B3
Almuñécar Spain 25 E5
Al Muqdādīyah Iraq 35 G4
Al Mūrītānīyah country Africa see Mauritania
Al Murūt well Saudi Arabia 35 E5
Almus Turkey 34 E2
Al Musannāh ridge Saudi Arabia 35 G5
Al Muwaqqar Jordan 39 C4
Almyros Greece 27 J5
Almyrou, Ormos b. Greece 27 K7
Alnwick U.K. 18 F3
Alofi Niue 53 J3
Aloja Latvia 15 N8
Along India 37 H3
Alongshan China 44 A2
Alonnisos i. Greece 27 J5
Alor i. Indon. 41 E8
Alor, Kepulauan is Indon. 41 E8
Alor Setar Malaysia 41 C7
Alor Star Malaysia see Alor Setar
Alost Belgium see Aalst
Aloysius, Mount Australia 55 E6
Alozero Rus. Fed. 14 Q4
Alpena U.S.A. 63 K2
Alpercatas, Serra das hills Brazil 69 J5
Alpha Australia 56 D4
Alpha Ridge sea feature Arctic Ocean 77 A1
Alpine NY U.S.A. 64 C1
Alpine TX U.S.A. 62 G5
Alpine National Park Australia 58 C6
Alps mts Europe 24 H4
Al Qa'āmīyāt reg. Saudi Arabia 32 G6
Al Qaddāḥīyah Libya 47 E1
Al Qadmūs Syria 39 C2
Al Qāhirah Egypt see Cairo
Al Qā'īyah Saudi Arabia 32 F5
Al Qal'a Beni Hammad tourist site Alg. 25 I6
Al Qalībah Saudi Arabia 34 E5
Al Qāmishlī Syria 35 F3
Al Qar'ah Libya 34 B5
Al Qar'ah lava field Syria 39 C3
Al Qardāḥah Syria 39 C2
Al Qarqar Saudi Arabia 39 C4
Al Qaryatayn Syria 39 C2
Al Qaṭn Yemen 32 G6
Al Qaṭrānah Jordan 39 C4
Al Qaṭrūn Libya 47 E2
Al Qayṣūmah well Saudi Arabia 35 F5
Al Qumur country Africa see Comoros
Al Qunayṭirah Syria 39 B3
Al Qunfidhah Saudi Arabia 32 F6
Al Qurayyāt Saudi Arabia 39 C4
Al Qurnah Iraq 35 G5
Al Quṣaymah Egypt 39 B4
Al Quṣayr Egypt 32 D4
Al Quṣayr Syria 39 C2
Al Qūṣīyah Egypt 34 C6
Al Quṭayfah Syria 39 C3
Al Quwayīyah Saudi Arabia 32 G5
Al Quwayrah Jordan 39 B5
Alroy Downs Australia 56 B3
Alsace reg. France 24 H2
Alsager U.K. 19 E5
Al Samīt well Iraq 35 F5
Alsatia reg. France see Alsace
Alston U.K. 18 E4
Alstonville Australia 58 F2
Alsunga Latvia 15 L8
Alta Norway 14 M2
Alta, Mount N.Z. 59 B7
Altaelva r. Norway 14 M2
Altafjorden sea chan. Norway 14 M1
Alta Floresta Brazil 69 G5
Altai Mountains Asia 42 F3
Altamaha r. U.S.A. 63 K5
Altamira Brazil 69 H4
Altamura Italy 26 G4
Altan Shiret China 43 J5
Altan Xiret China see Altan Shiret
Alta Paraiso de Goiás Brazil 71 B1
Altavista VA U.S.A. 64 B4
Altay China 42 F3
Altay Mongolia 42 G4
Altay Mongolia 42 H3
Altayskiy Khrebet mts Asia see Altai Mountains
Altdorf Switz. 24 I3
Altea Spain 25 F4
Alteidet Norway 14 M1
Altenqoke China 37 H1
Altin Köprü Iraq 35 G4
Altınoluk Turkey 27 L5
Altınözü Turkey 39 C1
Altıntaş Turkey 27 N5
Altiplano plain Bol. 68 E7
Altmühl r. Germany 17 M6
Alto, Monte h. Italy 26 D2
Alto Chicapa Angola 49 B5
Alto del Moncayo mt. Spain 25 F3
Alto de Pencoso hills Arg. 70 C4
Alto Garças Brazil 69 H7
Alto Madidi, Parque Nacional nat. park Bol. 68 E6
Alton NH U.S.A. 64 F1
Altoona PA U.S.A. 64 B2
Alto Parnaíba Brazil 69 I5
Alto Taquarí Mato Grosso Brazil 69 H7
Altötting Germany 17 N6
Altrincham U.K. 18 E5
Altūn Kūbrī Iraq see Altin Köprü
Altun Shan mts China 42 F5
Alturas U.S.A. 62 C3
Altus U.S.A. 62 H5
Al 'Ubaylah Saudi Arabia 48 F1
Alucra Turkey 34 E2
Alūksne Latvia 15 O8
Alūm Iran 35 H4
Alum Bridge WV U.S.A. 64 A3
Al 'Uqaylah Libya 47 E1
Al 'Uqaylah Saudi Arabia see An Nabk
Al Uqṣur Egypt see Luxor
Alur India 38 C3
Al 'Urayq des. Saudi Arabia 34 E5
Al 'Urdun country Asia see Jordan
Alur Setar Malaysia see Alor Setar
'Ālūt Iran 35 G4
Aluva India see Alwaye
Al 'Uwaynāt Libya 32 B5
Al 'Uwayqīlah Saudi Arabia 35 F5
Al 'Uzayr Iraq 35 G5
Alva U.S.A. 62 H4
Alvand, Kūh-e mt. Iran 35 H4
Alvarães Brazil 68 F4
Alvdal Norway 14 G5
Älvdalen Sweden 15 I6
Alvesta Sweden 15 I8
Ålvik Norway 15 E6
Alvik Sweden 14 J5
Alvorada do Norte Brazil 71 B1
Älvsbyn Sweden 14 L4
Al Wafrah Kuwait 35 G5
Al Wajh Saudi Arabia 32 E4
Al Waqbá well Saudi Arabia 35 G5
Alwar India 36 D4
Al Wari'ah Saudi Arabia 32 G4
Al Wāṭīyah well Egypt 34 B5
Alwaye India 38 C4
Al Widyān plat. Iraq/Saudi Arabia 35 F4
Al Wusayṭ well Saudi Arabia 35 G5
Alxa Youqi China see Ehen Hudag
Alxa Zuoqi China see Bayan Hot
Al Yaman country Asia see Yemen
Alyangula Australia 56 B2
Alyth U.K. 20 F4
Alytus Lith. 15 N9
Amacayacu, Parque Nacional nat. park Col. 68 D4
Amadeus, Lake imp. l. Australia 55 E6
Amadjuak Lake Canada 61 K3
Amadora Port. 25 B4
Amakusa-nada b. Japan 45 C6
Åmål Sweden 15 H7
Amalia S. Africa 51 G4
Amaliada Greece 27 I6
Amalner India 36 C5
Amamapare Indon. 41 F8
Amambaí Brazil 70 E2
Amambaí, Serra de hills Brazil/Para. 70 E2
Amami-Ō-shima i. Japan 45 C7
Amami-shotō is Japan 45 C8
Amamula Dem. Rep. Congo 48 C4
Amantea Italy 26 G5
Amanzimtoti S. Africa 51 J6
Amapá Brazil 69 H3
Amarante Brazil 69 J5
Amarapura Myanmar 37 I5
Amareleja Port. 25 C4
Amargosa Brazil 71 D1
Amargosa watercourse CA U.S.A. 65 D2
Amargosa Desert NV U.S.A. 65 D2
Amargosa Range mts CA U.S.A. 65 D2
Amargosa Valley NV U.S.A. 65 D2
Amarillo U.S.A. 62 G4
Amarillo, Cerro mt. Arg. 70 C4
Amarkantak India 37 E5
Amarpur Madh. Prad. India 36 E5
Amasia Turkey see Amasya
Amasine W. Sahara 46 B2
Amasra Turkey 34 D2
Amasya Turkey 34 D2
Amata Australia 55 E6
Amatulla India 37 H4
Amau P.N.G. 56 E1
Amazar Rus. Fed. 44 A1
Amazar r. Rus. Fed. 44 A1
Amazon r. S. America 68 F4
Amazon, Mouths of the Brazil 69 I3
Amazonas r. S. America 68 F4 see Amazon
Amazon Cone sea feature S. Atlantic Ocean 72 E5
Amazónia, Parque Nacional nat. park Brazil 69 G4
Ambajogai India 38 C2
Ambala India 36 D3
Ambalangoda Sri Lanka 38 D5
Ambalavao Madag. 49 E6
Ambam Cameroon 48 B3
Ambarchik Rus. Fed. 29 R3
Ambarnyy Rus. Fed. 14 R4
Ambasa India see Ambassa
Ambasamudram India 38 C4
Ambassa India 37 G5
Ambathala Australia 57 D5
Ambato Ecuador 68 C4
Ambato Boeny Madag. 49 E5
Ambato Finandrahana Madag. 49 E6
Ambatolampy Madag. 49 E5
Ambatomainty Madag. 49 E5
Ambatondrazaka Madag. 49 E5
Ambejogai India see Ambajogai
Ambeno enclave East Timor see Ocussi
Amberg Germany 17 M6
Ambergris Cay i. Belize 66 G5
Ambérieu-en-Bugey France 24 G4
Ambgaon India 38 D1
Ambianum France see Amiens
Ambikapur India 37 E5
Ambilobe Madag. 49 E5
Amble U.K. 18 F3
Ambler U.S.A. 60 C3
Ambleside U.K. 18 E4
Ambo India 37 F5
Amboasary Madag. 49 E6
Ambodifotatra Madag. 49 E5
Ambohimahasoa Madag. 49 E6
Ambohitra mt. Madag. 49 E5
Amboina Indon. see Ambon
Ambon Indon. 41 E8
Ambon i. Indon. 41 E8
Amboró, Parque Nacional nat. park Bol. 68 F7
Ambositra Madag. 49 E6
Ambovombe Madag. 49 E6
Amboy CA U.S.A. 65 E3
Ambre, Cap d' c. Madag. see Bobaomby, Tanjona
Ambrim i. Vanuatu see Ambrym
Ambriz Angola 49 B4
Ambrizete Angola see N'zeto
Ambrym i. Vanuatu 53 G3
Ambur India 38 C3
Am-Dam Chad 47 F3
Amded, Oued watercourse Alg. 46 D2
Amdo China see Lharigarbo
Amelia Court House VA U.S.A. 64 C4
Amenia NY U.S.A. 64 E2
Amer, Erg d' des. Alg. 48 A1
Amereli India see Amreli
American, North Fork r. CA U.S.A. 65 B1
Americana Brazil 71 B3
American-Antarctic Ridge sea feature S. Atlantic Ocean 72 G9
American Falls U.S.A. 62 E3
American Falls Reservoir U.S.A. 62 E3
American Fork U.S.A. 62 E3
American Samoa terr. S. Pacific Ocean 53 J3
Americus U.S.A. 63 K5
Amersfoort Neth. 16 J4
Amersfoort S. Africa 51 I4
Amersham U.K. 19 G7
Amery Ice Shelf Antarctica 76 E2
Ames U.S.A. 63 I3
Amesbury U.K. 19 F7
Amesbury MA U.S.A. 64 F1
Amet India 36 C4
Amethi India 37 E4
Amfissa Greece 27 J5
Amga Rus. Fed. 29 O3
Amgalang China 43 L3
Amgu Rus. Fed. 44 E3
Amguid Alg. 46 D2
Amgun' r. Rus. Fed. 44 E1
Amherst MA U.S.A. 64 E1
Amherst VA U.S.A. 64 B4
Amiata, Monte mt. Italy 26 D3
Amida Turkey see Diyarbakır
Amiens France 24 F2
'Amīj, Wādī watercourse Iraq 35 F4
Amik Ovası marsh Turkey 39 C1
'Amīnābād Iran 35 I5
Amindivi atoll India see Amini
Amindivi Islands India 38 B4
Amini atoll India 38 B4
Amino Eth. 48 E3
Aminuis Namibia 50 D2
Amīrābād Iran 35 G4
Amirante Islands Seychelles 73 L6
Amirante Trench sea feature Indian Ocean 73 L6
Amisk Lake Canada 62 G1
Amistad, Represa de resr Mex./U.S.A. see Amistad Reservoir
Amistad Reservoir Mex./U.S.A. 62 G6
Amisus Turkey see Samsun
Amity Point Australia 58 F1
Amla India 36 D5
Amlapura Indon. see Karangasem
Amlash Iran 35 H3
Amlekhganj Nepal 37 F4
Åmli Norway 15 F7
Amlia Island U.S.A. 60 A4
Amlwch U.K. 18 C5
'Ammān Jordan 39 B4
Ammanazar Turkm. 35 I3
Ammanford U.K. 19 D7
Ämmänsaari Fin. 14 P4
'Ammār, Tall h. Syria 39 C3
Ammarnäs Sweden 14 J4
Ammaroo Australia 56 A4
Ammassalik Greenland 77 J2
Ammochostos Cyprus see Famagusta
Ammochostos Bay Cyprus 39 B2
Am Nābiyah Yemen 32 F7
Amne Machin Range mts China see A'nyêmaqên Shan
Amnok-kang r. China/N. Korea see Yalu Jiang
Amol Iran 35 I3
Amorgos i. Greece 27 K6
Amory U.S.A. 63 J5
Amos Canada 63 L2
Amourj Mauritania 46 C3
Amoy China see Xiamen
Ampani India 38 D2
Ampanihy Madag. 49 E6
Amparai Sri Lanka 38 D5
Amparo Brazil 71 B3
Ampasimanolotra Madag. 49 E5
Amphitheatre Australia 58 A6
Amraoti India see Amravati
Amravati India 38 C1
Amrawad India 36 D5
Amreli India 36 B5
Amri Pak. 36 B4
Amring India 37 H4
'Amrīt Syria 39 B2
Amritsar India 36 C3
Amroha India 36 D3
Åmsele Sweden 14 K4
Amstelveen Neth. 16 J4
Amsterdam Neth. 16 J4
Amsterdam S. Africa 51 J4
Amsterdam NY U.S.A. 64 D1
Amsterdam, Île i. Indian Ocean 73 N8
Amstetten Austria 17 O6
Am Timan Chad 47 F3
Amudar'ya r. Asia 33 I1
Amudaryo r. Asia see Amudar'ya
Amund Ringnes Island Canada 61 I2
Amundsen, Mount Antarctica 76 F2
Amundsen Abyssal Plain sea feature Southern Ocean 76 J2
Amundsen Basin sea feature Arctic Ocean 77 H1
Amundsen Bay Antarctica 76 D2
Amundsen Coast Antarctica 76 J1
Amundsen Glacier Antarctica 76 I1
Amundsen Gulf Canada 60 F2
Amundsen Ridges sea feature Southern Ocean 76 J2
Amundsen-Scott research stn Antarctica 76 C1
Amundsen Sea Antarctica 76 K2
Amuntai Indon. 41 D8
Amur r. China/Rus. Fed. 40 F3
Amur r. Rus. Fed. 44 F1
'Amur, Wadi watercourse Sudan 32 D6
Amur Oblast admin. div. Rus. Fed. see Amurskaya Oblast'
Amursk Rus. Fed. 44 E2
Amurskaya Oblast' admin. div. Rus. Fed. 44 C1
Amurskiy Liman str. Rus. Fed. 44 F1
Amurzet Rus. Fed. 44 C3
Amvrosiyivka Ukr. 13 H7
Amyderya r. Asia see Amudar'ya
Am-Zoer Chad 47 F3
Anaa atoll Fr. Polynesia 75 K7
Anabanua Indon. 41 E8
Anabar r. Rus. Fed. 29 M2
Anacapa Islands CA U.S.A. 65 C3
Anaconda U.S.A. 62 E2
Anadolu reg. Turkey 34 D3
Anadolu Dağları mts Turkey 34 E2
Anadyr' Rus. Fed. 29 S3
Anadyr, Gulf of Rus. Fed. see Anadyrskiy Zaliv
Anadyrskiy Zaliv b. Rus. Fed. 29 T3
Anafi i. Greece 27 K6
Anagé Brazil 71 C1
'Ānah Iraq 35 F4
Anaheim CA U.S.A. 65 D4
Anaimalai Hills India 38 C4
Anaiteum i. Vanuatu see Anatom
Anajás Brazil 69 I4
Anakie Australia 56 D4
Analalava Madag. 49 E5
Anamã Brazil 68 F4
Anambas, Kepulauan is Indon. 41 C7
Anamur Turkey 39 A1
Anan Japan 45 D6
Anand India 36 C5
Anandapur India 37 F5
Anantapur India 38 C3
Ananthapur India see Anantapur
Anantnag India 36 C2
Anant Peth India 36 D4
Anantpur India see Anantapur
Ananyev Ukr. see Anan'yiv
Anan'yiv Ukr. 13 F7
Anapa Rus. Fed. 34 E1
Anápolis Brazil 71 A2
Anār Fin. see Inari
Anār Iran 35 I5
Anatom i. Vanuatu 53 G4
Añatuya Arg. 70 D3
Anaypazari Turkey see Gülnar
An Baile Breac Ireland 21 B6
An Bun Beag Ireland 21 D2
Anbyon N. Korea 45 B5
Ancenis France 24 D3
Anchorage U.S.A. 60 D3
Anchorage Island atoll Cook Is see Suwarrow
Anchuthengu India see Anjengo
Anci China see Langfang
An Clochán Liath Ireland 21 D3
An Cóbh Ireland see Cobh
Ancona Italy 26 E3
Ancud, Golfo de g. Chile 70 B6
Ancyra Turkey see Ankara
Anda Heilong. China 44 B3
Anda Heilong. China see Daqing
Andacollo Chile 70 B4
Andado Australia 56 A5
Andahuaylas Peru 68 D6
An Daingean Ireland 21 B5
Andal India 37 F5
Åndalsnes Norway 14 E5
Andalucía aut. comm. Spain 25 D5
Andalusia aut. comm. Spain see Andalucía
Andaman Basin sea feature Indian Ocean 73 O5
Andaman Islands India 31 I5
Andaman Sea Indian Ocean 41 B6
Andamooka Australia 57 B6
Andapa Madag. 49 E5
Andegavum France see Angers
Andelle r. France 19 I9
Andenes Norway 14 J2
Andenne Belgium 16 J5
Andéramboukane Mali 46 D3
Anderlecht Belgium 16 J5
Andermatt Switz. 24 I3
Andernos-les-Bains France 24 D4
Anderson r. Canada 60 F3
Anderson AK U.S.A. 60 D3
Anderson IN U.S.A. 63 J3
Anderson SC U.S.A. 63 K5
Anderson Bay Australia 57 [inset]
Andes mts S. America 70 C4
Andfjorden sea chan. Norway 14 J2
Andhíparos i. Greece see Antiparos
Andhra Lake India 38 B2
Andhra Pradesh state India 38 C2
Andijon Uzbek. 33 L1
Andikíthira i. Greece see Antikythira
Andilamena Madag. 49 E5
Andilanatoby Madag. 49 E5
Andīmeshk Iran 35 H4
Andímilos i. Greece see Antimilos
Andípsara i. Greece see Antipsara
Andırın Turkey 34 E3
Andirlangar China 37 E1
Andkhvoy Afgh. 36 A1
Andoany Madag. 49 E5
Andoas Peru 68 C4
Andogskaya Gryada hills Rus. Fed. 12 H4
Andol India 38 C2
Andong China see Dandong
Andong S. Korea 45 C5
Andoom Australia 56 C2
Andorra country Europe 25 G2
Andorra la Vella Andorra 25 G2
Andorra la Vieja Andorra see Andorra la Vella
Andover U.K. 19 F7
Andover NY U.S.A. 64 C1
Andover OH U.S.A. 64 A2
Andøya i. Norway 14 I2
Andrade CA U.S.A. 65 E4
Andradina Brazil 71 A3
Andranomavo Madag. 49 E5
Andranopasy Madag. 49 E6
Andreanof Islands U.S.A. 74 I2
Andreapol' Rus. Fed. 12 G4
Andreas Isle of Man 18 C4
André Félix, Parc National d' nat. park Cent. Afr. Rep. 48 C3
Andrelândia Brazil 71 B3
Andrews TX U.S.A. 62 G5
Andria Italy 26 G4
Androka Madag. 49 E6
Andropov Rus. Fed. see Rybinsk
Andros i. Bahamas 67 I4
Andros i. Greece 27 K6
Andros Town Bahamas 67 I4
Androtti i. India 38 B4
Andselv Norway 14 K2
Andújar Spain 25 D4
Andulo Angola 49 B5
Anec, Lake imp. l. Australia 55 E5
Āneen-Kio terr. N. Pacific Ocean see Wake Island
Anéfis Mali 46 D3
Anegada, Bahía b. Arg. 70 D6
Anegada Passage Virgin Is (U.K.) 67 L5
Aného Togo 46 D4
Aneityum i. Vanuatu see Anatom
'Aneiza, Jabal h. Iraq see 'Unayzah, Jabal
Anemourion tourist site Turkey 39 A1
Anetchom, Île i. Vanuatu see Anatom
Aneto mt. Spain 25 G2
Ānewetak atoll Marshall Is see Enewetak
Aney Niger 46 E3
Aneytioum, Île i. Vanuatu see Anatom
Angalarri r. Australia 54 E3
Angamos, Punta pt Chile 70 B2
Ang'angxi China 44 A3
Angara r. Rus. Fed. 42 G1
Angarsk Rus. Fed. 42 I2
Angas Downs Australia 55 F6
Angatuba Brazil 71 A3
Ånge Sweden 14 I5
Angel, Salto waterfall Venez. see Angel Falls
Ángel de la Guarda, Isla i. Mex. 66 B3
Angel Falls waterfall Venez. 68 F2
Ängelholm Sweden 15 H8
Angellala Creek r. Australia 58 C1
Angels Camp CA U.S.A. 65 B1
Ångermanälven r. Sweden 14 J5
Angers France 24 D3
Angikuni Lake Canada 61 I3
Angiola CA U.S.A. 65 C3
Anglesea Australia 58 B7
Anglesey i. U.K. 18 C5
Anglo-Egyptian Sudan country Africa see Sudan
Angmagssalik Greenland see Ammassalik
Ango Dem. Rep. Congo 48 C3
Angoche Moz. 49 D5
Angol Chile 70 B5
Angola country Africa 49 B5
Angola NY U.S.A. 64 B1
Angola Basin sea feature S. Atlantic Ocean 72 H7
Angora Turkey see Ankara
Angoulême France 24 E4
Angra dos Reis Brazil 71 B3

gren Uzbek. 33 L1
guang China 44 A3
guilla terr. West Indies 67 L5
gul India 38 E1
gutia Char i. Bangl. 37 G5
holt i. Denmark 15 G8
hui prov. China 43 L6
humas Brazil 69 H7
hwei prov. China see Anhui
iak U.S.A. 60 C3
iakchak National Monument and
Preserve nat. park U.S.A. 60 C4
itápolis Brazil 71 A4
ıtlı Turkey 39 A1
iva Rus. Fed. 44 F3
iva, Mys c. Rus. Fed. 44 F3
iva, Zaliv b. Rus. Fed. 44 F3
jadip i. India 38 B3
jalankoski Fin. 15 O6
jengo India 38 C4
jir Avand Iran 35 I4
jou reg. France 24 D3
jouan i. Comoros see Nzwani
jozorobe Madag. 49 E5
juthengu India see Anjengo
kang China 43 J6
kara Turkey 34 D3
karatra mt. Madag. 49 E5
kazoabo Madag. 49 E6
kleshwar India 36 C5
klesvar India see Ankleshwar
kola India 38 B3
lu China 43 K6
moore WV U.S.A. 64 A3
Muileann gCearr Ireland see Mullingar
myŏn-do i. S. Korea 45 B5
n, Cape Antarctica 76 D2
n, Cape MA U.S.A. 64 F1
na Rus. Fed. 13 I3
na, Lake VA U.S.A. 64 C3
naba Alg. 26 B6
Nabk Saudi Arabia 39 C4
Nabk Syria 39 C2
Nafūd des. Saudi Arabia 35 F5
nalee r. Ireland 21 E3
nalong U.K. 21 G3
nan U.K. 20 F6
nan r. U.K. 20 F6
nān, Wādī al watercourse Syria 39 D2
nandale VA U.S.A. 64 C3
na Plains Australia 54 C4
napolis MD U.S.A. 64 C3
napurna Conservation Area nature res.
Nepal 37 F3
napurna I mt. Nepal 37 E3
n Arbor U.S.A. 63 K3
na Regina Guyana 69 G2
Nās Ireland see Naas
Nașrānī, Jabal mts Syria 39 C3
nean, Lake imp. l. Australia 55 B6
necy France 24 H4
Nimārah Syria 39 C3
Nimāș Saudi Arabia 32 F6
niston U.S.A. 63 J5
nobón i. Equat. Guinea 46 D5
nonay France 24 G4
Nu'mānīyah Iraq 35 G4
Nușayrīyah, Jabal mts Syria 39 C2
noón de Sardinas, Bahía de b. Col. 68 C3
norontany, Tanjona hd Madag. 49 E5
nqing China 43 L6
nsbach Germany 17 M6
nser Group is Australia 58 C7
nshan China 44 A4
nshun China 42 J7
nshunchang China 42 I7
Sirḥān, Wādī watercourse Saudi Arabia
34 E5
nson Bay Australia 54 E3
nsongo Mali 46 D3
nsted WV U.S.A. 64 A3
ntabamba Peru 68 D6
ntakya Turkey 39 C1
ntalaha Madag. 49 F5
ntalya Turkey 27 N6
ntalya prov. Turkey 39 A1
ntalya Körfezi g. Turkey 27 N6
ntananarivo Madag. 49 E5
tAonach Ireland see Nenagh
ntarctica 76
ntarctic Peninsula Antarctica 76 L2
ntas r. Brazil 71 A5
Teallach mt. U.K. 20 D3
ntelope Range mts NV U.S.A. 65 D1
ntequera Spain 25 D5
nthony Lagoon Australia 56 A3
nti Atlas mts Morocco 22 C6
ntibes France 24 H5
nticosti, Île d' i. Canada 61 L5
nticosti Island Canada see Anticosti, Île d'
ntifer, Cap d' c. France 19 H9
ntigua i. Antigua and Barbuda 67 L5
ntigua country West Indies see
Antigua and Barbuda
ntigua and Barbuda country West Indies
67 L5
ntikythira i. Greece 27 J7
ntikythiro, Steno sea chan. Greece 27 J7
nti Lebanon mts Lebanon/Syria see
Sharqī, Jabal ash
ntimilos i. Greece 27 K6
tInbhear Mór Ireland see Arklow
ntioch Turkey see Antakya
ntioch CA U.S.A. 65 B1
ntiocheia ad Cragum tourist site Turkey
39 A1
ntiochia Turkey see Antakya
ntiparos i. Greece 27 K6
ntipodes Islands N.Z. 53 H6
ntipsara i. Greece 27 K5
ntium Italy see Anzio
ntofagasta Chile 70 B2
ntofagasta de la Sierra Arg. 70 C3
ntofalla, Volcán vol. Arg. 70 C3
ntónio Enes Moz. see Angoche
ntri India 36 D4
ntrim U.K. 21 F3
ntrim Hills U.K. 21 F2
ntrim Plateau Australia 54 E4
ntropovo Rus. Fed. 12 I4
ntsalova Madag. 49 E5
ntseranana Madag. see Antsirañana
ntsirabe Madag. 49 E5
ntsirañana Madag. 49 E5
ntsla Estonia 15 O8
ntsohihy Madag. 49 E5
nttis Sweden 14 M3
nttola Fin. 15 O6
ntwerp Belgium 16 J5
ntwerpen Belgium see Antwerp
Uaimh Ireland see Navan
nuchino Rus. Fed. 44 D4
nugul India see Angul
nupgarh India 36 C3
nuradhapura Sri Lanka 38 D4
nveh Iran 35 I6
nvers Island Antarctica 76 L2
nvik U.S.A. 60 B3
nxi Gansu China 42 H4
nxious Bay Australia 55 F8
nyang Henan China 43 K5
Anyang S. Korea 45 B5
A'nyêmaqên Shan mts China 42 H6
Anyuy r. Rus. Fed. 44 E2
Anyuysk Rus. Fed. 29 R3
Anzhero-Sudzhensk Rus. Fed. 28 J4
Anzi Dem. Rep. Congo 48 C4
Anzio Italy 26 E4
Aoba i. Vanuatu 53 G3
Aoga-shima i. Japan 45 E6
Aomen China see Macao
Aomori Japan 44 F4
Aoraki mt. N.Z. 59 C6
Aoraki/Mount Cook National Park N.Z.
59 C6
Aorangi mt. N.Z. see Aoraki
Aosta Italy 26 B2
Aotearoa country Oceania see New Zealand
Aouk, Bahr r. Cent. Afr. Rep./Chad 47 E4
Aoukâr reg. Mali/Mauritania 46 C2
Aoulef Alg. 46 D2
Aozou Chad 47 E2
Apa r. Brazil 70 E2
Apaiang atoll Kiribati see Abaiang
Apalachee Bay U.S.A. 63 K6
Apalachin NY U.S.A. 64 C1
Apamea Turkey see Dinar
Apaporis r. Col. 68 E4
Aparecida do Tabuado Brazil 71 A3
Aparima N.Z. see Riverton
Aparri Phil. 74 E4
Apatity Rus. Fed. 14 R3
Apatzingán Mex. 66 D5
Ape Latvia 15 O8
Apeldoorn Neth. 17 J4
Apennines mts Italy 26 C2
Api mt. Nepal 36 E3
Api i. Vanuatu see Epi
Apia atoll Kiribati see Abaiang
Apia Samoa 53 I3
Apiacas, Serra dos hills Brazil 69 G6
Apiaí Brazil 71 A4
Apiti N.Z. 59 E4
Aplao Peru 68 D7
Apoera Suriname 69 G2
Apollo Bay Australia 58 A7
Apollonia Bulg. see Sozopol
Apolo Bol. 68 E6
Aporé Brazil 71 A2
Aporé r. Brazil 71 A2
Apostolens Tommelfinger mt. Greenland
61 N3
Apostolos Andreas, Cape Cyprus 39 B2
Apoteri Guyana 69 G3
Apozai Pak. 36 B3
Appalachian Mountains U.S.A. 63 K4
Appalla i. Fiji see Kabara
Appennino mts Italy see Apennines
Appennino Abruzzese mts Italy 26 E3
Appennino Tosco-Emiliano mts Italy 26 D3
Appennino Umbro-Marchigiano mts Italy
26 E3
Applecross U.K. 20 D3
Appleton WI U.S.A. 63 J3
Apple Valley CA U.S.A. 65 D3
Appomattox VA U.S.A. 64 B4
Aprilia Italy 26 E4
Apsheronsk Rus. Fed. 13 H7
Apsheronskaya Rus. Fed. see Apsheronsk
Apt France 24 G5
Apucarana Brazil 71 A3
Apucarana, Serra da hills Brazil 71 A3
Apulum Romania see Alba Iulia
Aq"a Georgia see Sokhumi
'Aqaba Jordan see Al 'Aqabah
Aqaba, Gulf of Asia 34 D5
'Aqaba, Wādī el watercourse Egypt see
'Aqabah, Wādī al
'Aqabah, Wādī al watercourse Egypt 39 A4
Aqadyr Kazakh. see Agadyr'
Aqdoghmish r. Iran 35 G3
Aqköl Akmolinskaya Oblast' Kazakh. see
Akkol'
Aqköl Atyrauskaya Oblast' Kazakh. see
Akkol'
Aqmola Kazakh. see Astana
Aqqan China 37 F1
Aqqikkol Hu salt l. China 37 G1
Aqra', Jabal al mt. Syria/Turkey 39 B2
'Aqran h. Saudi Arabia 39 D4
Aqsay Kazakh. see Aksay
Aqsayqin Hit terr. Asia see Aksai Chin
Aqshuqyr Kazakh. see Akshukur
Aqsū Kazakh. see Aksu
Aqsūat Kazakh. see Aksuat
Aqsū-Ayuly Kazakh. see Aksu-Ayuly
Aqtaū Kazakh. see Aktau
Aqtōbe Kazakh. see Aktobe
Aqtoghay Kazakh. see Aktogay
Aquae Grani Germany see Aachen
Aquae Gratianae France see Aix-les-Bains
Aquae Sextiae France see Aix-en-Provence
Aquae Statiellae Italy see Acqui Terme
Aquarius Mountains AZ U.S.A. 65 F3
Aquaviva delle Fonti Italy 26 G4
Aquidauana Brazil 70 E2
Aquincum Hungary see Budapest
Aquiry r. Brazil see Acre
Aquisgranum Germany see Aachen
Aquitaine reg. France 24 D5
Aquitania reg. France see Aquitaine
Aqzhayqyn Köli salt l. Kazakh. see
Akzhaykyn, Ozero
Ara India 37 F4
Āra Ārba Eth. 48 E3
Arab, Bahr el watercourse Sudan 47 F4
'Arab, Khalīg el b. Egypt see 'Arab, Khalīj al
'Arab, Khalīj al b. Egypt 34 C5
'Arabah, Wādī al watercourse Israel/Jordan
39 B5
Arabian Basin sea feature Indian Ocean
73 M5
Arabian Gulf Asia see The Gulf
Arabian Peninsula Asia 32 G5
Arabian Sea Indian Ocean 33 K6
Araç Turkey 34 D2
Araça r. Brazil 68 F4
Aracaju Brazil 69 K6
Aracati Brazil 69 K4
Aracatu Brazil 71 C1
Araçatuba Brazil 71 A3
Aracena Spain 25 C5
Aracruz Brazil 71 C2
Araçuaí Brazil 71 C2
Araçuaí r. Brazil 71 C2
'Arad Israel 39 B4
Arad Romania 27 I1
Arafura Sea Australia/Indon. 52 D2
Arafura Shelf sea feature Australia/Indon.
74 E6
Aragarças Brazil 69 H7
Aragón r. Spain 25 F2
Araguaçu Brazil 71 A1
Araguaia r. Brazil 71 A1
Araguaia, Parque Nacional do nat. park
Brazil 69 H6
Araguaiana Brazil 71 A1
Araguaína Brazil 69 I5
Araguari Brazil 71 A2
Araguari r. Brazil 69 H3
Araguatins Brazil 69 I5
Arai Brazil 71 B1
'Arâif el Naga, Gebel h. Egypt see
'Urayf an Nāqah, Jabal
Araiosos Brazil 69 J4
Arak Alg. 46 D2
Arāk Iran 35 H4
Arak Syria 39 D2
Arakan Yoma mts Myanmar 37 H5
Arakkonam India 38 C3
Araks r. Azer. see Araz
Araku India 38 D2
Aral Kazakh. see Aral'sk
Aral Tajik. see Vose
Aral Sea salt l. Kazakh./Uzbek. 30 F2
Aral'sk Kazakh. 28 H5
Aral'skoye More salt l. Kazakh./Uzbek. see
Aral Sea
Aralsor, Ozero l. Kazakh. 13 K6
Aral Tengizi salt l. Kazakh./Uzbek. see
Aral Sea
Aramac Australia 56 D4
Aramac Creek watercourse Australia 56 D4
Aran r. India 38 C2
Aranda de Duero Spain 25 E3
Aranđelovac Serbia 27 I2
Arandis Namibia 50 B2
Arang India 37 E5
Arani India 38 C3
Aran Islands Ireland 21 C4
Aranjuez Spain 25 E3
Aranos Namibia 50 D3
Aransas Pass U.S.A. 63 H6
Arantangi India 38 C4
Aranuka atoll Kiribati 53 H1
Arao Japan 45 C6
Araouane Mali 46 C3
Arapgir Turkey 34 E3
Arapiraca Brazil 69 K5
Arapis, Akrotirio pt Greece 27 K4
Arapkir Turkey see Arapgir
Arapongas Brazil 71 A3
Araquari Brazil 71 A4
'Ar'ar Saudi Arabia 35 F5
Araracuara Col. 68 D4
Araranguá Brazil 71 A5
Araraquara Brazil 71 A3
Araras Brazil 69 H5
Ararat Armenia 35 G3
Ararat Australia 58 A6
Ararat, Mount Turkey 35 G3
Araria India 37 F4
Araripina Brazil 69 J5
Aras r. Azer. see Araz
Aras Turkey 35 F3
Arataca Brazil 71 D1
Arauca Col. 68 D2
Arauca r. Venez. 68 E2
Aravalli Range mts India 36 C4
Aravete Estonia 15 N7
Arawa P.N.G. 52 F2
Araxá Brazil 71 B2
Araxes r. Azer. see Araz
Arayıt Dağı mt. Turkey 27 N5
Araz r. Azer. 35 H2
Arbailu Iraq see Arbīl
Arbat Iraq 35 G4
Arbela Iraq see Arbīl
Arberth U.K. see Narberth
Arbīl Iraq 35 G3
Arboga Sweden 15 I7
Arbroath U.K. 20 G4
Arbuckle CA U.S.A. 65 A1
Arbu Lut, Dasht-e des. Afgh. 33 J4
Arcachon France 24 D4
Arcade NY U.S.A. 64 B1
Arcadia FL U.S.A. 63 K6
Arc Dome mt. NV U.S.A. 65 D1
Arcelia Mex. 66 D5
Archangel Rus. Fed. 12 I2
Archer r. Australia 41 G9
Archer Bend National Park Australia 56 C2
Archipiélago Los Roques nat. park Venez.
68 E1
Ārçivan Azer. 35 H3
Arckaringa watercourse Australia 57 A6
Arco U.S.A. 62 E3
Arcos Brazil 71 B3
Arcos de la Frontera Spain 25 D5
Arctic Bay Canada 61 J2
Arctic Institute Islands Rus. Fed. see
Arkticheskogo Instituta, Ostrova
Arctic Mid-Ocean Ridge sea feature
Arctic Ocean 77 H1
Arctic Ocean 77 B1
Arctic Red r. Canada 60 E3
Arctowski research stn Antarctica 76 A2
Arda r. Bulg. 27 L4
Ardabīl Iran 35 H3
Ardahan Turkey 35 F2
Ardakān Iran 35 I4
Årdalstangen Norway 15 E6
Ardara Ireland 21 D3
Ardas r. Bulg. see Arda
Arḍ aș Șawwān plain Jordan 39 C4
Ardatov Nizhegorodskaya Oblast' Rus. Fed.
13 I5
Ardatov Respublika Mordoviya Rus. Fed.
13 J5
Ardee Ireland 21 F4
Ardennes plat. Belgium 16 J6
Arden Town CA U.S.A. 65 B1
Arderin h. Ireland 21 E4
Ardestān Iran 35 I4
Ardglass U.K. 21 G3
Ardila r. Port. 25 C4
Ardlethan Australia 58 C5
Ardmore U.S.A. 63 H5
Ardnamurchan, Point of U.K. 20 C4
Ardon Rus. Fed. 35 G2
Ardrishaig U.K. 20 D4
Ardrossan U.K. 20 E5
Ardvasar U.K. 20 D3
Areia Branca Brazil 69 K4
Arel Belgium see Arlon
Arelas France see Arles
Arelate France see Arles
Arena, Point U.S.A. 62 C4
Arenas de San Pedro Spain 25 D3
Arendal Norway 15 F7
Areopoli Greece 27 J6
Arequipa Peru 68 D7
Arere Brazil 69 H4
Arévalo Spain 25 D3
Arezzo Italy 26 D3
'Arfajah well Saudi Arabia 39 D4
Argadargada Australia 56 B4
Arganda del Rey Spain 25 E3
Argel Alg. see Algiers
Argentan France 24 D2
Argentario, Monte h. Italy 26 D3
Argentera, Cima dell' mt. Italy 26 B2
Argentina country S. America 70 C5
Argentine Abyssal Plain sea feature
S. Atlantic Ocean 72 E9
Argentine Basin sea feature
S. Atlantic Ocean 72 F8
Argentine Republic country S. America see
Argentina
Argentine Rise sea feature S. Atlantic Ocean
72 E8
Argentino, Lago l. Arg. 70 B8
Argenton-sur-Creuse France 24 E3
Argentoratum France see Strasbourg
Argeș r. Romania 27 L2
Arghandab r. Afgh. 36 A3
Argi r. Rus. Fed. 44 C1
Argolikos Kolpos b. Greece 27 J6
Argos Greece 27 J6
Argostoli Greece 27 I5
Arguís Spain 25 F2
Argun' r. China/Rus. Fed. 43 M2
Argun Rus. Fed. 35 G2
Argungu Nigeria 46 D3
Argus Range mts CA U.S.A. 65 D3
Argyle, Lake Australia 54 E4
Argyrokastron Albania see Gjirokastër
Ar Horqin Qi China see Tianshan
Århus Denmark 15 G8
Ariah Park Australia 58 C5
Ariamsvlei Namibia 50 D5
Ariana Tunisia see L'Ariana
Ariano Irpino Italy 26 F4
Aribinda Burkina 46 C3
Arica Chile 68 D7
Arid, Cape Australia 55 C8
Arīḥā Syria 39 C2
Arīḥā West Bank see Jericho
Arima Trin. and Tob. 67 L6
Ariminum Italy see Rimini
Arinos Brazil 71 B1
Aripuanã Brazil 69 G6
Aripuanã r. Brazil 68 F5
Ariquemes Brazil 68 F5
Aris Namibia 50 C2
Arisaig U.K. 20 D4
Arisaig, Sound of sea chan. U.K. 20 D4
'Arīsh, Wādī al watercourse Egypt 39 A4
Arixang China see Wenquan
Ariyalur India 38 C4
Arizaro, Salar de salt flat Arg. 70 C2
Arizona Arg. 70 C5
Arizona state U.S.A. 62 E5
Arizpe Mex. 62 E5
'Arjah Saudi Arabia 32 F5
Arjeplog Sweden 14 J3
Arjuni Chhattisgarh India 38 D1
Arjuni India 36 E5
Arkadak Rus. Fed. 13 I6
Arkadelphia U.S.A. 63 I5
Arkaig, Loch l. U.K. 20 D4
Arkalyk Kazakh. 42 B2
Arkansas r. U.S.A. 63 I5
Arkansas state U.S.A. 63 I4
Arkansas City KS U.S.A. 63 H4
Arkatag Shan mts China 37 G1
Arkenu, Jabal mt. Libya 32 B5
Arkhangel'sk Rus. Fed. see Archangel
Arkhara Rus. Fed. 44 C2
Arkhipovka Rus. Fed. 44 D4
Arki i. Greece see Arkoi
Arklow Ireland 21 F5
Arkoi i. Greece 27 L6
Arkona Ont. Canada 64 A1
Arkona, Kap c. Germany 17 N3
Arkonam India see Arakkonam
Arkport NY U.S.A. 64 C1
Arkticheskogo Instituta, Ostrova is
Rus. Fed. 28 J2
Arkul' Rus. Fed. 12 K4
Arlandag mt. Turkm. 35 I3
Arles France 24 G5
Arlington S. Africa 51 H5
Arlington NY U.S.A. 64 E2
Arlington VA U.S.A. 64 C3
Arlit Niger 46 D3
Arlon Belgium 17 J6
Armadale Australia 55 A8
Armagh U.K. 21 F3
Armant Egypt 32 D4
Armavir Armenia 35 G2
Armavir Rus. Fed. 13 I7
Armenia country Asia 35 G2
Armenia Col. 68 C3
Armenopolis Romania see Gherla
Armeria Mex. 66 D5
Armidale Australia 58 E3
Armori India 38 D1
Armoy U.K. 21 F2
Armstrong r. Australia 54 E4
Armstrong Island Cook Is see Rarotonga
Armu r. Rus. Fed. 44 E3
Armur India 38 C2
Armutçuk Dağı mts Turkey 27 L5
Armyanskaya S.S.R. country Asia see
Armenia
Arnaoutis, Cape Cyprus see Arnauti, Cape
Arnauti, Cape Cyprus 39 A2
Årnes Norway 15 G6
Arnhem Neth. 17 J5
Arnhem, Cape Australia 56 B2
Arnhem Land reg. Australia 54 F3
Arno r. Italy 26 D3
Arno Bay Australia 57 B7
Arnold U.K. 19 F5
Arnon r. Jordan see Mawjib, Wādī al
Arnprior Canada 63 L2
Arnsberg Germany 17 L5
Aroab Namibia 50 D4
Aroma Sudan 32 E6
Arona Italy 26 C2
Arorae i. Kiribati 53 H2
Arore i. Kiribati see Arorae
Aros r. Mex. 62 F6
Arosi i. Solomon Is see San Cristobal
Arqalyq Kazakh. see Arkalyk
Arquipélago da Madeira aut. reg. Port. 46 B1
Arrabury Australia 57 C5
Arrah India see Ara
Arraias Brazil 71 B1
Arraias, Serra de hills Brazil 71 B1
Ar Ramlah Jordan 39 B5
Ar Ramthā Jordan 39 C3
Arran i. U.K. 20 D5
Arranmore Island Ireland 21 D3
Ar Raqqah Syria 39 D2
Arras France 24 F1
Ar Rass Saudi Arabia 32 F4
Ar Rastān Syria 39 C2
Ar Rayyān Qatar 32 H4
Arrecife Canary Is 46 B2
Arretium Italy see Arezzo
Arriagá Mex. 66 F5
Ar Rifā'ī Iraq 35 G5
Ar Rihāb salt flat Iraq 35 G5
Ar Rimāl reg. Saudi Arabia 48 F1
Arrington VA U.S.A. 64 B4
Ar Riyāḍ Saudi Arabia see Riyadh
Arrochar U.K. 20 E4
Arrojado r. Brazil 71 B1
Arrow, Lough l. Ireland 21 D3
Arrowsmith, Mount N.Z. 59 C6
Arroyo Grande CA U.S.A. 65 B3
Ar Rummān Jordan 39 B3
Ar Ruq'ī well Saudi Arabia 35 G5
Ar Ruṣāfah Syria 39 D2
Ar Ruṣayfah Jordan 39 C3
Ar Rustāq Oman 33 I5
Ar Ruṭbah Iraq 35 F4
Ar Ruwayḍah Syria 39 C2
Års Denmark see Aars
Ars Iran 35 G3
Arsen'yev Rus. Fed. 44 D3
Arsk Rus. Fed. 12 K4
Arta Greece 27 I5
Artem Rus. Fed. 44 D4
Artemivs'k Ukr. 13 H6
Artemovsk Ukr. see Artemivs'k
Artenay France 24 E2
Artesia NM U.S.A. 62 G5
Arthur, Lake PA U.S.A. 64 A2
Arthur's Pass National Park N.Z. 59 C6
Arti Rus. Fed. 11 R4
Artigas research stn Antarctica 76 A2
Artigas Uruguay 70 E4
Art'ik Armenia 35 F2
Artillery Lake Canada 60 H3
Artisia Botswana 51 H3
Artois reg. France 24 E1
Artos Dağı mt. Turkey 35 F3
Artova Turkey 34 E2
Artsakh aut. reg. Azer. see Dağlıq Qarabağ
Artsiz Ukr. see Artsyz
Artsyz Ukr. 27 M2
Artur de Paiva Angola see Kuvango
Artux China 42 D5
Artvin Turkey 35 F2
Aru, Kepulauan is Indon. 41 F8
Arua Uganda 48 D3
Aruanã Brazil 71 A1
Aruba terr. West Indies 67 K6
Arumã Brazil 68 F4
Arunachal Pradesh state India 37 H4
Arundel U.K. 19 G8
Arun Gol r. China 44 B3
Arun He r. China see Arun Gol
Arun Qi China see Naji
Aruppukkottai India 38 C4
Arusha Tanz. 48 D4
Aruwimi r. Dem. Rep. Congo 48 C3
Arvagh Ireland 21 E4
Arvayheer Mongolia 42 I3
Arviat Canada 61 I3
Arvidsjaur Sweden 14 K4
Arvika Sweden 15 H7
Arvonia VA U.S.A. 64 B4
Arwād i. Syria 39 B2
Arwala Indon. 54 D1
Arxan China 43 L3
Aryanah Tunisia see L'Ariana
Arys' Kazakh. 42 B4
Arzamas Rus. Fed. 13 I5
Arzew Alg. 25 F6
Arzgir Rus. Fed. 35 G1
Arzila Morocco see Asilah
Asaba Nigeria 46 D4
Asad, Buḥayrat al resr Syria 39 D1
Asadābād Afgh. 36 B2
Asadābād Iran 35 H4
Asahi-dake vol. Japan 44 F4
Asahikawa Japan 44 F4
'Asal Egypt 39 A5
Āsalē l. Eth. 48 E2
Asālem Iran 35 H3
'Asalūyeh Iran 35 I6
Asan-man b. S. Korea 45 B5
Asansol India 37 F5
Āsayita Eth. 48 E2
Asbestos Mountains S. Africa 50 F5
Asbury Park NJ U.S.A. 64 D2
Ascalon Israel see Ashqelon
Ascea Italy 26 F4
Ascensión Bol. 68 F7
Ascension atoll Micronesia see Pohnpei
Ascension i. S. Atlantic Ocean 72 H6
Aschaffenburg Germany 17 L6
Ascoli Piceno Italy 26 E3
Asculum Italy see Ascoli Piceno
Asculum Picenum Italy see Ascoli Piceno
Ascutney VT U.S.A. 64 E1
Āseb Eritrea see Assab
Åseda Sweden 15 I8
Åsele Sweden 14 J4
Asenovgrad Bulg. 27 K3
Aşfar, Jabal al mt. Jordan 39 C3
Aşfar, Tall al h. Syria 39 C3
Aşgabat Turkm. 30 E3
Aşgabat Turkm. see Aşgabat
Asha Rus. Fed. 11 R5
Ashburton watercourse Australia 54 A5
Ashburton N.Z. 59 C6
Ashburton Range hills Australia 54 F4
Ashdod Israel 39 B4
Asheville U.S.A. 63 K4
Ashford Australia 58 E2
Ashford U.K. 19 H7
Ashibetsu Japan 44 F4
Ashikaga Japan 45 E5
Ashington U.K. 18 F3
Ashizuri-misaki pt Japan 45 D6
Ashkelon Israel see Ashqelon
Ashkhabad Turkm. see Aşgabat
Ashland OR U.S.A. 62 C3
Ashland VA U.S.A. 64 C4
Ashland WI U.S.A. 63 I2
Ashley Australia 58 D2
Ashmore and Cartier Islands terr. Australia
54 C3
Ashmore Reef Australia 54 C3
Ashmore Reefs Australia 56 D1
Ashmyany Belarus 15 N9
Ashqelon Israel 39 B4
Ash Shabakah Iraq 35 F5
Ash Shaddādah Syria 35 F3
Ash Shallūfah Egypt 39 A4
Ash Sham Syria see Damascus
Ash Shanāfiyah Iraq 35 G5
Ash Shaqīq well Saudi Arabia 35 F5
Ash Sharāh reg. Jordan 39 B4
Ash Sharawrah Saudi Arabia 32 G6
Ash Shāriqah U.A.E. see Sharjah
Ash Sharqāṭ Iraq 35 F4
Ash Shaṭrah Iraq 35 G5
Ash Shaṭṭ Egypt 39 A5
Ash Shawbak Jordan 39 B4
Ash Shaybānī well Saudi Arabia 35 F5
Ash Shaykh Ibrāhīm Syria 39 D2
Ash Shiblīyāt h. Saudi Arabia 39 C5
Ash Shiḥr Yemen 32 G7
Ash Shu'aybah Saudi Arabia 35 F6
Ash Shu'bah Saudi Arabia 32 F4
Ash Shurayf Saudi Arabia see Khaybar
Ashta India 36 D5
Ashtabula OH U.S.A. 64 A2
Ashtarak Armenia 35 G2
Ashti Mahar. India 36 D5
Ashti Mahar. India 38 B2
Ashti Mahar. India 38 C2
Ashtīān Iran 35 H4
Ashton S. Africa 50 E7
Ashton-under-Lyne U.K. 18 E5
Ashuanipi Lake Canada 61 L4
Ashur Iraq see Ash Sharqāṭ
Asi r. Asia 34 E3 see 'Āṣī, Nahr al
'Āṣī r. Lebanon/Syria see Orontes
'Āṣī, Nahr al r. Asia 34 E3
Āsīā Bak Iran 35 H4
Asifabad India 38 C2
Asika India 38 E2
Asilah Morocco 25 C6
Asinara, Golfo dell' b. Sardegna Italy 26 C4
Asino Rus. Fed. 28 J4
Asipovichy Belarus 13 F5
Asīr Iran 35 I6
'Asīr reg. Saudi Arabia 32 F5
Asisium Italy see Assisi
Askale Pak. 36 C2
Aşkale Turkey 35 F3
Asker Norway 15 G7
Askersund Sweden 15 I7
Askim Norway 15 G7
Askī Mawşil Iraq 35 F3
Askino Rus. Fed. 11 R4
Askival h. U.K. 20 C4
Asl Egypt see 'Asal
Aslanköy r. Turkey 39 B1
Asmara Eritrea 32 E6
Āsmera Eritrea see Asmara
Åsnen l. Sweden 15 I8
Aso-Kuju Kokuritsu-kōen nat. park Japan
45 C6
Asop India 36 C4
Āsosa Eth. 48 D2
Aspang-Markt Austria 17 P7
Aspatria U.K. 18 D4
Aspen U.S.A. 62 F4
Aspiring, Mount N.Z. 59 B7
Aspro, Cape Cyprus 39 A2
Aspromonte, Parco Nazionale dell'
nat. park Italy 26 F5
Aspron, Cape Cyprus see Aspro, Cape
As Sa'an Syria 39 C2
Assab Eritrea 32 F7
Assad, Lake resr Syria see Asad, Buḥayrat al
Aş Şafā lava field Syria 39 C3
Aş Şafāqis Tunisia see Sfax
Aş Şaff Egypt 34 C5
As Safirah Syria 39 C1
Aş Şaḥrā' al Gharbīyah des. Egypt see
Western Desert
Aş Şaḥrā' ash Sharqīyah des. Egypt see
Eastern Desert
Aş Şaḥrā' ash Sharqīyah des. Egypt see
Eastern Desert
Assake-Audan, Vpadina depr.
Kazakh./Uzbek. 35 J2
'Assal, Lac l. Djibouti see Assal, Lake
Assal, Lake Djibouti 32 F7
Aş Şāliḥīyah Syria 35 F4
As Sallūm Egypt 34 B5
As Salmān Iraq 35 G5
As Salṭ Jordan 39 B3
Assam state India 37 G4
Assamakka Niger 46 D3
As Samāwah Iraq 35 G5
As Samrā' Jordan 39 C3
Aş Şanām reg. Saudi Arabia 32 H5
As Sarīr reg. Libya 47 F2
Assateague Island MD U.S.A. 64 D3
Assayeta Eth. see Āsayita
Assen Neth. 17 K4
As Sidrah Libya 47 E1
Assiniboia Canada 62 F2
Assiniboine r. Canada 62 H2
Assiniboine, Mount Canada 60 G4
Assis Brazil 71 A3
Assisi Italy 26 E3
Aş Şubayḥīyah Kuwait 35 G5
Aş Şufayrī well Saudi Arabia 35 G5
As Sukhnah Syria 39 D2
As Sulaymī Saudi Arabia 32 F4
As Sūq Saudi Arabia 32 F5
As Sūrīyah country Asia see Syria
Aş Şuwar Syria 35 F4
As Suwaydā' Syria 39 C3
As Suways Egypt see Suez
As Suways governorate Egypt 39 A4
Assynt, Loch l. U.K. 20 D2
Astacus Kocaeli Turkey see İzmit
Astakida i. Greece 27 L7
Astakos Greece 27 I5
Astana Kazakh. 42 C2
Astaneh Iran 35 H3
Astara Azer. 35 H3
Āstārā Iran 32 G2
Asterabad Iran see Gorgān
Asti Italy 26 C2
Astillero Peru 68 E6
Astin Tag mts China see Altun Shan
Astipálaia i. Greece see Astypalaia
Astor r. Pak. 36 C2
Astorga Spain 25 C2
Astoria U.S.A. 62 C2
Åstorp Sweden 15 H8
Astrabad Iran see Gorgān
Astrakhan' Rus. Fed. 13 K7
Astrakhan' Bazar Azer. see Cälilabad
Astravyets Belarus 15 N9
Astrida Rwanda see Butare
Asturias aut. comm. Spain 25 C2
Asturias, Principado de aut. comm. Spain
see Asturias
Asturica Augusta Spain see Astorga
Astypalaia i. Greece 27 L6
Asunción Para. 70 E3
Aswān Egypt 32 D5
Aswân Egypt see Aswān
Asyūṭ Egypt 34 C6
Asyûṭ Egypt see Asyūṭ
Ata i. Tonga 53 I4
Atacama, Desierto de des. Chile see
Atacama Desert
Atacama, Salar de salt flat Chile 70 C2
Atacama Desert Chile 70 C3
Atafu atoll Tokelau 53 I2
Atafu i. Tokelau 74 I6
'Aṭā'iṭah, Jabal al mt. Jordan 39 B4
Atakent Turkey 39 B1
Atakpamé Togo 46 D4
Atalándi Greece see Atalanti
Atalanti Greece 27 J5
Atalaya Peru 68 D6
Ataléia Brazil 71 C2
Atambua Indon. 54 D2
Atamyrat Turkm. 30 F3
Ataniya Turkey see Adana
'Ataq Yemen 32 G7
Atâr Mauritania 46 B2
Atari Pak. 36 C3
Atascadero CA U.S.A. 65 B3
Atasu Kazakh. 42 C3
Ataúro, Ilha de i. East Timor 54 D2
Atáviros mt. Greece see Attavyros
Atayurt Turkey 39 A1
Atbara Sudan 32 D6
Atbara r. Sudan 32 D6
Atbasar Kazakh. 28 H4
Atchison U.S.A. 63 H4
Atebubu Ghana 46 C4
Ateransk Kazakh. see Atyrau
Āteshān Iran 35 I4
Atessa Italy 26 F3
Athabasca r. Canada 60 G4
Athabasca, Lake Canada 60 H4
Atharan Hazari Pak. 36 C3
Athboy Ireland 21 F4
Athenae Greece see Athens
Athenry Ireland 21 D4
Athens Greece 27 J6
Athens GA U.S.A. 63 K5
Athens OH U.S.A. 63 K4
Athens PA U.S.A. 64 C2
Athens TN U.S.A. 63 K4
Atherstone U.K. 19 F6
Atherton Australia 56 D3
Athina Greece see Athens

83

Bennington NH U.S.A. 64 F1
Bennington VT U.S.A. 64 E1
Benoni S. Africa 51 I4
Ben Rinnes h. U.K. 20 F3
Benson AZ U.S.A. 62 E5
Benteng Indon. 41 E8
Bentiu Sudan 32 C8
Bent Jbaïl Lebanon 39 B3
Bentley U.K. 18 F5
Bento Gonçalves Brazil 71 A5
Benton CA U.S.A. 65 C2
Benton Harbor U.S.A. 63 J3
Bentonville U.S.A. 63 I4
Benue r. Nigeria 46 D4
Ben Vorlich h. U.K. 20 E4
Benwee Head hd Ireland 21 C3
Benwood WV U.S.A. 64 A2
Ben Wyvis mt. U.K. 20 E3
Benxi Liaoning China 44 A4
Benxi Liaoning China 44 B4
Beograd Serbia see Belgrade
Béoumi Côte d'Ivoire 46 C4
Beppu Japan 45 C6
Béqaa val. Lebanon see El Béqaa
Berach r. India 36 C4
Beraketa Madag. 49 E6
Berasia India 36 D5
Berat Albania 27 H4
Beravina Madag. 49 E5
Berber Sudan 32 D6
Berbera Somalia 48 E2
Berbérati Cent. Afr. Rep. 48 B3
Berchtesgaden, Nationalpark nat. park Germany 17 N7
Berck France 24 E1
Berdichev Ukr. see Berdychiv
Berdigestyakh Rus. Fed. 29 N3
Berdyans'k Ukr. 13 H7
Berdychiv Ukr. 13 F6
Beregovo Ukr. see Berehove
Beregovoy Rus. Fed. 44 B1
Berehove Ukr. 13 D6
Bereina P.N.G. 52 E2
Bere Island Ireland 21 C6
Bereket Turkm. 33 I3
Berekum Ghana 46 C4
Berenice Egypt see Baranīs
Berenice Libya see Benghazi
Berens River Canada 63 H1
Bereza Belarus see Byaroza
Berezino Belarus see Byerazino
Berezivka Ukr. 13 F7
Berezne Ukr. 13 E6
Bereznik Rus. Fed. 12 I3
Berezniki Rus. Fed. 11 R4
Berezov Rus. Fed. see Berezovo
Berezovka Rus. Fed. 44 B2
Berezovka Ukr. see Berezivka
Berezovo Rus. Fed. 11 T3
Berezovyy Rus. Fed. 44 D2
Berga Spain 25 G2
Bergama Turkey 27 L5
Bergamo Italy 26 C2
Bergby Sweden 15 J6
Bergen Mecklenburg-Vorpommern Germany 17 N3
Bergen Norway 15 D6
Bergen NY U.S.A. 64 C1
Bergerac France 24 E4
Bergheim (Erft) Germany 17 K5
Bergland Namibia 50 C2
Bergomum Italy see Bergamo
Bergoo WV U.S.A. 64 A3
Bergsjö Sweden 15 J6
Bergsviken Sweden 14 L4
Bergville S. Africa 51 I5
Berhampur India see Baharampur
Beringa, Ostrov i. Rus. Fed. 29 R4
Beringovskiy Rus. Fed. 29 S3
Bering Sea N. Pacific Ocean 29 S4
Bering Strait Rus. Fed./U.S.A. 29 U3
Berislav Ukr. see Beryslav
Berkåk Norway 14 G5
Berkane Morocco 25 E6
Berkeley CA U.S.A. 65 A2
Berkeley Springs WV U.S.A. 64 B3
Berkner Island Antarctica 76 A1
Berkovitsa Bulg. 27 J3
Berkshire Downs hills U.K. 19 F7
Berkshire Hills MA U.S.A. 64 E1
Berlevåg Norway 14 P1
Berlin Germany 17 N4
Berlin MD U.S.A. 64 D3
Berlin PA U.S.A. 64 B3
Berlin Lake OH U.S.A. 64 A2
Bermagui Australia 58 E6
Bermejo r. Arg./Bol. 70 E3
Bermejo Bol. 68 F8
Bermen, Lac l. Canada 61 L4
Bermuda terr. N. Atlantic Ocean 67 L2
Bermuda Rise sea feature N. Atlantic Ocean 72 D4
Bern Switz. 24 H3
Bernardino de Campos Brazil 71 A3
Bernardo O'Higgins, Parque Nacional nat. park Chile 70 B7
Bernasconi Arg. 70 D5
Berne Switz. see Bern
Berner Alpen mts Switz. 24 H3
Berneray i. Scotland U.K. 20 B3
Berneray i. Scotland U.K. 20 B4
Bernier Island Australia 55 A6
Bernina Pass Switz. 24 J3
Beroea Greece see Veroia
Beroea Syria see Aleppo
Beroroha Madag. 49 E6
Beroun Czech Rep. 17 O6
Berounka r. Czech Rep. 17 O6
Berovina Madag. see Beravina
Berri Australia 57 C7
Berriane Alg. 22 E5
Berridale Australia 58 D6
Berriedale U.K. 20 F2
Berrigan Australia 58 B5
Berrima Australia 58 E5
Berrouaghia Alg. 25 H5
Berry Australia 58 E5
Berryessa, Lake CA U.S.A. 65 A1
Berry Head hd U.K. 19 D8
Berry Islands Bahamas 67 I3
Berryville VA U.S.A. 64 C3
Berseba Namibia 50 C4
Berté, Lac l. Canada 63 N1
Berthoud Pass U.S.A. 62 F4
Bertolinía Brazil 69 J5
Bertoua Cameroon 46 E4
Bertraghboy Bay Ireland 21 C4
Beru atoll Kiribati 53 H2
Beruri Brazil 68 F4
Beruwala Sri Lanka 38 C5
Berwick Australia 58 B7
Berwick-upon-Tweed U.K. 18 E3
Berwyn hills U.K. 19 D6
Beryslav Ukr. 27 O1
Berytus Lebanon see Beirut
Besalampy Madag. 49 E5
Besançon France 24 H3
Beshneh Iran 35 I5
Besikama Indon. 54 D2
Beskra Alg. see Biskra
Beslan Rus. Fed. 35 G2
Besnard Lake Canada 60 H4
Besni Turkey 34 E3
Besor watercourse Israel 39 B4
Beşparmak Dağları mts Cyprus see Pentadaktylos Range
Bessbrook U.K. 21 F3
Bessemer U.S.A. 63 J5
Besshoky, Gora h. Kazakh. 35 I1
Besskorbnaya Rus. Fed. 13 I7
Bessonovka Rus. Fed. 13 J5
Betanzos Spain 25 B2
Bethal S. Africa 51 I4
Bethanie Namibia 50 C4
Bethel Park PA U.S.A. 64 A2
Bethesda U.K. 18 C5
Bethesda MD U.S.A. 64 C3
Bethesda OH U.S.A. 64 A2
Bethlehem S. Africa 51 I5
Bethlehem PA U.S.A. 64 D2
Bethlehem West Bank 39 B4
Bethulie S. Africa 51 G6
Beti Pak. 36 B3
Betim Brazil 71 B2
Bet Lehem West Bank see Bethlehem
Betma India 36 C5
Betoota Australia 56 C5
Betpak-Dala plain Kazakh. 42 C3
Betroka Madag. 49 E6
Bet She'an Israel 39 B3
Betsiamites Canada 63 N2
Bettiah India 37 F4
Bettyhill U.K. 20 E2
Bettystown Ireland 21 F4
Betul India 36 D5
Betwa r. India 36 D4
Betws-y-coed U.K. 19 D5
Beulah Australia 57 C7
Beult r. U.K. 19 H7
Beuthen Poland see Bytom
Beverley U.K. 18 G5
Beverly MA U.S.A. 64 F1
Beverly Hills CA U.S.A. 65 C3
Bexhill U.K. 19 H8
Bexley, Cape Canada 60 G3
Beyānlū Iran 35 G4
Beyce Turkey see Orhaneli
Bey Dağları mts Turkey 27 N6
Beykoz Turkey 27 M4
Beyla Guinea 46 C4
Beylagan Azer. see Beyläqan
Beyläqan Azer. 35 G3
Beyneu Kazakh. 30 E2
Beypazarı Turkey 27 N4
Beypınarı Turkey 34 E3
Beypore India 38 B4
Beyrouth Lebanon see Beirut
Beyşehir Turkey 34 C3
Beyşehir Gölü l. Turkey 34 C3
Beytonovo Rus. Fed. 44 B1
Beytüşşebap Turkey 35 F3
Bezbozhnik Rus. Fed. 12 K4
Bezhanitsy Rus. Fed. 12 F4
Bezhetsk Rus. Fed. 12 H4
Béziers France 24 F5
Bezmein Turkm. see Abadan
Bezwada India see Vijayawada
Bhabha India see Bhabhua
Bhabhar India 36 B4
Bhabhua India 37 E4
Bhabua India see Bhabhua
Bhachau India 36 B5
Bhachbhar India 36 B4
Bhadgaon Nepal see Bhaktapur
Bhadohi India 37 E4
Bhadra India 36 C3
Bhadrachalam Road Station India see Kottagudem
Bhadrak India 37 F5
Bhadrakh India see Bhadrak
Bhadravati India 38 B3
Bhag Pak. 36 A3
Bhagalpur India 37 F4
Bhainsa India 38 C2
Bhainsdehi India 36 D5
Bhairab Bazar Bangl. 37 G4
Bhaktapur Nepal 37 F4
Bhalki India 38 C2
Bhamo Myanmar 42 H8
Bhamragarh India 38 D2
Bhandara India 36 D5
Bhanjanagar India 38 E2
Bhanrer Range hills India 36 D5
Bhaptiahi India 37 F4
Bharat country Asia see India
Bharatpur India 36 D4
Bhareli r. India 37 H4
Bharuch India 36 C5
Bhatapara India 37 E5
Bhatarsaigh i. U.K. see Vatersay
Bhatghar Lake India 38 B2
Bhatinda India see Bathinda
Bhatnair India see Hanumangarh
Bhatpara India 37 G5
Bhaunagar India see Bhavnagar
Bhavani r. India 38 C4
Bhavani Sagar l. India 38 C4
Bhavnagar India 36 C5
Bhawana Pak. 36 C3
Bhawanipatna India 38 D2
Bhearnaraigh, Eilean i. U.K. see Berneray
Bheemavaram India see Bhimavaram
Bhekuzulu S. Africa 51 J4
Bhera Pak. 36 C2
Bhigvan India 38 B2
Bhikhna Thori Nepal 37 F4
Bhilai India 36 E5
Bhildi India 36 C4
Bhilwara India 36 C4
Bhima r. India 38 C2
Bhimar India 36 B4
Bhimavaram India 38 D2
Bhimlath India 36 E5
Bhind India 36 D4
Bhinga India 37 E4
Bhisho S. Africa 51 H7
Bhiwandi India 38 B2
Bhiwani India 36 D3
Bhogaipur India 36 D4
Bhojpur Nepal 37 F4
Bhola Bangl. 37 G5
Bhongweni S. Africa 51 I6
Bhopal India 36 D5
Bhopalpatnam India 38 D2
Bhrigukaccha India see Bharuch
Bhuban India 38 E1
Bhubaneshwar India 38 E1
Bhubaneswar India see Bhubaneshwar
Bhuj India 36 B5
Bhusawal India 36 C5
Bhutan country Asia 37 G4
Bhuttewala India 36 B4
Bia r. Ghana 46 C4
Bia, Phou mt. Laos 42 I9
Biafo Glacier Pak. 36 C2
Biafra, Bight of g. Africa see Benin, Bight of
Biak Indon. 41 F8
Biak i. Indon. 41 F8
Biała Podlaska Poland 13 D5
Białogard Poland 17 O4
Białystok Poland 13 D5
Bianco, Monte mt. France/Italy see Mont Blanc
Bianzhao China 44 A3
Biaora India 36 D5
Biarritz France 24 D5
Bibai Japan 44 F4
Bibbenluke Australia 58 D6
Bibbiena Italy 26 D3
Biberach an der Riß Germany 17 L6
Bibile Sri Lanka 38 D5
Biblos Lebanon see Jbail
Bicas Brazil 71 C3
Biçer Turkey 27 N5
Bicester U.K. 19 F7
Bichabhera India 36 C4
Bichevaya Rus. Fed. 44 D3
Bichi r. Rus. Fed. 44 E1
Bickerton Island Australia 56 B2
Bickleigh U.K. 19 D8
Bicuari, Parque Nacional do nat. park Angola 49 B5
Bid India 38 B2
Bida Nigeria 46 D4
Bidar India 38 C2
Biddeford ME U.S.A. 64 F1
Bidean nam Bian mt. U.K. 20 D4
Bideford U.K. 19 C7
Bideford Bay U.K. see Barnstaple Bay
Bidzhan Rus. Fed. 44 C3
Bié Angola see Kuito
Bié, Planalto do Angola 49 B5
Biebrzański Park Narodowy nat. park Poland 15 M10
Biel Switz. 24 H3
Bielawa Poland 17 P5
Bielefeld Germany 17 L4
Bielitz Poland see Bielsko-Biała
Biella Italy 26 C2
Bielsko-Biała Poland 17 Q6
Biên Hoa Vietnam 31 J5
Bienne Switz. see Biel
Bienville, Lac l. Canada 61 K4
Bierbank Australia 58 B1
Biesiesvlei S. Africa 51 G4
Bifoun Gabon 48 B4
Biga Turkey 27 L4
Bigadiç Turkey 27 M5
Biga Yarımadası pen. Turkey 27 L5
Big Bear Lake CA U.S.A. 65 D3
Big Bend Swaziland 51 J4
Bigbury-on-Sea U.K. 19 D8
Biger Nuur salt l. Mongolia 42 H3
Biggar Canada 62 F1
Biggar U.K. 20 F5
Bigge Island Australia 54 D3
Biggenden Australia 57 F5
Biggleswade U.K. 19 G6
Big Hole r. U.S.A. 62 E2
Bighorn r. U.S.A. 62 F2
Bighorn Mountains U.S.A. 62 F3
Big Island Nunavut Canada 61 K3
Big Lake U.S.A. 62 G5
Bignona Senegal 46 B3
Big Pine CA U.S.A. 65 C2
Big Pine Peak CA U.S.A. 65 C3
Big Rapids U.S.A. 63 J3
Big River Canada 62 F1
Big Smokey Valley val. NV U.S.A. 65 D1
Big Spring U.S.A. 62 G5
Bigstone Lake Canada 63 H1
Big Timber U.S.A. 62 F2
Big Trout Lake Canada 63 J1
Big Trout Lake Canada 63 I1
Bihać Bos.-Herz. 26 F2
Bihar state India 37 F4
Bihariganj India 37 F4
Bihar Sharif India 37 F4
Bihor, Vârful mt. Romania 27 J1
Bihoro Japan 44 G4
Bijagós, Arquipélago dos is Guinea-Bissau 46 B3
Bijainpur India 36 D4
Bijapur India 38 B2
Bījār Iran 35 G4
Bijbehara India 36 C2
Bijeljina Bos.-Herz. 27 H2
Bijelo Polje Montenegro 27 H3
Bijeraghogarh India 36 E5
Bijie China 42 J7
Bijji India 38 D2
Bijnor India 36 D3
Bijnore India see Bijnor
Bikampur India 36 C4
Bikaner India 36 C3
Bikin Rus. Fed. 44 D3
Bikin r. Rus. Fed. 44 D3
Bikini atoll Marshall Is 74 H5
Bikori Sudan 32 D7
Bikoro Dem. Rep. Congo 48 B4
Bikou China 42 J6
Bikramganj India 37 F4
Bilād Banī Bū 'Alī Oman 33 I5
Bilaigarh India 38 D1
Bilara India 36 C4
Bilaspur Chhattisgarh India 37 E5
Bilaspur Hima. Prad. India 36 D3
Biläsuvar Azer. 35 H3
Bila Tserkva Ukr. 13 F6
Bilbao Spain 25 E2
Bilbays Egypt 34 C5
Bilbeis Egypt see Bilbays
Bilbo Spain see Bilbao
Bilecik Turkey 27 M4
Biłgoraj Poland 13 D6
Bilharamulo Tanz. 48 D4
Bilhaur India 36 E4
Bilhorod-Dnistrovs'kyy Ukr. 27 N1
Bili Dem. Rep. Congo 48 C3
Bilibino Rus. Fed. 29 R3
Billabalong Australia 55 A6
Billabong Creek r. Australia see Moulamein Creek
Billericay U.K. 19 H7
Billiluna Australia 54 D4
Billingham U.K. 18 F4
Billings U.S.A. 62 F2
Billiton i. Indon. see Belitung
Bill of Portland hd U.K. 19 E8
Bill Williams r. AZ U.S.A. 65 E3
Bilma Niger 46 E3
Bilo r. Rus. Fed. see Belaya
Biloela Australia 56 E5
Bilohirs'k Ukr. 34 D1
Bilohir"ya Ukr. 13 E6
Biloku Guyana 69 G3
Biloli India 38 C2
Bilovods'k Ukr. 13 H6
Biloxi U.S.A. 63 J5
Bilpa Morea Claypan salt flat Australia 56 B5
Bilston U.K. 20 F5
Biltine Chad 47 F3
Bilto Norway 14 L2
Bilyayivka Ukr. 27 N1
Bima Indon. 54 B2
Bimberi, Mount Australia 58 D5
Bimbo Ombella-Mpoko 47 E4
Bimini Islands Bahamas 67 I3
Bimlipatam India 38 D2
Bīnāb Iran 35 H3
Bina-Etawa India 36 D4
Binaija, Gunung mt. Indon. 41 E8
Binboğa Dağı mt. Turkey 34 E3
Bincheng China see Binzhou
Bindebango Australia 58 C1
Bindle Australia 58 D1
Bindu Dem. Rep. Congo 49 B4
Bindura Zimbabwe 49 D5
Binefar Spain 25 G3
Binga Zimbabwe 49 C5
Binga, Monte mt. Moz. 49 D5
Bingara Australia 58 E2
Bingaram i. India 38 B4
Bing Bong Australia 56 B2
Binghamton NY U.S.A. 64 D1
Bingöl Turkey 35 F3
Bingol Dağı mt. Turkey 35 F3
Binika India 37 E5
Binnaway Australia 58 D3
Binpur India 37 F5
Bint Jbeil Lebanon see Bent Jbaïl
Bintulu Sarawak Malaysia 41 D7
Binxian Heilong. China 44 B3
Binxian Shaanxi China 43 J6
Binya Australia 58 C5
Bin-Yauri Nigeria 46 D3
Binzhou Heilong. China see Binxian
Binzhou Shandong China 43 L5
Bioco i. Equat. Guinea 46 D4
Biograd na Moru Croatia 26 F3
Bioko i. Equat. Guinea see Bioco
Biokovo mts Croatia 26 G3
Biquinhas Brazil 71 B2
Bir India see Bid
Bira Rus. Fed. 44 D2
Bi'r Abū Jady oasis Syria 39 D1
Birāk Libya 47 E2
Birakan Rus. Fed. 44 C2
Bi'r al 'Abd Egypt 39 A4
Bi'r al Ḥalbā well Syria 39 D2
Bi'r al Jifjāfah well Egypt 39 A4
Bi'r al Khamsah well Egypt 34 B5
Bi'r al Māliḥah well Egypt 39 A5
Bi'r al Mulūsi Iraq 35 F4
Bi'r al Munbaṭiḥ well Syria 39 D2
Bi'r al Qaṭrānī well Egypt 34 B5
Bi'r al Ubbayiḍ well Egypt 34 B6
Birandozero Rus. Fed. 12 H3
Bi'r an Nuşf well Egypt see Bi'r an Nuşş
Bi'r an Nuşş well Egypt 34 B5
Bir Anzarane W. Sahara 46 B2
Birao Cent. Afr. Rep. 48 C2
Bi'r ar Rābiyah well Egypt 34 B5
Birata Turkm. 33 J1
Biratnagar Nepal 37 F4
Bi'r aţ Ţarfāwī well Libya 34 B5
Bi'r Başīrī well Syria 39 C2
Bi'r Bayḍā' well Egypt 39 B4
Bi'r Baylī well Egypt 34 B5
Bîr Beida well Egypt see Bi'r Bayḍā'
Bi'r Buţaymān Syria 35 E3
Birch Mountains Canada 60 G4
Birch River WV U.S.A. 64 A3
Bircot Eth. 48 E3
Bîr Dignâsh well Egypt see Bi'r Diqnāsh
Bi'r Diqnāsh well Egypt 34 B5
Birdsville Australia 57 B5
Birecik Turkey 34 E3
Bîr el 'Abd Egypt see Bi'r al 'Abd
Bir el Arbi well Alg. 25 I6
Bîr el Istabl well Egypt see Bi'r Iṣṭabl
Bîr el Khamsa well Egypt see Bi'r al Khamsah
Bîr el Nuşş well Egypt see Bi'r an Nuşş
Bîr el Obeiyid well Egypt see Bi'r al Ubbayiḍ
Bîr el Qaṭrāni well Egypt see Bi'r al Qaṭrānī
Bîr el Râbia well Egypt see Bi'r ar Rābiyah
Birendranagar Nepal see Surkhet
Bir en Natrūn well Sudan 32 C6
Bireun Indon. 41 B7
Bi'r Fajr well Saudi Arabia 34 E5
Bi'r Fu'ad well Egypt 34 B5
Bîr Gifgâfa well Egypt see Bi'r al Jifjāfah
Bi'r Ḥajal well Syria 39 D2
Birhan mt. Eth. 48 D2
Bi'r Ḥasanah well Egypt 39 A4
Bi'r Ḥayzān well Saudi Arabia 34 E6
Bi'r Ibn Hirmās Saudi Arabia see Al Bi'r
Birigüi Brazil 71 A3
Bīrīn Syria 39 C2
Bi'r Iṣṭabl well Egypt 34 B5
Bīrjand Iran 33 I3
Bi'r Jubnī well Libya 34 B5
Birkāt Hamad well Iraq 35 G5
Birkenhead U.K. 18 D5
Birkirkara Malta 26 F7
Birksgate Range hills Australia 55 E6
Bîrlad Romania see Bârlad
Bi'r Lahfān well Egypt 39 A4
Birlik Kazakh. 42 C4
Birmingham U.K. 19 F6
Birmingham U.S.A. 63 J5
Bîr Mogreïn Mauritania 46 B2
Bi'r Muḥaymid al Wazwaz well Syria 39 D2
Bi'r Nāḥid oasis Egypt 34 C5
Birnin-Gwari Nigeria 46 D3
Birnin-Kebbi Nigeria 46 D3
Birnin Konni Niger 46 D3
Birobidzhan Rus. Fed. 44 D2
Bi'r Qaşīr as Sirr well Egypt 34 B5
Birr Ireland 21 E4
Bi'r Rawḍ Sālim well Egypt 39 A4
Birrie r. Australia 58 C2
Birrindudu Australia 54 E4
Bîr Rôḍ Sâlim well Egypt see Bi'r Rawḍ Sālim
Birsay U.K. 20 F1
Bi'r Shalatayn Egypt 32 E5
Bîr Shalatein Egypt see Bi'r Shalatayn
Birsk Rus. Fed. 11 R4
Birstall U.K. 19 F6
Birthday Mountain h. Australia 56 C2
Biru China 37 H3
Birur India 38 B3
Biruxiong China see Biru
Biržai Lith. 15 N8
Bisalpur India 36 D3
Bisau India 36 C3
Bisbee U.S.A. 62 F5
Biscay, Bay of sea France/Spain 24 B4
Biscay Abyssal Plain sea feature N. Atlantic Ocean 72 H3
Biscoe Islands Antarctica 76 L2
Biscotasi Lake Canada 63 K2
Bishbek Kyrg. see Bishkek
Bishenpur India see Bishnupur
Bishkek Kyrg. 42 C4
Bishnupur Manipur India 37 H4
Bishnupur W. Bengal India 37 F5
Bishop CA U.S.A. 65 C2
Bishop Auckland U.K. 18 F4
Bishop's Stortford U.K. 19 H7
Bishrī, Jabal hills Syria 39 D2
Bishui Heilong. China 44 A1
Biskra Alg. 22 F5
Bismarck U.S.A. 62 G2
Bismarck Archipelago is P.N.G. 52 E2
Bismarck Range mts P.N.G. 52 E2
Bismarck Sea P.N.G. 52 E2
Bismil Turkey 35 F3
Bismo Norway 14 F6
Bispgården Sweden 14 J5
Bissa, Djebel mt. Alg. 25 G5
Bissamcuttak India 38 D2
Bissau Guinea-Bissau 46 B3
Bissaula Nigeria 46 E4
Bissett Canada 63 H1
Bistcho Lake Canada 60 G4
Bistrița Romania 27 K1
Bistrița r. Romania 27 L1
Bitburg Germany 17 K6
Bitche France 24 H2
Bithur India 36 E4
Bithynia reg. Turkey 27 M4
Bitkine Chad 47 E3
Bitlis Turkey 35 F3
Bitola Macedonia 27 I4
Bitolj Macedonia see Bitola
Bitonto Italy 26 G4
Bitra Par rf India 38 B4
Bitterfontein S. Africa 50 D6
Bitter Lakes Egypt 34 D5
Bitterroot r. U.S.A. 62 E2
Bitterroot Range mts U.S.A. 62 D2
Bitterwater CA U.S.A. 65 B2
Biu Nigeria 46 E3
Biwa-ko l. Japan 45 D6
Biwmares U.K. see Beaumaris
Bīye K'obē Eth. 48 E2
Biysk Rus. Fed. 42 F2
Bizana S. Africa 51 I6
Bizerta Tunisia see Bizerte
Bizerte Tunisia 26 C6
Bjargtangar hd Iceland 14 [inset]
Bjästa Sweden 14 K5
Bjelovar Croatia 26 G2
Bjerkvik Norway 14 J2
Bjerringbro Denmark 15 F8
Bjørgan Norway 14 G5
Björkliden Sweden 14 K2
Björklinge Sweden 15 J6
Bjorli Norway 14 F5
Björna Sweden 14 K5
Björneborg Fin. see Pori
Bjørnøya i. Arctic Ocean 28 C2
Bjurholm Sweden 14 K5
Bla Mali 46 C3
Black r. Vietnam 42 J8
Blackadder Water r. U.K. 20 G5
Blackall Australia 56 D5
Black Bourton U.K. 19 F7
Blackbull Australia 56 C3
Blackburn U.K. 18 E5
Blackbutt Australia 58 F1
Black Canyon gorge AZ U.S.A. 65 E3
Black Combe h. U.K. 18 D4
Blackdown Tableland National Park Australia 56 E4
Black Forest mts Germany 17 L7
Black Hill h. U.K. 18 F5
Black Hills SD U.S.A. 62 G3
Black Lake Canada 60 H4
Black Lake Canada 60 H4
Black Mountain Pak. 36 C2
Black Mountain hills U.K. 19 D7
Black Mountain AK U.S.A. 60 B3
Black Mountain CA U.S.A. 65 D3
Black Mountains hills U.K. 19 D7
Black Mountains AZ U.S.A. 65 E3
Black Nossob watercourse Namibia 50 D2
Black Pagoda India see Konarka
Blackpool U.K. 18 D5
Black Rock h. Jordan see 'Unāb, Jabal al
Blacksburg VA U.S.A. 64 A4
Black Sea Asia/Europe 13 H8
Blacksod Bay Ireland 21 B3
Blackstairs Mountains hills Ireland 21 F5
Blackstone VA U.S.A. 64 B4
Black Sugarloaf mt. Australia 58 E3
Blackville Australia 58 E3
Blackwater Australia 56 E4
Blackwater Ireland 21 F5
Blackwater r. Ireland 21 E5
Blackwater r. Ireland/U.K. 21 F3
Blackwater Reservoir U.K. 20 E4
Blackwood r. Australia 55 A8
Blackwood National Park Australia 56 D4
Bladensburg National Park Australia 56 C4
Blaenavon U.K. 19 D7
Blagodarnyy Rus. Fed. 13 I7
Blagoevgrad Bulg. 27 J3
Blagoveshchensk Amurskaya Oblast' Rus. Fed. 44 B2
Blagoveshchensk Respublika Bashkortostan Rus. Fed. 11 R4
Blaine Lake Canada 62 F1
Blair Athol Australia 56 D4
Blair Atholl U.K. 20 F4
Blairgowrie U.K. 20 F4
Blakeney U.K. 19 I6
Blanc, Mont mt. France/Italy 24 H4
Blanca, Bahía b. Arg. 70 D5
Blanche, Lake imp. l. S.A. Australia 57 B6
Blanche, Lake imp. l. W.A. Australia 54 C5
Blanco r. Bol. 68 F6
Blanco, Cape U.S.A. 62 C3
Blanc-Sablon Canada 61 M4
Bland r. Australia 58 C4
Bland VA U.S.A. 64 A4
Blanda r. Iceland 14 [inset]
Blandford Forum U.K. 19 E8
Blanes Spain 25 H3
Blanquilla, Isla i. Venez. 68 F1
Blansko Czech Rep. 17 P6
Blantyre Malawi 49 D5
Blarney Ireland 21 D6
Blåviksjön Sweden 14 K4
Blaye France 24 D4
Blayney Australia 58 D4
Blaze, Point Australia 54 E3
Blenheim N.Z. 59 D5
Blenheim Palace tourist site U.K. 19 F7
Blessington Lakes Ireland 21 F4
Bletchley U.K. 19 G6
Blida Alg. 25 H5
Bligh Water b. Fiji 53 H3
Blitta Togo 46 D4
Block Island RI U.S.A. 64 F2
Block Island Sound sea chan. RI U.S.A. 64 F2
Bloemfontein S. Africa 51 H5
Bloemhof S. Africa 51 G4
Bloemhof Dam S. Africa 51 G4
Bloemhof Dam Nature Reserve S. Africa 51 G4
Blönduós Iceland 14 [inset]
Blongas Indon. 54 B2
Bloods Range mts Australia 55 E6
Bloodsworth Island MD U.S.A. 64 C3
Bloody Foreland pt Ireland 21 D2
Bloomington IL U.S.A. 63 J3
Bloomington IN U.S.A. 63 J4
Bloomsburg PA U.S.A. 64 C2
Blossburg PA U.S.A. 64 C2
Blosseville Kyst coastal area Greenland 61 P3
Blouberg S. Africa 51 I2
Blouberg Nature Reserve S. Africa 51 I2
Bloxham U.K. 19 F6
Blue Diamond NV U.S.A. 65 E2
Bluefield WV U.S.A. 64 A4
Bluefields Nicaragua 67 H6
Blue Knob h. PA U.S.A. 64 B2
Blue Mountain India 37 H5
Blue Mountain Pass Lesotho 51 H5
Blue Mountains Australia 58 D4
Blue Mountains U.S.A. 62 D2
Blue Mountains National Park Australia 58 E4
Blue Nile r. Eth./Sudan 32 D6
Bluenose Lake Canada 60 G3
Blue Ridge VA U.S.A. 64 B4
Blue Ridge mts VA U.S.A. 64 A4
Blue Stack h. Ireland 21 D3
Blue Stack Mts hills Ireland 21 D3
Bluestone Lake WV U.S.A. 64 A4
Bluff N.Z. 59 B8
Bluff Knoll mt. Australia 55 B8
Blumenau Brazil 71 A4
Blyde River Canyon Nature Reserve S. Africa 51 J3
Blyth England U.K. 18 F3
Blyth England U.K. 18 F5
Blythe CA U.S.A. 65 E4
Blytheville U.S.A. 63 J4
Bø Norway 15 F7
Bo Sierra Leone 46 B4
Boa Esperança Brazil 71 B3
Boali Cent. Afr. Rep. 48 B3
Boane Moz. 51 K4
Boa Nova Brazil 71 C1
Boatlaname Botswana 51 G2
Boa Viagem Brazil 69 K5
Boa Vista Brazil 68 F3
Boa Vista i. Cape Verde 46 [inset]
Bobadah Australia 58 C4
Bobai China 43 K8
Bobaomby, Tanjona c. Madag. 49 E5
Bobbili India 38 D2
Bobo-Dioulasso Burkina 46 C3
Bobotov Kuk mt. Montenegro see Durmitor
Bobriki Rus. Fed. see Novomoskovsk
Bobrinets Ukr. see Bobrynets'
Bobrov Rus. Fed. 13 I6
Bobrovitsa Ukr. see Bobrovytsya
Bobrovytsya Ukr. 13 F6
Bobruysk Belarus see Babruysk
Bobrynets' Ukr. 13 G6
Bobuk Sudan 32 D7
Bobures Venez. 68 D2
Boby mt. Madag. 49 E6
Boca de Macareo Venez. 68 F2
Boca do Acre Brazil 68 E5
Boca do Jari Brazil 69 H4
Bocaiúva Brazil 71 C2
Bocaranga Cent. Afr. Rep. 48 B3
Bocas del Toro Panama 67 H7
Bochnia Poland 17 R6
Bochum Germany 17 K5
Bocoio Angola 49 B5
Boda Cent. Afr. Rep. 48 B3
Bodalla Australia 58 E6
Bodallin Australia 55 B7
Bodaybo Rus. Fed. 29 M4
Boddam U.K. 20 H3
Bodega Head CA U.S.A. 65 A1
Bodélé reg. Chad 47 E3
Boden Sweden 14 L4
Bodenham U.K. 19 E6
Bodensee l. Germany/Switz. see Constance, Lake
Bodie (abandoned) CA U.S.A. 65 C1
Bodinayakkanur India 38 C4
Bodmin U.K. 19 C8
Bodmin Moor moorland U.K. 19 C8
Bodø Norway 14 I3
Bodoquena Brazil 69 G7
Bodoquena, Serra da hills Brazil 70 E2
Bodrum Turkey 27 L6
Bodträskfors Sweden 14 L3
Boende Dem. Rep. Congo 47 F5
Boffa Guinea 46 B3
Bogalusa U.S.A. 63 J5
Bogan r. Australia 58 C2
Bogandé Burkina 46 C3
Bogan Gate Australia 58 C4
Boğazlıyan Turkey 34 D3
Bogcang Zangbo r. China 37 F3
Bogd Övörhangay Mongolia 42 I4
Bogda Shan mts China 42 F4
Boggabilla Australia 58 E2
Boggabri Australia 58 E3
Boggeragh Mts hills Ireland 21 C5
Boghar Alg. 25 H6
Boghari Alg. see Ksar el Boukhari
Bognor Regis U.K. 19 G8
Bogodukhov Ukr. see Bohodukhiv
Bog of Allen reg. Ireland 21 E4
Bogong, Mount Australia 58 C6
Bogopol' Rus. Fed. 44 D3
Bogoroditsk Rus. Fed. 13 H5
Bogorodsk Rus. Fed. 12 I4
Bogorodskoye Khabarovskiy Kray Rus. Fed. 44 F1
Bogorodskoye Kirovskaya Oblast' Rus. Fed. 12 K4
Bogotá Col. 68 D3
Bogotol Rus. Fed. 28 J4
Bogoyavlenskoye Rus. Fed. see Pervomayskiy
Bogra Bangl. 37 G4
Boguchany Rus. Fed. 29 K4
Boguchar Rus. Fed. 13 I6
Bogué Mauritania 46 B3
Bo Hai g. China 43 L5
Bohai Wan b. China 40 D4
Bohemian Forest mts Germany see Böhmer Wald
Bohlokong S. Africa 51 I5
Böhmer Wald mts Germany 17 N6
Bohodukhiv Ukr. 13 G6
Bohol Sea Phil. 41 E7
Bohu China 42 F4
Boiaçu Brazil 68 F4
Boichoko S. Africa 50 F5
Boikhutso S. Africa 51 H4
Boileau, Cape Australia 54 C4
Boim Brazil 69 G4
Boipeba, Ilha i. Brazil 71 D1
Bois r. Brazil 71 A2
Boise U.S.A. 62 D3
Boise City U.S.A. 62 G4
Boitumelong S. Africa 51 G4
Bojnūrd Iran 33 I2
Bokaak atoll Marshall Is see Taongi
Bokajan India 37 H4
Bokaro India 37 F5
Bokaro Reservoir India 37 F5
Bokatola Dem. Rep. Congo 48 B4
Boké Guinea 46 B3
Bokele Dem. Rep. Congo 48 C4
Bokhara r. Australia 58 C2
Boknafjorden sea chan. Norway 15 D7
Bokoko Dem. Rep. Congo 48 C3
Bokoro Chad 47 E3
Bokovskaya Rus. Fed. 13 I6
Bokspits S. Africa 50 E4
Boktor Rus. Fed. 44 E2
Bokurdak Turkm. 33 I2
Bol Chad 47 E3
Bolaiti Dem. Rep. Congo 47 F5
Bolama Guinea-Bissau 46 B3

olangir India 38 D1
olan Pass Pak. 36 A3
olbec France 24 E2
ole China 42 E4
ole Ghana 46 C4
oleko Dem. Rep. Congo 48 B4
olen Rus. Fed. 44 D2
olgar Rus. Fed. 13 K5
olgatanga Ghana 46 C3
olgrad Ukr. see Bolhrad
olhrad Ukr. 27 M2
oli China 44 C3
olia Dem. Rep. Congo 48 B4
oliden Sweden 14 L4
olintin-Vale Romania 27 K2
olívar Peru 68 C5
olivar NY U.S.A. 64 B1
olívar, Pico mt. Venez. 68 D2
olivia country S. America 68 E7
olkhov Rus. Fed. 13 H5
ollène France 24 G4
ollnäs Sweden 15 J6
ollon Australia 58 C2
ollstabruk Sweden 14 J5
olmen l. Sweden 15 H8
olobo Dem. Rep. Congo 48 B4
ologna Italy 26 D2
olognesi Peru 68 D5
ologoye Rus. Fed. 12 G4
olokanang S. Africa 51 G5
olomba Dem. Rep. Congo 48 B3
olon' Rus. Fed. see Achan
olpur India 37 F5
olsena, Lago di l. Italy 26 D3
ol'shakovo Rus. Fed. 15 L9
ol'shaya Chernigovka Rus. Fed. 11 Q5
ol'shaya Glushitsa Rus. Fed. 13 K5
ol'shaya Imandra, Ozero l. Rus. Fed. 14 R3
ol'shaya Martinovka Rus. Fed. 13 I7
ol'shaya Tsarevshchina Rus. Fed. see Volzhskiy
ol'shenarymskoye Kazakh. 42 E3
ol'shevik, Ostrov i. Rus. Fed. 29 L2
ol'shezemel'skaya Tundra lowland Rus. Fed. 12 L2
ol'shiye Chirki Rus. Fed. 12 J3
ol'shiye Kozly Rus. Fed. 12 H2
ol'shoy Begichev, Ostrov i. Rus. Fed. 77 E2
ol'shoye Murashkino Rus. Fed. 12 J5
ol'shoy Irgiz r. Rus. Fed. 13 J6
ol'shoy Kamen' Rus. Fed. 44 D4
ol'shoy Kavkaz mts Asia/Europe see Caucasus
ol'shoy Kundysh r. Rus. Fed. 12 J4
ol'shoy Lyakhovskiy, Ostrov i. Rus. Fed. 29 P2
ol'shoy Tokmak Kyrg. see Tokmok
ol'shoy Tokmak Ukr. see Tokmak
olsón de Mapimí des. Mex. 66 D3
olton U.K. 18 E5
olu Turkey 27 N4
oluntay China 37 H1
olus Head hd Ireland 21 B6
olvadin Turkey 27 N5
olzano Italy 26 D1
oma Dem. Rep. Congo 49 B4
omaderry Australia 58 E5
ombala Australia 58 D6
ombay India see Mumbai
ombay Beach CA U.S.A. 65 E4
omberai, Semenanjung pen. Indon. 41 F8
omboma Dem. Rep. Congo 48 B3
om Comércio Brazil 68 E5
omdila India 37 H4
omi China 42 H7
omili Dem. Rep. Congo 48 C3
om Jardim Brazil 71 D1
om Jardim de Goiás Brazil 71 A2
om Jesus Brazil 71 A5
om Jesus da Gurgueia, Serra do hills Brazil 69 J5
om Jesus da Lapa Brazil 71 C1
om Jesus do Norte Brazil 71 C3
ømlo i. Norway 15 D7
omokandi r. Dem. Rep. Congo 48 C3
om Retiro Brazil 71 A4
om Sucesso Brazil 71 B3
on, Cap c. Tunisia 26 D6
ona Alg. see Annaba
onāb Iran 35 G3
on Air VA U.S.A. 64 C4
onaire i. Neth. Antilles 67 K6
onaparte Archipelago is Australia 54 D3
onar Bridge U.K. 20 E3
onavista Bay Canada 61 M5
onchester Bridge U.K. 20 G5
ondo Dem. Rep. Congo 48 C3
ondoukou Côte d'Ivoire 46 C4
ondyuzhskiy Rus. Fed. see Mendeleyevsk
ône Alg. see Annaba
one, Teluk b. Indon. 41 E8
onerate, Kepulauan is Indon. 41 E8
o'ness U.K. 20 F4
onete, Cerro mt. Arg. 70 C3
onga Eth. 48 D3
ongaigaon India 37 G4
ongandanga Dem. Rep. Congo 48 C3
ongani S. Africa 50 F5
ongba China 36 E2
ong Co l. China 37 G3
ongo, Massif des mts Cent. Afr. Rep. 48 C3
ongo, Serra do mts Angola 49 B4
ongolava mts Madag. 49 E5
ongor Chad 47 E3
oni Mali 46 C3
Bonifacio Corse France 24 I6
Bonifacio, Bocche di str. France/Italy see Bonifacio, Strait of
Bonifacio, Bouches de str. France/Italy see Bonifacio, Strait of
Bonifacio, Strait of France/Italy 24 I6
Bonin Islands Japan 45 F8
Bonn Germany 17 K5
Bonna Germany see Bonn
Bonnåsjøen Norway 14 I3
Bonners Ferry U.S.A. 62 D2
Bonneville France 24 H3
Bonnie Rock Australia 55 B7
Bonnyrigg U.K. 20 F5
Bonnyville Canada 62 E1
Bononia Italy see Bologna
Bonorva Sardegna Italy 26 C4
Bonshaw Australia 58 E2
Bontebok National Park S. Africa 50 E8
Bonthe Sierra Leone 46 B4
Bontoc Phil. 41 E6
Bontosunggu Indon. 52 B2
Bontrug S. Africa 51 G7
Bonvouloir Islands P.N.G. 56 E1
Bonwapitse Botswana 51 H2
Boolba Australia 58 D2
Booligal Australia 58 B4
Boomer WV U.S.A. 64 A3
Boomi Australia 58 D2
Boonah Australia 58 F1
Boones Mill VA U.S.A. 64 B4
Booneville MS U.S.A. 63 J5
Böön Tsagaan Nuur salt l. Mongolia 42 H3
Boonville CA U.S.A. 65 A1
Boonville NY U.S.A. 64 D1
Boorabin National Park Australia 55 C7
Boorama Somalia 48 E3
Booroorban Australia 58 B5
Boorowa Australia 58 D5
Boort Australia 58 A6
Boothby, Cape Antarctica 76 D2
Boothia, Gulf of Canada 61 J3
Boothia Peninsula Canada 61 I2
Bootle U.K. 18 E5
Booué Gabon 48 B4
Boqê China 37 G3
Boqueirão, Serra do hills Brazil 69 J6
Bor Rus. Fed. 12 J4
Bor Serbia 27 J2
Bor Sudan 47 G4
Bor Turkey 34 D3
Boraha, Nosy i. Madag. 49 F5
Borai India 38 D1
Borakalalo Nature Reserve S. Africa 51 H3
Boran Kazakh. see Buran
Borås Sweden 15 H8
Borasambar India 38 D1
Borāzjān Iran 35 H5
Borba Brazil 69 G4
Borborema, Planalto da plat. Brazil 69 K5
Borçka Turkey 35 F2
Bor Dağı mt. Turkey 27 M6
Bordeaux France 24 D4
Borden Island Canada 61 G2
Borden Peninsula Canada 61 J2
Border Ranges National Park Australia 58 F2
Borðeyri Iceland 14 [inset]
Bordj Bou Arréridj Alg. 25 I5
Bordj Bounaama Alg. 25 G6
Bordj Flye Ste-Marie Alg. 46 C2
Bordj Messaouda Alg. 22 F5
Bordj Mokhtar Alg. 46 D2
Bordj Omar Driss Alg. see Bordj Omer Driss
Bordj Omer Driss Alg. 46 D2
Boreas Abyssal Plain sea feature Arctic Ocean 77 H1
Borgå Fin. see Porvoo
Borgarfjörður Iceland 14 [inset]
Borgarnes Iceland 14 [inset]
Børgefjell Nasjonalpark nat. park Norway 14 H4
Borgholm Sweden 15 J8
Borgo San Lorenzo Italy 26 D3
Bori India 38 C1
Bori r. India 36 C5
Borislav Ukr. see Boryslav
Borisoglebsk Rus. Fed. 13 I6
Borisov Belarus see Barysaw
Borisovka Rus. Fed. 13 H6
Borispol' Ukr. see Boryspil'
Bo River Post Sudan 47 F4
Borja Peru 68 C4
Borkenes Norway 14 J2
Borkovskaya Rus. Fed. 12 K2
Borlänge Sweden 15 I6
Borlaug Norway 15 E6
Borlu Turkey 27 M5
Borneo i. Asia 41 D7
Bornholm i. Denmark 15 I9
Bornholm Denmark 77 H3
Bornova Turkey 27 L5
Borodino Rus. Fed. 28 J3
Borodinskoye Rus. Fed. 15 P6
Borogontsy Rus. Fed. 29 O3
Borohoro Shan mts China 42 E4
Borok-Sulezhskiy Rus. Fed. 12 H4
Boromo Burkina 46 C3
Boron CA U.S.A. 65 D3
Borondi India 38 D2
Boroughbridge U.K. 18 F4
Borovichi Rus. Fed. 12 G4
Borovoy Kirovskaya Oblast' Rus. Fed. 12 K4
Borovoy Respublika Kareliya Rus. Fed. 14 R4
Borovoy Respublika Komi Rus. Fed. 12 L3
Borpeta India see Barpeta
Borrisokane Ireland 21 D5
Borroloola Australia 56 B3
Børsa Norway 14 G5
Borşa Romania 13 E7
Borsakelmas sho'rxogi salt marsh Uzbek. 35 J2
Borshchiv Ukr. 13 E6
Borshchovochnyy Khrebet mts Rus. Fed. 43 J3
Bortala China see Bole
Borūjen Iran 35 H5
Borūjerd Iran 35 H4
Borve U.K. 20 C3
Boryslav Ukr. 13 D6
Boryspil' Ukr. 13 F6
Borzna Ukr. 13 G6
Borzya Rus. Fed. 43 L2
Bosanska Dubica Bos.-Herz. 26 G2
Bosanska Gradiška Bos.-Herz. 26 G2
Bosanska Krupa Bos.-Herz. 26 G2
Bosanski Novi Bos.-Herz. 26 G2
Bosansko Grahovo Bos.-Herz. 26 G2
Boscawen Island Tonga see Niuatoputopu
Bose China 42 J8
Boshof S. Africa 51 G5
Bosna i Hercegovina country Europe see Bosnia-Herzegovina
Bosna Saray Bos.-Herz. see Sarajevo
Bosnia-Herzegovina country Europe 26 G2
Bosobogolo Pan salt pan Botswana 50 F3
Bosobolo Dem. Rep. Congo 48 B3
Bōsō-hantō pen. Japan 45 F6
Bosporus str. Turkey 27 M4
Bossangoa Cent. Afr. Rep. 48 B3
Bossembélé Cent. Afr. Rep. 48 B3
Bossiesvlei Namibia 50 C3
Bossut, Cape Australia 54 C4
Bostan China 37 F1
Bostān Iran 35 G5
Bostan Pak. 36 A3
Bosten Hu l. China 42 F4
Boston U.K. 19 G6
Boston MA U.S.A. 64 F1
Boston Mountains U.S.A. 63 I4
Boston Spa U.K. 18 F5
Botad India 36 B5
Botany Bay Australia 58 E4
Botev mt. Bulg. 27 K3
Botevgrad Bulg. 27 J3
Bothaville S. Africa 51 H4
Bothnia, Gulf of Fin./Sweden 15 K6
Botlikh Rus. Fed. 35 G2
Botoşani Romania 13 E7
Botou China 43 L5
Botshabelo S. Africa 51 H5
Botswana country Africa 49 C6
Botte Donato, Monte mt. Italy 26 G5
Bottesford U.K. 18 G5
Bottrop Germany 17 K5
Botucatu Brazil 71 A3
Botuporã Brazil 71 C1
Bouaflé Côte d'Ivoire 46 C4
Bouaké Côte d'Ivoire 46 C4
Bouar Cent. Afr. Rep. 48 B3
Bouârfa Morocco 22 D5
Bouba Ndjida, Parc National de nat. park Cameroon 47 E4
Bouca Cent. Afr. Rep. 48 B3
Boucaut Bay Australia 54 F3
Boudh India 38 E1
Bougaa Alg. 25 I5
Bougainville, Cape Australia 54 D3
Bougainville Island P.N.G. 52 F2
Bougainville Reef Australia 56 D2
Boughessa Mali 46 D3
Bougie Alg. see Bejaïa
Bougouni Mali 46 C3
Bougtob Alg. 22 E5
Bouillon Belgium 16 J6
Bouira Alg. 25 H5
Bou Izakarn Morocco 46 C2
Boujdour W. Sahara 46 B2
Boulder Australia 55 C7
Boulder CO U.S.A. 62 F3
Boulder Canyon gorge NV U.S.A. 65 E2
Boulder City NV U.S.A. 65 E3
Boulevard CA U.S.A. 65 D4
Boulia Australia 56 B4
Boulogne France see Boulogne-sur-Mer
Boulogne-Billancourt France 24 F2
Boulogne-sur-Mer France 24 E1
Boumerdes Alg. 25 H5
Bouna Côte d'Ivoire 46 C4
Bou Naceur, Jbel mt. Morocco 22 D5
Boû Nâga Mauritania 46 B3
Boundary Peak NV U.S.A. 65 C2
Boundiali Côte d'Ivoire 46 C4
Boundji Congo 48 B4
Bounty Islands N.Z. 53 H6
Bounty Trough sea feature S. Pacific Ocean 74 H9
Bourail New Caledonia 53 G4
Bourbon reg. France see Bourbonnais
Bourbon terr. Indian Ocean see Réunion
Bourbonnais reg. France 24 F3
Bourem Mali 46 C3
Bouressa Mali see Boughessa
Bourg-Achard France 19 H9
Bourganeuf France 24 E4
Bourg-en-Bresse France 24 G3
Bourges France 24 F3
Bourgogne reg. France see Burgundy
Bourgogne, Canal de France 24 G3
Bourke Australia 58 B3
Bourne U.K. 19 G6
Bournemouth U.K. 19 F8
Bourtoutou Chad 47 F3
Bou Saâda Alg. 25 I6
Bou Salem Tunisia 26 C6
Bouse AZ U.S.A. 65 E4
Bouse Wash watercourse AZ U.S.A. 65 E3
Boutilimit Mauritania 46 B3
Bouvet Island terr. S. Atlantic Ocean see Bouvetøya
Bouvetøya terr. S. Atlantic Ocean 72 I9
Bova Marina Italy 26 F6
Bow r. Alta Canada 62 E2
Bowa China see Muli
Bowden WV U.S.A. 64 B3
Bowditch atoll Tokelau see Fakaofo
Bowen Australia 56 E4
Bowen, Mount Australia 58 D6
Bowenville Australia 58 E1
Bowers Ridge sea feature Bering Sea 74 H2
Bowie Australia 56 D4
Bow Island Canada 62 E2
Bowling Green KY U.S.A. 63 J4
Bowling Green OH U.S.A. 63 K3
Bowling Green VA U.S.A. 64 C3
Bowling Green Bay National Park Australia 56 D3
Bowman U.S.A. 62 G2
Bowman Island Antarctica 76 F2
Bowman Peninsula Antarctica 76 L2
Bowmore U.K. 20 C5
Bowo China see Bomi
Bowral Australia 58 E5
Boyabat Turkey 34 D2
Boyana tourist site Bulg. 27 J3
Boyd r. Australia 58 F2
Boyd Lagoon imp. l. Australia 55 D6
Boyers PA U.S.A. 64 B2
Boyle Ireland 21 D4
Boyne r. Ireland 21 F4
Boysun Uzbek. 33 K2
Boyuibe Bol. 68 F8
Böyük Qafqaz mts Asia/Europe see Caucasus
Bozcaada i. Turkey 27 L5
Bozdağ mt. Turkey 27 L5
Bozdağ mt. Turkey 39 C1
Boz Dağları mts Turkey 27 L5
Bozdoğan Turkey 27 M6
Bozeat U.K. 19 G6
Bozeman U.S.A. 62 E2
Bozen Italy see Bolzano
Bozoum Cent. Afr. Rep. 48 B3
Bozova Turkey 34 E3
Bozqūsh, Kūh-e mts Iran 35 G3
Bozüyük Turkey 27 N5
Bozyazı Turkey 39 A1
Bra Italy 26 B2
Brač i. Croatia 26 G3
Bracadale U.K. 20 C3
Bracadale, Loch b. U.K. 20 C3
Bracara Port. see Braga
Bracciano, Lago di l. Italy 26 E3
Bracebridge Canada 63 L2
Bräcke Sweden 14 I5
Bracknell U.K. 19 G7
Bradano r. Italy 26 G4
Bradenton U.S.A. 63 K6
Brades Germany 67 L5
Bradford U.K. 18 F5
Bradford PA U.S.A. 64 B2
Brady U.S.A. 62 H5
Brae U.K. 20 [inset]
Braemar U.K. 20 F3
Braga Port. 25 B3
Bragado Arg. 70 D5
Bragança Brazil 69 I4
Bragança Port. 25 C3
Bragança Paulista Brazil 71 B3
Brahin Belarus 13 F6
Brahmanbaria Bangl. 37 G5
Brahmapur India 38 E2
Brahmaputra r. China 42 F7
Brahmaputra r. China/India 40 B5
Brahmaputra r. India 37 H4
Brahmaur India 36 D2
Brăila Romania 27 L2
Brainerd U.S.A. 63 I2
Braintree U.K. 19 H7
Braithwaite Point Australia 54 F2
Brak r. S. Africa 51 I2
Brakwater Namibia 50 C2
Bramfield Australia 55 F8
Bramming Denmark 15 F9
Brämön i. Sweden 14 J5
Brampton England U.K. 18 E4
Brampton England U.K. 19 I6
Bramwell Australia 56 C2
Brancaster U.K. 19 H6
Branco r. Brazil 68 F4
Brandberg mt. Namibia 49 B6
Brandbu Norway 15 G6
Brande Denmark 15 F9
Brandenburg Germany 17 N4
Brandfort S. Africa 51 H5
Brandon Canada 62 H2
Brandon U.K. 19 H6
Brandon Head hd Ireland 21 B5
Brandon Mountain h. Ireland 21 B5
Brandvlei S. Africa 50 E6
Braniewo Poland 17 Q3
Bransfield Strait Antarctica 76 L2
Brantford Ont. Canada 64 A1
Branxton Australia 58 E4
Brasil country S. America see Brazil
Brasileia Brazil 68 E6
Brasília Brazil 71 B1
Brasília de Minas Brazil 71 B2
Braslav Belarus see Braslaw
Braslaw Belarus 15 O9
Braşov Romania 27 K2
Brassey, Mount Australia 55 F5
Brassey Range hills Australia 55 C6
Bratislava Slovakia 17 P6
Bratsk Rus. Fed. 42 I1
Bratskoye Vodokhranilishche resr Rus. Fed. 42 I1
Brattleboro VT U.S.A. 64 E1
Braunau am Inn Austria 17 N6
Braunschweig Germany 17 M4
Brava i. Cape Verde 46 [inset]
Brave PA U.S.A. 64 A3
Bråviken inlet Sweden 15 J7
Bravo, Cerro mt. Bol. 68 F7
Bravo del Norte, Río r. Mex. 62 H6
Bravo del Norte, Río r. Mex./U.S.A. see Rio Grande
Brawley CA U.S.A. 65 E4
Bray Ireland 21 F4
Bray Island Canada 61 K3
Brazil country S. America 69 G5
Brazil Basin sea feature S. Atlantic Ocean 72 G7
Brazilian Highlands plat. Brazil 69 J7
Brazos r. U.S.A. 63 H6
Brazzaville Congo 49 B4
Brčko Bos.-Herz. 26 H2
Bré Ireland see Bray
Breadalbane Australia 56 B4
Breaksea Sound inlet N.Z. 59 A7
Bream Bay N.Z. 59 E2
Brechfa U.K. 19 C7
Brechin U.K. 20 G4
Břeclav Czech Rep. 17 P6
Brecon U.K. 19 D7
Brecon Beacons reg. U.K. 19 D7
Brecon Beacons National Park U.K. 19 D7
Breda Neth. 16 J5
Bredasdorp S. Africa 50 E8
Bredbo Australia 58 D5
Bredviken Sweden 14 I3
Bregenz Austria 17 L7
Breiðafjörður b. Iceland 14 [inset]
Breiðdalsvík Iceland 14 [inset]
Breivikbotn Norway 14 M1
Breizh reg. France see Brittany
Brejo Velho Brazil 71 C1
Brekstad Norway 14 F5
Bremen Germany 17 L4
Bremer Bay Australia 55 B8
Bremerhaven Germany 17 L4
Bremer Range hills Australia 55 C8
Bremersdorp Swaziland see Manzini
Brenham U.S.A. 63 H5
Brenna Norway 14 H4
Brennero, Passo di pass Austria/Italy see Brenner Pass
Brenner Pass Austria/Italy 26 D1
Brennerpaß pass Austria/Italy see Brenner Pass
Brentwood U.K. 19 H7
Brescia Italy 26 D2
Breslau Poland see Wrocław
Bresle r. France 19 I8
Bressanone Italy 26 D1
Bressay i. U.K. 20 [inset]
Bressuire France 24 D3
Brest Belarus 15 M10
Brest France 24 B2
Brest-Litovsk Belarus see Brest
Bretagne reg. France see Brittany
Breton Sound b. U.S.A. 63 J6
Brett, Cape N.Z. 59 E2
Bretton U.K. 18 E5
Breves Brazil 69 H4
Brewarrina Australia 58 C2
Brewster OH U.S.A. 64 A2
Brewster, Kap c. Greenland see Kangikajik
Brewster, Lake imp. l. Australia 58 B4
Breyten S. Africa 51 I4
Breytovo Rus. Fed. 12 H4
Brezhnev Rus. Fed. see Naberezhnyye Chelny
Brezno Slovakia 17 Q6
Brezovo Bulg. 27 K3
Brezovo Polje plain Croatia 26 G2
Bria Cent. Afr. Rep. 48 C3
Briançon France 24 H4
Brian Head mt. UT U.S.A. 65 F2
Bribbaree Australia 58 C5
Bribie Island Australia 58 F1
Briceni Moldova 13 E6
Brichany Moldova see Briceni
Brichen' Moldova see Briceni
Bridgend U.K. 19 D7
Bridge of Orchy U.K. 20 E4
Bridgeport CA U.S.A. 65 C1
Bridgeport CT U.S.A. 64 E2
Bridgeport NE U.S.A. 62 G3
Bridgeton NJ U.S.A. 64 D3
Bridgetown Australia 55 B8
Bridgetown Barbados 67 M6
Bridgeville DE U.S.A. 64 D3
Bridgewater Canada 63 O3
Bridgewater NY U.S.A. 64 D1
Bridgnorth U.K. 19 E6
Bridgwater U.K. 19 D7
Bridgwater Bay U.K. 19 D7
Bridlington U.K. 18 G4
Bridlington Bay U.K. 18 G4
Bridport Australia 57 [inset]
Bridport U.K. 19 E8
Brie reg. France 24 F2
Brieg Poland see Brzeg
Briery Knob mt. WV U.S.A. 64 A3
Brig Switz. 24 H3
Brigg U.K. 18 G5
Brigham City U.S.A. 62 E3
Brightlingsea U.K. 19 I7
Brighton U.K. 19 G8
Brighton NY U.S.A. 64 C1
Brignoles France 24 H5
Brikama Gambia 46 B3
Brindisi Italy 26 G4
Brioude France 24 F4
Brisbane Australia 58 F1
Brisbane Ranges National Park Australia 58 B6
Bristol U.K. 19 E7
Bristol CT U.S.A. 64 E2
Bristol NH U.S.A. 64 F1
Bristol RI U.S.A. 64 F2
Bristol TN U.S.A. 63 K4
Bristol Bay U.S.A. 60 B4
Bristol Channel est. U.K. 19 C7
Bristol Lake CA U.S.A. 65 E3
Britannia Island New Caledonia see Maré
British Antarctic Territory Antarctica 76 L2
British Columbia prov. Canada 62 C1
British Empire Range mts Canada 61 J1
British Guiana country S. America see Guyana
British Honduras country Central America see Belize
British Indian Ocean Territory terr. Indian Ocean 73 M6
British Solomon Islands country S. Pacific Ocean see Solomon Islands
Brito Godins Angola see Kiwaba N'zogi
Brits S. Africa 51 H3
Britstown S. Africa 50 F6
Brittany reg. France 24 C2
Brive-la-Gaillarde France 24 E4
Briviesca Spain 25 E2
Brixham U.K. 19 D8
Brixia Italy see Brescia
Brlik Kazakh. see Birlik
Brno Czech Rep. 17 P6
Broach India see Bharuch
Broad r. U.S.A. 63 K5
Broadalbin NY U.S.A. 64 D1
Broad Arrow Australia 55 C7
Broadback r. Canada 63 L1
Broad Bay U.K. see Tuath, Loch a'
Broadford Australia 58 B6
Broadford Ireland 21 D5
Broadford U.K. 20 D3
Broad Law h. U.K. 20 F5
Broadmere Australia 56 A3
Broad Sound sea chan. Australia 56 E4
Broadstairs U.K. 19 I7
Broadus U.S.A. 62 F2
Broadway VA U.S.A. 64 B3
Broadwood N.Z. 59 D2
Brochet Canada 77 L3
Brochet, Lac l. Canada 61 H4
Brochet, Lac au l. Canada 63 N2
Brockman, Mount Australia 54 B5
Brockton MA U.S.A. 64 F1
Brockway PA U.S.A. 64 B2
Brodeur Peninsula Canada 61 J2
Brodick U.K. 20 D5
Brodnica Poland 17 Q4
Brody Ukr. 13 E6
Broken Arrow U.S.A. 63 H4
Broken Bay Australia 58 E4
Broken Hill Australia 57 C6
Broken Hill Zambia see Kabwe
Broken Plateau sea feature Indian Ocean 73 O8
Brokopondo Suriname 69 G2
Brokopondo Stuwmeer resr Suriname see Professor van Blommestein Meer
Bromberg Poland see Bydgoszcz
Bromsgrove U.K. 19 E6
Brønderslev Denmark 15 F8
Brønnøysund Norway 14 H4
Brooke U.K. 19 I6
Brookhaven U.S.A. 63 I5
Brookings OR U.S.A. 62 C3
Brookings SD U.S.A. 63 H3
Brookline MA U.S.A. 64 F1
Brookneal VA U.S.A. 64 B4
Brooks Canada 62 E1
Brooks Range mts U.S.A. 60 D3
Brookton Australia 55 B8
Brookville PA U.S.A. 64 B2
Broom, Loch inlet U.K. 20 D3
Broome Australia 54 C4
Brora U.K. 20 F2
Brora r. U.K. 20 F2
Brösarp Sweden 15 I9
Brosna r. Ireland 21 E4
Brough U.K. 18 E4
Brough Ness pt U.K. 20 G2
Broughshane U.K. 21 F3
Broughton Island Canada see Qikiqtarjuaq
Broughton Islands Australia 58 F4
Brovary Ukr. 13 F6
Brovinia Australia 57 E5
Brovst Denmark 15 F8
Browne Range hills Australia 55 D6
Brownfield U.S.A. 62 G5
Brown Mountain CA U.S.A. 65 D3
Brownsville PA U.S.A. 64 B2
Brownsville TN U.S.A. 63 J4
Brownsville TX U.S.A. 63 H6
Brownwood U.S.A. 62 H5
Browse Island Australia 54 C3
Bruay-la-Bussière France 24 F1
Bruce Rock Australia 55 B7
Bruck an der Mur Austria 17 O7
Brue r. U.K. 19 E7
Bruges Belgium see Brugge
Brugge Belgium 16 I5
Bruin PA U.S.A. 64 B2
Bruint India 37 I3
Brûk, Wâdi el watercourse Egypt see Burūk, Wādī al
Brukkaros Namibia 50 D3
Brûlé Canada 62 D1
Brumado Brazil 71 C1
Brumunddal Norway 15 G6
Brundisium Italy see Brindisi
Brunei country Asia 41 D7
Brunei Brunei see Bandar Seri Begawan
Brunette Downs Australia 56 A3
Brunflo Sweden 14 I5
Brunico Italy 26 D1
Brünn Czech Rep. see Brno
Brunner, Lake N.Z. 59 C6
Brunswick Germany see Braunschweig
Brunswick GA U.S.A. 63 K5
Brunswick MD U.S.A. 64 C3
Brunswick ME U.S.A. 63 N3
Brunswick, Península de pen. Chile 70 B8
Brunswick Bay Australia 54 D3
Bruntál Czech Rep. 17 P6
Brunt Ice Shelf Antarctica 76 B2
Bruntville S. Africa 51 J5
Bruny Island Australia 57 [inset]
Brusa Turkey see Bursa
Brusenets Rus. Fed. 12 I3
Brusque Brazil 71 A4
Brussel Belgium see Brussels
Brussels Belgium 16 J5
Bruthen Australia 58 C6
Bruxelles Belgium see Brussels
Bruzual Venez. 68 E2
Bryan TX U.S.A. 63 H5
Bryan, Mount h. Australia 57 B7
Bryan Coast Antarctica 76 L2
Bryansk Rus. Fed. 13 G5
Bryanskoye Rus. Fed. 35 G1
Brynbuga U.K. see Usk
Bryne Norway 15 D7
Bryukhovetskaya Rus. Fed. 13 H7
Brzeg Poland 17 P5
Brześć nad Bugiem Belarus see Brest
Bua r. Malawi 49 D5
Bu'aale Somalia 48 E3
Buala Solomon Is 53 F2
Būbīyān, Jazīrat Kuwait 35 H5
Bucak Turkey 27 N6
Bucaramanga Col. 68 D2
Buccaneer Archipelago is Australia 54 C4
Buchanan Liberia 46 B4
Buchanan VA U.S.A. 64 B4
Buchanan, Lake imp. l. Australia 56 D4
Buchan Gulf Canada 61 K2
Bucharest Romania 27 L2
Buchon, Point CA U.S.A. 65 B3
Buchy France 19 I9
Bucin, Pasul pass Romania 27 K1
Buckambool Mountain h. Australia 58 B3
Buckeye U.S.A. 62 E5
Buckhannon WV U.S.A. 64 A3
Buckhaven U.K. 20 F4
Buckie U.K. 20 G3
Buckingham U.K. 19 G6
Buckingham VA U.S.A. 64 B4
Buckingham Bay Australia 41 F9
Buckland Tableland reg. Australia 56 E5
Buckleboo Australia 55 G8
Buckle Island Antarctica 76 H2
Buckley watercourse Australia 56 B4
Buckley Bay Antarctica 76 G2
Buckskin Mountains AZ U.S.A. 65 F3
București Romania see Bucharest
Buda-Kashalyova Belarus 13 F5
Budalin Myanmar 37 H5
Budapest Hungary 27 H1
Budaun India 36 D3
Budawang National Park Australia 58 E5
Budda Australia 58 B3
Budd Coast Antarctica 76 F2
Buddusò Sardegna Italy 26 C4
Bude U.K. 19 C8
Budennovsk Rus. Fed. 13 J7
Buderim Australia 58 F1
Budīyah, Jabal mts Egypt 39 A5
Budongquan China 37 H2
Budoni Sardegna Italy 26 C4
Budweis Czech Rep. see České Budějovice
Buenaventura Col. 68 C3
Buena Vista i. N. Mariana Is see Tinian
Buena Vista VA U.S.A. 64 B4
Buendia, Embalse de resr Spain 25 E3
Buenos Aires Arg. 70 E4
Buenos Aires, Lago l. Arg./Chile 70 B7
Buerarema Brazil 71 D1
Buffalo NY U.S.A. 64 B1
Buffalo SD U.S.A. 62 G2
Buffalo WY U.S.A. 62 F3
Buffalo Narrows Canada 77 L3
Buffels watercourse S. Africa 50 C5
Buffels Drift S. Africa 51 H2
Buftea Romania 27 K2
Bug r. Poland 17 S5
Buga Col. 68 C3
Bugaldie Australia 58 D3
Bugdaýly Turkm. 35 I3
Bugojno Bos.-Herz. 26 G2
Bugrino Rus. Fed. 12 K1
Bugt China 44 A2
Bugul'ma Rus. Fed. 11 Q5
Büğür China see Luntai
Buguruslan Rus. Fed. 11 Q5
Buhera Zimbabwe 49 D5
Buhuşi Romania 27 L1
Builth Wells U.K. 19 D6
Bui National Park Ghana 46 C4
Buinsk Rus. Fed. 13 K5
Bu'in Zahrā Iran 35 H4
Buir Nur l. Mongolia 43 L3
Buitepos Namibia 50 D2
Bujanovac Serbia 27 I3
Bujumbura Burundi 48 C4
Bukachacha Rus. Fed. 43 L2
Buka Daban mt. China 37 G1
Buka Island P.N.G. 52 F2
Būkān Iran 35 G3
Būkand Iran 35 I5
Bukavu Dem. Rep. Congo 48 C4
Bukhoro Uzbek. see Buxoro
Bukittinggi Indon. 41 C8
Bukkapatnam India 38 C3
Bukoba Tanz. 48 D4
Bükreş Romania see Bucharest
Būl, Kūh-e mt. Iran 35 I5
Bülach Switz. 24 I3
Bulancak Turkey 34 E2
Bulandshahr India 36 D3
Bulanık Turkey 35 F3
Bulava Rus. Fed. 44 F2
Bulawayo Zimbabwe 49 C6
Buldan Turkey 27 M5
Buldana India see Buldhana
Buldhana India 38 C1
Bulembu Swaziland 51 J3
Bulgan Bulgan Mongolia 42 I3
Bulgan Mongolia 42 G3
Bulgan Hovd Mongolia see Bulgan
Bulgar Rus. Fed. see Bolgar
Bulgaria country Europe 27 K3
Bŭlgariya country Europe see Bulgaria
Bullawarra, Lake imp. l. Australia 58 A1
Buller r. N.Z. 59 C5
Buller, Mount Australia 58 C6
Bulleringa National Park Australia 56 C3
Bullfinch Australia 55 B7
Bullhead City AZ U.S.A. 65 E3
Bulli Australia 58 E5
Bullion Mountains CA U.S.A. 65 D3
Bullo r. Australia 54 E3
Bulloo Downs Australia 57 C6
Bulloo Lake imp. l. Australia 57 C6
Büllsport Namibia 50 C3
Bulman Australia 54 F3
Bulman Gorge Australia 54 F3
Buloke, Lake dry lake Australia 58 A6
Bulsar India see Valsad
Bultfontein S. Africa 51 H5
Bulukumba Indon. 41 E8
Bulun Rus. Fed. 29 N2
Bulungu Dem. Rep. Congo 49 C4
Bulung'ur Uzbek. 42 B5
Bumba Dem. Rep. Congo 48 C3
Būmbah Libya 34 A4
Bumbah, Khalīj b. Libya 34 A4
Bumpha Bum mt. Myanmar 37 I4
Buna Dem. Rep. Congo 48 B4
Buna Kenya 48 D3
Bunazi Tanz. 48 D4
Bunbury Australia 55 A8
Bunclody Ireland 21 F5
Buncrana Ireland 21 E2
Bunda Tanz. 48 D4
Bundaberg Australia 56 F5
Bundaleer Australia 58 C2
Bundarra Australia 58 E3
Bundi India 36 C4
Bundjalung National Park Australia 58 F2
Bundoran Ireland 21 D3
Bunduqiya Sudan 47 G4
Bungay U.K. 19 I6
Bungendore Australia 58 D5
Bunger Hills Antarctica 76 F2
Bungle Bungle National Park Australia see Purnululu National Park
Bungo-suidō sea chan. Japan 45 D6
Bunguran, Kepulauan is Indon. see Natuna, Kepulauan
Bunguran, Pulau i. Indon. see Natuna Besar
Bunia Dem. Rep. Congo 48 D3
Bunianga Dem. Rep. Congo 48 C4

Buningonia well Australia 55 C7
Bunji Pak. 36 C2
Bunker Group atolls Australia 56 F4
Bunkeya Dem. Rep. Congo 49 C5
Bünsum China 37 E3
Bunya Mountains National Park Australia 58 E1
Bünyan Turkey 34 D3
Buôn Ma Thuôt Vietnam 31 J5
Buorkhaya, Guba b. Rus. Fed. 29 O2
Bup r. China 37 F3
Buqayq Saudi Arabia see Abqaiq
Buqbuq Egypt 34 B5
Bura Kenya 48 D4
Buraan Somalia 48 E2
Buram Sudan 47 F3
Buran Kazakh. 42 F3
Buranhaém Brazil 71 C2
Buranhaém r. Brazil 71 D2
Burāq Syria 39 C3
Buray r. India 36 C5
Buraydah Saudi Arabia 32 F4
Burbank CA U.S.A. 65 C3
Burcher Australia 58 C4
Burco Somalia 48 E3
Burdigala France see Bordeaux
Burdur Turkey 27 N6
Burdur Gölü l. Turkey 27 N6
Burdwan India see Barddhaman
Burē Eth. 48 D2
Bure r. U.K. 19 I6
Bureå Sweden 14 L4
Bureinskiy Khrebet mts Rus. Fed. 44 D2
Bureinskiy Zapovednik nature res. Rus. Fed. 44 D2
Bureya r. Rus. Fed. 44 C2
Bureya Range mts Rus. Fed. see Bureinskiy Khrebet
Burford Ont. Canada 64 A1
Burgas Bulg. 27 L3
Burgeo Canada 61 M5
Burgersdorp S. Africa 51 H6
Burgersfort S. Africa 51 J3
Burges, Mount h. Australia 55 C7
Burgess Hill U.K. 19 G8
Burghausen Germany 17 N6
Burghead U.K. 20 F3
Burgio, Serra di h. Sicilia Italy 26 F6
Burgos Mex. 62 H7
Burgos Spain 25 E2
Burgsvik Sweden 15 K8
Burgundy reg. France 24 G3
Burhan Budai Shan mts China 42 G5
Burhaniye Turkey 27 L5
Burhanpur India 36 D5
Burhar-Dhanpuri India 37 E5
Buri Brazil 71 A3
Buritama Brazil 71 A3
Buriti Alegre Brazil 71 A2
Buriti Bravo Brazil 69 J5
Buritirama Brazil 69 J6
Buritis Brazil 71 B1
Burj Aziz Khan Pak. 36 A3
Burke Island Antarctica 76 K2
Burke Pass N.Z. see Burkes Pass
Burkes Pass N.Z. 59 C7
Burketown Australia 56 B3
Burkeville VA U.S.A. 64 B4
Burkina country Africa 46 C3
Burkina Faso country Africa see Burkina
Burley U.S.A. 62 E3
Burlington Ont. Canada 64 B1
Burlington CO U.S.A. 62 G4
Burlington IA U.S.A. 63 I3
Burlington VT U.S.A. 63 M3
Burma country Asia see Myanmar
Burmantovo Rus. Fed. 11 S3
Burney, Monte vol. Chile 70 B8
Burnie Australia 57 [inset]
Burniston U.K. 18 G4
Burnley U.K. 18 E5
Burns U.S.A. 62 D3
Burnside r. Canada 60 H3
Burnside, Lake imp. l. Australia 55 C6
Burns Lake Canada 60 F4
Burntisland U.K. 20 F4
Burntwood r. Canada 61 I4
Burog Co l. China 37 F2
Burqin China 42 F3
Burqu' Jordan 39 D3
Burra Australia 57 B7
Burra i. U.K. 20 [inset]
Burravoe U.K. 20 [inset]
Burrel Albania 27 I4
Burrel CA U.S.A. 65 C2
Burren reg. Ireland 21 C4
Burrendong, Lake Australia 58 D4
Burren Junction Australia 58 D3
Burrewarra Point Australia 58 E5
Burrinjuck Australia 58 D5
Burrinjuck Reservoir Australia 58 D5
Burro, Serranías del mts Mex. 66 D3
Burro Creek watercourse AZ U.S.A. 65 F3
Burrowa Pine Mountain National Park Australia 58 C6
Burrow Head hd U.K. 20 E6
Burrundie Australia 54 E3
Bursa Turkey 27 M4
Bûr Safâga Egypt see Būr Safājah
Būr Safājah Egypt 32 D4
Būr Sa'īd Egypt see Port Said
Bûr Sa'îd Egypt see Port Said
Būr Sa'īd governorate Egypt 39 A4
Bûr Sa'îd governorate Egypt see Būr Sa'īd
Bursinskoye Vodokhranilishche resr Rus. Fed. 44 C2
Būr Sudan Sudan see Port Sudan
Burton upon Trent U.K. 19 F6
Burträsk Sweden 14 L4
Burt Well Australia 55 F5
Buru i. Indon. 41 E8
Burūk, Wādī al watercourse Egypt 39 A4
Burullus, Bahra el lag. Egypt see Burullus, Lake
Burullus, Buḥayrat al lag. Egypt see Burullus, Lake
Burullus, Lake lag. Egypt 34 C5
Burultokay China see Fuhai
Burūn, Ra's pt Egypt 39 A4
Burundi country Africa 48 C4
Burunniy Rus. Fed. see Tsagan Aman
Bururi Burundi 48 C4
Burwash Landing Canada 60 E3
Burwick U.K. 20 G2
Buryn' Ukr. 13 G6
Bury St Edmunds U.K. 19 H6
Burzil Pass Pak. 36 C2
Busan S. Korea see Pusan
Busanga Dem. Rep. Congo 48 C4
Buseire Syria see Al Buşayrah
Bush r. U.K. 21 F2
Būshehr Iran 35 H5
Bushêngcaka China 37 E2
Bushenyi Uganda 48 D4
Bushire Iran see Būshehr
Bushmills U.K. 21 F2
Businga Dem. Rep. Congo 48 C3
Buşrá ash Shām Syria 39 C3
Busse Rus. Fed. 44 B2
Busselton Australia 55 A8
Busto Arsizio Italy 26 C2
Buta Dem. Rep. Congo 48 C3
Butare Rwanda 48 C4
Butaritari atoll Kiribati 74 H5
Bute Australia 57 B7
Bute i. U.K. 20 D5
Butha Buthe Lesotho 51 I5
Butha Qi China see Zalantun
Buthidaung Myanmar 37 H5
Butler PA U.S.A. 64 B2
Butlers Bridge Ireland 21 E3
Buton i. Indon. 41 E8
Butte MT U.S.A. 62 E2
Butterworth S. Africa 51 I7
Buttevant Ireland 21 D5
Butt of Lewis hd U.K. 20 C2
Button Bay Canada 61 I4
Butuan Phil. 41 E7
Buturlinovka Rus. Fed. 13 I6
Butwal Nepal 37 E4
Buulobarde Somalia 48 E3
Buur Gaabo Somalia 48 E4
Buurhabaka Somalia 48 E3
Buutsagaan Mongolia 42 H3
Buxar India 37 F4
Buxoro Uzbek. 33 J2
Buxton U.K. 18 F5
Buy Rus. Fed. 12 I4
Buynaksk Rus. Fed. 13 J8
Büyükçekmece Turkey 34 C2
Büyük Egri Dağ mt. Turkey 39 A1
Büyükmenderes r. Turkey 27 L6
Buzău Romania 27 L2
Buzdyak Rus. Fed. 11 Q5
Búzi Moz. 49 D5
Büzmeýin Turkm. see Abadan
Buzuluk Rus. Fed. 11 Q5
Buzuluk r. Rus. Fed. 13 I6
Buzzards Bay MA U.S.A. 64 F2
Byakar Bhutan see Jakar
Byala Bulg. 27 K3
Byala Slatina Bulg. 27 J3
Byalynichy Belarus 13 F5
Byarezina r. Belarus 13 F5
Byaroza Belarus 15 N10
Byblos tourist site Lebanon 39 B2
Bydgoszcz Poland 17 Q4
Byelorussia country Europe see Belarus
Byerazino Belarus 13 F5
Byeshankovichy Belarus 13 F5
Byesville OH U.S.A. 64 A3
Bygland Norway 15 E7
Bykhaw Belarus 13 F5
Bykhov Belarus see Bykhaw
Bykle Norway 15 E7
Bykovo Rus. Fed. 13 J6
Bylot Island Canada 61 K2
Byramgore Reef India 38 A4
Byrd Glacier Antarctica 76 H1
Byrkjelo Norway 15 E6
Byrock Australia 58 C3
Byron, Cape Australia 58 F2
Byron Bay Australia 58 F2
Byron Island Kiribati see Nikunau
Byrranga, Gory mts Rus. Fed. 29 K2
Byske Sweden 14 L4
Byssa Rus. Fed. 44 C1
Byssa r. Rus. Fed. 44 C1
Bytom Poland 17 Q5
Bytów Poland 17 P3
Byurgyutli Turkm. 35 I3
Byzantium Turkey see İstanbul

C

Caacupé Para. 70 E3
Caatinga Brazil 71 B2
Caazapá Para. 70 E3
Caballas Peru 68 C6
Caballococha Peru 68 D4
Caballos Mesteños, Llano de los plain Mex. 66 D3
Cabanaconde Peru 68 D7
Cabanatuan Phil. 41 E6
Cabdul Qaadir Somalia 48 E2
Cabeceira Rio Manso Brazil 69 G7
Cabeceiras Brazil 71 B1
Cabeza del Buey Spain 25 D4
Cabezas Bol. 68 F7
Cabimas Venez. 68 D1
Cabinda Angola 49 B4
Cabinda prov. Angola 49 B5
Cabinet Inlet Antarctica 76 L2
Cabistra Turkey see Ereğli
Cabo Frio Brazil 71 C3
Cabo Frio, Ilha do i. Brazil 71 C3
Cabonga, Réservoir resr Canada 63 L2
Caboolture Australia 58 F1
Cabo Orange, Parque Nacional de nat. park Brazil 69 H3
Cabo Pantoja Peru 68 C4
Cabora Bassa, Lake resr Moz. 49 D5
Cabo Raso Arg. 70 C6
Caborca Mex. 66 B2
Cabot Strait Canada 61 L5
Cabourg France 19 G9
Cabo Verde country N. Atlantic Ocean see Cape Verde
Cabo Verde, Ilhas do is N. Atlantic Ocean 46 [inset]
Cabo Yubi Morocco see Tarfaya
Cabral, Serra do mts Brazil 71 B2
Cābrayıl Azer. 35 G3
Cabrera, Illa de i. Spain 25 H4
Çaçador Brazil 71 A4
Čačak Serbia 27 I3
Caccia, Capo c. Sardegna Italy 26 C4
Cacequi Brazil 70 F3
Cáceres Brazil 69 G7
Cáceres Spain 25 C4
Cache Creek Canada 62 C1
Cacheu Guinea-Bissau 46 B3
Cachi, Nevados de mts Arg. 70 C2
Cachimbo, Serra do hills Brazil 69 H5
Cachoeira Brazil 71 D1
Cachoeira Alta Brazil 71 A2
Cachoeira de Goiás Brazil 71 A2
Cachoeira do Arari Brazil 69 I4
Cachoeiro de Itapemirim Brazil 71 C3
Cacine Guinea-Bissau 46 B3
Caciporé, Cabo c. Brazil 69 H3
Cacolo Angola 49 B5
Caconga Angola 49 B4
Caçu Brazil 71 A2
Caculé Brazil 71 C1
Čadca Slovakia 17 Q6
Cadereyta Mex. 62 G6
Cadibarrawirracanna, Lake imp. l. Australia 57 A6
Cadillac U.S.A. 63 J3
Cádiz Spain 25 C5
Cádiz OH U.S.A. 64 A2
Cádiz, Golfo de g. Spain 25 C5
Cadiz Lake CA U.S.A. 65 E3
Cadotte Lake Canada 60 G4
Caen France 24 D2
Caerdydd U.K. see Cardiff
Caerffili U.K. see Caerphilly
Caerfyrddin U.K. see Carmarthen
Caergybi U.K. see Holyhead
Caernarfon U.K. 19 C5
Caernarfon Bay U.K. 19 C5
Caernarvon U.K. see Caernarfon
Caerphilly U.K. 19 D7
Caesaraugusta Spain see Zaragoza
Caesarea Alg. see Cherchell
Caesarea Cappadociae Turkey see Kayseri
Caesarea Philippi Syria see Bāniyās
Caesarodunum France see Tours
Caesaromagus U.K. see Chelmsford
Caetité Brazil 71 C1
Cafayate Arg. 70 C3
Cafelândia Brazil 71 A3
Caffa Ukr. see Feodosiya
Cagayan de Oro Phil. 41 E7
Cagli Italy 26 E3
Cagliari Sardegna Italy 26 C5
Cagliari, Golfo di b. Sardegna Italy 26 C5
Çagyl Turkm. 35 I2
Cahama Angola 49 B5
Caha Mts hills Ireland 21 C6
Cahermore Ireland 21 B6
Cahersiveen Ireland see Cahirsiveen
Cahir Ireland 21 E5
Cahirsiveen Ireland 21 B6
Cahora Bassa, Lago de resr Moz. see Cabora Bassa, Lake
Cahore Point Ireland 21 F5
Cahors France 24 E4
Cahuapanas Peru 68 C5
Cahul Moldova 27 M2
Caia Moz. 49 D5
Caiabis, Serra dos hills Brazil 69 G6
Caianda Angola 49 C5
Caiapó r. Brazil 71 A1
Caiapó, Serra do mts Brazil 71 A2
Caiapônia Brazil 71 A2
Caicara Venez. 68 E2
Caicos Islands Turks and Caicos Is 67 J4
Caicos Passage Bahamas/Turks and Caicos Is 67 J4
Caiguna Australia 55 D8
Caimodorro mt. Spain 25 F3
Caipe Arg. 70 C2
Caird Coast Antarctica 76 B1
Cairngorm Mountains U.K. 20 F3
Cairnryan U.K. 20 D6
Cairns Australia 56 D3
Cairnsmore of Carsphairn h. U.K. 20 E5
Cairo Egypt 34 C5
Caisleán an Bharraigh Ireland see Castlebar
Caiundo Angola 49 B5
Caiwarro (abandoned) Australia 58 B2
Cajamarca Peru 68 C5
Cajati Brazil 71 A4
Çajuru Brazil 71 B3
Čakovec Croatia 26 G1
Çal Denizli Turkey 27 M5
Cala S. Africa 51 H6
Calabar Nigeria 46 D4
Calabria, Parco Nazionale della nat. park Italy 26 G5
Calafat Romania 27 J3
Calagurris Spain see Calahorra
Calahorra Spain 25 F2
Calai Angola 49 B5
Calais France 24 E1
Calais U.S.A. 63 N2
Calalasteo, Sierra de mts Arg. 70 C3
Calama Brazil 68 F5
Calama Chile 70 C2
Calamar Col. 68 D1
Calamian Group is Phil. 41 D6
Calamocha Spain 25 F3
Calandula Angola 49 B4
Calapan Phil. 41 E6
Călăraşi Romania 27 L2
Calatayud Spain 25 F3
Calayan i. Phil. 41 E6
Calbayog Phil. 41 E6
Calçoene Brazil 69 H3
Calcutta India see Kolkata
Caldas da Rainha Port. 25 B4
Caldas Novas Brazil 69 I7
Caldera Chile 70 B3
Caldervale Australia 56 D5
Caldew r. U.K. 18 E4
Caldwell ID U.S.A. 62 D3
Caldwell OH U.S.A. 64 A3
Caledon r. Lesotho/S. Africa 51 H6
Caledon S. Africa 50 D8
Caledon Bay Australia 56 B2
Caledonia Ont. Canada 64 B1
Caledonia admin. div. U.K. see Scotland
Caleta el Cobre Chile 70 B2
Calexico CA U.S.A. 65 E4
Calf of Man i. Isle of Man 18 C4
Calgary Canada 62 E1
Cali Col. 68 C3
Calicut India 38 B4
Caliente NV U.S.A. 65 E2
California PA U.S.A. 64 B2
California state U.S.A. 62 C3
California, Golfo de g. Mex. see California, Gulf of
California, Gulf of Mex. 66 B2
California Aqueduct canal CA U.S.A. 65 B2
Cälilabad Azer. 35 H3
Calingasta Arg. 70 C4
Calipatria CA U.S.A. 65 E4
Calistoga CA U.S.A. 65 A1
Calkiní Mex. 66 F4
Callabonna, Lake imp. l. Australia 57 C6
Callan Ireland 21 E5
Callan r. U.K. 21 F3
Callander U.K. 20 E4
Callao Peru 68 C6
Callicoon NY U.S.A. 64 D2
Callington U.K. 19 C8
Calliope Australia 56 E5
Callipolis Turkey see Gallipoli
Caloundra Australia 58 F1
Caltagirone Sicilia Italy 26 F6
Caltanissetta Sicilia Italy 26 F6
Calucinga Angola 49 B5
Calulo Angola 49 B4
Calunga Angola 49 B5
Caluquembe Angola 49 B5
Caluula Somalia 48 F2
Caluula, Raas pt Somalia 48 F2
Calvert Hills Australia 56 B3
Calvi Corse France 24 I5
Calvià Spain 25 H4
Calvinia S. Africa 50 D6
Calvo, Monte mt. Italy 26 F4
Cam r. U.K. 19 H6
Camaçari Brazil 71 D1
Camache Reservoir CA U.S.A. 65 B1
Camacho Mex. 66 D4
Camacuio Angola 49 B5
Camacupa Angola 49 B5
Camagüey Cuba 67 I4
Camagüey, Archipiélago de is Cuba 67 I4
Camamu Brazil 71 D1
Camana Peru 68 D7
Camanongue Angola 49 C5
Camapuã Brazil 69 H7
Camaquã Brazil 70 F4
Çamardı Turkey 34 D3
Camargo Bol. 68 E8
Camargue reg. France 24 G5
Camarillo CA U.S.A. 65 C3
Camarones Arg. 70 C6
Camarones, Bahía b. Arg. 70 C6
Ca Mau Vietnam 31 J6
Cambay India see Khambhat
Cambay, Gulf of India see Khambhat, Gulf of
Camberley U.K. 19 G7
Cambodia country Asia 31 J5
Camboriú Brazil 71 A4
Camborne U.K. 19 B8
Cambrai France 24 F1
Cambria admin. div. U.K. see Wales
Cambrian Mountains hills U.K. 19 D6
Cambridge Ont. Canada 64 A1
Cambridge N.Z. 59 E3
Cambridge U.K. 19 H6
Cambridge MA U.S.A. 64 F1
Cambridge MD U.S.A. 64 C3
Cambridge MN U.S.A. 63 I2
Cambridge NY U.S.A. 64 E1
Cambridge OH U.S.A. 63 K3
Cambridge Bay Canada 61 H3
Cambrien, Lac l. Canada 61 L4
Cambulo Angola 49 C4
Cambundi-Catembo Angola 49 B5
Cambuquira Brazil 71 B3
Cam Co l. China 37 E2
Camdeboo National Park S. Africa 50 G7
Camden AR U.S.A. 63 I5
Camden NJ U.S.A. 64 D3
Camden NY U.S.A. 64 D1
Cameia Angola 49 C5
Cameia, Parque Nacional da nat. park Angola 49 C5
Cameron Island Canada 61 H2
Cameron Park CA U.S.A. 65 B1
Cameroon country Africa 46 E4
Cameroon, Mount vol. Cameroon see Cameroun, Mont
Cameroon Highlands slope Cameroon/Nigeria 46 E4
Caméroun country Africa see Cameroon
Cameroun, Mont vol. Cameroon 46 D4
Cametá Brazil 69 I4
Camiña Chile 68 E7
Camiri Bol. 68 F8
Camisea Peru 68 D6
Camocim Brazil 69 J4
Camooweal Australia 56 B3
Camooweal Caves National Park Australia 56 B4
Campana, Isla i. Chile 70 A7
Campbell S. Africa 50 F5
Campbell, Cape N.Z. 59 E5
Campbell, Mount h. Australia 54 E5
Campbell Island N.Z. 74 H9
Campbell Plateau sea feature S. Pacific Ocean 74 H9
Campbell Range hills Australia 54 D3
Campbell River Canada 62 B1
Campbellton Canada 63 N2
Campbelltown Australia 58 E5
Campbeltown U.K. 20 D5
Campeche Mex. 66 F5
Campeche, Bahía de g. Mex. 66 F5
Camperdown Australia 58 A7
Câmpina Romania 27 K2
Campina Grande Brazil 69 K5
Campinas Brazil 71 B3
Campina Verde Brazil 71 A2
Campo Cameroon 46 D4
Campobasso Italy 26 F4
Campo Belo Brazil 71 B3
Campo Belo do Sul Brazil 71 A4
Campo de Diauarum Brazil 69 H6
Campo Florido Brazil 71 A2
Campo Gallo Arg. 70 D3
Campo Grande Brazil 70 F2
Campo Largo Brazil 71 A4
Campo Maior Brazil 69 J4
Campo Maior Port. 25 C4
Campo Mourão Brazil 70 F2
Campos Brazil 71 C3
Campos Altos Brazil 71 B2
Campos Novos Brazil 71 A4
Campos Sales Brazil 69 J5
Câmpulung Romania 27 K2
Câmpulung Moldovenesc Romania 27 K1
Camrose Canada 62 E1
Camrose U.K. 19 B7
Camsell Portage Canada 60 H4
Camulodunum U.K. see Colchester
Çan Turkey 27 L4
Canaan CT U.S.A. 64 E1
Canabrava Brazil 71 B2
Canacona India 38 B3
Canada country N. America 60 H4
Canada Basin sea feature Arctic Ocean 77 A1
Canadian U.S.A. 62 G4
Canadian r. U.S.A. 62 H4
Canadian Abyssal Plain sea feature Arctic Ocean 77 A1
Cañadón Grande, Sierra mts Arg. 70 C7
Canaima, Parque Nacional nat. park Venez. 68 F2
Çanakkale Turkey 27 L4
Çanakkale Boğazı str. Turkey see Dardanelles
Canalejas Arg. 70 C5
Cañamares Spain 25 E3
Canandaigua NY U.S.A. 64 C1
Cananea Mex. 66 B2
Cananéia Brazil 71 B4
Canápolis Brazil 71 A2
Cañar Ecuador 68 C4
Canarias terr. N. Atlantic Ocean see Canary Islands
Canárias, Ilha das i. Brazil 69 J4
Canarias, Islas terr. N. Atlantic Ocean see Canary Islands
Canary Islands terr. N. Atlantic Ocean 46 B2
Canastota NY U.S.A. 64 D1
Canastra, Serra da mts Brazil 71 A1
Canastra, Serra da mts Brazil 71 B2
Canatiba Brazil 71 C1
Canatlán Mex. 66 D4
Canaveral, Cape U.S.A. 63 K6
Cañaveras Spain 25 E3
Canavieiras Brazil 71 D1
Canbelego Australia 58 C3
Canberra Australia 58 D5
Cancún Mex. 67 G4
Çandar Turkey see Kastamonu
Çandarlı Turkey 27 L5
Candia Greece see Iraklion
Cândido de Abreu Brazil 71 A4
Çandır Turkey 34 D2
Candle Lake Canada 62 F1
Candlewood, Lake CT U.S.A. 64 E2
Cane r. Australia 54 A5
Canea Greece see Chania
Canela Brazil 71 A5
Canelones Uruguay 70 E4
Cangallo Peru 68 D6
Cangamba Angola 49 B5
Cangandala, Parque Nacional de nat. park Angola 49 B4
Cangbu r. China see Brahmaputra
Cango Caves S. Africa 50 F7
Cangola Angola 49 B4
Canguaretama Brazil 69 K5
Canguçu Brazil 70 F4
Canguçu, Serra do hills Brazil 70 F4
Cangzhou China 43 L5
Caniapiscau Canada 61 L4
Caniapiscau r. Canada 61 L4
Caniapiscau, Réservoir de resr Canada 61 K4
Caniçado Moz. see Guija
Canicatti Sicilia Italy 26 E6
Canindé Brazil 69 K4
Canisteo r. NY U.S.A. 64 C1
Canisteo Peninsula Antarctica 76 K2
Çankırı Turkey 34 D2
Canna Australia 55 A7
Canna i. U.K. 20 C3
Cannanore India 38 B4
Cannanore Islands India 38 B4
Cannes France 24 H5
Cannock U.K. 19 E6
Cann River Australia 58 D6
Canoas Brazil 71 A5
Canōas, Rio das r. Brazil 71 A4
Canoeiros Brazil 71 B2
Canoinhas Brazil 71 A4
Canoona Australia 56 E4
Canora Canada 62 G1
Canowindra Australia 58 D4
Cantabrian Mountains Spain see Cantábrica, Cordillera
Cantábrica, Cordillera mts Spain 25 D2
Cantábrico, Mar sea Spain 25 C2
Canterbury U.K. 19 I7
Canterbury Bight b. N.Z. 59 C7
Canterbury Plains N.Z. 59 C6
Cân Thơ Vietnam 31 J5
Cantil CA U.S.A. 65 D3
Canton MS U.S.A. 63 J5
Canton OH U.S.A. 64 A2
Canton PA U.S.A. 64 C2
Canton Island atoll Kiribati see Kanton
Cantuaria U.K. see Canterbury
Canunda National Park Australia 57 C8
Canutama Brazil 68 F5
Canvey Island U.K. 19 H7
Cany-Barville France 19 H9
Canyon U.S.A. 62 G4
Canyon Ferry Lake U.S.A. 62 E2
Cao Bằng Vietnam 31 J4
Caohu China 42 E4
Caoshi China 44 B4
Caozhou China see Heze
Çapakçur Turkey see Bingöl
Capanaparo r. Venez. 68 E2
Capanema Brazil 69 I4
Capão Bonito Brazil 71 A4
Caparaó, Serra do mts Brazil 71 C3
Cape r. Australia 56 D4
Cape Arid National Park Australia 55 C8
Cape Barren Island Australia 57 [inset]
Cape Basin sea feature S. Atlantic Ocean 72 I8
Cape Breton Island Canada 61 L5
Cape Charles VA U.S.A. 64 C4
Cape Coast Ghana 46 C4
Cape Coast Castle Ghana see Cape Coast
Cape Cod Bay MA U.S.A. 64 F2
Cape Cod National Seashore nature res. MA U.S.A. 64 G2
Cape Crawford Australia 56 A3
Cape Dorset Canada 61 K3
Cape Girardeau U.S.A. 63 J4
Cape Johnson Depth sea feature N. Pacific Ocean 74 E5
Cape Juby Morocco see Tarfaya
Cape Krusenstern National Monument nat. park U.S.A. 60 B3
Capel Australia 55 A8
Cape Le Grand National Park Australia 55 C8
Capelinha Brazil 71 C2
Capella Australia 56 E4
Capelongo Angola see Kuvango
Cape May NJ U.S.A. 64 D3
Cape May Court House NJ U.S.A. 64 D3
Cape May Point NJ U.S.A. 64 D3
Cape Melville National Park Australia 56 D2
Capenda-Camulemba Angola 49 B4
Cape Palmerston National Park Australia 56 E4
Cape Range National Park Australia 54 A5
Cape Town S. Africa 50 D7
Cape Tribulation National Park Australia 56 D2
Cape Upstart National Park Australia 56 D3
Cape Verde country N. Atlantic Ocean 46 [inset]
Cape Verde Basin sea feature N. Atlantic Ocean 72 F5
Cape Verde Plateau sea feature N. Atlantic Ocean 72 F4
Cape York Peninsula Australia 56 C2
Cap-Haïtien Haiti 67 J5
Capim r. Brazil 69 I4
Capitán Arturo Prat research stn Antarctica 76 A2
Capivara, Represa resr Brazil 71 A3
Čapljina Bos.-Herz. 26 G3
Cappoquin Ireland 21 E5
Capraia, Isola di i. Italy 26 C3
Caprara, Punta pt Sardegna Italy 26 C4
Capri, Isola di i. Italy 26 F4
Capricorn Channel Australia 56 E4
Capricorn Group atolls Australia 56 F4
Caprivi Strip reg. Namibia 49 C5
Capsa Tunisia see Gafsa
Captina r. OH U.S.A. 64 A3
Capuava Brazil 71 B4
Caquetá r. Col. 68 E4
Caracal Romania 27 K2
Caracas Venez. 68 E1
Caraguatatuba Brazil 71 B3
Caraí Brazil 71 C2
Carajás Brazil 69 H5
Carajás, Serra dos hills Brazil 69 H5
Carales Sardegna Italy see Cagliari
Caralis Sardegna Italy see Cagliari
Carandaí Brazil 71 C3
Caransebeş Romania 27 J2
Caraquet Canada 63 N2
Caratasca, Laguna de lag. Hond. 67 H5
Caratinga Brazil 71 C2
Carauari Brazil 68 E4
Caravaca de la Cruz Spain 25 F4
Caravelas Brazil 71 D2
Carbó Mex. 66 B3
Carbon, Cap c. Alg. 25 F6
Carbonara, Capo c. Sardegna Italy 26 C5
Carbondale PA U.S.A. 64 D2
Carbonia Sardegna Italy 26 C5
Carbonita Brazil 71 C2
Carcaixent Spain 25 F4
Carcassonne France 24 F5
Cardamom Hills India 38 C4
Cárdenas Cuba 67 H4
Cárdenas Mex. 66 E4
Cardenyabba watercourse Australia 58 A2
Çardi Turkey see Harmancık
Cardiel, Lago l. Arg. 70 B7
Cardiff U.K. 19 D7
Cardiff MD U.S.A. 64 C3
Cardigan U.K. 19 C6
Cardigan Bay U.K. 19 C6
Cardoso Brazil 71 A3
Cardoso, Ilha do i. Brazil 71 B4
Carei Romania 27 J1
Carentan France 24 D2
Carey, Lake imp. l. Australia 55 C7
Cargados Carajos Islands Mauritius 73 L7
Carhaix-Plouguer France 24 C2
Cariacica Brazil 71 C3
Cariamanga Ecuador 68 C4
Caribbean Sea N. Atlantic Ocean 67 H5
Caribou U.S.A. 63 N2
Caribou Lake Canada 61 J4
Caribou Mountains Canada 60 G4
Carinda Australia 58 C3
Cariñena Spain 25 F3
Carinhanha r. Brazil 71 C1
Carlabhagh U.K. see Carloway
Carletonville S. Africa 51 H4
Carlingford Lough inlet Ireland/U.K. 21 F3
Carlisle U.K. 18 E4
Carlisle NY U.S.A. 64 D1
Carlisle PA U.S.A. 64 C2
Carlisle Lakes imp. l. Australia 55 D7
Carlit, Pic mt. France 24 E5
Carlos Chagas Brazil 71 C2
Carlow Ireland 21 F5
Carloway U.K. 20 C2
Carlsbad Czech Rep. see Karlovy Vary
Carlsbad CA U.S.A. 65 D4
Carlsbad NM U.S.A. 62 G5
Carlsberg Ridge sea feature Indian Ocean 73 L5
Carlson Inlet Antarctica 76 L1
Carlton Hill Australia 54 E3
Carluke U.K. 20 F5
Carlyle Canada 62 G2
Carmacks Canada 60 E3
Carmagnola Italy 26 B2
Carman Canada 62 H2
Carmana Iran see Kermān
Carmarthen U.K. 19 C7
Carmarthen Bay U.K. 19 C7
Carmaux France 24 F4
Carmel NY U.S.A. 64 E2
Carmel, Mount h. Israel 39 B3
Carmel Head hd U.K. 18 C5
Carmel Valley CA U.S.A. 65 B2
Carmen, Isla i. Mex. 66 B3
Carmen de Patagones Arg. 70 D6
Carmichael CA U.S.A. 65 B1
Carmo da Cachoeira Brazil 71 B3
Carmo do Paranaíba Brazil 71 B2
Carmona Angola see Uíge
Carmona Spain 25 D5
Carnac France 24 C3
Carnamah Australia 55 A7
Carnarvon Australia 55 A6
Carnarvon S. Africa 50 F6
Carnarvon National Park Australia 56 D5
Carnarvon Range hills Australia 55 C6
Carnarvon Range mts Australia 56 E5
Carn Dearg h. U.K. 20 E3
Carndonagh Ireland 21 E2
Carnegie Australia 55 C6
Carnegie, Lake imp. l. Australia 55 C6
Carn Eige mt. U.K. 20 D3
Carnes Australia 55 F7
Carney Island Antarctica 76 J2
Carnforth U.K. 18 E4
Carn Glas-choire h. U.K. 20 F3
Carnlough U.K. 21 G3
Carn nan Gabhar mt. U.K. 20 F4
Carn Odhar h. U.K. 20 E3
Carnot Cent. Afr. Rep. 48 B3
Carnoustie U.K. 20 G4
Carnsore Point Ireland 21 F5
Carnwath U.K. 20 F5
Carola Cay rf Australia 56 F3
Carolina Brazil 69 I5
Carolina S. Africa 51 J4
Caroline Island atoll Kiribati 75 J6
Caroline Islands N. Pacific Ocean 41 G7
Caroline Peak N.Z. 59 A7
Caroline Range hills Australia 54 D4
Caroní r. Venez. 68 F2
Carpathian Mountains Europe 13 C6
Carpaţii mts Europe see Carpathian Mountains
Carpaţii Meridionali mts Romania see Transylvanian Alps
Carpaţii Occidentali mts Romania 27 J2
Carpentaria, Gulf of Australia 56 B2
Carpentras France 24 G4
Carpi Italy 26 D2
Carpinteria CA U.S.A. 65 C3
Carra, Lough l. Ireland 21 C4
Carraig na Siuire Ireland see Carrick-on-Suir
Carrantuohill mt. Ireland 21 C6
Carrara Italy 26 D2
Carrasco, Parque Nacional nat. park Bol. 68 F7
Carrathool Australia 58 B5
Carrhae Turkey see Harran
Carrickfergus U.K. 21 G3
Carrickmacross Ireland 21 F4
Carrick-on-Shannon Ireland 21 D4
Carrick-on-Suir Ireland 21 E5
Carrigallen Ireland 21 E4
Carrigtohill Ireland 21 D6
Carrington U.S.A. 62 H2
Carrizal Bajo Chile 70 B3
Carrizo Springs U.S.A. 62 H6
Carrizozo U.S.A. 62 F5
Carroll U.S.A. 63 I3
Carrollton GA U.S.A. 63 J5
Carrollton OH U.S.A. 64 A2
Carrolltown PA U.S.A. 64 B2
Carron r. U.K. 20 E3
Carrowmore Lake Ireland 21 C3
Çarşamba Turkey 34 E2
Carson City NV U.S.A. 65 C1
Carson Escarpment Australia 54 D3
Carson Lake NV U.S.A. 65 C1
Carstensz Pyramid mt. Indon. see Jaya, Puncak
Carstensz-top mt. Indon. see Jaya, Puncak
Cartagena Col. 68 C1
Cartagena Spain 25 F5
Carteret Group is P.N.G. see Kilinailau Islands
Carteret Island Solomon Is see Malaita
Carthage tourist site Tunisia 26 D6
Carthage MO U.S.A. 63 I4
Carthago tourist site Tunisia see Carthage
Carthago Nova Spain see Cartagena
Cartier Island Australia 54 C3
Cartmel U.K. 18 E4
Cartwright Nfld. and Lab. Canada 61 M4
Caruarú Brazil 69 K5
Carúpano Venez. 68 F1

Chinandega Nicaragua 66 G6
China Point CA U.S.A. 65 C4
Chincha Alta Peru 68 C6
Chinchaga r. Canada 60 G4
Chinchilla Australia 58 E1
Chincholi India 38 C2
Chinchorro, Banco sea feature Mex. 67 G5
Chincoteague Bay Maryland/Virginia U.S.A. 64 D4
Chinde Moz. 49 D5
Chindo S. Korea 45 B6
Chin-do i. S. Korea 45 B6
Chindwin r. Myanmar 37 H5
Chinese Turkestan aut. reg. China see Xinjiang Uygur Zizhiqu
Chinghai prov. China see Qinghai
Chingiz-Tau, Khrebet mts Kazakh. 42 D3
Chingleput India see Chengalpattu
Chingola Zambia 49 C5
Chinguar Angola 49 B5
Chinguetti Mauritania 46 B2
Chinhae S. Korea 45 C6
Chinhoyi Zimbabwe 49 D5
Chini India see Kalpa
Chining China see Jining
Chiniot Pak. 33 L3
Chinju S. Korea 45 C6
Chinle U.S.A. 62 F4
Chinnamp'o N. Korea see Namp'o
Chinnur India 38 C2
Chino Creek watercourse AZ U.S.A. 65 F3
Chinon France 24 E3
Chinook Trough sea feature N. Pacific Ocean 74 I3
Chino Valley U.S.A. 62 E5
Chintamani India 38 C3
Chioggia Italy 26 E2
Chios Greece 27 L5
Chios i. Greece 27 K5
Chipata Zambia 49 D5
Chipchihua, Sierra de mts Arg. 70 C6
Chipindo Angola 49 B5
Chipinga Zimbabwe see Chipinge
Chipinge Zimbabwe 49 D6
Chippenham U.K. 19 E7
Chipping Norton U.K. 19 F7
Chipping Sodbury U.K. 19 E7
Chipurupalle Andhra Prad. India 38 D2
Chipurupalle Andhra Prad. India 38 D2
Chiquinquira Col. 68 D2
Chir r. Rus. Fed. 13 I6
Chirada India 38 D3
Chirala India 38 D3
Chiras Afgh. 36 A2
Chirchiq Uzbek. 33 K1
Chiredzi Zimbabwe 49 D6
Chirfa Niger 46 E2
Chiricahua Peak U.S.A. 62 F5
Chirikof Island U.S.A. 60 C4
Chiriquí, Golfo de b. Panama 67 H7
Chiriquí, Volcán de vol. Panama see Barú, Volcán
Chiri-san mt. S. Korea 45 B6
Chirk U.K. 19 D6
Chirnside U.K. 20 G5
Chirripó mt. Costa Rica 67 H7
Chisamba Zambia 49 C5
Chisasibi Canada 61 K4
Chishima-retto is Rus. Fed. see Kuril Islands
Chishtian Mandi Pak. 33 L4
Chishui China 42 J7
Chisimaio Somalia see Kismaayo
Chişinău Moldova 27 M1
Chistopol' Rus. Fed. 12 K5
Chita Rus. Fed. 43 K2
Chitado Angola 49 B5
Chitaldrug India see Chitradurga
Chitalwana India 36 B4
Chitambo Zambia 49 D5
Chita Oblast Rus. Fed. see Chitinskaya Oblast'
Chitato Angola 49 C4
Chitembo Angola 49 B5
Chitina U.S.A. 60 D3
Chitinskaya Oblast' Rus. Fed. 44 A1
Chitipa Malawi 49 D4
Chitkul India see Chhitkul
Chitobe Moz. 49 D6
Chitoor India see Chittoor
Chitor India see Chittaurgarh
Chitose Japan 44 F4
Chitradurga India 38 C3
Chitrakoot India 36 E4
Chitrakut India see Chitrakoot
Chitral Pak. 33 L2
Chitral r. Pak. 36 B2
Chitravati r. India 38 C3
Chitré Panama 67 H7
Chitrod India 36 B5
Chittagong Bangl. 37 G5
Chittaurgarh India 36 C4
Chittoor India 38 C3
Chittor India see Chittoor
Chittorgarh India see Chittaurgarh
Chittur India 38 C4
Chitungwiza Zimbabwe 49 D5
Chiu Lung H.K. China see Kowloon
Chiume Angola 49 C5
Chivasso Italy 26 B2
Chivhu Zimbabwe 49 D5
Chizarira National Park Zimbabwe 49 C5
Chizha Vtoraya Kazakh. 13 K6
Chizu Japan 45 D6
Chkalov Rus. Fed. see Orenburg
Chkalovsk Rus. Fed. 12 I4
Chkalovskoye Rus. Fed. 44 D3
Chlef Alg. 25 G5
Chlef, Oued r. Alg. 25 G5
Chloride AZ U.S.A. 65 E3
Chlya, Ozero l. Rus. Fed. 44 F1
Chobe National Park Botswana 49 C5
Choele Choel Arg. 70 C5
Chogar r. Rus. Fed. 44 D1
Chogori Feng mt. China/Pakistan see K2
Chograyskoye Vodokhranilishche resr Rus. Fed. 13 J7
Choiseul i. Solomon Is 53 F2
Choix Mex. 66 C3
Chojnice Poland 17 P4
Chōkai-san vol. Japan 45 F5
Ch'ok'ē mts Eth. 48 D2
Ch'ok'ē Mountains Eth. see Ch'ok'ē
Chokola mt. China 36 E3
Choksum China 37 F3
Chokue Moz. see Chókwé
Chokurdakh Rus. Fed. 29 P2
Chókwé Moz. 51 K3
Cholame CA U.S.A. 65 B3
Cholet France 24 D3
Choluteca Hond. 67 G6
Choma Zambia 49 C5
Chomo Ganggar mt. China 37 G3
Chomo Lhari mt. China/Bhutan 37 G4
Chomutov Czech Rep. 17 N5
Ch'ŏnan S. Korea 45 B5
Chon Buri Thai. 31 J5
Ch'ŏnch'ŏn N. Korea 44 B4
Chone Ecuador 68 B4
Ch'ŏngch'ŏn-gang r. N. Korea 45 B5
Ch'ongdo S. Korea 45 C6
Chonggye China see Qonggyai
Ch'ŏngjin N. Korea 44 C4
Ch'ŏngju S. Korea 45 B5
Chongkü China 37 I3
Chongming Dao i. China 43 M6
Chongoroi Angola 49 B5
Chŏngp'yŏng N. Korea 45 B5
Chongqing China 42 J7
Chongqing mun. China 42 J6
Chonguene Moz. 51 K3
Chŏngŭp S. Korea 45 B6
Chŏnju S. Korea 45 B6
Cho Oyu mt. China/Nepal 37 F3
Chopda India 36 C5
Chor Pak. 36 B4
Chora Sfakion Greece 27 K7
Chorley U.K. 18 E5
Chornobyl' Ukr. 13 F6
Chornomors'ke Ukr. 27 O2
Chortkiv Ukr. 13 E6
Ch'osan N. Korea 44 B4
Chōshi Japan 45 F6
Chosŏn country Asia see South Korea
Chosŏn-minjujuŭi-inmin-konghwaguk country Asia see North Korea
Choszczno Poland 17 O4
Chota Peru 68 C5
Chota Sinchula mt. India 37 G4
Choti Pak. 36 B3
Choûm Mauritania 46 B2
Chowchilla CA U.S.A. 65 B2
Chowghat India 38 B4
Choybalsan Mongolia 43 K3
Choyr Mongolia 43 J3
Chřiby hills Czech Rep. 17 P6
Chrissiesmeer S. Africa 51 J4
Christchurch N.Z. 59 D6
Christchurch U.K. 19 F8
Christian, Cape Canada 61 L2
Christiana S. Africa 51 G4
Christiania Norway see Oslo
Christiansburg VA U.S.A. 64 A4
Christianshåb Greenland see Qasigiannguit
Christina, Mount N.Z. 59 B7
Christmas Island terr. Indian Ocean 41 C9
Christopher, Lake imp. l. Australia 55 D6
Chrudim Czech Rep. 17 O6
Chrysochou Bay Cyprus 39 A2
Chrysochous, Kolpos b. Cyprus see Chrysochou Bay
Chu Kazakh. see Shu
Chu r. Kazakh./Kyrg. 42 B4
Chuadanga Bangl. 37 G5
Chuali, Lago l. Moz. 51 K3
Chuanhui China see Zhoukou
Chubarovka Ukr. see Polohy
Chubartau Kazakh. see Barshatas
Chūbu-Sangaku Kokuritsu-kōen nat. park Japan 45 E5
Chuchkovo Rus. Fed. 13 I5
Chuckwalla Mountains CA U.S.A. 65 E4
Chudniv Ukr. 13 F6
Chudovo Rus. Fed. 12 F4
Chudskoye, Ozero l. Estonia/Rus. Fed. see Peipus, Lake
Chugach Mountains U.S.A. 60 D3
Chūgoku-sanchi mts Japan 45 D6
Chugqênsumdo China see Jigzhi
Chuguchak China see Tacheng
Chuguyev Ukr. see Chuhuyiv
Chuguyevka Rus. Fed. 44 D3
Chuhuyiv Ukr. 13 H6
Chu-Iliyskiye Gory mts Kazakh. 42 C4
Chujiang China see Shimen
Chukchagirskoye, Ozero l. Rus. Fed. 44 E1
Chukchi Abyssal Plain sea feature Arctic Ocean 77 B1
Chukchi Peninsula Rus. Fed. see Chukotskiy Poluostrov
Chukchi Plateau sea feature Arctic Ocean 77 B1
Chukchi Sea Rus. Fed./U.S.A. 29 T3
Chukhloma Rus. Fed. 12 I4
Chukotskiy, Mys c. Rus. Fed. 60 A3
Chukotskiy Poluostrov pen. Rus. Fed. 29 T3
Chulakkurgan Kazakh. see Sholakkorgan
Chulaktau Kazakh. see Karatau
Chulasa Rus. Fed. 12 J2
Chula Vista CA U.S.A. 65 D4
Chulucanas Peru 68 B5
Chulung Pass Pak. 36 D2
Chulym Rus. Fed. 28 J4
Chumar India 36 D2
Chumbicha Arg. 70 C3
Chumda China 37 I2
Chumikan Rus. Fed. 29 O4
Chumphon Thai. 31 I5
Chunar India 37 E4
Ch'unch'ŏn S. Korea 45 B5
Chunchura India 37 G5
Chundzha Kazakh. 42 D4
Chunga Zambia 49 C5
Chung-hua Jen-min Kung-ho-kuo country Asia see China
Chung-hua Min-kuo country Asia see Taiwan
Ch'ungju S. Korea 45 B5
Chungking China see Chongqing
Ch'ungmu S. Korea see T'ongyŏng
Chŭngsan N. Korea 45 B5
Chunskiy Rus. Fed. 42 H1
Chunya r. Rus. Fed. 29 K3
Chupa Rus. Fed. 14 R3
Chŭplŭ Iran 35 G3
Chuquicamata Chile 70 C2
Chur Switz. 24 I3
Churachandpur India 37 H4
Churapcha Rus. Fed. 29 O3
Churchill Canada 61 I4
Churchill r. Man. Canada 61 I4
Churchill r. Nfld. and Lab. Canada 61 L4
Churchill, Cape Canada 61 I4
Churchill Mountains Antarctica 76 H1
Churchville VA U.S.A. 64 B3
Churia Ghati Hills Nepal 37 F4
Churu India 36 C3
Churún-Merú waterfall Venez. see Angel Falls
Chushul India 36 D2
Chusovaya r. Rus. Fed. 11 R4
Chusovoy Rus. Fed. 11 R4
Chust Ukr. see Khust
Chute-des-Passes Canada 63 M2
Chutia Assam India 37 H4
Chutia Jharkhand India 37 F5
Chuuk is Micronesia 74 G5
Chuxiong China 42 I7
Chüy r. Kazakh./Kyrg. see Chu
Chymyshliya Moldova see Cimişlia
Chyulu Hills National Park Kenya 48 D4
Ciadâr-Lunga Moldova see Ciadîr-Lunga
Ciadîr-Lunga Moldova 27 M1
Cianorte Brazil 70 F2
Čićarija mts Croatia 26 E2
Cide Turkey 34 D2
Ciechanów Poland 17 R4
Ciego de Ávila Cuba 67 I4
Ciénaga Col. 68 D1
Cienfuegos Cuba 67 H4
Cieza Spain 25 F4
Çiftlik Turkey see Kelkit
Cifuentes Spain 25 E3
Cigüela r. Spain 25 E4
Cihanbeyli Turkey 34 D3
Cijara, Embalse de resr Spain 25 D4
Cilacap Indon. 41 C8
Çıldır Turkey 35 F2
Çıldır Gölü l. Turkey 35 F2
Çıldıroba Turkey 39 C1
Cilento e del Vallo di Diano, Parco Nazionale del nat. park Italy 26 F4
Cilician Gates pass Turkey see Gülek Boğazı
Cill Airne Ireland see Killarney
Cill Chainnigh Ireland see Kilkenny
Cill Mhantáin Ireland see Wicklow
Çilmämmetgum des. Turkm. 35 I2
Cilo Dağı mt. Turkey 35 G3
Çilov Adası i. Azer. 35 H2
Cimarron r. U.S.A. 62 H4
Cimişlia Moldova 27 M1
Cimone, Monte mt. Italy 26 D2
Cîmpina Romania see Câmpina
Cîmpulung Romania see Câmpulung
Cîmpulung Moldovenesc Romania see Câmpulung Moldovenesc
Çınar Turkey 35 F3
Cinaruco-Capanaparo, Parque Nacional nat. park Venez. 68 E2
Cinca r. Spain 25 G3
Cincinnati U.S.A. 63 K4
Cinco de Outubro Angola see Xá-Muteba
Cinderford U.K. 19 E7
Çine Turkey 27 M6
Cintalapa Mex. 66 F5
Cinto, Monte mt. France 24 I5
Ciping China see Jinggangshan
Circeo, Parco Nazionale del nat. park Italy 26 E4
Circle AK U.S.A. 60 D3
Cirebon Indon. 41 C8
Cirencester U.K. 19 F7
Cirò Marina Italy 26 G5
Cirta Alg. see Constantine
Cisne, Islas del is Caribbean Sea 67 H5
Citlaltépetl vol. Mex. see Orizaba, Pico de
Čitluk Bos.-Herz. 26 G3
Citrus Heights CA U.S.A. 65 B1
Città di Castello Italy 26 E3
Ciucaş, Vârful mt. Romania 27 K2
Ciudad Acuña Mex. 62 G6
Ciudad Altamirano Mex. 66 D5
Ciudad Bolívar Venez. 68 F2
Ciudad Camargo Mex. 66 C3
Ciudad Constitución Mex. 66 B3
Ciudad del Carmen Mex. 66 F5
Ciudad Delicias Mex. 66 C3
Ciudad de Panamá Panama see Panama City
Ciudad de Valles Mex. 66 E4
Ciudad Flores Guat. see Flores
Ciudad Guayana Venez. 68 F2
Ciudad Guzmán Mex. 66 D5
Ciudad Juárez Mex. 66 C2
Ciudad Mante Mex. 66 E4
Ciudad Obregón Mex. 66 C3
Ciudad Real Spain 25 E4
Ciudad Río Bravo Mex. 62 H6
Ciudad Rodrigo Spain 25 C3
Ciudad Trujillo Dom. Rep. see Santo Domingo
Ciudad Victoria Mex. 66 E4
Ciutadella Spain 25 H3
Civa Burnu pt Turkey 34 E2
Cividale del Friuli Italy 26 E1
Civitanova Marche Italy 26 E3
Civitavecchia Italy 26 D3
Çivril Turkey 27 M5
Cizre Turkey 35 F3
Clacton-on-Sea U.K. 19 I7
Clady U.K. 21 E3
Claire, Lake Canada 60 G4
Clairfontaine Alg. see El Aouinet
Clamecy France 24 F3
Clane Ireland 21 F4
Clanwilliam Dam S. Africa 50 D7
Clara Ireland 21 E4
Claraville Australia 56 C3
Clare N.S.W. Australia 58 A4
Clare S.A. Australia 57 B7
Clare r. Ireland 21 C4
Clarecastle Ireland 21 D5
Clare Island Ireland 21 B4
Claremont NH U.S.A. 64 E1
Claremorris Ireland 21 D4
Clarence r. Australia 58 F2
Clarence N.Z. 59 D6
Clarence Island Antarctica 76 A2
Clarence Town Bahamas 63 M7
Clarendon PA U.S.A. 64 B2
Clarenville Canada 61 M5
Claresholm Canada 62 E1
Clarie Coast Antarctica see Wilkes Coast
Clarington OH U.S.A. 64 A3
Clarion PA U.S.A. 64 B2
Clarion r. PA U.S.A. 64 B2
Clarión, Isla i. Mex. 66 B5
Clarkebury S. Africa 51 I6
Clarke Range mts Australia 56 D4
Clarke River Australia 56 D3
Clark Mountain CA U.S.A. 65 E3
Clarksburg WV U.S.A. 64 A3
Clarksdale U.S.A. 63 I5
Clarksville AR U.S.A. 63 I4
Clarksville TN U.S.A. 63 J4
Claro r. Goiás Brazil 71 A2
Claro r. Mato Grosso Brazil 71 A1
Clashmore Ireland 21 E5
Claudy U.K. 21 E3
Clay WV U.S.A. 64 A3
Clayhole Wash watercourse AZ U.S.A. 65 F2
Clayton DE U.S.A. 64 D3
Clayton NM U.S.A. 62 G4
Claytor Lake VA U.S.A. 64 A4
Clear, Cape Ireland 21 C6
Clearco WV U.S.A. 64 A3
Clear Creek Ont. Canada 64 A1
Cleare, Cape U.S.A. 60 D4
Clearfield PA U.S.A. 64 B2
Clear Island Ireland 21 C6
Clear Lake IA U.S.A. 63 I3
Clear Lake CA U.S.A. 65 A1
Clear Lake UT U.S.A. 65 F1
Clearwater r. Alberta/Saskatchewan Canada 60 G4
Clearwater U.S.A. 63 K6
Cleburne U.S.A. 63 H5
Cleethorpes U.K. 18 G5
Clendenin WV U.S.A. 64 A3
Clendening Lake OH U.S.A. 64 A2
Clères France 19 I9
Clerke Reef Australia 54 B4
Clermont Australia 56 D4
Clermont-Ferrand France 24 F4
Cles Italy 26 D1
Clevedon U.K. 19 E7
Cleveland MS U.S.A. 63 I5
Cleveland OH U.S.A. 64 A2
Cleveland TN U.S.A. 63 K4
Cleveland, Cape Australia 56 D3
Cleveland, Mount U.S.A. 62 E2
Cleveland Heights OH U.S.A. 64 A2
Cleveland Hills U.K. 18 F4
Cleveleys U.K. 18 D5
Clew Bay Ireland 21 C4
Clifden Ireland 21 B4
Cliffoney Ireland 21 D3
Clifton Australia 58 E1
Clifton U.S.A. 62 F5
Clifton Beach Australia 56 D3
Clifton Forge VA U.S.A. 64 B4
Clifton Park NY U.S.A. 64 E1
Clinton Ont. Canada 64 A1
Clinton IA U.S.A. 63 I3
Clinton OK U.S.A. 62 H4
Clipperton, Île terr. N. Pacific Ocean 75 M5
Clisham h. U.K. 20 C3
Clitheroe U.K. 18 E5
Cliza Bol. 68 E7
Clocolan S. Africa 51 H5
Cloghan Ireland 21 E4
Clonakilty Ireland 21 D6
Clonbern Ireland 21 D4
Cloncurry Australia 56 C4
Cloncurry r. Australia 56 C3
Clones Ireland 21 E3
Clonmel Ireland 21 E5
Clonygowan Ireland 21 E4
Cloonbannin Ireland 21 C5
Cloonfeagh Ireland 21 E4
Cloud Peak WY U.S.A. 62 F3
Cloverdale CA U.S.A. 65 A1
Clovis CA U.S.A. 65 C2
Clovis NM U.S.A. 62 G5
Cluain Meala Ireland see Clonmel
Cluanie, Loch l. U.K. 20 D3
Cluff Lake Mine Canada 60 H4
Cluj-Napoca Romania 27 J1
Clun U.K. 19 D6
Clunes Australia 58 A6
Cluny Australia 56 B5
Cluses France 24 H3
Clutterbuck Hills h. Australia 55 D6
Clwydian Range hills U.K. 18 D5
Clyde r. U.K. 20 E5
Clyde NY U.S.A. 64 C1
Clyde, Firth of est. U.K. 20 E5
Clydebank U.K. 20 E5
Clyde River Canada 61 L2
Côa r. Port. 25 C3
Coachella CA U.S.A. 65 D4
Coaldale NV U.S.A. 65 D1
Coalinga CA U.S.A. 65 B2
Coalport PA U.S.A. 64 B2
Coal River Canada 60 F4
Coal Valley val. NV U.S.A. 65 E2
Coalville U.K. 19 F6
Coari Brazil 68 F4
Coari r. Brazil 68 F4
Coarsegold CA U.S.A. 65 C2
Coastal Plain U.S.A. 63 I5
Coast Mountains Canada 60 F4
Coast Range hills Australia 57 E5
Coast Ranges mts CA U.S.A. 65 B2
Coatbridge U.K. 20 E5
Coatesville PA U.S.A. 64 D3
Coats Island Canada 61 J3
Coats Land reg. Antarctica 76 A1
Coatzacoalcos Mex. 66 F5
Cobar Australia 58 B3
Cobargo Australia 58 D6
Cobden Australia 58 A7
Cobh Ireland 21 D6
Cobija Bol. 68 E6
Coblenz Germany see Koblenz
Cobleskill NY U.S.A. 64 D1
Cobourg Peninsula Australia 54 F2
Cobra Australia 55 B6
Cobram Australia 58 B5
Coburg Germany 17 M5
Coburg Island Canada 61 K2
Coca Ecuador 68 C4
Coca Spain 25 D3
Cocalinho Brazil 71 A1
Cocanada India see Kakinada
Cochabamba Bol. 68 E7
Cochin India 38 C4
Cochrane Alta Canada 62 E1
Cochrane Ont. Canada 63 K2
Cockburn Australia 57 C7
Cockburnspath U.K. 20 G5
Cockburn Town Turks and Caicos Is see Grand Turk
Cockermouth U.K. 18 D4
Cocklebiddy Australia 55 D8
Cockscomb mt. S. Africa 50 G7
Coco r. Hond./Nicaragua 67 H6
Coco, Isla de i. N. Pacific Ocean 67 G7
Cocobeach Gabon 48 A3
Coconino Plateau AZ U.S.A. 65 F3
Cocopara National Park Australia 58 C5
Cocos Brazil 71 B1
Cocos Basin sea feature Indian Ocean 73 O5
Cocos Islands terr. Indian Ocean 41 B9
Cocos Ridge sea feature N. Pacific Ocean 75 O5
Cocuy, Sierra Nevada del mt. Col. 68 D2
Cod, Cape MA U.S.A. 64 F2
Codajás Brazil 68 F4
Codfish Island N.Z. 59 A8
Codigoro Italy 26 E2
Cod Island Canada 61 L4
Codlea Romania 27 K2
Codó Brazil 69 J4
Codsall U.K. 19 E6
Cod's Head hd Ireland 21 B6
Cody U.S.A. 62 F3
Coen Australia 56 C2
Coeur d'Alene U.S.A. 62 D2
Coffee Bay S. Africa 51 I6
Coffeyville U.S.A. 63 H4
Coffin Bay Australia 57 A7
Coffin Bay National Park Australia 57 A7
Coffs Harbour Australia 58 F3
Cofimvaba S. Africa 51 H7
Cognac France 24 D4
Cogo Equat. Guinea 46 D4
Coguno Moz. 51 L3
Cohoes NY U.S.A. 64 E1
Cohuna Australia 58 B5
Coiba, Isla de i. Panama 67 H7
Coigeach, Rubha pt U.K. 20 D2
Coihaique Chile 70 B7
Coimbatore India 38 C4
Coimbra Port. 25 B3
Coipasa, Salar de salt flat Bol. 68 E7
Coire Switz. see Chur
Colac Australia 58 A7
Colair Lake India see Kolleru Lake
Colatina Brazil 71 C2
Colby U.S.A. 62 G4
Colchester U.K. 19 H7
Colchester CT U.S.A. 64 E2
Cold Bay U.S.A. 60 B4
Coldingham U.K. 20 G5
Coldstream U.K. 20 G5
Coleambally Australia 58 B5
Coleman r. Australia 56 C2
Coleman U.S.A. 62 H5
Çölemerik Turkey see Hakkâri
Colenso S. Africa 51 I5
Cole Peninsula Antarctica 76 L2
Coleraine Australia 57 C8
Coleraine U.K. 21 F2
Coles, Punta de pt Peru 68 D7
Coles Bay Australia 57 [inset]
Colesberg S. Africa 51 G6
Colfax CA U.S.A. 65 B1
Colhué Huapí, Lago l. Arg. 70 C7
Coligny S. Africa 51 H4
Colima Mex. 66 D5
Colima, Nevado de vol. Mex. 66 D5
Coll i. U.K. 20 C4
Collado Villalba Spain 25 E3
Collarenebri Australia 58 D2
Collerina Australia 58 C2
Collie N.S.W. Australia 58 D3
Collie W.A. Australia 55 B8
Collier Bay Australia 54 D4
Collier Range National Park Australia 55 B6
Collingwood N.Z. 59 D5
Collins Glacier Antarctica 76 E2
Collinson Peninsula Canada 61 H2
Collipulli Chile 70 B5
Collooney Ireland 21 D3
Colmar France 24 H2
Colmenar Viejo Spain 25 E3
Colmonell U.K. 20 E5
Colne r. U.K. 19 H7
Cologne Germany 17 K5
Colomb-Béchar Alg. see Béchar
Colômbia Brazil 71 A3
Colombia country S. America 68 D3
Colombian Basin sea feature S. Atlantic Ocean 72 C5
Colombo Sri Lanka 38 C5
Colomiers France 24 E5
Colón Buenos Aires Arg. 70 D4
Colón Entre Ríos Arg. 70 E4
Colón Panama 67 I7
Colón, Archipiélago de is Ecuador see Galapagos Islands
Colona Australia 55 F7
Colonelganj India 37 E4
Colônia r. Brazil 71 D1
Colonia Agrippina Germany see Cologne
Colonia Julia Fenestris Italy see Fano
Colonia Las Heras Arg. 70 C7
Colonial Heights VA U.S.A. 64 C4
Colonna, Capo c. Italy 26 G5
Colonsay i. U.K. 20 C4
Colorado r. Arg. 70 D5
Colorado r. Mex./U.S.A. 65 F2
Colorado r. U.S.A. 62 H6
Colorado state U.S.A. 62 F4
Colorado City AZ U.S.A. 65 F2
Colorado Desert CA U.S.A. 65 D4
Colorado Plateau U.S.A. 62 F4
Colorado River Aqueduct canal CA U.S.A. 65 E3
Colorado Springs U.S.A. 62 G4
Colossae Turkey see Honaz
Colotlán Mex. 66 D4
Colquiri Bol. 68 E7
Colsterworth U.K. 19 G6
Colstrip U.S.A. 62 F2
Coltishall U.K. 19 I6
Colton CA U.S.A. 65 D3
Columbia MD U.S.A. 64 C3
Columbia MO U.S.A. 63 I4
Columbia PA U.S.A. 64 C2
Columbia SC U.S.A. 63 K5
Columbia TN U.S.A. 63 J4
Columbia r. U.S.A. 62 C2
Columbia, District of admin. dist. U.S.A. 64 C3
Columbia, Mount Canada 62 D1
Columbia Mountains Canada 62 C1
Columbia Plateau U.S.A. 62 D2
Columbine, Cape S. Africa 50 C7
Columbus GA U.S.A. 63 K5
Columbus IN U.S.A. 63 J4
Columbus MS U.S.A. 63 J5
Columbus NE U.S.A. 63 H3
Columbus NM U.S.A. 62 F5
Columbus OH U.S.A. 63 K4
Columbus Salt Marsh NV U.S.A. 65 C1
Colusa CA U.S.A. 65 A1
Colville N.Z. 59 E3
Colville r. U.S.A. 60 C2
Colville Channel N.Z. 59 E3
Colville Lake Canada 60 F3
Colwyn Bay U.K. 18 D5
Comacchio Italy 26 E2
Comacchio, Valli di lag. Italy 26 E2
Comai China 37 G3
Comalcalco Mex. 66 F5
Comandante Ferraz research stn Antarctica 76 A2
Comandante Salas Arg. 70 C4
Comănești Romania 27 L1
Combarbalá Chile 70 B4
Comber U.K. 21 G3
Combermere Bay Myanmar 37 H6
Combomune Moz. 51 K2
Comboyne Australia 58 F3
Comencho, Lac l. Canada 63 L1
Comendador Dom. Rep. see Elías Piña
Comendador Gomes Brazil 71 A2
Comeragh Mountains hills Ireland 21 E5
Comercinho Brazil 71 C2
Cometela Moz. 51 L1
Comilla Bangl. 37 G5
Comino, Capo c. Sardegna Italy 26 C4
Comitán de Domínguez Mex. 66 F5
Commack NY U.S.A. 64 E2
Commentry France 24 F3
Committee Bay Canada 61 J3
Commonwealth Territory admin. div. Australia see Jervis Bay Territory
Como Italy 26 C2
Como, Lago di Italy see Como, Lake
Como, Lake Italy 26 C2
Como Chamling l. China 37 G3
Comodoro Rivadavia Arg. 70 C7
Comores country Africa see Comoros
Comorin, Cape India 38 C4
Comoro Islands country Africa see Comoros
Comoros country Africa 49 E5
Compiègne France 24 F2
Comprida, Ilha i. Brazil 71 B4
Comrat Moldova 27 M1
Comrie U.K. 20 F4
Cona China 37 G4
Conakry Guinea 46 B4
Cona Niyeo Arg. 70 C6
Conceição r. Brazil 71 B2
Conceição da Barra Brazil 71 D2
Conceição do Araguaia Brazil 69 I5
Conceição do Mato Dentro Brazil 71 C2
Concepción Chile 70 B5
Concepción Mex. 66 D4
Concepción Para. 70 E2
Concepción de la Vega Dom. Rep. see La Vega
Conception, Point CA U.S.A. 65 B3
Conchos r. Mex. 66 D3
Conchos r. Nuevo León/Tamaulipas Mex. 66 E4
Concord CA U.S.A. 65 A2
Concord NH U.S.A. 64 F1
Concordia Arg. 70 E4
Concordia Peru 68 D4
Concordia S. Africa 50 C5
Concordia KS U.S.A. 62 H4
Concordia research stn 76 G2
Concord Peak Afgh. 36 C1
Condamine Australia 58 E1
Condamine r. Australia 58 D1
Condeúba Brazil 71 C1
Condobolin Australia 58 C4
Condom France 24 E5
Condor, Cordillera del mts Ecuador/Peru 68 C4
Conegliano Italy 26 E2
Conemaugh r. PA U.S.A. 64 B2
Conesus Lake NY U.S.A. 64 C1
Conflict Group is P.N.G. 56 E1
Confoederatio Helvetica country Europe see Switzerland
Confusion Range mts UT U.S.A. 65 F1
Congdü China 37 F3
Congleton U.K. 18 E5
Congo country Africa 48 B4
Congo r. Congo/Dem. Rep. Congo 48 B4
Congo (Brazzaville) country Africa see Congo
Congo (Kinshasa) country Africa see Congo, Democratic Republic of the
Congo, Democratic Republic of the country Africa 48 C4
Congo, Republic of country Africa see Congo
Congo Basin Dem. Rep. Congo 48 C4
Congo Cone sea feature S. Atlantic Ocean 72 I6
Congo Free State country Africa see Congo, Democratic Republic of the
Congonhas Brazil 71 C3
Congress AZ U.S.A. 65 F3
Conimbla National Park Australia 58 D4
Coningsby U.K. 19 G5
Coniston U.K. 18 D4
Conjuboy Australia 56 D3
Conn, Lough l. Ireland 21 C3
Connacht reg. Ireland see Connaught
Connaught reg. Ireland 21 C4
Conneaut OH U.S.A. 64 A2
Connecticut state U.S.A. 64 E2
Connemara reg. Ireland 21 C4
Connemara National Park Ireland 21 C4
Connors Range hills Australia 56 E4
Conoble Australia 58 B4
Conquista Brazil 71 B2
Conrad U.S.A. 62 E2
Conrad Rise sea feature Southern Ocean 73 K9
Conroe U.S.A. 63 H5
Conselheiro Lafaiete Brazil 71 C3
Consett U.K. 18 F4
Constance Germany see Konstanz
Constance, Lake Germany/Switz. 17 L7
Constância dos Baetas Brazil 68 F5
Constanța Romania 27 M2
Constantia tourist site Cyprus see Salamis
Constantia Germany see Konstanz
Constantina Spain 25 D5
Constantine Alg. 22 F4
Constantine, Cape U.S.A. 60 C4
Constantinople Turkey see İstanbul
Contagalo Brazil 71 C3
Contamana Peru 68 C5
Contas r. Brazil 71 D1
Contria Brazil 71 B2
Contwoyto Lake Canada 60 G3
Convención Col. 68 D2
Conway U.K. see Conwy
Conway AR U.S.A. 63 I4
Conway, Cape Australia 56 E4
Conway, Lake imp. l. Australia 57 A6
Conway National Park Australia 56 E4
Conway Reef Fiji see Ceva-i-Ra
Conwy U.K. 18 D5
Conwy r. U.K. 19 D5
Coober Pedy Australia 55 F7
Cooch Behar India see Koch Bihar
Coochbehar India see Koch Bihar
Cook Australia 55 E7
Cook, Grand Récif de rf New Caledonia 53 G3
Cook, Mount N.Z. see Aoraki
Cookhouse S. Africa 51 G7
Cook Ice Shelf Antarctica 76 H2
Cook Inlet sea chan. U.S.A. 60 C3
Cook Islands terr. S. Pacific Ocean 74 J7
Cooksburg NY U.S.A. 64 D1
Cooks Passage Australia 56 D2
Cookstown U.K. 21 F3
Cook Strait N.Z. 59 E5
Cooktown Australia 56 D2
Coolabah Australia 58 C3
Cooladdi Australia 58 B1
Coolah Australia 58 D3
Coolamon Australia 58 C5
Coolgardie Australia 55 C7
Coolibah Australia 54 E3
Cooloola National Park Australia 57 F5
Coolum Beach Australia 57 F5
Cooma Australia 58 D6
Coombah Australia 57 C7
Coonabarabran Australia 58 D3
Coonamble Australia 58 D3
Coondambo Australia 57 A6
Coondapoor India see Kundapura
Coongoola Australia 58 B1
Cooper Creek watercourse Australia 57 B6
Coopernook Australia 58 F3
Cooperstown NY U.S.A. 64 D1
Coopracambra National Park Australia 58 D6
Coorabie Australia 55 F7
Coorong National Park Australia 57 B8
Coorow Australia 55 B7
Coos Bay U.S.A. 62 C3
Cootamundra Australia 58 D5
Cootehill Ireland 21 E3
Cooyar Australia 58 E1
Copala Mex. 66 E5
Copenhagen Denmark 15 H9
Copertino Italy 26 H4
Copeton Reservoir Australia 58 E2
Copiapó Chile 70 B3
Copley Australia 57 B6
Copparo Italy 26 D2
Coppermine Canada see Kugluktuk
Coppermine r. Canada 77 L2
Copperton S. Africa 50 F5
Coqên China 37 F3
Coqên Xizang China 37 F3
Coquilhatville Dem. Rep. Congo see Mbandaka
Coquille i. Micronesia see Pikelot
Coquimbo Chile 70 B3
Corabia Romania 27 K3
Coração de Jesus Brazil 71 B2
Coracesium Turkey see Alanya
Coraki Australia 58 F2
Coral Bay Australia 55 A5
Coral Harbour Canada 61 J3

D

Dead Sea salt l. Asia 39 B4
Deakin Australia 55 E7
Deal U.K. 19 I7
Dealesville S. Africa 51 G5
Dean, Forest of U.K. 19 E7
Deán Funes Arg. 70 D4
Deanuvuotna inlet Norway see Tanafjorden
Dearne r. U.K. 18 F5
Dease Lake Canada 60 F4
Dease Strait Canada 60 H3
Death Valley depr. CA U.S.A. 65 D2
Death Valley Junction CA U.S.A. 65 D2
Death Valley National Park CA U.S.A. 65 D2
Deauville France 24 E2
De Baai S. Africa see Port Elizabeth
Debar Macedonia 27 I4
Debenham U.K. 19 I6
Débo, Lac l. Mali 46 C3
Deborah East, Lake imp. l. Australia 55 B7
Deborah West, Lake imp. l. Australia 55 B7
Debrecen Hungary 27 I1
Debre Markos Eth. 32 E7
Debre Tabor Eth. 32 E7
Debre Zeyit Eth. 48 D3
Decatur AL U.S.A. 63 J5
Decatur IL U.S.A. 63 J4
Deccan plat. India 38 C2
Deception Bay Australia 58 F1
Děčín Czech Rep. 17 O5
Decorah U.S.A. 63 I3
Deddington U.K. 19 F7
Dedegöl Dağları mts Turkey 27 N6
Dedo de Deus mt. Brazil 71 B4
Dédougou Burkina 46 C3
Dedovichi Rus. Fed. 12 F4
Dedu China see Wudalianchi
Dee r. Ireland 21 F4
Dee est. U.K. 18 D5
Dee r. England/Wales U.K. 19 D5
Dee r. Scotland U.K. 20 G3
Deel r. Ireland 21 D5
Deel r. Ireland 21 F4
Deep Creek Lake MD U.S.A. 64 B3
Deepwater Australia 58 E2
Deeri Somalia 48 E3
Deering U.S.A. 60 B3
Deering, Mount Australia 55 E6
Deer Island U.S.A. 60 B4
Deer Lodge U.S.A. 62 E2
Deesa India see Disa
Defensores del Chaco, Parque Nacional nat. park Para. 70 D2
Degana India 36 C4
Degeh Bur Eth. 48 E3
Degema Nigeria 46 D4
Deggendorf Germany 17 N6
Degh r. Pak. 36 C3
De Grey r. Australia 54 B5
Degtevo Rus. Fed. 13 I6
Deh-Dasht Iran 35 H5
Deheq Iran 35 H4
Deh Golān Iran 35 G4
Dehi Afgh. 36 A2
Dehküyeh Iran 35 I6
Dehlorān Iran 35 G4
De Hoop Nature Reserve S. Africa 50 E8
Dehra Dun India 36 D3
Dehradun India see Dehra Dun
Dehri India 37 F4
Deim Zubeir Sudan 47 F4
Deir-ez-Zor Syria see Dayr az Zawr
Dej Romania 27 J1
Deji China see Rinbung
Dejiang China 43 J7
De Kalb IL U.S.A. 63 J3
De-Kastri Rus. Fed. 44 F2
Dekemhare Eritrea 32 E6
Dekina Nigeria 46 D4
Dékoa Cent. Afr. Rep. 48 B3
Delaki Indon. 54 D2
Delamar Lake NV U.S.A. 65 E2
Delano CA U.S.A. 65 C3
Delano Peak UT U.S.A. 65 F1
Delap-Uliga-Djarrit Marshall Is 74 H5
Delārām Afgh. 33 J3
Delareyville S. Africa 51 G4
Delaronde Lake Canada 62 F1
Delaware r. New Jersey/Pennsylvania U.S.A. 64 D3
Delaware state U.S.A. 64 D3
Delaware, East Branch r. NY U.S.A. 64 D2
Delaware Bay Delaware/New Jersey U.S.A. 64 D3
Delaware Water Gap National Recreational Area park New Jersey/Pennsylvania U.S.A. 64 D2
Delêg China 37 F3
Delegate Australia 58 D6
Delémont Switz. 24 H3
Delfinópolis Brazil 71 B3
Delft Neth. 16 J4
Delfzijl Neth. 15 E10
Delgado, Cabo c. Moz. 49 E5
Delgerhaan Mongolia 42 I3
Delhi Ont. Canada 64 A1
Delhi China 42 H5
Delhi India 36 D3
Delhi NY U.S.A. 64 D1
Delice Turkey 34 D3
Delice r. Turkey 34 D2
Delījān Iran 35 H4
Déline Canada 60 F3
Delingha China see Delhi
Dellys Alg. 25 H5
Del Mar CA U.S.A. 65 D4
Delmenhorst Germany 17 L4
Delnice Croatia 26 F2
De-Longa, Ostrova is Rus. Fed. 29 Q2
De Long Islands Rus. Fed. see De-Longa, Ostrova
De Long Mountains U.S.A. 60 B3
De Long Strait Rus. Fed. see Longa, Proliv
Deloraine Canada 62 G2
Delportshoop S. Africa 50 G5
Del Rio U.S.A. 62 G6
Delsbo Sweden 15 J6
Delta CO U.S.A. 62 F4
Delta UT U.S.A. 62 E4
Delta Downs Australia 56 C3
Delta Junction U.S.A. 60 D3
Delungra Australia 58 E2
Delvin Ireland 21 E4
Delvinë Albania 27 I5
Delwara India 36 C4
Demavend mt. Iran see Damāvand, Qolleh-ye
Demba Dem. Rep. Congo 49 C4
Dembī Dolo Eth. 32 D8
Demerara Guyana see Georgetown
Demerara Abyssal Plain sea feature S. Atlantic Ocean 72 E5
Demidov Rus. Fed. 13 F5
Deming U.S.A. 62 F5
Demirci Turkey 27 M5
Demirköy Turkey 27 L4
Demirtaş Turkey 39 A1
Demmin Germany 17 N4
Dempo, Gunung vol. Indon. 41 C8
Dêmqog China 36 D2
Dem'yanovo Rus. Fed. 12 J3
De Naawte S. Africa 50 E6
Denakil reg. Africa 48 E2
Denali mt. U.S.A. see McKinley, Mount
Denali National Park and Preserve U.S.A. 60 C3
Denan Eth. 48 E3
Denbigh U.K. 18 D5
Den Bosch Neth. see 's-Hertogenbosch
Dendâra Mauritania 46 C3
Dendi mt. Eth. 48 D3
Dendron S. Africa see Mogwadi
Denezhkin Kamen', Gora mt. Rus. Fed. 11 R3
Dêngka China see Têwo
Dêngkagoin China see Têwo
Dengkou China 42 J4
Dêngqên China 37 H3
Den Haag Neth. see The Hague
Denham Australia 55 A6
Denham r. Australia 54 E3
Denham Range mts Australia 56 E4
Den Helder Neth. 16 J4
Denia Spain 25 G4
Denial Bay Australia 57 A7
Deniliquin Australia 58 B5
Denison IA U.S.A. 63 H3
Denison, Cape Antarctica 76 G2
Denison Plains Australia 54 E4
Deniyaya Sri Lanka 38 D5
Denizli Turkey 27 M6
Denman Australia 58 E4
Denman Glacier Antarctica 76 F2
Denmark Australia 52 B5
Denmark country Europe 15 G8
Denmark Strait Greenland/Iceland 10 A2
Dennis, Lake imp. l. Australia 54 E5
Denny U.K. 20 F4
Denpasar Indon. 41 D8
Denton MD U.S.A. 64 D3
Denton TX U.S.A. 63 H5
D'Entrecasteaux, Point Australia 55 A8
D'Entrecasteaux, Récifs rf New Caledonia 53 G3
D'Entrecasteaux Islands P.N.G. 52 F2
D'Entrecasteaux National Park Australia 55 A8
Denver CO U.S.A. 62 F4
Denver PA U.S.A. 64 C2
Deo India 37 F4
Deoband India 36 D3
Deogarh Jharkhand India see Deoghar
Deogarh Orissa India 37 F5
Deogarh Rajasthan India 36 C4
Deogarh Uttar Prad. India 36 D4
Deogarh mt. India 37 E5
Deoghar India 37 F4
Deolali India 38 B2
Deoli India 37 F5
Deori Madh. Prad. India 36 D5
Deoria India 37 E4
Deosai, Plains of Pak. 36 C2
Deosil India 37 E5
Deothang Bhutan 37 G4
Deposit NY U.S.A. 64 D1
Depsang Point h. Aksai Chin 36 D2
Deputatskiy Rus. Fed. 29 O3
Dêqên Xizang China see Dagzê
Dêqên Xizang China 37 G3
Dêqên Xizang China 37 G3
De Queen U.S.A. 63 I5
Dera Ghazi Khan Pak. 33 L3
Dera Ismail Khan Pak. 33 L3
Derawar Fort Pak. 36 B3
Derbent Rus. Fed. 35 H2
Derbesiye Turkey see Şenyurt
Derbur China 44 A2
Derby Australia 54 C4
Derby U.K. 19 F6
Derby CT U.S.A. 64 E2
Derby NY U.S.A. 64 B1
Dereham U.K. 19 H6
Derg r. Ireland/U.K. 21 E3
Derg, Lough l. Ireland 21 D5
Dergachi Rus. Fed. 13 K6
Dergachi Ukr. see Derhachi
Derhachi Ukr. 13 H6
De Ridder U.S.A. 63 I5
Derik Turkey 35 F3
Derm Namibia 50 D2
Derna Libya see Darnah
Dernberg, Cape Namibia 50 B4
Dêrong China 42 H7
Derravaragh, Lough l. Ireland 21 E4
Derry U.K. see Londonderry
Derry NH U.S.A. 64 F1
Derryveagh Mts hills Ireland 21 D3
Dêrub China 36 D2
Derudeb Sudan 32 E6
De Rust S. Africa 50 F7
Derventa Bos.-Herz. 26 G2
Derwent r. England U.K. 18 F6
Derwent r. England U.K. 18 G5
Derwent Water l. U.K. 18 D4
Derzhavinsk Kazakh. 28 H4
Derzhavinskiy Kazakh. see Derzhavinsk
Desaguadero r. Arg. 70 C4
Désappointement, Îles du is Fr. Polynesia 75 K6
Desē Eth. 48 D2
Deseado Arg. 70 C7
Deseado r. Arg. 70 C7
Desengaño, Punta pt Arg. 70 C7
Desert Canal Pak. 36 B3
Desert Center CA U.S.A. 65 E4
Desert Lake NV U.S.A. 65 E2
Des Moines IA U.S.A. 63 I3
Des Moines r. U.S.A. 63 I3
Desna r. Rus. Fed./Ukr. 13 F6
Desnogorsk Rus. Fed. 13 G5
Desolación, Isla i. Chile 70 B8
Dessau Germany 17 N5
Dessye Eth. see Desē
Destruction Bay Canada 77 A2
Dete Zimbabwe 49 C5
Detmold Germany 17 L5
Detrital Wash watercourse AZ U.S.A. 65 E2
Detroit U.S.A. 63 K3
Detroit Lakes U.S.A. 63 H2
Dett Zimbabwe see Dete
Deua National Park Australia 58 D5
Deutschland country Europe see Germany
Deutschlandsberg Austria 17 O7
Deva Romania 27 J2
Deva U.K. see Chester
Devana U.K. see Aberdeen
Devangere India see Davangere
Devanhalli India 38 C3
Deve Bair pass Bulg./Macedonia see Velbŭzhdki Prokhod
Develi Turkey 34 D3
Deventer Neth. 17 K4
Deveron r. U.K. 20 G3
Devét Skal h. Czech Rep. 17 P6
Devgarh India 38 B2
Devghar India see Deoghar
Devikot India 36 B4
Devil's Bridge U.K. 19 D6
Devil's Gate pass CA U.S.A. 65 C1
Devil's Lake U.S.A. 62 H2
Devil's Paw mt. U.S.A. 60 E4
Devil's Peak CA U.S.A. 65 C2
Devizes U.K. 19 F7
Devli India 36 C4
Devnya Bulg. 27 L3
Devon r. U.K. 20 F4
Devon Island Canada 61 I2
Devonport Australia 57 [inset]
Devrek Turkey 27 N4
Devrukh India 38 B2
Dewas India 36 D5
Dewetsdorp S. Africa 51 H5
Dewsbury U.K. 18 F5
Dexter MO U.S.A. 63 J4
Deyang China 42 I6
Dey-Dey Lake imp. l. Australia 55 E7
Deyhuk Iran 33 I3
Deyong, Tanjung pt Indon. 41 F8
Dez r. Iran 32 G3
Dezfūl Iran 35 H4
Dezhneva, Mys c. Rus. Fed. 29 T3
Dezhou Shandong China 43 L5
Dezh Shāhpūr Iran see Marīvān
Dhabarau India 37 E4
Dhahab, Wādī adh r. Syria 39 B3
Dhāhiriya West Bank 39 B4
Dhahran Saudi Arabia 30 E4
Dhaka Bangl. 37 G5
Dhalbhum reg. India 37 F5
Dhalgaon India 38 B2
Dhamār Yemen 32 F7
Dhamoni India 36 D4
Dhamtari India 38 D1
Dhana Pak. 36 B4
Dhana Sar Pak. 36 B3
Dhanbad India 37 F5
Dhanera India 36 C4
Dhang Range mts Nepal 37 E3
Dhankuta Nepal 37 F4
Dhansia India 36 C3
Dhar India 36 C5
Dhar Adrar hills Mauritania 46 B3
Dharampur India 38 B1
Dharan Bazar Nepal 37 F4
Dharashiv India see Osmanabad
Dhari India 36 B5
Dharmapuri India 38 C3
Dharmavaram India 38 C3
Dharmsala Hima. Prad. India see Dharmshala
Dharmsala Orissa India 37 F5
Dharmshala India 36 D2
Dharnaoda India 36 D4
Dhar Oualâta hills Mauritania 46 C3
Dhar Tîchît hills Mauritania 46 C3
Dharug National Park Australia 58 E4
Dharur India 38 C2
Dharwad India 38 B3
Dharwar India see Dharwad
Dharwas India 36 D2
Dhasan r. India 36 D4
Dhāt al Ḩājj Saudi Arabia 34 E5
Dhaulagiri mt. Nepal 37 E3
Dhaulpur India see Dholpur
Dhaura India 36 D4
Dhaurahra India 36 E4
Dhawlagiri mt. Nepal see Dhaulagiri
Dhebar Lake India see Jaisamand Lake
Dhekelia Sovereign Base Area military base Cyprus 39 A2
Dhemaji India 37 H4
Dhenkanal India 38 E1
Dhībān Jordan 39 B4
Dhidhimótikhon Greece see Didymoteicho
Dhing India 37 H4
Dhirwah, Wādī adh watercourse Jordan 39 C4
Dhodhekánisos is Greece see Dodecanese
Dhola India 36 B5
Dholera India 36 C5
Dholpur India 36 D4
Dhomokós Greece see Domokos
Dhone India 38 C3
Dhoraji India 36 B5
Dhori India 36 B5
Dhrangadhra India 36 B5
Dhubāb Yemen 32 F7
Dhubri India 37 G4
Dhuburi India see Dhubri
Dhudial Pak. 36 C2
Dhule India 38 B1
Dhulia India see Dhule
Dhulian India 37 F4
Dhulian Pak. 36 C2
Dhuma India 36 D5
Dhund r. India 36 D4
Dhurwai India 36 D4
Dhuusa Marreeb Somalia 48 E3
Dia i. Greece 27 K7
Diablo, Mount CA U.S.A. 65 B2
Diablo, Picacho del mt. Mex. 66 A2
Diablo Range mts CA U.S.A. 65 B2
Diagbe Dem. Rep. Congo 48 C3
Diamante Arg. 70 D4
Diamantina watercourse Australia 56 B5
Diamantina Brazil 71 C2
Diamantina, Chapada plat. Brazil 71 C1
Diamantina Deep sea feature Indian Ocean 73 O8
Diamantina Gates National Park Australia 56 C4
Diamantino Brazil 69 G6
Diamond Islets Australia 56 E3
Dian Chi l. China 42 I8
Diandioumé Mali 46 C3
Diane Bank sea feature Australia 56 E2
Dianópolis Brazil 69 I6
Diaobingshan China 44 A4
Diaoling China 44 C3
Diapaga Burkina 46 D3
Diarizos r. Cyprus 39 A2
Diaz Point Namibia 50 B4
Dibaya Dem. Rep. Congo 49 C4
Dibella well Niger 46 E3
Dibeng S. Africa 50 F4
Dibete Botswana 51 H2
Dibrugarh India 37 H4
Dibse Syria see Dibsī
Dibsī Syria 39 D2
Dickinson U.S.A. 62 G2
Dicle r. Asia see Tigris
Dicle r. Asia 35 F3 see Tigris
Didēsa Wenz r. Eth. 48 D3
Didiéni Mali 46 C3
Didwana India 36 C4
Didymoteicho Greece 27 L4
Die France 24 G4
Diébougou Burkina 46 C3
Diedenhofen France see Thionville
Diefenbaker, Lake Canada 62 F1
Diego de Almagro, Isla i. Chile 70 A8
Diégo Suarez Madag. see Antsirañana
Diéma Mali 46 C3
Dieppe France 24 E2
Di'er Songhua Jiang r. China 44 B3
Dietikon Switz. 24 I3
Diffa Niger 46 E3
Digby Canada 63 N3
Diggi India 36 C4
Diglur India 38 C2
Digne France see Digne-les-Bains
Digne-les-Bains France 24 H4
Digoin France 24 F3
Digras India 38 C1
Digri Pak. 36 B4
Digul r. Indon. 52 D2
Digya National Park Ghana 46 C4
Dihang r. India 37 H4 see Brahmaputra
Dihōk Iraq see Dahūk
Diinsoor Somalia 48 E3
Dijon France 24 G3
Dik Chad 47 E4
Diken India 36 C4
Dikhil Djibouti 32 F7
Dikili Turkey 27 L5
Diklosmta mt. Rus. Fed. 13 J8
Dikson Rus. Fed. 28 J2
Dīla Eth. 48 D3
Dili East Timor 54 D2
Dillingen an der Donau Germany 17 M6
Dillingham U.S.A. 60 C4
Dillon MT U.S.A. 62 E2
Dillwyn VA U.S.A. 64 B4
Dilolo Dem. Rep. Congo 49 C5
Dimapur India 37 H4
Dimashq Syria see Damascus
Dimbokro Côte d'Ivoire 46 C4
Dimboola Australia 57 C8
Dimitrov Ukr. see Dymytrov
Dimitrovgrad Bulg. 27 K3
Dimitrovgrad Rus. Fed. 13 K5
Dimitrovo Bulg. see Pernik
Dīmona Israel 39 B4
Dimpho Pan salt pan Botswana 50 E3
Dinajpur Bangl. 37 G4
Dinan France 24 C2
Dinant Belgium 16 J5
Dinapur India 37 F4
Dinar Turkey 27 N5
Dīnār, Kūh-e mt. Iran 35 H5
Dinara Planina mts Bos.-Herz./Croatia see Dinaric Alps
Dinaric Alps mts Bos.-Herz./Croatia 26 G2
Dinbych U.K. see Denbigh
Dinbych-y-pysgod U.K. see Tenby
Dinder National Park Sudan 47 G3
Dindi r. India 38 C2
Dindigul India 38 C4
Dindima Nigeria 46 E3
Dindiza Moz. 51 K2
Dindori India 36 E5
Dingla Nepal 37 F4
Dingle Bay Ireland 21 B5
Dingnan China 43 L8
Dingo Australia 56 E4
Dinguiraye Guinea 46 B3
Dingwall U.K. 20 E3
Dingxi China 42 I5
Dinngyê China 37 F3
Dinokwe Botswana 51 H2
Dinwiddie VA U.S.A. 64 C4
Dioïla Mali 46 C3
Dionísio Cerqueira Brazil 70 F3
Diorama Brazil 71 A2
Dioscurias Georgia see Sokhumi
Diouloulou Senegal 46 B3
Diourbel Senegal 46 B3
Dipayal Far Western 36 E3
Diphu India 37 H4
Dipkarpaz Cyprus see Rizokarpason
Diplo Pak. 36 B4
Dipperu National Park Australia 56 E4
Dirang India 37 H4
Diré Mali 46 C3
Direction, Cape Australia 56 C2
Dirē Dawa Eth. 48 E3
Dirico Angola 49 C5
Dirk Hartog Island Australia 55 A6
Dirranbandi Australia 58 D2
Dirs Saudi Arabia 48 E2
Dirschau Poland see Tczew
Disa India 36 C4
Disang r. India 37 H4
Disappointment, Cape S. Georgia 70 I8
Disappointment, Lake imp. l. Australia 55 C5
Disappointment Islands Fr. Polynesia see Désappointement, Îles du
Disaster Bay Australia 58 D6
Discovery Bay Australia 57 C8
Disko i. Greenland see Qeqertarsuaq
Disko Bugt b. Greenland see Qeqertarsuup Tunua
Dispur India 37 G4
Disputanta VA U.S.A. 64 C4
Diss U.K. 19 I6
Distrito Federal admin. dist. Brazil 71 B1
Disūq Egypt 34 C5
Ditloung S. Africa 50 F5
Dittaino r. Sicilia Italy 26 F6
Diu India 38 A1
Dīvān Darreh Iran 35 G4
Divehi country Indian Ocean see Maldives
Divi, Point India 38 D3
Divichi Azer. see Dāvāçi
Divinópolis Brazil 71 B3
Divnoye Rus. Fed. 13 I7
Divo Côte d'Ivoire 46 C4
Divriği Turkey 34 E3
Diwana Pak. 36 A4
Diwaniyah Iraq see Ad Dīwānīyah
Dixon CA U.S.A. 65 B1
Dixon IL U.S.A. 63 J3
Dixon Entrance sea chan. Canada/U.S.A. 60 E4
Diyadin Turkey 35 F3
Diyarbakır Turkey 35 F3
Diz Chah Iran 35 I4
Dize Turkey see Yüksekova
Djado Niger 46 E2
Djado, Plateau du Niger 46 E2
Djaja, Puntjak mt. Indon. see Jaya, Puncak
Djakarta Indon. see Jakarta
Djakovica Kosovo see Gjakovë
Djakovo Croatia see Đakovo
Djambala Congo 48 B4
Djanet Alg. 46 D2
Djarrit-Uliga-Dalap Marshall Is see Delap-Uliga-Djarrit
Djelfa Alg. 25 H6
Djéma Cent. Afr. Rep. 48 C3
Djenné Mali 46 C3
Djerdap nat. park Serbia 27 J2
Djibo Burkina 46 C3
Djibouti country Africa 32 F7
Djibouti Djibouti 32 F7
Djidjelli Alg. see Jijel
Djougou Benin 46 D4
Djoum Cameroon 46 E4
Djourab, Erg du des. Chad 47 E3
Djúpivogur Iceland 14 [inset]
Djurås Sweden 15 I6
Djurdjura, Parc National du Alg. 25 I5
Dmitriya Lapteva, Proliv sea chan. Rus. Fed. 29 P2
Dmitriyev-L'govskiy Rus. Fed. 13 G5
Dmitriyevsk Ukr. see Makiyivka
Dmitrov Rus. Fed. 12 H4
Dmytriyevs'k Ukr. see Makiyivka
Dnepr r. Europe 13 F5 see Dnieper
Dneprodzerzhinsk Ukr. see Dniprodzerzhyns'k
Dnepropetrovsk Ukr. see Dnipropetrovs'k
Dnieper r. Belarus 23 K1
Dnieper r. Europe 13 G7
Dnieper r. Ukr. 11 M6
Dniester r. Moldova 13 F7
Dniester r. Ukr. 13 F6
Dnipro r. Europe 13 G7 see Dnieper
Dnipro r. Ukr. see Dnieper
Dniprodzerzhyns'k Ukr. 13 G6
Dnipropetrovs'k Ukr. 13 G6
Dnister r. Ukr. 13 F6 see Dniester
Dno Rus. Fed. 12 F4
Dnyapro r. Belarus see Dnieper
Dnyapro r. Europe 13 F6 see Dnieper
Doāb Afgh. 36 A2
Doaba Pak. 36 B2
Doba Chad 47 E4
Doba China see Toiba
Dobele Latvia 15 M8
Doberai, Jazirah pen. Indon. 41 F8
Doberai Peninsula Indon. see Doberai, Jazirah
Dobo Indon. 41 F8
Doboj Bos.-Herz. 26 H2
Dobrich Bulg. 27 L3
Dobrinka Rus. Fed. 13 I5
Dobroye Rus. Fed. 13 H5
Dobrudja reg. Romania see Dobruja
Dobruja reg. Romania 27 L3
Dobrush Belarus 13 F5
Dobryanka Rus. Fed. 11 R4
Dobzha China 37 G3
Doce r. Brazil 71 D2
Dochart r. U.K. 20 E4
Do China Qala Afgh. 36 B3
Docking U.K. 19 H6
Doctor Hicks Range hills Australia 55 D7
Doctor Pedro P. Peña Para. 70 D2
Doda India 36 C2
Doda Betta mt. India 38 C4
Dod Ballapur India 38 C3
Dodecanese is Greece 27 L7
Dodekanisos is Greece see Dodecanese
Dodge City U.S.A. 62 G4
Dodman Point U.K. 19 C8
Dodoma Tanz. 49 D4
Dogai Coring salt l. China 37 G2
Dogaicoring Qangco salt l. China 37 G2
Doğanşehir Turkey 34 E3
Dogên Co l. Xizang China 37 G3
Dogên Co l. Xizang China see Bam Tso
Dōgo i. Japan 45 D5
Dogondoutchi Niger 46 D3
Doğubeyazıt Turkey 35 G3
Doğu Menteşe Dağları mts Turkey 27 M6
Dogxung Zangbo r. China 37 F3
Do'gyaling China 37 G3
Doha Qatar 32 H4
Dohad India see Dahod
Dohazari Bangl. 37 H5
Dohrighat India 37 E4
Doi i. Fiji 53 I4
Doire U.K. see Londonderry
Dois Irmãos, Serra dos hills Brazil 69 J5
Dokan, Sadd Iraq 35 G4
Dok-dō i. N. Pacific Ocean see Liancourt Rocks
Dokhara, Dunes de des. Alg. 22 F5
Dokka Norway 15 G6
Dokkum Neth. 17 J4
Dokri Pak. 36 B4
Dokshukino Rus. Fed. see Nartkala
Dokshytsy Belarus 15 O9
Dokuchayeva, Mys c. Rus. Fed. 44 G3
Dokuchayevs'k Ukr. 13 H7
Dolbenmaen U.K. 19 C6
Dol-de-Bretagne France 24 D2
Dole France 24 G3
Dolgellau U.K. 19 D6
Dolgiy, Ostrov i. Rus. Fed. 12 L1
Dolgorukovo Rus. Fed. 13 H5
Dolina Ukr. see Dolyna
Dolinsk Rus. Fed. 44 F3
Dolisie Congo see Loubomo
Dolleman Island Antarctica 76 L2
Dolok, Pulau i. Indon. 41 F8
Dolomites mts Italy 26 D2
Dolomiti mts Italy see Dolomites
Dolomiti Bellunesi, Parco Nazionale delle nat. park Italy 26 D1
Dolomitiche, Alpi mts Italy see Dolomites
Dolonnur China 43 L4
Dolo Odo Eth. 48 E3
Dolores Arg. 70 E5
Dolores Uruguay 70 E4
Dolphin and Union Strait Canada 60 G3
Dolphin Head hd Namibia 50 B3
Đô Lương Vietnam 42 J9
Dolyna Ukr. 13 D6
Domaila India 36 D3
Domaniç Turkey 27 M5
Domar China 42 E6
Domartang China 42 G6
Domažlice Czech Rep. 17 N6
Domba China 37 H2
Dom Bākh Iran 35 G4
Dombås Norway 14 F5
Dombóvár Hungary 26 H1
Dombrau Poland see Dąbrowa Górnicza
Dombrovitsa Ukr. see Dubrovytsya
Dombrowa Poland see Dąbrowa Górnicza
Domda China see Qingshuihe
Dome Argus Antarctica 76 E1
Dome Charlie Antarctica 76 F2
Dome Creek Canada 60 F4
Dome Rock Mountains AZ U.S.A. 65 E4
Domeyko Chile 70 B3
Domfront France 24 D2
Dominica country West Indies 67 L5
Dominicana, República country West Indies see Dominican Republic
Dominican Republic country West Indies 67 J5
Dominion, Cape Canada 61 K3
Dominique i. Fr. Polynesia see Hiva Oa
Dom Joaquim Brazil 71 C2
Domo Eth. 48 E3
Domokos Greece 27 J5
Dompu Indon. 41 D8
Domula China see Duomula
Domuyo, Volcán vol. Arg. 70 B5
Domville, Mount h. Australia 58 E2
Don r. Rus. Fed. 13 H7
Don r. U.K. 20 G3
Donaghadee U.K. 21 G3
Donaghmore U.K. 21 F3
Donald Australia 58 A6
Doñana, Parque Nacional de nat. park Spain 25 C5
Donau r. Austria/Germany see Danube
Donau r. Europe 17 P6 see Danube
Donauwörth Germany 17 M6
Don Benito Spain 25 D4
Doncaster U.K. 18 F5
Dondo Angola 49 B4
Dondo Moz. 49 D5
Dondra Head hd Sri Lanka 38 D5
Donegal Ireland 21 D3
Donegal Bay Ireland 21 D3
Donets'k Ukr. 13 H7
Donetsko-Amrovsiyevka Ukr. see Amvrosiyivka
Donets'kyy Kryazh hills Rus. Fed./Ukr. 13 H6
Donga r. Cameroon/Nigeria 46 D4
Dongane, Lagoa lag. Moz. 51 L3
Dongara Australia 55 A7
Dongbo China see Mêdog
Dongchuan Yunnan China 42 I7
Dongco China 37 F2
Dong Co l. China 37 F2
Dongfang China 43 J9
Dongfanghong China 44 D3
Donggang China 45 B5
Donggang Shandong China 43 L5
Donggi Conag l. China 37 I2
Donggou China see Donggang
Dong Hai sea N. Pacific Ocean see East China Sea
Đông Hơi Vietnam 31 J5
Dongjug China 37 H3
Dongliao He r. China 44 A4
Dongminzhutun China 44 A3
Dongning China 44 C3
Dongo Angola 49 B5
Dongo Dem. Rep. Congo 48 B3
Dongola Sudan 32 D6
Dongou Congo 48 B3
Dongqiao China 37 G3
Dongtai China 43 M6
Dongting Hu l. China 43 K7
Dong Ujimqin Qi China see Uliastai
Dongxing Heilong. China 44 B3
Dongying China 43 L5
Donnellys Crossing N.Z. 59 D2
Donner Pass U.S.A. 62 C4
Donostia-San Sebastián Spain 25 F2
Donousa i. Greece 27 K6
Donskoye Rus. Fed. 13 I7
Dooagh Ireland 21 B4
Doomadgee Australia 56 B3
Doon r. U.K. 20 E5
Doon, Loch l. U.K. 20 E5
Doonbeg r. Ireland 21 C5
Dooxo Nugaaleed val. Somalia 48 E3
Dor Israel 39 B3
Dora, Lake imp. l. Australia 54 C5
Dorah Pass Pak. 36 B1
Dorbiljin China see Emin
Dorbod China see Taikang
Dorbod Qi China see Ulan Hua
Dorchester U.K. 19 E8
Dordabis Namibia 50 C2
Dordogne r. France 24 D4
Dordrecht Neth. 16 J5
Dordrecht S. Africa 51 H6
Doreenville Namibia 50 D2
Doré Lake Canada 60 H4
Dores do Indaiá Brazil 71 B2
Dorgê Co l. China 37 H2
Dori r. Afgh. 36 A3
Dori Burkina 46 C3
Doring r. S. Africa 50 D6
Dorisvale Australia 54 E3
Dorking U.K. 19 G7
Dormidontovka Rus. Fed. 44 D3
Dornoch U.K. 20 E3
Dornoch Firth est. U.K. 20 E3
Doro Mali 46 C3
Dorogobuzh Rus. Fed. 13 G5
Dorogorskoye Rus. Fed. 12 J2
Dorohoi Romania 13 E7
Döröö Nuur salt l. Mongolia 42 G3
Dorostol Bulg. see Silistra
Dorotea Sweden 14 J4
Dorpat Estonia see Tartu
Dorre Island Australia 55 A6
Dorrigo Australia 58 F3
Dorsoidong Co l. China 37 G2
Dortmund Germany 17 K5
Dörtyol Turkey 39 C1
Doruma Dem. Rep. Congo 48 C3
Dorylaeum Turkey see Eskişehir
Dos Bahías, Cabo c. Arg. 70 C6
Dos de Mayo Peru 68 C5
Dos Palos CA U.S.A. 65 B2
Dosso Niger 46 D3
Dothan U.S.A. 63 J5
Douai France 24 F1
Douala Cameroon 46 D4
Douarnenez France 24 B2
Double Island Point Australia 57 F5
Double Peak CA U.S.A. 65 C3
Double Point Australia 56 D3
Doubs r. France/Switz. 24 G3
Doubtful Sound inlet N.Z. 59 A7
Doubtless Bay N.Z. 59 D2
Douentza Mali 46 C3
Dougga tourist site Tunisia 26 C6
Douglas Isle of Man 18 C4
Douglas S. Africa 50 F5
Douglas U.K. 20 F5
Douglas AZ U.S.A. 62 F5
Douglas GA U.S.A. 63 K5
Douglas WY U.S.A. 62 F3
Douglas Reef i. Japan see Okino-Tori-shima
Doulatpur Bangl. see Daulatpur
Doullens France 24 F1
Douna Mali 46 C3
Doune U.K. 20 E4
Dourada, Serra hills Brazil 71 A2
Dourada, Serra mts Brazil 71 A1
Dourados Brazil 70 F2
Douro r. Port. 25 B3
Douve r. France 19 F9
Dove r. U.K. 19 F6
Dover U.K. 19 I7
Dover DE U.S.A. 64 D3
Dover NH U.S.A. 64 F1
Dover NJ U.S.A. 64 D2
Dover OH U.S.A. 64 A2
Dover, Strait of France/U.K. 24 E1
Dover-Foxcroft U.S.A. 63 N2
Dovey r. U.K. 19 D6
Dovrefjell Nasjonalpark nat. park Norway 14 F5
Dowlaiswaram India 38 D2
Dowlatābād Fārs Iran 35 H5
Dowlatābād Fārs Iran 35 I5
Dowl at Yār Afgh. 36 A2
Downpatrick U.K. 21 G3
Downsville NY U.S.A. 64 D1
Dow Rūd Iran 35 H4
Doylestown PA U.S.A. 64 D2
Dōzen is Japan 45 D5
Dozois, Réservoir resr Canada 63 L2
Dozulé France 19 G9
Drâa, Hamada du plat. Alg. 22 C6
Dracena Brazil 71 A3
Drachten Neth. 17 K4
Drăgănești-Olt Romania 27 K2
Drăgășani Romania 27 K2
Dragonera, Isla i. Spain see Sa Dragonera
Dragsfjärd Fin. 15 M6
Draguignan France 24 H5
Drahichyn Belarus 15 N10
Drake Australia 58 F2
Drakensberg mts S. Africa 51 I3
Drake Passage S. Atlantic Ocean 72 D9
Drakes Bay CA U.S.A. 65 A2
Drama Greece 27 K4
Drammen Norway 15 G7

linders Island Australia 57 [inset]
linders Passage Australia 56 E3
linders Ranges mts Australia 57 B7
linders Ranges National Park Australia 57 B6
linders Reefs Australia 56 E3
in Flon Canada 62 G1
int U.K. 18 D5
int U.S.A. 63 K3
int Island Kiribati 75 J6
inton Australia 58 D1
isa Norway 15 H6
lissingskiy, Mys c. Rus. Fed. 28 H2
lodden U.K. 18 E3
lood Range mts Antarctica 76 J1
lora r. Australia 54 E3
lorac France 24 F4
lora Reef Australia 56 D3
lorence Italy 26 D3
lorence AL U.S.A. 63 J5
lorence AZ U.S.A. 62 E5
lorence SC U.S.A. 63 L5
lorencia Col. 68 C3
orentia Italy see Florence
orentino Ameghino, Embalse resr Arg. 70 C6
lores r. Arg. 70 E5
ores Guat. 66 G5
lores i. Indon. 41 E8
lores, Laut sea Indon. 41 D8
loresta Brazil 69 K5
loriano Brazil 69 J5
lorianópolis Brazil 71 A4
lorida Uruguay 70 E4
lorida state U.S.A. 63 K5
lorida, Straits of Bahamas/U.S.A. 67 H4
lorida Islands Solomon Is 53 G2
lorida Keys is U.S.A. 63 K7
lorin CA U.S.A. 65 B1
lorina Greece 27 I4
lorø Norway 15 D6
loyd VA U.S.A. 64 A4
loyd, Mount AZ U.S.A. 65 F3
lushing Neth. see Vlissingen
ly r. P.N.G. 52 E2
lying Fish, Cape Antarctica 76 K2
oam Lake Canada 62 G1
oča Bos.-Herz. 26 H3
oça Turkey 27 L5
ochabers U.K. 20 F3
ocșani Romania 27 L2
oggia Italy 26 F4
ogo i. Cape Verde 46 [inset]
oinaven h. U.K. 20 E2
oix France 24 E5
olda sea chan. Norway 14 I3
oldereid Norway 14 H4
oldfjorden sea chan. Norway 14 G4
olegandros i. Greece 27 K6
oleyet Canada 63 K2
oley Island Canada 61 K3
oligno Italy 26 E3
olkestone U.K. 19 I7
olkingham U.K. 19 G6
olkston U.S.A. 63 K5
olldal Norway 14 G5
ollonica Italy 26 D3
olsom Lake CA U.S.A. 65 B1
omboni Comoros 49 E5
omin Rus. Fed. 13 I7
ominskaya Rus. Fed. 12 K2
ominskoye Rus. Fed. 12 I4
onda NY U.S.A. 64 D1
ond-du-Lac Canada 60 H4
ond du Lac U.S.A. 63 J3
ondevila Spain 25 B3
ondi Italy 26 E4
onni Sardegna Italy 26 C4
onsagrada Spain see A Fonsagrada
onseca, Golfo do b. Central America 66 G6
onte Boa Brazil 68 E4
ontur pt Iceland 14 [inset]
oochow China see Fuzhou
oraker, Mount U.S.A. 60 C3
oraulep atoll Micronesia see Faraulep
orbes Australia 58 D4
orchheim Germany 17 M6
ord City CA U.S.A. 65 C3
ørde Norway 15 D6
ordham U.K. 19 H6
ordingbridge U.K. 19 F8
ord Range mts Antarctica 76 J1
ords Bridge Australia 58 B2
orécariah Guinea 46 B4
orel, Mont mt. Greenland 61 O3
oreland hd U.K. 19 F8
oreland Point U.K. 19 D7
orest MS U.S.A. 63 J5
orest Creek r. Australia 56 C3
orest Hill Australia 58 C5
orestville CA U.S.A. 65 A1
orfar U.K. 20 G4
orges-les-Eaux France 19 I9
orked River NJ U.S.A. 64 D3
ork Union VA U.S.A. 64 B4
orlì Italy 26 E2
ormby U.K. 18 D5
ormentera i. Spain 25 G4
ormentor, Cap de c. Spain 25 H4
ormer Yugoslav Republic of Macedonia country Europe see Macedonia
ormiga Brazil 71 B3
ormosa Arg. 70 E3
ormosa country Asia see Taiwan
ormosa Brazil 71 B1
ormosa, Serra hills Brazil 69 G6
ormosa Bay Kenya see Ungwana Bay
ormosa Strait China/Taiwan see Taiwan Strait
ormoso r. Bahia Brazil 71 B1
ormoso r. Tocantins Brazil 71 A1
ornos Moz. 51 L2
orres U.K. 20 F3
orrest Vic. Australia 58 A7
orrest W.A. Australia 55 E7
orrestal Range mts Antarctica 76 A1
orrest City U.S.A. 63 I4
orrest Lakes imp. l. Australia 55 E7
ors Sweden 14 J5
orsayth Australia 56 C3
orsnäs Sweden 14 M3
orssa Fin. 15 M6
orster Australia 58 F4
orsyth MT U.S.A. 62 F2
orsyth Range hills Australia 56 C4
ort Abbas Pak. 36 C3
ort Albany Canada 63 K1
ortaleza Brazil 69 K4
ort Archambault Chad see Sarh
ort Ashby WV U.S.A. 64 B3
ort Augustus U.K. 20 E3
ort Beaufort S. Africa 51 H7
ort Benton U.S.A. 62 E2
ort Brabant Canada see Tuktoyaktuk
ort Bragg U.S.A. 62 C4
ort Charlet Alg. see Djanet
ort Chimo Canada see Kuujjuaq
ort Chipewyan Canada 60 G4
Fort Crampel Cent. Afr. Rep. see Kaga Bandoro
Fort-Dauphin Madag. see Tôlañaro
Fort-de-France Martinique 67 L6
Fort de Kock Indon. see Bukittinggi
Fort de Polignac Alg. see Illizi
Fort Dodge U.S.A. 63 I3
Fort Edward NY U.S.A. 64 E1
Fortescue r. Australia 54 B5
Forte Veneza Brazil 69 H5
Fort Flatters Alg. see Bordj Omer Driss
Fort Foureau Cameroon see Kousséri
Fort Franklin Canada see Délįne
Fort Gardel Alg. see Zaouatallaz
Fort George Canada see Chisasibi
Fort Good Hope Canada 60 F3
Fort Gouraud Mauritania see Fdérik
Forth r. U.K. 20 F4
Forth, Firth of est. U.K. 20 F4
Fort Hertz Myanmar see Putao
Fortification Range mts NV U.S.A. 65 E1
Fortín General Mendoza Para. 70 D2
Fortín Leonida Escobar Para. 70 D2
Fortín Madrejón Para. 70 E2
Fortín Pilcomayo Arg. 70 D2
Fortín Ravelo Bol. 68 F7
Fortín Sargento Primero Leyes Arg. 70 E2
Fortín Suárez Arana Bol. 68 F7
Fortín Teniente Juan Echauri López Para. 70 D2
Fort Jameson Zambia see Chipata
Fort Johnston Malawi see Mangochi
Fort Lamy Chad see Ndjamena
Fort Laperrine Alg. see Tamanrasset
Fort Lauderdale U.S.A. 63 K6
Fort Liard Canada 60 F3
Fort Macleod Canada 62 E2
Fort Manning Malawi see Mchinji
Fort McMurray Canada 60 G4
Fort McPherson Canada 60 E3
Fort Munro Pak. 36 B3
Fort Myers U.S.A. 63 K6
Fort Nelson Canada 60 F4
Fort Payne U.S.A. 63 J5
Fort Peck Reservoir U.S.A. 62 F2
Fort Pierce U.S.A. 63 K6
Fort Portal Uganda 48 D3
Fort Providence Canada 60 G3
Fort Randall U.S.A. see Cold Bay
Fort Resolution Canada 60 G3
Fortrose N.Z. 59 B8
Fortrose U.K. 20 E3
Fort Rosebery Zambia see Mansa
Fort Rousset Congo see Owando
Fort Rupert Canada see Waskaganish
Fort Sandeman Pak. see Zhob
Fort Saskatchewan Canada 62 E1
Fort Scott U.S.A. 63 I4
Fort Severn Canada 61 J4
Fort-Shevchenko Kazakh. 30 E2
Fort Simpson Canada 60 F3
Fort Smith Canada 60 G3
Fort Smith U.S.A. 63 I4
Fort Stockton U.S.A. 62 G5
Fort Sumner U.S.A. 62 G5
Fort Trinquet Mauritania see Bîr Mogreïn
Fort Vermilion Canada 77 L3
Fort Victoria Zimbabwe see Masvingo
Fort Ware Canada see Ware
Fort Wayne U.S.A. 63 J3
Fort William U.K. 20 D4
Fort Worth U.S.A. 63 H5
Fort Yukon U.S.A. 60 D3
Forum Iulii France see Fréjus
Forvik Norway 14 H4
Fossano Italy 26 B2
Fossil Downs Australia 54 D4
Foster Australia 58 C7
Fotadrevo Madag. 49 E6
Fotherby U.K. 18 G5
Fotokol Cameroon 47 E3
Fotuna i. Vanuatu see Futuna
Fougères France 24 D2
Foula i. U.K. 20 [inset]
Foulness Point U.K. 19 H7
Foul Point Sri Lanka 38 D4
Foumban Cameroon 46 E4
Foundation Ice Stream glacier Antarctica 76 L1
Fountains Abbey and Royal Water Garden (NT) tourist site U.K. 18 F4
Fourches, Mont des h. France 24 G2
Four Corners CA U.S.A. 65 D3
Fouriesburg S. Africa 51 I5
Fournoi i. Greece 27 L6
Fourpeaked Mountain U.S.A. 60 C4
Fouta Djallon reg. Guinea 46 B3
Foveaux Strait N.Z. 59 A8
Fowey r. U.K. 19 C8
Fowler CO U.S.A. 62 G4
Fowler Ice Rise Antarctica 76 L1
Fowlers Bay Australia 52 D5
Fowlers Bay b. Australia 55 F8
Fox Creek Canada 60 G4
Foxdale Isle of Man 18 C4
Foxe Basin g. Canada 61 K3
Foxe Channel Canada 61 J3
Foxe Peninsula Canada 61 K3
Fox Glacier N.Z. 59 C6
Fox Islands U.S.A. 60 B4
Fox Mountain Canada 60 E3
Fox Valley Canada 62 F1
Foyers U.K. 20 E3
Foyle r. Ireland/U.K. 21 E3
Foyle, Lough b. Ireland/U.K. 21 E2
Foynes Ireland 21 C5
Foz de Areia, Represa de resr Brazil 71 A4
Foz do Cunene Angola 49 B5
Foz do Iguaçu Brazil 70 F3
Fraga Spain 25 G3
Frakes, Mount Antarctica 76 K1
Framingham MA U.S.A. 64 F1
Framnes Mountains Antarctica 76 E2
Franca Brazil 71 B3
Français, Récif des rf New Caledonia 53 G3
Francavilla Fontana Italy 26 G4
France country Europe 24 F3
Frances Australia 57 C8
Franceville Gabon 48 B4
Francis atoll Kiribati see Beru
Francisco de Orellana Ecuador see Coca
Francistown Botswana 49 C6
Francois Peron National Park Australia 55 A6
Frankenhöhe hills Germany 17 M6
Frankfort KY U.S.A. 63 K4
Frankfurt Germany see Frankfurt am Main
Frankfurt am Main Germany 17 L5
Frankfurt an der Oder Germany 17 O4
Frank Hann National Park Australia 55 C8
Fränkische Alb hills Germany 17 M6
Fränkische Schweiz reg. Germany 17 M6
Frankland, Cape Australia 57 [inset]
Franklin MA U.S.A. 64 F1
Franklin NH U.S.A. 64 F1
Franklin PA U.S.A. 64 B2
Franklin Bay Canada 77 A2
Franklin D. Roosevelt Lake resr U.S.A. 62 D2
Franklin-Gordon National Park Australia 57 [inset]
Franklin Island Antarctica 76 H1
Franklin Mountains Canada 60 F3
Franklin Strait Canada 61 I2
Franklinville NY U.S.A. 64 B1
Frankston Australia 58 B7
Fränsta Sweden 14 J5
Frantsa-Iosifa, Zemlya is Rus. Fed. 28 G2
Franz Josef Glacier N.Z. 59 C6
Frasca, Capo della c. Sardegna Italy 26 C5
Frascati Italy 26 E4
Fraser r. Australia 54 C4
Fraser r. B.C. Canada 62 C2
Fraser r. Nfld. and Lab. Canada 61 L4
Fraser, Mount h. Australia 55 B6
Fraserburg S. Africa 50 E6
Fraserburgh U.K. 20 G3
Fraserdale Canada 63 K2
Fraser Island Australia 56 F5
Fraser Island National Park Australia 56 F5
Fraser National Park Australia 58 B6
Fraser Range hills Australia 55 C8
Frauenfeld Switz. 24 I3
Fray Bentos Uruguay 70 E4
Freckleton U.K. 18 E5
Frederica DE U.S.A. 64 D3
Fredericia Denmark 15 F9
Frederick MD U.S.A. 64 C3
Frederick Reef Australia 56 F4
Fredericksburg TX U.S.A. 62 H5
Fredericksburg VA U.S.A. 64 C3
Fredericton Canada 61 L5
Frederikshåb Greenland see Paamiut
Frederikshavn Denmark 15 G8
Frederiksværk Denmark 15 H9
Fredonia AZ U.S.A. 65 F2
Fredonia NY U.S.A. 64 B1
Fredrika Sweden 14 K4
Fredrikshamn Fin. see Hamina
Fredrikstad Norway 15 G7
Freehold NJ U.S.A. 64 D2
Freeland PA U.S.A. 64 D2
Freeling Heights h. Australia 57 B6
Freel Peak CA U.S.A. 65 C1
Freeport TX U.S.A. 63 H6
Freeport City Bahamas 67 I3
Free State prov. S. Africa 51 H5
Freetown Sierra Leone 46 B4
Fregenal de la Sierra Spain 25 C4
Fregon Australia 55 F6
Fréhel, Cap c. France 24 C2
Frei (Chile) research stn Antarctica 76 A2
Freiburg Switz. see Fribourg
Freiburg im Breisgau Germany 17 K6
Freising Germany 17 M6
Freistadt Austria 17 O6
Fréjus France 24 H5
Fremantle Australia 55 A8
Fremont CA U.S.A. 65 B2
Fremont NE U.S.A. 63 H3
French Congo country Africa see Congo
French Guiana terr. S. America 69 H3
French Guinea country Africa see Guinea
French Island Australia 58 B7
Frenchman r. U.S.A. 62 F2
Frenchman Lake NV U.S.A. 65 E2
Frenchpark Ireland 21 D4
French Pass N.Z. 59 D5
French Polynesia terr. S. Pacific Ocean 75 K7
French Somaliland country Africa see Djibouti
French Southern and Antarctic Lands terr. Indian Ocean 73 M8
French Sudan country Africa see Mali
French Territory of the Afars and Issas country Africa see Djibouti
Frenda Alg. 25 G6
Fresco r. Brazil 69 H5
Freshford Ireland 21 E5
Fresnillo Mex. 66 D4
Fresno CA U.S.A. 65 C2
Fresno r. CA U.S.A. 65 B2
Freu, Cap des c. Spain 25 H4
Freudenstadt Germany 17 L6
Frew watercourse Australia 56 A4
Frewena Australia 56 A3
Freycinet Estuary inlet Australia 55 A6
Freycinet Peninsula Australia 57 [inset]
Freyming-Merlebach France 24 H2
Fria Guinea 46 B3
Fria, Cape Namibia 49 B5
Friant CA U.S.A. 65 C2
Frias Arg. 70 C3
Fribourg Switz. 24 H3
Friedens PA U.S.A. 64 B2
Friedland Rus. Fed. see Pravdinsk
Friedrichshafen Germany 17 L7
Friendly Islands country S. Pacific Ocean see Tonga
Frinton-on-Sea U.K. 19 I7
Frisco Mountain UT U.S.A. 65 F1
Frissell, Mount h. CT U.S.A. 64 E1
Frobisher Bay Canada see Iqaluit
Frobisher Bay b. Canada 61 L3
Frohavet b. Norway 14 F5
Frolovo Rus. Fed. 13 I6
Frome watercourse Australia 57 B6
Frome U.K. 19 E7
Frome r. U.K. 19 E8
Frome, Lake imp. l. Australia 57 B6
Frome Downs Australia 57 B6
Frontera Tabasco Mex. 66 F5
Fronteras Mex. 66 C2
Front Royal VA U.S.A. 64 B3
Frosinone Italy 26 E4
Frostburg MD U.S.A. 64 B3
Frøya i. Norway 14 F5
Frunze Kyrg. see Bishkek
Frusino Italy see Frosinone
Fruska Gora nat. park Serbia 27 H2
Frýdek-Místek Czech Rep. 17 Q6
Fucheng Shaanxi China see Fuxian
Fuding China 43 M7
Fuenlabrada Spain 25 E3
Fuerte Olimpo Para. 70 E2
Fuerteventura i. Canary Is 46 B2
Fuga i. Phil. 43 M9
Fuhai China 42 F3
Fuḩaymī Iraq 35 F4
Fujairah U.A.E. 33 I4
Fujeira U.A.E. see Fujairah
Fuji Japan 45 E6
Fujian prov. China 43 L7
Fuji-Hakone-Izu Kokuritsu-kōen nat. park Japan 45 E6
Fujin China 44 C3
Fujinomiya Japan 45 E6
Fuji-san vol. Japan 45 E6
Fujiyoshida Japan 45 E6
Fûka Egypt see Fūkah
Fūkah Egypt 34 B5
Fukien prov. China see Fujian
Fukuchiyama Japan 45 D6
Fukue-jima i. Japan 45 C6
Fukui Japan 45 E5
Fukuoka Japan 45 C6
Fukushima Japan 45 F5
Fukuyama Japan 45 C7
Fûl, Gebel h. Egypt see Fūl, Jabal
Fūl, Jabal h. Egypt 39 A5
Fulchhari Bangl. 37 G4
Fulda Germany 17 L5
Fulda r. Germany 17 L5
Fulham U.K. 19 G7
Fuli China see Jixian
Fulitun China see Jixian
Fullerton CA U.S.A. 65 D4
Fulton MO U.S.A. 63 I4
Fulton NY U.S.A. 64 C1
Fumane Moz. 51 K3
Fumay France 24 G2
Funabashi Japan 45 E6
Funafuti atoll Tuvalu 53 H2
Funchal Madeira 46 B1
Fundão Brazil 71 C2
Fundão Port. 25 C3
Fundi Italy see Fondi
Fundy, Bay of g. Canada 61 L5
Fünen i. Denmark see Fyn
Funeral Peak CA U.S.A. 65 D2
Fünfkirchen Hungary see Pécs
Funhalouro Moz. 51 L2
Funing Yunnan China 42 J8
Funtua Nigeria 46 D3
Funzie U.K. 20 [inset]
Fürgun, Kūh-e mt. Iran 33 I4
Furmanov Rus. Fed. 12 I4
Furmanovka Kazakh. see Moyynkum
Furmanovo Kazakh. see Zhalpaktal
Furnás h. Spain 25 G4
Furnas, Represa resr Brazil 71 B3
Furneaux Group is Australia 57 [inset]
Fürstenwalde Germany 17 O4
Fürth Germany 17 M6
Furukawa Japan 45 F5
Fury and Hecla Strait Canada 61 J3
Fusan S. Korea see Pusan
Fushun China 44 A4
Fushuncheng China see Shuncheng
Fusong China 44 B4
Futuna i. Vanuatu 53 H3
Futuna Islands Wallis and Futuna Is see Hoorn, Îles de
Fuxian Liaoning China see Wafangdian
Fuxian Shaanxi China 43 J5
Fuxin China 43 M4
Fuxing China see Wangmo
Fuxinzhen China see Fuxin
Fuyang Anhui China 43 L6
Fuyu Heilong. China 44 B3
Fuyu Jilin China see Songyuan
Fuyu Jilin China 44 B3
Fuyuan Heilong. China 44 D2
Fuyun China 42 F3
Fuzhou Fujian China 43 L7
Fuzhou Jiangxi China 31 K4
Füzuli Azer. 35 G3
Fyn i. Denmark 15 G9
Fyne, Loch inlet U.K. 20 D5
F.Y.R.O.M. (Former Yugoslav Republic of Macedonia) country Europe see Macedonia

G

Gaâfour Tunisia 26 C6
Gaalkacyo Somalia 48 E3
Gabakly Turkm. 33 J2
Gabbs NV U.S.A. 65 D1
Gabbs Valley Range mts NV U.S.A. 65 C1
Gabela Angola 49 B5
Gaberones Botswana see Gaborone
Gabès Tunisia 22 G5
Gabès, Golfe de g. Tunisia 22 G5
Gabo Island Australia 58 D6
Gabon country Africa 48 B4
Gaborone Botswana 51 G3
Gabrovo Bulg. 27 K3
Gabú Guinea-Bissau 46 B3
Gadag India 38 B3
Gadaisu P.N.G. 56 E1
Gadap Pak. 36 A4
Gadchiroli India 38 D1
Gäddede Sweden 14 I4
Gades Spain see Cádiz
Gadhra India 36 B5
Gadra Pak. 36 B4
Gadsden U.S.A. 63 J5
Gadwal India 38 C2
Gadyach Ukr. see Hadyach
Gaer U.K. 19 D7
Găești Romania 27 K2
Gaeta Italy 26 E4
Gaeta, Golfo di g. Italy 26 E4
Gaferut i. Micronesia 74 F5
Gafsa Tunisia 26 C7
Gagarin Rus. Fed. 13 G5
Gagnoa Côte d'Ivoire 46 C4
Gagnon Canada 63 N1
Gago Coutinho Angola see Lumbala N'guimbo
Gagra Georgia 13 I8
Gaiab watercourse Namibia 50 D5
Gaibanda Bangl. see Gaibandha
Gaibandha Bangl. 37 G4
Gaïdouronisi i. Greece 27 K7
Gaifi, Wâdi el watercourse Egypt see Jayfi, Wādī al
Gaillac France 24 E5
Gaillimh Ireland see Galway
Gaindainqoinkor China 37 G3
Gainesville FL U.S.A. 63 K6
Gainesville GA U.S.A. 63 K5
Gainesville TX U.S.A. 63 H5
Gainsborough U.K. 18 G5
Gairdner, Lake imp. l. Australia 57 A6
Gairloch U.K. 20 D3
Gair Loch b. U.K. 20 D3
Gajipur India see Ghazipur
Gajol India 37 G4
Gakarosa mt. S. Africa 50 F4
Gala China 37 G3
Gala Co l. China 37 G3
Galâla el Baharîya, Gebel el plat. Egypt see Jalālah al Baḩrīyah, Jabal
Galana r. Kenya 48 E4
Galanta Slovakia 17 P6
Galapagos Islands is Ecuador 75 O6
Galapagos Rise sea feature Pacific Ocean 75 N6
Galashiels U.K. 20 G5
Galați Romania 27 M2
Galatina Italy 26 H4
Gala Water r. U.K. 20 G5
Galaýmor Turkm. 33 J2
Galaymor Turkm. see Galaýmor
Galbally Ireland 21 D5
Galdhøpiggen mt. Norway 15 F6
Galeana Nuevo León Mex. 66 D4
Galena AK U.S.A. 60 C3
Galena MD U.S.A. 64 D3
Galera, Punta pt Chile 70 B6
Galesburg IL U.S.A. 63 I3
Galeshewe S. Africa 50 G5
Galeton PA U.S.A. 64 C2
Galey r. Ireland 21 C5
Galheirão r. Brazil 71 B1
Galich Rus. Fed. 12 I4
Galichskaya Vozvyshennost' hills Rus. Fed. 12 I4
Galicia aut. comm. Spain 25 C2
Galičica nat. park Macedonia 27 I4
Galilee, Lake imp. l. Australia 56 D4
Galilee, Sea of l. Israel 39 B3
Galizia aut. comm. Spain see Galicia
Gallabat Sudan 32 E7
Gallatin TN U.S.A. 63 J4
Galle Sri Lanka 38 D5
Gallego Rise sea feature Pacific Ocean 75 M6
Gallegos r. Arg. 70 C8
Gallia country Europe see France
Gallinas, Punta pt Col. 68 D1
Gallipoli Italy 26 H4
Gallipoli Turkey 27 L4
Gällivare Sweden 14 L3
Gällö Sweden 14 I5
Gallup U.S.A. 62 F4
Galmisdale U.K. 20 C4
Galong Australia 58 D5
Galoya Sri Lanka 38 D4
Gal Oya National Park Sri Lanka 38 D5
Galston U.K. 20 E5
Galt CA U.S.A. 65 B1
Galtat Zemmour W. Sahara 46 B2
Galtee Mountains hills Ireland 21 D5
Galtymore h. Ireland 16 C4
Galveston TX U.S.A. 63 I6
Galveston Bay U.S.A. 63 I6
Galwa Nepal 37 E3
Galway Ireland 21 C4
Galway Bay Ireland 21 C4
Gamalakhe S. Africa 51 J6
Gamba China see Gongbalou
Gamba Gabon 48 A4
Gambēla Eth. 48 D3
Gambēla National Park Eth. 48 D3
Gambell U.S.A. 60 A3
Gambella Eth. see Gambēla
Gambia, The country Africa 46 B3
Gambier, Îles is Fr. Polynesia 75 L7
Gambier Islands Australia 57 B7
Gambier Islands Fr. Polynesia see Gambier, Îles
Gamboma Congo 48 B4
Gamboola Australia 56 C3
Gamboula Cent. Afr. Rep. 48 B3
Gamda China see Zamtang
Gamêtì Canada 60 G3
Gamlakarleby Fin. see Kokkola
Gamleby Sweden 15 J8
Gammelstaden Sweden 14 M4
Gammon Ranges National Park Australia 57 B6
Gamova, Mys pt Rus. Fed. 44 C4
Gamtog China 42 H6
Gamud mt. Eth. 48 D3
Ganado U.S.A. 62 F4
Gäncä Azer. 35 G2
Ganda Angola 49 B5
Gandaingoin China 37 G3
Gandajika Dem. Rep. Congo 49 C4
Gandak Barrage Nepal 37 E4
Gandari Mountain Pak. 36 B3
Gandava Pak. 33 K4
Gander Canada 61 M5
Gandesa Spain 25 G3
Gandhidham India 36 B5
Gandhinagar India 36 C5
Gandhi Sagar resr India 36 C4
Gandia Spain 25 F4
Gandzha Azer. see Gäncä
Ganga r. Bangl./India 37 G5 see Ganges
Ganga Cone sea feature Indian Ocean see Ganges Cone
Gangán Arg. 70 C6
Ganganagar India 36 C3
Gangapur India 36 D4
Ganga Sera India 36 B4
Gangaw Myanmar 37 H5
Gangawati India 38 C3
Gangaw Range mts Myanmar 37 I5
Gangca China 42 I5
Gangdisê Shan mts China 37 E3
Ganges r. Bangl./India 37 G5
Ganges France 24 F5
Ganges, Mouths of the Bangl./India 37 G5
Ganges Cone sea feature Indian Ocean 73 N4
Gangouyi China 42 J5
Gangra Turkey see Çankırı
Gangtok India 37 G4
Ganjig China 43 M4
Ganmain Australia 58 C5
Gannan China 44 A3
Gannat France 24 F3
Gannett Peak U.S.A. 60 H5
Ganq China 42 G5
Gansu prov. China 42 H4
Gantheaume Point Australia 54 C4
Gantsevichi Belarus see Hantsavichy
Ganye Nigeria 46 E4
Ganyushkino Kazakh. 11 P6
Ganzhou China 43 K7
Ganzi Sudan 47 G4
Gao Mali 46 C3
Gaocheng China see Litang
Gaoleshan China see Xianfeng
Gaotai China 42 H5
Gaoth Dobhair Ireland 21 D2
Gaoua Burkina 46 C3
Gaoual Guinea 46 B3
Gaoxiong Taiwan see Kaohsiung
Gaoyao China see Zhaoqing
Gaoyou Hu l. China 43 L6
Gap France 24 H4
Gapuwiyak Australia 56 A2
Gaqoi China 37 E3
Gar China 36 E2
Gar' r. Rus. Fed. 44 C1
Gara, Lough l. Ireland 21 D4
Garabekewül Turkm. 33 J2
Garabil Belentligi hills Turkm. 33 J2
Garabogaz Turkm. 35 I2
Garabogaz Aylagy b. Turkm. see Garabogazköl Aylagy
Garabogazköl Aylagy b. Turkm. 35 I2
Garabogazköl Aylagy b. Turkm. see Garabogazköl Aylagy
Garabogazköl Bogazy sea chan. Turkm. 35 I2
Garagum des. Turkm. see Karakum Desert
Garagum Kanaly canal Turkm. 33 J2
Garah Australia 58 D2
Garalo Mali 46 C3
Garamba r. Dem. Rep. Congo 48 C3
Garanhuns Brazil 69 K5
Ga-Rankuwa S. Africa 51 H3
Garapuava Brazil 71 B2
Gárasavvon Sweden see Karesuando
Garautha India 36 D4
Garba China see Jiulong
Garbahaarrey Somalia 48 E3
Garba Tula Kenya 48 D3
Garbo China see Lhozhag
Garbsen Germany 17 L4
Garça Brazil 71 A3
Garco China 37 G2
Garda, Lago di Italy see Garda, Lake
Garda, Lake Italy 26 D2
Garde, Cap de c. Alg. 26 B6
Garden City U.S.A. 62 G4
Garden Hill Canada 63 I1
Garden Mountain VA U.S.A. 64 A4
Gardeyz Afgh. see Gardēz
Gardēz Afgh. 36 B2
Gardinas Belarus see Hrodna
Gardiner, Mount Australia 54 F5
Gardiner Range hills Australia 54 E4
Gardiners Island NY U.S.A. 64 E2
Gardīz Afgh. see Gardēz
Gardner atoll Micronesia see Faraulep
Gardner MA U.S.A. 64 F1
Gardner Inlet Antarctica 76 L1
Gardner Island atoll Kiribati see Nikumaroro
Gardner Pinnacles is U.S.A. 74 I4
Gáregasnjárga Fin. see Karigasniemi
Garelochhead U.K. 20 E4
Garet el Djenoun mt. Alg. 46 D2
Gargano, Parco Nazionale del nat. park Italy 26 F4
Gargunsa China see Gar
Gargždai Lith. 15 L9
Garhchiroli India see Gadchiroli
Garhi Madh. Prad. India 38 C1
Garhi Rajasthan India 36 C5
Garhi Khairo Pak. 36 A3
Garhwa India 37 E4
Gari Rus. Fed. 11 S4
Gariep Dam dam S. Africa 51 G6
Garies S. Africa 50 C6
Garigliano r. Italy 26 E4
Garissa Kenya 48 D4
Garkalne Latvia 15 N8
Garkung Caka l. China 37 F2
Garm Tajik. see Gharm
Garmī Iran 35 H3
Garmsar Iran 35 I4
Gampung Lake imp. l. Australia 58 A4
Garo Hills India 37 G4
Garonne r. France 24 D4
Garoowe Somalia 48 E3
Garopaba Brazil 71 A5
Garoua Cameroon 46 E4
Garoua Boulai Cameroon 47 E4
Garqêntang China see Sog
Garré Arg. 70 D5
Garruk Pak. 36 A3
Garry r. U.K. 20 E3
Garry Lake Canada 61 H3
Garrynahine U.K. 20 C2
Garsen Kenya 48 E4
Garshy Turkm. see Garşy
Garsila Sudan 47 F3
Garşy Turkm. 35 I2
Garth U.K. 19 D6
Gartok China see Garyarsa
Garub Namibia 50 C4
Garvagh U.K. 21 F3
Garve U.K. 20 E3
Garwa India see Garhwa
Garwha India see Garhwa
Gar Xincun China 36 E2
Gary IN U.S.A. 63 J3
Gary WV U.S.A. 64 A4
Garyarsa China 36 E3
Garyū-zan mt. Japan 45 D6
Garza García Mex. 66 D3
Garzê China 42 H6
Gasan-Kuli Turkm. see Esenguly
Gascogne reg. France see Gascony
Gascogne, Golfe de g. France see Gascony, Gulf of
Gascony reg. France 24 D5
Gascony, Gulf of France 24 C5
Gascoyne r. Australia 55 A6
Gascoyne Junction Australia 55 A6
Gasherbrum I mt. China/Pakistan 36 D2
Gashua Nigeria 46 E3
Gaspé Canada 63 O2
Gaspésie, Péninsule de la pen. Canada 63 N2
Gassan vol. Japan 45 F5
Gassaway WV U.S.A. 64 A3
Gasteiz Spain see Vitoria-Gasteiz
Gastello Rus. Fed. 44 F2
Gastonia U.S.A. 63 K4
Gata, Cabo de c. Spain 25 E5
Gata, Cape Cyprus 39 A2
Gata, Sierra de mts Spain 25 C3
Gatas, Akra c. Cyprus see Gata, Cape
Gatchina Rus. Fed. 12 F4
Gatehouse of Fleet U.K. 20 E6
Gateshead U.K. 18 F4
Gates of the Arctic National Park and Preserve U.S.A. 60 C3
Gatesville U.S.A. 62 H5
Gatineau r. Canada 63 L2
Gatong China see Jomda
Gatooma Zimbabwe see Kadoma
Gatton Australia 58 F1
Gatvand Iran 35 H4
Gatyana S. Africa see Willowvale
Gau i. Fiji 53 H3
Gauhati India see Guwahati
Gaujas nacionālais parks nat. park Latvia 15 N8
Gaul country Europe see France
Gaula r. Norway 14 G5
Gaurama Brazil 71 A4
Gauribidanur India 38 C3
Gauteng prov. S. Africa 51 I4
Gavarr Armenia 35 G2
Gāvbandī Iran 35 I6
Gāvbūs, Kūh-e mts Iran 35 I6
Gavdos i. Greece 27 K7
Gavião r. Brazil 71 C1
Gavīleh Iran 35 G4
Gav Khūnī Iran 35 I4
Gävle Sweden 15 J6
Gavrilovka Vtoraya Rus. Fed. 13 I5
Gavrilov-Yam Rus. Fed. 12 H4
Gawachab Namibia 50 C4
Gawan India 37 F4
Gawilgarh Hills India 36 D5
Gawler Australia 57 B7
Gawler Ranges hills Australia 57 A7
Gaxun Nur salt l. China 42 I4
Gaya India 37 F4
Gaya Niger 46 D3
Gaya He r. China 44 C4
Gayéri Burkina 46 D3
Gaylord U.S.A. 63 K2
Gayndah Australia 57 E5
Gayny Rus. Fed. 12 L3
Gaysin Ukr. see Haysyn
Gayutino Rus. Fed. 12 H4
Gaz Iran 35 H4
Gaza terr. Asia 39 B4
Gaza Gaza 39 B4
Gaza prov. Moz. 51 K2
Gazan Pak. 36 A3
Gazanjyk Turkm. see Bereket
Gaza Strip terr. Asia see Gaza
Gaziantep Turkey 34 E3
Gaziantep prov. Turkey 39 C1
Gazibenli Turkey see Yahyalı
Gazimağusa Cyprus see Famagusta

Gazimurskiy Khrebet mts Rus. Fed. 43 L2
Gazimurskiy Zavod Rus. Fed. 43 L2
Gazipaşa Turkey 39 A1
Gazli Uzbek. 33 J1
Gbarnga Liberia 46 C4
Gboko Nigeria 46 D4
Gcuwa S. Africa see Butterworth
Gdańsk Poland 17 Q3
Gdańsk, Gulf of Poland/Rus. Fed. 17 Q3
Gdańska, Zatoka g. Poland/Rus. Fed. see Gdańsk, Gulf of
Gdingen Poland see Gdynia
Gdov Rus. Fed. 12 E4
Gdynia Poland 17 Q3
Geaidnovuohppi Norway 14 M2
Gearraidh na h-Aibhne U.K. see Garrynahine
Geçitkale Cyprus see Lefkonikon
Gedaref Sudan 32 E7
Gediz r. Turkey 27 L5
Gedney Drove End U.K. 19 H6
Gedser Denmark 15 G9
Geelong Australia 58 B7
Geelvink Channel Australia 55 A7
Geel Vloer salt pan S. Africa 50 E5
Gees Gwardafuy c. Somalia see Gwardafuy, Gees
Geidam Nigeria 46 E3
Geikie r. Canada 60 H4
Geilo Norway 15 F6
Geiranger Norway 14 E5
Geisûm, Gezâ'ir is Egypt see Qaysūm, Juzur
Geita Tanz. 48 D4
Gejiu China 42 I8
Gela Sicilia Italy 26 F6
Gêladaindong mt. China 37 G2
Geladī Eth. 48 E3
Gelendzhik Rus. Fed. 34 E1
Gelibolu Turkey see Gallipoli
Gelidonya Burnu pt Turkey see Yardımcı Burnu
Gelincik Dağı mt. Turkey 27 N5
Gemena Dem. Rep. Congo 48 B3
Geminokağı Cyprus see Karavostasi
Gemlik Turkey 27 M4
Gemona del Friuli Italy 26 E1
Gemsa Egypt see Jamsah
Gemsbok National Park Botswana 50 E3
Gemsbokplein well S. Africa 50 E4
Genalē Wenz r. Eth. 48 E3
Genäveh Iran 35 H5
General Acha Arg. 70 D5
General Alvear Arg. 70 C5
General Belgrano II research stn Antarctica see Belgrano II
General Carrera, Lago l. Arg./Chile 70 B7
General Conesa Arg. 70 D6
General Freire Angola see Muxaluando
General Juan Madariaga Arg. 70 E5
General La Madrid Arg. 70 D5
General Machado Angola see Camacupa
General Pico Arg. 70 D5
General Pinedo Arg. 70 D3
General Roca Arg. 70 C5
General Salgado Brazil 71 A3
General San Martín research stn Antarctica see San Martín
General Santos Phil. 41 E7
General Villegas Arg. 70 D5
Genesee PA U.S.A. 64 C2
Geneseo NY U.S.A. 64 C1
Geneva S. Africa 51 H4
Geneva Switz. 24 H3
Geneva NY U.S.A. 64 C1
Geneva OH U.S.A. 64 A2
Geneva, Lake France/Switz. 24 H3
Genève Switz. see Geneva
Genf Switz. see Geneva
Genhe China 44 A2
Genichesk Ukr. see Heniches'k
Genji India 36 C5
Genk Belgium 17 J5
Genoa Australia 58 D6
Genoa Italy 26 C2
Genoa, Gulf of Italy 26 C2
Genova Italy see Genoa
Genova, Golfo di Italy see Genoa, Gulf of
Gent Belgium see Ghent
Gentioux, Plateau de France 24 F4
Genua Italy see Genoa
Geographe Bay Australia 55 A8
Geographical Society Ø i. Greenland 61 P2
George, Zemlya i. Rus. Fed. 28 F1
George r. Canada 61 L4
George S. Africa 50 F7
George, Lake Australia 58 D5
George, Lake NY U.S.A. 64 E1
George Land i. Rus. Fed. see Georga, Zemlya
Georges Mills NH U.S.A. 64 E1
George Sound inlet N.Z. 59 A7
Georgetown Australia 56 C3
George Town Cayman Is 67 H5
Georgetown Gambia 46 B3
Georgetown Guyana 69 G2
George Town Malaysia 41 C7
Georgetown DE U.S.A. 64 D3
Georgetown SC U.S.A. 63 L5
Georgetown TX U.S.A. 62 H5
George VI Sound sea chan. Antarctica 76 L2
George V Land reg. Antarctica 76 G2
Georgia country Asia 35 F2
Georgia state U.S.A. 63 K5
Georgian Bay Canada 63 K2
Georgienne, Baie b. Canada see Georgian Bay
Georgina watercourse Australia 56 B5
Georgiu-Dezh Rus. Fed. see Liski
Georgiyevka Vostochnyy Kazakhstan Kazakh. 42 E3
Georgiyevka Zhambylskaya Oblast' Kazakh. see Korday
Georgiyevsk Rus. Fed. 13 I7
Georgiyevskoye Rus. Fed. 12 J4
Georg von Neumayer research stn Antarctica see Neumayer
Gera Germany 17 N5
Geral, Serra mts Brazil 71 A4
Geral de Goiás, Serra hills Brazil 71 B1
Geraldine N.Z. 59 C7
Geral do Paraná, Serra hills Brazil 71 B1
Geraldton Australia 55 A7
Gerar watercourse Israel 39 B4
Gercüş Turkey 35 F3
Gerede Turkey 34 D2
Gereshk Afgh. 33 J3
Gerlachovský štít mt. Slovakia 17 R6
Germania country Europe see Germany
Germanicea Turkey see Kahramanmaraş
German South-West Africa country Africa see Namibia
Germany country Europe 17 L5
Germersheim Germany 17 L6
Gerona Spain see Girona
Gerrit Denys is P.N.G. see Lihir Group
Gers r. France 24 E4
Gersoppa India 38 B3
Géryville Alg. see El Bayadh
Gêrzê China 37 F2
Gerze Turkey 34 D2
Gesoriacum France see Boulogne-sur-Mer
Gettysburg PA U.S.A. 64 C3
Gettysburg SD U.S.A. 62 H2
Gettysburg National Military Park nat. park PA U.S.A. 64 C3
Getz Ice Shelf Antarctica 76 J2
Geurie Australia 58 D4
Gevaş Turkey 35 F3
Gevgelija Macedonia 27 J4
Gexto Spain see Algorta
Gey Iran see Nīkshahr
Geyikli Turkey 27 L5
Geylegphug Bhutan 37 G4
Geysdorp S. Africa 51 G4
Geyserville CA U.S.A. 65 A1
Geyve Turkey 27 N4
Ghaap Plateau S. Africa 50 F4
Ghāb, Wādī al r. Syria 39 C2
Ghabāghib Syria 39 C3
Ghabeish Sudan 32 C7
Ghadaf, Wādī al watercourse Jordan 39 C4
Ghadamés Libya see Ghadāmis
Ghadāmis Libya 46 D1
Gha'em Shahr Iran 35 I3
Ghaghara r. India 37 F4
Ghaibi Dero Pak. 36 A4
Ghana country Africa 46 C4
Ghantila India 36 B5
Ghanwā Saudi Arabia 32 G4
Ghanzi Botswana 49 C6
Ghanzi admin. dist. Botswana 50 F2
Ghap'an Armenia see Kapan
Ghardaïa Alg. 22 E5
Gharghoda India 38 D1
Ghârib, Gebel mt. Egypt see Ghārib, Jabal
Ghārib, Jabal mt. Egypt 34 D5
Gharm Tajik. 33 L2
Gharq Ābād Iran 35 H4
Gharwa India see Garhwa
Gharyān Libya 47 E1
Ghāt Libya 46 E2
Ghatgan India 37 F5
Ghatol India 36 C5
Ghawdex i. Malta see Gozo
Ghazal, Bahr el watercourse Chad 47 E3
Ghazaouet Alg. 25 F6
Ghaziabad India 36 D3
Ghazi Ghat Pak. 36 B3
Ghazipur India 37 E4
Ghazna Afgh. see Ghaznī
Ghaznī Afgh. 36 B2
Ghaznī r. Afgh. 36 A2
Ghazoor Afgh. 36 A2
Ghazzah Gaza see Gaza
Ghent Belgium 16 I5
Gheorghe Gheorghiu-Dej Romania see Onești
Gheorgheni Romania 27 K1
Gherla Romania 27 J1
Ghijduwon Uzbek. see G'ijduvon
Ghīnah, Wādī al watercourse Saudi Arabia 39 D4
Ghisonaccia Corse France 24 I5
Ghotaru India 36 B4
Ghotki Pak. 33 K4
Ghudamis Libya see Ghadāmis
Ghugri r. India 37 F4
Ghurayfah h. Saudi Arabia 39 C4
Ghūrī Iran 35 I5
Ghurian Afgh. 33 J3
Ghuzor Uzbek. see G'uzor
Giaginskaya Rus. Fed. 35 F1
Gialias r. Cyprus 39 A2
Gianisada i. Greece 27 L7
Giannitsa Greece 27 J4
Giant's Castle mt. S. Africa 51 I5
Giant's Causeway lava field U.K. 21 F2
Giarre Sicilia Italy 26 F6
Gibb r. Australia 54 D3
Gibeon Namibia 50 C3
Gibraltar terr. Europe 25 D5
Gibraltar Gibraltar 72 H3
Gibraltar, Strait of Morocco/Spain 25 C6
Gibraltar Range National Park Australia 58 F2
Gibson Australia 55 C8
Gibson Desert Australia 55 C6
Gichgeniyn Nuruu mts Mongolia 42 G3
Giddalur India 38 C3
Giddi, Gebel el h. Egypt see Jiddī, Jabal al
Gīdolē Eth. 47 G4
Gien France 24 F3
Gießen Germany 17 L5
Gifford r. Canada 61 J2
Gifu Japan 45 E6
Gigha i. U.K. 20 D5
Gigiga Eth. see Jijiga
G'ijduvon Uzbek. 33 J1
Gijón Spain see Gijón-Xixón
Gijón-Xixón Spain 25 D2
Gila r. AZ U.S.A. 65 E4
Gila Bend AZ U.S.A. 65 F4
Gila Bend Mountains AZ U.S.A. 65 F4
Gīlān-e Gharb Iran 35 G4
Gilbert r. Australia 56 C3
Gilbert Islands Kiribati 74 H5
Gilbert Islands country Pacific Ocean see Kiribati
Gilbert Ridge sea feature Pacific Ocean 74 H6
Gilbert River Australia 56 C3
Gilbués Brazil 69 I5
Gil Chashmeh Iran 35 J4
Gilé Moz. 49 D5
Giles Creek r. Australia 54 E4
Gilgai Australia 58 E2
Gilgandra Australia 58 D3
Gil Gil Creek r. Australia 58 D2
Gilgit Pak. 36 C2
Gilgit r. Pak. 33 L2
Gilgunnia Australia 58 C4
Gilindire Turkey see Aydıncık
Gillam Canada 61 I4
Gillen, Lake imp. l. Australia 55 D6
Gilles, Lake imp. l. Australia 57 B7
Gillett PA U.S.A. 64 C2
Gillette U.S.A. 62 F3
Gilliat Australia 56 C4
Gillingham England U.K. 19 E7
Gillingham England U.K. 19 H7
Gilling West U.K. 18 F4
Gilmour Island Canada 61 K4
Gilroy CA U.S.A. 65 B2
Gīmbī Eth. 48 D3
Gimhae S. Korea see Kimhae
Gimli Canada 63 H1
Gimol'skoye, Ozero l. Rus. Fed. 12 G3
Ginebra, Laguna l. Bol. 68 E6
Gineifa Egypt see Junayfah
Gin Gin Australia 56 E5
Gingin Australia 55 A7
Gīnīr Eth. 48 E3
Ginosa Italy 26 G4
Ginzo de Limia Spain see Xinzo de Limia
Gioia del Colle Italy 26 G4
Gippsland reg. Australia 58 B7
Girā, Wādī watercourse Egypt see Jirā', Wādī
Girard PA U.S.A. 64 A1
Giresun Turkey 34 E2
Girgenti Sicilia Italy see Agrigento
Giridh India see Giridih
Giridih India 37 F4
Girilambone Australia 58 C3
Girna r. India 36 C5
Gir National Park India 36 B5
Girne Cyprus see Kyrenia
Girón Ecuador 68 C4
Giron Sweden see Kiruna
Girona Spain 25 H3
Gironde est. France 24 D4
Girot Pak. 36 C2
Girral Australia 58 C4
Girraween National Park Australia 58 E2
Girvan U.K. 20 E5
Girvas Rus. Fed. 12 G3
Gisborne N.Z. 59 G4
Gislaved Sweden 15 H8
Gissar Range mts Tajik./Uzbek. 33 K2
Gissarskiy Khrebet mts Tajik./Uzbek. see Gissar Range
Gitarama Rwanda 48 C4
Gitega Burundi 48 C4
Giuba r. Somalia see Jubba
Giulianova Italy 26 E3
Giurgiu Romania 27 K3
Giuvala, Pasul pass Romania 27 K2
Givar Iran 35 J3
Givors France 24 G4
Giyani S. Africa 51 J2
Giza Egypt 34 C5
Gizhiga Rus. Fed. 29 R3
Gjakovë Kosovo 27 I3
Gjilan Kosovo 27 I3
Gjirokastër Albania 27 I4
Gjirokastra Albania see Gjirokastër
Gjoa Haven Canada 61 I3
Gjøra Norway 14 F5
Gjøvik Norway 15 G6
Gkinas, Akrotirio pt Greece 27 M6
Glace Bay Canada 61 M5
Glacier Bay National Park and Preserve U.S.A. 60 E4
Glacier Peak vol. U.S.A. 62 C2
Gladstad Norway 14 G4
Gladstone Australia 56 E4
Gladys VA U.S.A. 64 B4
Glamis U.K. 20 F4
Glamis CA U.S.A. 65 E4
Glamoč Bos.-Herz. 26 G2
Glanton U.K. 18 F3
Glasgow U.K. 20 E5
Glasgow KY U.S.A. 63 J4
Glasgow MT U.S.A. 62 F2
Glasgow VA U.S.A. 64 B4
Glass, Loch l. U.K. 20 E3
Glass Mountain CA U.S.A. 65 C2
Glastonbury U.K. 19 E7
Glazov Rus. Fed. 12 L4
Gleiwitz Poland see Gliwice
Glen Allen VA U.S.A. 64 C4
Glen Alpine Dam S. Africa 51 I2
Glenamaddy Ireland 21 D4
Glenamoy r. Ireland 21 C3
Glenbawn, Lake Australia 58 E4
Glencoe Ont. Canada 64 A1
Glencoe S. Africa 51 J5
Glendale AZ U.S.A. 62 E5
Glendale CA U.S.A. 65 C3
Glendale UT U.S.A. 65 F2
Glendale Lake PA U.S.A. 64 B2
Glen Davis Australia 58 E4
Glenden Australia 56 E4
Glendive U.S.A. 62 G2
Glenfield NY U.S.A. 64 D1
Glengavlen Ireland 21 E3
Glengyle Australia 56 B5
Glen Innes Australia 58 E2
Glenluce U.K. 20 E6
Glen More val. U.K. 20 E3
Glenmorgan Australia 58 D1
Glennallen U.S.A. 60 D3
Glenore Australia 56 C3
Glenormiston Australia 56 B4
Glenreagh Australia 58 F3
Glenrothes U.K. 20 F4
Glens Falls NY U.S.A. 64 E1
Glen Shee val. U.K. 20 F4
Glenties Ireland 21 D3
Glenveagh National Park Ireland 21 E2
Glenville WV U.S.A. 64 A3
Glenwood Springs U.S.A. 62 F4
Glevum U.K. see Gloucester
Glittertinden mt. Norway 15 F6
Gliwice Poland 17 Q5
Globe U.S.A. 62 E5
Glogau Poland see Głogów
Głogów Poland 17 P5
Glomfjord Norway 14 H3
Glomma r. Norway 14 G7
Glommersträsk Sweden 14 K4
Glorieuses, Îles is Indian Ocean 49 E5
Glorioso Islands Indian Ocean see Glorieuses, Îles
Gloucester Australia 58 E3
Gloucester U.K. 19 E7
Gloucester MA U.S.A. 64 F1
Gloucester VA U.S.A. 64 C4
Gloversville NY U.S.A. 64 D1
Glubinnoye Rus. Fed. 44 D3
Glubokiy Krasnoyarskiy Kray Rus. Fed. 42 H2
Glubokiy Rostovskaya Oblast' Rus. Fed. 13 I6
Glubokoye Belarus see Hlybokaye
Glubokoye Kazakh. 42 E2
Gluggarnir h. Faroe Is 14 [inset]
Glukhov Ukr. see Hlukhiv
Glusburn U.K. 18 F5
Glynebwy U.K. see Ebbw Vale
Gmelinka Rus. Fed. 13 J6
Gmünd Austria 17 O6
Gmunden Austria 17 N7
Gnarp Sweden 15 J5
Gnesen Poland see Gniezno
Gniezno Poland 17 P4
Gnjilane Kosovo see Gjilan
Gnowangerup Australia 55 B8
Gnows Nest Range hills Australia 55 B7
Goa India 38 B3
Goa state India 38 B3
Goageb Namibia 50 C4
Goalen Head hd Australia 58 E6
Goalpara India 37 G4
Goat Fell h. U.K. 20 D5
Goba Eth. 48 E3
Gobabis Namibia 50 D2
Gobannium U.K. see Abergavenny
Gobas Namibia 50 D4
Gobi Desert des. China/Mongolia 42 J4
Gobindpur India 37 F5
Gobō Japan 45 D6
Gochas Namibia 50 D3
Godalming U.K. 19 G7
Godavari r. India 38 D2
Godavari, Cape India 38 D2
Godda India 37 F4
Godē Eth. 48 E3
Godere Eth. 48 E3
Goderich Canada 63 K3
Goderville France 19 H9
Godhavn Greenland see Qeqertarsuaq
Godhra India 36 C5
Gods r. Canada 61 I4
Gods Lake Canada 63 I1
Godthåb Greenland see Nuuk
Godwin-Austen, Mount China/Pakistan see K2
Goedgegun Swaziland see Nhlangano
Goegap Nature Reserve S. Africa 50 D5
Goélands, Lac aux l. Canada 61 L4
Gogra r. India see Ghaghara
Goiana Brazil 69 L5
Goiandira Brazil 71 A2
Goianésia Brazil 71 A1
Goiânia Brazil 71 A2
Goiás Brazil 71 A1
Goiás state Brazil 71 A2
Goio-Erê Brazil 70 F2
Gojra Pak. 36 C3
Gokak India 38 B2
Gokarn India 38 B3
Gök Çay r. Turkey 39 A1
Gökçeada i. Turkey 27 K4
Gökdere r. Turkey 39 A1
Goklenkuy, Solonchak salt l. Turkm. 35 J2
Gökova Körfezi b. Turkey 27 L6
Göksun Turkey 34 E3
Goksu Parkı Turkey 39 A1
Gokwe Zimbabwe 49 C5
Gol Norway 15 F6
Golaghat India 37 H4
Gölbaşı Turkey 34 E3
Gölcük Turkey 27 M4
Gold PA U.S.A. 64 C2
Gołdap Poland 17 S3
Gold Coast country Africa see Ghana
Gold Coast Australia 58 F2
Golden Bay N.Z. 59 D5
Golden Gate Highlands National Park S. Africa 51 I5
Golden Hinde mt. Canada 62 B2
Goldfield NV U.S.A. 65 D2
Goldsboro U.S.A. 63 L4
Goldstone Lake CA U.S.A. 65 D3
Goldsworthy (abandoned) Australia 54 B5
Goldvein VA U.S.A. 64 C3
Göle Turkey 35 F2
Goleta CA U.S.A. 65 C3
Golets-Davydov, Gora mt. Rus. Fed. 43 J2
Golfo di Orosei Gennargentu e Asinara, Parco Nazionale del nat. park Sardegna Italy 26 C4
Gölgeli Dağları mts Turkey 27 M6
Golingka China see Gongbo'gyamda
Gölköy Turkey 34 E2
Gollel Swaziland see Lavumisa
Golmud China 42 G5
Golovnino Rus. Fed. 44 G4
Golpāyegān Iran 35 H4
Gölpazarı Turkey 27 N4
Golspie U.K. 20 F3
Golyama Syutkya mt. Bulg. 27 K4
Golyam Persenk mt. Bulg. 27 K4
Golyshi Rus. Fed. see Vetluzhskiy
Goma Dem. Rep. Congo 48 C4
Gomang Co salt l. China 37 G3
Gomati r. India 33 N4
Gombe Nigeria 46 E3
Gombe r. Tanz. 49 D4
Gombi Nigeria 46 E3
Gombroon Iran see Bandar-e 'Abbās
Gomel' Belarus see Homyel'
Gómez Palacio Mex. 66 D3
Gomīshān Iran 35 I3
Gomo Co salt l. China 37 F2
Gonaïves Haiti 67 J5
Gonarezhou National Park Zimbabwe 49 D6
Gonbad-e Kavus Iran 35 I3
Gonda India 37 E4
Gondal India 36 B5
Gondar Eth. see Gonder
Gonder Eth. 48 D2
Gondia India 36 E5
Gondiya India see Gondia
Gönen Turkey 27 L4
Gonfreville-l'Orcher France 19 H9
Gongbalou China 37 G3
Gongbo'gyamda China 37 H3
Gongchang China see Longxi
Gongga Shan mt. China 42 I7
Gonghe Qinghai China 42 I5
Gongogi r. Brazil 71 D1
Gongolgon Australia 58 C3
Gongtang China see Damxung
Gonjog China see Coqên
Gonzales CA U.S.A. 65 B2
Gonzales TX U.S.A. 63 H6
Gonzha Rus. Fed. 44 B1
Goochland VA U.S.A. 64 C4
Goodenough, Cape Antarctica 76 G2
Goodenough Island P.N.G. 52 F2
Good Hope, Cape of S. Africa 50 D8
Goodooga Australia 58 C2
Goodspeed Nunataks Antarctica 76 E2
Goole U.K. 18 G5
Goolgowi Australia 58 B5
Goolma Australia 58 D4
Gooloogong Australia 58 D4
Goomalling Australia 55 B7
Goombalie Australia 58 B2
Goondiwindi Australia 58 E2
Goongarrie, Lake imp. l. Australia 55 C7
Goongarrie National Park Australia 55 C7
Goonyella Australia 56 D4
Goorly, Lake imp. l. Australia 55 B7
Goose Bay Canada see Happy Valley-Goose Bay
Goose Lake U.S.A. 62 C3
Gooty India 38 C3
Gopalganj Bangl. 37 G5
Gopalganj India 37 F4
Gopeshwar India 36 D3
Göppingen Germany 17 L6
Gorakhpur India 37 E4
Goražde Bos.-Herz. 26 H3
Gorczański Park Narodowy nat. park Poland 17 R6
Gördes Turkey 27 M5
Gordil Cent. Afr. Rep. 48 C3
Gordon U.K. 20 G5
Gordon, Lake Australia 57 [inset]
Gordon Downs (abandoned) Australia 54 E4
Gordon Lake PA U.S.A. 64 B3
Gordonsville VA U.S.A. 64 B3
Goré Chad 47 E4
Gorē Eth. 48 D3
Gore N.Z. 59 B8
Gore VA U.S.A. 64 B3
Gorebridge U.K. 20 F5
Gore Point U.S.A. 60 C4
Gorey Ireland 21 F5
Gorgān Iran 35 I3
Gorgān, Khalīj-e Iran 35 I3
Gorge Range hills Australia 54 B5
Gorgona, Isla i. Col. 68 C3
Gori Georgia 32 F1
Goris Armenia 35 G3
Gorizia Italy 26 E2
Gorki Belarus see Horki
Gor'kiy Rus. Fed. see Nizhniy Novgorod
Gor'kovskoye Vodokhranilishche resr Rus. Fed. 12 I4
Gorlice Poland 13 D6
Görlitz Germany 17 O5
Gorlovka Ukr. see Horlivka
Gorna Dzhumaya Bulg. see Blagoevgrad
Gorna Oryakhovitsa Bulg. 27 K3
Gornji Milanovac Serbia 27 I2
Gornji Vakuf Bos.-Herz. 26 G3
Gorno-Altaysk Rus. Fed. 42 F2
Gornotrakiyska Nizina lowland Bulg. 27 K3
Gornozavodsk Permskiy Kray Rus. Fed. 11 R4
Gornozavodsk Sakhalinskaya Oblast' Rus. Fed. 44 F3
Gornyak Rus. Fed. 42 E2
Gornyy Rus. Fed. 13 K6
Gornyye Klyuchi Rus. Fed. 44 D3
Goro i. Fiji see Koro
Gorodenka Ukr. see Horodenka
Gorodets Rus. Fed. 12 I4
Gorodishche Penzenskaya Oblast' Rus. Fed. 13 J5
Gorodishche Volgogradskaya Oblast' Rus. Fed. 13 J6
Gorodok Belarus see Haradok
Gorodok Rus. Fed. see Zakamensk
Gorodok Khmel'nyts'ka Oblast' Ukr. see Horodok
Gorodok L'vivs'ka Oblast' Ukr. see Horodok
Gorodovikovsk Rus. Fed. 13 I7
Goroka P.N.G. 52 E2
Gorokhovets Rus. Fed. 12 I4
Gorom Gorom Burkina 46 C3
Gorongosa mt. Moz. 49 D5
Gorongosa, Parque Nacional de nat. park Moz. 49 D5
Gorontalo Indon. 41 E7
Gorshechnoye Rus. Fed. 13 H6
Gort Ireland 21 D4
Gort an Choirce Ireland 21 D2
Gorutuba r. Brazil 71 C1
Goryachiy Klyuch Rus. Fed. 35 E1
Gorzów Wielkopolski Poland 17 O4
Gosainthan mt. China see Xixabangma Feng
Gosforth U.K. 18 F3
Goshen CA U.S.A. 65 C2
Goshen NH U.S.A. 64 E1
Goshen NY U.S.A. 64 D2
Goshen VA U.S.A. 64 B4
Goshoba Turkm. see Goşoba
Goşoba Turkm. 35 I2
Gospić Croatia 26 F2
Gosport U.K. 19 F8
Gossi Mali 46 C3
Gostivar Macedonia 27 I4
Göteborg Sweden see Gothenburg
Götene Sweden 15 H7
Gotenhafen Poland see Gdynia
Gotha Germany 17 M5
Gothenburg Sweden 15 G8
Gotland i. Sweden 15 K8
Gotō-rettō is Japan 45 C6
Gotse Delchev Bulg. 27 J4
Gotska Sandön i. Sweden 15 K7
Gōtsu Japan 45 D6
Göttingen Germany 17 L5
Gott Peak Canada 62 C1
Gottwaldow Czech Rep. see Zlín
Gouda Neth. 16 J4
Goudiri Senegal 46 B3
Goudoumaria Niger 46 E3
Gouǧaram Niger 46 D3
Gough Island S. Atlantic Ocean 72 H8
Gouin, Réservoir resr Canada 63 M2
Goulburn Australia 58 D5
Goulburn r. N.S.W. Australia 58 E4
Goulburn r. Vic. Australia 58 B6
Goulburn Islands Australia 54 F2
Goulburn River National Park Australia 58 E4
Gould Coast Antarctica 76 J1
Goulou atoll Micronesia see Ngulu
Goundam Mali 46 C3
Goundi Chad 47 E4
Gouraya Alg. 25 G5
Gourcy Burkina 46 C3
Gourdon France 24 E4
Gouré Niger 46 E3
Gouripur Bangl. 37 G4
Gourits r. S. Africa 50 E8
Gourma-Rharous Mali 46 C3
Gournay-en-Bray France 24 E2
Governador Valadares Brazil 71 C2
Governor's Harbour Bahamas 67 I3
Govĭ Altayn Nuruu mts Mongolia 42 H4
Govind Ballash Pant Sagar resr India 37 E4
Gowanda NY U.S.A. 64 B1
Gowan Range hills Australia 56 D5
Gowārān Afgh. 36 A3
Gowd-e Mokh l. Iran 35 I5
Gowd-e Zereh depr. Afgh. 33 J4
Gowmal Kalay Afgh. 36 B2
Gowna, Lough l. Ireland 21 E4
Goya Arg. 70 E3
Göyçay Azer. 35 G2
Goyder watercourse Australia 55 F6
Goymatdag hills Turkm. 35 I2
Goýmatdag hills Turkm. see Goymatdag
Göynük Turkey 27 N4
Goyoum Cameroon 46 E4
Goz-Beïda Chad 47 F3
Gozha Co salt l. China 36 E2
Gözkaya Turkey 39 C1
Gozo i. Malta 26 F6
Graaff-Reinet S. Africa 50 G7
Grabo Côte d'Ivoire 46 C4
Grabouw S. Africa 50 D8
Gračac Croatia 26 F2
Gradaús, Serra dos hills Brazil 69 H5
Gradiška Bos.-Herz. see Bosanska Gradiška
Grafton Australia 58 F2
Grafton WV U.S.A. 64 A3
Grafton, Cape Australia 56 D3
Grafton, Mount NV U.S.A. 65 E1
Grafton Passage Australia 56 D3
Graham TX U.S.A. 62 H5
Graham Bell Island Rus. Fed. see Greem-Bell, Ostrov
Graham Island B.C. Canada 60 E4
Graham Island Nunavut Canada 61 I2
Graham Land pen. Antarctica 76 L2
Grahamstown S. Africa 51 H7
Grahovo Bos.-Herz. see Bosansko Grahovo
Graigue Ireland 21 F5
Grajaú Brazil 69 I5
Grajaú r. Brazil 69 J4
Grammos mt. Greece 27 I4
Grampian Mountains U.K. 20 E4
Grampians National Park Australia 57 C8
Granada Nicaragua 67 G6
Granada Spain 25 E5
Granard Ireland 21 E4
Granby Canada 63 M2
Gran Canaria i. Canary Is 46 B2
Gran Chaco reg. Arg./Para. 70 D3
Grand r. MO U.S.A. 62 J3
Grand Atlas mts Morocco see Haut Atlas
Grand Bahama i. Bahamas 67 I3
Grand Ballon mt. France 17 K7
Grand Bank Canada 61 M5
Grand Banks of Newfoundland sea feature N. Atlantic Ocean 72 E3
Grand-Bassam Côte d'Ivoire 46 C4
Grand Bend Ont. Canada 64 A1
Grand Canal Ireland 21 E4
Grand Canary i. Canary Is see Gran Canaria
Grand Canyon U.S.A. 62 E4
Grand Canyon gorge AZ U.S.A. 65 F2
Grand Canyon National Park AZ U.S.A. 65 F2
Grand Cayman i. Cayman Is 67 H5
Grand Drumont mt. France 17 K7
Grande r. Bahia Brazil 71 B1
Grande r. São Paulo Brazil 71 A3
Grande r. Nicaragua 67 H6
Grande, Bahía b. Arg. 70 C8
Grande, Ilha i. Brazil 71 B3
Grande Comore i. Comoros see Njazidja
Grande Prairie Canada 60 G4
Grand Erg de Bilma des. Niger 46 E3
Grand Erg Occidental des. Alg. 22 D5
Grand Erg Oriental des. Alg. 22 F6
Grande-Rivière Canada 63 O2
Grandes, Salinas salt flat Arg. 70 C4
Grand Falls N.B. Canada 63 N2
Grand Falls-Windsor Nfld. and Lab. Canada 61 M5
Grand Forks U.S.A. 63 H2
Grand Gorge NY U.S.A. 64 D1
Grandioznyy, Pik mt. Rus. Fed. 42 H2
Grand Island U.S.A. 62 H3
Grand Isle U.S.A. 63 I6
Grand Junction U.S.A. 62 F4
Grand-Lahou Côte d'Ivoire 46 C4
Grand Lake N.B. Canada 63 N2
Grand Manan Island Canada 63 N3
Grand Marais MN U.S.A. 63 I2
Grândola Port. 25 B4
Grand Passage New Caledonia 53 G3
Grand Rapids Canada 62 H1
Grand Rapids MI U.S.A. 63 J3
Grand Rapids MN U.S.A. 63 I2
Grand-Sault Canada see Grand Falls
Grand St-Bernard, Col du pass Italy/Switz. see Great St Bernard Pass
Grand Teton mt. U.S.A. 62 E3
Grand Turk Turks and Caicos Is 67 J4
Grand Wash Cliffs mts AZ U.S.A. 65 E3
Grange Ireland 21 E6
Grängesberg Sweden 15 I6
Grangeville U.S.A. 62 D2
Granite Mountains CA U.S.A. 65 E3
Granite Mountains CA U.S.A. 65 E4
Granite Peak MT U.S.A. 62 F2
Granitola, Capo c. Sicilia Italy 26 E6
Granja Brazil 69 J4
Gran Laguna Salada l. Arg. 70 C6
Gränna Sweden 15 I7
Gran Paradiso mt. Italy 26 B2
Gran Paradiso, Parco Nazionale del nat. park Italy 26 B2
Gran Pilastro mt. Austria/Italy 17 M7
Gran San Bernardo, Colle del pass Italy/Switz. see Great St Bernard Pass
Gran Sasso e Monti della Laga, Parco Nazionale del nat. park Italy 26 E3
Grantham U.K. 19 G6
Grant Island Antarctica 76 J2
Grantown-on-Spey U.K. 20 F3
Grant Range mts NV U.S.A. 65 E1
Grants U.S.A. 62 F4
Grants Pass U.S.A. 62 C3
Grantsville WV U.S.A. 64 A3
Grantville PA U.S.A. 64 C2
Granville France 24 D2
Granville NY U.S.A. 64 E1
Granville Lake Canada 61 H4
Grão Mogol Brazil 71 C2
Grapevine Mountains NV U.S.A. 65 D2
Graskop S. Africa 51 J3
Grasplatz Namibia 50 B4
Grasse France 24 H5
Grassflat PA U.S.A. 64 B2
Grassington U.K. 18 F4
Grass Valley CA U.S.A. 65 B1
Grästorp Sweden 15 H7
Graudenz Poland see Grudziądz
Graus Spain 25 G2
Gravataí Brazil 71 A5
Grave, Pointe de pt France 24 D4
Gravelotte S. Africa 51 J2
Gravesend Australia 58 E2
Gravesend U.K. 19 H7
Gravina in Puglia Italy 26 G4
Gray France 24 G3
Grays U.K. 19 H7
Graz Austria 17 O7
Great Abaco i. Bahamas 67 I3
Great Australian Bight g. Australia 55 E8
Great Baddow U.K. 19 H7
Great Bahama Bank sea feature Bahamas 67 I3
Great Barrier Island N.Z. 59 E3
Great Barrier Reef Australia 56 D1
Great Barrier Reef Marine Park (Cairns Section) Australia 56 D3
Great Barrier Reef Marine Park (Capricorn Section) Australia 56 E4
Great Barrier Reef Marine Park (Central Section) Australia 56 E3
Great Barrier Reef Marine Park (Far North Section) Australia 56 D2
Great Barrington MA U.S.A. 64 E1
Great Basalt Wall National Park Australia 56 D3
Great Basin U.S.A. 62 D4
Great Basin National Park NV U.S.A. 65 E1
Great Bear Lake Canada 60 G3
Great Belt sea chan. Denmark 15 G9
Great Bend U.S.A. 62 H4
Great Bitter Lake Egypt 39 A4
Great Blasket Island Ireland 21 B5
Great Britain i. U.K. 16 G4
Great Clifton U.K. 18 D4
Great Cumbrae i. U.K. 20 E5
Great Dividing Range mts Australia 58 B6
Great Eastern Erg des. Alg. see Grand Erg Oriental
Greater Antarctica reg. Antarctica see East Antarctica
Greater Antilles is Caribbean Sea 67 H4
Greater Khingan Mountains China see Da Hinggan Ling
Great Exuma i. Bahamas 67 I4
Great Falls U.S.A. 62 E2
Great Fish r. S. Africa 51 H7
Great Fish Point S. Africa 51 H7
Great Fish River Reserve Complex nature res. S. Africa 51 H7
Great Gandak r. India 37 F4
Great Ganges atoll Cook Is see Manihiki
Great Inagua i. Bahamas 67 J4
Great Karoo plat. S. Africa 50 F7
Great Kei r. S. Africa 51 I7
Great Lake Australia 57 [inset]

Great Malvern U.K. 19 E6
Great Meteor Tablemount sea feature N. Atlantic Ocean 72 G4
Great Namaqualand reg. Namibia 50 C4
Great Nicobar i. India 31 I6
Great Ormes Head hd U.K. 18 D5
Great Ouse r. U.K. 19 H6
Great Oyster Bay Australia 57 [inset]
Great Palm Islands Australia 56 D3
Great Plain of the Koukdjuak Canada 61 K3
Great Point MA U.S.A. 64 F2
Great Rift Valley Africa 48 D4
Great Ruaha r. Tanz. 49 D4
Great Sacandaga Lake NY U.S.A. 64 D1
Great St Bernard Pass Italy/Switz. 26 B2
Great Salt Lake U.S.A. 62 E3
Great Salt Lake Desert U.S.A. 62 E3
Great Sand Sea des. Egypt/Libya 34 B5
Great Sandy Desert Australia 54 C5
Great Sandy Island Australia see Fraser Island
Great Sea Reef Fiji 53 H3
Great Slave Lake Canada 60 G3
Greatstone-on-Sea U.K. 19 H8
Great Stour r. U.K. 19 I7
Great Torrington U.K. 19 C8
Great Victoria Desert Australia 55 E7
Great Wall research stn Antarctica 76 A2
Great Wall tourist site China 43 L4
Great Waltham U.K. 19 H7
Great Western Erg des. Alg. see Grand Erg Occidental
Great Whernside h. U.K. 18 F4
Great Yarmouth U.K. 19 I6
Grebenkovskiy Ukr. see Hrebinka
Grebyonka Ukr. see Hrebinka
Greco, Cape Cyprus see Greko, Cape
Gredos, Sierra de mts Spain 25 D3
Greece country Europe 27 I5
Greece NY U.S.A. 64 C1
Greeley U.S.A. 62 G3
Greem-Bell, Ostrov i. Rus. Fed. 28 H1
Green r. WY U.S.A. 62 F4
Green Bay U.S.A. 63 J3
Green Bay U.S.A. 63 J2
Greenbrier r. WV U.S.A. 64 A4
Green Cape Australia 58 E6
Greencastle U.K. 21 F3
Greene NY U.S.A. 64 D1
Greeneville U.S.A. 63 K4
Greenfield CA U.S.A. 65 B2
Greenfield MA U.S.A. 64 E1
Green Head hd Australia 55 A7
Greenhill Island Australia 54 F2
Green Lake Canada 62 F1
Greenland terr. N. America 61 N3
Greenland Basin sea feature Arctic Ocean 77 I2
Greenland Fracture Zone sea feature Arctic Ocean 77 I1
Greenland Sea Greenland/Svalbard 28 A2
Greenlaw U.K. 20 G5
Greenock U.K. 20 E5
Greenore Ireland 21 F3
Greenport NY U.S.A. 64 E2
Green River WY U.S.A. 62 F3
Greensburg PA U.S.A. 64 B2
Greenstone Point U.K. 20 D3
Greenville Liberia 46 C4
Greenville AL U.S.A. 63 J5
Greenville MS U.S.A. 63 I5
Greenville NH U.S.A. 64 F1
Greenville PA U.S.A. 64 A2
Greenville SC U.S.A. 63 K5
Greenville TX U.S.A. 63 H5
Greenwich atoll Micronesia see Kapingamarangi
Greenwich CT U.S.A. 64 E2
Greenwood SC U.S.A. 63 K5
Gregory r. Australia 56 B3
Gregory, Lake imp. l. S.A. Australia 57 B6
Gregory, Lake imp. l. W.A. Australia 54 D5
Gregory, Lake imp. l. W.A. Australia 55 B6
Gregory Downs Australia 56 B3
Gregory National Park Australia 54 E4
Gregory Range hills Qld Australia 56 C3
Gregory Range hills W.A. Australia 54 C5
Greifswald Germany 17 N3
Greko, Cape Cyprus 39 B2
Gremikha Rus. Fed. 77 G2
Gremyachinsk Rus. Fed. 11 R4
Grenå Denmark 15 G8
Grenaa Denmark see Grenå
Grenada U.S.A. 63 J5
Grenada country West Indies 67 L6
Grenade France 24 E5
Grenen spit Denmark 15 G8
Grenfell Australia 58 D4
Grenfell Canada 62 G1
Grenoble France 24 G4
Grense-Jakobselv Norway 14 Q2
Grenville, Cape Australia 56 C1
Grenville Island Fiji see Rotuma
Greshak Pak. 36 A4
Gressåmoen Nasjonalpark nat. park Norway 14 H4
Greta r. U.K. 18 E4
Gretna U.K. 20 F6
Gretna VA U.S.A. 64 B4
Grevena Greece 27 I4
Grevesmühlen Germany 17 M4
Grey, Cape Australia 56 B2
Greybull U.S.A. 62 F3
Grey Hunter Peak Canada 60 E3
Greylock, Mount MA U.S.A. 64 E1
Greymouth N.Z. 59 C6
Grey Range hills Australia 58 A2
Grey's Plains Australia 55 A6
Greytown S. Africa 51 J5
Gribanovskiy Rus. Fed. 13 I6
Griffin U.S.A. 63 K5
Griffith Australia 58 C5
Grim, Cape Australia 57 [inset]
Grimari Cent. Afr. Rep. 48 C3
Grimmen Germany 17 N3
Grimsby U.K. 18 G5
Grímsey i. Iceland 14 [inset]
Grimshaw Canada 60 G4
Grímsstaðir Iceland 14 [inset]
Grimstad Norway 15 F7
Grindavík Iceland 14 [inset]
Grindsted Denmark 15 F9
Grindul Chituc spit Romania 27 M2
Grinnell Peninsula Canada 61 I2
Griqualand East reg. S. Africa 51 I6
Griqualand West reg. S. Africa 50 F5
Griquatown S. Africa 50 F5
Grise Fiord Canada 61 J2
Grishino Ukr. see Krasnoarmiys'k
Gris Nez, Cap c. France 19 I8
Gritley U.K. 20 G2
Grmeč mts Bos.-Herz. 26 G2
Groblersdal S. Africa 51 I3
Groblershoop S. Africa 50 F5
Grodno Belarus see Hrodna
Groen watercourse S. Africa 50 F6
Groen watercourse S. Africa 50 C6
Groix, Île de i. France 24 C3
Grombalia Tunisia 26 D6
Grong Norway 14 H4
Groningen Neth. 17 K4
Grønland terr. N. America see Greenland
Groom Lake NV U.S.A. 65 E2
Groot-Aar Pan salt pan S. Africa 50 E4
Groot Berg r. S. Africa 50 D7
Groot Brakrivier S. Africa 50 F8
Grootdraaidam dam S. Africa 51 I4
Grootdrink S. Africa 50 E5
Groote Eylandt i. Australia 56 B2
Grootfontein Namibia 49 B5
Groot Karas Berg plat. Namibia 50 D4
Groot Letaba r. S. Africa 51 J2
Groot Marico S. Africa 51 H3
Groot Swartberge mts S. Africa 50 E7
Grootvloer salt pan S. Africa 50 E5
Groot Winterberg mt. S. Africa 51 H7
Gross Barmen Namibia 50 C2
Großer Rachel mt. Germany 17 N6
Grosser Speikkogel mt. Austria 17 O7
Grosseto Italy 26 D3
Grossevichi Rus. Fed. 44 E3
Groß-Gerau Germany 17 L6
Großglockner mt. Austria 17 N7
Gross Ums Namibia 50 D2
Großvenediger mt. Austria 17 N7
Grottoes VA U.S.A. 64 B3
Groundhog r. Canada 63 K2
Grove Mountains Antarctica 76 E2
Grover Beach CA U.S.A. 65 B3
Growler Mountains AZ U.S.A. 65 F4
Groznyy Rus. Fed. 13 J8
Grubišno Polje Croatia 26 G2
Grudovo Bulg. see Sredets
Grudziądz Poland 17 Q4
Grünau Namibia 50 D4
Grünberg Poland see Zielona Góra
Grundarfjörður Iceland 14 [inset]
Gruzinskaya S.S.R. country Asia see Georgia
Gryazi Rus. Fed. 13 H5
Gryazovets Rus. Fed. 12 I4
Gryfice Poland 17 O4
Gryfino Poland 17 O4
Gryfów Śląski Poland 17 O5
Gryllefjord Norway 14 J2
Grytviken S. Georgia 70 I8
Gua India 37 F5
Guacanayabo, Golfo de b. Cuba 67 I4
Guadajoz r. Spain 25 D5
Guadalajara Mex. 66 D4
Guadalajara Spain 25 E3
Guadalcanal i. Solomon Is 53 G2
Guadalete r. Spain 25 C5
Guadalope r. Spain 25 F3
Guadalquivir r. Spain 25 C5
Guadalupe i. Mex. 66 A3
Guadalupe CA U.S.A. 65 B3
Guadalupe, Sierra de mts Spain 25 D4
Guadalupe Peak U.S.A. 62 G5
Guadalupe Victoria Durango Mex. 62 G7
Guadarrama, Sierra de mts Spain 25 D3
Guadeloupe terr. West Indies 67 L5
Guadeloupe Passage Caribbean Sea 67 L5
Guadiana r. Port./Spain 25 C5
Guadix Spain 25 E5
Guafo, Isla i. Chile 70 B6
Guaíba Brazil 71 A5
Guaiçuí Brazil 71 B2
Guaíra Brazil 70 F2
Gualala CA U.S.A. 65 A1
Gualeguay Arg. 70 E4
Gualeguaychu Arg. 70 E4
Gualicho, Salina salt flat Arg. 70 C6
Guam terr. N. Pacific Ocean 41 G6
Guamblin, Isla i. Chile 70 A6
Guampí, Sierra de mts Venez. 68 E2
Guamúchil Mex. 66 C3
Guanajuato Mex. 66 D4
Guanambi Brazil 71 C1
Guanare Venez. 68 E2
Guane Cuba 67 H4
Guangdong prov. China 43 K8
Guanghua China see Laohekou
Guangxi aut. reg. China see Guangxi Zhuangzu Zizhiqu
Guangxi Zhuangzu Zizhiqu aut. reg. China 43 J8
Guangyuan China 42 J6
Guangzhou China 43 K8
Guanhães Brazil 71 C2
Guanipa r. Venez. 68 F2
Guanshui China 44 B4
Guantánamo Cuba 67 I4
Guapé Brazil 71 B3
Guapí Col. 68 C3
Guaporé r. Bol./Brazil 68 E6
Guaporé Brazil 71 A5
Guaqui Bol. 68 E7
Guará r. Brazil 71 B1
Guarabira Brazil 69 K5
Guaranda Ecuador 68 C4
Guarapari Brazil 71 C3
Guarapuava Brazil 71 A4
Guararapes Brazil 71 A3
Guaratinguetá Brazil 71 B3
Guaratuba Brazil 71 A4
Guaratuba, Baía de b. Brazil 71 A4
Guarda Port. 25 C3
Guardafui, Cape Somalia see Gwardafuy, Gees
Guardiagrele Italy 26 F3
Guardo Spain 25 D2
Guárico, del Embalse resr Venez. 68 E2
Guarujá Brazil 71 B3
Guasave Mex. 62 F6
Guasdualito Venez. 68 D2
Guatemala country Central America 66 F5
Guatemala Guat. 66 F6
Guatemala Guat. see Guatemala
Guaviare r. Col. 68 E3
Guaxupé Brazil 71 B3
Guayaquil Ecuador 68 C4
Guayaquil, Golfo de g. Ecuador 68 B4
Guaymas Mex. 66 B3
Guba Eth. 48 D2
Gubakha Rus. Fed. 11 R4
Gubbi India 38 C3
Gubio Nigeria 46 E3
Gubkin Rus. Fed. 13 H6
Gucheng China 43 K6
Gudari India 38 D2
Gudbrandsdalen val. Norway 15 F6
Gudermes Rus. Fed. 13 J8
Gudivada India 38 D2
Gudiyattam India 38 C3
Gudur Andhra Prad. India 38 C3
Gudur Andhra Prad. India 38 C3
Gudvangen Norway 15 E6
Gudzhal r. Rus. Fed. 44 D2
Guecho Spain see Algorta
Guéckédou Guinea 46 B4
Guelma Alg. 26 B6
Guelmine Morocco 46 B2
Guelph Ont. Canada 64 A1
Guerara Alg. 22 E5
Guercif Morocco 22 D5
Guéret France 24 E3
Guernsey terr. Channel Is 19 E9
Guérou Mauritania 46 B3
Guerrah Et-Tarf salt pan Alg. 26 B7
Guerrero Negro Mex. 62 E6
Guers, Lac l. Canada 61 L4
Gueugnon France 24 G3
Gugē mt. Eth. 48 D3
Gügerd, Küh-e mts Iran 35 I4
Guiana Basin sea feature N. Atlantic Ocean 72 E5
Guiana Highlands mts S. America 68 E2
Guidan-Roumji Niger 46 D3
Guider Cameroon 47 E4
Guidonia-Montecelio Italy 26 E4
Guigang China 43 J8
Guiglo Côte d'Ivoire 46 C4
Guija Moz. 51 K3
Guildford U.K. 19 G7
Guilherme Capelo Angola see Cacongo
Guilin China 43 K7
Guillaume-Delisle, Lac l. Canada 61 K4
Guimarães Brazil 69 J4
Guimarães Port. 25 B3
Guinea country Africa 46 B3
Guinea, Gulf of Africa 46 D4
Guinea Basin sea feature N. Atlantic Ocean 72 H5
Guinea-Bissau country Africa 46 B3
Guinea-Conakry country Africa see Guinea
Guinea Ecuatorial country Africa see Equatorial Guinea
Guiné-Bissau country Africa see Guinea-Bissau
Guinée country Africa see Guinea
Güines Cuba 67 H4
Guingamp France 24 C2
Guipavas France 24 B2
Guiratinga Brazil 69 H7
Guiyang Guizhou China 42 J7
Guizhou prov. China 42 J7
Gujarat state India 36 C5
Gujar Khan Pak. 36 C2
Gujerat state India see Gujarat
Gujranwala Pak. 33 L3
Gujrat Pak. 33 L3
Gukovo Rus. Fed. 13 H6
Gulabgarh India 36 D2
Gulbarga India 38 C2
Gulbene Latvia 15 O8
Gul'cha Kyrg. see Gülchö
Gülchö Kyrg. 42 C4
Gülcihan Turkey 39 B1
Gülek Boğazı pass Turkey 34 D3
Gulf, The Asia 32 H4
Gulfport U.S.A. 63 J5
Gulian China 44 A1
Guliston Uzbek. 33 K1
Guliya Shan mt. China 44 A2
Gulja China see Yining
Gul Kach Pak. 36 B3
Gul'kevichi Rus. Fed. 35 F1
Gull Lake Canada 62 F1
Gullträsk Sweden 14 L3
Güllük Körfezi b. Turkey 27 L6
Gülnar Turkey 39 A1
Gulu Uganda 48 D3
Guluwuru Island Australia 56 B1
Gulyayevskiye Koshki, Ostrova is Rus. Fed. 12 L1
Guma China see Pishan
Gumal r. Pak. 33 L3
Gumare Botswana 49 C5
Gumbaz Pak. 36 B3
Gumbinnen Rus. Fed. see Gusev
Gumdag Turkm. 35 I3
Gumel Nigeria 46 D3
Gümgüm Turkey see Varto
Gumla India 37 F5
Gümüşhacıköy Turkey 34 D2
Gümüşhane Turkey 35 E2
Guna India 36 D4
Guna Terara mt. Eth. 32 E7
Gunbar Australia 58 B5
Gunbower Australia 58 B5
Güncang China 37 H3
Gundagai Australia 58 D5
Güney Turkey 27 M5
Güneydoğu Toroslar mts Turkey 34 F3
Gungu Dem. Rep. Congo 49 B4
Gunib Rus. Fed. 35 G2
Gunnaur India 36 D3
Gunnbjørn Fjeld nunatak Greenland 61 P3
Gunnedah Australia 58 E3
Gunning Australia 58 D5
Gunnison U.S.A. 62 F4
Güns Hungary see Kőszeg
Guntakal India 38 C3
Guntur India 38 D2
Gunungsitoli Indon. 41 B7
Günyüzü Turkey 34 C3
Gunza Angola see Porto Amboim
Günzburg Germany 17 M6
Guovdageaidnu Norway see Kautokeino
Gupis Pak. 36 C1
Gurbantünggüt Shamo des. China 42 F4
Gurdaspur India 36 C2
Gurdzhaani Georgia see Gurjaani
Güre Turkey 27 M5
Gurgan Iran see Gorgān
Gurgaon India 36 D3
Gurgei, Jebel mt. Sudan 47 F3
Gurha India 36 B4
Guri, Embalse de resr Venez. 68 F2
Gurig National Park Australia 54 F2
Gurinhatã Brazil 71 A2
Gurjaani Georgia 35 G2
Guro Moz. 49 D5
Guru China 37 G3
Gürün Turkey 34 E3
Gurupá Brazil 69 H4
Gurupi Brazil 69 I6
Gurupi r. Brazil 69 I4
Gurupi, Serra do hills Brazil 69 I4
Guru Sikhar mt. India 36 C4
Guruzala India 38 C2
Gur'yev Kazakh. see Atyrau
Gur'yevsk Rus. Fed. 15 L9
Gur'yevskaya Oblast' admin. div. Kazakh. see Atyrauskaya Oblast'
Gusau Nigeria 46 D3
Gusev Rus. Fed. 15 M9
Gushan China 45 A5
Gusino Rus. Fed. 13 F5
Gusinoozersk Rus. Fed. 42 J2
Gus'-Khrustal'nyy Rus. Fed. 12 I5
Guspini Sardegna Italy 26 C5
Gustav Holm, Kap c. Greenland see Tasiilap Karra
Gustine CA U.S.A. 65 B2
Güstrow Germany 17 N4
Gütersloh Germany 17 L5
Gutsuo China 37 F3
Guwahati India 37 G4
Guwēr Iraq 35 F3
Guwlumaýak Turkm. 35 I2
Guwlumayak Turkm. see Guwlumaýak
Guyana country S. America 69 G2
Guyane Française terr. S. America see French Guiana
Guyang Nei Mongol China 43 K4
Guyenne reg. France 24 D4
Guy Fawkes River National Park Australia 58 F3
Guymon U.S.A. 62 G4
Guyra Australia 58 E3
Guyuan Hebei China 43 L4
Guyuan Ningxia China 42 J5
Güzelolük Turkey 39 B1
Güzelyurt Cyprus see Morfou
Guzmán Mex. 66 C2
Guzmán, Lago de l. Mex. 66 C2
G'uzor Uzbek. 33 K2
Gvardeysk Rus. Fed. 15 L9
Gvasyugi Rus. Fed. 44 E3
Gwa Myanmar 42 G9
Gwabegar Australia 58 D3
Gwaii Haanas National Park Reserve Canada 60 E4
Gwal Haidarzai Pak. 36 B3
Gwalior India 36 D4
Gwanda Zimbabwe 49 C6
Gwane Dem. Rep. Congo 48 C3
Gwardafuy, Gees c. Somalia 48 F2
Gweebarra Bay Ireland 21 D3
Gwelo Zimbabwe see Gweru
Gweru Zimbabwe 49 C5
Gweta Botswana 49 C6
Gwoza Nigeria 46 E3
Gwydir r. Australia 58 D2
Gyablung China 37 H3
Gyaca China 37 H3
Gya'gya China see Saga
Gyaijêpozhanggê China see Zhidoi
Gyai Qu r. China 37 H3
Gyairong China 37 I2
Gyaisi China see Jiulong
Gyali i. Greece 27 L6
Gyamotang China see Dêngqên
Gyamug China 36 E2
Gyandzha Azer. see Gäncä
Gyangkar China see Dinngyê
Gyangnyi Caka salt l. China 37 F2
Gyangrang China 37 F3
Gyangtse China see Gyangzê
Gyangzê China 37 G3
Gyaring China 37 I2
Gyaring Co l. China 37 G3
Gyaring Hu l. China 42 H6
Gyaros i. Greece 27 K6
Gyarubtang China 42 G6
Gydan, Khrebet mts Rus. Fed. see Kolymskiy, Khrebet
Gydan Peninsula Rus. Fed. 28 I2
Gydanskiy Poluostrov pen. Rus. Fed. see Gydan Peninsula
Gyêgu China see Yushu
Gyêmdong China 37 H3
Gyigang China 42 H7
Gyimda China 37 H3
Gyirong Xizang China 37 F3
Gyirong Xizang China 37 F3
Gyiza China 37 H2
Gyldenløve Fjord inlet Greenland see Umiiviip Kangertiva
Gympie Australia 57 F5
Gyöngyös Hungary 17 Q7
Győr Hungary 26 G1
Gypsumville Canada 62 H1
Gyrfalcon Islands Canada 61 L4
Gytheio Greece 27 J6
Gyula Hungary 27 I1
Gyulafehérvár Romania see Alba Iulia
Gyümai China see Darlag
Gyumri Armenia 35 F2
Gzhatsk Rus. Fed. see Gagarin

H

Ha Bhutan 37 G4
Haa-Alif Atoll Maldives see Ihavandhippolhu Atoll
Ha'apai Group is Tonga 53 I3
Haapajärvi Fin. 14 N5
Haapavesi Fin. 14 N4
Haapsalu Estonia 15 M7
Ha 'Arava watercourse Israel/Jordan see 'Arabah, Wādī al
Ha'Arava, Nahal watercourse Israel/Jordan see Jayb, Wādī al
Haarlem Neth. 16 J4
Haarlem S. Africa 50 F7
Hab r. Pak. 36 A4
Habahe China 42 F3
Habana Cuba see Havana
Habarane Sri Lanka 38 D4
Habaswein Kenya 48 D3
Habbān Yemen 32 G7
Ḩabbānīyah, Hawr al l. Iraq 35 F4
Hab Chauki Pak. 36 A4
Habiganj Bangl. 37 G4
Habra India 37 G5
Hachijō-jima i. Japan 45 E6
Hachinohe Japan 44 F4
Hacıköy Turkey see Çekerek
Hack, Mount Australia 57 B6
Hackberry AZ U.S.A. 65 F3
Hackensack NJ U.S.A. 64 D2
Hacufera Moz. 49 D6
Ḩaḑabat al Jilf al Kabīr plat. Egypt see Jilf al Kabīr, Haḑabat al
Hadagalli India 38 B3
Hada Mountains Afgh. 36 A3
Hadayang China 44 B2
Ḩadd, Ra's al pt Oman 33 I5
Haddington U.K. 20 G5
Hadejia Nigeria 46 E3
Ḩadera Israel 39 B3
Ḩadera r. Israel 39 B3
Haderslev Denmark 15 F9
Hadhramaut reg. Yemen see Ḩaḑramawt
Ḩādī, Jabal al mts Jordan 39 C4
Hadım Turkey 34 D3
Hadleigh U.K. 19 H6
Hadong S. Korea 45 B6
Ḩadraj, Wādī watercourse Saudi Arabia 39 C4
Ḩaḑramawt reg. Yemen 48 E2
Hadranum Sicilia Italy see Adrano
Hadrian's Wall tourist site U.K. 18 E3
Hadrumetum Tunisia see Sousse
Hadsund Denmark 15 G8
Hadyach Ukr. 13 G6
Haeju N. Korea 45 B5
Haeju-man b. N. Korea 45 B5
Haenam S. Korea 45 B6
Haenertsburg S. Africa 51 I2
Ha'erbin China see Harbin
Ḩafar al Bāţin Saudi Arabia 32 G4
Hafik Turkey 34 E3
Ḩafīrah, Qā' al salt pan Jordan 39 C4
Hafizabad Pak. 36 C2
Haflong India 37 H4
Hafnarfjörður Iceland 14 [inset]
Hafren r. U.K. see Severn
Haft Gel Iran 35 H5
Hafursfjörður b. Iceland 14 [inset]
Haga Myanmar see Haka
Hagar Nish Plateau Eritrea 32 E6
Hagåtña Guam 41 G6
Hagen Germany 17 K5
Hagerstown MD U.S.A. 64 C3
Hagfors Sweden 15 H6
Hagi Japan 45 C6
Ha Giang Vietnam 31 J4
Hagley U.K. 19 E6
Hag's Head hd Ireland 21 C5
Haguenau France 24 H2
Hahajima-rettō is Japan 45 F8
Hai Tanz. 47 G5
Haib watercourse Namibia 50 C5
Haibowan China see Wuhai
Haicheng Liaoning China 43 M4
Haifa Israel 39 B3
Haifa, Bay of Israel 39 B3
Haig Australia 55 D7
Haikakan country Asia see Armenia
Haikou China 43 K8
Ḩā'il Saudi Arabia 35 F6
Ḩā'il, Wādī watercourse Saudi Arabia 35 F6
Hailin China 44 C3
Hailong China see Meihekou
Hailsham U.K. 19 H8
Hailun China 44 B3
Hailuoto Fin. 14 N4
Hainan i. China 43 K9
Hainan prov. China 43 J9
Hainan Strait China 43 J9
Haines U.S.A. 60 E4
Haines Junction Canada 60 E3
Hai Phong Vietnam 31 J4
Haiphong Vietnam see Hai Phong
Haiqing China 44 D3
Haitan Dao i. China 43 L7
Haiti country West Indies 67 J5
Haiwee Reservoir CA U.S.A. 65 D2
Haiya Sudan 32 E6
Haiyan Qinghai China 42 I5
Haiyang Dao i. China 45 A5
Haizhou Wan b. China 43 L6
Hāj Ali Qoli, Kavīr-e salt pan Iran 35 I4
Hajdúböszörmény Hungary 27 I1
Hajeb El Ayoun Tunisia 26 C7
Ḩajhir mt. Yemen 33 H7
Haji Mahesar Pak. 36 A3
Hajipur India 37 F4
Ḩajjah Yemen 32 F6
Ḩājjīābād Fārs Iran 35 I5
Ḩājjīābād Iran 35 I4
Haka Myanmar 37 H5
Hakha Myanmar see Haka
Hakkârı Turkey 35 F3
Hakkas Sweden 14 L3
Hakken-zan mt. Japan 45 D6
Hako-dake mt. Japan 44 F3
Hakodate Japan 44 F4
Hakos Mountains Namibia 50 C2
Hakseen Pan salt pan S. Africa 50 E4
Hakui Japan 45 E5
Haku-san vol. Japan 45 E5
Hala Pak. 36 B4
Ḩalab Syria see Aleppo
Ḩalabja Iraq 35 G4
Halaç Turkm. 33 J2
Halaç Turkm. see Halaç
Halaha China 44 B3
Halahai China 44 B3
Halaib Sudan 32 E5
Halaib Triangle terr. Egypt/Sudan 32 E5
Ḩalāl, Gebel h. Egypt see Hilāl, Jabal
Ḩalāniyāt, Juzur al is Oman 33 I6
Halba Lebanon 39 C2
Halberstadt Germany 17 M5
Halden Norway 15 G7
Haldensleben Germany 17 M4
Haldwani India 36 D3
Hale watercourse Australia 56 A5
Hāleh Iran 35 I6
Haleparki Deresi r. Syria/Turkey see Quwayq, Nahr
Halesowen U.K. 19 E6
Halesworth U.K. 19 I6
Half Assini Ghana 46 C4
Halfmoon Bay N.Z. 59 B8
Halfway Ireland 21 D6
Halhgol Mongolia 43 L3
Halia India 37 E4
Ḩalībīyah Syria 35 E4
Halicarnassus Turkey see Bodrum
Halifax Canada 61 L5
Halifax U.K. 18 F5
Halifax, Mount Australia 56 D3
Ḩalīmah mt. Lebanon/Syria 39 C2
Halkirk U.K. 20 F2
Hälla Sweden 14 J5
Halladale r. U.K. 20 F2
Halla-san National Park S. Korea 45 B6
Hall Beach Canada 61 J3
Halle (Saale) Germany 17 M5
Hällefors Sweden 15 I7
Hallein Austria 17 N7
Hallett, Cape Antarctica 76 H2
Halley research stn Antarctica 76 B1
Hallgreen, Mount Antarctica 76 B2
Hall Islands Micronesia 74 G5
Hällnäs Sweden 14 K4
Hallock U.S.A. 63 H2
Hall Peninsula Canada 61 L3
Hallsberg Sweden 15 I7
Halls Creek Australia 54 D4
Hallstead PA U.S.A. 64 D2
Hallviken Sweden 14 I5
Halmahera i. Indon. 41 E7
Halmstad Sweden 15 H8
Hals Denmark 15 G8
Hälsingborg Sweden see Helsingborg
Halsua Fin. 14 N5
Haltwhistle U.K. 18 E4
Haly, Mount h. Australia 58 E1
Hamada Japan 45 D6
Hamâda El Ḩaricha des. Mali 46 C2
Hamadān Iran 35 H4
Ḩamādat Murzuq plat. Libya 48 B1
Ḩamāh Syria 39 C2
Hamam Turkey 39 C1
Hamamatsu Japan 45 E6
Hamar Norway 15 G6
Hamarøy Norway 14 I2
Ḩamāţa, Gebel mt. Egypt see Ḩamāţah, Jabal
Ḩamāţah, Jabal mt. Egypt 32 D5
Hamatonbetsu Japan 44 F3
Hambantota Sri Lanka 38 D5
Hambleton Hills U.K. 18 F4
Hamburg Germany 17 L4
Hamburg S. Africa 51 H7
Hamburg NY U.S.A. 64 B1
Hamburgisches Wattenmeer, Nationalpark nat. park Germany 17 L4
Ḩamḑ, Wādī al watercourse Saudi Arabia 32 E4
Hamden CT U.S.A. 64 E2
Hämeenlinna Fin. 15 N6
HaMelaḩ, Yam salt l. Asia see Dead Sea
Hamelin Australia 55 A6
Hameln Germany 17 L4
Hamersley Lakes imp. l. Australia 55 B7
Hamersley Range mts Australia 54 B5
Hamhŭng N. Korea 45 B5
Hami China 42 G4
Hamid Sudan 32 D5
Hamilton Qld Australia 56 C4
Hamilton S.A. Australia 57 A5
Hamilton Vic. Australia 57 C8
Hamilton watercourse Qld Australia 56 B4
Hamilton watercourse S.A. Australia 57 A5
Hamilton Bermuda 67 L2
Hamilton Ont. Canada 64 B1
Hamilton r. Canada see Churchill
Hamilton N.Z. 59 E3
Hamilton U.K. 20 E5
Hamilton MT U.S.A. 62 E2
Hamilton NY U.S.A. 64 D1
Hamilton OH U.S.A. 63 K4
Hamilton, Mount CA U.S.A. 65 B2
Hamilton, Mount NV U.S.A. 65 E1
Hamilton Mountain h. NY U.S.A. 64 D1
Hamīm, Wādī al watercourse Libya 23 I5
Hamina Fin. 15 O6
Hamirpur Hima. Prad. India 36 D3
Hamirpur Uttar Prad. India 36 E4
Hamitabat Turkey see Isparta
Hamju N. Korea 45 B5
Hamm Germany 17 K5
Ḩammām al 'Alīl Iraq 35 F3
Hammam Boughrara Alg. 25 F6
Hammamet Tunisia 26 D6
Hammamet, Golfe de g. Tunisia 26 D6
Ḩammār, Hawr al imp. l. Iraq 35 G5
Hammarstrand Sweden 14 J5
Hammerdal Sweden 14 I5
Hammerfest Norway 14 M1
Hammonton NJ U.S.A. 64 D3
Hampden Sydney VA U.S.A. 64 B4
Hampshire Downs hills U.K. 19 F7
Hampton NH U.S.A. 64 F1
Hampton VA U.S.A. 64 C4
Hampton Tableland reg. Australia 55 D8
Ḩamrā, Birkat al well Saudi Arabia 35 F5
Hamra, Vâdii watercourse Syria/Turkey see Ḩimār, Wādī al
Hamrat esh Sheikh Sudan 32 C7
Hamta Pass India 36 D2
Hāmūn-e Jaz Mūrīān imp. l. Iran 33 I4
Hāmūn-e Lowrah dry lake Afgh./Pak. see Hamun-i-Lora
Hamun-i-Lora dry lake Afgh./Pak. 33 K4
Hamun-i-Mashkel salt flat Pak. 33 J4
Hamur Turkey 35 F3
Hamwic U.K. see Southampton
Hanahai watercourse Botswana/Namibia 50 F2
Ḩanak Saudi Arabia 32 E4
Hanakpınar Turkey see Çınar
Hanamaki Japan 45 F5
Hanang mt. Tanz. 49 D4
Hanbin China see Ankang
Hancheng China 43 K5
Hancock MD U.S.A. 64 B3
Hancock NY U.S.A. 64 D2
Handa Island U.K. 20 D2
Handan China 43 K5
Handeni Tanz. 49 D4
HaNegev des. Israel see Negev
HaNeqarot watercourse Israel 39 B4
Hanford CA U.S.A. 65 C2
Hangayn Nuruu mts Mongolia 42 H3
Hangchow China see Hangzhou
Hangö Fin. see Hanko
Hangu China 43 L5
Hangya China 42 H5
Hangzhou China 43 M6
Hangzhou Wan b. China 43 M6
Hani Turkey 35 F3
Hanish Kabir i. Yemen see Suyūl Ḩanīsh
Hankey S. Africa 50 G7
Hanko Fin. 15 M7
Hanle India 36 D2
Hann, Mount h. Australia 54 D3
Hanna Canada 62 E1
Hannibal MO U.S.A. 63 I4
Hannibal NY U.S.A. 64 C1
Hannover Germany 17 L4
Hann Range mts Australia 55 F5
Hanöbukten b. Sweden 15 I9
Ha Nôi Vietnam 31 J4
Hanoi Vietnam see Ha Nôi
Hanover Germany see Hannover
Hanover S. Africa 50 G6
Hanover PA U.S.A. 64 C3
Hanover VA U.S.A. 64 C4
Hansen Mountains Antarctica 76 D2
Hansi India 36 D3
Hansnes Norway 14 K2
Hanstholm Denmark 15 F8
Hantsavichy Belarus 15 O10
Hanumangarh India 36 C3
Hanwood Australia 58 C5
Hanzhong China 42 J6
Hao atoll Fr. Polynesia 75 K7
Haora India 37 G5
Haparanda Sweden 14 N4
Happy Valley-Goose Bay Canada 61 L4
Ḩaql Saudi Arabia 39 B5
Ḩarad, Jabal al mt. Jordan 39 B5
Ḩaraḑh Saudi Arabia 32 G5
Haradok Belarus 13 F5
Haramachi Japan 45 F5
Haramukh mt. India 36 C2
Haran Turkey see Harran
Harappa Road Pak. 36 C3
Harar Eth. see Hārer
Harare Zimbabwe 49 D5
Ḩarāsīs, Jiddat al des. Oman 33 I6
Harāt Iran 35 I5
Har-Ayrag Mongolia 43 J3
Haraze-Mangueigne Chad 47 F3
Harb, Jabal mt. Saudi Arabia 34 D6
Harbin China 44 B3
Harboi Hills Pak. 36 A3
Harchoka India 37 E5
Harda India 36 D5
Harda Khas India see Harda
Hardangerfjorden sea chan. Norway 15 D7
Hardangervidda plat. Norway 15 E6
Hardangervidda Nasjonalpark nat. park Norway 15 E6
Hardap admin. reg. Namibia 50 C3
Hardap nature res. Namibia 50 C3
Hardap Dam Namibia 50 C3
Hardeveld mts S. Africa 50 D6
Hardin U.S.A. 62 F2
Harding S. Africa 51 I6
Harding Range hills Australia 55 B6
Hardoi India 36 E4
Hardwar India see Haridwar
Ḩareidīn, Wādī watercourse Egypt see Ḩurayḑin, Wādī
Hārer Eth. 48 E3
Harf el Mreffi mt. Lebanon 39 B3
Hargeisa Somalia see Hargeysa
Hargele Eth. 48 E3
Hargeysa Somalia 48 E3
Harghita-Mădăraş, Vârful mt. Romania 27 K1
Harhorin Mongolia 42 I3
Har Hu l. China 42 H5
Haridwar India 36 D3
Ḩarif, Har mt. Israel 39 B4
Harihar India 38 B3
Harihari N.Z. 59 C6
Hariharpur India 38 B3
Ḩārim Syria 39 C1
Harima-nada b. Japan 45 D6
Haringhat r. Bangl. 37 G5
Ḩārīr, Wādī adh r. Syria 39 C3
Hari Rūd r. Afgh./Iran 33 J2

Hudson Bay Canada 62 G1
Hudson Bay sea Canada 61 J4
Hudson Falls NY U.S.A. 64 E1
Hudson Island Tuvalu see Nanumanga
Hudson Mountains Antarctica 76 K2
Hudson Strait Canada 61 K3
Huê Vietnam 31 J5
Huehuetenango Guat. 66 F5
Huehueto, Cerro mt. Mex. 66 C4
Huelva Spain 25 C5
Huentelauquén Chile 70 B4
Huércal-Overa Spain 25 F5
Huesca Spain 25 F2
Huéscar Spain 25 E5
Hughenden Australia 56 D4
Hughes (abandoned) Australia 55 E7
Hughson CA U.S.A. 65 B2
Hugli r. mouth India 37 F5
Hugo OK U.S.A. 63 H5
Huhehot China see Hohhot
Huhhot China see Hohhot
Huhudi S. Africa 50 G4
Hui'anpu China 42 J5
Huiarau Range mts N.Z. 59 F4
Huib-Hoch Plateau Namibia 50 C4
Huila, Nevado de vol. Col. 68 C3
Huíla, Planalto da Angola 49 B5
Huili China 42 I7
Huimanguillo Mex. 66 F5
Huiten Nur l. China 37 G2
Huittinen Fin. 15 M6
Huiyang China see Huizhou
Huize China 42 I7
Huizhou China 43 K8
Hujr Saudi Arabia 32 F4
Hukawng Valley Myanmar 37 I4
Hukuntsi Botswana 50 E2
Hulan China 44 B3
Hulan Ergi China 44 A3
Hulayfah Saudi Arabia 32 F4
Hulayḥilah well Syria 39 D2
Hulin China 44 D3
Hulin Gol r. China 44 B3
Hull Canada 63 L2
Hull U.K. see Kingston upon Hull
Hull Island atoll Kiribati see Orona
Hultsfred Sweden 15 I8
Hulun China see Hulun Buir
Hulun Buir China 43 L3
Hulun Nur l. China 43 L3
Hulwān Egypt 34 C5
Huma China 44 B2
Humahuaca Arg. 70 C2
Humaitá Brazil 68 F5
Humber, Mouth of the U.K. 18 H5
Humboldt Canada 62 F1
Humboldt r. U.S.A. 60 G5
Humeburn Australia 58 B1
Hume Reservoir Australia 58 C5
Humphrey Island atoll Cook Is see Manihiki
Humphreys, Mount CA U.S.A. 65 C2
Humphreys Peak U.S.A. 62 E4
Hūn Libya 47 E2
Húnaflói b. Iceland 14 [inset]
Hunan prov. China 43 K7
Hunedoara Romania 27 J2
Hungary country Europe 23 H2
Hungerford Australia 58 B2
Hŭngnam N. Korea 45 B5
Hunjiang China see Baishan
Huns Mountains Namibia 50 C4
Hunstanton U.K. 19 H6
Hunte r. Germany 17 L4
Hunter r. Australia 58 E4
Hunter Island Australia 57 [inset]
Hunter Island S. Pacific Ocean 53 H4
Hunter Islands Australia 57 [inset]
Huntingdon U.K. 19 G6
Huntingdon PA U.S.A. 64 C2
Huntington IN U.S.A. 63 J3
Huntington WV U.S.A. 63 K4
Huntington Beach CA U.S.A. 65 C4
Huntly N.Z. 59 E3
Huntly U.K. 20 G3
Huntsville Canada 63 L2
Huntsville AL U.S.A. 63 J5
Huntsville TX U.S.A. 63 H5
Hunza reg. Pak. 36 C1
Huolin He r. China see Hulin Gol
Huolongmen China 44 B2
Huonville Australia 57 [inset]
Hupeh prov. China see Hubei
Hupnik r. Turkey 39 C1
Huraydīn, Wādī watercourse Egypt 39 A4
Hurd Island Kiribati see Arorae
Hurghada Egypt see Al Ghurdaqah
Hurler's Cross Ireland 21 D5
Huron CA U.S.A. 65 B2
Huron SD U.S.A. 62 H3
Huron, Lake Canada/U.S.A. 64 A1
Hurricane UT U.S.A. 65 F2
Hursley U.K. 19 F7
Hurst Green U.K. 19 H7
Husain Nika Pak. 36 B3
Húsavík Norðurland eystra Iceland 14 [inset]
Húsavík Vestfirðir Iceland 14 [inset]
Huseyinabat Turkey see Alaca
Huseyinli Turkey see Kızılırmak
Huşi Romania 27 M1
Huskvarna Sweden 15 I8
Husn Jordan see Al Ḥiṣn
Ḥusn Āl 'Abr Yemen 32 G6
Husnes Norway 15 D7
Husum Germany 17 L3
Husum Sweden 14 K5
Hutag-Öndör Mongolia 42 I3
Hutchinson KS U.S.A. 62 H4
Hutou China 44 D3
Hutton, Mount h. Australia 57 E5
Hutton Range hills Australia 55 C6
Hüvek Turkey see Bozova
Huwaytat reg. Saudi Arabia 39 C5
Huzhong China 44 A2
Huzhou China 43 M6
Hvannadalshnúkur vol. Iceland 14 [inset]
Hvar i. Croatia 26 G3
Hvide Sande Denmark 15 F8
Hvítá r. Iceland 14 [inset]
Hwange Zimbabwe 49 C5
Hwange National Park Zimbabwe 49 C5
Hwang Ho r. China see Yellow
Hwedza Zimbabwe 49 D5
Hwlffordd U.K. see Haverfordwest
Hyannis MA U.S.A. 64 F2
Hyargas Nuur salt l. Mongolia 42 G3
Hyde N.Z. 59 C7
Hyden Australia 55 B8
Hyderabad India 38 C2
Hyderabad Pak. 33 K4
Hydra i. Greece see Ydra
Hyères France 24 H5
Hyères, Îles d' is France 24 H5
Hyesan N. Korea 44 C4
Hyland, Mount Australia 58 F3
Hyland Post Canada 60 F4
Hyllestad Norway 15 D6
Hyltebruk Sweden 15 H8
Hyōno-sen mt. Japan 45 D6
Hyrcania Iran see Gorgān
Hyrynsalmi Fin. 14 P4
Hythe U.K. 19 I7
Hyūga Japan 45 C6
Hyvinkää Fin. 15 N6

I

Iaciara Brazil 71 B1
Iaco r. Brazil 68 E5
Iaçu Brazil 71 C1
Iadera Croatia see Zadar
Iakora Madag. 49 E6
Ialomiţa r. Romania 27 L2
Ianca Romania 27 L2
Iaşi Romania 27 L1
Ibadan Nigeria 46 D4
Ibagué Col. 68 C3
Ibaiti Brazil 71 A3
Ibarra Ecuador 68 C3
Ibb Yemen 32 F7
Iberá, Esteros del marsh Arg. 70 E3
Iberia Peru 68 E6
Iberian Peninsula Europe 25
Ibeto Nigeria 46 D3
iBhayi S. Africa see Port Elizabeth
Ibi Nigeria 46 D4
Ibiá Brazil 71 B2
Ibiaí Brazil 71 B2
Ibiapaba, Serra da hills Brazil 69 J4
Ibiassucê Brazil 71 C1
Ibicaraí Brazil 71 D1
Ibiquera Brazil 71 C1
Ibirama Brazil 71 A4
Ibiranhém Brazil 71 C2
Ibitinga Brazil 71 A3
Ibiza Spain 25 G4
Ibiza i. Spain 25 G4
Iblei, Monti mts Sicilia Italy 26 F6
Ibn Buşayyiş well Saudi Arabia 35 G6
Ibotirama Brazil 69 J6
Iboundji, Mont h. Gabon 48 B4
Ibrā' Oman 33 I5
Ibradı Turkey 34 C3
Ibrī Oman 33 I5
Ica r. Col. see Putumayo
Ica Peru 68 C6
Içana Brazil 68 E3
Içana r. Brazil 68 E3
Icaria i. Greece see Ikaria
Icatu Brazil 69 J4
Iceberg Canyon gorge NV U.S.A. 65 E2
İçel Mersin Turkey see Mersin
Iceland country Europe 14 [inset]
Iceland Basin sea feature N. Atlantic Ocean 72 G2
Icelandic Plateau sea feature N. Atlantic Ocean 77 I2
Ichalkaranji India 38 B2
Ichifusa-yama mt. Japan 45 C6
Ichinomiya Japan 45 E6
Ichinoseki Japan 45 F5
Ichinskaya Sopka vol. Rus. Fed. 29 Q4
Ichkeul, Parc National de l' Tunisia 26 C6
Ichnya Ukr. 13 G6
Icó Brazil 69 K5
Iconha Brazil 71 C3
Iconium Turkey see Konya
Icosium Alg. see Algiers
Iculisma France see Angoulême
Icy Cape U.S.A. 60 B2
Id Turkey see Narman
Idah Nigeria 46 D4
Idaho state U.S.A. 62 E3
Idaho Falls U.S.A. 62 E3
Idalia National Park Australia 56 D5
Idar India 36 C5
Idar-Oberstein Germany 17 K6
Ideriyn Gol r. Mongolia 42 I3
Idfū Egypt 32 D5
Idhān Awbārī des. Libya 46 E2
Idhān Murzūq des. Libya 46 E2
Idhra i. Greece see Ydra
Idi Amin Dada, Lake Dem. Rep. Congo/Uganda see Edward, Lake
Idiofa Dem. Rep. Congo 49 B4
Idivuoma Sweden 14 M2
Idkū Egypt 34 C5
Idle r. U.K. 18 G5
Idlib Syria 39 C2
Idra i. Greece see Ydra
Idre Sweden 15 H6
Idutywa S. Africa 51 I7
Idzhevan Armenia see Ijevan
Iecava Latvia 15 N8
Iepê Brazil 71 A3
Ierapetra Greece 27 K7
Ierissou, Kolpos b. Greece 27 J4
Iešjávri l. Norway 14 N2
Ifakara Tanz. 49 D4
Ifanadiana Madag. 49 E6
Ife Nigeria 46 D4
Ifenat Chad 47 E3
Iferouâne Niger 46 D3
Iffley Australia 56 C3
Ifjord Norway 14 O1
Ifôghas, Adrar des hills Mali 46 D3
Iforas, Adrar des hills Mali see Ifôghas, Adrar des
Igan Sarawak Malaysia 41 D7
Iganga Uganda 47 G4
Igarapava Brazil 71 B3
Igarka Rus. Fed. 28 J3
Igatpuri India 38 B2
Igbeti Nigeria see Igbetti
Igbetti Nigeria 46 D4
Igdir Iran 35 G3
Iğdır Turkey 35 G3
Iggesund Sweden 15 J6
Igikpak, Mount U.S.A. 60 C3
Iglesias Sardegna Italy 26 C5
Iglesiente reg. Sardegna Italy 26 C5
Igloolik Canada 61 J3
Igluligaarjuk Canada see Chesterfield Inlet
Ignace Canada 63 I2
Ignalina Lith. 15 O9
İğneada Turkey 27 L4
İğneada Burnu pt Turkey 27 M4
iGoli S. Africa see Johannesburg
Igoumenitsa Greece 27 I5
Igra Rus. Fed. 11 Q4
Igrim Rus. Fed. 11 S3
Iguaçu r. Brazil 71 A4
Iguaçu, Saltos do waterfall Arg./Brazil see Iguaçu Falls
Iguaçu Falls Arg./Brazil 70 F3
Iguaí Brazil 71 C1
Iguala Mex. 66 E5
Igualada Spain 25 G3
Iguape Brazil 71 B4
Iguaraçu Brazil 71 A3
Iguatama Brazil 71 B3
Iguatemi Brazil 70 F2
Iguatu Brazil 69 K5
Iguazú, Cataratas do waterfall Arg./Brazil see Iguaçu Falls
Iguéla Gabon 48 A4
Iguidi, Erg des. Alg./Mauritania 46 C2
Igunga Tanz. 49 D4
Iharaña Madag. 49 E5
Ihavandhippolhu Atoll Maldives 38 B5
Ihavandiffulu Atoll Maldives see Ihavandhippolhu Atoll
Ih Bogd Uul mt. Mongolia 42 I4
Ihosy Madag. 49 E6
Iide-san mt. Japan 45 E5
Iijärvi l. Fin. 14 O2
Iijoki r. Fin. 14 N4
Iisalmi Fin. 14 O5
Iizuka Japan 45 C6
Ijebu-Ode Nigeria 46 D4
Ijevan Armenia 35 G2
IJssel r. Neth. 17 J4
IJsselmeer l. Neth. 22 F1
Ikaahuk Canada see Sachs Harbour
Ikaalinen Fin. 15 M6
Ikageleng S. Africa 51 H3
Ikageng S. Africa 51 H4
iKapa S. Africa see Cape Town
Ikare Nigeria 46 D4
Ikaria i. Greece 27 L6
Ikast Denmark 15 F8
Ikeda Japan 44 F4
Ikela Dem. Rep. Congo 48 C4
Ikhtiman Bulg. 27 J3
Ikhutseng S. Africa 50 G5
Iki-Burul Rus. Fed. 13 J7
Ikom Nigeria 46 D4
Iksan S. Korea 45 B6
Ikungu Tanz. 49 D4
Ilagan Phil. 41 E6
Ilaisamis Kenya 48 D3
Īlām Iran 35 G4
Ilam Nepal 37 F4
Ilan Taiwan 43 M8
Ilave Peru 68 E7
Iława Poland 17 Q4
Ilazārān, Kūh-e mt. Iran 33 I4
Ilebo Dem. Rep. Congo 49 C4
Île Europa i. Indian Ocean see Europa, Île
Ilek Kazakh. 11 Q5
Ilen r. Ireland 21 C6
Ileret Kenya 48 D3
Ileza Rus. Fed. 12 I3
Ilfeld Germany 17 M5
Ilford U.K. 19 H7
Ilfracombe Australia 56 D4
Ilfracombe U.K. 19 C7
Ilgaz Turkey 34 D2
Ilgın Turkey 34 C3
Ilha Grande, Represa resr Brazil 70 F2
Ilha Solteíra, Represa resr Brazil 71 A3
Ílhavo Port. 25 B3
Ilhéus Brazil 71 D1
Ili Kazakh. see Kapchagay
Iliamna Lake U.S.A. 60 C4
İliç Turkey 34 E3
Il'ichevsk Azer. see Şärur
Il'ichevsk Ukr. see Illichivs'k
Ilici Spain see Elche-Elx
Ilimananngip Nunaa i. Greenland 61 P2
Il'inka Rus. Fed. 13 J7
Il'inskiy Permskiy Kray Rus. Fed. 11 R4
Il'inskiy Sakhalinskaya Oblast' Rus. Fed. 44 F3
Il'insko-Podomskoye Rus. Fed. 12 J3
Ilion NY U.S.A. 64 D1
Ilium tourist site Turkey see Troy
Iliysk Kazakh. see Kapchagay
Ilkal India 38 C3
Ilkeston U.K. 19 F6
Ilkley U.K. 18 F5
Illapel Chile 70 B4
Illéla Niger 46 D3
Iller r. Germany 17 L6
Illichivs'k Ukr. 27 N1
Illimani, Nevado de mt. Bol. 68 E7
Illinois r. U.S.A. 63 I4
Illinois state U.S.A. 63 J4
Illizi Alg. 46 D2
Illogwa watercourse Australia 56 A5
Ilmajoki Fin. 14 M5
Il'men', Ozero l. Rus. Fed. 12 F4
Ilminster U.K. 19 E8
Ilo Peru 68 D7
Iloilo Phil. 41 E6
Ilomantsi Fin. 14 Q5
Ilorin Nigeria 46 D4
Ilovlya Rus. Fed. 13 I6
Iluka Australia 58 F2
Ilulissat Greenland 61 M3
Iluppur India 38 C4
Ilva i. Italy see Elba, Isola d'
Imabari Japan 45 D6
Imaichi Japan 45 E5
Imala Moz. 49 D5
İmamoğlu Turkey 34 D3
Iman Rus. Fed. see Dal'nerechensk
Iman r. Rus. Fed. 44 D3
Imari Japan 45 C6
Imaruí Brazil 71 A5
Imataca, Serranía de mts Venez. 68 F2
Imatra Fin. 15 P6
Imbituva Brazil 71 A4
imeni 26 Bakinskikh Komissarov Azer. see Uzboy
imeni Babushkina Rus. Fed. 12 I4
imeni Kirova Kazakh. see Kopbirlik
imeni Petra Stuchki Latvia see Aizkraukle
imeni Poliny Osipenko Rus. Fed. 44 E1
imeni Tel'mana Rus. Fed. 44 D2
Īmī Eth. 48 E3
İmishli Azer. see İmişli
İmişli Azer. 35 H3
Imit Pak. 36 C1
Imja-do i. S. Korea 45 B6
Imola Italy 26 D2
iMonti S. Africa see East London
Impendle S. Africa 51 I5
Imperatriz Brazil 69 I5
Imperia Italy 26 C3
Imperial CA U.S.A. 65 E4
Imperial Beach CA U.S.A. 65 D4
Imperial Dam Arizona/California U.S.A. 65 E4
Imperial Valley plain CA U.S.A. 65 E4
Imperieuse Reef Australia 54 B4
Impfondo Congo 48 B3
Imphal India 37 H4
İmralı Adası i. Turkey 27 M4
İmroz Turkey 27 K4
İmroz i. Turkey see Gökçeada
Imtān Syria 39 C3
In r. Rus. Fed. 44 D2
Ina Japan 45 E6
Inambari r. Peru 68 E6
Inari Fin. 14 O2
Inarijärvi l. Fin. 14 O2
Inarijoki r. Fin./Norway 14 N2
Inca Spain 25 H4
İnce Burnu pt Turkey 27 L4
İnce Burun pt Turkey 34 D2
Inch Ireland 21 F5
Inchard, Loch b. U.K. 20 D2
Incheon S. Korea see Inch'ŏn
Inchicronan Lough l. Ireland 21 D5
Inch'ŏn S. Korea 45 B5
Incirli Turkey see Karasu
Indaal, Loch b. U.K. 20 C5
Indalsälven r. Sweden 14 J5
Indalstø Norway 15 D6
Inda Silasē Eth. 48 D2
Indé Mex. 66 C3
Indefatigable Island Galápagos Ecuador see Santa Cruz, Isla
Independence CA U.S.A. 65 C2
Independence MO U.S.A. 63 I4
Inder China 44 A3
Inderborskiy Kazakh. 30 E2
Indi India 38 C2
India country Asia 31 I4
Indiana PA U.S.A. 64 B2
Indiana state U.S.A. 63 J3
Indian-Antarctic Ridge sea feature Southern Ocean 74 D9
Indianapolis U.S.A. 63 J4
Indian Desert India/Pak. see Thar Desert
Indian Head Canada 62 G1
Indian Lake NY U.S.A. 64 D1
Indian Lake PA U.S.A. 64 B2
Indian Ocean 73
Indianola IA U.S.A. 63 I3
Indianola MS U.S.A. 63 I5
Indian Peak UT U.S.A. 65 F1
Indian Springs NV U.S.A. 65 E2
Indiga Rus. Fed. 12 K2
Indigirka r. Rus. Fed. 29 P2
Indigskaya Guba b. Rus. Fed. 12 K2
Inđija Serbia 27 I2
Indio CA U.S.A. 65 D4
Indira Priyadarshini Pench National Park India 36 D5
Indispensable Reefs Solomon Is 53 G3
Indjija Serbia see Inđija
Indonesia country Asia 41 D8
Indore India 36 C5
Indrapura, Gunung vol. Indon. see Kerinci, Gunung
Indravati r. India 38 D2
Indre r. France 24 E3
Indulkana Australia 55 F6
Indur India see Nizamabad
Indus r. China/Pakistan 31 F4
Indus, Mouths of the Pak. 33 K5
Indus Cone sea feature Indian Ocean 73 M4
Indwe S. Africa 51 H6
İnebolu Turkey 34 D2
İnegöl Turkey 27 M4
Inevi Turkey see Cihanbeyli
Infantes Spain see Villanueva de los Infantes
Infiernillo, Presa resr Mex. 66 D5
Inga Rus. Fed. 14 S3
Ingersoll Ont. Canada 64 A1
Ingham Australia 56 D3
Ingleborough h. U.K. 18 E4
Inglefield Land reg. Greenland 61 K2
Ingleton U.K. 18 E4
Inglewood Qld Australia 58 E2
Inglewood Vic. Australia 58 A6
Inglewood CA U.S.A. 65 C4
Ingoka Pum mt. Myanmar 37 I4
Ingoldmells U.K. 18 H5
Ingolstadt Germany 17 M6
Ingomar Australia 55 F7
Ingraj Bazar India 37 G4
Ingrid Christensen Coast Antarctica 76 E2
Ingwavuma S. Africa 51 K4
Ingwavuma r. S. Africa/Swaziland see Ngwavuma
Inhaca Moz. 51 K3
Inhaca, Península pen. Moz. 51 K4
Inhambane Moz. 51 L2
Inhambane prov. Moz. 51 L2
Inhaminga Moz. 49 D5
Inharrime Moz. 51 L3
Inhassoro Moz. 49 D6
Inhaúmas Brazil 71 B1
Inhobim Brazil 71 C1
Inhumas Brazil 71 A2
Inis Ireland see Ennis
Inis Córthaidh Ireland see Enniscorthy
Inishark i. Ireland 21 B4
Inishbofin i. Ireland 21 B4
Inisheer i. Ireland 21 C4
Inishkea North i. Ireland 21 B3
Inishkea South i. Ireland 21 B3
Inishmaan i. Ireland 21 C4
Inishmore i. Ireland 21 C4
Inishmurray i. Ireland 21 D3
Inishowen pen. Ireland 21 E2
Inishowen Head hd Ireland 21 F2
Inishtrahull i. Ireland 21 E2
Inishturk i. Ireland 21 B4
Injune Australia 57 E5
Inkerman Australia 56 C3
Inland Kaikoura Range mts N.Z. 59 D6
Inland Sea Japan see Seto-naikai
Inlet NY U.S.A. 64 D1
Inn r. Europe 17 M7
Innaanganeq c. Greenland 61 L2
Innamincka Australia 57 C5
Innamincka Regional Reserve nature res. Australia 57 C5
Inndyr Norway 14 I3
Inner Sound sea chan. U.K. 20 D3
Innes National Park Australia 57 B7
Innisfail Australia 56 D3
Innokent'yevka Rus. Fed. 44 C2
Innoko r. U.S.A. 60 C3
Innsbruck Austria 17 M7
Inny r. Ireland 21 E4
Inocência Brazil 71 A2
Inongo Dem. Rep. Congo 48 B4
İnönü Turkey 27 N5
Inowrocław Poland 17 Q4
In Salah Alg. 46 D2
Insch U.K. 20 G3
Inscription, Cape Australia 56 B3
Insterburg Rus. Fed. see Chernyakhovsk
Inta Rus. Fed. 11 S2
Interamna Italy see Teramo
Interlaken Switz. 24 H3
International Falls U.S.A. 63 I2
Intutu Peru 68 D4
Inubō-zaki pt Japan 45 F6
Inuvik Canada 60 E3
Inveraray U.K. 20 D4
Inverbervie U.K. 20 G4
Invercargill N.Z. 59 B8
Inverell Australia 58 E2
Invergordon U.K. 20 E3
Inverkeithing U.K. 20 F4
Inverleigh Australia 56 C3
Inverness U.K. 20 E3
Inverness CA U.S.A. 65 A1
Inverurie U.K. 20 G3
Investigator Group is Australia 55 F8
Investigator Ridge sea feature Indian Ocean 73 O6
Investigator Strait Australia 57 B7
Inwood WV U.S.A. 64 B3
Inya Rus. Fed. 42 F2
Inyanga Zimbabwe see Nyanga
Inyangani mt. Zimbabwe 49 D5
Inyokern CA U.S.A. 65 D3
Inyo Mountains CA U.S.A. 65 C2
Inyonga Tanz. 49 D4
Inza Rus. Fed. 13 J5
Inzhavino Rus. Fed. 13 I5
Ioannina Greece 27 I5
Iokanga r. Rus. Fed. 12 H2
Iola U.S.A. 63 H4
Iolgo, Khrebet mts Rus. Fed. 42 F2
Iolotan' Turkm. see Ýolöten
Iona i. U.K. 20 C4
Iona, Parque Nacional do nat. park Angola 49 B5
Ione NV U.S.A. 65 D1
Iongo Angola 49 B4
Ionian Islands Greece 27 H5
Ionian Sea Greece/Italy 26 H5
Ionioi Nisoi is Greece see Ionian Islands
Ios i. Greece 27 K6
Iowa state U.S.A. 63 I3
Iowa City U.S.A. 63 I3
Ipameri Brazil 71 A2
Ipanema Brazil 71 C2
Iparía Peru 68 D5
Ipatinga Brazil 71 C2
Ipatovo Rus. Fed. 13 I7
Ipelegeng S. Africa 51 G4
Ipiales Col. 68 C3
Ipiaú Brazil 71 D1
Ipirá Brazil 71 D1
Ipiranga Brazil 71 A4
iPitoli S. Africa see Pretoria
Ipixuna r. Brazil 68 F5
Ipoh Malaysia 41 C7
Iporá Brazil 71 A2
Ippy Cent. Afr. Rep. 48 C3
İpsala Turkey 27 L4
Ipswich Australia 58 F1
Ipswich U.K. 19 I6
Ipu Brazil 69 J4
Iqaluit Canada 61 L3
Iquique Chile 70 B2
Iquiri r. Brazil see Ituxi
Iquitos Peru 68 D4
Irai Brazil 70 F3
Irakleio Greece see Iraklion
Iraklion Greece 27 K7
Iramaia Brazil 71 C1
Iran country Asia 32 I3
Īrānshahr Iran 33 J4
Irapuato Mex. 66 D4
Iraq country Asia 35 F4
Irara Brazil 71 D1
Irati Brazil 71 A4
Irayel' Rus. Fed. 12 L2
Irazú, Volcán vol. Costa Rica 67 H7
Irbid Jordan 39 B3
Irbil Iraq see Arbīl
Irbit Rus. Fed. 28 H4
Irecê Brazil 69 J6
Ireland country Europe 21 E4
Ireland i. Ireland/U.K. 21
Irema Dem. Rep. Congo 48 C4
Irgiz Kazakh. 42 A3
Irgiz r. Kazakh. 42 A3
Iri S. Korea see Iksan
Irian, Teluk b. Indon. see Cenderawasih, Teluk
Iriba Chad 47 F3
Īrī Dāgh mt. Iran 35 G3
Irîgui reg. Mali/Mauritania 46 C3
Iringa Tanz. 49 D4
Iriri r. Brazil 69 H4
Irish Sea Ireland/U.K. 21 G4
Irituia Brazil 69 I4
Irkutsk Rus. Fed. 42 I2
Irmak Turkey 34 D3
Irminger Basin sea feature N. Atlantic Ocean 72 F2
Iron Baron Australia 57 B7
Irondequoit NY U.S.A. 64 C1
Iron Mountain U.S.A. 63 J2
Iron Mountain UT U.S.A. 65 F2
Iron Range National Park Australia 56 C2
Irosin Phil. 41 E6
Irpen' Ukr. see Irpin'
Irpin' Ukr. 13 F6
Irrawaddy r. Myanmar 37 H6
Irrawaddy, Mouths of the Myanmar 31 I5
Irshad Pass Afgh./Pak. 36 C1
Irta Rus. Fed. 12 K3
Irthing r. U.K. 18 E4
Irtysh r. Kazakh./Rus. Fed. 31 G1
Irun Spain 25 F2
Iruña Spain see Pamplona
Iruñea Spain see Pamplona
Irvine U.K. 20 E5
Irvine CA U.S.A. 65 D4
Irvine Glacier Antarctica 76 L2
Irwin r. Australia 55 A7
Isa Nigeria 46 D3
Isaac r. Australia 56 E4
Isabela Phil. 41 E7
Isabela, Isla i. Galápagos Ecuador 68 [inset]
Isabelia, Cordillera mts Nicaragua 67 G6
Isabella Lake CA U.S.A. 65 C3
Isachsen, Cape Canada 61 H2
Ísafjarðardjúp est. Iceland 14 [inset]
Ísafjörður Iceland 14 [inset]
Isa Khel Pak. 36 B2
Isar r. Germany 17 N6
Isbister U.K. 20 [inset]
Ischia, Isola d' i. Italy 26 E4
Ise Japan 45 E6
Isère r. France 24 G4
Isère, Pointe pt Fr. Guiana 69 H2
Isernia Italy 26 F4
Ise-shima Kokuritsu-kōen nat. park Japan 45 E6
Ise-wan b. Japan 45 E6
Iseyin Nigeria 46 D4
Isfahan Iran see Eşfahān
Isheyevka Rus. Fed. 13 K5
Ishigaki Japan 43 M8
Ishikari-wan b. Japan 44 F4
Ishim r. Kazakh./Rus. Fed. 30 G1
Ishinomaki Japan 45 F5
Ishinomaki-wan b. Japan 43 Q5
Ishioka Japan 45 F5
Ishkoshim Tajik. 36 B1
Ishurdi Bangl. 37 G4
Ishwardi Bangl. see Ishurdi
Isiboro Sécure, Parque Nacional nat. park Bol. 68 E7
Isigny-sur-Mer France 19 F9
Işıklar Dağı mts Turkey 27 L4
Işıklı Turkey 27 M5
Isil'kul' Rus. Fed. 28 I4
Isimangaliso Wetland Park nature res. S. Africa 51 K4
Isipingo S. Africa 51 J5
Isiro Dem. Rep. Congo 48 C3
Isisford Australia 56 D5
İskateley Rus. Fed. 12 L2
İskenderun Turkey 39 C1
İskenderun Körfezi b. Turkey 39 B1
İskilip Turkey 34 D2
Iskitim Rus. Fed. 28 J4
Iskŭr r. Bulg. 27 K3
Iskushuban Somalia 48 F2
Isla r. Scotland U.K. 20 F4
Isla r. Scotland U.K. 20 G3
Isla Gorge National Park Australia 56 E5
İslahiye Turkey 34 E3
Islamabad India see Anantnag
Islamabad Pak. 33 L3
Islamgarh Pak. 36 B4
Islamkot Pak. 36 B4
Ísland country Europe see Iceland
Island Lagoon imp. l. Australia 57 B6
Island Lake Canada 63 I1
Island Magee pen. U.K. 21 G3
Islands, Bay of N.Z. 59 E2
Islay i. U.K. 20 C5
Isle of Man terr. Irish Sea 18 C4
Isle of Wight VA U.S.A. 64 C4
Ismail Ukr. see Izmayil
Ismâ'ilîya Egypt see Al Ismā'īlīyah
Ismâ'ilîya governorate Egypt see Al Ismā'īlīyah
Ismailly Azer. see İsmayıllı
İsmayıllı Azer. 35 H2
Isojoki Fin. 14 L5
Isoka Zambia 49 D5
Isokylä Fin. 14 O3
Isokyrö Fin. 14 M5
Isola di Capo Rizzuto Italy 26 G5
Ispahan Iran see Eşfahān
Isparta Turkey 27 N6
Isperikh Bulg. 27 L3
İspir Turkey 35 F2
Ispisar Tajik. see Khŭjand
Isplinji Pak. 36 A3
Israel country Asia 39 B4
Israelite Bay Australia 55 C8
Isra'īl country Asia see Israel
Issia Côte d'Ivoire 46 C4
Issoire France 24 F4
Issyk-Kul' Kyrg. see Balykchy
Issyk-Kul', Ozero salt l. Kyrg. see Ysyk-Köl
Istalif Afgh. 36 B2
İstanbul Turkey 27 M4
İstanbul Boğazı str. Turkey see Bosporus
Īstgāh-e Eznā Iran 35 H4
Istiaia Greece 27 J5
Istik r. Tajik. 36 C1
Istočni Drvar Bos.-Herz. 26 G2
Istra pen. Croatia see Istria
Istres France 24 G5
Istria pen. Croatia 26 E2
Iswardi Bangl. see Ishurdi
Itabapoana r. Brazil 71 C3
Itaberá Brazil 71 A3
Itaberaba Brazil 71 C1
Itaberaí Brazil 71 A2
Itabira Brazil 71 C2
Itabirito Brazil 71 C3
Itabuna Brazil 71 D1
Itacajá Brazil 69 I5
Itacarambi Brazil 71 B1
Itacoatiara Brazil 69 G4
Itaetê Brazil 71 C1
Itagmatana Iran see Hamadān
Itaguaçu Brazil 71 C2
Itaí Brazil 71 A3
Itaiópolis Brazil 71 A4
Itäisen Suomenlahden kansallispuisto nat. park Fin. 15 O6
Itaituba Brazil 69 G4
Itajaí Brazil 71 A4
Itajubá Brazil 71 B3
Itajuípe Brazil 71 D1
Italia country Europe see Italy
Italia, Laguna l. Bol. 68 F6
Italy country Europe 26 E3
Itamarandiba Brazil 71 C2
Itambé Brazil 71 C1
Itambé, Pico de mt. Brazil 71 C2
Itampolo Madag. 49 E6
Itanagar India 37 H4
Itanguari r. Brazil 71 B1
Itanhaém Brazil 71 B4
Itanhém Brazil 71 C2
Itanhém r. Brazil 71 D2
Itaobím Brazil 71 C2
Itapaci Brazil 71 A1
Itapajipe Brazil 71 A2
Itapebi Brazil 71 D1
Itapecerica Brazil 71 B3
Itapemirim Brazil 71 C3
Itaperuna Brazil 71 C3
Itapetinga Brazil 71 C1
Itapetininga Brazil 71 A3
Itapeva Brazil 71 A3
Itapeva, Lago l. Brazil 71 A5
Itapicuru Brazil 69 J6
Itapicuru, Serra de hills Brazil 69 I5
Itapicuru Mirim Brazil 69 J4
Itapipoca Brazil 69 K4
Itapira Brazil 71 B3
Itaporanga Brazil 71 A3
Itapuã Brazil 71 A5
Itaqui Brazil 70 E3
Itararé Brazil 71 A4
Itarsi India 36 D5
Itarumã Brazil 71 A2
Itatiba Brazil 71 B3
Itatuba Brazil 68 F5
Itaúna Brazil 71 B3
Itaúnas Brazil 71 D2
Itbayat i. Phil. 43 M8
Itea Greece 27 J5
Ithaca NY U.S.A. 64 C1
iThekweni S. Africa see Durban
Ithrah Saudi Arabia 39 C4
Itilleq Greenland 61 M3
Itimbiri r. Dem. Rep. Congo 48 C3
Itinga Brazil 71 C2
Itiquira Brazil 69 H7
Itiruçu Brazil 71 C1
Itiúba, Serra de hills Brazil 69 K6
Itō Japan 45 E6
iTswane S. Africa see Pretoria
Ittiri Sardegna Italy 26 C4
Ittoqqortoormiit Greenland 61 P2
Itu Brazil 71 B3
Ituaçu Brazil 71 C1
Ituberá Brazil 71 D1
Ituí r. Brazil 68 D4
Ituiutaba Brazil 71 A2
Itumbiara Brazil 71 A2
Itumbiara, Barragem resr Brazil 71 A2
Ituni Guyana 69 G2
Itupiranga Brazil 69 I5
Ituporanga Brazil 71 A4
Iturama Brazil 71 A2
Ituri r. Dem. Rep. Congo 48 C3
Iturup, Ostrov i. Rus. Fed. 44 G3
Itutinga Brazil 71 B3
Ituxi r. Brazil 68 F5
Ityop'ia country Africa see Ethiopia
Itzehoe Germany 17 L4
Iul'tin Rus. Fed. 29 T3
Ivalo Fin. 14 O2
Ivalojoki r. Fin. 14 O2
Ivanava Belarus 15 N10
Ivanhoe Australia 58 B4
Ivankiv Ukr. 13 F6
Ivankovtsy Rus. Fed. 44 D2
Ivano-Frankivs'k Ukr. 13 E6
Ivano-Frankovsk Ukr. see Ivano-Frankivs'k
Ivanovka Rus. Fed. 44 B2
Ivanovo Belarus see Ivanava
Ivanovo tourist site Bulg. 27 K3
Ivanovo Rus. Fed. 12 I4
Ivanteyevka Rus. Fed. 13 K5
Ivantsevichi Belarus see Ivatsevichy
Ivatsevichy Belarus 15 N10

Ivaylovgrad Bulg. 27 L4
Ivdel' Rus. Fed. 11 S3
Ivittuut Greenland 61 N3
Iviza i. Spain see Ibiza
Ivory Coast country Africa see Côte d'Ivoire
Ivrea Italy 26 B2
İvrindi Turkey 27 L5
Ivris Ugheltekhili pass Georgia 35 G2
Ivugivik Canada see Ivujivik
Ivujivik Canada 61 K3
Ivyanyets Belarus 15 O10
Ivydale WV U.S.A. 64 A3
Iwaki Japan 45 F5
Iwaki-san vol. Japan 44 F4
Iwakuni Japan 45 D6
Iwamizawa Japan 44 F4
Iwo Nigeria 46 D4
Iwye Belarus 15 N10
Ixiamas Bol. 68 E6
Ixmiquilpán Mex. 66 E4
Ixopo S. Africa 51 J6
Ixtlán Mex. 66 D4
Ixworth U.K. 19 H6
İyirmi Altı Bakı Komissarı Azer. see Uzboy
Izabal, Lago de l. Guat. 66 G5
Izberbash Rus. Fed. 35 G2
Īzeh Iran 35 H5
Izgal Pak. 36 C2
Izhevsk Rus. Fed. 11 Q4
Izhma Respublika Komi Rus. Fed. 12 L2
Izhma Respublika Komi Rus. Fed. see Sosnogorsk
Izhma r. Rus. Fed. 12 L2
Izmail Ukr. see Izmayil
Izmayil Ukr. 27 M2
İzmir Turkey 27 L5
İzmir Körfezi g. Turkey 27 L5
İzmit Turkey 27 M4
İzmit Körfezi b. Turkey 27 M4
Izozog Bol. 68 F7
Izra' Syria 39 C3
Iztochni Rodopi mts Bulg. 27 K4
Izu-hantō pen. Japan 45 E6
Izuhara Japan 45 C6
Izumo Japan 45 D6
Izu-Ogasawara Trench sea feature N. Pacific Ocean 74 F3
Izu-shotō is Japan 45 E6
Izyaslav Ukr. 13 E6
Iz"yayu Rus. Fed. 12 M2
Izyum Ukr. 13 H6

Jabalón r. Spain 25 D4
Jabalpur India 36 D5
Jabbūl, Sabkhat al salt flat Syria 39 C2
Jabiru Australia 54 F3
Jablah Syria 39 B2
Jablanica Bos.-Herz. 26 G3
Jaboatão Brazil 69 L5
Jaboticabal Brazil 71 A3
Jacaraci Brazil 71 C1
Jacareacanga Brazil 69 G5
Jacareí Brazil 71 B3
Jacarézinho Brazil 71 A3
Jacinto Brazil 71 C2
Jack r. Australia 56 D2
Jackson Australia 58 D1
Jackson AL U.S.A. 63 J5
Jackson CA U.S.A. 65 B1
Jackson MI U.S.A. 63 K3
Jackson MS U.S.A. 63 I5
Jackson TN U.S.A. 63 J4
Jackson WY U.S.A. 62 E3
Jackson, Mount Antarctica 76 L2
Jackson Head hd N.Z. 59 B6
Jacksonville FL U.S.A. 63 K5
Jacksonville IL U.S.A. 63 I4
Jacksonville NC U.S.A. 63 L5
Jack Wade U.S.A. 60 D3
Jacmel Haiti 67 J5
Jacobabad Pak. 33 K4
Jacobina Brazil 69 J6
Jacobsdal S. Africa 50 G5
Jacques-Cartier, Mont mt. Canada 63 N2
Jacuí Brazil 71 B3
Jacuípe r. Brazil 69 K6
Jacunda Brazil 69 I4
Jaddangi India 38 D2
J. A. D. Jensen Nunatakker nunataks Greenland 61 N3
Jadotville Dem. Rep. Congo see Likasi
Jādū Libya 46 E1
Jaén Spain 25 E5
Jaffa, Cape Australia 57 B8
Jaffna Sri Lanka 38 C4
Jafr, Qā' al imp. l. Jordan 39 C4
Jagadhri India 36 D3
Jagalur India 38 C3
Jagatsinghapur India see Jagatsinghpur
Jagatsinghpur India 37 F5
Jagdalpur India 38 D2
Jagdaqi China 44 B2
Jagersfontein S. Africa 51 G5
Jaggang China 36 D2
Jaggayyapeta India 38 D2
Jaghīn Iran 33 I4
Jagok Tso salt l. China see Urru Co
Jagtial India 38 C2
Jaguariaíva Brazil 71 A4
Jaguaripe Brazil 71 D1
Jahanabad India see Jehanabad
Jahmah well Iraq 35 G5
Jahrom Iran 35 I5
Jaicós Brazil 69 J5
Jaigarh India 38 B2
Jailolo Gilolo i. Indon. see Halmahera
Jainpur India 37 E4
Jaintapur Bangl. see Jaintiapur
Jaintiapur Bangl. 37 H4
Jaipur India 36 C4
Jaipurhat Bangl. see Joypurhat
Jais India 37 E4
Jaisalmer India 36 B4
Jaisamand Lake India 36 C4
Jaitaran India 36 C4
Jaitgarh h. India 38 C1
Jajapur India see Jajpur
Jajarkot Nepal 33 N4
Jajce Bos.-Herz. 26 G2
Jajnagar state India see Orissa
Jajpur India 37 F5
Jakar Bhutan 37 G4
Jakarta Indon. 41 C8
Jakhau India 36 B5
Jakin mt. Afgh. 36 A3
Jäkkvik Sweden 14 J3
Jakliat India 36 C3
Jakobshavn Greenland see Ilulissat
Jakobstad Fin. 14 M5
Jalaid China see Inder
Jalālābād Afgh. 36 B2
Jalal-Abad Kyrg. 42 C4
Jalālah al Baḩrīyah, Jabal plat. Egypt 34 C5
Jalalpur Pirwala Pak. 36 B3
Jalāmīd, Ḩazm al ridge Saudi Arabia 35 E5
Jalandhar India 36 C3
Jalapa Mex. 66 E5
Jalapa Enríquez Mex. see Jalapa
Jalasjärvi Fin. 14 M5
Jalaun India 36 D4
Jalawlā' Iraq 35 G4
Jaldak Afgh. 36 A3
Jaldrug India 38 C2
Jales Brazil 71 A3
Jalesar India 36 D4
Jalgaon India 36 C5
Jalībah Iraq 35 G5
Jalingo Nigeria 46 E4
Jalna India 38 B2
Jalón r. Spain 25 F3
Jalor India see Jalore
Jalore India 36 C4
Jalpa Mex. 66 D4
Jalpaiguri India 37 G4
Jālū Libya 47 F2
Jalūlā Iraq see Jalawlā'
Jamaica country West Indies 67 I5
Jamaica Channel Haiti/Jamaica 67 I5
Jamalpur Bangl. 37 G4
Jamalpur India 37 F4
Jamanxim r. Brazil 69 G4
Jambi Indon. 41 C8
Jambin Australia 56 E5
Jambo India 36 C4
Jamda India 37 F5
Jamekunte India 38 C2
James r. N. Dakota/S. Dakota U.S.A. 62 H3
James r. VA U.S.A. 64 C4
James, Baie b. Canada see James Bay
Jamesabad Pak. 36 B4
James Bay Canada 63 K1
James Island Galápagos Ecuador see San Salvador, Isla
Jameson Land reg. Greenland 61 P2
James Peak N.Z. 59 B7
James Ranges mts Australia 55 F6
James Ross Island Antarctica 76 A2
James Ross Strait Canada 61 I3
Jamestown Australia 57 B7
Jamestown S. Africa 51 H6
Jamestown St Helena 72 H7
Jamestown ND U.S.A. 62 H2
Jamestown NY U.S.A. 64 B1
Jamkhed India 38 B2
Jammu India 36 C2
Jammu and Kashmir terr. Asia 36 D2
Jamnagar India 36 B5
Jampur Pak. 36 B3
Jamrud Pak. 36 B2
Jämsä Fin. 15 N6
Jamsah Egypt 34 D6
Jämsänkoski Fin. 14 N6
Jamshedpur India 37 F5
Jamtari Nigeria 46 E4
Jamui India 37 F4
Jamuna r. Bangl. see Raimangal
Jamuna r. India see Yamuna
Janā i. Saudi Arabia 35 H6
Janāb, Wādī al watercourse Jordan 39 C4
Janakpur India 37 E5
Janaúba Brazil 71 C1
Jandaia Brazil 71 A2
Jandaq Iran 35 I4
Jandola Pak. 36 B2
Jandowae Australia 58 E1
Janesville WI U.S.A. 63 J3
Jangada Brazil 71 A4
Jangamo Moz. 51 L3
Jangaon India 38 C2
Jangipur India 37 G4
Jangnga Turkm. see Jaňňa
Jangngai Ri mts China 37 F2
Jan Mayen terr. Arctic Ocean 77 I2
Jan Mayen Fracture Zone sea feature Arctic Ocean 77 I2
Jaňňa Turkm. 35 I2
Jansenville S. Africa 50 G7
Januária Brazil 71 B1
Janūb Sīnā' governorate Egypt 39 A5
Janūb Sīnā' governorate Egypt see Janūb Sīnā'
Japan country Asia 45 D5
Japan, Sea of N. Pacific Ocean 45 D5
Japan Alps National Park Japan see Chūbu-Sangaku Kokuritsu-kōen
Japan Trench sea feature N. Pacific Ocean 74 F3
Japiim Brazil 68 D5
Japurá r. Brazil 68 F4
Japvo Mount India 37 H4
Jarābulus Syria 39 D1
Jaraguá Brazil 71 A1
Jaraguá, Serra mts Brazil 71 A4
Jaraguá do Sul Brazil 71 A4
Jarash Jordan 39 B3
Jardine River National Park Australia 56 C1
Jardinésia Brazil 71 A2
Jardinópolis Brazil 71 B3
Jargalang China 44 A4
Jargalant Bayanhongor Mongolia 42 H3
Jargalant Hovd Mongolia see Hovd
Jari r. Brazil 69 H4
Järna Sweden 15 J7
Jarocin Poland 17 P5
Jarosław Poland 13 D6
Järpen Sweden 14 H5
Jarrettsville MD U.S.A. 64 C3
Jarú Brazil 68 F6
Jarud China see Lubei
Järvakandi Estonia 15 N7
Järvenpää Fin. 15 N6
Jarvis Island terr. S. Pacific Ocean 74 J6
Jarwa India 37 E4
Jashpurnagar India 37 F5
Jāsk Iran 33 I4
Jasliq Uzbek. 35 J2
Jasło Poland 13 D6
Jasol India 36 C4
Jason Islands Falkland Is 70 D8
Jason Peninsula Antarctica 76 L2
Jasper Canada 62 D1
Jasper NY U.S.A. 64 C1
Jasper TX U.S.A. 63 I5
Jasrasar India 36 C4
Jaşşān Iraq 35 G4
Jassy Romania see Iaşi
Jastrzębie-Zdrój Poland 17 Q6
Jaswantpura India 36 C4
Jászberény Hungary 27 H1
Jataí Brazil 71 A2
Jatapu r. Brazil 69 G4
Jath India 38 B2
Jati Pak. 33 K5
Játiva Spain see Xàtiva
Jatoi Pak. 36 B3
Jat Poti Afgh. 36 A3
Jaú Brazil 71 A3
Jaú r. Brazil 68 F4
Jaú, Parque Nacional do nat. park Brazil 68 F4
Jaua Sarisariñama, Parque Nacional nat. park Venez. 68 F3
Jauja Peru 68 C6
Jaunlutriņi Latvia 15 M8
Jaunpiebalga Latvia 15 O8
Jaunpur India 37 E4
Java Georgia 35 F2
Java i. Indon. 41 C8
Javaés r. Brazil see Formoso
Javari r. Brazil/Peru see Yavari
Java Ridge sea feature Indian Ocean 73 P6
Java Sea Indon. see Jawa, Laut
Java Trench sea feature Indian Ocean 74 C6
Jävre Sweden 14 L4
Jawa i. Indon. see Java
Jawa, Laut sea Indon. 41 D8
Jawhar India 38 B2
Jawhar Somalia 48 E3
Jawor Poland 17 P5
Jaya, Puncak mt. Indon. 41 F8
Jayakusumu mt. Indon. see Jaya, Puncak
Jayakwadi Sagar l. India 38 B2
Jayantiapur Bangl. see Jaintiapur
Jayapura Indon. 41 G8
Jayb, Wādī al watercourse Israel/Jordan 39 B4
Jayfi, Wādī al watercourse Egypt 39 B4
Jaypur India 38 D2
Jayrūd Syria 39 C3
Jazīreh-ye Shīf Iran 35 H5
Jbail Lebanon 39 B2
Jean NV U.S.A. 65 E3
Jeannin, Lac l. Canada 61 L4
Jebel, Bahr el r. Sudan/Uganda see White Nile
Jebel, Bahr el r. Sudan/Uganda see White Nile
Jebel Abyad Plateau Sudan 32 C6
Jech Doab lowland Pak. 36 C3
Jedburgh U.K. 20 G5
Jeddah Saudi Arabia 32 E5
Jedeida Tunisia 26 C6
Jefferson OH U.S.A. 64 A2
Jefferson, Mount NV U.S.A. 65 D1
Jefferson City U.S.A. 63 I4
Jeffreys Bay S. Africa 50 G8
Jehanabad India 37 F4
Jeju S. Korea see Cheju
Jejuí Guazú r. Para. 70 E2
Jēkabpils Latvia 15 N8
Jelbart Ice Shelf Antarctica 76 B2
Jelenia Góra Poland 17 O5
Jelep La pass China/India 37 G4
Jelgava Latvia 15 M8
Jember Indon. 41 D8
Jena Germany 17 M5
Jendouba Tunisia 26 C6
Jengish Chokusu mt. China/Kyrg. see Pobeda Peak
Jenīn West Bank 39 B3
Jenne Mali see Djenné
Jennings U.S.A. 63 I5
Jenolan Caves Australia 58 E4
Jens Munk Island Canada 61 K3
Jeparit Australia 57 C8
Jequié Brazil 71 C1
Jequitaí r. Brazil 71 B2
Jequitinhonha Brazil 71 C2
Jequitinhonha r. Brazil 71 D1
Jerba, Île de i. Tunisia 22 G5
Jerbar Sudan 47 G4
Jereh Iran 35 H5
Jérémie Haiti 67 J5
Jerez Mex. 66 D4
Jerez de la Frontera Spain 25 C5
Jergol Norway 14 N2
Jergucat Albania 27 I5
Jericho Australia 56 D4
Jericho West Bank 39 B4
Jerid, Chott el salt l. Tunisia 22 F5
Jerilderie Australia 58 B5
Jerimoth Hill RI U.S.A. 64 F2
Jeroaquara Brazil 71 A1
Jerome U.S.A. 62 D3
Jerruck Pak. 36 B4
Jersey terr. Channel Is 19 E9
Jersey City NJ U.S.A. 64 D2
Jersey Shore PA U.S.A. 64 C2
Jerumenha Brazil 69 J5
Jerusalem Israel/West Bank 39 B4
Jervis Bay Australia 58 E5
Jervis Bay b. Australia 58 E5
Jervis Bay Territory admin. div. Australia 58 E5
Jesenice Slovenia 26 F1
Jesi Italy 26 E3
Jesselton Sabah Malaysia see Kota Kinabalu
Jessheim Norway 15 G6
Jessore Bangl. 37 G5
Jesu Maria Island P.N.G. see Rambutyo Island
Jesup U.S.A. 63 K5
Jetpur India 36 B5
Jewish Autonomous Oblast admin. div. Rus. Fed. see Yevreyskaya Avtonomnaya Oblast'
Jeypur India see Jaypur
Jezzine Lebanon 39 B3
Jhabua India 36 C5
Jhajhar India see Jhajjar
Jhajjar India 36 D3
Jhal Pak. 36 A3
Jhalawar India 36 D4
Jhang Pak. 33 L3
Jhansi India 36 D4
Jhapa Nepal 37 F4
Jharia India 37 F5
Jharkhand state India 37 F5
Jharsuguda India 37 F5
Jhawani Nepal 37 F4
Jhelum r. India/Pak. 36 C3
Jhelum Pak. 33 L3
Jhenaidah Bangl. 37 G5
Jhenaidaha Bangl. see Jhenaidah
Jhenida Bangl. see Jhenaidah
Jhimpir Pak. 36 B4
Jhudo Pak. 36 B4
Jhumritilaiya India 37 F4
Jhund India 36 B5
Jhunjhunun India 36 C3
Jiamusi China 44 C3
Ji'an Jiangxi China 43 K7
Ji'an Jilin China 44 B4
Jiangcheng China 42 I8
Jiangjunmiao China 42 F4
Jiangmen China 43 K8
Jiangna China see Yanshan
Jiangsi China see Dejiang
Jiangsu prov. China 43 L6
Jiangxi prov. China 43 L7
Jiangzhesongrong China 37 F3
Jianshui Hu l. China 37 E2
Jianyang Fujian China 43 L7
Jiaohe China 44 B4
Jiaojiang China see Taizhou
Jia Tsuo La pass China 37 F3
Jiaxing China 43 M6
Jiayi Taiwan see Chiai
Jiayin China 44 C2
Jiayuguan China 42 H5
Jibūti country Africa see Djibouti
Jibuti Djibouti see Djibouti
Jiddah Saudi Arabia see Jeddah
Jiddī, Jabal al h. Egypt 39 A4
Jidong China 44 C3
Jiehkkevárri mt. Norway 14 K2
Jiexiu China 43 K5
Jieyang China 43 L8
Jieznas Lith. 15 N9
Jigzhi China 42 I6
Jiḩār, Wādī al watercourse Syria 39 C2
Jihlava Czech Rep. 17 O6
Jijel Alg. 22 F4
Jijiga Eth. 48 E3
Jījīrud Iran 35 H4
Jil'ād reg. Jordan 39 B3
Jilf al Kabīr, Haḑabat al plat. Egypt 32 C5
Jilib Somalia 48 E3
Jilin China 44 B4
Jilin prov. China 44 B4
Jilin Hada Ling mts China 44 B4
Jiliu He r. China 44 A2
Jilo India 36 C4
Jilong Taiwan see Chilung
Jīma Eth. 48 D3
Jiménez Chihuahua Mex. 66 D3
Jiménez Tamaulipas Mex. 66 E4
Jimía, Cerro mt. Hond. 66 G5
Jimsar China 42 F4
Jim Thorpe PA U.S.A. 64 D2
Jinan China 43 L5
Jin'an China see Songpan
Jinbi China see Dayao
Jinchang China 42 I5
Jincheng Shanxi China 43 K5
Jinchengjiang China see Hechi
Jinchuan Gansu China see Jinchang
Jind India 36 D3
Jindřichův Hradec Czech Rep. 17 O6
Jingbian China 43 J5
Jingdezhen China 43 L7
Jingellic Australia 58 C5
Jinggangshan China 43 K7
Jinghong China 42 I8
Jingle China 43 K5
Jingmen China 43 K6
Jingpo China 44 C4
Jingpo Hu l. China 44 C4
Jingsha China see Jingzhou
Jingtai China 42 I5
Jingtieshan China 42 H5
Jingxian Hunan China see Jingzhou
Jingyu China 44 B4
Jingyuan China 42 I5
Jingzhou Hubei China 43 K6
Jingzhou Hunan China 43 J7
Jinhe Nei Mongol China 44 A2
Jinhua Zhejiang China 43 L7
Jining Nei Mongol China 43 K4
Jining Shandong China 43 L5
Jinja Uganda 48 D3
Jinka Eth. 48 D3
Jinotepe Nicaragua 67 G6
Jinping Guizhou China 43 J7
Jinsen S. Korea see Inch'ŏn
Jinsha Jiang r. China see Yangtze
Jinshan Nei Mongol China see Guyang
Jinshi Hunan China 43 K7
Jintur India 38 C2
Jinxi Jiangxi China 43 L7
Jinxi Liaoning China see Lianshan
Jinxian China 43 L7
Jinz, Qā' al salt flat Jordan 39 C4
Jinzhong China 43 K5
Jinzhou China 43 M4
Ji-Paraná Brazil 68 F6
Jipijapa Ecuador 68 B4
Ji Qu r. China 37 I3
Jiquiriçá Brazil 71 D1
Jiquitaia Brazil 71 D2
Jirā', Wādī watercourse Egypt 39 A5
Jirānīyāt, Shi'bān al watercourse Saudi Arabia 39 D4
Jīroft Iran 33 I4
Jirriiban Somalia 48 E3
Jishou China 43 J7
Jisr ash Shughūr Syria 39 C2
Jiu r. Romania 27 J3
Jiuding Shan mt. China 42 I6
Jiujiang Jiangxi China 43 L7
Jiulian China see Mojiang
Jiulong H.K. China see Kowloon
Jiulong Sichuan China 42 I7
Jiwani Pak. 33 J4
Jiwen China 44 A2
Jixi Heilong. China 44 C3
Jixian China 44 C3
Jīzah, Ahrāmāt al tourist site Egypt see Pyramids of Giza
Jīzān Saudi Arabia 32 F6
Jizzakh Uzbek. see Jizzax
Jizzax Uzbek. 33 K1
Joaçaba Brazil 71 A4
Joaíma Brazil 71 C2
João Belo Moz. see Xai-Xai
João de Almeida Angola see Chibia
João Pessoa Brazil 69 L5
João Pinheiro Brazil 71 B2
Joaquin V. González Arg. 70 D3
Joda India 37 F5
Jodhpur India 36 C4
Jodiya India 36 B5
Joensuu Fin. 14 P5
Jōetsu Japan 45 E5
Jofane Moz. 49 D6
Jogbura Nepal 36 E3
Jõgeva Estonia 15 O7
Jogjakarta Indon. see Yogyakarta
Johannesburg S. Africa 51 H4
Johannesburg CA U.S.A. 65 D3
Johan Peninsula Canada 61 K2
Johi Pak. 36 A4
John Day U.S.A. 62 D3
John Day r. U.S.A. 62 C2
John F. Kennedy airport NY U.S.A. 64 E2
John o'Groats U.K. 20 F2
Johnsonburg PA U.S.A. 64 B2
Johnsondale CA U.S.A. 65 C3
Johnston, Lake imp. l. Australia 55 C8
Johnston and Sand Islands terr. N. Pacific Ocean see Johnston Atoll
Johnston Atoll terr. N. Pacific Ocean 74 I4
Johnstone U.K. 20 E5
Johnstone Lake Canada see Old Wives Lake
Johnston Range hills Australia 55 B7
Johnstown Ireland 21 E5
Johnstown NY U.S.A. 64 D1
Johnstown PA U.S.A. 64 B2
Johor Bahru Malaysia 41 C7
Johore Bahru Malaysia see Johor Bahru
Jōhvi Estonia 15 O7
Joinville Brazil 71 A4
Joinville France 24 G2
Joinville Island Antarctica 76 A2
Jokkmokk Sweden 14 K3
Jökulsá r. Iceland 14 [inset]
Jökulsá á Fjöllum r. Iceland 14 [inset]
Jökulsá í Fljótsdal r. Iceland 14 [inset]
Jolfa Iran 35 G3
Joliet U.S.A. 63 J3
Jolo i. Phil. 41 E7
Jomda China 42 H6
Jonava Lith. 15 N9
Jonesboro AR U.S.A. 63 I4
Jones Sound sea chan. Canada 61 J2
Jonglei Canal Sudan 32 D8
Jönköping Sweden 15 I8
Jonquière Canada 63 M2
Joplin U.S.A. 63 I4
Joppa Israel see Tel Aviv-Yafo
Jora India 36 D4
Jordan country Asia 39 C4
Jordan r. Asia 39 B4
Jordan U.S.A. 62 F2
Jordânia Brazil 71 C1
Jordet Norway 15 H6
Jorhat India 37 H4
Jorm Afgh. 36 B1
Jörn Sweden 14 L4
Joroinen Fin. 14 O5
Jørpeland Norway 15 E7
Jos Nigeria 46 D4
José de San Martín Arg. 70 B6
Joseph, Lac l. Canada 61 L4
Joseph Bonaparte Gulf Australia 54 E3
Joshimath India 36 D3
Joshipur India 38 E1
Joshua Tree National Park CA U.S.A. 65 E4
Jos Plateau Nigeria 46 D4
Jostedalsbreen Nasjonalpark nat. park Norway 15 E6
Jotunheimen Nasjonalpark nat. park Norway 15 F6
Jouaiya Lebanon 39 B3
Joubertina S. Africa 50 F7
Jouberton S. Africa 51 H4
Jõuga Estonia 15 O7
Joûnié Lebanon 39 B3
Joutsa Fin. 15 O6
Joutseno Fin. 15 P6
Jowai India 37 H4
Jowr Deh Iran 35 H3
Joyce's Country reg. Ireland 21 C4
Joypurhat Bangl. 37 G4
Juan Aldama Mex. 66 D4
Juan de Fuca Strait Canada/U.S.A. 62 C2
Juan Fernández, Archipiélago is S. Pacific Ocean 75 O8
Juan Fernández Islands S. Pacific Ocean see Juan Fernández, Archipiélago
Juanjuí Peru 68 C5
Juankoski Fin. 14 P5
Juàzeiro Brazil 69 J5
Juàzeiro do Norte Brazil 69 K5
Juba r. Somalia see Jubba
Juba Sudan 47 G4
Jubany research stn Antarctica 76 A2
Jubba r. Somalia 48 E4
Jubbah Saudi Arabia 35 F5
Jubbulpore India see Jabalpur
Jubilee Lake imp. l. Australia 55 D7
Juby, Cap c. Morocco 46 B2
Juchitán Mex. 66 E5
Jucuruçu Brazil 71 D2
Jucuruçu r. Brazil 71 D2
Judaberg Norway 15 D7
Judaidat al Hamir Iraq 35 F5
Judayyidat 'Ar'ar well Iraq 35 F5
Judenburg Austria 17 O7
Juelsminde Denmark 15 G9
Juerana Brazil 71 D2
Jugar China see Sêrxü
Juigalpa Nicaragua 67 G6
Juína Brazil 69 G6
Juiz de Fora Brazil 71 C3
Julaca Bol. 68 E8
Julia Brazil 68 E4
Juliaca Peru 68 D7
Julia Creek Australia 56 C4
Julian CA U.S.A. 65 D4
Julian Alps mts Slovenia see Julijske Alpe
Julianatop mt. Indon. see Mandala, Puncak
Juliana Top mt. Suriname 69 G3
Julianehåb Greenland see Qaqortoq
Julijske Alpe mts Slovenia 26 E1
Juliomagus France see Angers
Julius, Lake Australia 56 B4
Jullundur India see Jalandhar
Jumbilla Peru 68 C5
Jumilla Spain 25 F4
Jumla Nepal 37 E3
Jumna r. India see Yamuna
Junagadh India 36 B5
Junagarh India 38 D2
Junayfah Egypt 39 A4
Junction TX U.S.A. 62 H5
Junction City KS U.S.A. 63 H4
Jundiaí Brazil 71 B3
Juneau AK U.S.A. 60 E4
Junee Australia 58 C5
Jūn el Khudr b. Lebanon 39 B3
Jungar Qi China see Shagedu
Jungfrau mt. Switz. 24 H3
Junggar Pendi basin China 42 F3
Juniata r. PA U.S.A. 64 C2
Junín Arg. 70 D4
Junín Peru 68 C6
Junior WV U.S.A. 64 B3
Juniper Mountains AZ U.S.A. 65 F3
Junipero Serro Peak CA U.S.A. 65 B2
Junlian China 42 I7
Junsele Sweden 14 J5
Junxian China see Danjiangkou
Juodupė Lith. 15 N8
Jupiá Brazil 71 A3
Jupía, Represa resr Brazil 71 A3
Juquiá r. Brazil 71 B4
Jur r. Sudan 32 C8
Jura mts France/Switz. 24 G4
Jura i. U.K. 20 D4
Jura, Sound of sea chan. U.K. 20 D5
Juracî Brazil 71 C1
Jurbarkas Lith. 15 M9
Jurf ad Darāwīsh Jordan 39 B4
Jūrmala Latvia 15 M8
Jurmu Fin. 14 O4
Juruá r. Brazil 68 E4
Juruena r. Brazil 69 G5
Juruti Brazil 69 G4
Jurva Fin. 14 L5
Jūsīyah Syria 39 C2
Jussara Brazil 71 A1
Jutaí Brazil 68 E5
Jutaí r. Brazil 68 E4
Jutiapa Guat. 66 G6
Juticalpa Hond. 66 G6
Jutis Sweden 14 J3
Jutland pen. Denmark 15 F8
Juuka Fin. 14 P5
Juva Fin. 14 O6
Jūyom Iran 35 I5
Južnoukrajinsk Ukr. see Yuzhnoukrayinsk
Jwaneng Botswana 50 G3
Jylland pen. Denmark see Jutland
Jyväskylä Fin. 14 N5

K

K2 mt. China/Pakistan 36 D2
Ka r. Nigeria 46 D3
Kaafu Atoll Maldives see Male Atoll
Kaa-Iya del Gran Chaco, Parque Nacional nat. park Bol. 68 F7
Kaakhka Turkm. see Kaka
Kaapstad S. Africa see Cape Town
Kaarina Fin. 15 M6
Kaavi Fin. 14 P5
Kaba China see Habahe
Kabala Sierra Leone 46 B4
Kabale Uganda 48 C4
Kabalega Falls National Park Uganda see Murchison Falls National Park
Kabalo Dem. Rep. Congo 49 C4
Kabambare Dem. Rep. Congo 49 C4
Kabangu Dem. Rep. Congo 49 C5
Kabara i. Fiji 53 I3
Kabarega National Park Uganda see Murchison Falls National Park
Kabaw Valley Myanmar 37 H5
Kabbani r. India 38 C3
Kåbdalis Sweden 14 L3
Kabinakagami Lake Canada 63 K2
Kabinda Dem. Rep. Congo 49 C4
Kabīr r. Syria 39 B2
Kabīrkūh mts Iran 35 G4
Kabo Cent. Afr. Rep. 48 B3
Kābol Afgh. see Kābul
Kabompo r. Zambia 49 C5
Kabongo Dem. Rep. Congo 49 C4
Kabūd Rāhang Iran 35 H4
Kābul Afgh. 36 B2
Kābul r. Afgh. 36 C2
Kabunda Dem. Rep. Congo 49 C5
Kabunduk Indon. 54 B2
Kabwe Zambia 49 C5
Kachalinskaya Rus. Fed. 13 J6
Kachchh, Great Rann of marsh India see Kachchh, Rann of
Kachchh, Gulf of India 36 B5
Kachchh, Little Rann of marsh India 36 B5
Kachchh, Rann of marsh India 36 B4
Kachia Nigeria 46 D4
Kachiry Kazakh. 42 D2
Kachkanar Rus. Fed. 11 R4
Kachret'i Georgia 35 G2
Kachug Rus. Fed. 42 J2
Kaçkar Dağı mt. Turkey 35 F2
Kadaiyanallur India 38 C4
Kadanai r. Afgh./Pak. 36 A3
Kadavu i. Fiji 53 H3
Kadavu Passage Fiji 53 H3
Kaddam l. India 38 C2
Kade Ghana 46 C4
Kādhimain Iraq 35 G4
Kādhimain Iraq see Kādhimain
Kadi India 36 C5
Kadıköy Turkey 27 M4
Kadınhanı Turkey 34 D3
Kadiolo Mali 46 C3
Kadiri India 38 C3
Kadirli Turkey 34 E3
Kadirpur Pak. 36 C3
Kadiyevka Ukr. see Stakhanov
Kadmat atoll India 38 B4
Ka-do i. N. Korea 45 B5
Kadoma Zimbabwe 49 C5
Kadu Myanmar 37 I4
Kadugli Sudan 32 C7
Kaduna Nigeria 46 D3
Kaduna r. Nigeria 46 D4
Kadusam mt. China/India 37 I3
Kaduy Rus. Fed. 12 H4
Kadyy Rus. Fed. 12 I4
Kadzherom Rus. Fed. 12 L2
Kaédi Mauritania 46 B3
Kaélé Cameroon 47 E3
Kaesŏng N. Korea 45 B5
Kāf Saudi Arabia 39 C4
Kafa Ukr. see Feodosiya
Kafakumba Dem. Rep. Congo 49 C4
Kafan Armenia see Kapan
Kafanchan Nigeria 46 D4
Kafr ash Shaykh Egypt 34 C5
Kafr el Sheikh Egypt see Kafr ash Shaykh
Kafue Zambia 49 C5
Kafue r. Zambia 49 C5
Kafue National Park Zambia 49 C5
Kaga Japan 45 E5
Kaga Bandoro Cent. Afr. Rep. 48 B3
Kagan Pak. 36 C2
Kaganovichabad Tajik. see Kolkhozobod
Kaganovichi Pervyye Ukr. see Polis'ke
Kagarlyk Ukr. see Kaharlyk
Kåge Sweden 14 L4
Kağızman Turkey 35 F2
Kagmar Sudan 32 D7
Kagoshima Japan 45 C7
Kagoshima pref. Japan 45 C7
Kagul Moldova see Cahul
Kahama Tanz. 48 D4
Kaharlyk Ukr. 13 F6
Kaherekoau Mountains N.Z. 59 A7
Kahperusvaarat mts Fin. 14 L2
Kahramanmaraş Turkey 34 E3
Kahror Pak. 36 B3
Kâhta Turkey 34 E3
Kahurangi National Park N.Z. 59 D5
Kahurangi Point N.Z. 59 D5
Kahuta Pak. 36 C2
Kahuzi-Biega, Parc National du nat. park Dem. Rep. Congo 48 C4
Kai, Kepulauan is Indon. 41 F8
Kaiapoi N.Z. 59 D6
Kaibab AZ U.S.A. 65 F2
Kai Besar i. Indon. 41 F8
Kaifeng Henan China 43 K6
Kaihua Yunnan China see Wenshan
Kaiingveld reg. S. Africa 50 E5
Kai Kecil i. Indon. 41 F8
Kaikoura N.Z. 59 D6
Kailas mt. China see Kangrinboqê Feng
Kailasahar India see Kailashahar
Kailashahar India 37 H4
Kailas Range mts China see Gangdisê Shan
Kaili China 43 J7
Kailu China 43 M4
Kaimana Indon. 41 F8
Kaimanawa Mountains N.Z. 59 E4
Kaimar China 37 H2
Kaimur Range hills India 36 E4
Käina Estonia 15 M7
Kainan Japan 45 D6
Kainji Lake National Park Nigeria 46 D4
Kaipara Harbour N.Z. 59 E3
Kairana India 36 D3
Kairouan Tunisia 26 D7
Kaiser Wilhelm II Land reg. Antarctica 76 E2
Kaitaia N.Z. 59 D2
Kaitangata N.Z. 59 B8
Kaitawa N.Z. 59 F4
Kaithal India 36 D3
Kaitum Sweden 14 L3
Kaiwatu Indon. 54 D2
Kaiyuan Liaoning China 44 B4
Kaiyuan Yunnan China 42 I8
Kajaani Fin. 14 O4
Kajabbi Australia 56 C4
Kajaki Afgh. 36 A2
Kajarabie, Lake Australia 58 D1
Kajrān Afgh. 36 A2
Kaka Turkm. 33 I2
Kakadu National Park Australia 54 F3

akamas S. Africa 50 E5
akamega Kenya 48 D3
akar Pak. 36 A4
akata Liberia 46 B4
akenge Dem. Rep. Congo 49 C4
akhi Azer. see Qax
akhovka Ukr. 27 O1
akhovs'ke Vodoskhovyshche resr Ukr. 13 G7
akhul Moldova see Cahul
ākī Iran 35 H5
akinada India 38 D2
akogawa Japan 45 D6
akori India 36 E4
akshaal-Too mts China/Kyrg. 42 D4
aktovik U.S.A. 60 D2
ala Pak. 36 B3
ala Tanz. 49 D4
alaâ Kebira Tunisia 26 D7
alaallit Nunaat terr. N. America see Greenland
alabahi Indon. 41 E8
alabáka Greece see Kalampaka
alabgur India 38 C2
alabo Zambia 49 C5
alach Rus. Fed. 13 I6
alacha Dida Kenya 48 D3
alach-na-Donu Rus. Fed. 13 I6
aladan r. India/Myanmar 37 H5
alagwe Myanmar 37 I5
alahari Desert Africa 50 F2
alahari Gemsbok National Park S. Africa 50 E3
alajoki Fin. 14 M4
alalé Benin 46 D3
alam India 38 C1
alam Pak. 33 L2
alámai Greece see Kalamata
alamare Botswana 51 H2
alamaria Greece 27 J4
alamata Greece 27 J6
alamazoo U.S.A. 63 J3
alampaka Greece 27 I5
alanchak Ukr. 27 O1
alandula Angola see Calandula
alannie Australia 55 B7
alanshiyū ar Ramlī al Kabīr, Sarīr des. Libya 32 B3
alār Iraq 35 G4
alāt Afgh. 36 A2
alāt Sīstān va Balūchestān Iran 33 I4
alat Balochistan Pak. 36 A3
alaus r. Rus. Fed. 13 J7
alaw Myanmar 37 I5
älbäcär Azer. 35 G2
albarri Australia 55 A6
albarri National Park Australia 55 A6
ale Turkey 27 M6
alecik Turkey 34 D2
alemie Dem. Rep. Congo 49 C4
alemyo Myanmar 37 H5
āl-e Namak Iran 35 I4
alevala Rus. Fed. 12 F2
alewa Myanmar 37 H5
aleybar Iran 35 G3
algan China see Zhangjiakou
alghatgi India 38 B3
algoorlie Australia 55 C7
ali Croatia 26 F2
ali r. India/Nepal 36 E3
aliakra, Nos pt Bulg. 27 M3
ali Gandaki r. Nepal 37 F4
aligiri India 38 C3
alikata India see Kolkata
alima Dem. Rep. Congo 48 C4
álimnos i. Greece see Kalymnos
alinin Rus. Fed. see Tver'
aliningrad Rus. Fed. 12 D5
alinino Armenia see Tashir
alinino Rus. Fed. 12 I4
alininsk Rus. Fed. 13 J6
alininskaya Rus. Fed. 13 H7
alinjara India 36 C5
alinkavichy Belarus 13 F5
alinkovichi Belarus see Kalinkavichy
alisch Poland see Kalisz
alispell U.S.A. 62 E2
alisz Poland 17 Q5
alitva r. Rus. Fed. 13 I6
aliua Tanz. 49 D4
aliujar India 36 E4
alix Sweden 14 M4
alkalighat India 37 H4
alkalpen, Nationalpark nat. park Austria 17 O7
alkan Turkey 27 M6
alkfeld Namibia 49 B6
alkfonteindam dam S. Africa 51 G5
alkudah Sri Lanka 38 D5
allaste Estonia 15 O7
allavesi l. Fin. 14 O5
allsedet Sweden 14 H5
allsjön l. Sweden 14 H5
allur India 38 C2
almar Sweden 15 J8
almarsund sea chan. Sweden 15 J8
almūkh Qal'eh Iran 35 J3
almunai Sri Lanka 38 D5
almykia aut. rep. Rus. Fed. see Kalmykiya-Khalm'g-Tangch, Respublika
almykiya-Khalm'g-Tangch, Respublika aut. rep. Rus. Fed. 35 G1
almykovo Kazakh. see Taypak
almytskaya Avtonomnaya Oblast' aut. rep. Rus. Fed. see Kalmykiya-Khalm'g-Tangch, Respublika
alnai India 37 E5
alodnaye Belarus 15 O11
alol India 36 C5
alomo Zambia 49 C5
alone Peak Canada 60 F4
alpa India 36 D3
alpeni atoll India 38 B4
alpetta India 38 C4
alpi India 36 D4
altag U.S.A. 60 C3
altukatjara Australia 55 E6
aluga Rus. Fed. 13 H5
alundborg Denmark 15 G9
alush Ukr. 13 E6
alvakol India 38 C2
älviä Fin. 14 M5
al'ya Rus. Fed. 11 R3
alyan India 38 B2
alyandurg India 33 M7
alyansingapuram India 38 D2
alyazin Rus. Fed. 12 H4
alymnos i. Greece 27 L6
ama Dem. Rep. Congo 48 C4
ama r. Rus. Fed. 12 L4
amaishi Japan 45 F5
amalia Pak. 36 C3
aman Turkey 34 D3
amanjab Namibia 49 B5
amarān i. Yemen 32 F6
amaran Island Yemen see Kamarān
amaron Sierra Leone 46 B4
amasin India 36 E4
ambalda Australia 55 C7
ambam India 38 C4
ambara i. Fiji see Kabara
Kambia Sierra Leone 46 B4
Kambing, Pulau i. East Timor see Ataúro, Ilha de
Kambo-san mt. N. Korea see Kwanmo-bong
Kambove Dem. Rep. Congo 49 C5
Kambūt Libya 34 B5
Kamchatka, Poluostrov pen. Rus. Fed. see Kamchatka Peninsula
Kamchatka Basin sea feature Bering Sea 74 H2
Kamchatka Peninsula Rus. Fed. 29 Q4
Kamchiya r. Bulg. 27 L3
Kameia, Parque Nacional de nat. park Angola see Cameia, Parque Nacional da
Kamelik r. Rus. Fed. 13 K5
Kamen', Gory mts Rus. Fed. 28 K3
Kamenets-Podol'skiy Ukr. see Kam"yanets'-Podil's'kyy
Kamenitsa mt. Bulg. 27 J4
Kamenjak, Rt pt Croatia 26 E2
Kamenka Kazakh. 11 Q5
Kamenka Arkhangel'skaya Oblast' Rus. Fed. 12 J2
Kamenka Penzenskaya Oblast' Rus. Fed. 13 J5
Kamenka Primorskiy Kray Rus. Fed. 44 E3
Kamenka-Bugskaya Ukr. see Kam"yanka-Buz'ka
Kamenka-Strumilovskaya Ukr. see Kam"yanka-Buz'ka
Kamen'-na-Obi Rus. Fed. 42 E2
Kamennogorsk Rus. Fed. 15 P6
Kamennomostskiy Rus. Fed. 35 F1
Kamenolomni Rus. Fed. 13 I7
Kamenongue Angola see Camanongue
Kamen'-Rybolov Rus. Fed. 44 D3
Kamenskoye Rus. Fed. 29 R3
Kamenskoye Ukr. see Dniprodzerzhyns'k
Kamensk-Shakhtinskiy Rus. Fed. 13 I6
Kamensk-Ural'skiy Rus. Fed. 28 H4
Kamet mt. China 36 D3
Kamiesberge mts S. Africa 50 D6
Kamieskroon S. Africa 50 C6
Kamileroi Australia 56 C3
Kamina Dem. Rep. Congo 49 C4
Kaminak Lake Canada 61 I3
Kaminuriak Lake Canada see Qamanirjuaq Lake
Kamishihoro Japan 44 F4
Kamloops Canada 62 C1
Kamo Armenia see Gavarr
Kamoke Pak. 36 C3
Kamonia Dem. Rep. Congo 49 C4
Kampala Uganda 48 D3
Kampara India 38 D1
Kampene Dem. Rep. Congo 48 C4
Kampinoski Park Narodowy nat. park Poland 17 R4
Kâmpóng Cham Cambodia 31 J5
Kâmpóng Saôm Cambodia see Sihanoukville
Kâmpóng Spœ Cambodia 31 J5
Kâmpóng Thum Cambodia 31 J5
Kâmpôt Cambodia 31 J5
Kampuchea country Asia see Cambodia
Kamrau, Teluk b. Indon. 41 F8
Kamsack Canada 62 G1
Kamskoye Vodokhranilishche resr Rus. Fed. 11 R4
Kamsuuma Somalia 48 E3
Kamuli Uganda 48 D3
Kam"yanets'-Podil's'kyy Ukr. 13 E6
Kam"yanka-Buz'ka Ukr. 13 E6
Kamyanyets Belarus 15 M10
Kāmyārān Iran 35 G4
Kamyshin Rus. Fed. 13 J6
Kamyzyak Rus. Fed. 13 K7
Kanab U.S.A. 62 E4
Kanab Creek r. AZ U.S.A. 65 F2
Kanak Pak. 36 A3
Kananga Dem. Rep. Congo 49 C4
Kanangra-Boyd National Park Australia 58 E4
Kanarak India see Konarka
Kanarraville UT U.S.A. 65 F2
Kanas watercourse Namibia 50 C4
Kanash Rus. Fed. 12 J5
Kanauj India see Kannauj
Kanazawa Japan 45 E5
Kanbalu Myanmar 37 H5
Kanchanjanga mt. India/Nepal see Kangchenjunga
Kanchipuram India 38 C3
Kand mt. Pak. 36 A3
Kanda Pak. 36 A3
Kandahār Afgh. 36 A3
Kandalaksha Rus. Fed. 12 G2
Kandalakshskiy Zaliv g. Rus. Fed. 12 G2
Kandar Indon. 54 E2
Kandavu i. Fiji see Kadavu
Kandavu Passage Fiji see Kadavu Passage
Kandé Togo 46 D4
Kandh Kot Pak. 36 B3
Kandi Benin 46 D3
Kandi India 38 C2
Kandiaro Pak. 36 B4
Kandıra Turkey 27 N4
Kandos Australia 58 D4
Kandreho Madag. 49 E5
Kandukur India 38 C3
Kandy Sri Lanka 38 D5
Kandyagash Kazakh. 28 G5
Kane PA U.S.A. 64 B2
Kane Bassin b. Greenland 77 K1
Kaneh watercourse Iran 35 I6
Kaneti Pak. 36 A3
Kanevskaya Rus. Fed. 13 H7
Kang Botswana 50 F2
Kangaamiut Greenland 61 M3
Kangaarsussuaq c. Greenland 61 K2
Kangaba Mali 46 C3
Kangal Turkey 34 E3
Kangān Būshehr Iran 35 I6
Kangandala, Parque Nacional de nat. park Angola see Cangandala, Parque Nacional de
Kangar Malaysia 41 C7
Kangaroo Island Australia 57 B7
Kangaroo Point Australia 56 B3
Kangaslampi Fin. 14 P5
Kangasniemi Fin. 14 O6
Kangāvar Iran 35 G4
Kangchenjunga mt. India/Nepal 37 G4
Kangding China 42 I6
Kangean, Kepulauan is Indon. 41 D8
Kangen r. Sudan 47 G4
Kangerlussuaq Greenland 61 M3
Kangerlussuaq inlet Greenland 61 M3
Kangerlussuaq inlet Greenland 77 J2
Kangersuatsiaq Greenland 61 M2
Kangertittivaq sea chan. Greenland 61 P2
Kanggye N. Korea 44 B4
Kanghwa S. Korea 45 B5
Kangikajik c. Greenland 61 P2
Kangirsuk Canada 61 K3
Kangmar China 37 F3
Kangnŭng S. Korea 45 C5
Kango Gabon 48 B3
Kangping China 44 A4
Kangri Karpo Pass China/India 37 I3
Kangrinboqê Feng mt. China 36 E3
Kangsangdobdê China see Xainza
Kangto mt. China/India 37 H4
Kangtog China 37 F2
Kanifing Gambia 46 B3
Kanigiri India 38 C3
Kanin, Poluostrov pen. Rus. Fed. 12 J2
Kanin Nos Rus. Fed. 77 G2
Kanin Nos, Mys c. Rus. Fed. 12 I1
Kaninskiy Bereg coastal area Rus. Fed. 12 I2
Kanjiroba mt. Nepal 37 E3
Kankaanpää Fin. 15 M6
Kankakee U.S.A. 63 J3
Kankan Guinea 46 C3
Kanker India 38 D1
Kankesanturai Sri Lanka 38 D4
Kankossa Mauritania 46 B3
Kannauj India 36 D4
Kanniya Kumari c. India see Comorin, Cape
Kannonkoski Fin. 14 N5
Kannur India see Cannanore
Kannus Fin. 14 M5
Kano Nigeria 46 D3
Kanonpunt pt S. Africa 50 E8
Kanosh UT U.S.A. 65 F1
Kanovlei Namibia 49 B5
Kanoya Japan 45 C7
Kanpur Orissa India 38 E1
Kanpur Uttar Prad. India 36 E4
Kansai airport Japan 45 D6
Kansas r. U.S.A. 62 I4
Kansas state U.S.A. 62 H4
Kansas City KS U.S.A. 63 I4
Kansk Rus. Fed. 29 K4
Kansu prov. China see Gansu
Kantara h. Cyprus 39 A2
Kantavu i. Fiji see Kadavu
Kantchari Burkina 46 D3
Kantemirovka Rus. Fed. 13 H6
Kanthi India 37 F5
Kantishna r. U.S.A. 60 C3
Kanton atoll Kiribati 53 I2
Kanturk Ireland 21 D5
Kanuku Mountains Guyana 69 G3
Kanur India 38 C3
Kanus Namibia 50 D4
Kanyakubja India see Kannauj
Kanyamazane S. Africa 51 J3
Kanye Botswana 51 G3
Kaohsiung Taiwan 43 M8
Kaokoveld plat. Namibia 49 B5
Kaolack Senegal 46 B3
Kaoma Zambia 49 C5
Kaouadja Cent. Afr. Rep. 48 C3
Kapa S. Africa see Cape Town
Kapan Armenia 35 G3
Kapanga Dem. Rep. Congo 49 C4
Kaparhā Iran 35 H5
Kapatu Zambia 49 D4
Kapchagay Kazakh. 42 D4
Kapchagayskoye Vodokhranilishche resr Kazakh. 42 D4
Kap Dan Greenland see Kulusuk
Kapello, Akrotirio pt Greece 27 J6
Kapellskär Sweden 15 K7
Kapelskär Sweden see Kapellskär
Kapili r. India 37 G4
Kapingamarangi atoll Micronesia 74 G5
Kapingamarangi Rise sea feature N. Pacific Ocean 74 G5
Kapıorman Dağları mts Turkey 27 N4
Kapip Pak. 36 B3
Kapiri Mposhi Zambia 49 C5
Kapisillit Greenland 61 M3
Kapiskau r. Canada 63 K1
Kapiti Island N.Z. 59 E5
Kaplankyr, Chink esc. Asia 35 I2
Kaplankyr Döwlet Gorugy nature res. Turkm. 35 J2
Kapoeta Sudan 47 G4
Kaposvár Hungary 26 G1
Kappeln Germany 17 L3
Kapsukas Lith. see Marijampolė
Kaptai Bangl. 37 H5
Kapuriya India 36 C4
Kapurthala India 36 C3
Kapuskasing Canada 63 K2
Kapustin Yar Rus. Fed. 13 J6
Kaputar mt. Australia 58 E3
Kaputir Kenya 48 D3
Kapuvár Hungary 26 G1
Kapydzhik, Gora mt. Armenia/Azer. see Qazangödağ
Kapyl' Belarus 15 O10
Kara India 36 E4
Kara Togo 46 D4
Kara r. Turkey 35 F3
Kara-Balta Kyrg. 42 C4
Karabalyk Kazakh. 30 F1
Karabekaul' Turkm. see Garabekewül
Karabiga Turkey 27 L4
Kara-Bogaz-Gol, Proliv sea chan. Turkm. see Garabogazköl Bogazy
Kara-Bogaz-Gol'skiy Zaliv b. Turkm. see Garabogazköl Aýlagy
Karabük Turkey 34 D2
Karaburun Turkey 27 L5
Karabutak Kazakh. 28 H5
Karacabey Turkey 27 M4
Karacaköy Turkey 27 M4
Karacalı Dağ mt. Turkey 35 E3
Karaçal Tepe mt. Turkey 39 A1
Karacasu Turkey 27 M6
Karaca Yarımadası pen. Turkey 27 N6
Karachayevsk Rus. Fed. 13 I8
Karachev Rus. Fed. 13 G5
Karachi Pak. 33 K5
Karacurun Turkey see Hilvan
Karad India 38 B2
Kara Dağ h. Turkey 39 D1
Kara Dağ mt. Turkey 34 D3
Kara Deniz sea Asia/Europe see Black Sea
Karagan Rus. Fed. 44 A1
Karaganda Kazakh. 42 C3
Karagayly Kazakh. 42 D3
Karaginskiy Zaliv b. Rus. Fed. 29 R4
Karagiye, Vpadina depr. Kazakh. 35 H2
Karagola India 37 F4
Karahallı Turkey 27 M5
Karahasanlı Turkey 34 D3
Karaikal India 38 C4
Karaikkudi India 38 C4
Karaisalı Turkey 34 D3
Karaj Iran 35 H4
Karak Jordan see Al Karak
Karakalli Turkey see Özalp
Karakax China see Moyu
Karakax He r. China 36 E1
Karakax Shan mts China 36 E2
Karaki China 36 E1
Karaklis Armenia see Vanadzor
Karakoçan Turkey 35 F3
Kara-Köl Kyrg. 31 G2
Karakol Kyrg. 42 D4
Karakoram Pass China/India 36 D2
Karakoram Range mts Asia 33 M2
Kara K'orē Eth. 48 D2
Karakorum Range mts Asia see Karakoram Range
Karaköse Turkey see Ağrı
Kara Kul' Kyrg. see Kara-Köl
Karakul', Ozero l. Tajik. see Qarokŭl
Kara Kum des. Turkm. see Karakum Desert
Karakum, Peski Kazakh. see Karakum Desert
Karakum Desert Kazakh. 30 E2
Karakum Desert Turkm. 30 F3
Karakurt Turkey 35 F2
Karakuş Dağı ridge Turkey 27 N5
Karal Chad 47 E3
Karala Estonia 15 L7
Karalundi Australia 55 B6
Karaman Turkey 34 D3
Karaman prov. Turkey 39 A1
Karamanlı Turkey 27 M6
Karamay China 42 E3
Karambar Pass Afgh./Pak. 36 C1
Karamea N.Z. 59 D5
Karamea Bight b. N.Z. 59 C5
Karamiran China 37 F1
Karamiran Shankou pass China 37 F1
Karamürsel Turkey 27 M4
Karamyshevo Rus. Fed. 15 P8
Karān i. Saudi Arabia 35 H6
Karangasem Indon. 54 A2
Karanja India 38 C1
Karanjia India 36 E5
Karapınar Gaziantep Turkey 39 C1
Karapınar Konya Turkey 34 D3
Karas admin. reg. Namibia 50 C4
Karasay China 37 E1
Karasburg Namibia 50 D5
Kara Sea Rus. Fed. 28 I2
Kárášjohka Finnmark Norway see Karasjok
Karasjok Norway 14 N2
Kara Strait Rus. Fed. see Karskiye Vorota, Proliv
Karasu r. Syria/Turkey 39 C1
Karasu Bitlis Turkey see Hizan
Karasu Sakarya Turkey 27 N4
Karasu r. Turkey 35 F3
Karasubazar Ukr. see Bilohirs'k
Karasuk Rus. Fed. 28 I4
Karataş Turkey 39 B1
Karataş Burnu hd Turkey see Fener Burnu
Karatau Kazakh. 42 C4
Karatau, Khrebet mts Kazakh. 42 B4
Karatepe Turkey 39 A1
Karativu i. Sri Lanka 38 C4
Karatsu Japan 45 C6
Karaudanawa Guyana 69 G3
Karauli India 36 D4
Karavan Kyrg. see Kerben
Karavostasi Cyprus 39 A2
Karayılan Turkey 39 C1
Karayulgan China 42 E4
Karazhal Kazakh. 42 C3
Karbalā' Iraq 35 G4
Karcag Hungary 27 I1
Kardhítsa Greece see Karditsa
Karditsa Greece 27 I5
Kärdla Estonia 15 M7
Karee S. Africa 51 H5
Kareeberge mts S. Africa 50 E6
Kareima Sudan 32 D6
Kareli India 36 D5
Karelia aut. rep. Rus. Fed. see Kareliya, Respublika
Kareliya, Respublika aut. rep. Rus. Fed. 14 R5
Karel'skaya A.S.S.R. aut. rep. Rus. Fed. see Kareliya, Respublika
Karel'skiy Bereg coastal area Rus. Fed. 12 G2
Karema Tanz. 49 D4
Karera India 36 D4
Karesuando Sweden 14 M2
Kargalinskaya Rus. Fed. 35 G2
Kargalinski Rus. Fed. see Kargalinskaya
Kargapazarı Dağları mts Turkey 35 F3
Karghalik China see Yecheng
Kargı Turkey 34 D2
Kargil India 36 D2
Kargilik China see Yecheng
Kargıpınarı Turkey 39 B1
Kargopol' Rus. Fed. 12 H3
Kari Nigeria 46 E3
Kariba Zimbabwe 49 C5
Kariba, Lake resr Zambia/Zimbabwe 49 C5
Kariba Dam Zambia/Zimbabwe 49 C5
Kariba-yama vol. Japan 44 E4
Karibib Namibia 50 B1
Karigasniemi Fin. 14 N2
Karijini National Park Australia 55 B5
Karijoki Fin. 14 L5
Karikachi-tōge pass Japan 44 F4
Karikari, Cape N.Z. 59 D2
Karimata, Selat str. Indon. 41 C8
Karimganj India 37 H4
Karimnagar India 38 C2
Káristos Greece see Karystos
Karjat Mahar. India 38 B2
Karjat Mahar. India 38 B2
Karkaralinsk Kazakh. 42 D3
Karkar Island P.N.G. 52 E2
Karkh Pak. 36 A4
Karkinits'ka Zatoka g. Ukr. 27 O2
Kärkölä Fin. 15 N6
Karkonoski Park Narodowy nat. park Czech Rep./Poland see Krkonošský narodní park
Karksi-Nuia Estonia 15 N7
Karkūk Iraq see Kirkūk
Karlachi Pak. 36 B2
Karlholmsbruk Sweden 15 J6
Karlik Shan mts China 42 G4
Karlıova Turkey 35 F3
Karlivka Ukr. 13 G6
Karl Marks, Qullai mt. Tajik. 36 C1
Karl-Marx-Stadt Germany see Chemnitz
Karlovac Croatia 26 F2
Karlovka Ukr. see Karlivka
Karlovo Bulg. 27 K3
Karlovy Vary Czech Rep. 17 N5
Karlsborg Sweden 15 I7
Karlsburg Romania see Alba Iulia
Karlshamn Sweden 15 I8
Karlskoga Sweden 15 I7
Karlskrona Sweden 15 I8
Karlsruhe Germany 17 L6
Karlstad Sweden 15 H7
Karluk U.S.A. 60 C4
Karmala India 38 B2
Karmel, Har h. Israel see Carmel, Mount
Karmona Spain see Córdoba
Karmøy i. Norway 15 D7
Karmpur Pak. 36 C3
Karnafuli Reservoir Bangl. 37 H5
Karnal India 36 D3
Karnataka state India 38 B3
Karnavati India see Ahmadabad
Karnobat Bulg. 27 L3
Karodi Pak. 36 A4
Karoi Zimbabwe 49 C5
Karo La pass China 37 G3
Karong India 37 H4
Karonga Malawi 49 D4
Karonie Australia 55 C7
Karoo National Park S. Africa 50 F7
Karoonda Australia 57 B7
Karora Eritrea 32 E6
Káros i. Greece see Keros
Karossa, Tanjung pt Indon. 54 B2
Karpasia pen. Cyprus 39 B2
Karpas Peninsula Cyprus see Karpasia
Karpathos i. Greece 27 L7
Karpathou, Steno sea chan. Greece 27 L6
Karpaty mts Europe see Carpathian Mountains
Karpenisi Greece 27 I5
Karpilovka Belarus see Aktsyabrski
Karpinsk Rus. Fed. 11 S4
Karpogory Rus. Fed. 12 J2
Karpuz r. Turkey 39 A1
Karratha Australia 54 B5
Karroo plat. S. Africa see Great Karoo
Kars Turkey 35 F2
Kärsämäki Fin. 14 N5
Kārsava Latvia 15 O8
Karshi Qashqadaryo Uzbek. see Qarshi
Karskiye Vorota, Proliv str. Rus. Fed. 28 G3
Karskoye More sea Rus. Fed. see Kara Sea
Karstula Fin. 14 N5
Karsu Turkey 39 C1
Karsun Rus. Fed. 13 J5
Kartal Turkey 27 M4
Kartaly Rus. Fed. 28 H4
Kartayel' Rus. Fed. 12 L2
Karttula Fin. 14 O5
Karumba Australia 56 C3
Karumbhar Island India 36 B5
Kārūn, Rūd-e r. Iran 35 H5
Karuni Indon. 54 B2
Karur India 38 C4
Karvia Fin. 14 M5
Karviná Czech Rep. 17 Q6
Karwar India 38 B3
Karyagino Azer. see Füzuli
Karymskoye Rus. Fed. 43 K2
Karynzharyk, Peski des. Kazakh. 35 I2
Karystos Greece 27 K5
Kaş Turkey 27 M6
Kasa India 38 B2
Kasaba Turkey see Turgutlu
Kasaï r. Dem. Rep. Congo 48 B4
Kasaï, Plateau du Dem. Rep. Congo 49 C4
Kasaji Dem. Rep. Congo 49 C5
Kasama Zambia 49 D5
Kasane Botswana 49 C5
Kasaragod India 38 B3
Kasargod India see Kasaragod
Kasargode India see Kasaragod
Kasatkino Rus. Fed. 44 C2
Kasba Lake Canada 61 H3
Kasba Tadla Morocco 22 C5
Kasenga Dem. Rep. Congo 49 C5
Kasengu Dem. Rep. Congo 49 C4
Kasese Dem. Rep. Congo 48 C4
Kasese Uganda 48 D3
Kasevo Rus. Fed. see Neftekamsk
Kasganj India 36 D4
Kāshān Iran 35 H4
Kashary Rus. Fed. 13 I6
Kashgar China see Kashi
Kashi China 42 D5
Kashihara Japan 45 D6
Kashima-nada b. Japan 45 F5
Kashin Rus. Fed. 12 H4
Kashipur India 36 D3
Kashira Rus. Fed. 13 H5
Kashiwazaki Japan 45 E5
Kashkarantsy Rus. Fed. 12 H2
Kāshmar Iran 33 I2
Kashmir terr. Asia see Jammu and Kashmir
Kashmir, Vale of reg. India 36 C2
Kashyukulu Dem. Rep. Congo 49 C4
Kasi India see Varanasi
Kasigar Afgh. 36 B2
Kasimov Rus. Fed. 13 I5
Kaskinen Fin. 14 L5
Kaskö Fin. see Kaskinen
Kasongo Dem. Rep. Congo 49 C4
Kasongo-Lunda Dem. Rep. Congo 49 B4
Kasos i. Greece 27 L7
Kaspīy Mangy Oypaty lowland Kazakh./Rus. Fed. see Caspian Lowland
Kaspiysk Rus. Fed. 35 G2
Kaspiyskiy Rus. Fed. see Lagan'
Kaspiyskoye More l. Asia/Europe see Caspian Sea
Kassa Slovakia see Košice
Kassala Sudan 32 E6
Kassandras, Akrotirio pt Greece 27 J5
Kassandras, Kolpos b. Greece 27 J4
Kassel Germany 17 L5
Kasserine Tunisia 26 C7
Kastamonu Turkey 34 D2
Kastéllion Greece see Kissamos
Kastellorizon i. Greece see Megisti
Kastoria Greece 27 I4
Kastornoye Rus. Fed. 13 H6
Kastsyukovichy Belarus 13 G5
Kasulu Tanz. 49 D4
Kasumkent Rus. Fed. 35 H2
Kasungu Malawi 49 D5
Kasungu National Park Malawi 49 D5
Kasur Pak. 36 C3
Katâdtlit Nunât terr. N. America see Greenland
Katahdin, Mount U.S.A. 63 N2
Kataklik India 36 D2
Katako-Kombe Dem. Rep. Congo 48 C4
Katakwi Uganda 48 D3
Katana India 36 C5
Katangi India 36 D5
Katanning Australia 55 B8
Katavi National Park Tanz. 49 D4
Katea Dem. Rep. Congo 49 C4
Katerini Greece 27 J4
Katesh Tanz. 49 D4
Kate's Needle mt. Canada/U.S.A. 60 E4
Katete Zambia 49 D5
Katherîna, Gebel mt. Egypt see Kātrīnā, Jabal
Katherine Australia 54 F3
Katherine Gorge National Park Australia see Nitmiluk National Park
Kathiawar pen. India 36 B5
Kathihar India see Katihar
Kathiraveli Sri Lanka 38 D4
Kathiwara India 36 C5
Kathleen Falls Australia 54 E3
Kathmandu Nepal 37 F4
Kathu S. Africa 50 F4
Kathua India 36 C2
Kati Mali 46 C3
Katihar India 37 F4
Katikati S. Africa 51 H7
Katima Mulilo Namibia 49 C5
Katiola Côte d'Ivoire 46 C4
Kā Tiritiri o te Moana mts N.Z. see Southern Alps
Katkop Hills S. Africa 50 E6
Katlehong S. Africa 51 I4
Katmai National Park and Preserve U.S.A. 60 C4
Katmandu Nepal see Kathmandu
Kato Achaïa Greece 27 I5
Katoomba Australia 58 E4
Katowice Poland 17 Q5
Katoya India 37 G5
Katrancık Dağı mts Turkey 27 M6
Kātrīnā, Jabal mt. Egypt 34 D5
Katrine, Loch l. U.K. 20 E4
Katrineholm Sweden 15 J7
Katse Dam Lesotho 51 I5
Katsina Nigeria 46 D3
Katsina-Ala Nigeria 46 D4
Katsuura Japan 45 F6
Kattamudda Well Australia 54 D5
Kattaqo'rg'on Uzbek. 33 K2
Kattaqŭrghon Uzbek. see Kattaqo'rg'on
Kattasang Hills Afgh. 36 A2
Kattegat str. Denmark/Sweden 15 G8
Kattowitz Poland see Katowice
Katumbar India 36 D4
Katunino Rus. Fed. 12 J4
Katuri Pak. 36 B3
Katwa India see Katoya
Kaua'i i. U.S.A. 75 J4
Kauhajoki Fin. 14 M5
Kauhava Fin. 14 M5
Kaukkwè Hills Myanmar 37 I4
Kaukonen Fin. 14 N3
Kaunas Lith. 15 M9
Kaunata Latvia 15 O8
Kaundy, Vpadina depr. Kazakh. 35 I2
Kaunia Bangl. 37 G4
Kaura-Namoda Nigeria 46 D3
Kaustinen Fin. 14 M5
Kautokeino Norway 14 M2
Kavadarci Macedonia 27 J4
Kavak Turkey 34 E2
Kavaklıdere Turkey 27 M6
Kavala Greece 27 K4
Kavalas, Kolpos b. Greece 27 K4
Kavalerovo Rus. Fed. 44 D3
Kavali India 38 D3
Kavār Iran 35 I5
Kavaratti India 38 B4
Kavaratti atoll India 38 B4
Kavarna Bulg. 27 M3
Kavendou, Mont mt. Guinea 46 B3
Kaveri r. India 38 C4
Kavīr Iran 35 H4
Kavīr, Dasht-e des. Iran 35 I4
Kavkasioni mts Asia/Europe see Caucasus
Kawagoe Japan 45 E6
Kawaguchi Japan 45 E6
Kawakawa N.Z. 59 E2
Kawambwa Zambia 49 C4
Kawana Zambia 49 C5
Kawardha India 36 E5
Kawasaki Japan 45 E6
Kawau Island N.Z. 59 E3
Kawerau N.Z. 59 F4
Kawhia N.Z. 59 E4
Kawhia Harbour N.Z. 59 E4
Kawich Peak NV U.S.A. 65 D2
Kawich Range mts NV U.S.A. 65 D2
Kawlin Myanmar 37 H5
Kawm Umbū Egypt 32 D5
Kaxgar China see Kashi
Kaxgar He r. China 33 M2
Kax He r. China 42 E4
Kaxtax Shan mts China 37 E1
Kaya Burkina 46 C3
Kayadibi Turkey 34 E3
Kayankulam India 38 C4
Kayar India 38 C2
Kaydak, Sor dry lake Kazakh. 35 I1
Kaydanovo Belarus see Dzyarzhynsk
Kayembe-Mukulu Dem. Rep. Congo 49 C4
Kayenta U.S.A. 62 E4
Kayes Mali 46 B3
Kaymaz Turkey 27 N5
Kaynar Kazakh. 42 D3
Kaynar Turkey 34 E3
Kayseri Turkey 34 D3
Kayuyu Dem. Rep. Congo 48 C4
Kazach'ye Rus. Fed. 29 O2
Kazakh Azer. see Qazax
Kazakhskaya S.S.R. country Asia see Kazakhstan
Kazakhskiy Melkosopochnik plain Kazakh. 42 C2
Kazakhskiy Zaliv b. Kazakh. 35 I2
Kazakhstan country Asia 30 F2
Kazakhstan Kazakh. see Aksay
Kazakstan country Asia see Kazakhstan
Kazan' Rus. Fed. 12 K5
Kazandzhik Turkm. see Bereket
Kazanka r. Rus. Fed. 12 K5
Kazanlı Turkey 39 B1
Kazanlŭk Bulg. 27 K3
Kazan-rettō is Japan see Volcano Islands
Kazatin Ukr. see Kozyatyn
Kazbek mt. Georgia/Rus. Fed. 13 J8
Kaz Dağı mts Turkey 27 L5
Kāzerūn Iran 35 H5
Kazhim Rus. Fed. 12 K3
Kazidi Tajik. see Qozideh
Kazi Magomed Azer. see Qazımämmäd
Kazincbarcika Hungary 13 D6
Kaziranga National Park India 37 H4
Kazret'i Georgia 35 G2
Kaztalovka Kazakh. 11 P6
Kazym r. Rus. Fed. 11 T3
Kazymskiy Mys Rus. Fed. 11 T3
Keady U.K. 21 F3
Kéamu i. Vanuatu see Anatom
Kearney U.S.A. 62 H3
Keban Turkey 34 E3
Keban Barajı resr Turkey 34 E3
Kébémèr Senegal 46 B3
Kebili Tunisia 22 F5
Kebīr, Nahr al r. Lebanon/Syria 39 B2
Kebkabiya Sudan 47 F3
Kebnekaise mt. Sweden 14 K3
Kebock Head hd U.K. 20 C2
K'ebrī Dehar Eth. 48 E3
Kechika r. Canada 77 A3
Keçiborlu Turkey 27 N6
Kecskemét Hungary 27 H1
K'eda Georgia 35 F2
Kėdainiai Lith. 15 M9
Kedairu Passage Fiji see Kadavu Passage
Kedong China 44 B3
Kedva r. Rus. Fed. 12 L2
Kędzierzyn-Koźle Poland 17 Q5
Keele r. Canada 60 F3
Keele Peak Canada 60 E3
Keeler CA U.S.A. 65 D2
Keeling Islands terr. Indian Ocean see Cocos Islands
Keen, Mount h. U.K. 20 G4
Keene CA U.S.A. 65 C3
Keene NH U.S.A. 64 E1
Keeper Hill h. Ireland 21 D5
Keepit, Lake resr Australia 58 E3
Keep River National Park Australia 54 E3
Keer-weer, Cape Australia 56 C2
Keetmanshoop Namibia 50 D4
Keewatin Canada 63 I2
Kefallinía i. Greece see Cephalonia
Kefallonia i. Greece see Cephalonia
Kefamenanu Indon. 41 E8
Kefe Ukr. see Feodosiya
Keffi Nigeria 46 D4
Keflavík Iceland 14 [inset]
Kegalla Sri Lanka 38 D5
Kegen Kazakh. 42 D4

Keg River Canada 60 G4
Kegul'ta Rus. Fed. 13 J7
Kehra Estonia 15 N7
Keighley U.K. 18 F5
Keila Estonia 15 N7
Keimoes S. Africa 50 E5
Keitele Fin. 14 O5
Keitele *l.* Fin. 14 O5
Keith Australia 57 C8
Keith U.K. 20 G3
Kékes *mt.* Hungary 17 R7
Kekri India 36 C4
K'elafo Eth. 48 E3
Kelai *i.* Maldives 38 B5
Kelibia Tunisia 26 D6
Kelif Uzboýy *marsh* Turkm. 33 J2
Kelkit Turkey 35 E2
Kelkit *r.* Turkey 34 E2
Kéllé Congo 48 B4
Keller Lake Canada 60 F3
Kellett, Cape Canada 60 F2
Kelloselkä Fin. 14 P3
Kells Ireland 21 F4
Kells *r.* U.K. 21 F3
Kelly Range *hills* Australia 55 C6
Kelmė Lith. 15 M9
Kélo Chad 47 E4
Kelowna Canada 62 D2
Kelseyville *CA* U.S.A. 65 A1
Kelso U.K. 20 G5
Kelso *CA* U.S.A. 65 E3
Keluang Malaysia 41 C7
Kelvington Canada 62 G1
Kem' Rus. Fed. 12 G2
Kem' *r.* Rus. Fed. 12 G2
Ke Macina Mali *see* Massina
Kemah Turkey 34 E3
Kemaliye Turkey 34 E3
Kemalpaşa Turkey 27 L5
Kemano (abandoned) Canada 60 F4
Kembé Cent. Afr. Rep. 48 C3
Kemeneshát *hills* Hungary 26 G1
Kemer *Antalya* Turkey 27 N6
Kemer *Muğla* Turkey 27 M6
Kemer Barajı *resr* Turkey 27 M6
Kemerovo Rus. Fed. 28 J4
Kemi Fin. 14 N4
Kemijärvi Fin. 14 O3
Kemijärvi *l.* Fin. 14 O3
Kemijoki *r.* Fin. 14 N4
Kemiö Fin. *see* Kimito
Kemir Turkm. *see* Keymir
Kemmerer U.S.A. 62 E3
Kemnay U.K. 20 G3
Kemp Coast *reg.* Antarctica *see* Kemp Land
Kempele Fin. 14 N4
Kemp Land *reg.* Antarctica 76 D2
Kemp Peninsula Antarctica 76 A2
Kempsey Australia 58 F3
Kempt, Lac *l.* Canada 63 M2
Kempten (Allgäu) Germany 17 M7
Kempton Park S. Africa 51 I4
Ken *r.* India 36 E4
Kenai U.S.A. 60 C3
Kenai Fiords National Park U.S.A. 60 C4
Kenai Mountains U.S.A. 60 C4
Kenâyis, Râs el *pt* Egypt *see* Ḥikmah, Ra's al
Kenbridge *VA* U.S.A. 64 B4
Kendal U.K. 18 E4
Kendall Australia 58 F3
Kendall, Cape Canada 61 J3
Kendari Indon. 41 E8
Kendawangan Indon. 41 D8
Kendégué Chad 47 E3
Kendrapara India 37 F5
Kendraparha India *see* Kendrapara
Kendujhar India *see* Keonjhar
Kendujhargarh India *see* Keonjhar
Kendyrli-Kayasanskoye, Plato *plat.* Kazakh. 35 I2
Kendyrlisor, Solonchak *salt l.* Kazakh. 35 I2
Kenebri Australia 58 D3
Kenema Sierra Leone 46 B4
Kenge Dem. Rep. Congo 49 B4
Kenhardt S. Africa 50 E5
Kéniéba Mali 46 B3
Kénitra Morocco 22 C5
Kenmare Ireland 21 C6
Kenmare River *inlet* Ireland 21 B6
Kenmore *NY* U.S.A. 64 B1
Kennebunkport *ME* U.S.A. 64 F1
Kennedy, Cape U.S.A. *see* Canaveral, Cape
Kennedy Range National Park Australia 55 A6
Kennet *r.* U.K. 19 G7
Kenneth Range *hills* Australia 55 B5
Kennewick U.S.A. 62 D2
Kenn Reef Australia 56 F4
Kenora Canada 63 I2
Kenosha U.S.A. 63 J3
Kenozero, Ozero *l.* Rus. Fed. 12 H3
Kent *r.* U.K. 18 E4
Kent *OH* U.S.A. 64 A2
Kent *VA* U.S.A. 64 A4
Kentani S. Africa 51 I7
Kent Group *is* Australia 57 [inset]
Kent Peninsula Canada 60 H3
Kentucky *state* U.S.A. 63 K4
Kenya *country* Africa 48 D3
Kenya, Mount Kenya 48 D4
Keokuk U.S.A. 63 I3
Keoladeo National Park India 36 D4
Keonjhar India 37 F5
Keonjhargarh India *see* Keonjhar
Kepina *r.* Rus. Fed. 12 I2
Keppel Bay Australia 56 E4
Kepsut Turkey 27 M5
Kera India 37 F5
Kerala *state* India 38 B4
Kerang Australia 58 A5
Kerava Fin. 15 N6
Kerba Alg. 25 G5
Kerbela Iraq *see* Karbalā'
Kerben Kyrg. 42 C4
Kerbi *r.* Rus. Fed. 44 E1
Kerch Ukr. 34 E1
Kerchem'ya Rus. Fed. 12 L3
Kerema P.N.G. 52 E2
Kerempe Burun *pt* Turkey 34 D2
Keren Eritrea 32 E6
Kerewan Gambia 46 B3
Kerguélen, Îles *is* Indian Ocean 73 M9
Kerguelen Islands Indian Ocean *see* Kerguélen, Îles
Kerguelen Plateau *sea feature* Indian Ocean 73 M9
Kericho Kenya 48 D4
Kerikeri N.Z. 59 D2
Kerimäki Fin. 14 P6
Kerinci, Gunung *vol.* Indon. 41 C8
Kerintji *vol.* Indon. *see* Kerinci, Gunung
Keriya He *watercourse* China 42 E5
Keriya Shankou *pass* China 37 E2
Kerkennah, Îles *is* Tunisia 26 D7
Kerkini, Limni *l.* Greece 27 J4
Kérkira *i.* Greece *see* Corfu
Kerkouane *tourist site* Tunisia 26 D6
Kerkyra Greece 27 H5
Kerkyra *i.* Greece *see* Corfu
Kerma Sudan 32 D6
Kermadec Islands S. Pacific Ocean 53 I5
Kermadec Trench *sea feature* S. Pacific Ocean 74 I8
Kermān Iran 33 I3
Kerman *CA* U.S.A. 65 B2
Kermānshāh Iran 35 G4
Kermānshāhān Iran 35 I5
Kermine Uzbek. *see* Navoiy
Kermit U.S.A. 62 G5
Kern *r. CA* U.S.A. 65 C3
Keros *i.* Greece 27 K6
Keros Rus. Fed. 12 L3
Kérouané Guinea 46 C4
Kerr, Cape Antarctica 76 H1
Kerrville U.S.A. 62 H5
Kerry Head *hd* Ireland 21 C5
Kerteminde Denmark 15 G9
Kerulen *r.* China/Mongolia *see* Herlen Gol
Kerur India 38 B2
Keryneia Cyprus *see* Kyrenia
Kerzaz Alg. 46 C2
Kerzhenets *r.* Rus. Fed. 12 J4
Kesagami Lake Canada 63 K1
Kesälahti Fin. 14 P6
Keşan Turkey 27 L4
Keşap Turkey 13 H8
Kesariya India 37 F4
Kesennuma Japan 45 F5
Keshan China 44 B2
Keshem Afgh. 36 B1
Keshendeh-ye Bala Afgh. 36 A1
Keshod India 36 B5
Keshvar Iran 35 H4
Keskin Turkey 34 D3
Keskozero Rus. Fed. 12 G3
Kesova Gora Rus. Fed. 12 H4
Kestell S. Africa 51 I5
Kesten'ga Rus. Fed. 14 Q4
Kestilä Fin. 14 O4
Keswick U.K. 18 D4
Keszthely Hungary 26 G1
Ketapang Indon. 41 D8
Keti Bandar Pak. 36 A4
Ketmen', Khrebet *mts* China/Kazakh. 42 E4
Kettering U.K. 19 G6
Kettle Creek *r. PA* U.S.A. 64 C2
Kettleman City *CA* U.S.A. 65 C2
Keuka *NY* U.S.A. 64 C1
Keuka Lake *NY* U.S.A. 64 C1
Keumgang, Mount N. Korea *see* Kumgang-san
Keumsang, Mount N. Korea *see* Kumgang-san
Keuruu Fin. 14 N5
Keweenaw Peninsula U.S.A. 63 J2
Key, Lough *l.* Ireland 21 D3
Keyala Sudan 47 G4
Keyihe China 44 A2
Key Largo U.S.A. 63 K6
Keymir Turkm. 35 I3
Keynsham U.K. 19 E7
Keyser *WV* U.S.A. 64 B3
Keysville *VA* U.S.A. 64 B4
Keyvy, Vozvyshennost' *hills* Rus. Fed. 12 H2
Key West U.S.A. 63 K7
Kez Rus. Fed. 11 Q4
Kezi Zimbabwe 49 C6
Kgalagadi *admin. dist.* Botswana 50 E3
Kgalazadi *admin. dist.* Botswana *see* Kgalagadi
Kgatlen *admin. dist.* Botswana *see* Kgatleng
Kgatleng *admin. dist.* Botswana 51 H3
Kgomofatshe Pan *salt pan* Botswana 50 E2
Kgoro Pan *salt pan* Botswana 50 G3
Kgotsong S. Africa 51 H4
Khabab Syria 39 C3
Khabar Iran 35 I5
Khabarikha Rus. Fed. 12 L2
Khabarovsk Rus. Fed. 44 D2
Khabarovskiy Kray *admin. div.* Rus. Fed. 44 D2
Khabarovsk Kray *admin. div.* Rus. Fed. *see* Khabarovskiy Kray
Khabary Rus. Fed. 42 D2
Khachmas Azer. *see* Xaçmaz
Khadro Pak. 36 B4
Khagaria India 37 F4
Khagrachari Bangl. 37 G5
Khagrachhari Bangl. *see* Khagrachari
Khairgarh Pak. 36 B3
Khairpur *Punjab* Pak. 36 C3
Khairpur *Sindh* Pak. 33 K4
Khāīz, Kūh-e *mt.* Iran 35 H5
Khaja Du Koh *h.* Afgh. 36 A1
Khajuha India 36 E4
Khāk-e Jabbar Afgh. 36 B2
Khakhea Botswana 50 F3
Khak-rēz Afgh. 36 A3
Khalatse India 36 D2
Khalifat *mt.* Pak. 33 K3
Khalīj Surt *g.* Libya *see* Sirte, Gulf of
Khalilabad India 37 E4
Khalīlī Iran 35 I6
Khalkhāl Iran 35 H3
Khálki *i.* Greece *see* Chalki
Khalkís Greece *see* Chalkida
Khallikot India 38 E2
Khalturin Rus. Fed. *see* Orlov
Khamar-Daban, Khrebet *mts* Rus. Fed. 42 I2
Khamaria India 38 D1
Khambhat India 36 C5
Khambhat, Gulf of India 38 A2
Khamgaon India 38 C1
Khamir Yemen 32 F6
Khamis Mushayṭ Saudi Arabia 32 F6
Khammam India 38 D2
Khammouan Laos *see* Thakèk
Khamra Rus. Fed. 29 M3
Khan Afgh. 36 B2
Khānābād Afgh. 36 B1
Khān al Baghdādī Iraq 35 F4
Khān al Mashāhidah Iraq 35 G4
Khān al Muşallá Iraq 35 G4
Khanapur India 38 B2
Khān ar Raḥbah Iraq 35 G5
Khanasur Pass Iran/Turkey 35 G3
Khanbalik China *see* Beijing
Khānch Iran 35 G3
Khandwa India 36 D5
Khandyga Rus. Fed. 29 O3
Khanewal Pak. 33 L3
Khaniá Greece *see* Chania
Khānī Yek Iran 35 I5
Khanka, Lake China/Rus. Fed. 44 D3
Khanka, Ozero *l.* China/Rus. Fed. *see* Khanka, Lake
Khankendi Azer. *see* Xankändi
Khanna India 36 D3
Khannā, Qā' *salt pan* Jordan 39 C3
Khanpur Pak. 36 B3
Khanpur Pak. 33 L4
Khān Ruḥābah Iraq *see* Khān ar Raḥbah
Khansar Pak. 36 B3
Khān Shaykhūn Syria 39 C2
Khantayskoye, Ozero *l.* Rus. Fed. 28 K3
Khanthabouli Laos *see* Savannakhét
Khanty-Mansiysk Rus. Fed. 28 H3
Khān Yūnis Gaza 39 B4
Khanzi *admin. dist.* Botswana *see* Ghanzi
Khaplu Pak. 33 M2
Khaptad National Park Nepal 36 E3
Kharabali Rus. Fed. 13 J7
Kharagpur *Bihar* India 37 F4
Kharagpur *W. Bengal* India 37 F5
Khārān *r.* Iran 33 I4
Kharari India *see* Abu Road
Kharda India 38 B2
Khardi India 36 C6
Khardong La *pass* India *see* Khardung La
Khardung La *pass* India 36 D2
Kharfiyah Iraq 35 G5
Kharga Egypt *see* Al Khārijah
Kharga *r.* Rus. Fed. 44 D1
Khârga, El Wâḥât el *oasis* Egypt *see* Khārijah, Wāḥāt al
Kharga Oasis Egypt *see* Khārijah, Wāḥāt al
Kharg Islands Iran 35 H5
Khargon India 36 C5
Khari *r. Rajasthan* India 36 C4
Khari *r. Rajasthan* India 36 C4
Kharian Pak. 36 C2
Khariar India 38 D1
Khārijah, Wāḥāt al *oasis* Egypt 32 D5
Kharīm, Gebel *h.* Egypt *see* Kharīm, Jabal
Kharīm, Jabal *h.* Egypt 39 A4
Kharkhara *r.* India 36 E5
Kharkiv Ukr. 13 H6
Khar'kov Ukr. *see* Kharkiv
Khār Kūh *mt.* Iran 35 I5
Kharlovka Rus. Fed. 12 H1
Kharlu Rus. Fed. 14 Q6
Kharmanli Bulg. 27 K4
Kharovsk Rus. Fed. 12 I4
Kharsia India 37 E5
Khartoum Sudan 32 D6
Khasavyurt Rus. Fed. 13 J8
Khāsh Iran 33 J4
Khashgort Rus. Fed. 11 T2
Khashm el Girba Sudan 32 E7
Khashm Şana' Saudi Arabia 34 E6
Khashuri Georgia 35 F2
Khasi Hills India 37 G4
Khaskovo Bulg. 27 K4
Khatanga Rus. Fed. 29 L2
Khatanga, Gulf of Rus. Fed. *see* Khatangskiy Zaliv
Khatangskiy Zaliv *b.* Rus. Fed. 29 L2
Khatayakha Rus. Fed. 12 M2
Khatinza Pass Pak. 36 B1
Khatyrka Rus. Fed. 29 S3
Khāvāk, Khowtal-e Afgh. 36 B2
Khavda India 36 B5
Khayamnandi S. Africa 51 G6
Khaybar Saudi Arabia 32 E4
Khayelitsha S. Africa 50 D8
Khayrān, Ra's al *pt* Oman 33 I5
Khefa Israel *see* Haifa
Khehuene, Ponta *pt* Moz. 51 L2
Khemis Miliana Alg. 25 H5
Khenchela Alg. 26 B7
Khenifra Morocco 22 C5
Kherāmeh Iran 35 I5
Kherrata Alg. 25 I5
Kherreh Iran 35 I6
Khersan *r.* Iran 35 H5
Kherson Ukr. 27 O1
Kheta *r.* Rus. Fed. 29 L2
Khezerābād Iran 35 I3
Khiching India 37 F5
Khilok Rus. Fed. 43 K2
Khilok *r.* Rus. Fed. 43 J2
Khinganskiy Zapovednik *nature res.* Rus. Fed. 44 C2
Khíos *i.* Greece *see* Chios
Khipro Pak. 33 K4
Khirbat Isrīyah Syria 39 C2
Khitai Dawan Aksai Chin 36 D2
Khīyāv Iran 35 G3
Khiytola Rus. Fed. 15 P6
Khlevnoye Rus. Fed. 13 H5
Khmel'nik Ukr. *see* Khmil'nyk
Khmel'nitskiy Ukr. *see* Khmel'nyts'kyy
Khmel'nyts'kyy Ukr. 13 E6
Khmer Republic *country* Asia *see* Cambodia
Khmil'nyk Ukr. 13 E6
Khobi Georgia 35 F2
Khodzha-Kala Turkm. *see* Hojagala
Khodzhent Tajik. *see* Khŭjand
Khojand Tajik. *see* Khŭjand
Khokhowe Pan *salt pan* Botswana 50 E3
Khokhropar Pak. 36 B4
Khoksar India 36 D2
Kholm Afgh. 36 A1
Kholm Poland *see* Chełm
Kholm Rus. Fed. 12 F4
Kholmsk Rus. Fed. 44 F3
Kholon Israel *see* Ḥolon
Khomas *admin. reg.* Namibia 50 C2
Khomas Highland *hills* Namibia 50 B2
Khomeyn Iran 35 H4
Khomeynīshahr Iran 35 H4
Khong, Mae Nam *r.* Asia *see* Mekong
Khong, Mae Nam *r.* China/Myanmar *see* Salween
Khonj Iran 35 I6
Khonj, Kūh-e *mts* Iran 35 I6
Khon Kaen Thai. 31 J5
Khonsa India 37 H4
Khonuu Rus. Fed. 29 P3
Khoper *r.* Rus. Fed. 13 I6
Khor Rus. Fed. 44 D3
Khor *r.* Rus. Fed. 44 D3
Khorda India *see* Khurda
Khordha India *see* Khurda
Khoreyver Rus. Fed. 12 M2
Khorinsk Rus. Fed. 43 J2
Khorixas Namibia 49 B6
Khormūj, Kūh-e *mt.* Iran 35 H5
Khorog Tajik. *see* Khorugh
Khorol Rus. Fed. 44 D3
Khorol Ukr. 13 G6
Khoroslū Dāgh *hills* Iran 35 G3
Khorramābād Iran 35 H4
Khorramshahr Iran 35 H5
Khorugh Tajik. 33 L2
Khosheutovo Rus. Fed. 13 J7
Khosūyeh Iran 35 I5
Khotan China *see* Hotan
Khouribga Morocco 22 C5
Khowrjān Iran 35 I5
Khownag, Kūh-e *mt.* Iran 35 I4
Khreum Myanmar 37 H5
Khroma *r.* Rus. Fed. 29 P2
Khromtau Kazakh. 28 G4
Khrushchev Ukr. *see* Svitlovods'k
Khrysokhou Bay Cyprus *see* Chrysochou Bay
Khrystynivka Ukr. 13 F6
Khudumelapye Botswana 50 G2
Khudzhand Tajik. *see* Khŭjand
Khuis Botswana 50 E4
Khŭjand Tajik. 33 K1
Khŭjayli Uzbek. *see* Xo'jayli
Khulays Saudi Arabia 32 E5
Khulkhuta Rus. Fed. 13 J7
Khulm *r.* Afgh. 36 A1
Khulna Bangl. 37 G5
Khulo Georgia 35 F2
Khuma S. Africa 51 H4
Khunayzīr, Jabal al *mts* Syria 39 C2
Khūnīnshahr Iran *see* Khorramshahr
Khunjerab Pass China/Pakistan 36 C1
Khunsar Iran 35 H4
Khurayş Saudi Arabia 32 G4
Khurd, Koh-i- *mt.* Afgh. 36 A2
Khurda India 38 E1
Khurdha India *see* Khurda
Khurja India 36 D3
Khurmuli Rus. Fed. 44 E2
Khūrrāb Iran 35 I5
Khurz Iran 35 I4
Khushab Pak. 33 L3
Khushalgarh Pak. 36 B2
Khushshah, Wādī al *watercourse* Jordan/Saudi Arabia 39 C5
Khust Ukr. 13 D6
Khutse Game Reserve *nature res.* Botswana 50 G2
Khutsong S. Africa 51 H4
Khutu *r.* Rus. Fed. 44 E2
Khuzdar Pak. 33 K4
Khvāf Iran 33 J3
Khvājeh Iran 35 G3
Khvalynsk Rus. Fed. 13 K5
Khvormūj Iran 35 H5
Khvoy Iran 35 G3
Khvoynaya Rus. Fed. 12 G4
Khwaja Amran *mt.* Pak. 36 A3
Khwaja Muhammad Range *mts* Afgh. 36 B1
Khyber Pass Afgh./Pak. 33 L3
Kiama Australia 58 E5
Kiangsi *prov.* China *see* Jiangxi
Kiangsu *prov.* China *see* Jiangsu
Kiantajärvi *l.* Fin. 14 P4
Kīāseh Iran 35 I3
Kiatassuaq *i.* Greenland 61 M2
Kibaha Tanz. 49 D4
Kibali *r.* Dem. Rep. Congo 48 C3
Kibangou Congo 48 B4
Kibaya Tanz. 49 D4
Kiboga Uganda 48 D3
Kibombo Dem. Rep. Congo 48 C4
Kibondo Tanz. 48 D4
Kibre Mengist Eth. 47 G4
Kıbrıs *country* Asia *see* Cyprus
Kibungo Rwanda 48 D4
Kičevo Macedonia 27 I4
Kichmengskiy Gorodok Rus. Fed. 12 J4
Kiçik Qafqaz *mts* Asia *see* Lesser Caucasus
Kicking Horse Pass Canada 62 D1
Kidal Mali 46 D3
Kidderminster U.K. 19 E6
Kidepo Valley National Park Uganda 48 D3
Kidira Senegal 46 B3
Kidmang India 36 D2
Kidnappers, Cape N.Z. 59 F4
Kidsgrove U.K. 19 E5
Kiel Germany 17 M3
Kiel Canal Germany 17 L3
Kielce Poland 17 R5
Kielder Water *resr* U.K. 18 E3
Kieler Bucht *b.* Germany 17 M3
Kienge Dem. Rep. Congo 49 C5
Kiev Ukr. 13 F6
Kiffa Mauritania 46 B3
Kifisia Greece 27 J5
Kifrī Iraq 35 G4
Kigali Rwanda 48 D4
Kiğı Turkey 35 F3
Kigoma Tanz. 49 C4
Kihlanki Fin. 14 M3
Kihniö Fin. 14 M5
Kiiminki Fin. 14 N4
Kii-sanchi *mts* Japan 45 D6
Kii-suidō *sea chan.* Japan 45 D6
Kikerino Rus. Fed. 15 P7
Kikinda Serbia 27 I2
Kikládhes *is* Greece *see* Cyclades
Kiknur Rus. Fed. 12 J4
Kikonai Japan 44 F4
Kikori P.N.G. 52 E2
Kikwit Dem. Rep. Congo 49 B4
Kilafors Sweden 15 J6
Kilar India 36 D2
Kilchu N. Korea 44 C4
Kilcoole Ireland 21 F4
Kilcormac Ireland 21 E4
Kilcoy Australia 58 F1
Kildare Ireland 21 F4
Kil'dinstroy Rus. Fed. 14 R2
Kilemary Rus. Fed. 12 J4
Kilembe Dem. Rep. Congo 49 B4
Kilfinan U.K. 20 D5
Kilham U.K. 18 E3
Kilia Ukr. *see* Kiliya
Kılıç Dağı *mt.* Syria/Turkey *see* Aqra', Jabal al
Kilifi Kenya 48 D4
Kilik Pass China 36 C1
Kilimanjaro *vol.* Tanz. 48 D4
Kilimanjaro National Park Tanz. 48 D4
Kilinailau Islands P.N.G. 52 F2
Kilindoni Tanz. 49 D4
Kilingi-Nõmme Estonia 15 N7
Kilis Turkey 39 C1
Kilis *prov.* Turkey 39 C1
Kiliya Ukr. 27 M2
Kilkee Ireland 21 C5
Kilkeel U.K. 21 G3
Kilkenny Ireland 21 E5
Kilkhampton U.K. 19 C8
Kilkis Greece 27 J4
Killala Ireland 21 C3
Killala Bay Ireland 21 C3
Killaloe Ireland 21 D5
Killarney *N.T.* Australia 54 E4
Killarney *Qld* Australia 58 F2
Killarney Ireland 21 C5
Killarney National Park Ireland 21 C6
Killary Harbour *b.* Ireland 21 C4
Killeen U.S.A. 62 H5
Killenaule Ireland 21 E5
Killimor Ireland 21 D4
Killin U.K. 20 E4
Killinchy U.K. 21 G3
Killíni *mt.* Greece *see* Kyllini
Killinick Ireland 21 F5
Killorglin Ireland 21 C5
Killurin Ireland 21 F5
Killybegs Ireland 21 D3
Kilmacrenan Ireland 21 E2
Kilmaine Ireland 21 C4
Kilmallock Ireland 21 D5
Kilmaluag U.K. 20 C3
Kilmarnock U.K. 20 E5
Kilmelford U.K. 20 D4
Kil'mez' Rus. Fed. 12 K4
Kil'mez' *r.* Rus. Fed. 12 K4
Kilmona Ireland 21 D6
Kilmore Australia 58 B6
Kilmore Quay Ireland 21 F5
Kilosa Tanz. 49 D4
Kilpisjärvi Fin. 14 L2
Kilrea U.K. 21 F3
Kilrush Ireland 21 C5
Kilsyth U.K. 20 E5
Kiltan *atoll* India 38 B4
Kiltullagh Ireland 21 D4
Kilwa Masoko Tanz. 49 D4
Kilwinning U.K. 20 E5
Kimba Australia 55 G8
Kimba Congo 48 B4
Kimball U.S.A. 62 G3
Kimball, Mount U.S.A. 60 D3
Kimbe P.N.G. 52 F2
Kimberley S. Africa 50 G5
Kimberley Plateau Australia 54 D4
Kimberley Range *hills* Australia 55 B6
Kimch'aek N. Korea 45 C4
Kimch'ŏn S. Korea 45 C5
Kimhae S. Korea 45 C6
Kimhandu *mt.* Tanz. 49 D4
Kimhwa S. Korea 45 B5
Kími Greece *see* Kymi
Kimito Fin. 15 M6
Kimmirut Canada 61 L3
Kimolos *i.* Greece 27 K6
Kimovsk Rus. Fed. 13 H5
Kimpese Dem. Rep. Congo 49 B4
Kimpoku-san *mt.* Japan *see* Kinpoku-san
Kimry Rus. Fed. 12 H4
Kimvula Dem. Rep. Congo 49 B4
Kinabalu, Gunung *mt. Sabah* Malaysia 41 D7
Kinango Kenya 49 D4
Kinbasket Lake Canada 62 D1
Kinbrace U.K. 20 F2
Kincardine U.K. 20 F4
Kinchega National Park Australia 57 C7
Kinda Dem. Rep. Congo 49 C4
Kindat Myanmar 37 H5
Kinder Scout *h.* U.K. 18 F5
Kindersley Canada 62 F1
Kindia Guinea 46 B3
Kindu Dem. Rep. Congo 48 C4
Kinel' Rus. Fed. 13 K5
Kineshma Rus. Fed. 12 I4
Kingaroy Australia 58 E1
King Christian Island Canada 61 H2
King City *CA* U.S.A. 65 B2
King Edward VII Land *pen.* Antarctica *see* Edward VII Peninsula
King George *VA* U.S.A. 64 C3
King George Island Antarctica 76 A2
King George Islands Canada 61 K4
King George Islands Fr. Polynesia *see* Roi Georges, Îles du
King Hill *h.* Australia 54 C5
Kingisepp Rus. Fed. 12 F4
King Island Australia 57 [inset]
Kingisseppa Estonia *see* Kuressaare
Kinglake National Park Australia 58 B6
King Leopold and Queen Astrid Coast Antarctica 76 E2
King Leopold Range National Park Australia 54 D4
King Leopold Ranges *hills* Australia 54 D4
Kingman *AZ* U.S.A. 65 E3
Kingman Reef *terr.* N. Pacific Ocean 74 J5
Kingoonya Australia 57 A6
King Peak Antarctica 76 L1
King Peninsula Antarctica 76 K2
Kingri Pak. 36 B3
Kings *r.* Ireland 21 E5
Kings *r. CA* U.S.A. 65 B2
King Salmon U.S.A. 60 C4
Kingsbridge U.K. 19 D8
Kingsburg *CA* U.S.A. 65 C2
Kings Canyon National Park *CA* U.S.A. 65 C2
Kingscliff Australia 58 F2
Kingscote Australia 57 B7
Kingscourt Ireland 21 F4
King Sejong *research stn* Antarctica 76 A2
King's Lynn U.K. 19 H6
Kingsmill Group *is* Kiribati 53 H2
Kingsnorth U.K. 19 H7
King Sound *b.* Australia 54 C4
Kings Peak U.S.A. 62 E3
Kingsport U.S.A. 63 K4
Kingston Australia 57 [inset]
Kingston Canada 63 L3
Kingston Jamaica 67 I5
Kingston Norfolk I. 53 G4
Kingston *NY* U.S.A. 64 D2
Kingston *PA* U.S.A. 64 D2
Kingston Peak *CA* U.S.A. 65 E3
Kingston South East Australia 57 B8
Kingston upon Hull U.K. 18 G5
Kingstown St Vincent 67 L6
Kingsville U.S.A. 62 H6
Kingswood U.K. 19 E7
Kington U.K. 19 D6
Kingungi Dem. Rep. Congo 49 B4
Kingussie U.K. 20 E3
King William *VA* U.S.A. 64 C4
King William Island Canada 61 I3
King William's Town S. Africa 51 H7
Kingwood *WV* U.S.A. 64 B3
Kinloch N.Z. 59 B7
Kinloss U.K. 20 F3
Kinna Sweden 15 H8
Kinnegad Ireland 21 E4
Kinneret, Yam *l.* Israel *see* Galilee, Sea of
Kinniyai Sri Lanka 38 D4
Kinnula Fin. 14 N5
Kinpoku-san *mt.* Japan 45 E5
Kinross U.K. 20 F4
Kinsale Ireland 21 D6
Kinsale *VA* U.S.A. 64 C3
Kinshasa Dem. Rep. Congo 49 B4
Kinston U.S.A. 63 L4
Kintore U.K. 20 G3
Kintyre *pen.* U.K. 20 D5
Kin-U Myanmar 37 H5
Kinyeti *mt.* Sudan 47 G4
Kiparissía Greece *see* Kyparissia
Kipawa, Lac *l.* Canada 63 L2
Kipnuk U.S.A. 60 B4
Kiptopeke *VA* U.S.A. 64 D4
Kipungo Angola *see* Quipungo
Kipushi Dem. Rep. Congo 49 C5
Kirakira Solomon Is 53 G3
Kirandul India 38 D2
Kircubbin U.K. 21 G3
Kirdimi Chad 47 E3
Kirenga *r.* Rus. Fed. 43 J1
Kirensk Rus. Fed. 29 L4
Kireyevsk Rus. Fed. 13 H5
Kirghizia *country* Asia *see* Kyrgyzstan
Kirghiz Range *mts* Kazakh./Kyrg. 42 C4
Kirgizskaya S.S.R. *country* Asia *see* Kyrgyzstan
Kirgizskiy Khrebet *mts* Kazakh./Kyrg. *see* Kirghiz Range
Kirgizstan *country* Asia *see* Kyrgyzstan
Kiri Dem. Rep. Congo 48 B4
Kiribati *country* Pacific Ocean 74 I6
Kırıkhan Turkey 39 C1
Kırıkkale Turkey 34 D3
Kirillov Rus. Fed. 12 H4
Kirillovo Rus. Fed. 44 F3
Kirin China *see* Jilin
Kirin *prov.* China *see* Jilin
Kirinda Sri Lanka 38 D5
Kirinyaga *mt.* Kenya *see* Kenya, Mount
Kirishi Rus. Fed. 12 G4
Kirishima-Yaku Kokuritsu-kōen *nat. park* Japan 45 C7
Kirishima-yama *vol.* Japan 45 C7
Kiritimati *atoll* Kiribati 75 J5
Kiriwina Islands P.N.G. *see* Trobriand Islands
Kırkağaç Turkey 27 L5
Kirk Bulāg Dāgi *mt.* Iran 35 G3
Kirkby U.K. 18 E5
Kirkby in Ashfield U.K. 19 F5
Kirkby Lonsdale U.K. 18 E4
Kirkby Stephen U.K. 18 E4
Kirkcaldy U.K. 20 F4
Kirkcolm U.K. 20 D6
Kirkcudbright U.K. 20 E6
Kirkenær Norway 15 H6
Kirkenes Norway 14 Q2
Kirkintilloch U.K. 20 E5
Kirkkonummi Fin. 15 N6
Kirkland *AZ* U.S.A. 65 F3
Kirkland Lake Canada 63 K2
Kırklareli Turkey 27 L4
Kirk Michael Isle of Man 18 C4
Kirkoswald U.K. 18 E4
Kirkpatrick, Mount Antarctica 76 H1
Kirksville U.S.A. 63 I3
Kirkūk Iraq 35 G4
Kirkwall U.K. 20 G2
Kirkwood S. Africa 51 G7
Kirman Iran *see* Kermān
Kirov *Kaluzhskaya Oblast'* Rus. Fed. 13 G5
Kirov *Kirovskaya Oblast'* Rus. Fed. 12 K4
Kirovabad Azer. *see* Gäncä
Kirovabad Tajik. *see* Panj
Kirovakan Armenia *see* Vanadzor
Kirovo Ukr. *see* Kirovohrad
Kirovo-Chepetsk Rus. Fed. 12 K4
Kirovo-Chepetskiy Rus. Fed. *see* Kirovo-Chepetsk
Kirovograd Ukr. *see* Kirovohrad
Kirovohrad Ukr. 13 G6
Kirovsk *Leningradskaya Oblast'* Rus. Fed. 12 F4
Kirovsk *Murmanskaya Oblast'* Rus. Fed. 12 G2
Kirovs'ke Ukr. 34 D1
Kirovskiy Rus. Fed. 44 D3
Kirovskoye Ukr. *see* Kirovs'ke
Kırpaşa *pen.* Cyprus *see* Karpasia
Kirpili Turkm. 35 J3
Kirriemuir U.K. 20 F4
Kirs Rus. Fed. 12 L4
Kirsanov Rus. Fed. 13 I5
Kırşehir Turkey 34 D3
Kirthar National Park Pak. 36 A4
Kirthar Range *mts* Pak. 33 K4
Kiruna Sweden 14 L3
Kirundu Dem. Rep. Congo 48 C4
Kirwan Escarpment Antarctica 76 B2
Kiryū Japan 45 E5
Kisa Sweden 15 I8
Kisama, Parque Nacional de *nat. park* Angola *see* Quiçama, Parque Nacional do
Kisandji Dem. Rep. Congo 49 B4
Kisangani Dem. Rep. Congo 48 C3
Kisantu Dem. Rep. Congo 49 B4
Kisar *i.* Indon. 54 D2
Kiselevsk Rus. Fed. 42 F2
Kisel'ovka Rus. Fed. 44 E2
Kishanganj India 37 F4
Kishangarh *Madh. Prad.* India 36 D4
Kishangarh *Rajasthan* India 36 B4
Kishangarh *Rajasthan* India 36 C4
Kishangarh *Rajasthan* India 36 D4
Kishi Nigeria 46 D4
Kishinev Moldova *see* Chişinău
Kishkenekol' Kazakh. 31 G1
Kishoreganj Bangl. 37 G4
Kishorganj Bangl. *see* Kishoreganj
Kisi Nigeria *see* Kishi
Kisii Kenya 48 D4
Kiska Island U.S.A. 29 S4
Kiskunfélegyháza Hungary 27 H1
Kiskunhalas Hungary 27 H1
Kiskunsági *nat. park* Hungary 27 H1
Kislovodsk Rus. Fed. 35 F2
Kismaayo Somalia 48 E4
Kismayu Somalia *see* Kismaayo
Kisoro Uganda 47 F5
Kissamos Greece 27 J7
Kissidougou Guinea 46 B4
Kissimmee U.S.A. 63 K6
Kissimmee, Lake U.S.A. 63 K6
Kistendey Rus. Fed. 13 I5
Kistna *r.* India *see* Krishna
Kisumu Kenya 48 D4
Kisykkamys Kazakh. *see* Dzhangala
Kita Mali 46 C3
Kita-Daitō-jima *i.* Japan 43 O7
Kitaibaraki Japan 45 F5
Kitakami Japan 45 F5
Kita-Kyūshū Japan 45 C6
Kitale Kenya 48 D3
Kitami Japan 44 F4
Kitchener *Ont.* Canada 64 A1
Kitee Fin. 14 Q5
Kitgum Uganda 48 D3
Kíthira *i.* Greece *see* Kythira
Kíthnos *i.* Greece *see* Kythnos
Kiti, Cape Cyprus *see* Kition, Cape
Kitinen *r.* Fin. 14 O3
Kition, Cape Cyprus 39 A2
Kitiou, Akra *c.* Cyprus *see* Kition, Cape
Kittanning *PA* U.S.A. 64 B2
Kittatinny Mountains *hills NJ* U.S.A. 64 D2
Kittery *ME* U.S.A. 64 F1
Kittilä Fin. 14 N3
Kittur India 38 B3
Kitui Kenya 48 D4
Kitwe Zambia 49 C5
Kitzbüheler Alpen *mts* Austria 17 N7
Kiuruvesi Fin. 14 O5
Kivalina U.S.A. 60 B3
Kivijärvi Fin. 14 N5
Kiviõli Estonia 15 O7
Kivu, Lake Dem. Rep. Congo/Rwanda 48 C4
Kiwaba N'zogi Angola 49 B4
Kiyev Ukr. *see* Kiev
Kiyevskoye Vodokhranilishche *resr* Ukr. *see* Kyyivs'ke Vodoskhovyshche
Kıyıköy Turkey 27 M4
Kizel Rus. Fed. 11 R4
Kizema Rus. Fed. 12 J3
Kızılcadağ Turkey 27 M6
Kızılca Dağ *mt.* Turkey 34 C3
Kızılcahamam Turkey 34 D2
Kızıldağ *mt.* Turkey 39 A1
Kızıldağ *mt.* Turkey 39 B1
Kızıl Dağı *mt.* Turkey 34 E3
Kızılırmak Turkey 34 D2
Kızılırmak *r.* Turkey 34 D2
Kızıltepe Turkey 35 F3
Kizilyurt Rus. Fed. 13 J8
Kızkalesi Turkey 39 B1
Kizlyar Rus. Fed. 13 J8
Kizlyarskiy Zaliv *b.* Rus. Fed. 35 G1
Kizner Rus. Fed. 12 K4
Kizyl-Arbat Turkm. *see* Serdar
Kizyl-Atrek Turkm. *see* Etrek
Kjøllefjord Norway 14 O1
Kjøpsvik Norway 14 J2
Kladno Czech Rep. 17 O5

Klagenfurt Austria 17 O7
Klaipėda Lith. 15 L9
Klaksvig Faroe Is see Klaksvík
Klaksvík Faroe Is 14 [inset]
Klamath r. U.S.A. 60 F5
Klamath Falls U.S.A. 62 C3
Klarälven r. Sweden 15 H7
Klatovy Czech Rep. 17 N6
Klawer S. Africa 50 D6
Kleides Islands Cyprus 39 B2
Kleinbegin S. Africa 50 E5
Klein Karas Namibia 50 D4
Klein Nama Land reg. S. Africa see Namaqualand
Klein Roggeveldberge mts S. Africa 50 E7
Kleinsee S. Africa 50 C5
Klerksdorp S. Africa 51 H4
Kletnya Rus. Fed. 13 G5
Kletsk Belarus see Klyetsk
Kletskaya Rus. Fed. 13 I6
Kletskiy Rus. Fed. see Kletskaya
Klidhes Islands Cyprus see Kleides Islands
Klimkovka Rus. Fed. 12 K4
Klimovo Rus. Fed. 13 G5
Klin Rus. Fed. 12 H4
Klínovec mt. Czech Rep. 17 N5
Klintehamn Sweden 15 K8
Klintsy Rus. Fed. 13 G5
Ključ Bos.-Herz. 26 G2
Kłodzko Poland 17 P5
Klosterneuburg Austria 17 P6
Kluane National Park Canada 60 E3
Kluang Malaysia see Keluang
Kluczbork Poland 17 Q5
Klukhori Rus. Fed. see Karachayevsk
Klukhorskiy, Pereval Georgia/Rus. Fed. 35 F2
Klukwan U.S.A. 60 E4
Klyetsk Belarus 15 O10
Klyuchevskaya, Sopka vol. Rus. Fed. 29 R4
Klyuchi Rus. Fed. 44 B2
Knåda Sweden 15 I6
Knaresborough U.K. 18 F4
Knighton U.K. 19 D6
Knights Landing CA U.S.A. 65 B1
Knin Croatia 26 G2
Knittelfeld Austria 17 O7
Knjaževac Serbia 27 J3
Knob Lake Canada see Schefferville
Knob Peak h. Australia 54 E3
Knock Ireland 21 D4
Knockalongy h. Ireland 21 D3
Knockalough Ireland 21 C5
Knockanaffrin h. Ireland 21 E5
Knockboy h. Ireland 21 C6
Knock Hill h. U.K. 20 G3
Knockmealdown Mts hills Ireland 21 D5
Knocknaskagh h. Ireland 21 D5
Knowle U.K. 19 F6
Knox PA U.S.A. 64 B2
Knox Coast Antarctica 76 F2
Knoxville TN U.S.A. 63 K4
Knud Rasmussen Land reg. Greenland 61 L2
Knysna S. Africa 50 F8
Ko, Gora mt. Rus. Fed. 44 E3
Koartac Canada see Quaqtaq
Kobbfoss Norway 14 P2
Kōbe Japan 45 D6
København Denmark see Copenhagen
Kobenni Mauritania 46 C3
Koblenz Germany 17 K5
Koboldo Rus. Fed. 44 D1
Kobrin Belarus see Kobryn
Kobroör i. Indon. 41 F8
Kobryn Belarus 15 N10
Kobuk Valley National Park U.S.A. 60 C3
K'obulet'i Georgia 35 F2
Kocaeli Kocaeli Turkey see İzmit
Kocaeli Yarımadası pen. Turkey 27 M4
Kočani Macedonia 27 J4
Kocasu r. Turkey 27 M4
Kočevje Slovenia 26 F2
Koch Bihar India 37 G4
Kochevo Rus. Fed. 11 Q4
Kochi India see Cochin
Kōchi Japan 45 D6
Koçhisar Turkey see Kızıltepe
Koch Island Canada 61 K3
Kochkor Kyrg. 42 D4
Kochkorka Kyrg. see Kochkor
Kochkurovo Rus. Fed. 13 J5
Kochubeyevskoye Rus. Fed. 35 F1
Kod India 38 B3
Kodala India 38 E2
Kodarma India 37 F4
Koderma India see Kodarma
Kodiak U.S.A. 60 C4
Kodiak Island U.S.A. 60 C4
Kodibeleng Botswana 51 H2
Kodino Rus. Fed. 12 H3
Kodiyakkarai India 38 C4
Kodok Sudan 32 D8
Kodyma Ukr. 13 F6
Kodzhaele mt. Bulg./Greece 27 K4
Koedoesberg mts S. Africa 50 E7
Koegrabie S. Africa 50 E5
Koekenaap S. Africa 50 D6
Koës Namibia 50 D3
Kofa Mountains AZ U.S.A. 65 F4
Koffiefontein S. Africa 50 G5
Koforidua Ghana 46 C4
Kōfu Japan 45 E6
Kogaluk r. Canada 61 L4
Kogan Australia 58 E1
Køge Denmark 15 H9
Kogon r. Guinea 46 B3
Kohat Pak. 33 L3
Kohestānāt Afgh. 36 A2
Kohila Estonia 15 N7
Kohima India 37 H4
Kohler Range mts Antarctica 76 K2
Kohlu Pak. 36 B3
Kohtla-Järve Estonia 15 O7
Kohŭng S. Korea 45 B6
Koidu Sierra Leone see Sefadu
Koilkonda India 38 C2
Koin N. Korea 45 B4
Koin r. Rus. Fed. 12 K3
Koi Sanjaq Iraq 35 G3
Kŏje-do i. S. Korea 45 C6
Kojonup Australia 55 B8
Kökar Fin. 15 L7
Kokchetav Kazakh. see Kokshetau
Kokemäenjoki r. Fin. 15 L6
Kokerboom Namibia 50 D5
Kokkilai Sri Lanka 38 D4
Kokkola Fin. 14 M5
Koko Nigeria 46 D3
Kokomo U.S.A. 63 J3
Kokong Botswana 50 F3
Kokosi S. Africa 51 H4
Kokpekti Kazakh. 42 E3
Koksan N. Korea 45 B5
Kokshaal-Tau, Khrebet mts China/Kyrg. see Kakshaal-Too
Koksharka Rus. Fed. 12 J4
Kokshetau Kazakh. 31 F1
Kokstad S. Africa 51 I6
Kokterek Kazakh. 13 K6
Koktokay China see Fuyun
Kola Rus. Fed. 14 R2
Kolachi r. Pak. 36 A4
Kolahoi mt. India 36 C2
Kolaka Indon. 41 E8
Kola Peninsula Rus. Fed. 12 H2
Kolar Chhattisgarh India 38 D2
Kolar Karnataka India 38 C3
Kolaras India 36 D4
Kolar Gold Fields India 38 C3
Kolari Fin. 14 M3
Kolarovgrad Bulg. see Shumen
Kolasib India 37 H4
Kolayat India 36 C4
Kolberg Poland see Kołobrzeg
Kol'chugino Rus. Fed. 12 H4
Kolda Senegal 46 B3
Kolding Denmark 15 F9
Kole Kasaï-Oriental Dem. Rep. Congo 48 C4
Kole Orientale Dem. Rep. Congo 48 C3
Koléa Alg. 25 H5
Koler Sweden 14 L4
Kolguyev, Ostrov i. Rus. Fed. 12 K1
Kolhan reg. India 37 F5
Kolhapur India 38 B2
Kolikata India see Kolkata
Kõljala Estonia 15 M7
Kolkasrags pt Latvia 15 M8
Kolkata India 37 G5
Kolkhozabad Khatlon Tajik. see Kolkhozobod
Kolkhozabad Khatlon Tajik. see Vose
Kolkhozobod Tajik. 33 K2
Kollam India see Quilon
Kolleru Lake India 38 D2
Kolmanskop (abandoned) Namibia 50 B4
Köln Germany see Cologne
Kołobrzeg Poland 17 O3
Kologriv Rus. Fed. 12 J4
Kolokani Mali 46 C3
Kolombangara i. Solomon Is 53 F2
Kolomea Ukr. see Kolomyya
Kolomna Rus. Fed. 13 H5
Kołomyja Ukr. see Kolomyya
Kolomyya Ukr. 13 E6
Kolondiéba Mali 46 C3
Kolonedale Indon. 52 C2
Koloni Cyprus 39 A2
Kolonkwaneng Botswana 50 E4
Kolozsvár Romania see Cluj-Napoca
Kolpashevo Rus. Fed. 28 J4
Kolpos Messaras b. Greece 27 K7
Kol'skiy Poluostrov pen. Rus. Fed. see Kola Peninsula
Kölük Turkey see Kâhta
Koluli Eritrea 32 F7
Kolva r. Rus. Fed. 12 M2
Kolvan India 38 B2
Kolvereid Norway 14 G4
Kolvik Norway 14 N1
Kolvitskoye, Ozero l. Rus. Fed. 14 R3
Kolwezi Dem. Rep. Congo 49 C5
Kolyma r. Rus. Fed. 29 R3
Kolyma Lowland Rus. Fed. see Kolymskaya Nizmennost'
Kolyma Range mts Rus. Fed. see Kolymskiy, Khrebet
Kolymskaya Nizmennost' lowland Rus. Fed. 29 Q3
Kolymskiy, Khrebet mts Rus. Fed. 29 R3
Kolyshley Rus. Fed. 13 J5
Kom mt. Bulg. 27 J3
Komadugu-gana watercourse Nigeria 46 E3
Komaggas S. Africa 50 C5
Komaki Japan 45 E6
Komandnaya, Gora mt. Rus. Fed. 44 E2
Komandorskiye Ostrova is Rus. Fed. 29 R4
Komárno Slovakia 17 Q7
Komati r. Swaziland 51 J3
Komatipoort S. Africa 51 J3
Komatsu Japan 45 E5
Komba i. Indon. 54 C1
Komga S. Africa 51 H7
Komintern Ukr. see Marhanets'
Kominternivs'ke Ukr. 27 N1
Komiža Croatia 26 G3
Komló Hungary 26 H1
Kommunarsk Ukr. see Alchevs'k
Komodo, Taman Nasional Indon. 54 B2
Kôm Ombo Egypt see Kawm Umbū
Komono Congo 48 B4
Komotini Greece 27 K4
Kompong Cham Cambodia see Kâmpóng Cham
Kompong Som Cambodia see Sihanoukville
Kompong Speu Cambodia see Kâmpóng Spœ
Kompong Thom Cambodia see Kâmpóng Thum
Komrat Moldova see Comrat
Komsberg mts S. Africa 50 E7
Komsomol Kazakh. see Karabalyk
Komsomolets Kazakh. see Karabalyk
Komsomolets, Ostrov i. Rus. Fed. 28 K1
Komsomol's'k Ukr. 13 G6
Komsomol'skiy Chukotskiy Avtonomnyy Okrug Rus. Fed. 77 C2
Komsomol'skiy Khanty-Mansiyskiy Avtonomnyy Okrug-Yugra Rus. Fed. see Yugorsk
Komsomol'skiy Respublika Kalmykiya-Khalm'g-Tangch Rus. Fed. 13 J7
Komsomol'sk-na-Amure Rus. Fed. 44 E2
Komsomol'skoye Rus. Fed. 13 J6
Kömürlü Turkey 35 F2
Kon India 37 E4
Konacık Turkey 39 B1
Konada India 38 D2
Konarak India see Konarka
Konarka India 37 F6
Konch India 36 D4
Kondagaon India 38 D2
Kondinin Australia 55 B8
Kondinskoye Rus. Fed. see Oktyabr'skoye
Kondoa Tanz. 49 D4
Kondol' Rus. Fed. 13 J5
Kondopoga Rus. Fed. 12 G3
Kondoz Afgh. see Kunduz
Kondrovo Rus. Fed. 13 G5
Köneürgenç Turkm. 33 I1
Köneürgenç Turkm. see Köneürgenç
Kong Cameroon 46 E4
Kong Christian IX Land reg. Greenland 61 O3
Kong Christian X Land reg. Greenland 61 P2
Kongelab atoll Marshall Is see Rongelap
Kong Frederik IX Land reg. Greenland 61 M3
Kong Frederik VI Kyst coastal area Greenland 61 N3
Kongolo Dem. Rep. Congo 49 C4
Kongor Sudan 47 G4
Kong Oscars Fjord inlet Greenland 61 P2
Kongoussi Burkina 46 C3
Kongsberg Norway 15 F7
Kongsvinger Norway 15 H6
Kongur Shan mt. China 42 D5
Königsberg Rus. Fed. see Kaliningrad
Konin Poland 17 Q4
Konjic Bos.-Herz. 26 G3
Konkiep watercourse Namibia 50 C5
Konnevesi Fin. 14 O5
Konosha Rus. Fed. 12 I3
Konotop Ukr. 13 G6
Konpara India 37 E5
Konqi He r. China 42 F4
Konso Eth. 48 D3
Konstantinograd Ukr. see Krasnohrad
Konstantinovka Rus. Fed. 44 B2
Konstantinovka Ukr. see Kostyantynivka
Konstanz Germany 17 L7
Kontiolahti Fin. 14 P5
Konttila Fin. 14 O4
Könugard Ukr. see Kiev
Konushin, Mys pt Rus. Fed. 12 I2
Konya Turkey 34 D3
Konzhakovskiy Kamen', Gora mt. Rus. Fed. 11 R4
Kooch Bihar India see Koch Bihar
Kookynie Australia 55 C7
Koolyanobbing Australia 55 B7
Koondrook Australia 58 B5
Koorawatha Australia 58 D5
Koordarrie Australia 54 A5
Kootenay Lake Canada 62 D2
Kootjieskolk S. Africa 50 E6
Kópasker Iceland 14 [inset]
Kopbirlik Kazakh. 42 D3
Koper Slovenia 26 E2
Kopet Dag mts Iran/Turkm. 33 I2
Kopet-Dag, Khrebet mts Iran/Turkm. see Kopet Dag
Köpetdag Gershi mts Iran/Turkm. see Kopet Dag
Köping Sweden 15 J7
Köpmanholmen Sweden 14 K5
Kopong Botswana 51 G3
Koppal India 38 C3
Koppang Norway 15 G6
Kopparberg Sweden 15 I7
Koppeh Dāgh mts Iran/Turkm. see Kopet Dag
Koppi r. Rus. Fed. 44 F2
Koppies S. Africa 51 H4
Koppieskraal Pan salt pan S. Africa 50 E4
Koprivnica Croatia 26 G1
Köprülü Turkey 39 A1
Köprülü Kanyon Milli Parkı nat. park Turkey 27 N6
Kopyl' Belarus see Kapyl'
Kora India 36 E4
Korablino Rus. Fed. 13 I5
K'orahē Eth. 48 E3
Koramlik China 37 F1
Korangal India 38 C2
Korangi Pak. 36 A4
Korān va Monjan Afgh. 36 B1
Koraput India 38 D2
Korat Thai. see Nakhon Ratchasima
Koratla India 38 C2
Korba India 37 E5
Korçë Albania 27 I4
Korčula Croatia 26 G3
Korčula i. Croatia 26 G3
Korčulanski Kanal sea chan. Croatia 26 G3
Korday Kazakh. 42 C4
Kord Küy Iran 35 I3
Korea, North country Asia 45 B5
Korea, South country Asia 45 B5
Korea Bay g. China/N. Korea 45 B5
Korea Strait Japan/S. Korea 45 C6
Koregaon India 38 B2
Korenovsk Rus. Fed. 35 E1
Korenovskaya Rus. Fed. see Korenovsk
Korepino Rus. Fed. 11 R3
Korets' Ukr. 13 E6
Körfez Turkey 27 M4
Korff Ice Rise Antarctica 76 L1
Korfovskiy Rus. Fed. 44 D2
Korgalzhyn Kazakh. 42 C2
Korgen Norway 14 H3
Korhogo Côte d'Ivoire 46 C4
Koribundu Sierra Leone 46 B4
Kori Creek inlet India 36 B5
Korinthiakos Kolpos sea chan. Greece see Corinth, Gulf of
Korinthos Greece see Corinth
Kőris-hegy h. Hungary 26 G1
Koritnik mt. Albania 27 I3
Koritsa Albania see Korçë
Kōriyama Japan 45 F5
Korkuteli Turkey 27 N6
Korla China 42 F4
Kormakitis, Cape Cyprus 39 A2
Körmend Hungary 26 G1
Kornat nat. park Croatia 26 F3
Korneyevka Rus. Fed. 13 K6
Koro Côte d'Ivoire 46 C4
Koro i. Fiji 53 H3
Koro Mali 46 C3
Köroğlu Dağları mts Turkey 27 O4
Köroğlu Tepesi mt. Turkey 34 D2
Korogwe Tanz. 49 D4
Koroneia, Limni l. Greece 27 J4
Korong Vale Australia 58 A6
Koror Palau 41 F7
Koro Sea sea Fiji 53 H3
Korosten' Ukr. 13 F6
Korostyshiv Ukr. 13 F6
Koro Toro Chad 47 E3
Korpilahti Fin. 14 N5
Korpo Fin. 15 L6
Korppoo Fin. see Korpo
Korsakov Rus. Fed. 44 F3
Korsnäs Fin. 14 L5
Korsør Denmark 15 G9
Korsun'-Shevchenkivs'kyy Ukr. 13 F6
Korsun'-Shevchenkovskiy Ukr. see Korsun'-Shevchenkivs'kyy
Korsze Poland 17 R3
Kortesjärvi Fin. 14 M5
Korti Sudan 32 D6
Kortkeros Rus. Fed. 12 K3
Kortrijk Belgium 16 I5
Korvala Fin. 14 O3
Koryakskaya, Sopka vol. Rus. Fed. 29 Q4
Koryakskoye Nagor'ye mts Rus. Fed. 29 S3
Koryazhma Rus. Fed. 12 J3
Koryŏng S. Korea 45 C6
Kos i. Greece 27 L6
Kosa Rus. Fed. 11 Q4
Kosam India 36 E4
Kosan N. Korea 45 B5
Kościan Poland 17 P4
Kosciusko, Mount Australia see Kosciuszko, Mount
Kosciuszko, Mount Australia 58 D6
Kosciuszko National Park Australia 58 D6
Köse Turkey 35 E2
Köseçobanlı Turkey 39 A1
Kosgi India 38 C2
Kosh-Agach Rus. Fed. 42 F3
Koshikijima-rettō is Japan 45 C7
Koshki Rus. Fed. 13 K5
Kosi Bay S. Africa 51 K4
Košice Slovakia 13 D6
Kosigi India 38 C3
Koskullskulle Sweden 14 L3
Köslin Poland see Koszalin
Kosma r. Rus. Fed. 12 K2
Kosŏng N. Korea 45 C5
Kosova country Europe see Kosovo
Kosovo country Europe 27 I3
Kosovo-Metohija country Europe see Kosovo
Kosovska Mitrovica Kosovo see Mitrovicë
Kosrae atoll Micronesia 74 G5
Kosta-Khetagurovo Rus. Fed. see Nazran'
Kostanay Kazakh. 30 F1
Kostenets Bulg. 27 J3
Kosti Sudan 32 D7
Kostinbrod Bulg. 27 J3
Kostino Rus. Fed. 28 J3
Kostomuksha Rus. Fed. 12 F2
Kostopil' Ukr. 13 E6
Kostopol' Ukr. see Kostopil'
Kostroma Rus. Fed. 12 I4
Kostrzyn Poland 17 O4
Kostyantynivka Ukr. 13 H6
Kostyukovichi Belarus see Kastsyukovichy
Kos'yu Rus. Fed. 11 R2
Koszalin Poland 17 P3
Kőszeg Hungary 26 G1
Kota Andhra Prad. India 38 D3
Kota Chhattisgarh India 37 E5
Kota Rajasthan India 36 C4
Kota Baharu Malaysia see Kota Bharu
Kotabaru Kalimantan Selatan Indon. 41 D8
Kota Bharu Malaysia 41 C7
Kot Addu Pak. 36 B3
Kota Kinabalu Sabah Malaysia 41 D7
Kotaparh India 38 D2
Kot Diji Pak. 36 B4
Kotel'nich Rus. Fed. 12 K4
Kotel'nikovo Rus. Fed. 13 I7
Kotel'nyy, Ostrov i. Rus. Fed. 29 O2
Kotgar India 38 D2
Kotgarh India 36 D3
Kothagudem India see Kottagudem
Kotido Uganda 47 G4
Kotikovo Rus. Fed. 44 D3
Kotka Fin. 15 O6
Kot Kapura India 36 C3
Kotkino Rus. Fed. 12 K2
Kotlas Rus. Fed. 12 J3
Kotli Pak. 36 C2
Kotlik U.S.A. 60 B3
Kötlutangi pt Iceland 14 [inset]
Kotly Rus. Fed. 15 P7
Kotorkoshi Nigeria 46 D3
Kotovo Rus. Fed. 13 J6
Kotovsk Rus. Fed. 13 I5
Kotra India 36 C4
Kotra Pak. 36 A3
Kotri r. India 38 D2
Kot Sarae Pak. 36 A5
Kottagudem India 38 D2
Kottarakara India 38 C4
Kottayam India 38 C4
Kotte Sri Lanka see Sri Jayewardenepura Kotte
Kotto r. Cent. Afr. Rep. 48 C3
Kotturu India 38 C3
Kotuy r. Rus. Fed. 29 L2
Kotzebue U.S.A. 60 B3
Kotzebue Sound sea chan. U.S.A. 60 B3
Kouango Cent. Afr. Rep. 48 C3
Koubia Guinea 46 B3
Koudougou Burkina 46 C3
Kouebokkeveld mts S. Africa 50 D7
Koufey Niger 46 E3
Koufonisi i. Greece 27 L7
Kougaberge mts S. Africa 50 F7
Koukourou r. Cent. Afr. Rep. 48 B3
Koulikoro Mali 46 C3
Koumac New Caledonia 53 G4
Koumpentoum Senegal 46 B3
Koundâra Guinea 46 B3
Koupéla Burkina 46 C3
Kourou Fr. Guiana 69 H2
Kouroussa Guinea 46 C3
Kousséri Cameroon 47 E3
Koutiala Mali 46 C3
Kouvola Fin. 15 O6
Kovallberget Sweden 14 J4
Kovdor Rus. Fed. 12 F2
Kovdozero, Ozero l. Rus. Fed. 14 R3
Kovel' Ukr. 13 E6
Kovernino Rus. Fed. 12 I4
Kovilpatti India 38 C4
Kovno Lith. see Kaunas
Kovriga, Gora h. Rus. Fed. 12 K2
Kovrov Rus. Fed. 12 I4
Kovylkino Rus. Fed. 13 I5
Kovzhskoye, Ozero l. Rus. Fed. 12 H3
Kowanyama Australia 56 C2
Kowloon H.K. China 73 P4
Kowŏn N. Korea 45 B5
Kōyama-misaki pt Japan 45 C6
Köyceğiz Turkey 27 M6
Koygorodok Rus. Fed. 12 K3
Koyna Reservoir India 38 B2
Köytendag Turkm. 33 K2
Koyuk U.S.A. 60 B3
Koyukuk r. U.S.A. 60 C3
Koyulhisar Turkey 34 E2
Kozağacı Turkey see Günyüzü
Kō-zaki pt Japan 45 C6
Kozan Turkey 34 D3
Kozani Greece 27 I4
Kozara mts Bos.-Herz. 26 G2
Kozara nat. park Bos.-Herz. 26 G2
Kozarska Dubica Bos.-Herz. see Bosanska Dubica
Kozelets' Ukr. 13 F6
Kozel'sk Rus. Fed. 13 G5
Kozhikode India see Calicut
Kozhva Rus. Fed. 12 M2
Kozlu Turkey 27 N4
Koz'modem'yansk Rus. Fed. 12 J4
Kožuf mts Greece/Macedonia 27 J4
Kōzu-shima i. Japan 45 E6
Kozyatyn Ukr. 13 F6
Kpalimé Togo 46 D4
Kpandae Ghana 46 C4
Kpungan Pass India/Myanmar 37 I4
Krabi Thai. 31 I6
Krâchéh Cambodia 31 J5
Kraddsele Sweden 14 J4
Kragerø Norway 15 F7
Kragujevac Serbia 27 I2
Krakau Poland see Kraków
Kraków Poland 17 Q5
Kralendijk Neth. Antilles 67 K6
Kramators'k Ukr. 13 H6
Kramfors Sweden 14 J5
Kranidi Greece 27 J6
Kranj Slovenia 26 F1
Kranskop S. Africa 51 J5
Krasavino Rus. Fed. 12 J3
Krasilov Ukr. see Krasyliv
Krasino Rus. Fed. 28 G2
Kraskino Rus. Fed. 44 C4
Krāslava Latvia 15 O9
Krasnaya Gorbatka Rus. Fed. 12 I5
Krasnaya Zarya Rus. Fed. 13 H5
Krasnoarmeysk Rus. Fed. 13 J6
Krasnoarmeysk Ukr. see Krasnoarmiys'k
Krasnoarmiys'k Ukr. 13 H6
Krasnoborsk Rus. Fed. 12 J3
Krasnodar Rus. Fed. 13 H7
Krasnodar Kray admin. div. Rus. Fed. see Krasnodarskiy Kray
Krasnodarskiy Kray admin. div. Rus. Fed. 34 E1
Krasnodon Ukr. 13 H6
Krasnogorodskoye Rus. Fed. 15 P8
Krasnogorsk Rus. Fed. 44 F2
Krasnogorskoye Rus. Fed. 12 L4
Krasnograd Ukr. see Krasnohrad
Krasnogvardeyskiy Uzbek. see Bulung'ur
Krasnogvardeyskoye Rus. Fed. 13 I7
Krasnohrad Ukr. 13 G6
Krasnohvardiys'ke Ukr. 13 G7
Krasnokamsk Rus. Fed. 11 R4
Krasnoperekops'k Ukr. 13 G7
Krasnopol'ye Rus. Fed. 44 F2
Krasnorechenskiy Rus. Fed. 44 D3
Krasnoslobodsk Rus. Fed. 13 I5
Krasnotur'insk Rus. Fed. 11 S4
Krasnoufimsk Rus. Fed. 11 R4
Krasnovishersk Rus. Fed. 11 R3
Krasnovodsk Turkm. see Türkmenbaşy
Krasnovodsk, Mys pt Turkm. 35 I3
Krasnovodskoye Plato plat. Turkm. 35 I2
Krasnovodsk Aylagy b. Turkm. see Türkmenbaşy Aylagy
Krasnoyarovo Rus. Fed. 44 C2
Krasnoyarsk Rus. Fed. 28 K4
Krasnoyarskoye Vodokhranilishche resr Rus. Fed. 42 G2
Krasnoye Lipetskaya Oblast' Rus. Fed. 13 H5
Krasnoye Respublika Kalmykiya-Khalm'g-Tangch Rus. Fed. see Ulan Erge
Krasnoznamenskiy Kazakh. see Yegindykol'
Krasnoznamenskoye Kazakh. see Yegindykol'
Krasnyy Rus. Fed. 13 F5
Krasnyy Chikoy Rus. Fed. 43 J2
Krasnyye Baki Rus. Fed. 12 J4
Krasnyy Kamyshanik Rus. Fed. see Komsomol'skiy
Krasnyy Kholm Rus. Fed. 12 H4
Krasnyy Kut Rus. Fed. 13 J6
Krasnyy Luch Ukr. 13 H6
Krasnyy Lyman Ukr. 13 H6
Krasnyy Yar Rus. Fed. 13 K7
Krasyliv Ukr. 13 E6
Kratie Cambodia see Krâchéh
Kraulshavn Greenland see Nuussuaq
Kraynovka Rus. Fed. 13 J8
Krefeld Germany 17 K5
Kremenchug Ukr. see Kremenchuk
Kremenchugskoye Vodokhranilishche resr Ukr. see Kremenchuts'ka Vodoskhovyshche
Kremenchuk Ukr. 13 G6
Kremenchuts'ka Vodoskhovyshche resr Ukr. 13 G6
Křemešník h. Czech Rep. 17 O6
Kremges Ukr. see Svitlovods'k
Kremmydi, Akrotirio pt Greece 27 J6
Krems Austria see Krems an der Donau
Krems an der Donau Austria 17 O6
Kresta, Zaliv g. Rus. Fed. 29 T3
Kresttsy Rus. Fed. 12 G4
Kretinga Lith. 15 L9
Kreva Belarus 15 O9
Kribi Cameroon 46 D4
Krichev Belarus see Krychaw
Kriel S. Africa 51 I4
Krikellos Greece 27 I5
Kril'on, Mys c. Rus. Fed. 44 F3
Krishna India 38 C2
Krishna r. India 38 D2
Krishnanagar India 37 G5
Krishnaraja Sagara l. India 38 C3
Kristiania Norway see Oslo
Kristiansand Norway 15 E7
Kristianstad Sweden 15 I8
Kristiansund Norway 14 E5
Kristiinankaupunki Fin. see Kristinestad
Kristinehamn Sweden 15 I7
Kristinestad Fin. 14 L5
Kristinopol' Ukr. see Chervonohrad
Kriti i. Greece see Crete
Kritiko Pelagos sea Greece 27 K6
Krivoy Rog Ukr. see Kryvyy Rih
Križevci Croatia 26 G1
Krk i. Croatia 26 F2
Krkonošský narodní park nat. park Czech Rep./Poland 17 O5
Krokom Sweden 14 I5
Krokstadøra Norway 14 F5
Krokstranda Norway 14 I3
Krolevets' Ukr. 13 G6
Kronoby Fin. 14 M5
Kronprins Christian Land reg. Greenland 77 I1
Kronprins Frederik Bjerge nunataks Greenland 61 O3
Kronshtadt Rus. Fed. 15 P7
Kronstadt Romania see Braşov
Kronstadt Rus. Fed. see Kronshtadt
Kroonstad S. Africa 51 H4
Kropotkin Rus. Fed. 13 I7
Krosno Poland 13 D6
Krotoszyn Poland 17 P5
Kruger National Park S. Africa 51 J2
Kruglikovo Rus. Fed. 44 D2
Kruglyakov Rus. Fed. see Oktyabr'skiy
Krui Indon. 41 C8
Kruisfontein S. Africa 50 G8
Kruja Albania see Krujë
Krujë Albania 27 H4
Krumovgrad Bulg. 27 K4
Krungkao Thai. see Ayutthaya
Krung Thep Thai. see Bangkok
Krupa Bos.-Herz. see Bosanska Krupa
Krupa na Uni Bos.-Herz. see Bosanska Krupa
Krupki Belarus 13 F5
Krusenstern, Cape U.S.A. 60 B3
Kruševac Serbia 27 I3
Krychaw Belarus 13 F5
Krylov Seamount sea feature N. Atlantic Ocean 72 G4
Krym' pen. Ukr. see Crimea
Krymsk Rus. Fed. 34 E1
Krymskaya Rus. Fed. see Krymsk
Kryms'kyy Pivostriv pen. Ukr. see Crimea
Krystynopol Ukr. see Chervonohrad
Kryvyy Rih Ukr. 13 G7
Ksabi Alg. 22 D6
Ksar Chellala Alg. 25 H6
Ksar el Boukhari Alg. 25 H6
Ksar el Kebir Morocco 22 C5
Ksar-es-Souk Morocco see Er Rachidia
Ksenofontova Rus. Fed. 11 R3
Kshirpai India 37 F5
Ksour Essaf Tunisia 26 D7
Kstovo Rus. Fed. 12 J4
Kū', Jabal al h. Saudi Arabia 32 G4
Kuaidamao China see Tonghua
Kuala Dungun Malaysia see Dungun
Kuala Lipis Malaysia 41 C7
Kuala Lumpur Malaysia 41 C7
Kuala Terengganu Malaysia 41 C7
Kuandian China 44 B4
Kuantan Malaysia 41 C7
Kuba Azer. see Quba
Kuban' r. Rus. Fed. 13 H7
Kubār Syria 35 E4
Kubaybāt Syria 39 C2
Kubaysah Iraq 35 F4
Kubenskoye, Ozero l. Rus. Fed. 12 H4
Kubrat Bulg. 27 L3
Kuchema Rus. Fed. 12 I2
Kuching Sarawak Malaysia 41 D7
Kucing Sarawak Malaysia see Kuching
Kuçovë Albania 27 H4
Kuda India 36 B5
Kudal India 38 B3
Kudat Sabah Malaysia 41 D7
Kudligi India 38 C3
Kudremukh mt. India 38 B3
Kudymkar Rus. Fed. 11 Q4
Kūfah Iraq 35 G4
Kufstein Austria 17 N7
Kugaaruk Canada 61 J3
Kugesi Rus. Fed. 12 J4
Kugka Lhai China 37 G3
Kugluktuk Canada 60 G3
Kugmallit Bay Canada 77 A2
Kuhanbokano mt. China 37 E3
Kūhdasht Iran 35 G4
Kūhhā-ye Zagros mts Iran see Zagros Mountains
Kūhīn Iran 35 H3
Kuhmo Fin. 14 P4
Kuhmoinen Fin. 15 N6
Kūhrān, Kūh-e mt. Iran 33 I4
Kuis Namibia 50 C3
Kuiseb watercourse Namibia 50 B2
Kuito Angola 49 B5
Kuitun China see Kuytun
Kuivaniemi Fin. 14 N4
Kujang N. Korea 45 B5
Kuji Japan 45 F4
Kujū-san vol. Japan 45 C6
Kukan Rus. Fed. 44 D2
Kukës Albania 27 I3
Kukesi Albania see Kukës
Kukmor Rus. Fed. 12 K4
Kukshi India 36 C5
Kukunuru India 38 D2
Kula Turkey 27 M5
Kulaisila India 37 F5
Kula Kangri mt. China/Bhutan 37 G3
Kulandy Kazakh. 28 G5
Kular Rus. Fed. 29 O2
Kuldīga Latvia 15 L8
Kuldja China see Yining
Kul'dur Rus. Fed. 44 C2
Kule Botswana 50 E2
Kulebaki Rus. Fed. 13 I5
Kulgera Australia 55 F6
Kulikovo Rus. Fed. 12 J3
Kulin Australia 55 B8
Kulja Australia 55 B7
Kulkyne watercourse Australia 58 B3
Kullu India 36 D3
Kulmbach Germany 17 M5
Kŭlob Tajik. 33 K2
Kuloy Rus. Fed. 12 I3
Kuloy r. Rus. Fed. 12 I2
Kulp Turkey 35 F3
Kul'sary Kazakh. 30 E2
Kulu India see Kullu
Kulu Turkey 34 D3
Kulunda Rus. Fed. 42 D2
Kulundinskaya Step' plain Kazakh./Rus. Fed. 42 D2
Kulundinskoye, Ozero salt l. Rus. Fed. 42 D2
Kulusuk Greenland 61 O3
Kulwin Australia 57 C7
Kulyab Tajik. see Kŭlob
Kuma r. Rus. Fed. 13 J7
Kumagaya Japan 45 E5
Kumalar Dağı mts Turkey 27 N5
Kumamoto Japan 45 C6
Kumano Japan 45 E6
Kumanovo Macedonia 27 I3
Kumara Rus. Fed. 44 B2
Kumasi Ghana 46 C4
Kumayri Armenia see Gyumri
Kumba Cameroon 46 D4
Kumbakonam India 38 C4
Kümbet Turkey 27 N5
Kumbharli Ghat mt. India 38 B2
Kumbla India 38 B3
Kumchuru Botswana 50 F2
Kum-Dag Turkm. see Gumdag
Kumdah Saudi Arabia 32 G5
Kumel well Iran 35 I4
Kumeny Rus. Fed. 12 K4
Kumertau Rus. Fed. 28 G4
Kumgang-san mt. N. Korea 45 C5
Kumguri India 37 G4
Kumi S. Korea 45 C5
Kumi Uganda 47 G4
Kumla Sweden 15 I7
Kumluca Turkey 39 C1
Kumo Nigeria 46 E3
Kŭmō-do i. S. Korea 45 B6
Kumon Range mts Myanmar 42 H7
Kums Namibia 50 D5
Kumta India 38 B3
Kumu Dem. Rep. Congo 48 C3
Kumukh Rus. Fed. 35 G2
Kumul China see Hami
Kumund India 38 D1
Kumylzhenskaya Rus. Fed. see Kumylzhenskiy
Kumylzhenskiy Rus. Fed. 13 I6
Kunar r. Afgh. 36 B2
Kunashir, Ostrov i. Rus. Fed. 44 G3
Kunashirskiy Proliv sea chan. Japan/Rus. Fed. see Nemuro-kaikyō
Kunchuk Tso salt l. China 37 E2
Kunda Estonia 15 O7
Kunda India 37 E4
Kundapura India 38 B3
Kundelungu, Parc National de nat. park Dem. Rep. Congo 49 C5
Kundelungu Ouest, Parc National de nat. park Dem. Rep. Congo 49 C5
Kundia India 36 C4
Kunduz Afgh. 36 B1
Kunene r. Angola see Cunene
Kuneneng admin. dist. Botswana see Kweneng
Künes China see Xinyuan
Kungälv Sweden 15 G8
Kungsbacka Sweden 15 H8
Kungshamn Sweden 15 G7
Kungu Dem. Rep. Congo 48 B3
Kungur mt. China see Kongur Shan
Kungur Rus. Fed. 11 R4
Kunhi r. India 38 C2
Kunié i. New Caledonia see Pins, Île des
Kunigai India 38 C3
Kunimi-dake mt. Japan 45 C6
Kunkavav India 36 B5
Kunlun Shan mts China 36 D1
Kunlun Shankou pass China 37 H2
Kunming China 42 I7
Kunsan S. Korea 45 B6

Kununurra Australia 54 E3
Kun'ya Rus. Fed. 12 F4
Kunya-Urgench Turkm. see Köneürgenç
Kuohijärvi l. Fin. 15 N6
Kuolayarvi Rus. Fed. 14 P3
Kuopio Fin. 14 O5
Kuortane Fin. 14 M5
Kupa r. Croatia/Slovenia 26 G2
Kupang Indon. 41 E9
Kupari India 37 F5
Kupiškis Lith. 15 N9
Kupreanof Island U.S.A. 60 E4
Kupwara India 36 C2
Kup"yans'k Ukr. 13 H6
Kuqa China 42 E4
Kur r. Rus. Fed. 44 D2
Kura r. Georgia 35 G2
Kuragino Rus. Fed. 42 G2
Kurakh Rus. Fed. 13 J8
Kurama Range mts Asia 33 K1
Kuraminskiy Khrebet mts Asia see Kurama Range
Kurashiki Japan 45 D6
Kurasia India 37 E5
Kurayn i. Saudi Arabia 35 H6
Kurayoshi Japan 45 D6
Kurchatov Rus. Fed. 13 G6
Kurchum Kazakh. 42 E3
Kürdämir Azer. 35 H2
Kŭrdzhali Bulg. 27 K4
Kure Japan 45 D6
Küre Turkey 34 D2
Kure Atoll U.S.A. 74 I4
Kuressaare Estonia 15 M7
Kurgal'dzhino Kazakh. see Korgalzhyn
Kurgal'dzhinskiy Kazakh. see Korgalzhyn
Kurgan Rus. Fed. 28 H4
Kurganinsk Rus. Fed. 35 F1
Kurgannaya Rus. Fed. see Kurganinsk
Kurgantyube Tajik. see Qŭrghonteppa
Kuri India 36 B4
Kuria Muria Islands Oman see Ḩalāniyāt, Juzur al
Kuridala Australia 56 C4
Kurigram Bangl. 37 G4
Kurikka Fin. 14 M5
Kuril Basin sea feature Sea of Okhotsk 74 F2
Kuril Islands Rus. Fed. 44 H3
Kurilovka Rus. Fed. 13 K6
Kuril'sk Rus. Fed. 44 G3
Kuril'skiye Ostrova is Rus. Fed. see Kuril Islands
Kuril Trench sea feature N. Pacific Ocean 74 F3
Kurkino Rus. Fed. 13 H5
Kurmashkino Kazakh. see Kurchum
Kurmuk Sudan 32 D7
Kurnool India 38 C3
Kuroiso Japan 45 F5
Kurovskiy Rus. Fed. 44 B1
Kurow N.Z. 59 C7
Kurram Pak. 36 B2
Kurri Kurri Australia 58 E4
Kursavka Rus. Fed. 35 F1
Kürshim Kazakh. see Kurchum
Kurshskiy Zaliv b. Lith./Rus. Fed. see Courland Lagoon
Kuršių marios b. Lith./Rus. Fed. see Courland Lagoon
Kursk Rus. Fed. 13 H6
Kurskaya Rus. Fed. 35 G1
Kurskiy Zaliv b. Lith./Rus. Fed. see Courland Lagoon
Kurşunlu Turkey 34 D2
Kurtalan Turkey 35 F3
Kurtoğlu Burnu pt Turkey 27 M6
Kurtpınar Turkey 39 B1
Kurucaşile Turkey 34 D2
Kuruçay Turkey 34 E3
Kurukshetra India 36 D3
Kuruktag mts China 42 F4
Kuruman S. Africa 50 F4
Kuruman watercourse S. Africa 50 E4
Kurume Japan 45 C6
Kurumkan Rus. Fed. 43 K2
Kurunegala Sri Lanka 38 D5
Kurupam India 38 D2
Kurush, Jebel hills Sudan 32 D5
Kur'ya Rus. Fed. 11 R3
Kuryk Kazakh. 35 H2
Kuşadası Turkey 27 L6
Kuşadası Körfezi b. Turkey 27 L6
Kusaie atoll Micronesia see Kosrae
Kusary Azer. see Qusar
Kuşcenneti nat. park Turkey 39 B1
Kuschke Nature Reserve S. Africa 51 I3
Kuş Gölü l. Turkey 27 L4
Kushalgarh India 36 C5
Kushchevskaya Rus. Fed. 13 H7
Kushimoto Japan 45 D6
Kushiro Japan 44 G4
Kushka Turkm. see Serhetabat
Kushkopola Rus. Fed. 12 J3
Kushmurun Kazakh. 30 F1
Kushtagi India 38 C3
Kushtia Bangl. 37 G5
Kuskan Turkey 39 A1
Kuskokwim r. U.S.A. 60 B3
Kuskokwim Bay U.S.A. 60 B4
Kuskokwim Mountains U.S.A. 60 C3
Kuşluyan Turkey see Gölköy
Kusŏng N. Korea 45 B5
Kustanay Kazakh. see Kostanay
Küstence Romania see Constanța
Kustia Bangl. see Kushtia
Kut Iran 35 H5
Kūt 'Abdollāh Iran 35 H5
Kütahya Turkey 27 M5
K'ut'aisi Georgia 35 F2
Kut-al-Imara Iraq see Al Kūt
Kutan Rus. Fed. 13 J7
Kutaraja Indon. see Banda Aceh
Kutayfat Turayf vol. Saudi Arabia 39 D4
Kutch, Gulf of India see Kachchh, Gulf of
Kutch, Rann of marsh India see Kachchh, Rann of
Kutchan Japan 44 F4
Kutina Croatia 26 G2
Kutjevo Croatia 26 G2
Kutno Poland 17 Q4
Kutru India 38 D2
Kutu Dem. Rep. Congo 48 B4
Kutubdia Island Bangl. 37 G5
Kutum Sudan 47 F3
Kutztown PA U.S.A. 64 D2
Kuujjua r. Canada 60 G2
Kuujjuaq Canada 61 L4
Kuujjuarapik Canada 61 K4
Kuusamo Fin. 14 P4
Kuusankoski Fin. 15 O6
Kuvango Angola 49 B5
Kuvshinovo Rus. Fed. 12 G4
Kuwait country Asia 32 G4
Kuwait Kuwait 35 G5
Kuwajleen atoll Marshall Is see Kwajalein
Kuybyshev Novosibirskaya Oblast' Rus. Fed. 28 I4
Kuybyshev Respublika Tatarstan Rus. Fed. see Bolgar
Kuybyshev Samarskaya Oblast' Rus. Fed. see Samara
Kuybysheve Ukr. 13 H7
Kuybyshevka-Vostochnaya Rus. Fed. see Belogorsk
Kuybyshevskoye Vodokhranilishche resr Rus. Fed. 13 K5
Kuyeda Rus. Fed. 11 R4
Kuygan Kazakh. 42 C3
Kuytun China 42 E4
Kuytun Rus. Fed. 42 I2
Kuyucak Turkey 27 M6
Kuzino Rus. Fed. 11 R4
Kuznechnoye Rus. Fed. 15 P6
Kuznetsk Rus. Fed. 13 J5
Kuznetsovo Rus. Fed. 44 E3
Kuznetsovs'k Ukr. 13 E6
Kuzovatovo Rus. Fed. 13 J5
Kvænangen sea chan. Norway 14 L1
Kvaløya i. Norway 14 K2
Kvalsund Norway 14 M1
Kvarnerić sea chan. Croatia 26 F2
Kvitøya i. Svalbard 28 E2
Kwa r. Dem. Rep. Congo see Kasaï
Kwabhaca S. Africa see Mount Frere
Kwadelen atoll Marshall Is see Kwajalein
Kwajalein atoll Marshall Is 74 H5
Kwale Nigeria 46 D4
KwaMashu S. Africa 51 J5
KwaMhlanga S. Africa 51 I3
Kwa Mtoro Tanz. 49 D4
Kwangch'ŏn S. Korea 45 B5
Kwangchow China see Guangzhou
Kwangju S. Korea 45 B6
Kwangsi Chuang Autonomous Region aut. reg. China see Guangxi Zhuangzu Zizhiqu
Kwangtung prov. China see Guangdong
Kwanmo-bong mt. N. Korea 44 C4
Kwanobuhle S. Africa 51 G7
KwaNojoli S. Africa 51 G7
Kwanonqubela S. Africa 51 H7
KwaNonzame S. Africa 50 G6
Kwanza r. Angola see Cuanza
Kwatinidubu S. Africa 51 H7
KwaZamokuhle S. Africa 51 I4
KwaZamukucinga S. Africa 50 G7
Kwazamuxolo S. Africa 50 G6
KwaZanele S. Africa 51 I4
KwaZulu-Natal prov. S. Africa 51 J5
Kweichow prov. China see Guizhou
Kweiyang China see Guiyang
Kwekwe Zimbabwe 49 C5
Kweneng admin. dist. Botswana 50 G2
Kwenge r. Dem. Rep. Congo 49 B4
Kwezi-Naledi S. Africa 51 H6
Kwidzyn Poland 17 Q4
Kwikila P.N.G. 52 E2
Kwilu r. Angola/Dem. Rep. Congo 49 B4
Kwoka mt. Indon. 41 F8
Kyabra Australia 57 C5
Kyabram Australia 58 B6
Kyakhta Rus. Fed. 42 J2
Kyalite Australia 58 A5
Kyancutta Australia 55 F8
Kyangin Myanmar 37 I6
Kyangngoin China 37 H3
Kyaukpadaung Myanmar 37 H5
Kyaukpyu Myanmar 37 H6
Kyaukse Myanmar 37 I5
Kyauktaw Myanmar 37 H5
Kybartai Lith. 15 M9
Kyêbxang Co l. China 37 G2
Kyela Tanz. 49 D4
Kyelang India 36 D2
Kyidaunggan Myanmar 37 I6
Kyiv Ukr. see Kiev
Kyklades is Greece see Cyclades
Kyle of Lochalsh U.K. 20 D3
Kyllini mt. Greece 27 J6
Kymi Greece 27 K5
Kymis, Akrotirio pt Greece 27 K5
Kyneton Australia 58 B6
Kynuna Australia 56 C4
Kyoga, Lake Uganda 48 D3
Kyōga-misaki pt Japan 45 D6
Kyogle Australia 58 F2
Kyŏngju S. Korea 45 C6
Kyōto Japan 45 D6
Kyparissia Greece 27 I6
Kypros country Asia see Cyprus
Kypshak, Ozero salt l. Kazakh. 31 F1
Kyra Rus. Fed. 43 K3
Kyra Panagia i. Greece 27 K5
Kyrenia Cyprus 39 A2
Kyrenia Mountains Cyprus see Pentadaktylos Range
Kyrgyz Ala-Too mts Kazakh./Kyrg. see Kirghiz Range
Kyrgyzstan country Asia 31 G2
Kyrksæterøra Norway 14 F5
Kyrta Rus. Fed. 11 R3
Kyssa Rus. Fed. 12 J2
Kytalyktakh Rus. Fed. 29 O3
Kythira i. Greece 27 J6
Kythnos i. Greece 27 K6
Kyunglung China 36 E3
Kyunhla Myanmar 37 H5
Kyuquot Canada 62 B1
Kyurdamir Azer. see Kürdämir
Kyūshū i. Japan 45 C7
Kyushu-Palau Ridge sea feature N. Pacific Ocean 74 F4
Kyustendil Bulg. 27 J3
Kywong Australia 58 C5
Kyyev Ukr. see Kiev
Kyyiv Ukr. see Kiev
Kyyivs'ke Vodoskhovyshche resr Ukr. 13 F6
Kyyjärvi Fin. 14 N5
Kyzyl Rus. Fed. 42 G2
Kyzyl-Burun Azer. see Siyäzän
Kyzyl-Kiya Kyrg. see Kyzyl-Kyya
Kyzylkum, Peski des. Kazakh./Uzbek. see Kyzylkum Desert
Kyzylkum Desert Kazakh./Uzbek. 30 F2
Kyzyl-Kyya Kyrg. 42 C4
Kyzyl-Mazhalyk Rus. Fed. 42 G2
Kyzylorda Kazakh. 42 B4
Kyzylrabot Tajik. see Qizilrabot
Kyzylsay Kazakh. 35 I2
Kyzylysor Kazakh. 35 H1
Kyzylzhar Kazakh. 42 B3
Kzyl-Dzhar Kazakh. see Kyzylzhar
Kzyl-Orda Kazakh. see Kyzylorda
Kzyltu Kazakh. see Kishkenekol'

L

Laagri Estonia 15 N7
La Angostura, Presa de resr Mex. 66 F5
Laanila Fin. 14 O2
Laascaanood Somalia 48 E3
La Ascensión, Bahía de b. Mex. 67 G5
Laasgoray Somalia 48 E2
Laâyoune W. Sahara 46 B2
La Banda Arg. 70 D3
Labasa Fiji 53 H3
La Baule-Escoublac France 24 C3
Labazhskoye Rus. Fed. 12 L2
Labé Guinea 46 B3
La Bénoué, Parc National de nat. park Cameroon 47 E4
Labinsk Rus. Fed. 13 I7
La Boucle du Baoulé, Parc National de nat. park Mali 46 C3
Labouheyre France 24 D4
Laboulaye Arg. 70 D4
Labrador reg. Canada 61 L4
Labrador City Canada 61 L4
Labrador Sea Canada/Greenland 61 M3
Lábrea Brazil 68 F5
Labudalin China see Ergun
Labuhanbilik Indon. 41 C7
Labuna Indon. 41 E8
Labyrinth, Lake imp. l. Australia 57 A6
Labytnangi Rus. Fed. 28 H3
Laç Albania 27 H4
La Cabrera, Sierra de mts Spain 25 C2
La Calle Alg. see El Kala
La Cañiza Spain see A Cañiza
La Capelle France 24 F2
La Carlota Arg. 70 D4
La Carolina Spain 25 E4
Lăcăuți, Vârful mt. Romania 27 L2
Laccadive, Minicoy and Amindivi Islands union terr. India see Lakshadweep
Laccadive Islands India 38 B4
Lac du Bonnet Canada 63 H1
Lacedaemon Greece see Sparti
La Ceiba Hond. 67 G5
Lacepede Bay Australia 57 B8
Lacepede Islands Australia 54 C4
Lacha, Ozero l. Rus. Fed. 12 H3
Lachlan r. Australia 58 A5
La Chorrera Panama 67 I7
Lachute Canada 63 M2
Laçın Azer. 35 G3
La Ciotat France 24 G5
Lac La Biche Canada 60 G4
Lac la Martre Canada see Whatî
Lacombe Canada 62 E1
La Comoé, Parc National de nat. park Côte d'Ivoire 46 C4
Laconi Sardegna Italy 26 C5
Laconia NH U.S.A. 64 F1
La Coruña Spain see A Coruña
La Coubre, Pointe de pt France 24 D4
La Crosse WI U.S.A. 63 I3
La Cruz Mex. 66 C4
La Cuesta Mex. 62 G6
La Culebra, Sierra de mts Spain 25 C3
Ladainha Brazil 71 C2
Ladakh reg. India/Pak. 36 D2
Ladakh Range mts India 36 D2
La Demanda, Sierra de mts Spain 25 E2
La Déroute, Passage de str. Channel Is/France 19 E9
Ladik Turkey 34 D2
Ladnun India 36 C4
Ladoga, Lake Rus. Fed. 12 F3
Ladozhskoye Ozero l. Rus. Fed. see Ladoga, Lake
Ladrones terr. N. Pacific Ocean see Northern Mariana Islands
Ladu mt. India 37 H4
Ladva-Vetka Rus. Fed. 12 G3
Ladybank U.K. 20 F4
Ladybrand S. Africa 51 H5
Lady Frere S. Africa 51 H6
Lady Grey S. Africa 51 H6
Ladysmith S. Africa 51 I5
Ladzhanurges Georgia see Lajanurpekhi
Lae P.N.G. 52 E2
Lærdalsøyri Norway 15 E6
La Esmeralda Bol. 68 F8
Læsø i. Denmark 15 G8
Lafayette Alg. see Bougaa
Lafayette IN U.S.A. 63 J3
Lafayette LA U.S.A. 63 I5
Lafia Nigeria 46 D4
Lafiagi Nigeria 46 D4
La Flèche France 24 D3
Laforge Canada 61 K4
Lāft Iran 33 I4
La Galite i. Tunisia 26 C6
La Galite, Canal de sea chan. Tunisia 26 C6
Lagan' Rus. Fed. 13 J7
Lagan r. U.K. 21 G3
La Garamba, Parc National de nat. park Dem. Rep. Congo 48 C3
Lagarto Brazil 69 K6
Lågen r. Norway 15 G7
Lagg U.K. 20 D5
Laggan U.K. 20 E3
Lagh Bor watercourse Kenya/Somalia 48 E3
Laghouat Alg. 22 E5
Lagkor Co salt l. China 37 F2
Lago Agrio Ecuador 68 C3
Lagoa Santa Brazil 71 C2
Lagoa Vermelha Brazil 71 A5
Lagodekhi Georgia 35 G2
Lagolândia Brazil 71 A1
La Gomera i. Canary Is 46 B2
La Gonâve, Île de i. Haiti 67 J5
Lagos Nigeria 46 D4
Lagos Port. 25 B5
Lagosa Tanz. 49 C4
La Grande U.S.A. 62 D2
La Grande 3, Réservoir resr Canada 61 K4
La Grande 4, Réservoir resr Que. Canada 61 K4
La Grange Australia 54 C4
La Grange CA U.S.A. 65 B2
La Grange GA U.S.A. 63 J5
La Gran Sabana plat. Venez. 68 F2
La Grita Venez. 68 D2
La Guajira, Península de pen. Col. 68 D1
Laguna Brazil 71 A5
Laguna, Picacho de la mt. Mex. 66 B4
Laguna Dam Arizona/California U.S.A. 65 E4
Laguna Mountains CA U.S.A. 65 D4
Lagunas Chile 70 C2
Laguna San Rafael, Parque Nacional nat. park Chile 70 B7
Laha China 44 B2
La Habana Cuba see Havana
La Habra CA U.S.A. 65 D4
Lahad Datu Sabah Malaysia 41 D7
La Hague, Cap de c. France 24 D2
Laharpur India 36 E4
Lahat Indon. 41 C8
Lahe Myanmar 37 H4
Lahemaa rahvuspark nat. park Estonia 15 N7
La Hève, Cap de c. France 19 H9
Laḩij Yemen 32 F7
Lāhījān Iran 35 H3
Laholm Sweden 15 H8
Lahore Pak. 33 L3
Lahri Pak. 36 B3
Lahti Fin. 15 N6
Laï Chad 47 E4
Laibach Slovenia see Ljubljana
Laidley Australia 58 F1
L'Aigle France 24 E2
Laihia Fin. 14 M5
Laimakuri India 37 H4
Laimos, Akrotirio pt Greece 27 J5
Laingsburg S. Africa 50 E7
Lainioälven r. Sweden 14 M3
L'Aïr, Massif de mts Niger 46 D3
Lairg U.K. 20 E2
Laishevo Rus. Fed. 12 K5
Laitila Fin. 15 L6
Laives Italy 26 D1
Laiwu China 43 L5
Laiyang China 43 M5
Laizhou China 43 L5
Laizhou Wan b. China 43 L5
Lajamanu Australia 54 E4
Lajanurpekhi Georgia 35 F2
Lajeado Brazil 71 A5
Lajes Rio Grande do Norte Brazil 69 K5
Lajes Santa Catarina Brazil 71 A4
La Junta Mex. 62 F6
La Junta U.S.A. 62 G4
La Juventud, Isla de i. Cuba 67 H4
Lakadiya India 36 B5
L'Akagera, Parc National de nat. park Rwanda see Akagera National Park
La Kagera, Parc National de nat. park Rwanda see Akagera National Park
Lakeba i. Fiji 53 I3
Lake Bardawil Reserve nature res. Egypt 39 A4
Lake Bolac Australia 58 A6
Lake Cargelligo Australia 58 C4
Lake Cathie Australia 58 F3
Lake Charles U.S.A. 63 I5
Lake City FL U.S.A. 63 K5
Lake Clark National Park and Preserve U.S.A. 60 C3
Lake District National Park U.K. 18 D4
Lake Eyre National Park Australia 57 B6
Lakefield Australia 56 D2
Lakefield National Park Australia 56 D2
Lake Gairdner National Park Australia 57 B7
Lake George NY U.S.A. 64 E1
Lake Grace Australia 55 B8
Lake Harbour Canada see Kimmirut
Lake Havasu City AZ U.S.A. 65 E3
Lakehurst NJ U.S.A. 64 D2
Lake Isabella CA U.S.A. 65 C3
Lake King Australia 55 B8
Lakeland FL U.S.A. 63 K6
Lakemba i. Fiji see Lakeba
Lake Nash Australia 56 B4
Lake Paringa N.Z. 59 B6
Lake Pleasant NY U.S.A. 64 D1
Lakeport CA U.S.A. 65 A1
Lake Providence U.S.A. 63 I5
Lakes Entrance Australia 58 D6
Lakeside VA U.S.A. 64 C4
Lake Tabourie Australia 58 E5
Lake Tekapo N.Z. 59 C7
Lake Torrens National Park Australia 57 B6
Lakeview OR U.S.A. 62 C3
Lakewood NJ U.S.A. 64 D2
Lakewood NY U.S.A. 64 B1
Lakha India 36 B4
Lakhdenpokh'ya Rus. Fed. 14 Q6
Lakhimpur Assam India see North Lakhimpur
Lakhimpur Uttar Prad. India 36 E4
Lakhisarai India 37 F4
Lakhish r. Israel 39 B4
Lakhnadon India 36 D5
Lakhpat India 36 B5
Lakhtar India 36 B5
Lakki Marwat Pak. 33 L3
Lakonikos Kolpos b. Greece 27 J6
Lakor i. Indon. 54 E2
Lakota Côte d'Ivoire 46 C4
Laksefjorden sea chan. Norway 14 O1
Lakselv Norway 14 N1
Lakshadweep is India see Laccadive Islands
Lakshadweep union terr. India 38 B4
Lakshettipet India 38 C2
Lakshmipur Bangl. 37 G5
Laksmipur Bangl. see Lakshmipur
Lalaghat India 37 H4
Lalbara India 38 D1
L'Alcora Spain 25 F3
Lalganj India 37 F4
Lālī Iran 35 H4
La Ligua Chile 70 B4
Laliki Indon. 54 D1
Lalin China 44 B3
Lalín Spain 25 B2
La Línea de la Concepción Spain 25 D5
Lalin He r. China 44 B3
Lalitpur India 36 D4
Lalitpur Nepal see Patan
Lalmanirhat Bangl. see Lalmonirhat
Lalmonirhat Bangl. 37 G4
La Loche Canada 60 H4
La Louvière Belgium 16 J5
Lal'sk Rus. Fed. 12 J3
Lalung La pass China 37 F3
Lama Bangl. 37 H5
La Macarena, Parque Nacional nat. park Col. 68 D3
La Maddalena Sardegna Italy 26 C4
La Madeleine, Îles de is Canada 63 O2
La Madeleine, Monts de mts France 24 F3
Lamadian China 44 B3
Lamadianzi China see Lamadian
La Maiko, Parc National de nat. park Dem. Rep. Congo 48 C4
La Mancha reg. Spain 25 E4
La Manche str. France/U.K. see English Channel
Lamar CO U.S.A. 62 G4
Lamard Iran 35 I6
La Margeride, Monts de mts France 24 F4
La Marmora, Punta mt. Sardegna Italy 26 C5
La Martre, Lac l. Canada 60 G3
Lamas r. Turkey 39 B1
Lambaréné Gabon 48 B4
Lambasa Fiji see Labasa
Lambayeque Peru 68 C5
Lambay Island Ireland 21 G4
Lambert atoll Marshall Is see Ailinglaplap
Lambert Glacier Antarctica 76 E2
Lambert's Bay S. Africa 50 D7
Lambeth Ont. Canada 64 A1
Lambi India 36 C3
Lambourn Downs hills U.K. 19 F7
La Medjerda, Monts de mts Alg. 26 B6
Lamego Port. 25 C3
La Merced Arg. 70 C3
La Merced Peru 68 C6
Lameroo Australia 57 C7
La Mesa CA U.S.A. 65 D4
Lamesa U.S.A. 62 G5
Lamia Greece 27 J5
Lamington National Park Australia 58 F2
Lammerlaw Range mts N.Z. 59 B7
Lammermuir Hills U.K. 20 G5
Lammhult Sweden 15 I8
Lammi Fin. 15 N6
Lamont CA U.S.A. 65 C3
La Montagne d'Ambre, Parc National de nat. park Madag. 49 E5
La Montaña de Covadonga, Parque Nacional de nat. park Spain see Los Picos de Europa, Parque Nacional de
Lampang Thai. 31 I5
Lampazos Mex. 62 G6
Lampedusa, Isola di i. Sicilia Italy 26 E7
Lampeter U.K. 19 C6
Lampsacus Turkey see Lâpseki
Lamu Kenya 48 E4
Lamu Myanmar 37 H6
La Nao, Cabo de c. Spain 25 G4
Lanark U.K. 20 F5
Lancang Jiang r. Xizang/Yunnan China see Mekong
Lancaster U.K. 18 E4
Lancaster CA U.S.A. 65 C3
Lancaster PA U.S.A. 64 C2
Lancaster SC U.S.A. 63 K5
Lancaster VA U.S.A. 64 C4
Lancaster Canal U.K. 18 E5
Lancaster Sound str. Canada 61 J2
Lanchow China see Lanzhou
Landana Angola see Cacongo
Landau an der Isar Germany 17 N6
Landeck Austria 17 M7
Lander watercourse Australia 54 E5
Lander U.S.A. 62 F3
Landhi Pak. 36 A4
Landor Australia 55 B6
Landsberg Poland see Gorzów Wielkopolski
Landsberg am Lech Germany 17 M6
Land's End pt U.K. 19 B8
Landshut Germany 17 N6
Landskrona Sweden 15 H9
Lanesborough Ireland 21 E4
La'nga Co l. China 36 E3
Langar Afgh. 36 B2
Langberg mts S. Africa 50 F5
Langdon U.S.A. 62 H2
Langeac France 24 F4
Langeberg mts S. Africa 50 D7
Langeland i. Denmark 15 G9
Längelmäki Fin. 15 N6
Langenthal Switz. 24 H3
Langesund Norway 15 F7
Langfang China 43 L5
Langgar China 37 H3
Langjan Nature Reserve S. Africa 51 I2
Langjökull Iceland 14 [inset]
Langklip S. Africa 50 E5
Langlo Crossing Australia 57 D5
Langøya i. Norway 14 I2
Langphu mt. China 37 F3
Langport U.K. 19 E7
Langqên Zangbo r. China 36 D3
Langres France 24 G3
Langres, Plateau de France 24 G3
Langru China 36 D1
Langsa Indon. 41 B7
Långsele Sweden 14 J5
Lang Sơn Vietnam 42 J8
Langtang National Park Nepal 37 F3
Langting India 37 H4
Langtoft U.K. 18 G4
Languedoc reg. France 24 E5
Långvattnet Sweden 14 L4
Lanigan Canada 62 F1
Lanín, Parque Nacional nat. park Arg. 70 B5
Lanín, Volcán vol. Arg./Chile 70 B5
Lanji India 36 E5
Lanka country Asia see Sri Lanka
Länkäran Azer. 35 H3
Lannion France 24 C2
Lansån Sweden 14 M3
Lansing U.S.A. 63 K3
Lanxi Heilong. China 44 B3
Lan Yü i. Taiwan 43 M8
Lanzarote i. Canary Is 46 B2
Lanzhou China 42 I5
Lanzijing China 44 A3
Laoag Phil. 41 E6
Lao Cai Vietnam 31 J4
Laodicea Syria see Latakia
Laodicea Turkey see Denizli
Laodicea ad Lycum Turkey see Denizli
Laodicea ad Mare Syria see Latakia
Laohekou China 43 K6
Laojunmiao China see Yumen
La Okapi, Parc National de nat. park Dem. Rep. Congo 48 C3
Lao Ling mts China 44 B4
Laon France 24 F2
La Oroya Peru 68 C6
Laos country Asia 41 C6
Laotougou China 44 C4
Laotuding Shan mt. China 44 B4
Laowohi pass India see Khardung La
Laoye Ling mts Heilongjiang/Jilin China 44 C4
Laoye Ling mts Jilin China 44 B4
Lapa Brazil 71 A4
La Palma i. Canary Is 46 B2
La Palma Panama 67 I7
La Palma del Condado Spain 25 C5
La Panza Range mts CA U.S.A. 65 B3
La Paragua Venez. 68 F2
La Paya, Parque Nacional nat. park Col. 68 D3
La Paz Arg. 70 E4
La Paz Bol. 68 E7
La Paz Hond. 66 G6
La Paz Mex. 66 B4
La Pedrera Col. 68 E4
La Pendjari, Parc National de nat. park Benin 46 D3
La Pérouse Strait Japan/Rus. Fed. 44 F3
La Pesca Mex. 66 E4
Lapinlahti Fin. 14 O5
Lapithos Cyprus 39 A2
La Plata Arg. 70 E4
La Plata MD U.S.A. 64 C3
La Plata, Isla i. Ecuador 68 B4
La Plata, Río de sea chan. Arg./Uruguay 70 E4
Lapmežciems Latvia 15 M8
Lapominka Rus. Fed. 12 I2
Laporte PA U.S.A. 64 C2
Lappajärvi Fin. 14 M5
Lappajärvi l. Fin. 14 M5
Lappeenranta Fin. 15 P6
Lappi Fin. 15 L6
Lappland reg. Europe 14 K3
Lâpseki Turkey 27 L4
Laptevo Rus. Fed. see Yasnogorsk
Laptev Sea Rus. Fed. 29 N2
Lapua Fin. 14 M5
Lapurdum France see Bayonne
Laqiya Arbain well Sudan 32 C5
La Quiaca Arg. 70 C2
L'Aquila Italy 26 E3
La Quinta CA U.S.A. 65 D4
Lār Iran 35 I6
Larache Morocco 25 C6
Laramie U.S.A. 62 F3
Laramie Mountains U.S.A. 62 F3
Laranda Turkey see Karaman
Laranjal Paulista Brazil 71 B3
Laranjeiras do Sul Brazil 70 F3
Laranjinha r. Brazil 71 A3
Larantuka Indon. 41 E8
Larat Indon. 54 E1
Larat i. Indon. 41 F8
Larba Alg. 25 H5
Lärbro Sweden 15 K8
L'Ardenne, Plateau de plat. Belgium see Ardennes
Laredo Spain 25 E2
Laredo U.S.A. 62 H6
La Reina Adelaida, Archipiélago de is Chile 70 B8
Largeau Chad see Faya
Largs U.K. 20 E5
Lārī Iran 35 G3
L'Ariana Tunisia 26 D6
La Rioja Arg. 70 C3
La Rioja aut. comm. Spain 25 E2
Larisa Greece 27 J5
Larissa Greece see Larisa
Larkana Pak. 33 K4
Lark Passage Australia 56 D2
L'Arli, Parc National de nat. park Burkina 46 D3
Larnaca Cyprus 39 A2
Larnaka Cyprus see Larnaca
Larnaka Bay Cyprus 39 A2
Larnakos, Kolpos b. Cyprus see Larnaka Bay
Larne U.K. 21 G3
La Robla Spain 25 D2
La Rochelle France 24 D3
La Roche-sur-Yon France 24 D3
La Roda Spain 25 E4
La Romana Dom. Rep. 67 K5
La Ronge Canada 60 H4
La Ronge, Lac l. Canada 60 H4
Larrey Point Australia 54 B4
Larrimah Australia 54 F3
Lars Christensen Coast Antarctica 76 E2
Larsen Ice Shelf Antarctica 76 L2
Larsmo Fin. 14 M5
Larvik Norway 15 G7
La Salonga Nord, Parc National de nat. park Dem. Rep. Congo 48 C4
Las Anod Somalia see Laascaanood
La Sarre Canada 63 L2
Las Cruces CA U.S.A. 65 B3
Las Cruces NM U.S.A. 62 F5
La Selle, Pic mt. Haiti 67 J5
La Serena Chile 70 B3
La Seu d'Urgell Spain 25 G2
Las Flores Arg. 70 E5
Las Heras Arg. 70 C4
Lashio Myanmar 42 H8
Lashkar India 36 D4
Lashkar Gāh Afgh. 33 J3
Las Juntas Chile 70 C3
Las Lomitas Arg. 70 D2
Las Marismas marsh Spain 25 C5
Las Martinetas Arg. 70 C7
Las Minas, Cerro de mt. Hond. 66 G6
La Société, Archipel de la is Fr. Polynesia see Society Islands
Las Palmas de Gran Canaria Canary Is 46 B2
Las Petas Bol. 69 G7
La Spezia Italy 26 C2
Las Piedras, Río de r. Peru 68 E6
Las Plumas Arg. 70 C6
Laspur Pak. 36 C1
Lassance Brazil 71 B2
Las Tablas Panama 67 H7
Las Tablas de Daimiel, Parque Nacional de nat. park Spain 25 E4
Las Termas Arg. 70 D3
Last Mountain Lake Canada 62 F1
Las Tórtolas, Cerro mt. Chile 70 C3
Lastoursville Gabon 48 B4
Lastovo i. Croatia 26 G3
Las Tres Vírgenes, Volcán vol. Mex. 66 B3
Las Tunas Cuba 67 I4
Las Varas Chihuahua Mex. 66 C3
Las Varas Nayarit Mex. 66 C4
Las Varillas Arg. 70 D4
Las Vegas NM U.S.A. 62 F4
Las Vegas NV U.S.A. 65 E2
Las Viajas, Isla de i. Peru 68 C6
Las Villuercas mt. Spain 25 D4
Latacunga Ecuador 68 C4
Latady Island Antarctica 76 L2
Latakia Syria 39 B2
La Teste-de-Buch France 24 D4
Latham Australia 55 B7
Latheron U.K. 20 F2
Lathi India 36 B4
Latho India 36 D2
Lathrop CA U.S.A. 65 B2
Latina Italy 26 E4
La Tortuga, Isla i. Venez. 68 E1
Latrun West Bank 39 B4
Lattaquié Syria see Latakia
La Tuque Canada 63 M2
Latur India 38 C2
Latvia country Europe 15 N8
Latvija country Europe see Latvia
Latviyskaya S.S.R. country Europe see Latvia
Lauca, Parque Nacional nat. park Chile 68 E7
Lauchhammer Germany 17 N5
Lauder U.K. 20 G5
Laudio Spain see Llodio
Laufen Switz. 24 H3
Lauge Koch Kyst reg. Greenland 61 L2
Laughlen, Mount Australia 55 F5
Lauka Estonia 15 M7
Launceston Australia 57 [inset]
Launceston U.K. 19 C8
Laune r. Ireland 21 C5
La Unión Bol. 68 F7
Laura Australia 56 D2
Laurel DE U.S.A. 64 D3
Laurel MS U.S.A. 63 J5
Laureldale PA U.S.A. 64 D2
Laurel Hill hills PA U.S.A. 64 B3
Laurencekirk U.K. 20 G4
Laurieton Australia 58 F3
Laurinburg U.S.A. 63 L5
Lauru i. Solomon Is see Choiseul
Lausanne Switz. 24 H3
Laut i. Indon. 41 D8
Laut Bali sea Indon. see Bali, Laut
Lautem East Timor 54 D2
Laut Flores sea Indon. see Flores, Laut
Lautoka Fiji 53 H3
Laut Sawu sea Indon. see Sawu, Laut
Lauvuskylä Fin. 14 P5
Laval France 24 D2
La Vall d'Uixó Spain 25 F4
Lāvān i. Iran 35 I6
La Vanoise, Massif de mts France 24 H4
La Vanoise, Parc National de nat. park France 24 H4
Lavapié, Punta pt Chile 70 B5
Lāvar Iran 35 H5
Laveaga Peak CA U.S.A. 65 B2
La Vega Dom. Rep. 67 J5
Laverton Australia 55 C7
La Vila Joíosa Spain see Villajoyosa-La Vila Joíosa
La Viña Peru 68 C5
Lavongai i. P.N.G. see New Hanover
Lavras Brazil 71 B3
Lavumisa Swaziland 51 J4
Lavushi-Manda National Park Zambia 49 D5

Longhurst, Mount Antarctica 76 H1
Long Island Bahamas 67 I4
Long Island P.N.G. 52 E2
Long Island NY U.S.A. 64 E2
Long Island Sound sea chan. Connecticut/New York U.S.A. 64 E2
Longjiang China 44 A3
Longlac Canada 63 J2
Longmeadow MA U.S.A. 64 E1
Long Melford U.K. 19 H6
Longmen Heilong. China 44 B2
Longmont U.S.A. 62 F3
Longnan China 42 I6
Long Point Ont. Canada 64 A1
Long Point Ont. Canada 64 A1
Long Point N.Z. 59 B8
Long Point Bay Ont. Canada 64 A1
Long Preston U.K. 18 E4
Long Range Mountains Nfld. and Lab. Canada 61 M5
Longreach Australia 56 D4
Long Stratton U.K. 19 I6
Longtown U.K. 18 E3
Longuyon France 24 G2
Longview TX U.S.A. 63 I5
Longwangmiao China 44 D3
Longwei Co l. China 37 G2
Longxi China 42 I6
Longxingchang China see Wuyuan
Long Xuyên Vietnam 31 J5
Longyan China 43 L7
Longyearbyen Svalbard 28 C2
Longzhen China 44 B2
Lönsboda Sweden 15 I8
Lons-le-Saunier France 24 G3
Lonton Myanmar 37 I4
Loochoo Islands Japan see Ryukyu Islands
Lookout, Cape U.S.A. 63 L5
Lookout, Point Australia 58 F1
Lookout Point Australia 55 B8
Loolmalasin vol. crater Tanz. 48 D4
Loongana Australia 55 D7
Loop Head hd Ireland 21 C5
Lop China 36 E1
Lopasnya Rus. Fed. see Chekhov
Lopatina, Gora mt. Rus. Fed. 44 F2
Lop Buri Thai. 31 J5
Lopez, Cap c. Gabon 48 A4
Lop Nur salt flat China 42 G4
Lopphavet b. Norway 14 L1
Loptyuga Rus. Fed. 12 K3
Lora r. Venez. 68 D2
Lora del Río Spain 25 D5
Lorain U.S.A. 61 J5
Loralai Pak. 33 K3
Loralai r. Pak. 36 B3
Lorca Spain 25 F5
Lordegān Iran 35 H5
Lord Howe Atoll Solomon Is see Ontong Java Atoll
Lord Howe Island Australia 53 F5
Lord Howe Rise sea feature S. Pacific Ocean 74 G7
Lordsburg U.S.A. 62 F5
Lore East Timor 54 D2
Lorena Brazil 71 B3
Loreto Brazil 69 I5
Loreto Mex. 62 E6
Lorient France 24 C3
Lorn, Firth of est. U.K. 20 D4
Lorne Australia 56 D5
Lorne watercourse Australia 56 B3
Lorrain, Plateau France 24 H2
Lorraine Australia 56 B3
Lorraine reg. France 24 G2
Losal India 36 C4
Los Alamos CA U.S.A. 65 B3
Los Alamos NM U.S.A. 62 F4
Los Alerces, Parque Nacional nat. park Arg. 70 B6
Los Ángeles Chile 70 B5
Los Angeles CA U.S.A. 65 C3
Los Angeles Aqueduct canal CA U.S.A. 65 C3
Los Banos CA U.S.A. 65 B2
Los Blancos Arg. 70 D2
Los Canarreos, Archipiélago de is Cuba 67 H4
Los Chonos, Archipiélago de is Chile 70 A6
Los Desventurados, Islas de is S. Pacific Ocean 75 O7
Los Estados, Isla de i. Arg. 70 D8
Los Glaciares, Parque Nacional nat. park Arg. 70 B8
Lošinj i. Croatia 26 F2
Los Jardines de la Reina, Archipiélago de is Cuba 67 I4
Los Juríes Arg. 70 D3
Los Katios, Parque Nacional nat. park Col. 67 I7
Loskop Dam S. Africa 51 I3
Los Menucos Arg. 70 C6
Los Mochis Mex. 66 C3
Losombo Dem. Rep. Congo 48 B3
Los Picos de Europa, Parque Nacional de nat. park Spain 25 D2
Los Roques, Islas is Venez. 68 E1
Lossie r. U.K. 20 F3
Lossiemouth U.K. 20 F3
Lost Creek WV U.S.A. 64 A3
Los Teques Venez. 68 E1
Los Testigos is Venez. 68 F1
Lost Hills CA U.S.A. 65 C3
Lostwithiel U.K. 19 C8
Los Vilos Chile 70 B4
Lot r. France 24 E4
Lota Chile 70 B5
Lothringen reg. France see Lorraine
Lotikipi Plain Kenya/Sudan 48 D3
Loto Dem. Rep. Congo 48 C4
Lotsane r. Botswana 51 I2
Lot's Wife i. Japan see Sōfu-gan
Lotta r. Fin./Rus. Fed. 14 Q2
Louangnamtha Laos 40 C5
Louangphabang Laos 41 C6
Loubomo Congo 49 B4
Loudéac France 24 C2
Louga Senegal 46 B3
Loughborough U.K. 19 F6
Lougheed Island Canada 61 H2
Loughor r. U.K. 19 C7
Loughrea Ireland 21 D4
Loughton U.K. 19 H7
Louhans France 24 G3
Louisa VA U.S.A. 64 C3
Louisburgh Ireland 21 C4
Louis-Gentil Morocco see Youssoufia
Louisiade Archipelago is P.N.G. 52 F3
Louisiana state U.S.A. 63 I5
Louis Trichardt S. Africa see Makhado
Louisville KY U.S.A. 63 J4
Louisville Ridge sea feature S. Pacific Ocean 74 I8
Loukhi Rus. Fed. 12 G2
Loukoléla Congo 48 B4
Loukouo Congo 47 E5
Loulé Port. 25 B5
Loum Cameroon 46 D4
Louny Czech Rep. 17 N5
Loups Marins, Lacs des lakes Canada 61 K4
Lourdes France 24 D5
Lourenço Marques Moz. see Maputo
Lousã Port. 25 B3
Loushan China 44 C3
Louth Australia 58 B3
Louth U.K. 18 G5
Loutra Aidipsou Greece 27 J5
Louvain Belgium see Leuven
Louviers France 19 I9
Louwater-Suid Namibia 50 C2
Louwsburg S. Africa 51 J4
Lövånger Sweden 14 L4
Lovat' r. Rus. Fed. 12 F4
Lovech Bulg. 27 K3
Lovelock U.S.A. 62 D3
Loviisa Fin. 15 O6
Lovington U.S.A. 62 G5
Lovozero Rus. Fed. 12 G1
Lóvua Angola 49 C4
Lôvua Angola 49 C5
Low, Cape Canada 61 J3
Lowa Dem. Rep. Congo 48 C4
Lowa r. Dem. Rep. Congo 48 C4
Lowarai Pass Pak. 36 B2
Lowell MA U.S.A. 64 F1
Lower California pen. Mex. see Baja California
Lower Glenelg National Park Australia 57 C8
Lower Granite Gorge AZ U.S.A. 65 F3
Lower Hutt N.Z. 59 E5
Lower Lake CA U.S.A. 65 A1
Lower Lough Erne l. U.K. 21 E3
Lower Tunguska r. Rus. Fed. see Nizhnyaya Tunguska
Lower Zambezi National Park Zambia 49 C5
Lowestoft U.K. 19 I6
Łowicz Poland 17 Q4
Low Island Kiribati see Starbuck Island
Lowther Hills U.K. 20 F5
Lowville U.S.A. 63 L3
Loxton Australia 57 C7
Loyal, Loch l. U.K. 20 E2
Loyalsock Creek r. PA U.S.A. 64 C2
Loyalty Islands New Caledonia see Loyauté, Îles
Loyang China see Luoyang
Loyauté, Îles is New Caledonia 53 G4
Loyev Belarus see Loyew
Loyew Belarus 13 F6
Lozère, Mont mt. France 24 F4
Loznica Serbia 27 H2
Lozova Ukr. 13 H6
Lozovaya Ukr. see Lozova
Lua r. Dem. Rep. Congo 48 B3
Luacano Angola 49 C5
Lu'an China 43 L6
Luanda Angola 49 B4
Luang Namtha Laos see Louangnamtha
Luang Prabang Laos see Louangphabang
Luanhaizi China 37 H2
Luanshya Zambia 49 C5
Luanza Dem. Rep. Congo 49 C4
Luao Angola see Luau
Luarca Spain 25 C2
Luashi Dem. Rep. Congo 49 C5
Luau Angola 49 C5
Luba Equat. Guinea 46 D4
Lubaczów Poland 13 D6
Lubalo Angola 49 B4
Lubānas ezers l. Latvia 15 O8
Lubango Angola 49 B5
Lubao Dem. Rep. Congo 49 C4
Lubartów Poland 13 D6
Lubbeskolk salt pan S. Africa 50 D5
Lubbock U.S.A. 62 G5
Lübeck Germany 17 M4
Lubefu Dem. Rep. Congo 49 C4
Lubei China 43 M4
Lüben Poland see Lubin
Lubersac France 24 E4
Lubin Poland 17 P5
Lublin Poland 13 D6
Lubnān country Asia see Lebanon
Lubnān, Jabal mts Lebanon see Liban, Jebel
Lubny Ukr. 13 G6
Lubok Antu Sarawak Malaysia 41 D7
Lubudi Dem. Rep. Congo 49 C4
Lubumbashi Dem. Rep. Congo 49 C5
Lubutu Dem. Rep. Congo 48 C4
Lucala Angola 49 B4
Lucan Ont. Canada 64 A1
Lucan Ireland 21 F4
Lucapa Angola 49 C4
Lucca Italy 26 D3
Luce Bay U.K. 20 E6
Lucélia Brazil 71 A3
Lucena Phil. 41 E6
Lucena Spain 25 D5
Lučenec Slovakia 17 Q6
Lucera Italy 26 F4
Lucerne Switz. 24 I3
Lucerne Valley CA U.S.A. 65 D3
Luchegorsk Rus. Fed. 44 D3
Lucheng Sichuan China see Kangding
Łuck Ukr. see Luts'k
Luckeesarai India see Lakhisarai
Luckenwalde Germany 17 N4
Luckhoff S. Africa 50 G5
Lucknow India 36 E4
Lucrecia, Cabo c. Cuba 67 I4
Lucusse Angola 49 C5
Lucy Creek Australia 56 B4
Lüda China see Dalian
Lüdenscheid Germany 17 K5
Lüderitz Namibia 50 B4
Ludewa Tanz. 49 D5
Ludhiana India 36 C3
Ludlow U.K. 19 E6
Ludlow CA U.S.A. 65 D3
Ludogorie reg. Bulg. 27 L3
Ludvika Sweden 15 I6
Ludwigsburg Germany 17 L6
Ludwigshafen am Rhein Germany 17 L6
Ludwigslust Germany 17 M4
Ludza Latvia 15 O8
Luebo Dem. Rep. Congo 49 C4
Luena Angola 49 B5
Luena Flats plain Zambia 49 C5
Lufeng Guangdong China 43 L8
Lufkin U.S.A. 63 I5
Luga Rus. Fed. 12 F4
Luga r. Rus. Fed. 15 P7
Lugano Switz. 24 I3
Lugansk Ukr. see Luhans'k
Lugdunum France see Lyon
Lugg r. U.K. 19 E6
Lugguudontsen mt. China 37 G3
Lugnaquilla h. Ireland 21 F5
Lugo Italy 26 D2
Lugo Spain 25 C2
Lugoj Romania 27 I2
Luhans'k Ukr. 13 H6
Luḥfi, Wādī watercourse Jordan 39 C3
Luhit r. China/India see Zayü Qu
Luhit r. India 37 H4
Luhuo China 42 I6
Luhyny Ukr. 13 F6
Luia Angola 49 C4
Luiana Angola 49 C5
Luichow Peninsula China see Leizhou Bandao
Luik Belgium see Liège
Luimneach Ireland see Limerick
Luiro r. Fin. 14 O3
Luis Echeverría Álvarez Baja California Mex. 65 D4
Luitpold Coast Antarctica 76 A1
Luiza Dem. Rep. Congo 49 C4
Lukachek Rus. Fed. 44 D1
Lukapa Angola see Lucapa
Lukavac Bos.-Herz. 26 H2
Lukenga, Lac l. Dem. Rep. Congo 49 C4
Lukenie r. Dem. Rep. Congo 48 B4
Lukh r. Rus. Fed. 12 I4
Lukhovitsy Rus. Fed. 13 H5
Lukovit Bulg. 27 K3
Łuków Poland 13 D6
Lukoyanov Rus. Fed. 13 J5
Lukusuzi National Park Zambia 49 D5
Luleå Sweden 14 M4
Luleälven r. Sweden 14 M4
Lüleburgaz Turkey 27 L4
Lüliang Shan mts China 43 K5
Lulimba Dem. Rep. Congo 49 C4
Lulonga r. Dem. Rep. Congo 48 B3
Luluabourg Dem. Rep. Congo see Kananga
Lülung China 37 F3
Lumachomo China 37 F3
Lumajangdong Co salt l. China 36 E2
Lumbala Moxico Angola see Lumbala Kaquengue
Lumbala Moxico Angola see Lumbala N'guimbo
Lumbala Kaquengue Angola 49 C5
Lumbala N'guimbo Angola 49 C5
Lumberton U.S.A. 63 L5
Lumbini Nepal 37 E4
Lumbrales Spain 25 C3
Lumezzane Italy 26 D2
Lumsden Canada 62 G1
Lumsden N.Z. 59 B7
Lunan Bay U.K. 20 G4
Lund Sweden 15 H9
Lund NV U.S.A. 65 E1
Lund UT U.S.A. 65 F1
Lundy U.K. 19 C7
Lune r. U.K. 18 E4
Lüneburg Germany 17 M4
Lunenburg VA U.S.A. 64 B4
Lunéville France 24 H2
Lunga r. Zambia 49 C5
Lungdo China 37 E2
Lunggar China 37 E3
Lungleh India see Lunglei
Lunglei India 37 H5
Lungmari mt. China 37 F3
Lungmu Co salt l. China 36 E2
Lungwebungu r. Zambia 49 C5
Lunh Nepal 37 E3
Luni India 36 C4
Luni r. India 36 B4
Luni r. Pak. 36 B3
Luninets Belarus see Luninyets
Luning NV U.S.A. 65 C1
Luninyets Belarus 15 O10
Lunkaransar India 36 C3
Lunkha India 36 C3
Lunsar Sierra Leone 46 B4
Lunsklip S. Africa 51 I3
Luntai China 42 E4
Luobei China 44 C3
Luobuzhuang China 42 F5
Luohe China 43 K6
Luoto Fin. see Larsmo
Luoyang Henan China 43 K6
Luozigou China 44 C4
Lupane Zimbabwe 49 C5
Lupanshui China 42 I7
L'Upemba, Parc National de nat. park Dem. Rep. Congo 49 C4
Lupeni Romania 27 J2
Lupilichi Moz. 49 D5
Luray VA U.S.A. 64 B3
Luremo Angola 49 B4
Lurgan U.K. 21 F3
Luring China see Oma
Lúrio Moz. 49 E5
Lurio r. Moz. 49 E5
Lusaka Zambia 49 C5
Lusambo Dem. Rep. Congo 49 C4
Lusancay Islands and Reefs P.N.G. 52 F2
Lusangi Dem. Rep. Congo 49 C4
Lush, Mount h. Australia 54 D4
Lushnja Albania see Lushnjë
Lushnjë Albania 27 H4
Lushuihe China 44 B4
Lusikisiki S. Africa 51 I6
Lusk U.S.A. 62 G3
Luso Angola see Luena
Lussvale Australia 58 C1
Lut, Bahrat salt l. Asia see Dead Sea
Lut, Dasht-e des. Iran 33 I3
Lutetia France see Paris
Lutherstadt Wittenberg Germany 17 N5
Luton U.K. 19 G7
Łutselk'e Canada 60 G3
Luts'k Ukr. 13 E6
Lutto r. Fin./Rus. Fed. see Lotta
Lützow-Holm Bay Antarctica 76 D2
Lutzputs S. Africa 50 E5
Lutzville S. Africa 50 D6
Luumäki Fin. 15 O6
Luuq Somalia 48 E3
Luverne MN U.S.A. 63 H3
Luvuei Angola 49 C5
Luvuvhu r. S. Africa 51 J2
Luwero Uganda 48 D3
Luwingu Zambia 49 C5
Luwuk Indon. 41 E8
Luxembourg country Europe 17 K6
Luxembourg Lux. 17 K6
Luxemburg country Europe see Luxembourg
Luxeuil-les-Bains France 24 H3
Luxi Yunnan China 42 H8
Luxolweni S. Africa 51 G6
Luxor Egypt 32 D4
Luza Rus. Fed. 12 J3
Luza r. Rus. Fed. 12 J3
Luza r. Rus. Fed. 12 M2
Luzern Switz. see Lucerne
Luzhou China 42 J7
Luziânia Brazil 71 B2
Luzon i. Phil. 41 E6
Luzon Strait Phil. 41 E5
Luzy France 24 F3
L'viv Ukr. 13 E6
L'vov Ukr. see L'viv
Lwów Ukr. see L'viv
Lyady Rus. Fed. 15 P7
Lyakhavichy Belarus 15 O10
Lyakhovichi Belarus see Lyakhavichy
Lyallpur Pak. see Faisalabad
Lyamtsa Rus. Fed. 12 H2
Lycia reg. Turkey 27 M6
Lyck Poland see Ełk
Lycksele Sweden 14 K4
Lycopolis Egypt see Asyūṭ
Lydd U.K. 19 H8
Lydda Israel see Lod
Lyddan Island Antarctica 76 B2
Lydia reg. Turkey 27 L5
Lydney U.K. 19 E7
Lyel'chytsy Belarus 13 F6
Lyell, Mount CA U.S.A. 65 C2
Lyell Brown, Mount h. Australia 55 E5
Lyepyel' Belarus 15 P9
Lykens PA U.S.A. 64 C2
Lyme Bay U.K. 19 E8
Lyme Regis U.K. 19 E8
Lymington U.K. 19 F8
Lynchburg VA U.S.A. 64 B4
Lyndhurst N.S.W. Australia 58 D4
Lyndhurst Qld Australia 56 D3
Lyndhurst S.A. Australia 57 B6
Lyndon Australia 55 A5
Lyndon r. Australia 55 A5
Lyne r. U.K. 18 D4
Lyness U.K. 20 F2
Lyngdal Norway 15 E7
Lynn U.K. see King's Lynn
Lynn MA U.S.A. 64 F1
Lynn Lake Canada 61 H4
Lynton U.K. 19 D7
Lynx Lake Canada 60 H3
Lyon France 24 G4
Lyon r. U.K. 20 F4
Lyons Australia 55 F7
Lyons France see Lyon
Lyons NY U.S.A. 64 C1
Lyons Falls NY U.S.A. 64 D1
Lyozna Belarus 13 F5
Lyra Reef P.N.G. 52 F2
Lysekil Sweden 15 G7
Lyskovo Rus. Fed. 12 J4
Lys'va Rus. Fed. 11 R4
Lysychans'k Ukr. 13 H6
Lysyye Gory Rus. Fed. 13 J6
Lytham St Anne's U.K. 18 D5
Lyuban' Belarus 15 P10
Lyubertsy Rus. Fed. 11 N4
Lyubeshiv Ukr. 13 E6
Lyubim Rus. Fed. 12 I4
Lyubytino Rus. Fed. 12 G4
Lyudinovo Rus. Fed. 13 G5
Lyunda r. Rus. Fed. 12 J4
Lyzha r. Rus. Fed. 12 M2

M

Ma'agan Israel 39 B3
Maale Maldives see Male
Maale Atholhu atoll Maldives see Male Atoll
Maalhosmadulu Atholhu Uthuruburi atoll Maldives see North Maalhosmadulu Atoll
Maalhosmadulu Atoll Maldives 38 B5
Ma'ān Jordan 39 B4
Maan Turkey see Nusratiye
Maaninka Fin. 14 O5
Maaninkavaara Fin. 14 P3
Maardu Estonia 15 N7
Maarianhamina Fin. see Mariehamn
Ma'arrat an Nu'mān Syria 39 C2
Maas-Schwalm-Nette nat. park Germany/Neth. 17 J5
Maastricht Neth. 17 J5
Maaza Plateau Egypt 34 C6
Mabalane Moz. 51 K2
Mabana Dem. Rep. Congo 48 C3
Mabaruma Guyana 68 G2
Mabein Myanmar 37 I5
Mabel Creek Australia 55 F7
Mabel Downs Australia 54 D4
Mablethorpe U.K. 18 H5
Mabopane S. Africa 51 I3
Mabote Moz. 51 L2
Mabrak, Jabal mt. Jordan 39 B4
Mabuasehube Game Reserve nature res. Botswana 50 F3
Mabule Botswana 50 G3
Mabutsane Botswana 50 F3
Macá, Monte mt. Chile 70 B7
Macadam Plains Australia 55 B6
Macaé Brazil 71 C3
Macajuba Brazil 71 C1
Macaloge Moz. 49 D5
MacAlpine Lake Canada 61 H3
Macandze Moz. 51 K2
Macao China 43 K8
Macapá Brazil 69 H3
Macará Ecuador 68 C4
Macarani Brazil 71 C1
Macas Ecuador 68 C4
Macassar Indon. see Makassar
Macau Brazil 69 K5
Macaúba Brazil 69 H6
Macauley Island N.Z. 53 I5
Maccaretane Moz. 51 K3
Macclesfield U.K. 18 E5
Macdonald, Lake imp. l. Australia 55 E5
Macdonald Range hills Australia 54 D3
Macdonnell Ranges mts Australia 55 E5
MacDowell Lake Canada 63 I1
Macduff U.K. 20 G3
Macedo de Cavaleiros Port. 25 C3
Macedon mt. Australia 58 B6
Macedon country Europe see Macedonia
Macedonia country Europe 27 I4
Maceió Brazil 69 K5
Macenta Guinea 46 C4
Macerata Italy 26 E3
Macfarlane, Lake imp. l. Australia 57 B7
Macgillycuddy's Reeks mts Ireland 21 C6
Machachi Ecuador 68 C4
Machaila Moz. 51 K2
Machakos Kenya 48 D4
Machala Ecuador 68 C4
Machali China see Madoi
Machanga Moz. 49 D6
Machar Marshes Sudan 32 D8
Machattie, Lake imp. l. Australia 56 B5
Machatuine Moz. 51 K3
Machaze Moz. see Chitobe
Macherla India 38 C2
Machhagan India 37 F5
Machias ME U.S.A. 63 N3
Machias NY U.S.A. 64 B1
Machilipatnam India 38 D2
Machiques Venez. 68 D1
Machrihanish U.K. 20 D5
Machu Picchu tourist site Peru 68 D6
Machynlleth U.K. 19 D6
Macia Moz. 51 K3
Macias Nguema i. Equat. Guinea see Bioco
Măcin Romania 27 M2
Macintyre r. Australia 58 E2
Macintyre Brook r. Australia 58 E2
Maçka Turkey 35 E2
Mackay Australia 56 E4
Mackay, Lake imp. l. Australia 54 E5
MacKay Lake Canada 60 G3
Mackenzie r. Australia 56 E4
Mackenzie Canada 60 F4
Mackenzie r. Canada 60 E3
Mackenzie Guyana see Linden
Mackenzie atoll Micronesia see Ulithi
Mackenzie Bay Antarctica 76 E2
Mackenzie Bay Canada 60 E3
Mackenzie King Island Canada 61 G2
Mackenzie Mountains Canada 60 E3
Mackenzie-Peace-Finlay r. Canada 60 E3
Mackillop, Lake imp. l. Australia see Yamma Yamma, Lake
Mackintosh Range hills Australia 55 D6
Macklin Canada 62 F1
Macksville Australia 58 F3
Maclean Australia 58 F2
Maclear S. Africa 51 I6
MacLeod Canada see Fort Macleod
MacLeod, Lake dry lake Australia 55 A6
Macmillan Pass Canada 60 F3
Macomb U.S.A. 63 I3
Macomer Sardegna Italy 26 C4
Mâcon France 24 G3
Macon GA U.S.A. 63 K5
Macon MO U.S.A. 63 I4
Macondo Angola 49 C5
Macpherson Robertson Land reg. Antarctica see Mac. Robertson Land
Macquarie r. Australia 58 C3
Macquarie, Lake b. Australia 58 E4
Macquarie Island S. Pacific Ocean 74 G9
Macquarie Marshes Australia 58 C3
Macquarie Mountain Australia 58 D4
Macquarie Ridge sea feature S. Pacific Ocean 74 G9
Mac. Robertson Land reg. Antarctica 76 E2
Macroom Ireland 21 D6
Macumba Australia 57 A5
Macumba watercourse Australia 57 B5
Macuzari, Presa resr Mex. 66 C3
Mādabā Jordan 39 B4
Madadeni S. Africa 51 J4
Madagascar country Africa 49 E6
Madagascar Basin sea feature Indian Ocean 73 L7
Madagascar Ridge sea feature Indian Ocean 73 K8
Madagasikara country Africa see Madagascar
Madakasira India 38 C3
Madama Niger 47 E2
Madan Bulg. 27 K4
Madanapalle India 38 C3
Madang P.N.G. 52 E2
Madaoua Niger 46 D3
Madaripur Bangl. 37 G5
Madau Turkm. see Madaw
Madaw Turkm. 35 I3
Madaya Myanmar 37 I5
Madded India 38 D2
Madeira r. Brazil 68 G4
Madeira terr. N. Atlantic Ocean 46 B1
Madeira, Arquipélago da terr. N. Atlantic Ocean see Madeira
Maden Turkey 35 E3
Madera Mex. 66 C3
Madera CA U.S.A. 65 B2
Madgaon India 38 B3
Madha India 38 B2
Madhavpur India 36 B5
Madhepura India 37 F4
Madhipura India see Madhepura
Madhubani India 37 F4
Madhya Pradesh state India 36 D5
Madibogo S. Africa 51 G4
Madidi r. Bol. 68 E6
Madikeri India 38 B3
Madikwe Game Reserve nature res. S. Africa 51 H3
Madīnat ath Thawrah Syria 39 D2
Madingo-Kayes Congo 49 B4
Madingou Congo 49 B4
Madison IN U.S.A. 63 J4
Madison SD U.S.A. 63 H3
Madison VA U.S.A. 64 B3
Madison WI U.S.A. 63 J3
Madison r. U.S.A. 62 E2
Madison Heights VA U.S.A. 64 B4
Madisonville KY U.S.A. 63 J4
Madley, Mount h. Australia 55 C6
Mado Gashi Kenya 48 D3
Madoi China 37 I2
Madona Latvia 15 O8
Madpura India 36 B4
Madra Dağı mts Turkey 27 L5
Madrakah Saudi Arabia 32 E5
Madrakah, Ra's c. Oman 33 I6
Madras India see Chennai
Madras state India see Tamil Nadu
Madras U.S.A. 62 C3
Madre, Laguna lag. Mex. 66 E3
Madre de Dios r. Peru 68 E6
Madre de Dios, Isla i. Chile 70 A8
Madre del Sur, Sierra mts Mex. 66 D5
Madre Occidental, Sierra mts Mex. 66 C3
Madre Oriental, Sierra mts Mex. 66 D3
Madrid Spain 25 E3
Madridejos Spain 25 E4
Madugula India 38 D2
Madura i. Indon. 41 D8
Madurai India 38 C4
Madurantakam India 38 C3
Madvār, Kūh-e mt. Iran 35 I5
Madwas India 37 E4
Maé i. Vanuatu see Émaé
Maebashi Japan 45 E5
Mae Hong Son Thai. 42 H9
Mae Sai Thai. 42 H8
Mae Sariang Thai. 42 H9
Maevatanana Madag. 49 E5
Maéwo i. Vanuatu 53 G3
Mafeking S. Africa see Mafikeng
Mafeteng Lesotho 51 H5
Maffra Australia 58 C6
Mafia Island Tanz. 49 D4
Mafikeng S. Africa 51 G3
Mafinga Tanz. 49 D4
Mafra Brazil 71 A4
Mafraq Jordan see Al Mafraq
Magabeni S. Africa 51 J6
Magadan Rus. Fed. 29 Q4
Magadi Kenya 48 D4
Magaiza Moz. 51 K2
Magallanes Chile see Punta Arenas
Magallanes, Estrecho de Chile see Magellan, Strait of
Magangue Col. 68 D2
Mağara Dağı mt. Turkey 39 A1
Magaramkent Rus. Fed. 35 H2
Magaria Niger 46 D3
Magarida P.N.G. 56 E1
Magas Rus. Fed. 13 I8
Magdagachi Rus. Fed. 44 B1
Magdalena Bol. 68 F6
Magdalena r. Col. 68 D1
Magdalena Sonora Mex. 66 B2
Magdalena, Bahía b. Mex. 66 B4
Magdalena, Isla i. Chile 70 B6
Magdeburg Germany 17 M4
Magdelaine Cays atoll Australia 56 E3
Magellan, Strait of Chile 70 B8
Magellan Seamounts sea feature N. Pacific Ocean 74 F4
Magenta, Lake imp. l. Australia 55 B8
Magerøya i. Norway 14 N1
Maggiorasca, Monte mt. Italy 26 C2
Maggiore, Lago Italy see Maggiore, Lake
Maggiore, Lake Italy 26 C2
Maghāgha Egypt see Maghāghah
Maghāghah Egypt 34 C5
Maghama Mauritania 46 B3
Maghâra, Gebel h. Egypt see Magharah, Jabal
Magharah, Jabal h. Egypt 39 A4
Maghera U.K. 21 F3
Magherafelt U.K. 21 F3
Maghnia Alg. 25 F6
Maghull U.K. 18 E5
Magilligan Point U.K. 21 F2
Magna Grande mt. Sicilia Italy 26 F6
Magnetic Island Australia 56 D3
Magnetic Passage Australia 56 D3
Magnetity Rus. Fed. 14 R2
Magnitogorsk Rus. Fed. 28 G4
Magnolia AR U.S.A. 63 I5
Mago Rus. Fed. 44 F1
Màgoé Moz. 49 D5
Mago National Park Eth. 48 D3
Magosa Cyprus see Famagusta
Magpie, Lac l. Canada 63 O1
Magta' Lahjar Mauritania 46 B3
Magu Tanz. 48 D4
Magu, Khrebet mts Rus. Fed. 44 E1
Magude Moz. 51 K3
Magura Bangl. 37 G5
Magway Myanmar see Magwe
Magwe Myanmar 37 H5
Magyar Köztársaság country Europe see Hungary
Magyichaung Myanmar 37 H5
Mahābād Iran 35 G3
Mahabharat Range mts Nepal 37 F4
Mahaboobnagar India see Mahbubnagar
Mahad India 38 B2
Mahadeo Hills India 36 D5
Mahaffey PA U.S.A. 64 B2
Mahajan India 36 C3
Mahajanga Madag. 49 E5
Mahalapye Botswana 51 H2
Mahale Mountains National Park Tanz. 49 C4
Mahalevona Madag. 49 E5
Mahallāt Iran 35 H4
Māhān Iran 33 I3
Mahanadi r. India 38 E1
Mahanoro Madag. 49 E5
Maha Oya Sri Lanka 38 D5
Maharashtra state India 38 B2
Maha Sarakham Thai. 31 J5
Mahasham, Wādi el watercourse Egypt see Muhashsham, Wādī al
Mahbubabad India 38 D2
Mahbubnagar India 38 C2
Mahd adh Dhahab Saudi Arabia 32 F5
Mahdia Alg. 25 G6
Mahdia Guyana 69 G2
Mahdia Tunisia 26 D7
Mahé i. Seychelles 73 L6
Mahendragiri mt. India 38 E2
Mahenge Tanz. 49 D4
Mahesana India 36 C5
Mahi r. India 36 C5
Mahia Peninsula N.Z. 59 F4
Mahilyow Belarus 13 F5
Mahim India 38 B2
Mah Jān Iran 35 I5
Mahlabatini S. Africa 51 J5
Maḥmūdābād Iran 35 I3
Maḥmūd-e 'Erāqī Afgh. see Maḥmūd-e Rāqī
Maḥmūd-e Rāqī Afgh. 36 B2
Maho Sri Lanka 38 D5
Mahoba India 36 D4
Maholi India 36 E4
Mahón Spain 25 I4
Mahrauni India 36 D4
Mahrès Tunisia 26 D7
Māhrūd Iran 33 J3
Mahsana India see Mahesana
Mahudaung mts Myanmar 37 H5
Mahur India 38 C2
Mahuva India 36 B5
Mahwa India 36 D4
Mahya Dağı mt. Turkey 27 L4
Mai i. Vanuatu see Émaé
Maiaia Moz. see Nacala
Maicao Col. 68 D1
Maidenhead U.K. 19 G7
Maidstone Canada 62 F1
Maidstone U.K. 19 H7
Maiduguri Nigeria 46 E3
Maiella, Parco Nazionale della nat. park Italy 26 F3
Mai Gudo mt. Eth. 48 D3
Maigue r. Ireland 21 D5
Maihar India 36 E4
Maikala Range hills India 36 E5
Maiko r. Dem. Rep. Congo 48 C3
Mailan Hill mt. India 37 E5
Mailsi Pak. 36 C3
Main r. U.K. 21 F3
Maindargi India 38 C2
Mai-Ndombe, Lac l. Dem. Rep. Congo 48 B4
Maindong Xizang China see Coqên
Maine state U.S.A. 63 N2
Maine, Gulf of Canada/U.S.A. 61 L5
Mainé Hanari, Cerro h. Col. 68 D4
Mainé-Soroa Niger 46 E3
Maingkaing Myanmar 37 H4
Maingkwan Myanmar 37 I4
Mainland i. Scotland U.K. 20 F1
Mainland i. Scotland U.K. 20 [inset]
Mainoru Australia 54 F3
Mainpat reg. India 37 E5
Mainpuri India 36 D4
Main Range National Park Australia 58 F2
Maintirano Madag. 49 E5
Mainz Germany 17 L5
Maio i. Cape Verde 46 [inset]
Maipú Arg. 70 E5
Maiskhal Island Bangl. 37 G5
Maitengwe Botswana 49 C6
Maitland N.S.W. Australia 58 E4
Maitland S.A. Australia 57 B7
Maitland r. Australia 54 B5
Maitri research stn Antarctica 76 C2
Maiwo i. Vanuatu see Maéwo
Maiyu, Mount h. Australia 54 E4
Maíz, Islas del is Nicaragua 67 H6
Maizar Pak. 36 B2
Maizuru Japan 45 D6
Maja Jezercë mt. Albania 27 H3
Majdel Aanjar tourist site Lebanon 39 B3
Majene Indon. 41 D8
Majī Eth. 48 D3
Majiazi China 44 B2
Majōl country N. Pacific Ocean see Marshall Islands
Major, Puig mt. Spain 25 H4
Majorca i. Spain 25 H4
Mājro atoll Marshall Is see Majuro
Majunga Madag. see Mahajanga
Majuro atoll Marshall Is 74 H5
Majwemasweu S. Africa 51 H5
Makabana Congo 48 B4
Makale Indon. 41 D8

Northern prov. S. Africa see Limpopo
Northern Areas admin. div. Pak. 36 C1
Northern Cape prov. S. Africa 50 D5
Northern Donets r. Rus. Fed./Ukr. see Severskiy Donets
Northern Dvina r. Rus. Fed. see Severnaya Dvina
Northern Ireland prov. U.K. 21 F3
Northern Lau Group is Fiji 53 I3
Northern Mariana Islands terr. N. Pacific Ocean 41 G6
Northern Rhodesia country Africa see Zambia
Northern Sporades is Greece see Voreies Sporades
Northern Territory admin. div. Australia 52 D3
Northern Transvaal prov. S. Africa see Limpopo
North Esk r. U.K. 20 G4
North Foreland c. U.K. 19 I7
North Fork CA U.S.A. 65 C2
North Fork Pass Canada 60 E3
North Frisian Islands Germany 17 L3
North Geomagnetic Pole Arctic Ocean 61 K2
North Grimston U.K. 18 G4
North Haven CT U.S.A. 64 E2
North Head hd N.Z. 59 E3
North Horr Kenya 48 D3
North Island India 38 B4
North Island N.Z. 59 D4
North Kingsville OH U.S.A. 64 A2
North Knife Lake Canada 61 I4
North Korea country Asia 45 B5
North Lakhimpur India 37 H4
North Las Vegas NV U.S.A. 65 E2
North Luangwa National Park Zambia 49 D5
North Maalhosmadulu Atoll Maldives 38 B5
North Magnetic Pole Canada 77 A1
North Malosmadulu Atoll Maldives see North Maalhosmadulu Atoll
North Palisade mt. CA U.S.A. 65 C2
North Perry OH U.S.A. 64 A2
North Platte U.S.A. 62 G3
North Platte r. U.S.A. 62 G3
North Pole Arctic Ocean 77 I1
North Rona i. U.K. see Rona
North Ronaldsay i. U.K. 20 G1
North Ronaldsay Firth sea chan. U.K. 20 G1
North Saskatchewan r. Canada 62 F1
North Sea Europe 16 H2
North Shields U.K. 18 F3
North Shoshone Peak NV U.S.A. 65 D1
North Siberian Lowland Rus. Fed. 28 L2
North Siberian Lowland Rus. Fed. 77 E2
North Simlipal National Park India 37 F5
North Sinai governorate Egypt see Shamāl Sīnā'
North Slope plain U.S.A. 60 D3
North Somercotes U.K. 18 H5
North Spirit Lake Canada 63 I1
North Stradbroke Island Australia 58 F1
North Sunderland U.K. 18 F3
North Syracuse NY U.S.A. 64 C1
North Taranaki Bight b. N.Z. 59 E4
Northton U.K. 20 B3
North Tonawanda NY U.S.A. 64 B1
North Trap rf N.Z. 59 A8
North Tyne r. U.K. 18 E4
North Uist i. U.K. 20 B3
Northumberland National Park U.K. 18 E3
Northumberland Strait Canada 63 O2
Northville NY U.S.A. 64 D1
North Walsham U.K. 19 I6
Northwest prov. S. Africa 50 G4
Northwest Atlantic Mid-Ocean Channel N. Atlantic Ocean 72 E1
North West Cape Australia 54 A5
North West Frontier prov. Pak. 36 B2
North West Nelson Forest Park nat. park N.Z. see Kahurangi National Park
Northwest Pacific Basin sea feature N. Pacific Ocean 74 G3
Northwest Territories admin. div. Canada 60 H3
Northwich U.K. 18 E5
North Wildwood NJ U.S.A. 64 D3
Northwind Ridge sea feature Arctic Ocean 77 B1
Northwood NH U.S.A. 64 F1
North York Moors moorland U.K. 18 G4
North York Moors National Park U.K. 18 G4
Norton U.K. 18 G4
Norton de Matos Angola see Balombo
Norton Sound sea chan. U.S.A. 60 B3
Norvegia, Cape Antarctica 76 B2
Norwalk CT U.S.A. 64 E2
Norwalk OH U.S.A. 63 K3
Norway country Europe 14 E6
Norway House Canada 62 H1
Norwegian Basin sea feature N. Atlantic Ocean 72 H1
Norwegian Bay Canada 61 I2
Norwegian Sea N. Atlantic Ocean 77 H2
Norwich Ont. Canada 64 A1
Norwich U.K. 19 I6
Norwich CT U.S.A. 64 E2
Norwich NY U.S.A. 64 D1
Noshiro Japan 45 F4
Nosovaya Rus. Fed. 12 L1
Noşratābād Iran 33 I4
Noss, Isle of i. U.K. 20 [inset]
Nossebro Sweden 15 H7
Nossob watercourse Africa 50 D2
Nossob watercourse Africa 50 D2
Notch Peak UT U.S.A. 65 F1
Noteć r. Poland 17 O4
Noto, Golfo di g. Sicilia Italy 26 F6
Notodden Norway 15 F7
Noto-hantō pen. Japan 45 E5
Notre-Dame, Monts mts Canada 63 N2
Notre Dame Bay Canada 61 M5
Notre-Dame-de-Koartac Canada see Quaqtaq
Nottaway r. Canada 63 L1
Nottingham U.K. 19 F6
Nottingham Island Canada 61 K3
Nottoway r. VA U.S.A. 64 C4
Nouabalé-Ndoki, Parc National nat. park Congo 48 B3
Nouâdhibou Mauritania 46 B2
Nouâdhibou, Râs c. Mauritania 46 B2
Nouakchott Mauritania 46 B3
Nouâmghâr Mauritania 46 B3
Nouméa New Caledonia 53 G4
Nouna Burkina 46 C3
Noupoort S. Africa 50 G6
Nousu Fin. 14 P3
Nouveau-Brunswick prov. Canada see New Brunswick
Nouveau-Comptoir Canada see Wemindji
Nouvelle Calédonie i. S. Pacific Ocean 53 G4
Nouvelle Calédonie terr. S. Pacific Ocean see New Caledonia
Nouvelle-France, Cap de c. Canada 61 K3
Nouvelles Hébrides country S. Pacific Ocean see Vanuatu
Nova América Brazil 71 A1
Nova Chaves Angola see Muconda
Nova Freixa Moz. see Cuamba
Nova Friburgo Brazil 71 C3
Nova Gaia Angola see Cambundi-Catembo
Nova Goa India see Panaji
Nova Gradiška Croatia 26 G2
Nova Iguaçu Brazil 71 C3
Nova Kakhovka Ukr. 27 O1
Nova Lima Brazil 71 C2
Nova Lisboa Angola see Huambo
Novalukoml' Belarus 13 F5
Nova Mambone Moz. 49 D6
Nova Nabúri Moz. 49 D5
Nova Odesa Ukr. 13 F7
Nova Paraiso Brazil 68 F3
Nova Pilão Arcado Brazil 69 J5
Nova Ponte Brazil 71 B2
Nova Ponte, Represa resr Brazil 71 B2
Novara Italy 26 C2
Nova Roma Brazil 71 B1
Nova Scotia prov. Canada 63 N3
Nova Sento Sé Brazil 69 J5
Novato CA U.S.A. 65 A1
Nova Trento Brazil 71 A4
Nova Venécia Brazil 71 C2
Nova Xavantino Brazil 69 H6
Novaya Kakhovka Ukr. see Nova Kakhovka
Novaya Kazanka Kazakh. 11 P6
Novaya Ladoga Rus. Fed. 12 G3
Novaya Lyalya Rus. Fed. 11 S4
Novaya Odessa Ukr. see Nova Odesa
Novaya Sibir', Ostrov i. Rus. Fed. 29 P2
Novaya Ussura Rus. Fed. 44 E2
Novaya Zemlya is Rus. Fed. 28 G2
Nova Zagora Bulg. 27 L3
Novelda Spain 25 F4
Nové Zámky Slovakia 17 Q7
Novgorod Rus. Fed. see Velikiy Novgorod
Novgorod-Severskiy Ukr. see Novhorod-Sivers'kyy
Novgorod-Volynskiy Ukr. see Novohrad-Volyns'kyy
Novhorod-Sivers'kyy Ukr. 13 G6
Novi Grad Bos.-Herz. see Bosanski Novi
Novi Iskŭr Bulg. 27 J3
Novikovo Rus. Fed. 44 F3
Novi Kritsim Bulg. see Stamboliyski
Novi Ligure Italy 26 C2
Novi Pazar Bulg. 27 L3
Novi Pazar Serbia 27 I3
Novi Sad Serbia 27 H2
Novo Acre Brazil 71 C1
Novoaltaysk Rus. Fed. 42 E2
Novoanninskiy Rus. Fed. 13 I6
Novo Aripuanã Brazil 68 F5
Novoazovs'k Ukr. 13 H7
Novocheboksarsk Rus. Fed. 12 J4
Novocherkassk Rus. Fed. 13 I7
Novo Cruzeiro Brazil 71 C2
Novodugino Rus. Fed. 12 G5
Novodvinsk Rus. Fed. 12 I2
Novoekonomicheskoye Ukr. see Dymytrov
Novogeorgiyevka Rus. Fed. 44 B2
Novogrudok Belarus see Navahrudak
Novo Hamburgo Brazil 71 A5
Novohradské hory mts Czech Rep. 17 O6
Novohrad-Volyns'kyy Ukr. 13 E6
Novokhopersk Rus. Fed. 13 I6
Novokiyevskiy Uval Rus. Fed. 44 C2
Novokubansk Rus. Fed. 35 F1
Novokubanskiy Rus. Fed. see Novokubansk
Novokuybyshevsk Rus. Fed. 13 K5
Novokuznetsk Rus. Fed. 42 F2
Novolazarevskaya research stn Antarctica 76 C2
Novolukoml' Belarus see Novalukoml'
Novo Mesto Slovenia 26 F2
Novomikhaylovskiy Rus. Fed. 34 E1
Novomoskovsk Rus. Fed. 13 H5
Novomoskovs'k Ukr. 13 G6
Novonikolayevsk Rus. Fed. see Novosibirsk
Novonikolayevskiy Rus. Fed. 13 I6
Novooleksiyivka Ukr. 13 G7
Novopashiyskiy Rus. Fed. see Gornozavodsk
Novopokrovka Rus. Fed. 44 D3
Novopokrovskaya Rus. Fed. 13 I7
Novopolotsk Belarus see Navapolatsk
Novopskov Ukr. 13 H6
Novo Redondo Angola see Sumbe
Novorossiyka Rus. Fed. 44 C1
Novorossiysk Rus. Fed. 13 H7
Novorybnaya Rus. Fed. 29 L2
Novorzhev Rus. Fed. 12 F4
Novoselovo Rus. Fed. 42 G1
Novoselskoye Rus. Fed. see Achkhoy-Martan
Novosel'ye Rus. Fed. 15 P7
Novosergiyevka Rus. Fed. 11 Q5
Novoshakhtinsk Rus. Fed. 13 H7
Novosheshminsk Rus. Fed. 12 K5
Novosibirsk Rus. Fed. 28 J4
Novosibirskiye Ostrova is Rus. Fed. see New Siberia Islands
Novosil' Rus. Fed. 13 H5
Novosokol'niki Rus. Fed. 12 F4
Novospasskoye Rus. Fed. 13 J5
Novotroyits'ke Ukr. 13 G7
Novoukrainka Ukr. see Novoukrayinka
Novoukrayinka Ukr. 13 F6
Novouzensk Rus. Fed. 13 K6
Novovolyns'k Ukr. 13 E6
Novovoronezh Rus. Fed. 13 H6
Novovoronezhskiy Rus. Fed. see Novovoronezh
Novovoskresenovka Rus. Fed. 44 B1
Novozybkov Rus. Fed. 13 F5
Nový Jičín Czech Rep. 17 P6
Novyy Afon Georgia see Akhali Ap'oni
Novyy Bor Rus. Fed. 12 L2
Novyy Donbass Ukr. see Dymytrov
Novyye Petushki Rus. Fed. see Petushki
Novyy Kholmogory Rus. Fed. see Archangel
Novyy Margelan Uzbek. see Farg'ona
Novyy Nekouz Rus. Fed. 12 H4
Novyy Oskol Rus. Fed. 13 H6
Novyy Port Rus. Fed. 28 I3
Novyy Urengoy Rus. Fed. 28 I3
Novyy Urgal Rus. Fed. 44 D2
Novyy Uzen' Kazakh. see Zhanaozen
Novyy Zay Rus. Fed. 12 L5
Now Iran 35 I5
Nowabganj Bangl. see Nawabganj
Nowdī Iran 35 H3
Nowgong India see Nagaon
Now Kharegan Iran 35 I3
Nowogard Poland 17 O4
Noworadomsk Poland see Radomsko
Nowra Australia 58 E5
Nowrangapur India see Nabarangapur
Nowshera Pak. 33 L3
Nowy Sącz Poland 17 R6
Nowy Targ Poland 17 R6
Noxen PA U.S.A. 64 C2
Noyabr'sk Rus. Fed. 28 I3
Noyon Mongolia 42 I4
Nozizwe S. Africa 51 G6
Nqamakwe S. Africa 51 H7
Nqutu S. Africa 51 J5
Nsanje Malawi 49 D5
Nsombo Zambia 49 C5
Nsukka Nigeria 46 D4
Nsumbu National Park Zambia see Sumbu National Park
Ntambu Zambia 49 C5
Ntha S. Africa 51 H4
Ntoro, Kavo pt Greece 27 K5
Ntoum Gabon 48 A3
Ntungamo Uganda 48 D4
Nuanetsi Zimbabwe see Mwenezi
Nuba Mountains Sudan 32 D7
Nubian Desert Sudan 32 D5
Nudo Coropuna mt. Peru 68 D7
Nueltin Lake Canada 61 I3
Nueva Gerona Cuba 67 H4
Nueva Harberton Arg. 70 C8
Nueva Imperial Chile 70 B5
Nueva Loja Ecuador see Lago Agrio
Nueva Rosita Mex. 62 G6
Nueva San Salvador El Salvador 66 G6
Nueve de Julio Arg. see 9 de Julio
Nuevitas Cuba 67 I4
Nuevo, Golfo g. Arg. 70 D6
Nuevo Casas Grandes Mex. 66 C2
Nuevo Ideal Mex. 66 C4
Nuevo Laredo Mex. 66 E3
Nuevo Rocafuerte Ecuador 68 C4
Nugaal watercourse Somalia 48 E3
Nugget Point N.Z. 59 B8
Nugur India 38 D2
Nuguria Islands P.N.G. 52 F2
Nuhaka N.Z. 59 F4
Nui atoll Tuvalu 53 H2
Nui Con Voi r. Vietnam see Red
Nuiqsut U.S.A. 60 C2
Nujiang China 37 I3
Nu Jiang r. China/Myanmar see Salween
Nu Jiang r. China/Myanmar see Salween
Nukey Bluff h. Australia 57 A7
Nukha Azer. see Şäki
Nuku'alofa Tonga 53 I4
Nukufetau atoll Tuvalu 53 H2
Nukuhiva i. Fr. Polynesia see Nuku Hiva
Nuku Hiva i. Fr. Polynesia 75 K6
Nukulaelae atoll Tuvalu 53 H2
Nukulailai atoll Tuvalu see Nukulaelae
Nukumanu Islands P.N.G. 53 F2
Nukunau i. Kiribati see Nikunau
Nukunono atoll Tokelau see Nukunonu
Nukunonu atoll Tokelau 53 I2
Nukus Uzbek. 33 I1
Nulato U.S.A. 60 C3
Nullagine Australia 54 C5
Nullarbor Australia 55 E7
Nullarbor National Park Australia 55 E7
Nullarbor Plain Australia 55 E7
Nullarbor Regional Reserve nature res. Australia 55 E7
Nulu'erhu Shan mts China 43 L4
Numalla, Lake imp. l. Australia 58 B2
Numan Nigeria 48 B3
Numanuma P.N.G. 56 E1
Numazu Japan 45 E6
Numbulwar Australia 56 A2
Numedal val. Norway 15 F6
Numfoor i. Indon. 41 F8
Numin He r. China 44 B3
Numurkah Australia 58 B6
Nunakuluut i. Greenland 61 N3
Nunap Isua c. Greenland see Farewell, Cape
Nunarsuit i. Greenland see Nunakuluut
Nunavut admin. div. Canada 61 J2
Nunda NY U.S.A. 64 C1
Nundle Australia 58 E3
Nuneaton U.K. 19 F6
Nungba India 37 H4
Nungnain Sum China 43 L3
Nunivak Island U.S.A. 60 B4
Nunkapasi India 38 E1
Nunkun mt. India 36 D2
Nunligran Rus. Fed. 29 T3
Nuñomoral Spain 25 C3
Nuoro Sardegna Italy 26 C4
Nupani i. Solomon Is 53 G3
Nuqrah Saudi Arabia 32 F4
Nūrābād Iran 35 H5
Nurakita i. Tuvalu see Niulakita
Nur Dağları mts Turkey 39 B1
Nuremberg Germany 17 M6
Nurla India 36 D2
Nurlat Rus. Fed. 13 K5
Nurmes Fin. 14 P5
Nurmo Fin. 14 M5
Nürnberg Germany see Nuremberg
Nurota Uzbek. 33 K1
Nurri, Mount h. Australia 58 C3
Nusaybin Turkey 35 F3
Nu Shan mts China 42 H7
Nushki Pak. 36 A3
Nusratiye Turkey 39 D1
Nuttal Pak. 36 B3
Nutwood Downs Australia 54 F3
Nuuk Greenland 61 M3
Nuupas Fin. 14 O3
Nuussuaq Greenland 61 M2
Nuussuaq pen. Greenland 61 M2
Nuwaybi' al Muzayyinah Egypt 34 D5
Nuweiba el Muzeina Egypt see Nuwaybi' al Muzayyinah
Nuwerus S. Africa 50 D6
Nuweveldberge mts S. Africa 50 E7
Nuyts, Point Australia 55 B8
Nuyts Archipelago is Australia 55 F8
Nuzvid India 38 D2
Nwanedi Nature Reserve S. Africa 51 J2
Nxai Pan National Park Botswana 49 C5
Nyagan' Rus. Fed. 11 T3
Nyahururu Kenya 48 D3
Nyah West Australia 58 A5
Nyainqêntanglha Feng mt. China 37 G3
Nyainqêntanglha Shan mts China 37 G3
Nyainrong China 42 G6
Nyainronglung China see Nyainrong
Nyåker Sweden 14 K5
Nyakh Rus. Fed. see Nyagan'
Nyaksimvol' Rus. Fed. 11 S3
Nyala Sudan 47 F3
Nyalam China see Congdü
Nyalikungu Tanz. see Maswa
Nyamandhlovu Zimbabwe 49 C5
Nyamtumbo Tanz. 49 D5
Nyande Zimbabwe see Masvingo
Nyandoma Rus. Fed. 12 I3
Nyandomskiy Vozvyshennost' hills Rus. Fed. 12 H3
Nyanga Congo 48 B4
Nyanga Zimbabwe 49 D5
Nyasa, Lake Africa 49 D4
Nyasaland country Africa see Malawi
Nyashabozh Rus. Fed. 12 L2
Nyasvizh Belarus 15 O10
Nyborg Denmark 15 G9
Nyborg Norway 14 P1
Nybro Sweden 15 I8
Nyeboe Land reg. Greenland 61 M1
Nyêmo China 37 G3
Nyenchen Tanglha Range mts China see Nyainqêntanglha Shan
Nyeri Kenya 48 D4
Nyi, Co l. China 37 F2
Nyika National Park Zambia 49 D5
Nyima China 37 F3
Nyimba Zambia 49 D5
Nyingchi China 37 H3
Nyíregyháza Hungary 13 D7
Nyiru, Mount Kenya 48 D3
Nykarleby Fin. 14 M5
Nykøbing Denmark 15 G9
Nykøbing Sjælland Denmark 15 G9
Nyköping Sweden 15 J7
Nyland Sweden 14 J5
Nylsvley nature res. S. Africa 51 I3
Nymagee Australia 58 C4
Nymboida National Park Australia 58 F2
Nynäshamn Sweden 15 J7
Nyngan Australia 58 C3
Nyogzê China 37 E3
Nyoman r. Belarus/Lith. 15 M10
Nyon Switz. 24 H3
Nyons France 24 G4
Nyrob Rus. Fed. 11 R3
Nysa Poland 17 P5
Nysh Rus. Fed. 44 F2
Nystad Fin. see Uusikaupunki
Nytva Rus. Fed. 11 R4
Nyuksenitsa Rus. Fed. 12 J3
Nyunzu Dem. Rep. Congo 49 C4
Nyurba Rus. Fed. 29 M3
Nyyskiy Zaliv b. Rus. Fed. 44 F1
Nzambi Congo 48 B4
Nzega Tanz. 49 D4
Nzérékoré Guinea 46 C4
N'zeto Angola 49 B4
Nzwani i. Comoros 49 E5

O

Oahe, Lake U.S.A. 62 G3
O'ahu i. U.S.A. 75 J4
Oaitupu i. Tuvalu see Vaitupu
Oak Bluffs MA U.S.A. 64 F2
Oakey Australia 58 E1
Oakham U.K. 19 G6
Oak Hill WV U.S.A. 64 A4
Oakhurst CA U.S.A. 65 C2
Oakland CA U.S.A. 65 A2
Oakland MD U.S.A. 64 B3
Oakland airport CA U.S.A. 65 A2
Oaklands Australia 58 C5
Oakover r. Australia 54 C5
Oakridge U.S.A. 62 C3
Oakvale Australia 57 C7
Oak View CA U.S.A. 65 C3
Oakville Ont. Canada 64 B1
Oamaru N.Z. 59 C7
Oaro N.Z. 59 D6
Oasis CA U.S.A. 65 D2
Oates Coast reg. Antarctica see Oates Land
Oates Land reg. Antarctica 76 H2
Oaxaca Mex. 66 E5
Oaxaca de Juárez Mex. see Oaxaca
Ob' r. Rus. Fed. 42 E2
Ob, Gulf of sea chan. Rus. Fed. see Obskaya Guba
Oba i. Vanuatu see Aoba
Obala Cameroon 46 E4
Obama Japan 45 D6
Oban U.K. 20 D4
O Barco Spain 25 C2
Obbia Somalia see Hobyo
Obdorsk Rus. Fed. see Salekhard
Óbecse Serbia see Bečej
Oberon Australia 58 D4
Oberpfälzer Wald mts Germany 17 N6
Obi i. Indon. 41 E8
Óbidos Brazil 69 G4
Obihiro Japan 44 F4
Obil'noye Rus. Fed. 13 J7
Ob'-Irtysh r. Rus. Fed. 28 H3
Obluch'ye Rus. Fed. 44 C2
Obninsk Rus. Fed. 13 H5
Obo Cent. Afr. Rep. 48 C3
Obock Djibouti 32 F7
Ŏbŏk N. Korea 44 C4
Obokote Dem. Rep. Congo 48 C4
Obo Liang China 42 G5
Obouya Congo 48 B4
Oboyan' Rus. Fed. 13 H6
Obozerskiy Rus. Fed. 12 I3
Obrenovac Serbia 27 I2
Obruk Turkey 34 D3
Observatory Hill h. Australia 55 F7
Obshchiy Syrt hills Rus. Fed. 11 Q5
Obskaya Guba sea chan. Rus. Fed. 28 I3
Obuasi Ghana 46 C4
Ob"yachevo Rus. Fed. 12 K3
Ocala U.S.A. 63 K6
Ocaña Col. 68 D2
Ocaña Spain 25 E4
Occidental, Cordillera mts Chile 68 E7
Occidental, Cordillera mts Col. 68 C3
Occidental, Cordillera mts Peru 68 D7
Ocean City MD U.S.A. 64 D3
Ocean City NJ U.S.A. 64 D3
Ocean Falls Canada 60 F4
Ocean Island Kiribati see Banaba
Ocean Island atoll U.S.A. see Kure Atoll
Oceanside CA U.S.A. 65 D4
Ochakiv Ukr. 27 N1
Och'amch'ire Georgia 35 F2
Ocher Rus. Fed. 11 Q4
Ochiishi-misaki pt Japan 44 G4
Ochil Hills U.K. 20 F4
Ochrida, Lake Albania/Macedonia see Ohrid, Lake
Ochsenfurt Germany 17 M6
Ockelbo Sweden 15 J6
Ocolaşul Mare, Vârful mt. Romania 27 K1
Octeville-sur-Mer France 19 H9
October Revolution Island Rus. Fed. see Oktyabr'skoy Revolyutsii, Ostrov
Ocussi enclave East Timor 54 D2
Ocussi-Ambeno enclave East Timor see Ocussi
Oda, Jebel mt. Sudan 32 E5
Ódáðahraun lava field Iceland 14 [inset]
Ŏdaejin N. Korea 44 C4
Odae-san National Park S. Korea 45 C5
Ōdate Japan 45 F4
Odawara Japan 45 E6
Odda Norway 15 E6
Odemira Port. 25 B5
Ödemiş Turkey 27 L5
Ödenburg Hungary see Sopron
Odense Denmark 15 G9
Odenwald reg. Germany 17 L6
Oderbucht b. Germany 17 O3
Ödeshog Sweden 15 I7
Odessa Ukr. 27 N1
Odessa Ukr. see Odessa
Odessa TX U.S.A. 62 G5
Odessus Bulg. see Varna
Odiel r. Spain 25 C5
Odienné Côte d'Ivoire 46 C4
Odintsovo Rus. Fed. 12 H5
Odra r. Germany/Pol. 17 Q6
Odzala, Parc National d' nat. park Congo 48 B3
Oea Libya see Tripoli
Oé-Cusse enclave East Timor see Ocussi
Oecussi enclave East Timor see Ocussi
Oeiras Brazil 69 J5
Oekussi enclave East Timor see Ocussi
Oenpelli Australia 54 F3
Oesel i. Estonia see Hiiumaa
Of Turkey 35 F2
Ofanto r. Italy 26 G4
Ofaqim Israel 39 B4
Offa Nigeria 46 D4
Offenbach am Main Germany 17 L5
Offenburg Germany 17 K6
Oga Japan 45 E5
Ogadēn reg. Eth. 48 E3
Oga-hantō pen. Japan 45 E5
Ōgaki Japan 45 E6
Ogallala U.S.A. 62 G3
Ogasawara-shotō is Japan see Bonin Islands
Ogbomosho Nigeria 46 D4
Ogbomoso Nigeria see Ogbomosho
Ogden UT U.S.A. 62 E3
Ogilvie r. Canada 60 E3
Ogilvie Mountains Canada 60 D3
Oglio r. Italy 26 D2
Oglongi Rus. Fed. 44 E1
Ogmore Australia 56 E4
Ogodzha Rus. Fed. 44 D1
Ogoja Nigeria 46 D4
Ogoki Reservoir Canada 63 J1
Ogoron Rus. Fed. 44 C1
Ogosta r. Bulg. 27 J3
Ogre Latvia 15 N8
Ogulin Croatia 26 F2
Ogurchinskiy, Ostrov i. Turkm. see Ogurjaly Adasy
Ogurjaly Adasy i. Turkm. 35 I3
Oğuzeli Turkey 39 C1
Ohai N.Z. 59 A7
Ohakune N.Z. 59 E4
Ohanet Alg. 46 D2
Ōhata Japan 44 F4
Ohcejohka Fin. see Utsjoki
O'Higgins (Chile) research stn Antarctica 76 A2
O'Higgins, Lago l. Chile 70 B7
Ohio r. Ohio/West Virginia U.S.A. 64 A3
Ohio state U.S.A. 64 A2
Ohrid Macedonia 27 I4
Ohrid, Lake Albania/Macedonia 27 I4
Ohridsko Ezero l. Albania/Macedonia see Ohrid, Lake
Ohrigstad S. Africa 51 J3
Ohrit, Liqeni i l. Albania/Macedonia see Ohrid, Lake
Ohura N.Z. 59 E4
Oich r. U.K. 20 E3
Oiga China 37 H3
Oil City PA U.S.A. 64 B2
Oise r. France 24 F2
Ōita Japan 45 C6
Oiti mt. Greece 27 J5
Ojai CA U.S.A. 65 C3
Ojalava i. Samoa see 'Upolu
Ojinaga Mex. 66 D3
Ojiya Japan 45 E5
Ojos del Salado, Nevado mt. Arg./Chile 70 C3
Oka r. Rus. Fed. 13 I4
Oka r. Rus. Fed. 42 I1
Okahandja Namibia 50 C1
Okahukura N.Z. 59 E4
Okakarara Namibia 49 B6
Okanagan Lake Canada 62 D2
Okanda Sri Lanka 38 D5
Okano r. Gabon 48 B4
Okanogan U.S.A. 62 D2
Okanogan r. U.S.A. 62 D2
Okara Pak. 33 L3
Okarem Turkm. see Ekerem
Okataina vol. N.Z. see Tarawera, Mount
Okaukuejo Namibia 49 B5
Okavango r. Africa 49 C5
Okavango Delta swamp Botswana 49 C5
Okavango Swamps Botswana see Okavango Delta
Okaya Japan 45 E5
Okayama Japan 45 D6
Okazaki Japan 45 E6
Okeechobee, Lake U.S.A. 63 K6
Okefenokee Swamp U.S.A. 63 K5
Okehampton U.K. 19 C8
Okha India 36 B5
Okha Rus. Fed. 44 F1
Okha Rann marsh India 36 B5
Okhotsk Rus. Fed. 29 P4
Okhotsk, Sea of Japan/Rus. Fed. 44 G3
Okhotskoye More sea Japan/Rus. Fed. see Okhotsk, Sea of
Okhtyrka Ukr. 13 G6
Okinawa i. Japan 45 B8
Okinawa-guntō is Japan see Okinawa-shotō
Okinawa-shotō is Japan 45 B8
Okino-Daitō-jima i. Japan 43 O8
Okino-Tori-shima i. Japan 43 P8
Oki-shotō is Japan 43 O5
Oki-shotō is Japan 45 D5
Oklahoma state U.S.A. 62 H4
Oklahoma City U.S.A. 63 H4
Okmulgee U.S.A. 63 H4
Okondja Gabon 48 B4
Okovskiy Les for. Rus. Fed. 12 G5
Okoyo Congo 48 B4
Øksfjord Norway 14 M1
Oktemberyan Armenia see Armavir
Oktyabr' Kazakh. see Kandyagash
Oktyabr'sk Kazakh. see Kandyagash
Oktyabr'skiy Belarus see Aktsyabrski
Oktyabr'skiy Amurskaya Oblast' Rus. Fed. 44 C1
Oktyabr'skiy Arkhangel'skaya Oblast' Rus. Fed. 12 I3
Oktyabr'skiy Kamchatskiy Kray Rus. Fed. 29 Q4
Oktyabr'skiy Respublika Bashkortostan Rus. Fed. 11 Q5
Oktyabr'skiy Volgogradskaya Oblast' Rus. Fed. 13 I7
Oktyabr'skoye Rus. Fed. 11 T3
Oktyabr'skoy Revolyutsii, Ostrov i. Rus. Fed. 29 K2
Okulovka Rus. Fed. 12 G4
Okushiri-tō i. Japan 44 E4
Okusi enclave East Timor see Ocussi
Okuta Nigeria 46 D4
Okwa watercourse Botswana 50 G1
Ólafsvík Iceland 14 [inset]
Olakkur India 38 C3
Olancha CA U.S.A. 65 C2
Olancha Peak CA U.S.A. 65 C2
Öland i. Sweden 15 J8
Olary Australia 57 C7
Olavarría Arg. 70 D5
Oława Poland 17 P5
Olbia Sardegna Italy 26 C4
Old Bastar India 38 D2
Oldcastle Ireland 21 E4
Old Cork Australia 56 C4
Old Crow Canada 60 E3
Oldenburg Germany 17 L4
Oldenburg in Holstein Germany 17 M3
Olderdalen Norway 14 L2
Old Gidgee Australia 55 B6
Oldham U.K. 18 E5
Old Harbor U.S.A. 60 C4
Old Head of Kinsale hd Ireland 21 D6
Oldmeldrum U.K. 20 G3
Old River CA U.S.A. 65 C3
Olds Canada 62 E1
Old Wives Lake Canada 62 F1
Olean NY U.S.A. 64 B1
Olecko Poland 17 S3
Olekma r. Rus. Fed. 29 N3
Olekminsk Rus. Fed. 29 N3
Olekminskiy Stanovik mts Rus. Fed. 43 M
Oleksandrivs'k Ukr. see Zaporizhzhya
Oleksandriya Ukr. 13 G6
Ølen Norway 15 D7
Olenegorsk Rus. Fed. 12 G1
Olenek Rus. Fed. 29 M3
Olenek r. Rus. Fed. 29 M2
Olenek Bay Rus. Fed. see Olenekskiy Zali
Olenekskiy Zaliv b. Rus. Fed. 29 N2
Olenino Rus. Fed. 12 G4
Olenitsa Rus. Fed. 12 G2
Olenivs'ki Kar"yery Ukr. see Dokuchayevs
Olenya Rus. Fed. see Olenegorsk
Oleshky Ukr. see Tsyurupyns'k
Olevs'k Ukr. 13 E6
Ol'ga Rus. Fed. 44 D4
Olga, Mount Australia 55 E6
Ol'ginsk Rus. Fed. 44 D1
Olginskoye Rus. Fed. see Kochubeyevskoye
Ölgiy Mongolia 42 F3
Olhão Port. 25 C5
Olia Chain mts Australia 55 E6
Olifants r. Moz./S. Africa 51 J3
Olifants watercourse Namibia 50 D3
Olifants S. Africa 51 J2
Olifants r. W. Cape S. Africa 50 D6
Olifants r. W. Cape S. Africa 50 E7
Olifantshoek S. Africa 50 F4
Olifantsrivierberge mts S. Africa 50 D7
Olimbos h. Cyprus see Olympos
Olimbos mt. Greece see Olympus, Mount
Olimpos Beydağları Milli Parkı nat. park Turkey 27 N6
Olinda Brazil 69 L5
Olinga Moz. 49 D5
Olio Australia 56 C4
Oliphants Drift S. Africa 51 H3
Olisipo Port. see Lisbon
Oliva Spain 25 F4
Oliva, Cordillera de mts Arg./Chile 70 C3
Olivares, Cerro de mt. Arg./Chile 70 C4
Olivehurst CA U.S.A. 65 B1
Oliveira dos Brejinhos Brazil 71 C1
Olivença Moz. see Lupilichi
Olivenza Spain 25 C4
Ol'khovka Rus. Fed. 13 J6
Ollagüe Chile 70 C2
Ollombo Congo 48 B4
Olmaliq Uzbek. 42 B4
Olmos Peru 68 C5
Olmütz Czech Rep. see Olomouc
Olney U.K. 19 G6
Olney MD U.S.A. 64 C3
Olofström Sweden 15 I8
Olomouc Czech Rep. 17 P6
Olonets Rus. Fed. 12 G3
Oloron-Ste-Marie France 24 D5
Olosenga atoll American Samoa see Swains Island
Olot Spain 25 H2
Olovyannaya Rus. Fed. 43 L2
Oloy r. Rus. Fed. 29 Q3
Oloy, Qatorkŭhi mts Asia see Alai Range
Olsztyn Poland 17 R4
Olt r. Romania 27 K3
Olten Switz. 24 H3
Olteniţa Romania 27 L2
Oltu Turkey 35 F2
Ol'viopol' Ukr. see Pervomays'k
Olymbos h. Cyprus see Olympos
Olympia U.S.A. 62 C2
Olympos h. Cyprus 39 A2
Olympos Greece see Olympus, Mount
Olympou, Ethnikos Drymos nat. park Greece 27 J4
Olympus, Mount Greece 27 J4
Olympus, Mount U.S.A. 62 C2
Olyutorskiy Rus. Fed. 29 R3
Olyutorskiy, Mys c. Rus. Fed. 29 S4
Olyutorskiy Zaliv b. Rus. Fed. 29 R4
Olzheras Rus. Fed. see Mezhdurechensk
Oma China 37 E2
Oma r. Rus. Fed. 12 J2
Omagh U.K. 21 E3
Omaha U.S.A. 63 H3
Omaheke admin. reg. Namibia 50 D2
Omal'skiy Khrebet mts Rus. Fed. 44 E1
Oman country Asia 33 I6
Oman, Gulf of Asia 33 I4
Omaruru Namibia 49 B6
Omate Peru 68 D7
Omaweneno Botswana 50 F3
Omba i. Vanuatu see Aoba
Ombai, Selat sea chan. Indon. 54 D2
Ombalantu Namibia see Uutapi
Omboué Gabon 48 A4
Ombu China 37 F3
Omdraaisvlei S. Africa 50 F6
Omdurman Sudan 32 D6
Omeo Australia 58 C6
Ometepec Mex. 66 E5
Om Hajēr Eritrea 32 E7
Omīdīyeh Iran 35 H5
Omineca Mountains Canada 60 F4
Omitara Namibia 50 C2
Ōmiya Japan 45 E6
Omolon Rus. Fed. 29 R3
Omo National Park Eth. 48 D3
Omsk Rus. Fed. 28 I4
Omsukchan Rus. Fed. 29 Q3
Ōmū Japan 44 F3
Omu, Vârful mt. Romania 27 K2
Ōmura Japan 45 C6
Omutninsk Rus. Fed. 12 L4
Onancock VA U.S.A. 64 D4
Onangué, Lac l. Gabon 48 B4
Onaping Lake Canada 63 K2
Oncativo Arg. 70 D4
Onchan Isle of Man 18 C4
Oncócua Angola 49 B5
Öncül Turkey 39 D1
Ondal India see Andal
Ondangwa Namibia 49 B5
Onderstedorings S. Africa 50 E6
Ondjiva Angola 49 B5
Ondo Nigeria 46 D4
Öndörhaan Mongolia 43 K3
Öndörshil Mongolia 43 J3
Ondozero Rus. Fed. 12 G3
One Botswana 50 E2
Onega Rus. Fed. 12 H3
Onega r. Rus. Fed. 12 H3
Onega, Lake l. Rus. Fed. see Onezhskoye Ozero

Paraná, Serra do hills Brazil 71 B1
Paranaguá Brazil 71 A4
Paranaíba Brazil 71 A2
Paranaíba r. Brazil 71 A3
Paranapiacaba, Serra mts Brazil 71 A4
Paranavaí Brazil 70 F2
Parangi Aru r. Sri Lanka 38 D4
Parang Pass India 36 D2
Parângul Mare, Vârful mt. Romania 27 J2
Paranthan Sri Lanka 38 D4
Paraopeba Brazil 71 B2
Pārapāra Iraq 35 G4
Paraparaumu N.Z. 59 E5
Paras Pak. 36 C2
Paraspori, Akrotirio pt Greece 27 L7
Parateca Brazil 71 C1
Paratinga Brazil 71 C1
Parāū, Kūh-e mt. Iraq 35 G4
Paraúna Brazil 71 A2
Parbhani India 38 C2
Parchim Germany 17 M4
Parding China 37 G2
Pardo r. Bahia Brazil 71 D1
Pardo r. Mato Grosso do Sul Brazil 70 F2
Pardo r. São Paulo Brazil 71 A3
Pardoo Australia 54 B5
Pardubice Czech Rep. 17 O5
Parece Vela i. Japan see Okino-Tori-shima
Parecis, Serra dos hills Brazil 68 F6
Pareh Iran 35 G3
Parenda India 38 B2
Parent, Lac l. Canada 63 L2
Pareora N.Z. 59 C7
Parepare Indon. 41 D8
Parga Greece 27 I5
Pargas Fin. 15 M6
Parghelia Italy 26 F5
Pargi India 38 C2
Paria, Gulf of Trin. and Tob./Venez. 67 L6
Paria, Península de pen. Venez. 68 F1
Parikkala Fin. 15 P6
Parikud Islands India 38 E2
Parima, Serra mts Brazil 68 F3
Parima-Tapirapecó, Parque Nacional nat. park Venez. 68 F3
Parintins Brazil 69 G4
Paris Ont. Canada 64 A1
Paris France 24 F2
Paris TX U.S.A. 63 H5
Park U.K. 21 E3
Parkano Fin. 15 M5
Parker AZ U.S.A. 65 E3
Parker Dam CA U.S.A. 65 E3
Parker Range hills Australia 55 B8
Parkersburg WV U.S.A. 64 A3
Parkes Australia 58 D4
Park Falls U.S.A. 63 I2
Parkhill Ont. Canada 64 A1
Parkutta Pak. 36 D2
Parla Kimedi India see Paralakhemundi
Parlakimidi India see Paralakhemundi
Parli Vaijnath India 38 C2
Parlung Zangbo r. China 37 H3
Parma Italy 26 D2
Parma OH U.S.A. 64 A2
Parnaíba Brazil 69 J4
Parnaíba r. Brazil 69 J4
Parnassus N.Z. 59 D6
Parner India 38 B2
Parnonas mts Greece 27 J6
Pärnu Estonia 15 N7
Pärnu-Jaagupi Estonia 15 N7
Paro Bhutan 37 G4
Paroikia Greece 27 K6
Paroo watercourse Australia 58 A3
Paroo Channel watercourse Australia 58 A3
Paros i. Greece 27 K6
Parowan UT U.S.A. 65 F2
Parral Chile 70 B5
Parramatta Australia 58 E4
Parramore Island VA U.S.A. 64 D4
Parras Mex. 66 D3
Parrett r. U.K. 19 D7
Parry, Cape Canada 77 A2
Parry, Kap c. Greenland see Kangaarsussuaq
Parry Bay Canada 61 J3
Parry Channel Canada 61 G2
Parry Islands Canada 61 G2
Parry Range hills Australia 54 A5
Parry Sound Canada 63 K2
Parsnip Peak NV U.S.A. 65 E1
Parsons KS U.S.A. 63 H4
Parsons WV U.S.A. 64 B3
Parsons Range hills Australia 54 F3
Partabgarh India 38 B2
Partabpur India 37 E5
Parthenay France 24 D3
Partizansk Rus. Fed. 44 D4
Partney U.K. 18 H5
Partry Ireland 21 C4
Partry Mts hills Ireland 21 C4
Paru r. Brazil 69 H4
Paryang China 37 E3
Parys S. Africa 51 H4
Pasa Dağı mt. Turkey 34 D3
Pasadena CA U.S.A. 65 C3
Pasado, Cabo c. Ecuador 68 B4
Pascagoula U.S.A. 63 J5
Paşcani Romania 27 L1
Pascoal, Monte h. Brazil 71 D2
Pascua, Isla de i. S. Pacific Ocean see Easter Island
Pas de Calais str. France/U.K. see Dover, Strait of
Pasewalk Germany 17 O4
Pasha Rus. Fed. 12 G3
Pashih Haihsia sea chan. Phil./Taiwan see Bashi Channel
Pashkovo Rus. Fed. 44 C2
Pashkovskiy Rus. Fed. 13 H7
Pasighat India 37 H3
Pasinler Turkey 35 F3
Pasni Pak. 73 M4
Paso de los Toros Uruguay 70 E4
Pasok Myanmar 37 H5
Paso Robles CA U.S.A. 65 B3
Passaic NJ U.S.A. 64 D2
Passa Tempo Brazil 71 B3
Passau Germany 17 N6
Passo del San Gottardo Switz. see St Gotthard Pass
Passo Fundo Brazil 70 F3
Passos Brazil 71 B3
Passur r. Bangl. see Pusur
Passuri Nadi r. Bangl. see Pusur
Pastavy Belarus 15 O9
Pastaza r. Peru 68 C4
Pasto Col. 68 C3
Pastos Bons Brazil 69 J5
Pasu Pak. 36 C1
Pasur Turkey see Kulp
Pasvalys Lith. 15 N8
Pasvikelva r. Europe see Patsoyoki
Patache, Punta pt Chile 70 B2
Patagonia reg. Arg. 70 B8
Pataliputra India see Patna
Patan Gujarat India see Somnath
Patan Gujarat India 36 C5
Patan Mahar. India 38 B2
Patan Nepal 37 F4
Patan Pak. 36 C2
Patavium Italy see Padua
Patea N.Z. 59 E4
Patea inlet N.Z. see Doubtful Sound
Pate Island Kenya 48 E4
Pateley Bridge U.K. 18 F4
Patensie S. Africa 50 G7
Patera India 36 D4
Paterson Australia 58 E4
Paterson r. Australia 58 C2
Paterson NJ U.S.A. 64 D2
Paterson Range hills Australia 54 C5
Pathanamthitta India 38 C4
Pathankot India 36 C2
Pathari India 36 D5
Pathein Myanmar see Bassein
Patía r. Col. 68 C3
Patiala India 36 D3
Patkai Bum mts India/Myanmar 37 H4
Patkaklik China 37 F1
Patmos i. Greece 27 L6
Patna India 37 F4
Patna Orissa India 37 F5
Patnagarh India 37 E5
Patnos Turkey 35 F3
Pato Branco Brazil 70 F3
Patoda India 38 B2
Patos Albania 27 H4
Patos Brazil 69 K5
Patos, Lagoa dos l. Brazil 70 F4
Patos de Minas Brazil 71 B2
Patquía Arg. 70 C4
Patra Greece see Patras
Patrae Greece see Patras
Pátrai Greece see Patras
Patras Greece 27 I5
Patreksfjörður Iceland 14 [inset]
Patricio Lynch, Isla i. Chile 70 A7
Patrick Creek watercourse Australia 56 D4
Patrimônio Brazil 71 A2
Patrocínio Brazil 71 B2
Patsoyoki r. Europe 14 Q2
Pattadakal tourist site India 38 B2
Patterson CA U.S.A. 65 B2
Patti India 37 E4
Pattijoki Fin. 14 N4
Pättikkä Fin. 14 L2
Patton PA U.S.A. 64 B2
Pattullo, Mount Canada 60 F4
Patu Brazil 69 K5
Patuakhali Bangl. 37 G5
Patuca, Punta pt Hond. 67 H5
Patur India 38 C1
Patuxent r. MD U.S.A. 64 C3
Patuxent Range mts Antarctica 76 L1
Patvinsuon kansallispuisto nat. park Fin. 14 Q5
Pau France 24 D5
Pauhunri mt. China/India 37 G4
Pauillac France 24 D4
Pauini Brazil 68 E5
Pauiní r. Brazil 68 E5
Pauk Myanmar 37 H5
Paulatuk Canada 77 A2
Paulicéia Brazil 71 A3
Paulis Dem. Rep. Congo see Isiro
Paulo Afonso Brazil 69 K5
Paulo de Faria Brazil 71 A3
Paulpietersburg S. Africa 51 J4
Paul Roux S. Africa 51 H5
Paumotu, Îles is Fr. Polynesia see Tuamotu Islands
Paungbyin Myanmar 37 H4
Pauni India 38 C1
Pauri India 36 D3
Pavagada India 38 C3
Pavão Brazil 71 C2
Pāveh Iran 35 G4
Pavia Italy 26 C2
Pāvilosta Latvia 15 L8
Pavino Rus. Fed. 12 J4
Pavlikeni Bulg. 27 K3
Pavlodar Kazakh. 42 D2
Pavlof Volcano U.S.A. 60 B4
Pavlograd Ukr. see Pavlohrad
Pavlohrad Ukr. 13 G6
Pavlovka Rus. Fed. 13 J5
Pavlovo Rus. Fed. 12 I5
Pavlovsk Altayskiy Kray Rus. Fed. 42 E2
Pavlovsk Voronezhskaya Oblast' Rus. Fed. 13 I6
Pavlovskaya Rus. Fed. 13 H7
Pawai India 36 E4
Paw Paw WV U.S.A. 64 B3
Pawtucket RI U.S.A. 64 F2
Paxson U.S.A. 60 D3
Payakumbuh Indon. 41 C8
Payette U.S.A. 62 D3
Pay-Khoy, Khrebet hills Rus. Fed. 28 H3
Payne Canada see Kangirsuk
Payne, Lac l. Canada 61 K4
Payne's Find Australia 55 B7
Paysandú Uruguay 70 E4
Pazar Turkey 35 F2
Pazarcık Turkey 34 E3
Pazardzhik Bulg. 27 K3
Pazin Croatia 26 E2
Peabody MA U.S.A. 64 F1
Peace r. Canada 60 G4
Peace River Canada 77 L3
Peach Springs AZ U.S.A. 65 F3
Peak Charles h. Australia 55 C8
Peak Charles National Park Australia 55 C8
Peak District National Park U.K. 18 F5
Peake watercourse Australia 57 B6
Peak Hill N.S.W. Australia 58 D4
Peak Hill W.A. Australia 55 B6
Peale, Mount U.S.A. 62 F4
Pearce Point Australia 54 E3
Pearisburg VA U.S.A. 64 A4
Pearl r. U.S.A. 63 J5
Pearsall U.S.A. 62 H6
Pearston S. Africa 51 G7
Peary Channel Canada 61 I2
Peary Land reg. Greenland 77 J1
Pebane Moz. 49 D5
Pebas Peru 68 D4
Peć Kosovo see Pejë
Peçanha Brazil 71 C2
Peças, Ilha das i. Brazil 71 A4
Pechenga Rus. Fed. 14 Q2
Pechora Rus. Fed. 12 M2
Pechora r. Rus. Fed. 12 L1
Pechora Sea Rus. Fed. see Pechorskoye More
Pechorskaya Guba b. Rus. Fed. 12 L1
Pechorskoye More sea Rus. Fed. 77 G2
Pechory Rus. Fed. 15 O8
Pecos U.S.A. 62 G5
Pecos r. U.S.A. 62 G6
Pécs Hungary 26 H1
Pedda Vagu r. India 38 C2
Pedder, Lake Australia 57 [inset]
Peddie S. Africa 51 H7
Pedernales Dom. Rep. 67 J5
Pedersöre Fin. 14 M5
Pediaios r. Cyprus 39 A2
Pediva Angola 49 B5
Pedra Azul Brazil 71 C1
Pedra Preta, Serra da mts Brazil 71 A1
Pedras de Maria da Cruz Brazil 71 B1
Pedregulho Brazil 71 B3
Pedreiras Brazil 69 J4
Pedro, Point Sri Lanka 38 D4
Pedro II, Ilha reg. Brazil/Venez. 68 E3
Pedro Juan Caballero Para. 70 E2
Peebles U.K. 20 F5
Pee Dee r. U.S.A. 63 L5
Peekskill NY U.S.A. 64 E2
Peel r. Australia 58 E3
Peel r. Canada 60 E3
Peel Isle of Man 18 C4
Peera Peera Poolanna Lake imp. l. Australia 57 B5
Peery Lake salt l. Australia 58 A3
Pegasus Bay N.Z. 59 D6
Pegu Myanmar 42 H9
Pegu Yoma mts Myanmar 37 H6
Pegysh Rus. Fed. 12 K3
Pehuajó Arg. 70 D5
Peine Chile 70 C2
Peint India 38 B1
Peipsi järv l. Estonia/Rus. Fed. see Peipus, Lake
Peipus, Lake Estonia/Rus. Fed. 15 O7
Peiraias Greece see Piraeus
Pei Shan mts China see Bei Shan
Peixe Brazil 69 I6
Peixe r. Brazil 71 A1
Peixoto de Azevedo Brazil 69 H6
Pejë Kosovo 27 I3
Pèk Laos see Phônsavan
Peka Lesotho 51 H5
Peking China see Beijing
Pekinga Benin 46 D3
Pelagie, Isole is Sicilia Italy 26 E7
Peleaga, Vârful mt. Romania 27 J2
Peles Rus. Fed. 12 K3
Pelkosenniemi Fin. 14 O3
Pella S. Africa 50 D5
Pello Fin. 14 M3
Pelly Crossing Canada 60 E3
Pelly Mountains Canada 60 E3
Peloponnese admin. reg. Greece 27 J6
Pelopónnesos admin. reg. Greece see Peloponnese
Peloponnisos admin. reg. Greece see Peloponnese
Pelotas Brazil 70 F4
Pelotas, Rio das r. Brazil 71 A4
Pelusium tourist site Egypt 39 A4
Pelusium, Bay of Egypt see Ţīnah, Khalīj aţ
Pemba Moz. 49 E5
Pemba Island Tanz. 49 D4
Pemberton Canada 62 C1
Pembina r. Canada 62 D1
Pembroke Canada 63 L2
Pembroke U.K. 19 C7
Pembrokeshire Coast National Park U.K. 19 B7
Pen India 38 B2
Peña Cerredo mt. Spain see Torrecerredo
Peñalara mt. Spain 25 E3
Penamar Brazil 71 C1
Peña Nevada, Cerro mt. Mex. 66 E4
Penang Malaysia see George Town
Penápolis Brazil 71 A3
Peñaranda de Bracamonte Spain 25 D3
Penarie Australia 58 A5
Penarlâg U.K. see Hawarden
Peñarroya mt. Spain 25 F3
Peñarroya-Pueblonuevo Spain 25 D4
Penarth U.K. 19 D7
Peñas, Cabo de c. Spain 25 D2
Penas, Golfo de g. Chile 70 A7
Peña Ubiña mt. Spain 25 D2
Pendle Hill h. U.K. 18 E5
Pendleton U.S.A. 62 D2
Pend Oreille Lake U.S.A. 62 D2
Pendra India 37 E5
Penduv India 38 B2
Peneda Gerês, Parque Nacional da nat. park Port. 25 B3
Penfro U.K. see Pembroke
Penganga r. India 38 C2
Penge Dem. Rep. Congo 49 C4
Penge S. Africa 51 J3
P'enghu Ch'üntao is Taiwan 43 L8
P'enghu Liehtao is Taiwan see P'enghu Ch'üntao
Penha Brazil 71 A4
Penhoek Pass S. Africa 51 H6
Penhook VA U.S.A. 64 B4
Peniche Port. 25 B4
Penicuik U.K. 20 F5
Peninga Rus. Fed. 14 R5
Peninsular Malaysia Malaysia 41 C7
Penitente, Serra do hills Brazil 69 I5
Pennell Coast Antarctica 76 H2
Penn Hills PA U.S.A. 64 B2
Pennine, Alpi mts Italy/Switz. 26 B2
Pennine Alps mts Italy/Switz. see Pennine, Alpi
Pennines hills U.K. 18 E4
Pennsburg PA U.S.A. 64 D2
Penns Grove NJ U.S.A. 64 D3
Pennsville NJ U.S.A. 64 D3
Pennsylvania state U.S.A. 64 B2
Penn Yan NY U.S.A. 64 C1
Penny Icecap Canada 61 L3
Penny Point Antarctica 76 H1
Penola Australia 57 C8
Penong Australia 55 F7
Penonomé Panama 67 H7
Penrhyn atoll Cook Is 75 J6
Penrhyn Basin sea feature S. Pacific Ocean 75 J6
Penrith Australia 58 E4
Penrith U.K. 18 E4
Pensacola U.S.A. 63 J5
Pensacola Mountains Antarctica 76 L1
Pensi La pass India 36 D2
Pentadaktylos Range mts Cyprus 39 A2
Pentakota India 38 D2
Pentecost Island Vanuatu 53 G3
Pentecôte, Île i. Vanuatu see Pentecost Island
Penticton Canada 62 D2
Pentire Point U.K. 19 B8
Pentland Australia 56 D4
Pentland Firth sea chan. U.K. 20 F2
Pentland Hills U.K. 20 F5
Pen-y-Bont ar Ogwr U.K. see Bridgend
Penygadair h. U.K. 19 D6
Penza Rus. Fed. 13 J5
Penzance U.K. 19 B8
Penzhinskaya Guba b. Rus. Fed. 29 R3
Peoria IL U.S.A. 63 J3
Peradeniya Sri Lanka 38 D5
Pera Head hd Australia 56 C2
Perales del Alfambra Spain 25 F3
Perambalur India 38 C4
Perämeren kansallispuisto nat. park Fin. 14 N4
Peräseinäjoki Fin. 14 M5
Percival Lakes imp. l. Australia 54 D5
Percy Isles Australia 56 E4
Perdizes Brazil 71 B2
Peregrebnoye Rus. Fed. 11 T3
Pereira Col. 68 C3
Pereira Barreto Brazil 71 A3
Pereira de Eça Angola see Ondjiva
Peremul Par rf India 38 B4
Peremyshlyany Ukr. 13 E6
Perenjori Australia 55 B7
Pereslavl'-Zalesskiy Rus. Fed. 12 H4
Pereslavskiy Natsional'nyy Park nat. park Rus. Fed. 12 H4
Pereyaslavka Rus. Fed. 44 D3
Pereyaslav-Khmel'nitskiy Ukr. see Pereyaslav-Khmel'nyts'kyy
Pereyaslav-Khmel'nyts'kyy Ukr. 13 F6
Pergamino Arg. 70 D4
Perho Fin. 14 N5
Perico Arg. 70 C2
Pericos Mex. 66 C3
Périgueux France 24 E4
Perijá, Parque Nacional nat. park Venez. 68 D2
Perija, Sierra de mts Venez. 68 D2
Periyar India see Erode
Perlas, Punta de pt Nicaragua 67 H6
Perleberg Germany 17 M4
Perm' Rus. Fed. 11 R4
Permas Rus. Fed. 12 J4
Pernambuco Brazil see Recife
Pernambuco Plain sea feature S. Atlantic Ocean 72 G6
Pernatty Lagoon imp. l. Australia 57 B6
Pernem India 38 B3
Pernik Bulg. 27 J3
Pernov Estonia see Pärnu
Perojpur Bangl. see Pirojpur
Peron Islands Australia 54 E3
Péronne France 24 F2
Perpignan France 24 F5
Perranporth U.K. 19 B8
Perrégaux Alg. see Mohammadia
Perris CA U.S.A. 65 D4
Perros-Guirec France 24 C2
Perry FL U.S.A. 63 K5
Perryton U.S.A. 62 G4
Perryville AK U.S.A. 60 C4
Perryville MO U.S.A. 63 J4
Perseverancia Bol. 68 F6
Pershore U.K. 19 E6
Persia country Asia see Iran
Persian Gulf Asia see The Gulf
Pertek Turkey 35 E3
Perth Australia 55 A7
Perth Canada 63 L3
Perth U.K. 20 F4
Perth Amboy NJ U.S.A. 64 D2
Perth Basin sea feature Indian Ocean 73 P7
Pertominsk Rus. Fed. 12 H2
Pertunmaa Fin. 15 O6
Pertusato, Capo c. Corse France 24 I6
Peru atoll Kiribati see Beru
Peru country S. America 68 D6
Peru-Chile Trench sea feature S. Pacific Ocean 75 O6
Perugia Italy 26 E3
Peruru India 38 C3
Perusia Italy see Perugia
Pervomaysk Rus. Fed. 13 I5
Pervomays'k Ukr. 13 F6
Pervomayskiy Kazakh. 42 E2
Pervomayskiy Arkhangel'skaya Oblast' Rus. Fed. see Novodvinsk
Pervomayskiy Tambovskaya Oblast' Rus. Fed. 13 I5
Pervomays'kyy Ukr. 13 H6
Pervorechenskiy Rus. Fed. 29 R3
Pesaro Italy 26 E3
Pescadores is Taiwan see P'enghu Ch'üntao
Pescara Italy 26 F3
Pescara r. Italy 26 F3
Peschanokopskoye Rus. Fed. 13 I7
Peschanoye Rus. Fed. see Yashkul'
Peschanyy, Mys pt Kazakh. 35 H2
Pesha r. Rus. Fed. 12 J2
Peshawar Pak. 33 L3
Peshkopi Albania 27 I4
Peshtera Bulg. 27 K3
Peski Karakumy des. Turkm. see Karakum Desert
Peskovka Rus. Fed. 12 L4
Pesnica Slovenia 26 F1
Pessac France 24 D4
Pestovo Rus. Fed. 12 G4
Pestravka Rus. Fed. 13 K5
Petah Tiqwa Israel 39 B3
Petäjävesi Fin. 14 N5
Petalion, Kolpos sea chan. Greece 27 K5
Petaluma CA U.S.A. 65 A1
Petatlán Mex. 66 D5
Petauke Zambia 49 D5
Peterborough Australia 57 B7
Peterborough Canada 63 L3
Peterborough U.K. 19 G6
Peterborough NH U.S.A. 64 F1
Peterculter U.K. 20 G3
Peterhead U.K. 20 H3
Peter I Island Antarctica 76 K2
Peter I Øy i. Antarctica see Peter I Island
Peterlee U.K. 18 F4
Petermann Bjerg nunatak Greenland 61 P2
Petermann Ranges mts Australia 55 E6
Peter Pond Lake Canada 60 H4
Petersburg NY U.S.A. 64 E1
Petersburg VA U.S.A. 64 C4
Petersburg WV U.S.A. 64 B3
Petersfield U.K. 19 G7
Petersville U.S.A. 60 C3
Peter the Great Bay Rus. Fed. see Petra Velikogo, Zaliv
Peth India 38 B2
Petilia Policastro Italy 26 G5
Petit Atlas mts Morocco see Anti Atlas
Petitjean Morocco see Sidi Kacem
Petit Lac Manicouagan l. Canada 61 L4
Petit Mécatina r. Nfld. and Lab./Que. Canada 61 M4
Petit St-Bernard, Col du pass France 24 H4
Petit Saut, Barrage du dam Fr. Guiana 69 H3
Peto Mex. 66 G4
Petoskey U.S.A. 63 K2
Petra tourist site Jordan 39 B4
Petra Velikogo, Zaliv b. Rus. Fed. 44 C4
Petre, Point Ont. Canada 64 C1
Petrich Bulg. 27 J4
Petrikau Poland see Piotrków Trybunalski
Petrikov Belarus see Pyetrykaw
Petrinja Croatia 26 G2
Petroaleksandrovsk Uzbek. see To'rtko'l
Petrograd Rus. Fed. see St Petersburg
Petrokhanski Prokhod pass Bulg. 27 J3
Petrokov Poland see Piotrków Trybunalski
Petrolina Brazil 69 J5
Petrolina de Goiás Brazil 71 A2
Petropavl Kazakh. see Petropavlovsk
Petropavlovsk Kazakh. 31 F1
Petropavlovsk Rus. Fed. see Petropavlovsk-Kamchatskiy
Petropavlovsk-Kamchatskiy Rus. Fed. 29 Q4
Petrópolis Brazil 71 C3
Petroşani Romania 27 J2
Petrovsk Rus. Fed. 13 J5
Petrovskoye Rus. Fed. see Svetlograd
Petrovsk-Zabaykal'skiy Rus. Fed. 43 J2
Petrozavodsk Rus. Fed. 12 G3
Petrus Steyn S. Africa 51 I4
Petrusville S. Africa 50 G6
Petsamo Rus. Fed. see Pechenga
Pettau Slovenia see Ptuj
Pettigo U.K. 21 E3
Petukhovo Rus. Fed. 28 H4
Petushki Rus. Fed. 12 H5
Petzeck mt. Austria 17 N7
Pevek Rus. Fed. 29 S3
Pêxung China 37 H2
Peza r. Rus. Fed. 12 J2
Pezinok Slovakia 17 P6
Pezu Pak. 36 B2
Pforzheim Germany 17 L6
Phagameng Limpopo S. Africa 51 I3
Phagwara India 36 C3
Phahameng Free State S. Africa 51 H5
Phalaborwa S. Africa 51 J2
Phalodi India 36 C4
Phalsund India 36 B4
Phalta India 37 G5
Phalut Peak India/Nepal 37 G4
Phangnga Thai. 31 I6
Phăng Xi Păng mt. Vietnam 42 I8
Phan Rang-Thap Cham Vietnam 31 J5
Phan Thiêt Vietnam 31 J5
Phatthalung Thai. 31 J6
Phayao Thai. 42 H9
Phek India 37 H4
Phenix VA U.S.A. 64 B4
Phenix City U.S.A. 63 J5
Phet Buri Thai. 31 I5
Philadelphia Jordan see 'Ammān
Philadelphia Turkey see Alaşehir
Philadelphia PA U.S.A. 64 D3
Philip U.S.A. 62 G3
Philip Atoll Micronesia see Sorol
Philippeville Alg. see Skikda
Philippi WV U.S.A. 64 A3
Philippi, Lake imp. l. Australia 56 B5
Philippine Basin sea feature N. Pacific Ocean 74 E4
Philippines country Asia 41 E6
Philippine Sea N. Pacific Ocean 41 E6
Philippine Trench sea feature N. Pacific Ocean 74 E4
Philippolis S. Africa 51 G6
Philippopolis Bulg. see Plovdiv
Philipsburg PA U.S.A. 64 B2
Philip Smith Mountains U.S.A. 60 D3
Philipstown S. Africa 50 G6
Phillip Island Australia 58 B7
Phillipsburg U.S.A. 62 H4
Phillips Range hills Australia 54 D4
Philmont NY U.S.A. 64 E1
Philomelium Turkey see Akşehir
Phiritona S. Africa 51 H4
Phitsanulok Thai. 31 J5
Phnom Penh Cambodia 31 J5
Phnum Pénh Cambodia see Phnom Penh
Phoenicia NY U.S.A. 64 D1
Phoenix U.S.A. 62 E5
Phoenix Island Kiribati see Rawaki
Phoenix Islands Kiribati 53 I2
Phôngsali Laos 40 C5
Phong Saly Laos see Phôngsali
Phônsavan Laos 41 C6
Phosphate Hill Australia 56 C4
Phrae Thai. 31 J5
Phra Nakhon Si Ayutthaya Thai. see Ayutthaya
Phuket Thai. 31 I6
Phulabani India see Phulbani
Phulbani India 38 E1
Phulchhari Ghat Bangl. see Fulchhari
Phulji Pak. 36 A4
Phyu Myanmar 42 H9
Piaca Brazil 69 I5
Piacenza Italy 26 C2
Pian r. Australia 58 D3
Pianosa, Isola i. Italy 26 D3
Piatra Neamţ Romania 27 L1
Piave r. Italy 26 E2
Pibor Post Sudan 47 G4
Picardie admin. reg. France 19 J9
Picardie reg. France see Picardy
Picardy admin. reg. France see Picardie
Picardy reg. France 24 E2
Picauville France 19 F9
Picayune U.S.A. 63 J5
Pichanal Arg. 70 D2
Pichhor India 36 D4
Pichilemu Chile 70 B4
Pichilingue Mex. 66 B4
Pickens WV U.S.A. 64 A3
Pickering U.K. 18 G4
Pickering, Vale of val. U.K. 18 G4
Pickle Lake Canada 61 I4
Pico da Neblina, Parque Nacional do nat. park Brazil 68 E3
Picos Brazil 69 J5
Pico Truncado Arg. 70 C7
Picton Australia 58 E5
Picton N.Z. 59 E5
Pidurutalagala mt. Sri Lanka 38 D5
Piedade Brazil 71 B3
Piedra de Águila Arg. 70 B6
Piedras, Punta pt Arg. 70 E5
Piedras Blancas Point CA U.S.A. 65 B3
Piedras Negras Mex. 66 D3
Pieksämäki Fin. 14 O5
Pielavesi Fin. 14 O5
Pielinen l. Fin. 14 P5
Pieljekaise nationalpark nat. park Sweden 14 J3
Pienaarsrivier S. Africa 51 I3
Pieniński Park Narodowy nat. park Poland 17 R6
Pieninský nat. park Slovakia 17 R6
Pieria mts Greece 27 J4
Pierowall U.K. 20 G1
Pierpont OH U.S.A. 64 A2
Pierre U.S.A. 62 G3
Pierrelatte France 24 G4
Pietermaritzburg S. Africa 51 J5
Pietersaari Fin. see Jakobstad
Pietra Spada, Passo di pass Italy 26 G5
Piet Retief S. Africa 51 J4
Pietrosa mt. Romania 27 K1
Pigeon Lake Canada 62 E1
Pigg's Peak Swaziland 51 J3
Pihij India 36 C5
Pihkva järv l. Estonia/Rus. Fed. see Pskov, Lake
Pihlajavesi l. Fin. 14 P6
Pihlava Fin. 15 L6
Pihtipudas Fin. 14 N5
Piippola Fin. 14 N4
Piispajärvi Fin. 14 P4
Pikalevo Rus. Fed. 12 G4
Pike WV U.S.A. 64 A3
Pikelot i. Micronesia 74 F5
Pikes Peak U.S.A. 62 G4
Pikeville KY U.S.A. 63 K4
Pikinni atoll Marshall Is see Bikini
Piła Poland 17 P4
Pilanesberg National Park S. Africa 51 H3
Pilar Arg. 70 E4
Pilar Para. 70 E3
Pilar de Goiás Brazil 71 A1
Pilaya r. Bol. 68 F8
Pilcomayo r. Bol./Para. 68 F8
Piler India 38 C3
Pili, Cerro mt. Chile 70 C2
Pilibangan India 36 C3
Pilibhit India 36 D3
Pilipinas country Asia see Philippines
Pillau Rus. Fed. see Baltiysk
Pillcopata Peru 68 D6
Pilliga Australia 58 D3
Pil'na Rus. Fed. 12 J5
Pil'nya, Ozero l. Rus. Fed. 12 M1
Pilões, Serra dos mts Brazil 71 B2
Pílos Greece see Pylos
Pilot Peak NV U.S.A. 65 D1
Pilot Station U.S.A. 60 B3
Pilsen Czech Rep. see Plzeň
Piltene Latvia 15 L8
Pil'tun, Zaliv b. Rus. Fed. 44 F1
Pilu Pak. 36 B4
Pimenta Bueno Brazil 68 F6
Pimpalner India 38 B1
Pin r. India 36 D2
Pin r. Myanmar 37 H5
Pinahat India 36 D4
Pinamar Arg. 70 E5
Pinang Malaysia see George Town
Pınarbaşı Turkey 34 E3
Pinar del Río Cuba 67 H4
Pinarhisar Turkey 27 L4
Piñas Ecuador 68 C4
Pińczów Poland 17 R5
Pindaí Brazil 71 C1
Pindamonhangaba Brazil 71 B3
Pindar Australia 55 A7
Pindaré r. Brazil 69 J4
Píndhos Óros mts Greece see Pindus Mountains
Pindos mts Greece see Pindus Mountains
Pindrei India 36 E5
Pindus Mountains Greece 27 I5
Pine watercourse Australia 57 C7
Pine Bluff U.S.A. 63 I5
Pine Creek Australia 54 E3
Pine Creek r. PA U.S.A. 64 C2
Pinecrest CA U.S.A. 65 B1
Pinedale WY U.S.A. 62 F3
Pine Flat Lake CA U.S.A. 65 C2
Pinega Rus. Fed. 12 I2
Pinega r. Rus. Fed. 12 I2
Pinegrove Australia 55 A6
Pine Grove PA U.S.A. 64 C2
Pineios r. Greece 27 J5
Pine Island Bay Antarctica 75 N10
Pine Island Glacier Antarctica 76 K1
Pine Mountain CA U.S.A. 65 B3
Pine Peak AZ U.S.A. 65 F3
Pine Point (abandoned) Canada 60 G3
Pineridge CA U.S.A. 65 C2
Pine Ridge U.S.A. 62 G3
Pinerolo Italy 26 B2
Pines, Akrotirio pt Greece 27 K4
Pines, Isle of i. Cuba see La Juventud, Isla de
Pines, Isle of i. New Caledonia see Pins, Île des
Pinetown S. Africa 51 J5
Pine Valley NY U.S.A. 64 C1
Ping'an China 42 I5
Ping'anyi China see Ping'an
Pingdingbu China see Guyuan
Pingdingshan China 43 K6
Pingdong Taiwan see P'ingtung
Pingdu Shandong China 43 L5
Pinggang China 44 B4
Pingliang China 42 J5
Pingtan Dao i. China see Haitan Dao
P'ingtung Taiwan 43 M8
Pingxiang Guangxi China 42 J8
Pingxiang Jiangxi China 43 K7
Pingyang Heilong. China 44 B2
Pinhal Brazil 71 B3
Pinheiro Brazil 69 I4
Pinhoe U.K. 19 D8
Piniós r. Greece see Pineios
Pinjin Australia 55 C7
Pinlebu Myanmar 37 H4
Pinnacle h. Virginia/West Virginia U.S.A. 64 B3
Pinnacles National Monument nat. park CA U.S.A. 65 B2
Pinon Hills CA U.S.A. 65 D3
Pinos, Isla de i. Cuba see La Juventud, Isla de
Pinos, Mount CA U.S.A. 65 C3
Pinotepa Nacional Mex. 66 E5
Pins, Île des i. New Caledonia 53 G4
Pins, Pointe aux pt Ont. Canada 64 A1
Pinsk Belarus 15 O10
Pintados Chile 70 C2
Pintura UT U.S.A. 65 F2
Pioche NV U.S.A. 65 E2
Piodi Dem. Rep. Congo 49 C4
Pioner, Ostrov i. Rus. Fed. 28 K2
Pionerskiy Kaliningradskaya Oblast' Rus. Fed. 15 L9
Pionerskiy Khanty-Mansiyskiy Avtonomnyy Okrug-Yugra Rus. Fed. 11 S3
Pionki Poland 17 R5
Piopio N.Z. 59 E4
Piopiotahi inlet N.Z. see Milford Sound
Piorini, Lago l. Brazil 68 F4
Piotrków Trybunalski Poland 17 Q5
Pipa Dingzi mt. China 44 C4
Pipar India 36 C4
Pipar Road India 36 C4
Piperi i. Greece 27 K5
Piper Peak NV U.S.A. 65 D2
Pipli India 36 C3
Pipmuacan, Réservoir resr Canada 63 M2
Piquiri r. Brazil 71 A4
Pira Benin 46 D4
Piracanjuba Brazil 71 A2
Piracicaba Brazil 71 B3
Piracicaba r. Brazil 71 C2
Piraçununga Brazil 71 B3
Piracuruca Brazil 69 J4
Piraeus Greece 27 J6
Piraí do Sul Brazil 71 A4
Piráievs Greece see Piraeus
Piraju Brazil 71 A3
Pirajuí Brazil 71 A3
Pirallahı Adası Azer. 35 H2
Piranhas Bahia Brazil 71 C1
Piranhas Goiás Brazil 69 H7
Piranhas r. Brazil 71 A2
Piranhas r. Rio Grande do Norte Brazil 69 K
Pirapora Brazil 71 B2
Pirawa India 36 D4
Pirenópolis Brazil 71 A1
Pires do Rio Brazil 71 A2
Pírgos Greece see Pyrgos
Pirin nat. park Bulg. 27 J4
Pirineos mts Europe see Pyrenees
Piripiri Brazil 69 J4
Pirlerkondu Turkey see Taşkent
Pirojpur Bangl. 37 G5
Pir Panjal Pass India 36 C2
Pir Panjal Range mts India/Pak. 36 C2
Piryatin Ukr. see Pyryatyn
Pisa Italy 26 D3

isae Italy see Pisa
isagua Chile 68 D7
saurum Italy see Pesaro
sco Peru 68 C6
sek Czech Rep. 17 O6
sha China see Ningnan
shan China 36 D1
shīn Iran 33 J4
shin Pak. 36 A3
shpek Kyrg. see Bishkek
sidia reg. Turkey 34 C3
ssis, Cerro mt. Arg. 70 C3
sté Mex. 66 G4
sticci Italy 26 G4
stoia Italy 26 D3
storiae Italy see Pistoia
suerga r. Spain 25 D3
ta Guinea 46 B3
tanga Brazil 71 A4
tangui Brazil 71 B2
tar India 36 B5
tarpunga Lake imp. l. Australia 58 A5
tcairn, Henderson, Ducie and Oeno Islands terr. S. Pacific Ocean see Pitcairn Islands
tcairn Island Pitcairn Is 75 L7
tcairn Islands terr. S. Pacific Ocean 75 L7
teå Sweden 14 L4
teälven r. Sweden 14 L4
telino Rus. Fed. 13 I5
terka Rus. Fed. 13 J6
teşti Romania 27 K2
thoragarh India 36 E3
tihra India 36 D5
tkyaranta Rus. Fed. 12 F3
tlochry U.K. 20 F4
tsane Siding Botswana 51 G3
tti i. India 38 B4
tt Island N.Z. 53 I6
tt Islands Solomon Is see Vanikoro Islands
ttsburgh PA U.S.A. 64 B2
ttsfield MA U.S.A. 64 E1
ttsworth Australia 58 E1
umhí Brazil 71 B3
ura Peru 68 B5
ute Mountains CA U.S.A. 65 E3
ute Peak CA U.S.A. 65 C3
uthan Nepal 37 E3
vka Slovenia 26 F2
xariá mt. Greece see Pyxaria
xley CA U.S.A. 65 C3
z Bernina mt. Italy/Switz. 26 C1
z Buin mt. Austria/Switz. 17 M7
zhanka Rus. Fed. 12 K4
zhi Nigeria 46 D4
zhma Rus. Fed. 12 J4
zhma r. Rus. Fed. 12 K4
zhma r. Rus. Fed. 12 L2
acentia Italy see Piacenza
acerville CA U.S.A. 65 B1
ácido de Castro Brazil 68 E6
ainfield CT U.S.A. 64 F2
ainview U.S.A. 62 G5
aka, Akrotirio pt Greece 27 L7
akoti, Cape Cyprus 39 B2
anada CA U.S.A. 65 B2
analtina Brazil 71 B1
anura Brazil 71 A3
aquemine U.S.A. 63 I5
asencia Spain 25 C3
aster City CA U.S.A. 65 E4
astun Rus. Fed. 44 E3
atani r. Sicilia Italy 26 E6
atberg mt. S. Africa 51 I5
atinum U.S.A. 77 B3
ato Col. 68 D2
atte r. U.S.A. 62 H3
attsburgh U.S.A. 63 M3
auen Germany 17 N5
avsk Rus. Fed. 13 H5
ayas Ecuador 68 B4
easant Bay MA U.S.A. 64 G2
easanton U.S.A. 66 E3
easant Point N.Z. 59 C7
easantville NJ U.S.A. 64 D3
eaux France 24 F4
edger Lake Canada 63 K1
enty watercourse Australia 56 B5
enty, Bay of g. N.Z. 59 F3
entywood U.S.A. 62 G2
esetsk Rus. Fed. 12 I3
eshchentsy Belarus see Plyeshchanitsy
étipi, Lac l. Canada 63 M1
ettenberg Bay S. Africa 50 F8
even Bulg. 27 K3
evna Bulg. see Pleven
evlja Montenegro 27 H3
ock Poland 17 Q4
očno mt. Bos.-Herz. 26 G3
odovoye Rus. Fed. 12 F3
oemeur France 24 C3
oeşti Romania see Ploieşti
oieşti Romania 27 L2
omb du Cantal mt. France 24 F4
oskoye Rus. Fed. see Stanovoye
oty Poland 17 O4
oudalmézeau France 24 B2
ouzané France 24 B2
ovdiv Bulg. 27 K3
ozk Poland see Płock
umridge Lakes imp. l. Australia 55 D7
ungė Lith. 15 L9
yeshchanitsy Belarus 15 O9
ymouth Montserrat 67 L5
ymouth U.K. 19 C8
ymouth CA U.S.A. 65 B1
ymouth IN U.S.A. 63 J3
ymouth MA U.S.A. 64 F2
ymouth Bay MA U.S.A. 64 F2
ynlimon h. U.K. 19 D6
yussa Rus. Fed. 15 P7
zeň Czech Rep. 17 N6
Burkina 46 C3
r. Italy 26 E2
, Parc National de nat. park Burkina 46 C3
beda Peak China/Kyrg. 31 H2
bedy, Pik mt. China/Kyrg. see Pobeda Peak
catello U.S.A. 62 E3
chala Sudan 47 G4
chayiv Ukr. 13 E6
chep Rus. Fed. 13 G5
chinki Rus. Fed. 13 J5
chinok Rus. Fed. 13 G5
chutla Mex. 66 E5
cking Germany 17 N6
cklington U.K. 18 G5
ções Brazil 71 C1
comoke City MD U.S.A. 64 D3
comoke Sound b. Maryland/Virginia U.S.A. 64 D4
coné Brazil 69 G7
cono Mountains hills PA U.S.A. 64 D2
ços de Caldas Brazil 71 B3
danur India 38 C4
ddor'ye Rus. Fed. 12 F4
dgorenskiy Rus. Fed. 13 H6
dgorica Montenegro 27 H3
Podgornoye Rus. Fed. 28 J4
Podile India 38 C3
Podişul Transilvaniei plat. Romania see Transylvanian Basin
Podkamennaya Tunguska r. Rus. Fed. 29 K3
Podocarpus, Parque Nacional nat. park Ecuador 68 C4
Podol'sk Rus. Fed. 13 H5
Podporozh'ye Rus. Fed. 12 G3
Podujevë Kosovo 27 I3
Podujevo Kosovo see Podujevë
Podz' Rus. Fed. 12 K3
Poelela, Lagoa l. Moz. 51 L3
Poeppel Corner imp. l. Australia 57 B5
Poetovio Slovenia see Ptuj
Pofadder S. Africa 50 D5
Pogar Rus. Fed. 13 G5
Poggibonsi Italy 26 D3
Poggio di Montieri mt. Italy 26 D3
Pogradec Albania 27 I4
Pogranichnyy Rus. Fed. 44 C3
Po Hai g. China see Bo Hai
P'ohang S. Korea 45 C5
Pohnpei atoll Micronesia 74 G5
Pohri India 36 D4
Poi India 37 H4
Poiana Mare Romania 27 J3
Poinsett, Cape Antarctica 76 F2
Point Arena CA U.S.A. 65 A1
Pointe-à-Pitre Guadeloupe 67 L5
Pointe-Noire Congo 49 B4
Point Hope U.S.A. 60 B3
Point Lake Canada 60 G3
Point Pleasant NJ U.S.A. 64 D2
Poitiers France 24 E3
Poitou reg. France 24 E3
Pojuca r. Brazil 71 D1
Pokaran India 36 B4
Pokataroo Australia 58 D2
Pokcha Rus. Fed. 11 R3
Pokhara Nepal 37 E3
Pokhran Landi Pak. 36 A4
Pokhvistnevo Rus. Fed. 11 Q5
Poko Dem. Rep. Congo 48 C3
Pokosnoye Rus. Fed. 42 I1
P'ok'r Kovkas mts Asia see Lesser Caucasus
Pokrovka Primorskiy Kray Rus. Fed. 44 C4
Pokrovka Zabaykal'skiy Kray Rus. Fed. 44 A1
Pokrovsk Respublika Sakha (Yakutiya) Rus. Fed. 29 N3
Pokrovsk Saratovskaya Oblast' Rus. Fed. see Engel's
Pokrovskoye Rus. Fed. 13 H7
Pokshen'ga r. Rus. Fed. 12 J3
Pol India 36 C5
Pola Croatia see Pula
Pola de Lena Spain 25 D2
Pola de Siero Spain 25 D2
Poland country Europe 10 J5
Poland NY U.S.A. 64 D1
Polar Plateau Antarctica 76 A1
Polatlı Turkey 34 D3
Polatsk Belarus 15 P9
Polavaram India 38 D2
Polcirkeln Sweden 14 L3
Pol-e Fāsā Iran 35 I5
Pol-e Khomrī Afgh. 36 B2
Polessk Rus. Fed. 15 L9
Poles'ye marsh Belarus/Ukr. see Pripet Marshes
Polgahawela Sri Lanka 38 D5
Poli Cyprus see Polis
Políaigos i. Greece see Polyaigos
Police Poland 17 O4
Policoro Italy 26 G4
Poligny France 24 G3
Polikastron Greece see Polykastro
Polillo Islands Phil. 41 E6
Polis Cyprus 39 A2
Polis'ke Ukr. 13 F6
Polis'kyy Zapovidnyk nat. park Ukr. 13 F6
Politovo Rus. Fed. 12 K2
Políyiros Greece see Polygyros
Polkowice Poland 17 P5
Pollachi India 38 C4
Pollard Islands U.S.A. see Gardner Pinnacles
Pollino, Monte mt. Italy 26 G5
Pollino, Parco Nazionale del nat. park Italy 26 G5
Pollock Pines CA U.S.A. 65 B1
Pollock Reef Australia 55 C8
Polmak Norway 14 O1
Polnovat Rus. Fed. 11 T3
Polo Fin. 14 P4
Pologi Ukr. see Polohy
Polohy Ukr. 13 H7
Polokwane S. Africa 51 I2
Polonne Ukr. 13 E6
Polonnoye Ukr. see Polonne
Polotsk Belarus see Polatsk
Polperro U.K. 19 C8
Polska country Europe see Poland
Polson U.S.A. 62 E2
Polta r. Rus. Fed. 12 I2
Poltava Ukr. 13 G6
Poltoratsk Turkm. see Aşgabat
Põltsamaa Estonia 15 N7
Polunochnoye Rus. Fed. 11 S3
Põlva Estonia 15 O7
Polvijärvi Fin. 14 P5
Polyaigos i. Greece 27 K6
Polyanovgrad Bulg. see Karnobat
Polyarnyy Chukotskiy Avtonomnyy Okrug Rus. Fed. 29 S3
Polyarnyy Murmanskaya Oblast' Rus. Fed. 12 G1
Polyarnyye Zori Rus. Fed. 12 G2
Polyarnyy Ural mts Rus. Fed. 11 S2
Polygyros Greece 27 J4
Polykastro Greece 27 J4
Polynesia is Pacific Ocean 74 I6
Polynésie Française terr. S. Pacific Ocean see French Polynesia
Pomarkku Fin. 15 M6
Pombal Pará Brazil 69 H4
Pombal Paraíba Brazil 69 K5
Pombal Port. 25 B4
Pomene Moz. 51 L2
Pomeranian Bay Poland 17 O3
Pomeroy S. Africa 51 J5
Pomeroy U.K. 21 F3
Pomezia Italy 26 E4
Pomfret S. Africa 50 F3
Pomona Namibia 50 B4
Pomona CA U.S.A. 65 D3
Pomorie Bulg. 27 L3
Pomorskie, Pojezierze reg. Poland 17 O4
Pomorskiy Bereg coastal area Rus. Fed. 12 G2
Pomorskiy Proliv sea chan. Rus. Fed. 12 K1
Pomos Point Cyprus 39 A2
Pomo Tso l. China see Puma Yumco
Pomou, Akra pt Cyprus see Pomos Point
Pomozdino Rus. Fed. 12 L3
Pompain China 37 H3
Pompei Italy 26 F4
Pompéia Brazil 71 A3
Pompeyevka Rus. Fed. 44 C2
Ponape atoll Micronesia see Pohnpei
Ponazyrevo Rus. Fed. 12 J4
Ponca City U.S.A. 63 H4
Ponce Puerto Rico 67 K5
Pondicherry India see Puducherry
Pond Inlet Canada 77 K2
Ponds Bay Canada see Pond Inlet
Ponente, Riviera di coastal area Italy 26 B3
Ponferrada Spain 25 C2
Pongara, Pointe pt Gabon 48 A3
Pongaroa N.Z. 59 F5
Pongo watercourse Sudan 47 F4
Pongola r. S. Africa 51 K4
Pongolapoort Dam dam S. Africa 51 J4
Ponnagyun Myanmar 37 H5
Ponnaivar r. India 38 C4
Ponnampet India 38 B3
Ponnani India 38 B4
Ponnyadaung Range mts Myanmar 37 H5
Ponoka Canada 62 E1
Ponoy r. Rus. Fed. 12 I2
Ponta Delgada Arquipélago dos Açores 72 G3
Ponta Grossa Brazil 71 A4
Pontal Brazil 71 A3
Pontalina Brazil 71 A2
Pont-à-Mousson France 24 H2
Ponta Porã Brazil 70 E2
Pontarfynach U.K. see Devil's Bridge
Pont-Audemer France 19 H9
Ponte Alta do Norte Brazil 69 I6
Ponte de Sor Port. 25 B4
Ponte Firme Brazil 71 B2
Pontefract U.K. 18 F5
Ponteix Canada 62 F2
Ponteland U.K. 18 F3
Ponte Nova Brazil 71 C3
Pontes-e-Lacerda Brazil 69 G7
Pontevedra Spain 25 B2
Ponthierville Dem. Rep. Congo see Ubundu
Pontiac IL U.S.A. 63 J3
Pontiac MI U.S.A. 63 K3
Pontiae is Italy see Ponziane, Isole
Pontianak Indon. 41 C8
Pontine Islands is Italy see Ponziane, Isole
Pont-l'Abbé France 24 B3
Pontoise France 24 F2
Ponton watercourse Australia 55 C7
Ponton Canada 62 H1
Pontypool U.K. 19 D7
Pontypridd U.K. 19 D7
Ponza, Isola di i. Italy 26 E4
Ponziane, Isole is Italy 26 E4
Poochera Australia 55 F8
Poole U.K. 19 F8
Poolowanna Lake imp. l. Australia 57 B5
Poona India see Pune
Pooncarie Australia 57 C7
Poonch India see Punch
Poopelloe Lake salt l. Australia 58 B3
Poopó, Lago de l. Bol. 68 E7
Poor Knights Islands N.Z. 59 E2
Popayán Col. 68 C3
Popigay r. Rus. Fed. 29 L2
Popiltah Australia 57 C7
Popilta Lake imp. l. Australia 57 C7
Poplar r. Canada 63 H1
Poplar Bluff U.S.A. 63 I4
Poplar Camp VA U.S.A. 64 A4
Popocatépetl, Volcán vol. Mex. 66 E5
Popokabaka Dem. Rep. Congo 49 B4
Popovichskaya Rus. Fed. see Kalininskaya
Popovo Bulg. 27 L3
Popovo Polje plain Bos.-Herz. 26 G3
Poprad Slovakia 17 R6
Poquoson VA U.S.A. 64 C4
Porangahau N.Z. 59 F5
Porangatu Brazil 71 A1
Porbandar India 36 B5
Porcos r. Brazil 71 B1
Porcupine Abyssal Plain sea feature N. Atlantic Ocean 72 G2
Porcupine Gorge National Park Australia 56 D4
Poreč Croatia 26 E2
Porecatu Brazil 71 A3
Poretskoye Rus. Fed. 13 J5
Pori Fin. 15 L6
Porirua N.Z. 59 E5
Porkhov Rus. Fed. 12 F4
Porlamar Venez. 68 F1
Pormpuraaw Australia 56 C2
Pornic France 24 C3
Poronaysk Rus. Fed. 44 F2
Porong China 37 G3
Poros Greece 27 J6
Porosozero Rus. Fed. 12 G3
Porpoise Bay Antarctica 76 G2
Porsangerfjorden sea chan. Norway 14 N1
Porsangerhalvøya pen. Norway 14 N1
Porsgrunn Norway 15 F7
Porsuk r. Turkey 27 N5
Portadown U.K. 21 F3
Portaferry U.K. 21 G3
Portage PA U.S.A. 64 B2
Portage WI U.S.A. 63 J3
Portage la Prairie Canada 62 H2
Port Alberni Canada 62 C2
Port Albert Australia 58 C7
Portalegre Port. 25 C4
Portales U.S.A. 62 G5
Port Alfred S. Africa 51 H7
Port Allegany PA U.S.A. 64 B2
Port Alma Australia 56 E4
Port Angeles U.S.A. 62 C2
Port Antonio Jamaica 67 I5
Portarlington Ireland 21 E4
Port Arthur Australia 57 [inset]
Port Arthur U.S.A. 63 I6
Port Askaig U.K. 20 C5
Port Augusta Australia 57 B7
Port-au-Prince Haiti 67 J5
Portavogie U.K. 21 G3
Port Beaufort S. Africa 50 E8
Port Blair India 31 I5
Portbou Spain 25 H2
Port Burwell Ont. Canada 64 A1
Port Campbell Australia 58 A7
Port Campbell National Park Australia 58 A7
Port Chalmers N.Z. 59 C7
Port Charlotte U.S.A. 63 K6
Port-de-Paix Haiti 67 J5
Port Douglas Australia 56 D3
Port Edward S. Africa 51 J6
Porteira Brazil 69 G4
Porteirinha Brazil 71 C1
Portel Brazil 69 H4
Port Elizabeth S. Africa 51 G7
Port Ellen U.K. 20 C5
Port Erin Isle of Man 18 C4
Porterville S. Africa 50 D7
Porterville CA U.S.A. 65 C2
Port Étienne Mauritania see Nouâdhibou
Port Everglades U.S.A. see Fort Lauderdale
Port Fitzroy N.Z. 59 E3
Port Francqui Dem. Rep. Congo see Ilebo
Port-Gentil Gabon 48 A4
Port Glasgow U.K. 20 E5
Port Harcourt Nigeria 46 D4
Porthcawl U.K. 19 D7
Port Hedland Australia 54 B5
Port Herald Malawi see Nsanje
Porthleven U.K. 19 B8
Porthmadog U.K. 19 C6
Port Hope Simpson Canada 61 M4
Port Hueneme CA U.S.A. 65 C3
Port Huron U.S.A. 63 K3
Portimão Port. 25 B5
Port Jackson Australia see Sydney
Port Jackson inlet Australia 58 E4
Port Keats Australia see Wadeye
Port Láirge Ireland see Waterford
Portland N.S.W. Australia 58 D4
Portland Vic. Australia 57 C8
Portland ME U.S.A. 63 M3
Portland OR U.S.A. 62 C2
Portland, Isle of pen. U.K. 19 E8
Portland Bill hd U.K. see Bill of Portland
Portland Roads Australia 56 C2
Port-la-Nouvelle France 24 F5
Portlaoise Ireland 21 E4
Port Lavaca U.S.A. 63 H6
Portlaw Ireland 21 E5
Portlethen U.K. 20 G3
Port Lincoln Australia 57 A7
Port Loko Sierra Leone 46 B4
Port Louis Mauritius 73 L7
Port-Lyautrey Morocco see Kénitra
Port Macquarie Australia 58 F3
Portmadoc U.K. see Porthmadog
Port McNeill Canada 62 B1
Port-Menier Canada 63 O2
Port Moresby P.N.G. 52 E2
Portnaguran U.K. 20 C2
Portnahaven U.K. 20 C5
Port nan Giúran U.K. see Portnaguran
Port Neill Australia 57 B7
Port Nis U.K. see Port of Ness
Port Noarlunga Australia 57 B7
Port Nolloth S. Africa 50 C5
Port Norris NJ U.S.A. 64 D3
Porto Port. see Oporto
Porto Acre Brazil 68 E5
Porto Alegre Brazil 71 A5
Porto Alexandre Angola see Tombua
Porto Amboim Angola 49 B5
Porto Amélia Moz. see Pemba
Porto Artur Brazil 69 G6
Porto Belo Brazil 71 A4
Porto de Moz Brazil 69 H4
Porto de Santa Cruz Brazil 71 C1
Porto dos Gaúchos Óbidos Brazil 69 G6
Porto Esperança Brazil 69 G7
Porto Esperidião Brazil 69 G7
Portoferraio Italy 26 D3
Port of Ness U.K. 20 C2
Porto Franco Brazil 69 I5
Port of Spain Trin. and Tob. 67 L6
Porto Grande Brazil 69 H3
Portogruaro Italy 26 E2
Porto Jofre Brazil 69 G7
Portomaggiore Italy 26 D2
Porto Mendes Brazil 70 F2
Porto Murtinho Brazil 70 E2
Porto Nacional Brazil 69 I6
Porto-Novo Benin 46 D4
Porto Novo Cape Verde 46 [inset]
Porto Primavera, Represa resr Brazil 70 F2
Porto Rico Angola 49 B4
Porto Santo, Ilha de i. Madeira 46 B1
Porto Seguro Brazil 71 D2
Porto Tolle Italy 26 E2
Porto Torres Sardegna Italy 26 C4
Porto União Brazil 71 A4
Porto-Vecchio Corse France 24 I6
Porto Velho Brazil 68 F5
Portoviejo Ecuador 68 B4
Porto Wálter Brazil 68 D5
Portpatrick U.K. 20 D6
Port Phillip Bay Australia 58 B7
Port Pirie Australia 57 B7
Portreath U.K. 19 B8
Portree U.K. 20 C3
Port Royal VA U.S.A. 64 C3
Portrush U.K. 21 F2
Port Safaga Egypt see Būr Safājah
Port Said Egypt 39 A4
Port St Joe U.S.A. 63 J6
Port St Mary Isle of Man 18 C4
Portsalon Ireland 21 E2
Port Shepstone S. Africa 51 J6
Portsmouth U.K. 19 F8
Portsmouth NH U.S.A. 64 F1
Portsmouth OH U.S.A. 63 K4
Portsmouth VA U.S.A. 64 C4
Portsoy U.K. 20 G3
Port Stanley Falkland Is see Stanley
Port Stephens b. Australia 58 F4
Portstewart U.K. 21 F2
Port Sudan Sudan 32 E6
Port Talbot U.K. 19 D7
Porttipahdan tekojärvi resr Fin. 14 O2
Portugal country Europe 25 C4
Portugália Angola see Chitato
Portuguese East Africa country Africa see Mozambique
Portuguese Guinea country Africa see Guinea-Bissau
Portuguese Timor country Asia see East Timor
Portuguese West Africa country Africa see Angola
Portumna Ireland 21 D4
Portus Herculis Monoeci country Europe see Monaco
Port-Vendres France 24 F5
Port Vila Vanuatu 53 G3
Portville NY U.S.A. 64 B1
Port Vladimir Rus. Fed. 14 R2
Port Waikato N.Z. 59 E3
Port William U.K. 20 E6
Porvenir Bol. 68 E6
Porvenir Chile 70 B8
Porvoo Fin. 15 N6
Posada Spain 25 D2
Posada de Llanera Spain see Posada
Posadas Arg. 70 E3
Posen Poland see Poznań
Poshekhon'ye Rus. Fed. 12 H4
Poshekon'ye-Volodarsk Rus. Fed. see Poshekhon'ye
Posht-e Badam Iran 35 I4
Posht-e Kūh mts Iran 35 G4
Posht Kūh h. Iran 35 H3
Posio Fin. 14 P3
Poso Indon. 41 E8
Posof Turkey 35 F2
Posŏng S. Korea 45 B6
Possession Island Namibia 50 B4
Post U.S.A. 62 G5
Postavy Belarus see Pastavy
Poste-de-la-Baleine Canada see Kuujjuarapik
Poste Weygand Alg. 46 D2
Postmasburg S. Africa 50 F5
Poston AZ U.S.A. 65 E3
Postysheve Ukr. see Krasnoarmiys'k
Pota Indon. 54 C2
Poté Brazil 71 C2
Potegaon India 38 D2
Potentia Italy see Potenza
Potenza Italy 26 F4
P'ot'i Georgia 35 F2
Potikal India 38 D2
Potiraguá Brazil 71 D1
Potiskum Nigeria 46 E3
Potomac r. Maryland/Virginia U.S.A. 64 C3
Potosí Bol. 68 E7
Potosi Mountain NV U.S.A. 65 E3
Potrerillos Chile 70 C3
Potsdam Germany 17 N4
Potterne U.K. 19 E7
Potters Bar U.K. 19 G7
Pottstown PA U.S.A. 64 D2
Pottsville PA U.S.A. 64 C2
Pottuvil Sri Lanka 38 D5
Poughkeepsie NY U.S.A. 64 E2
Poulton-le-Fylde U.K. 18 E5
Pouso Alegre Brazil 71 B3
Poŭthĭsăt Cambodia 31 J5
Považská Bystrica Slovakia 17 Q6
Povenets Rus. Fed. 12 G3
Poverty Bay N.Z. 59 F4
Povlen mt. Serbia 27 H2
Póvoa de Varzim Port. 25 B3
Povorino Rus. Fed. 13 I6
Povorotnyy, Mys hd Rus. Fed. 44 D4
Poway CA U.S.A. 65 D4
Powell, Lake resr U.S.A. 62 E4
Powell Mountain NV U.S.A. 65 C1
Powell River Canada 62 C2
Powhatan VA U.S.A. 64 C4
Poxoréu Brazil 69 H7
Poyang Hu l. China 43 L7
Poyarkovo Rus. Fed. 44 C2
Pozantı Turkey 34 D3
Požarevac Serbia 27 I2
Poza Rica Mex. 66 E4
Pozdeyevka Rus. Fed. 44 C2
Požega Croatia 26 G2
Požega Serbia 27 I3
Pozharskoye Rus. Fed. 44 D3
Poznań Poland 17 P4
Pozoblanco Spain 25 D4
Pozo Colorado Para. 70 E2
Pozsony Slovakia see Bratislava
Pozzuoli Italy 26 F4
Prachatice Czech Rep. 17 O6
Prachi r. India 37 F6
Prachuap Khiri Khan Thai. 31 I5
Prades France 24 F5
Prado Brazil 71 D2
Prague Czech Rep. 17 O5
Praha Czech Rep. see Prague
Praia Cape Verde 46 [inset]
Praia do Bilene Moz. 51 K3
Prainha Brazil 69 H4
Prairie Australia 56 D4
Prairie du Chien U.S.A. 63 I3
Prasonisi, Akrotirio pt Greece 27 L7
Prata Brazil 71 A2
Prata r. Brazil 71 A2
Prat de Llobregat Spain see El Prat de Llobregat
Prathes Thai country Asia see Thailand
Prato Italy 26 D3
Pratt U.S.A. 62 H4
Pravdinsk Rus. Fed. 15 L9
Praya Indon. 54 B2
Preble NY U.S.A. 64 C1
Prechistoye Smolenskaya Oblast' Rus. Fed. 13 G5
Prechistoye Yaroslavskaya Oblast' Rus. Fed. 12 I4
Precipice National Park Australia 56 E5
Preeceville Canada 62 G1
Pregolya r. Rus. Fed. 15 L9
Preiļi Latvia 15 O8
Premer Australia 58 D3
Prémery France 24 F3
Prenzlau Germany 17 N4
Přerov Czech Rep. 17 P6
Prescelly Mts hills U.K. see Preseli, Mynydd
Prescott AZ U.S.A. 62 E5
Preseli, Mynydd hills U.K. 19 C7
Preševo Serbia 27 I3
Presidencia Roque Sáenz Peña Arg. 70 D3
Presidente Dutra Brazil 69 J5
Presidente Hermes Brazil 68 F6
Presidente Olegário Brazil 71 B2
Presidente Prudente Brazil 71 A3
Presidente Venceslau Brazil 71 A3
Presidio U.S.A. 62 G6
Preslav Bulg. see Veliki Preslav
Prešov Slovakia 13 D6
Prespa, Lake Europe 27 I4
Prespansko Ezero l. Europe see Prespa, Lake
Prespes nat. park Greece 27 I4
Prespës, Liqeni i l. Europe see Prespa, Lake
Presque Isle ME U.S.A. 63 N2
Pressburg Slovakia see Bratislava
Presteigne U.K. 19 D6
Preston U.K. 18 E5
Preston ID U.S.A. 62 E3
Preston, Cape Australia 54 B5
Prestonpans U.K. 20 G5
Prestwick U.K. 20 E5
Preto r. Bahia Brazil 69 J6
Preto r. Minas Gerais Brazil 71 B2
Preto r. Brazil 71 D1
Pretoria S. Africa 51 I3
Pretoria-Witwatersrand-Vereeniging prov. S. Africa see Gauteng
Preussisch-Eylau Rus. Fed. see Bagrationovsk
Preußisch Stargard Poland see Starogard Gdański
Preveza Greece 27 I5
Priargunsk Rus. Fed. 43 L2
Pribilof Islands U.S.A. 60 A4
Priboj Serbia 27 H3
Price r. Australia 54 E3
Price UT U.S.A. 62 E4
Pridorozhnoye Rus. Fed. see Khulkhuta
Priekule Latvia 15 L8
Priekuļi Latvia 15 N8
Priel'brus'ye, Natsional'nyy Park nat. park Rus. Fed. 13 I8
Prienai Lith. 15 M9
Prieska S. Africa 50 F5
Prievidza Slovakia 17 Q6
Prijedor Bos.-Herz. 26 G2
Prijepolje Serbia 27 H3
Prikaspiyskaya Nizmennost' lowland Kazakh./Rus. Fed. see Caspian Lowland
Prilep Macedonia 27 I4
Priluki Ukr. see Pryluky
Primorsk Rus. Fed. 15 P6
Primorsk Ukr. see Prymors'k
Primorskiy Kray admin. div. Rus. Fed. 44 D3
Primorsko-Akhtarsk Rus. Fed. 13 H7
Prince Albert Canada 60 H4
Prince Albert S. Africa 50 F7
Prince Albert Mountains Antarctica 76 H1
Prince Albert Peninsula Canada 60 G2
Prince Albert Road S. Africa 50 E7
Prince Alfred, Cape Canada 60 F2
Prince Alfred Hamlet S. Africa 50 D7
Prince Charles Island Canada 61 K3
Prince Charles Mountains Antarctica 76 E2
Prince Edward Island prov. Canada 63 O2
Prince Edward Islands Indian Ocean 73 K9
Prince Frederick MD U.S.A. 64 C3
Prince George Canada 60 F4
Prince Harald Coast Antarctica 76 D2
Prince of Wales, Cape U.S.A. 60 B3
Prince of Wales Island Australia 56 C1
Prince of Wales Island Canada 61 I2
Prince of Wales Island U.S.A. 60 E4
Prince of Wales Strait Canada 60 G2
Prince Patrick Island Canada 60 G2
Prince Regent Inlet sea chan. Canada 61 I2
Prince Rupert Canada 60 E4
Princess Anne MD U.S.A. 64 D3
Princess Astrid Coast Antarctica 76 C2
Princess Charlotte Bay Australia 56 C2
Princess Elizabeth Land reg. Antarctica 76 E2
Princess Ragnhild Coast Antarctica 76 C2
Princess Royal Island Canada 60 F4
Princeton Canada 62 C2
Princeton NJ U.S.A. 64 D2
Princeton WV U.S.A. 64 A4
Prince William Sound b. U.S.A. 60 D3
Príncipe i. São Tomé and Príncipe 46 D4
Prins Harald Kyst coastal area Antarctica see Prince Harald Coast
Prinzapolca Nicaragua 67 H6
Priozersk Rus. Fed. 12 F3
Priozyorsk Rus. Fed. see Priozersk
Pripet r. Belarus 23 J1
Pripet r. Belarus/Ukr. 13 F6
Pripet Marshes Belarus/Ukr. 13 E6
Pirechnyy Rus. Fed. 14 Q2
Prishtinë Kosovo 27 I3
Priština Kosovo see Prishtinë
Pritzwalk Germany 17 N4
Privas France 24 G4
Privlaka Croatia 26 F2
Privolzhsk Rus. Fed. 12 I4
Privolzhskaya Vozvyshennost' hills Rus. Fed. 13 J6
Privolzhskiy Rus. Fed. 13 J6
Privolzh'ye Rus. Fed. 13 K5
Priyutnoye Rus. Fed. 13 I7
Prizren Kosovo 27 I3
Probus U.K. 19 C8
Proddatur India 38 C3
Professor van Blommestein Meer resr Suriname 69 G3
Progreso Hond. see El Progreso
Progress Rus. Fed. 44 C2
Prokhladnyy Rus. Fed. 13 J8
Prokop'yevsk Rus. Fed. 42 F2
Prokuplje Serbia 27 I3
Proletarsk Rus. Fed. 13 I7
Proletarskaya Rus. Fed. see Proletarsk
Prome Myanmar see Pyè
Promissão Brazil 71 A3
Promissão, Represa resr Brazil 71 A3
Prophet r. Canada 77 A3
Prophet River Canada 60 F4
Propriá Brazil 69 K6
Proskurov Ukr. see Khmel'nyts'kyy
Protem S. Africa 50 E8
Provadiya Bulg. 27 L3
Prøven Greenland see Kangersuatsiaq
Provence reg. France 24 G5
Providence RI U.S.A. 64 F2
Providence, Cape N.Z. 59 A8
Providencia, Isla de i. Caribbean Sea 67 H6
Provideniya Rus. Fed. 29 T3
Provincetown MA U.S.A. 64 F1
Provo U.S.A. 62 E3
Prudentópolis Brazil 71 A4
Prudhoe Bay U.S.A. 60 D2
Prunelli-di-Fiumorbo Corse France 24 I5
Prusa Turkey see Bursa
Prushkov Poland see Pruszków
Pruszków Poland 17 R4
Prut r. Europe 13 F7
Prydz Bay Antarctica 76 E2
Pryluky Ukr. 13 G6
Prymors'k Ukr. 13 H7
Prymors'ke Ukr. see Sartana
Pryp"yat' r. Belarus/Ukr. 13 F6 see Pripet
Prypyats' r. Belarus see Pripet
Prypyats' r. Belarus/Ukr. 11 L5 see Pripet
Przemyśl Poland 13 D6
Przheval'sk Kyrg. see Karakol
Psara i. Greece 27 K5
Pskov Rus. Fed. 12 F4
Pskov, Lake Estonia/Rus. Fed. 15 O7
Pskov Oblast admin. div. Rus. Fed. see Pskovskaya Oblast'
Pskovskaya Oblast' admin. div. Rus. Fed. 15 P8
Pskovskoye Ozero l. Estonia/Rus. Fed. see Pskov, Lake
Ptolemaïda Greece 27 I4
Ptolemais Israel see 'Akko
Ptuj Slovenia 26 F1
Puan S. Korea 45 B6
Pucallpa Peru 68 D5
Puchezh Rus. Fed. 12 I4
Puch'ŏn S. Korea 45 B5
Puck Poland 17 Q3
Pudasjärvi Fin. 14 O4
Pudimoe S. Africa 50 G4
Pudozh Rus. Fed. 12 H3
Pudsey U.K. 18 F5
Pudu China see Suizhou
Puduchcheri India see Puducherry
Puducherry India 38 C4
Puducherry union terr. India 38 C4
Pudukkottai India 38 C4
Puebla Baja California Mex. 65 E4
Puebla Puebla Mex. 66 E5
Puebla de Sanabria Spain 25 C2
Puebla de Zaragoza Mex. see Puebla
Pueblo U.S.A. 62 G4
Puelches Arg. 70 C5
Puelén Arg. 70 C5
Puente-Genil Spain 25 D5
Puerto Acosta Bol. 68 E7
Puerto Alegre Bol. 68 F6
Puerto Ángel Mex. 66 E5
Puerto Armuelles Panama 67 H7
Puerto Ayacucho Venez. 68 E2
Puerto Bahía Negra Para. see Bahía Negra
Puerto Baquerizo Moreno Galápagos Ecuador 68 [inset]
Puerto Barrios Guat. 66 G5
Puerto Cabello Venez. 68 E1
Puerto Cabezas Nicaragua 67 H6
Puerto Carreño Col. 68 E2
Puerto Casado Para. 70 E2
Puerto Cavinas Bol. 68 E6
Puerto Coig Arg. 70 C8
Puerto Cortés Mex. 66 B4
Puerto Escondido Mex. 66 E5
Puerto Francisco de Orellana Ecuador see Coca
Puerto Frey Bol. 68 F6
Puerto Génova Bol. 68 E6
Puerto Guarani Para. 70 E2
Puerto Heath Bol. 68 E6
Puerto Huitoto Col. 68 D3
Puerto Inírida Col. 68 E3
Puerto Isabel Bol. 69 G7

Rāwah Iraq 35 F4
Rawaki i. Kiribati 53 I2
Rawalpindi Pak. 33 L3
Rawāndiz Iraq 35 G3
Rawicz Poland 17 P5
Rawlinna Australia 55 D7
Rawlins U.S.A. 62 F3
Rawlinson Range hills Australia 55 E6
Rawson Arg. 70 C6
Rawu China 42 H7
Raxón, Cerro mt. Guat. 66 G5
Rayachoti India 38 C3
Rayadurg India 38 C3
Rayagada India 38 D2
Rayagarha India see Rayagada
Rayak Lebanon 39 C3
Raychikhinsk Rus. Fed. 44 C2
Raydah Yemen 32 F6
Rayes Peak CA U.S.A. 65 C3
Rayevskiy Rus. Fed. 11 Q5
Rayleigh U.K. 19 H7
Raymond NH U.S.A. 64 F1
Raymond Terrace Australia 58 E4
Raymondville U.S.A. 62 H6
Rayner Glacier Antarctica 76 D2
Raystown Lake PA U.S.A. 64 B2
Raz, Pointe du pt France 24 B2
Razan Iran 35 H4
Rāzān Iran 35 H4
Razani Pak. 36 B2
Razāzah, Buḩayrat ar l. Iraq 35 F4
Razdan Armenia see Hrazdan
Razdel'naya Ukr. see Rozdil'na
Razdol'noye Rus. Fed. 44 C4
Razeh Iran 35 H4
Razgrad Bulg. 27 L3
Razim, Lacul lag. Romania 27 M2
Razlog Bulg. 27 J4
Razmak Pak. 36 B2
Raz"yezd 3km Rus. Fed. see Novyy Urgal
Ré, Île de i. France 24 D3
Reading U.K. 19 G7
Reading PA U.S.A. 64 D2
Reagile S. Africa 51 H3
Realicó Arg. 70 D5
Réalmont France 24 F5
Reate Italy see Rieti
Rebecca, Lake imp. l. Australia 55 C7
Rebiana Sand Sea des. Libya 47 F2
Reboly Rus. Fed. 14 Q5
Rebrikha Rus. Fed. 42 E2
Rebun-tō i. Japan 44 F3
Recherche, Archipelago of the is Australia 55 C8
Rechitsa Belarus see Rechytsa
Rechna Doab lowland Pak. 36 C3
Rechytsa Belarus 13 F5
Recife Brazil 69 L5
Recife, Cape S. Africa 51 G8
Recklinghausen Germany 17 K5
Reconquista Arg. 70 E3
Recreo Arg. 70 C3
Red r. Australia 56 C3
Red r. U.S.A. 63 I5
Red r. Vietnam 42 J8
Red Bank NJ U.S.A. 64 D2
Red Basin China see Sichuan Pendi
Red Bluff U.S.A. 62 C3
Redcar U.K. 18 F4
Redcliffe, Mount h. Australia 55 C7
Red Cliffs Australia 57 C7
Red Deer Canada 62 E1
Red Deer r. Alberta/Saskatchewan Canada 62 E1
Red Deer Lake Canada 62 G1
Reddersburg S. Africa 51 H5
Redding U.S.A. 62 C3
Redditch U.K. 19 F6
Rede r. U.K. 18 E3
Redenção Brazil 69 H5
Redeyef Tunisia 26 C7
Redfield U.S.A. 62 H3
Red Hook NY U.S.A. 64 E2
Redkino Rus. Fed. 12 H4
Red Lake Canada 63 I1
Red Lakes U.S.A. 63 I2
Redlands CA U.S.A. 65 D3
Red Lion PA U.S.A. 64 C3
Red Oak U.S.A. 63 H3
Redondo Port. 25 C4
Redondo Beach CA U.S.A. 65 C4
Red Rock PA U.S.A. 64 C2
Red Sea Africa/Asia 32 D4
Red Wing U.S.A. 63 I3
Redwood City CA U.S.A. 65 A2
Redwood Falls U.S.A. 63 H3
Ree, Lough l. Ireland 21 E4
Reedley CA U.S.A. 65 C2
Reedville VA U.S.A. 64 C4
Reedy WV U.S.A. 64 A3
Reedy Glacier Antarctica 76 J1
Reefton N.Z. 59 C6
Refahiye Turkey 34 E3
Regen Germany 17 N6
Regência Brazil 71 D2
Regensburg Germany 17 N6
Reggane Alg. 46 D2
Reggio Calabria Italy see Reggio di Calabria
Reggio Emilia-Romagna Italy see Reggio nell'Emilia
Reggio di Calabria Italy 26 F5
Reggio Emilia Italy see Reggio nell'Emilia
Reggio nell'Emilia Italy 26 D2
Reghin Romania 27 K1
Regina Canada 62 G1
Régina Fr. Guiana 69 H3
Registro Brazil 70 G2
Registro do Araguaia Brazil 71 A1
Regium Lepidum Italy see Reggio nell'Emilia
Regozero Rus. Fed. 14 Q4
Rehli India 36 D5
Rehoboth Namibia 50 C2
Rehoboth Bay DE U.S.A. 64 D3
Rehovot Israel 39 B4
Reibell Alg. see Ksar Chellala
Reichshoffen France 24 H2
Reid Australia 55 E7
Reidh, Rubha pt U.K. 20 D3
Reigate U.K. 19 G7
Reims France 24 G2
Reinbek Germany 17 M4
Reindeer r. Canada 60 H4
Reindeer Island Canada 62 H1
Reindeer Lake Canada 61 H4
Reine Norway 14 H3
Reinosa Spain 25 D2
Reiphólsfjöll h. Iceland 14 [inset]
Reisaelva r. Norway 14 L2
Reisa Nasjonalpark nat. park Norway 14 M2
Reisjärvi Fin. 14 N5
Reitz S. Africa 51 I4
Rekapalle India 38 D2
Relizane Alg. 25 G6
Remarkable, Mount h. Australia 57 B7
Remeshk Iran 33 I4
Remhoogte Pass Namibia 50 C2
Remi France see Reims
Rena Norway 15 G6
Renapur India 38 C2
Rendsburg Germany 17 L3
Renfrew U.K. 20 E5
Rengali Reservoir India 37 F5
Rengo Chile 70 B4
Reni Ukr. 27 M2
Renick WV U.S.A. 64 A4
Renland reg. Greenland see Tuttut Nunaat
Rennell i. Solomon Is 53 G3
Rennes France 24 D2
Rennick Glacier Antarctica 76 H2
Reno r. Italy 26 E2
Reno U.S.A. 62 D4
Renovo PA U.S.A. 64 C2
Réo Burkina 46 C3
Reo Indon. 54 C2
Repalle India 38 D2
Repolka Rus. Fed. 15 P7
Republican r. U.S.A. 62 H4
Republic of South Africa country Africa 50 F5
Repulse Bay b. Australia 56 E4
Repulse Bay Canada 61 J3
Requena Peru 68 D5
Requena Spain 25 F4
Reşadiye Turkey 34 E2
Reserva Brazil 71 A4
Reshteh-ye Alborz mts Iran see Elburz Mountains
Resistencia Arg. 70 E3
Reşiţa Romania 27 I2
Resolute Canada 61 I2
Resolution Island Canada 61 L3
Resolution Island N.Z. 59 A7
Resplendor Brazil 71 C2
Resülayn Turkey see Ceylanpınar
Retalhuleu Guat. 66 F6
Retezat, Parcul Naţional nat. park Romania 27 J2
Retford U.K. 18 G5
Rethel France 24 G2
Réthimnon Greece see Rethymno
Rethymno Greece 27 K7
Retreat Australia 56 C5
Réunion terr. Indian Ocean 73 L7
Reus Spain 25 G3
Reutlingen Germany 17 L6
Reval Estonia see Tallinn
Revda Rus. Fed. 12 G2
Revel Estonia see Tallinn
Revel France 24 F5
Revillagigedo, Islas is Mex. 66 B5
Revillagigedo Island U.S.A. 60 E4
Revivim Israel 39 B4
Rewa India 36 E4
Rewari India 36 D3
Rexburg U.S.A. 62 E3
Reyes, Point CA U.S.A. 65 A1
Reyhanlı Turkey 39 C1
Reykir Iceland 14 [inset]
Reykjanes Ridge sea feature N. Atlantic Ocean 72 F2
Reykjanestá pt Iceland 14 [inset]
Reykjavík Iceland 14 [inset]
Reyneke, Ostrov i. Rus. Fed. 44 E1
Reynolds Range mts Australia 54 F5
Reynosa Mex. 66 E3
Rezā Iran 35 I4
Rezā'īyeh Iran see Urmia
Rezā'īyeh, Daryācheh-ye salt l. Iran see Urmia, Lake
Rēzekne Latvia 15 O8
Rezvāndeh Iran see Rezvānshahr
Rezvānshahr Iran 35 H3
Rhaeader Gwy U.K. see Rhayader
Rhayader U.K. 19 D6
Rhegium Italy see Reggio di Calabria
Rheims France see Reims
Rhein r. Germany see Rhine
Rheine Germany 17 K4
Rhemilès well Alg. 46 C2
Rhin r. France see Rhine
Rhine r. France 24 I2
Rhine r. Germany 17 K5
Rhinebeck NY U.S.A. 64 E2
Rhinelander U.S.A. 63 J2
Rhiwabon U.K. see Ruabon
Rho Italy 26 C2
Rhode Island state U.S.A. 64 F2
Rhodes Greece 27 M6
Rhodes i. Greece 27 M6
Rhodesia country Africa see Zimbabwe
Rhodope Mountains Bulg./Greece 27 J4
Rhodus i. Greece see Rhodes
Rhône r. France/Switz. 24 G5
Rhum i. U.K. see Rum
Rhuthun U.K. see Ruthin
Rhydaman U.K. see Ammanford
Rhyl U.K. 18 D5
Riachão Brazil 69 I5
Riacho Brazil 71 C2
Riacho de Santana Brazil 71 C1
Riacho dos Machados Brazil 71 C1
Rialma Brazil 71 A1
Rialto CA U.S.A. 65 D3
Riasi India 36 C2
Riau, Kepulauan is Indon. 41 C7
Ribadeo Spain 25 C2
Ribadesella Spain 25 D2
Ribas do Rio Pardo Brazil 70 F2
Ribat Afgh. 36 B1
Ribáuè Moz. 49 D5
Ribble r. U.K. 18 E5
Ribblesdale val. U.K. 18 E4
Ribe Denmark 15 F9
Ribeira r. Brazil 71 B4
Ribeirão Preto Brazil 71 B3
Ribérac France 24 E4
Riberalta Bol. 68 E6
Rîbniţa Moldova 13 F7
Ribnitz-Damgarten Germany 17 N3
Říčany Czech Rep. 17 O6
Rice VA U.S.A. 64 B4
Richards Bay S. Africa 51 K5
Richards Inlet Antarctica 76 H1
Richards Island Canada 60 E3
Richardson Mountains Canada 60 E3
Richardson Mountains N.Z. 59 B7
Richfield U.S.A. 62 E4
Richfield Springs NY U.S.A. 64 D1
Richford NY U.S.A. 64 C1
Richgrove CA U.S.A. 65 C3
Richland U.S.A. 62 D2
Richmond N.S.W. Australia 58 E4
Richmond Qld Australia 56 C4
Richmond N.Z. 59 D5
Richmond KwaZulu-Natal S. Africa 51 J5
Richmond N. Cape S. Africa 50 F6
Richmond U.K. 18 F4
Richmond CA U.S.A. 65 A2
Richmond IN U.S.A. 63 K4
Richmond KY U.S.A. 63 K4
Richmond VA U.S.A. 64 C4
Richmond Range hills Australia 58 F2
Richtersveld National Park S. Africa 50 C5
Richwood WV U.S.A. 64 A3
Ricomagus France see Riom
Riddell Nunataks Antarctica 76 E2
Rideau Lakes Canada 63 L3
Ridgecrest CA U.S.A. 65 D3
Ridgway PA U.S.A. 64 B2
Riecito Venez. 68 E1
Riesa Germany 17 N5
Riesco, Isla i. Chile 70 B8
Riet watercourse S. Africa 50 E6
Rietavas Lith. 15 L9
Rietfontein S. Africa 50 E4
Rieti Italy 26 E3
Rifā'ī, Tall mt. Jordan/Syria 39 C3
Rifstangi pt Iceland 14 [inset]
Rift Valley Lakes National Park Eth. see Abijatta-Shalla National Park
Riga Latvia 15 N8
Riga, Gulf of Estonia/Latvia 15 M8
Rigain Pünco l. China 37 F2
Rīgān Iran 33 I4
Rīgas jūras līcis b. Estonia/Latvia see Riga, Gulf of
Rigby U.S.A. 62 E3
Rigside U.K. 20 F5
Riia laht b. Estonia/Latvia see Riga, Gulf of
Riihimäki Fin. 15 N6
Riiser-Larsen Ice Shelf Antarctica 76 B2
Rijau Nigeria 46 D3
Rijeka Croatia 26 F2
Rikuchū-kaigan Kokuritsu-kōen nat. park Japan 45 F5
Rikuzen-takata Japan 45 F5
Rila mts Bulg. 27 J3
Rila China 37 F3
Rileyville VA U.S.A. 64 B3
Rillieux-la-Pape France 24 G4
Rimah, Wādī al watercourse Saudi Arabia 32 F4
Rimavská Sobota Slovakia 17 R6
Rimini Italy 26 E2
Râmnicu Sărat Romania see Râmnicu Sărat
Râmnicu Vâlcea Romania see Râmnicu Vâlcea
Rimouski Canada 63 N2
Rimsdale, Loch l. U.K. 20 E2
Rinbung China 37 G3
Rincão Brazil 71 A3
Rindal Norway 14 F5
Ringarooma Bay Australia 57 [inset]
Ringas India 36 C4
Ringebu Norway 15 G6
Ringkøbing Denmark 15 F8
Ringsend U.K. 21 F2
Ringsted Denmark 15 G9
Ringtor China 37 E3
Ringvassøya i. Norway 14 K2
Ringwood Australia 58 B6
Ringwood U.K. 19 F8
Rinns Point U.K. 20 C5
Rinqênzê China 37 G3
Río Abiseo, Parque Nacional nat. park Peru 68 C5
Rio Azul Brazil 71 A4
Riobamba Ecuador 68 C4
Rio Bonito Brazil 71 C3
Rio Branco Brazil 68 E6
Rio Branco, Parque Nacional do nat. park Brazil 68 F3
Rio Brilhante Brazil 70 F2
Río Casca Brazil 71 C3
Rio Claro Brazil 71 B3
Río Colorado Arg. 70 D5
Río Cuarto Arg. 70 D4
Rio das Pedras Moz. 51 L2
Rio de Contas Brazil 71 C1
Rio de Janeiro Brazil 71 C3
Rio de Janeiro state Brazil 71 C3
Río de la Plata-Paraná r. S. America 70 E4
Rio do Sul Brazil 71 A4
Río Gallegos Arg. 70 C8
Río Grande Arg. 70 C8
Rio Grande Brazil 70 F4
Río Grande Mex. 66 D4
Rio Grande r. Mex./U.S.A. 62 H6
Rio Grande City U.S.A. 62 H6
Rio Grande do Sul state Brazil 71 A5
Rio Grande Rise sea feature S. Atlantic Ocean 72 F8
Ríohacha Col. 68 D1
Río Hondo, Embalse resr Arg. 70 C3
Rioja Peru 68 C5
Río Lagartos Mex. 66 G4
Rio Largo Brazil 69 K5
Riom France 24 F4
Rio Manso, Represa do resr Brazil 69 G6
Río Mulatos Bol. 68 E7
Río Muni reg. Equat. Guinea 46 E4
Río Negro, Embalse del resr Uruguay 70 E4
Rioni r. Georgia 35 F2
Rio Novo Brazil 71 C3
Rio Pardo de Minas Brazil 71 C1
Rio Preto Brazil 71 C3
Rio Preto, Serra do hills Brazil 71 B2
Río Rancho U.S.A. 62 F4
Río Tigre Ecuador 68 C4
Rio Verde Brazil 71 A2
Rio Verde de Mato Grosso Brazil 69 H7
Rio Vista CA U.S.A. 65 B1
Ripky Ukr. 13 F6
Ripley England U.K. 18 F4
Ripley England U.K. 19 F5
Ripley WV U.S.A. 64 B1
Ripoll Spain 25 H2
Ripon U.K. 18 F4
Ripon CA U.S.A. 65 B2
Ripu India 37 G4
Risca U.K. 19 D7
Rishiri-tō i. Japan 44 F3
Rishon LeZiyyon Israel 39 B4
Rising Sun MD U.S.A. 64 C3
Risle r. France 19 H9
Risør Norway 15 F7
Rissa Norway 14 F5
Ristiina Fin. 15 O6
Ristijärvi Fin. 14 P4
Ristikent Rus. Fed. 12 F1
Risum China 36 D2
Ritchie S. Africa 50 G5
Ritscher Upland mts Antarctica 76 B2
Ritsem Sweden 14 J3
Ritter, Mount CA U.S.A. 65 C2
Ritzville U.S.A. 62 D2
Riva del Garda Italy 26 D2
Rivas Nicaragua 67 G6
Rivera Arg. 70 D5
Rivera Uruguay 70 E4
River Cess Liberia 46 C4
Riverhead NY U.S.A. 64 E2
Riverhurst Canada 62 F1
Riverina Australia 55 C7
Riverina reg. Australia 58 B5
Riversdale S. Africa 50 E8
Riverside S. Africa 51 I6
Riverside CA U.S.A. 65 D4
Riversleigh Australia 56 B3
Riverton N.Z. 59 B8
Riverton VA U.S.A. 64 B3
Riverton WY U.S.A. 62 F3
Riverview Canada 63 O2
Rivesaltes France 24 F5
Rivière-du-Loup Canada 63 N2
Rivne Ukr. 13 E6
Rivungo Angola 49 C5
Riwaka N.Z. 59 D5
Riwoqê China see Racaka
Riyadh Saudi Arabia 32 G5
Riza well Iran 35 I4
Rize Turkey 35 F2
Rizokarpaso Cyprus see Rizokarpason
Rizokarpason Cyprus 39 B2
Rjukan Norway 15 F7
Rjuvbrokkene mt. Norway 15 E7
Rkîz Mauritania 46 B3
Roa Norway 15 G6
Roach Lake NV U.S.A. 65 E3
Roade U.K. 19 G6
Road Town Virgin Is (U.K.) 67 L5
Roan Norway 14 G4
Roan Fell h. U.K. 20 G5
Roanne France 24 G3
Roanoke VA U.S.A. 64 B4
Roanoke Rapids U.S.A. 63 L4
Roaring Spring PA U.S.A. 64 B2
Roaringwater Bay Ireland 21 C6
Roatán Hond. 67 G5
Röbäck Sweden 14 L5
Robāţe Tork Iran 35 H4
Robāţ Karīm Iran 35 H4
Robbins Island Australia 57 [inset]
Robe Australia 57 B8
Robe r. Australia 54 A5
Robe r. Ireland 21 C4
Robert-Bourassa, Réservoir resr Canada 61 K4
Robert Glacier Antarctica 76 D2
Roberts, Mount Australia 58 F2
Roberts Butte mt. Antarctica 76 H2
Robertsfors Sweden 14 L4
Robertsganj India 37 E4
Robertson S. Africa 50 D7
Robertson Bay Antarctica 76 H2
Robertson Island Antarctica 76 A2
Robertson Range hills Australia 55 C5
Robertsport Liberia 46 B4
Roberval Canada 63 M2
Robhanais, Rubha hd U.K. see Butt of Lewis
Robin Hood's Bay U.K. 18 G4
Robinson Range hills Australia 55 B6
Robinson River Australia 56 B3
Robson, Mount Canada 62 D1
Roçadas Angola see Xangongo
Rocca Busambra mt. Sicilia Italy 26 E6
Rocha Uruguay 70 F4
Rochdale U.K. 18 E5
Rochechouart France 24 E4
Rochefort France 24 D4
Rochegda Rus. Fed. 12 I3
Rochester Australia 58 B6
Rochester U.K. 19 H7
Rochester MN U.S.A. 63 I3
Rochester NH U.S.A. 64 F1
Rochester NY U.S.A. 64 C1
Rochford U.K. 19 H7
Roc'h Trévezel h. France 24 C2
Rockall i. N. Atlantic Ocean 10 D4
Rockall Bank sea feature N. Atlantic Ocean 72 G2
Rock Creek OH U.S.A. 64 A2
Rockefeller Plateau Antarctica 76 J1
Rockford IL U.S.A. 63 J3
Rockhampton Australia 56 E4
Rockhampton Downs Australia 54 F4
Rockingham Australia 55 A8
Rockingham Bay Australia 56 D3
Rock Island U.S.A. 63 I3
Rockland MA U.S.A. 64 F1
Rocksprings U.S.A. 62 G6
Rockstone Guyana 69 G2
Rockville CT U.S.A. 64 E2
Rockville MD U.S.A. 64 C3
Rockwood PA U.S.A. 64 B3
Rocky Mount VA U.S.A. 64 B4
Rocky Mountains Canada/U.S.A. 62 F3
Rodberg Norway 15 F6
Rødbyhavn Denmark 15 G9
Rodeio Brazil 71 A4
Rodel U.K. 20 C3
Rodeo Arg. 70 C4
Rodez France 24 F4
Ródhos i. Greece see Rhodes
Rodi i. Greece see Rhodes
Rodney, Cape U.S.A. 60 B3
Rodniki Rus. Fed. 12 I4
Rodopi Planina mts Bulg./Greece see Rhodope Mountains
Rodos Greece see Rhodes
Rodos i. Greece see Rhodes
Rodosto Turkey see Tekirdağ
Rodrigues Island Mauritius 73 M7
Roe r. U.K. 21 F2
Roebourne Australia 54 B5
Roebuck Bay Australia 54 C4
Roedtan S. Africa 51 I3
Roe Plains Australia 55 D7
Roeselare Belgium 16 I5
Roes Welcome Sound sea chan. Canada 61 J3
Rogachev Belarus see Rahachow
Rogers Lake CA U.S.A. 65 D3
Roggeveen Basin sea feature S. Pacific Ocean 75 O8
Roggeveld plat. S. Africa 50 E7
Roggeveldberge esc. S. Africa 50 E7
Roghadal U.K. see Rodel
Rognan Norway 14 I3
Roha India 38 B2
Rohnert Park CA U.S.A. 65 A1
Rohrbach in Oberösterreich Austria 17 N6
Rohri Sangar Pak. 36 B4
Rohtak India 36 D3
Roi Georges, Îles du is Fr. Polynesia 75 K6
Rois-Bheinn h. U.K. 20 D4
Roja Latvia 15 M8
Rojas Arg. 70 D4
Rokeby Australia 56 C2
Rokeby National Park Australia 56 C2
Rokiškis Lith. 15 N9
Roknäs Sweden 14 L4
Rokytne Ukr. 13 E6
Rolagang China 37 G2
Rola Kangri mt. China 37 G2
Rolândia Brazil 71 A3
Rolim de Moura Brazil 68 F6
Roll AZ U.S.A. 65 F4
Rolla MO U.S.A. 63 I4
Rollag Norway 15 F6
Rolleston Australia 56 E5
Roma Australia 57 E5
Roma Italy see Rome
Roma Lesotho 51 H5
Roma Sweden 15 K8
Romain, Cape U.S.A. 63 L5
Roman Romania 27 L1
Români, Câmpia plain Romania 27 J2
Romanche Gap sea feature S. Atlantic Ocean 72 G6
Romang, Pulau i. Indon. 41 E8
Romania country Europe 27 K2
Roman-Kosh mt. Ukr. 34 D1
Romanovka Rus. Fed. 43 K2
Romans-sur-Isère France 24 G4
Romanzof, Cape U.S.A. 60 B3
Rombas France 24 H2
Romblon Phil. 41 E6
Rome Italy 26 E4
Rome GA U.S.A. 63 J5
Rome NY U.S.A. 64 D1
Romford U.K. 19 H7
Romilly-sur-Seine France 24 F2
Romney WV U.S.A. 64 B3
Romney Marsh reg. U.K. 19 H7
Romny Ukr. 13 G6
Rømø i. Denmark 15 F9
Romodanovo Rus. Fed. 13 J5
Romorantin-Lanthenay France 24 E3
Romsey U.K. 19 F8
Ron India 38 B3
Rona i. U.K. 20 D1
Ronas Hill h. U.K. 20 [inset]
Roncador, Serra do hills Brazil 69 H6
Roncador Reef Solomon Is 53 F2
Ronda Spain 25 D5
Ronda, Serranía de mts Spain 25 D5
Rondane Nasjonalpark nat. park Norway 15 F6
Rondon Brazil 70 F2
Rondonópolis Brazil 69 H7
Rondout Reservoir NY U.S.A. 64 D2
Rong Chu r. China 37 G3
Rongelap atoll Marshall Is 74 H5
Rongklang Range mts Myanmar 37 H5
Rongwo China see Tongren
Rongyul China 37 I3
Rönlap atoll Marshall Is see Rongelap
Rønne Denmark 15 I9
Ronneby Sweden 15 I8
Ronne Entrance str. Antarctica 76 L2
Ronne Ice Shelf Antarctica 76 L1
Rooke Island P.N.G. see Umboi
Roorkee India 36 D3
Roosendaal Neth. 16 J5
Roosevelt, Mount Canada 60 F4
Roosevelt Island Antarctica 76 I1
Ropar India see Rupnagar
Roper r. Australia 56 A2
Roper Bar Australia 54 F3
Roquefort France 24 D4
Roraima, Mount Guyana 68 F2
Rori India 36 C3
Røros Norway 14 G5
Rørvik Norway 14 G4
Rosamond CA U.S.A. 65 C3
Rosamond Lake CA U.S.A. 65 C3
Rosario Arg. 70 D4
Rosário Brazil 69 J4
Rosario Baja California Mex. 66 A2
Rosario Sinaloa Mex. 66 C4
Rosario Sonora Mex. 62 F6
Rosario Venez. 68 D1
Rosário do Sul Brazil 70 F4
Rosário Oeste Brazil 69 G6
Rosarito Baja California Mex. 62 E6
Rosarno Italy 26 F5
Roscoff France 24 C2
Roscommon Ireland 21 D4
Roscrea Ireland 21 E5
Rose r. Australia 56 A2
Rose Atoll American Samoa see Rose Island
Roseau Dominica 67 L5
Roseberth Australia 57 B5
Roseburg U.S.A. 62 C3
Rosedale Abbey U.K. 18 G4
Roseires Reservoir Sudan 32 D7
Rose Island atoll American Samoa 53 J3
Rosenberg U.S.A. 63 H6
Rosendal Norway 15 E7
Rosendal S. Africa 51 H5
Rosenheim Germany 17 N7
Roseto degli Abruzzi Italy 26 F3
Rosetown Canada 62 F1
Rosetta Egypt see Rashid
Roseville CA U.S.A. 65 B1
Rosewood Australia 58 F1
Roshchino Rus. Fed. 15 P6
Rosh Pinah Namibia 50 C4
Roshtkala Tajik. see Roshtqal'a
Roshtqal'a Tajik. 36 B1
Rosignano Marittimo Italy 26 D3
Roşiori de Vede Romania 27 K2
Roskilde Denmark 15 H9
Roslavl' Rus. Fed. 13 G5
Roslyakovo Rus. Fed. 14 R2
Roslyatino Rus. Fed. 12 J4
Ross N.Z. 59 C6
Ross, Mount h. N.Z. 59 E5
Rossano Italy 26 G5
Rossan Point Ireland 21 D3
Rosscarbery Ireland 21 C6
Ross Dependency Antarctica 76 I2
Rossel Island P.N.G. 56 F1
Ross Ice Shelf Antarctica 76 I1
Rössing Namibia 50 B2
Ross Island Antarctica 76 H1
Rossiyskaya Sovetskaya Federativnaya Sotsialisticheskaya Respublika country Asia/Europe see Russian Federation
Rosslare Ireland 21 F5
Rosslare Harbour Ireland 21 F5
Rosso Mauritania 46 B3
Ross-on-Wye U.K. 19 E7
Rossony Belarus see Rasony
Rossosh' Rus. Fed. 13 H6
Ross River Canada 60 E3
Ross Sea Antarctica 76 H1
Røssvatnet l. Norway 14 I4
Rostāq Afgh. 36 B1
Rostāq Iran 35 I6
Rosthern Canada 62 F1
Rostock Germany 17 N3
Rostov Rus. Fed. 12 H4
Rostov-na-Donu Rus. Fed. 13 H7
Rostov-on-Don Rus. Fed. see Rostov-na-Donu
Rosvik Sweden 14 L4
Roswell U.S.A. 62 G5
Rota i. N. Mariana Is 41 G6
Rotch Island Kiribati see Tamana
Rote i. Indon. 41 E9
Roth Germany 17 M6
Rothbury U.K. 18 F3
Rothenburg ob der Tauber Germany 17 M6
Rother r. U.K. 19 G8
Rothera research stn Antarctica 76 L2
Rotherham U.K. 18 F5
Rothes U.K. 20 F3
Rothesay U.K. 20 D5
Rothwell U.K. 19 G6
Roti Indon. 54 C2
Roti i. Indon. see Rote
Roto Australia 58 B4
Rotomagus France see Rouen
Rotomanu N.Z. 59 C6
Rotondo, Monte mt. Corse France 24 I5
Rotorua N.Z. 59 F4
Rotorua, Lake N.Z. 59 F4
Rottenmann Austria 17 O7
Rotterdam Neth. 16 J5
Rottnest Island Australia 55 A8
Rottweil Germany 17 L6
Rotuma i. Fiji 53 H3
Rötviken Sweden 14 I5
Roubaix France 24 F1
Rouen France 24 E2
Roulers Belgium see Roeselare
Roumania country Europe see Romania
Round Hill h. U.K. 18 F4
Round Mountain Australia 58 F3
Roundup U.S.A. 62 F2
Rousay i. U.K. 20 F1
Rouxville S. Africa 51 H6
Rouyn-Noranda Canada 63 L2
Rovaniemi Fin. 14 N3
Roven'ki Rus. Fed. 13 H6
Rovereto Italy 26 D2
Rovigo Italy 26 D2
Rovinj Croatia 26 E2
Rovno Ukr. see Rivne
Rovnoye Rus. Fed. 13 J6
Rovuma r. Moz./Tanz. see Ruvuma
Rowena Australia 58 D2
Rowley Island Canada 61 K3
Rowley Shoals sea feature Australia 54 B4
Równe Ukr. see Rivne
Roxburgh N.Z. 59 B7
Roxburgh Island Cook Is see Rarotonga
Roxby Downs Australia 57 B6
Roxo, Cabo c. Senegal 46 B3
Royal Canal Ireland 21 E4
Royal Chitwan National Park Nepal 37 F4
Royale, Île i. Canada see Cape Breton Island
Royale, Isle i. U.S.A. 63 J2
Royal Natal National Park S. Africa 51 I5
Royal National Park Australia 58 E5
Royal Sukla Phanta Wildlife Reserve Nepal 36 E3
Royan France 24 D4
Roy Hill Australia 54 B5
Royston U.K. 19 G6
Rozdil'na Ukr. 27 N1
Rozivka Ukr. 13 H7
Rtishchevo Rus. Fed. 13 I5
Ruabon U.K. 19 D6
Ruaha National Park Tanz. 49 D4
Ruahine Range mts N.Z. 59 F5
Ruanda country Africa see Rwanda
Ruapehu, Mount vol. N.Z. 59 E4
Ruapuke Island N.Z. 59 B8
Ruatoria N.Z. 59 G3
Ruba Belarus 13 F5
Rub' al Khālī des. Saudi Arabia 32 G6
Rubtsovsk Rus. Fed. 42 E2
Ruby U.S.A. 60 C3
Ruckersville VA U.S.A. 64 B3
Rudall River National Park Australia 54 C5
Rudarpur India 37 E4
Ruda Śląska Poland 17 Q5
Rudauli India 37 E4
Rūdbār Iran 35 H3
Rudkøbing Denmark 15 G9
Rudnaya Pristan' Rus. Fed. 44 D3
Rudnichnyy Rus. Fed. 12 L4
Rudnya Smolenskaya Oblast' Rus. Fed. 13 F5
Rudnya Volgogradskaya Oblast' Rus. Fed. 13 J6
Rudnyy Kazakh. 30 F1
Rudolf, Lake salt l. Eth./Kenya see Turkana, Lake
Rudol'fa, Ostrov i. Rus. Fed. 28 G1
Rudolph Island Rus. Fed. see Rudol'fa, Ostrov
Rüdsar Iran 35 H3
Rue France 19 I8
Rufiji r. Tanz. 49 D4
Rufino Arg. 70 D4
Rufisque Senegal 46 B3
Rufunsa Zambia 49 C5
Rugao China 43 M6
Rugby U.K. 19 F6
Rugby U.S.A. 62 G2
Rugeley U.K. 19 F6
Rügen i. Germany 17 N3
Ruhengeri Rwanda 48 C4
Ruhnu i. Estonia 15 M8
Ruhuna National Park Sri Lanka 38 D5
Rui Barbosa Brazil 71 C1
Ruijin China 43 L7
Ruipa Tanz. 49 D4
Ruiz Mex. 66 C4
Ruiz, Nevado del vol. Col. 68 C3
Rujaylah, Ḩarrat ar lava field Jordan 39 C3
Rūjiena Latvia 15 N8
Ruk is Micronesia see Chuuk
Rukumkot Nepal 37 E3
Rukwa, Lake Tanz. 49 D4
Rum i. U.K. 20 C4
Rum, Jebel mts Jordan see Ramm, Jabal
Ruma Serbia 27 H2
Rumāh Saudi Arabia 32 G4
Rumania country Europe see Romania
Rumbek Sudan 47 F4
Rum Cay i. Bahamas 67 J4
Rum Jungle Australia 54 E3
Rummānā h. Syria 39 D3
Rumphi Malawi 49 D5
Runaway, Cape N.Z. 59 F3
Runcorn U.K. 18 E5
Rundu Namibia 49 B5
Rundvik Sweden 14 K5
Rungwa Tanz. 49 D4
Rungwa r. Tanz. 49 D4
Runton Range hills Australia 55 C5
Ruokolahti Fin. 15 P6
Ruoqiang China 42 F5
Rupa India 37 H4
Rupert r. Canada 63 L1
Rupert WV U.S.A. 64 A4
Rupert Bay Canada 63 L1
Rupert Coast Antarctica 76 J1
Rupert House Canada see Waskaganish
Rupnagar India 36 D3
Rupshu reg. India 36 D2
Ruqqād, Wādī ar watercourse Israel 39 B3
Rural Retreat VA U.S.A. 64 A4
Rusaddir N. Africa see Melilla
Rusape Zimbabwe 49 D5
Ruschuk Bulg. see Ruse
Ruse Bulg. 27 K3
Rusera India 37 F4
Rushden U.K. 19 G6
Rushinga Zimbabwe 49 D5
Rushville NE U.S.A. 62 G3
Rushworth Australia 58 B6
Russell N.Z. 59 E2
Russell PA U.S.A. 64 B2
Russell Bay Antarctica 76 J2
Russell Range hills Australia 55 C8
Russellville AR U.S.A. 63 I4
Rüsselsheim Germany 17 L5
Russia country Asia/Europe see Russian Federation
Russian r. CA U.S.A. 65 A1
Russian Federation country Asia/Europe 28 I3
Russian Soviet Federal Socialist Republic country Asia/Europe see Russian Federation
Russkiy, Ostrov i. Rus. Fed. 44 C4
Russkiy Kameshkir Rus. Fed. 13 J5
Rust'avi Georgia 35 G2
Rustburg VA U.S.A. 64 B4
Rustenburg S. Africa 51 H3
Ruston U.S.A. 63 I5
Rutanzige, Lake Dem. Rep. Congo/Uganda see Edward, Lake
Ruteng Indon. 41 E8

Stafford Springs *CT* U.S.A. 64 E2
Staicele Latvia 15 N8
Staines U.K. 19 G7
Stakhanov Ukr. 13 H6
Stakhanovo Rus. Fed. *see* **Zhukovskiy**
Stalbridge U.K. 19 E8
Stalham U.K. 19 I6
Stalin Bulg. *see* **Varna**
Stalinabad Tajik. *see* **Dushanbe**
Stalingrad Rus. Fed. *see* **Volgograd**
Staliniri Georgia *see* **Ts'khinvali**
Stalino Ukr. *see* **Donets'k**
Stalinogorsk Rus. Fed. *see* **Novomoskovsk**
Stalinogród Poland *see* **Katowice**
Stalinsk Rus. Fed. *see* **Novokuznetsk**
Stalowa Wola Poland 13 D6
Stamboliyski Bulg. 27 K3
Stamford Australia 56 C4
Stamford U.K. 19 G6
Stamford *CT* U.S.A. 64 E2
Stamford *NY* U.S.A. 64 D1
Stampalia *i.* Greece *see* **Astypalaia**
Stampriet Namibia 50 D3
Stamsund Norway 14 H2
Stanardsville *VA* U.S.A. 64 B3
Stancomb-Wills Glacier Antarctica 76 B1
Standerton S. Africa 51 I4
Standish U.S.A. 63 K3
Stanger S. Africa 51 J5
Stanislaus *r. CA* U.S.A. 65 B2
Stanislav Ukr. *see* **Ivano-Frankivs'k**
Stanke Dimitrov Bulg. *see* **Dupnitsa**
Stanley Australia 57 [inset]
Stanley Falkland Is 70 E8
Stanley U.K. 18 F4
Stanley *ND* U.S.A. 62 G2
Stanley *VA* U.S.A. 64 B3
Stanley, Mount *h. N.T.* Australia 54 E5
Stanley, Mount *h. Tas.* Australia 57 [inset]
Stanley, Mount Dem. Rep. Congo/Uganda *see* **Margherita Peak**
Stanleyville Dem. Rep. Congo *see* **Kisangani**
Stann Creek Belize *see* **Dangriga**
Stannington U.K. 18 F3
Stanovoye Rus. Fed. 13 H5
Stanovoye Nagor'ye *mts* Rus. Fed. 43 L1
Stanovoy Khrebet *mts* Rus. Fed. 29 N4
Stansmore Range *hills* Australia 54 E5
Stanthorpe Australia 58 E2
Stanton U.K. 19 H6
Starachowice Poland 17 R5
Stara Planina *mts* Bulg./Serbia *see* **Balkan Mountains**
Staraya Russa Rus. Fed. 12 F4
Stara Zagora Bulg. 27 K3
Starbuck Island Kiribati 75 J6
Starcke National Park Australia 56 D2
Stargard in Pommern Poland *see* **Stargard Szczeciński**
Stargard Szczeciński Poland 17 O4
Staritsa Rus. Fed. 12 G4
Starkville U.S.A. 63 J5
Starnberger See *l.* Germany 17 M7
Starobel'sk Ukr. *see* **Starobil's'k**
Starobil's'k Ukr. 13 H6
Starogard Gdański Poland 17 Q4
Starokonstantinov Ukr. *see* **Starokostyantyniv**
Starokostyantyniv Ukr. 13 E6
Starominskaya Rus. Fed. 13 H7
Staroshcherbinovskaya Rus. Fed. 13 H7
Start Point U.K. 19 D8
Starve Island Kiribati *see* **Starbuck Island**
Staryya Darohi Belarus 13 F5
Staryye Dorogi Belarus *see* **Staryya Darohi**
Staryy Kayak Rus. Fed. 29 L2
Staryy Oskol Rus. Fed. 13 H6
State College *PA* U.S.A. 64 C2
Staten Island Arg. *see* **Los Estados, Isla de**
Statesboro U.S.A. 63 K5
Statia *i.* Neth. Antilles *see* **Sint Eustatius**
Station Nord Greenland 77 I1
Staunton *VA* U.S.A. 64 B3
Stavanger Norway 15 D7
Staveley U.K. 18 F5
Stavropol' Rus. Fed. 13 I7
Stavropol Kray *admin. div.* Rus. Fed. *see* **Stavropol'skiy Kray**
Stavropol'-na-Volge Rus. Fed. *see* **Tol'yatti**
Stavropol'skaya Vozvyshennost' *hills* Rus. Fed. 13 I7
Stavropol'skiy Kray *admin. div.* Rus. Fed. 35 F1
Steadville S. Africa 51 I5
Steamboat Springs U.S.A. 62 F3
Stebbins U.S.A. 60 B3
Steele Island Antarctica 76 L2
Steenkampsberge *mts* S. Africa 51 J3
Steen River Canada 60 G4
Steens Mountain U.S.A. 62 D3
Steenstrup Gletscher *glacier* Greenland *see* **Sermersuaq**
Stefansson Island Canada 61 H2
Stegi Swaziland *see* **Siteki**
Steigerwald *mts* Germany 17 M6
Steinhausen Namibia 49 B6
Steinkjer Norway 14 G4
Steinkopf S. Africa 50 C5
Steinsdalen Norway 14 G4
Stella S. Africa 50 G4
Stellenbosch S. Africa 50 D7
Stello, Monte *mt. Corse* France 24 I5
Stelvio, Parco Nazionale dello *nat. park* Italy 26 D1
Stendal Germany 17 M4
Stenhousemuir U.K. 20 F4
Stenungsund Sweden 15 G7
Steornabhagh U.K. *see* **Stornoway**
Stepanakert Azer. *see* **Xankändi**
Stephens, Cape N.Z. 59 D5
Stephens City *VA* U.S.A. 64 B3
Stephenville U.S.A. 62 H5
Stepnoy Rus. Fed. *see* **Elista**
Stepnoye Rus. Fed. 13 J6
Sterkfontein Dam *dam* S. Africa 51 I5
Sterkstroom S. Africa 51 H6
Sterlibashevo Rus. Fed. 11 R5
Sterling S. Africa 50 E6
Sterling *CO* U.S.A. 62 G3
Sterlitamak Rus. Fed. 28 G4
Stettin Poland *see* **Szczecin**
Steubenville *OH* U.S.A. 64 A2
Stevenage U.K. 19 G7
Stevenson Lake Canada 63 H1
Stevens Village U.S.A. 60 D3
Stevensville *PA* U.S.A. 64 C2
Stewart *r.* Canada 60 E3
Stewart, Isla *i.* Chile 70 B8
Stewart Island N.Z. 59 A8
Stewart Islands Solomon Is 53 G2
Stewart Lake Canada 61 J3
Stewarton U.K. 20 E5
Stewarts Point *CA* U.S.A. 65 A1
Steynsburg S. Africa 51 G6
Steyr Austria 17 O6
Steytlerville S. Africa 50 G7
Stif Alg. *see* **Sétif**
Stikine *r.* Canada 60 E4
Stikine Plateau Canada 60 E4
Stilbaai S. Africa 50 E8
Stillwater *OK* U.S.A. 63 H4
Stilton U.K. 19 G6
Štip Macedonia 27 J4
Stirling Australia 54 F5
Stirling U.K. 20 F4
Stirling Creek *r.* Australia 54 E4
Stirling Range National Park Australia 55 B8
Stjørdalshalsen Norway 14 G5
Stockerau Austria 17 P6
Stockholm Sweden 15 K7
Stockinbingal Australia 58 C5
Stockport U.K. 18 E5
Stockton *CA* U.S.A. 65 B2
Stockton-on-Tees U.K. 18 F4
Stoer, Point of U.K. 20 D2
Stoke-on-Trent U.K. 19 E5
Stokesley U.K. 18 F4
Stokes Point Australia 57 [inset]
Stokes Range *hills* Australia 54 E4
Stokkseyri Iceland 14 [inset]
Stokkvågen Norway 14 H3
Stokmarknes Norway 14 I2
Stolac Bos.-Herz. 26 G3
Stolbovoy Rus. Fed. 77 G2
Stolbtsy Belarus *see* **Stowbtsy**
Stolin Belarus 15 O11
Stolp Poland *see* **Słupsk**
Stone U.K. 19 E6
Stoneboro *PA* U.S.A. 64 A2
Stonehaven U.K. 20 G4
Stonehenge Australia 56 C5
Stonehenge *tourist site* U.K. 19 F7
Stonewall Jackson Lake *WV* U.S.A. 64 A3
Stony Creek *VA* U.S.A. 64 C4
Stony River U.S.A. 60 C3
Stora Lulevatten *l.* Sweden 14 K3
Stora Sjöfallets nationalpark *nat. park* Sweden 14 J3
Storavan *l.* Sweden 14 K4
Store Bælt *sea chan.* Denmark *see* **Great Belt**
Støren Norway 14 G5
Storfjordbotn Norway 14 O1
Storforshei Norway 14 I3
Storjord Norway 14 I3
Storkerson Peninsula Canada 61 H2
Storm Bay Australia 57 [inset]
Stormberg S. Africa 51 H6
Storm Lake U.S.A. 63 H3
Stornosa *mt.* Norway 14 E6
Stornoway U.K. 20 C2
Storozhevsk Rus. Fed. 12 L3
Storozhynets' Ukr. 13 E6
Storrs *CT* U.S.A. 64 E2
Storseleby Sweden 14 J4
Storsjön *l.* Sweden 14 I5
Storskrymten *mt.* Norway 14 F5
Storslett Norway 14 L2
Storuman Sweden 14 J4
Storuman *l.* Sweden 14 J4
Storvik Sweden 15 J6
Storvorde Denmark 15 G8
Storvreta Sweden 15 J7
Stotfold U.K. 19 G6
Stour *r. England* U.K. 19 F6
Stour *r. England* U.K. 19 F8
Stour *r. England* U.K. 19 I7
Stour *r. England* U.K. 19 I7
Stourbridge U.K. 19 E6
Stourport-on-Severn U.K. 19 E6
Stout Lake Canada 63 I1
Stowbtsy Belarus 15 O10
Stowmarket U.K. 19 H6
Stoyba Rus. Fed. 44 C1
Strabane U.K. 21 E3
Stradbally Ireland 21 E4
Stradbroke U.K. 19 I6
Stradella Italy 26 C2
Strakonice Czech Rep. 17 N6
Stralsund Germany 17 N3
Strand S. Africa 50 D8
Stranda Norway 14 E5
Strangford U.K. 21 G3
Strangford Lough *inlet* U.K. 21 G3
Strangways *r.* Australia 54 F3
Stranraer U.K. 20 D6
Strasbourg France 24 H2
Strasburg *VA* U.S.A. 64 B3
Strassburg France *see* **Strasbourg**
Stratford Australia 58 C6
Stratford *Ont.* Canada 64 A1
Stratford *CA* U.S.A. 65 C2
Stratford *TX* U.S.A. 62 G4
Stratford-upon-Avon U.K. 19 F6
Strathaven U.K. 20 E5
Strathmore *r.* U.K. 20 E2
Strathroy *Ont.* Canada 64 A1
Strathspey *val.* U.K. 20 F3
Strathy U.K. 20 F2
Stratton U.K. 19 C8
Stratton Mountain *VT* U.S.A. 64 E1
Straubing Germany 17 N6
Straumnes *pt* Iceland 14 [inset]
Streaky Bay Australia 55 F8
Streaky Bay *b.* Australia 55 F8
Street U.K. 19 E7
Streetsboro *OH* U.S.A. 64 A2
Strehaia Romania 27 J2
Streich Mound *h.* Australia 55 C7
Strelka Rus. Fed. 29 Q3
Strel'na *r.* Rus. Fed. 12 H2
Strenči Latvia 15 N8
Streymoy *i.* Faroe Is 14 [inset]
Strichen U.K. 20 G3
Stroeder Arg. 70 D6
Strokestown Ireland 21 D4
Stroma, Island of U.K. 20 F2
Stromboli, Isola *i.* Italy 26 F5
Stromness S. Georgia 70 I8
Stromness U.K. 20 F2
Strömstad Sweden 15 G7
Strömsund Sweden 14 I5
Stronsay *i.* U.K. 20 G1
Stroud Australia 58 E4
Stroud U.K. 19 E7
Stroud Road Australia 58 E4
Stroudsburg *PA* U.S.A. 64 D2
Struer Denmark 15 F8
Struga Macedonia 27 I4
Strugi-Krasnyye Rus. Fed. 15 P7
Struis Bay S. Africa 50 E8
Struma *r.* Bulg. 27 J4
Strumble Head *hd* U.K. 19 B6
Strumica Macedonia 27 J4
Struthers *OH* U.S.A. 64 A2
Stryama *r.* Bulg. 27 K3
Strydenburg S. Africa 50 F5
Strymonas *r.* Greece 27 J4
Stryn Norway 14 E6
Stryy Ukr. 13 D6
Strzelecki, Mount *h.* Australia 54 F5
Strzelecki Desert Australia 57 C6
Strzelecki Regional Reserve *nature res.* Australia 57 B6
1st Three Mile Opening *sea chan.* Australia 56 D2
Stuart Lake Canada 60 F4
Stuart Range *hills* Australia 57 A6
Stuarts Draft *VA* U.S.A. 64 B3
Stuart Town Australia 58 D4
Stuchka Latvia *see* **Aizkraukle**
Stučka Latvia *see* **Aizkraukle**
Studholme Junction N.Z. 59 C7
Studsviken Sweden 14 K5
Stupino Rus. Fed. 13 H5
Sturge Island Antarctica 76 H2
Sturgis *SD* U.S.A. 62 G3
Sturt, Mount *h.* Australia 57 C6
Sturt Creek *watercourse* Australia 54 D4
Sturt National Park Australia 57 C6
Sturt Stony Desert Australia 57 C6
Stutterheim S. Africa 51 H7
Stuttgart Germany 17 L6
Stuttgart U.S.A. 63 I5
Stykkishólmur Iceland 14 [inset]
Styr *r.* Belarus/Ukr. 13 E5
Suaçuí Grande *r.* Brazil 71 C2
Suai East Timor 54 D2
Suakin Sudan 32 E6
Suau P.N.G. 56 E1
Subačius Lith. 15 N9
Subankhata India 37 G4
Subarnapur India *see* **Sonapur**
Sūbāshī Iran 35 H4
Şubayḩah Saudi Arabia 39 D4
Subei China 42 G5
Subotica Serbia 27 H1
Success, Lake *CA* U.S.A. 65 C2
Succiso, Alpi di *mts* Italy 26 D2
Suceava Romania 13 E7
Suchan Rus. Fed. *see* **Partizansk**
Suck *r.* Ireland 21 D4
Suckling, Mount P.N.G. 56 E1
Sucre Bol. 68 E7
Suczawa Romania *see* **Suceava**
Sud, Grand Récif du *rf* New Caledonia 53 G4
Suda Rus. Fed. 12 H4
Sudak Ukr. 34 D1
Sudan *country* Africa 47 F3
Suday Rus. Fed. 12 I4
Sudbury Canada 63 K2
Sudbury U.K. 19 H6
Sudd *swamp* Sudan 32 C8
Sudest Island P.N.G. *see* **Tagula Island**
Sudetenland *mts* Czech Rep./Poland *see* **Sudety**
Sudety *mts* Czech Rep./Poland 17 O5
Sudislavl' Rus. Fed. 12 I4
Sudlersville *MD* U.S.A. 64 D3
Sudogda Rus. Fed. 12 I5
Sudr Egypt 39 A5
Suðuroy *i.* Faroe Is 14 [inset]
Sue *watercourse* Sudan 47 F4
Sueca Spain 25 F4
Suez Egypt 39 A5
Suez, Gulf of Egypt 39 A5
Suez Bay Egypt 39 A5
Suez Canal Egypt 39 A4
Suffolk U.S.A. 63 L4
Sugarloaf Point Australia 58 F4
Sugun China 42 D5
Sūhāj Egypt 32 D4
Şuḩār Oman 33 I5
Suhaymī, Wādī as *watercourse* Egypt 39 A4
Sühbaatar Mongolia 42 J2
Suheli Par *atoll* India 38 B4
Suhl Germany 17 M5
Şuhut Turkey 27 N5
Sui Pak. 36 B3
Suibin China 44 C3
Suid-Afrika *country* Africa *see* **Republic of South Africa**
Suide China 43 K5
Suidzhikurmsy Turkm. *see* **Madaw**
Suifenhe China 44 C3
Suihua China 44 B3
Suileng China 44 B3
Suining *Sichuan* China 42 J6
Suir *r.* Ireland 21 E5
Suisse *country* Europe *see* **Switzerland**
Sui Vehar Pak. 36 B3
Suixian *Hubei* China *see* **Suizhou**
Suiza *country* Europe *see* **Switzerland**
Suizhong China 43 M4
Suizhou China 43 K6
Sujangarh India 36 C4
Sujawal Pak. 36 B4
Sukabumi Indon. 41 C8
Sukagawa Japan 45 F5
Sukarnapura Indon. *see* **Jayapura**
Sukarno, Puncak *mt.* Indon. *see* **Jaya, Puncak**
Sukchŏn N. Korea 45 B5
Sukhinichi Rus. Fed. 13 G5
Sukhona *r.* Rus. Fed. 12 J3
Sukhumi Georgia *see* **Sokhumi**
Sukhum-Kale Georgia *see* **Sokhumi**
Sukkertoppen Greenland *see* **Maniitsoq**
Sukkozero Rus. Fed. 12 G3
Sukkur Pak. 33 K4
Sukma India 38 D2
Sukpay Rus. Fed. 44 E3
Sukpay *r.* Rus. Fed. 44 E3
Sukri *r.* India 36 C4
Sukri *r.* India 36 C4
Suktel *r.* India 38 D1
Sukun *i.* Indon. 54 C2
Sula *i.* Norway 15 D6
Sula *r.* Rus. Fed. 12 K2
Sula, Kepulauan *is* Indon. 41 E8
Sulaiman Range *mts* Pak. 33 K3
Sulak Rus. Fed. 35 G2
Sūlār Iran 35 H5
Sula Sgeir *i.* U.K. 20 C1
Sulawesi *i.* Indon. *see* **Celebes**
Sulaymān Beg Iraq 35 G4
Sulaymānīyah Iraq 35 G4
Sulci *Sardegna* Italy *see* **Sant'Antioco**
Sulcis *Sardegna* Italy *see* **Sant'Antioco**
Suledeh Iran 35 H3
Sule Skerry *i.* U.K. 20 E1
Sule Stack *i.* U.K. 20 E1
Sulitjelma Norway 14 J3
Sulkava Fin. 14 P6
Sullana Peru 68 B4
Sulmo Italy *see* **Sulmona**
Sulmona Italy 26 E3
Sulphur Springs U.S.A. 63 H5
Sultanabad India *see* **Osmannagar**
Sultanabad Iran *see* **Arāk**
Sultan Dağları *mts* Turkey 27 N5
Sultanıye Turkey *see* **Karapınar**
Sultanpur India 37 E4
Sulu Archipelago *is* Phil. 41 E7
Sulu Basin *sea feature* N. Pacific Ocean 74 E5
Sülüklü Turkey 34 D3
Sulusaray Turkey 34 E3
Sulu Sea N. Pacific Ocean 41 D7
Sulzberger Bay Antarctica 76 I1
Sumāil Oman 33 I5
Sumampa Arg. 70 D3
Sumapaz, Parque Nacional *nat. park* Col. 68 D3
Sūmār Iran 35 G4
Sumatera *i.* Indon. *see* **Sumatra**
Sumatra *i.* Indon. 41 B7
Šumava *nat. park* Czech Rep. 17 N6
Sumba *i.* Indon. 41 E8
Sumba, Selat *sea chan.* Indon. 41 D8
Sumbar *r.* Turkm. 35 I3
Sumbawa *i.* Indon. 41 D8
Sumbawabesar Indon. 54 B2
Sumbawanga Tanz. 49 D4
Sumbe Angola 49 B5
Sumbu National Park Zambia 49 D4
Sumburgh U.K. 20 [inset]
Sumburgh Head *hd* U.K. 20 [inset]
Sume'eh Sarā Iran 35 H3
Sumeih Sudan 32 C8
Sumgait Azer. *see* **Sumqayıt**
Sumisu-jima *i.* Japan 43 Q6
Summēl Iraq 35 F3
Summer Isles U.K. 20 D2
Summersville *WV* U.S.A. 64 A3
Summit Lake Canada 60 F4
Sumnal Aksai Chin 36 D2
Sumner N.Z. 59 D6
Sumner, Lake N.Z. 59 D6
Sumon-dake *mt.* Japan 45 E5
Šumperk Czech Rep. 17 P6
Sumpu Japan *see* **Shizuoka**
Sumqayıt Azer. 35 H2
Sumskiy Posad Rus. Fed. 12 G2
Sumter U.S.A. 63 K5
Sumur India 36 D2
Sumy Ukr. 13 G6
Sumzom China 37 I3
Suna Rus. Fed. 12 K4
Sunaj India 36 D4
Sunam India 36 C3
Sunamganj Bangl. 37 G4
Sunart, Loch *inlet* U.K. 20 D4
Sunbury Australia 58 B6
Sunbury *PA* U.S.A. 64 C2
Sunch'ŏn S. Korea 45 B6
Sun City S. Africa 51 H3
Sun City *CA* U.S.A. 65 D4
Sunda, Selat *str.* Indon. 41 C8
Sunda Kalapa Indon. *see* **Jakarta**
Sundance U.S.A. 62 G3
Sundarbans *coastal area* Bangl./India 37 G5
Sundarbans National Park Bangl./India 37 G5
Sundargarh India 37 F5
Sunda Shelf *sea feature* Indian Ocean 73 P5
Sunda Strait Indon. *see* **Sunda, Selat**
Sunda Trench *sea feature* Indian Ocean *see* **Java Trench**
Sunderland U.K. 18 F4
Sündiken Dağları *mts* Turkey 27 N5
Sundown National Park Australia 58 E2
Sundsvall Sweden 14 J5
Sundumbili S. Africa 51 J5
Sungari *r.* China *see* **Songhua Jiang**
Sungqu China *see* **Songpan**
Sungurlu Turkey 34 D2
Sun Kosi *r.* Nepal 37 F4
Sunndal Norway 15 E6
Sunndalsøra Norway 14 F5
Sunne Sweden 15 H7
Sunnyside U.S.A. 62 D2
Sunnyvale *CA* U.S.A. 65 A2
Suntar Rus. Fed. 29 M3
Suntsar Pak. 33 J4
Sunwi-do *i.* N. Korea 45 B5
Sunwu China 44 B2
Sunyani Ghana 46 C4
Suolijärvet *l.* Fin. 14 P3
Suomi *country* Europe *see* **Finland**
Suomussalmi Fin. 14 P4
Suō-nada *b.* Japan 45 C6
Suonenjoki Fin. 14 O5
Suoyarvi Rus. Fed. 12 G3
Supa India 38 B3
Supaul India 37 F4
Superior *NE* U.S.A. 62 H3
Superior *WI* U.S.A. 63 I2
Superior, Lake Canada/U.S.A. 63 J2
Süphan Dağı *mt.* Turkey 35 F3
Suponevo Rus. Fed. 13 G5
Support Force Glacier Antarctica 76 A1
Sūq ash Shuyūkh Iraq 35 G5
Suqian China 43 L6
Suquṭrá *i.* Yemen *see* **Socotra**
Şūr Oman 33 I5
Sur, Point *CA* U.S.A. 65 B2
Sur, Punta *pt* Arg. 70 E5
Sura *r.* Rus. Fed. 13 J4
Şuraabad Azer. 35 H2
Surabaya Indon. 41 D8
Surakarta Indon. 41 D8
Şūrān Syria 39 C2
Surat Australia 58 D1
Surat India 36 C5
Suratgarh India 36 C3
Surat Thani Thai. 31 I6
Surazh Rus. Fed. 13 G5
Surbiton Australia 56 D4
Surdulica Serbia 27 J3
Surendranagar India 36 B5
Surf *CA* U.S.A. 65 B3
Surgut Rus. Fed. 28 I3
Suri India *see* **Siuri**
Suriapet India 38 C2
Surigao Phil. 41 E7
Surin Thai. 31 J5
Surinam *country* S. America *see* **Suriname**
Suriname *country* S. America 69 G3
Surkhet Nepal 37 E3
Sürmene Turkey 35 F2
Surovikino Rus. Fed. 13 I6
Surpura India 36 C4
Surry *VA* U.S.A. 64 C4
Surskoye Rus. Fed. 13 J5
Surt Libya *see* **Sirte**
Surtsey *i.* Iceland 14 [inset]
Suruç Turkey 39 D1
Surud, Raas *pt* Somalia 48 E2
Surud Ad *mt.* Somalia *see* **Shimbiris**
Suruga-wan *b.* Japan 45 E6
Suryapet India *see* **Suriapet**
Şuşa Azer. 35 G3
Susah Tunisia *see* **Sousse**
Susaki Japan 45 D6
Susan *VA* U.S.A. 64 C4
Süsangerd Iran 35 H5
Susanino Rus. Fed. 44 F1
Susanville U.S.A. 62 C3
Suşehri Turkey 34 E2
Susquehanna *PA* U.S.A. 64 D2
Susquehanna *r. PA* U.S.A. 64 C3
Susquehanna, West Branch *r. PA* U.S.A. 64 C2
Susques Arg. 70 C2
Sussex *VA* U.S.A. 64 C4
Susuman Rus. Fed. 29 P3
Susurluk Turkey 27 M5
Sutak India 36 D2
Sutherland Australia 58 E5
Sutherland S. Africa 50 E7
Sutherland Range *hills* Australia 55 D6
Sutjeska *nat. park* Bos.-Herz. 26 H3
Sutlej *r.* India/Pak. 36 B3
Sütlüce Turkey 39 A1
Sutter *CA* U.S.A. 65 B1
Sutterton U.K. 19 G6
Sutton U.K. 19 H6
Sutton *WV* U.S.A. 64 A3
Sutton Coldfield U.K. 19 F6
Sutton in Ashfield U.K. 19 F5
Sutton Lake *WV* U.S.A. 64 A3
Suttor *r.* Australia 56 D4
Suttsu Japan 44 F4
Sutwik Island U.S.A. 60 C4
Sutyr' *r.* Rus. Fed. 44 D2
Suva Fiji 53 H3
Suvalki Poland *see* **Suwałki**
Suvorov *atoll* Cook Is *see* **Suwarrow**
Suvorov Rus. Fed. 13 H5
Suwa Japan 45 E5
Suwałki Poland 13 D5
Suwanose-jima *i.* Japan 45 C7
Suwarrow *atoll* Cook Is 53 J3
Suwayliḩ Jordan 39 B3
Suwayr *well* Saudi Arabia 35 F5
Suways, Khalīj as *g.* Egypt *see* **Suez, Gulf of**
Suways, Qanāt as *canal* Egypt *see* **Suez Canal**
Suweilih Jordan *see* **Suwayliḩ**
Suweis, Khalîg el *g.* Egypt *see* **Suez, Gulf of**
Suweis, Qanâ el *canal* Egypt *see* **Suez Canal**
Suwŏn S. Korea 45 B5
Suyūl Ḩanīsh *i.* Yemen 32 F7
Suz, Mys *pt* Kazakh. 35 I2
Suzaka Japan 45 E5
Suzdal' Rus. Fed. 12 I4
Suzhou *Anhui* China 43 L6
Suzhou *Jiangsu* China 43 M6
Suzi He *r.* China 44 B4
Suzuka Japan 45 E6
Suzu-misaki *pt* Japan 45 E5
Sværholthalvøya *pen.* Norway 14 O1
Svalbard *terr.* Arctic Ocean 28 C2
Svappavaara Sweden 14 L3
Svartenhuk Halvø *pen.* Greenland *see* **Sigguup Nunaa**
Svatove Ukr. 13 H6
Svecha Rus. Fed. 12 J4
Sveg Sweden 15 I5
Sveki Latvia 15 O8
Svelgen Norway 14 D6
Svellingen Norway 14 F5
Švenčionėliai Lith. 15 N9
Švenčionys Lith. 15 O9
Svendborg Denmark 15 G9
Svensbu Norway 14 K2
Svenstavik Sweden 14 I5
Sverdlovsk Rus. Fed. *see* **Yekaterinburg**
Sverdlovs'k Ukr. 13 H6
Sverdrup Islands Canada 61 I2
Sverige *country* Europe *see* **Sweden**
Sveti Nikole Macedonia 27 I4
Svetlaya Rus. Fed. 44 E3
Svetlogorsk Belarus *see* **Svyetlahorsk**
Svetlogorsk *Kaliningradskaya Oblast'* Rus. Fed. 15 L9
Svetlogorsk *Krasnoyarskiy Kray* Rus. Fed. 28 J3
Svetlograd Rus. Fed. 13 I7
Svetlovodsk Ukr. *see* **Svitlovods'k**
Svetlyy *Kaliningradskaya Oblast'* Rus. Fed. 15 L9
Svetlyy Yar Rus. Fed. 13 J6
Svetogorsk Rus. Fed. 12 F3
Svíahnúkar *vol.* Iceland 14 [inset]
Svilaja *mts* Croatia 26 G3
Svilengrad Bulg. 27 L4
Svinecea Mare, Vârful *mt.* Romania 27 J2
Svir Belarus 15 O9
Svir' *r.* Rus. Fed. 12 G3
Svishtov Bulg. 27 K3
Svitava *r.* Czech Rep. 17 P6
Svitavy Czech Rep. 17 P6
Svitlovods'k Ukr. 13 G6
Sviyaga *r.* Rus. Fed. 12 K5
Svizzer, Parc Naziunal Switz. 26 D1
Svizzera *country* Europe *see* **Switzerland**
Svobodnyy Rus. Fed. 44 C2
Svolvær Norway 14 I2
Svrljiške Planine *mts* Serbia 27 J3
Svyatoy Nos, Mys *c.* Rus. Fed. 12 K2
Svyetlahorsk Belarus 13 F5
Swadlincote U.K. 19 F6
Swaffham U.K. 19 H6
Swain Reefs Australia 56 F4
Swains Island *atoll* American Samoa 53 I3
Swakop *watercourse* Namibia 50 B2
Swakopmund Namibia 50 B2
Swale *r.* U.K. 18 F4
Swallow Islands Solomon Is 53 G3
Swamihalli India 38 C3
Swan *r.* Australia 55 A7
Swanage U.K. 19 F8
Swandale *WV* U.S.A. 64 A3
Swan Hill Australia 58 A5
Swan Lake *Man.* Canada 62 G1
Swanley U.K. 19 H7
Swan Reach Australia 57 B7
Swan River Canada 62 G1
Swansea U.K. 19 D7
Swansea Bay U.K. 19 D7
Swanton *CA* U.S.A. 65 A2
Swartbergpas *pass* S. Africa 50 F7
Swart Nossob *watercourse* Namibia *see* **Black Nossob**
Swartruggens S. Africa 51 H3
Swatow China *see* **Shantou**
Swaziland *country* Africa 51 J4
Sweden *country* Europe 14 I5
Sweet Springs *WV* U.S.A. 64 A4
Sweetwater U.S.A. 62 G5
Sweetwater *r.* U.S.A. 62 F3
Swellendam S. Africa 50 E8
Świdnica Poland 17 P5
Świdwin Poland 17 O4
Świebodzin Poland 17 O4
Świecie Poland 17 Q4
Swift Current Canada 62 F1
Swilly *r.* Ireland 21 E3
Swilly, Lough *inlet* Ireland 21 E2
Swindon U.K. 19 F7
Swinford Ireland 21 D4
Świnoujście Poland 17 O4
Swinton U.K. 20 G5
Swiss Confederation *country* Europe *see* **Switzerland**
Switzerland *country* Europe 24 I3
Swords Ireland 21 F4
Swords Range *hills* Australia 56 C4
Syamozero, Ozero *l.* Rus. Fed. 12 G3
Syamzha Rus. Fed. 12 I3
Syang Nepal 37 E3
Syas'troy Rus. Fed. 12 G3
Sychevka Rus. Fed. 12 G5
Sydenham *atoll* Kiribati *see* **Nonouti**
Sydney Australia 58 E4
Sydney Island Kiribati *see* **Manra**
Syedra *tourist site* Turkey 39 A1
Syeverodonets'k Ukr. 13 H6
Sykesville *PA* U.S.A. 64 B2
Syktyvkar Rus. Fed. 12 K3
Sylarna *mt.* Norway/Sweden 14 H5
Sylhet Bangl. 37 G4
Syloga Rus. Fed. 12 I3
Sylt *i.* Germany 17 L3
Sylvester, Lake *imp. l.* Australia 56 A3
Symi *i.* Greece 27 L6
Synel'nykove Ukr. 13 G6
Syngyrli, Mys *pt* Kazakh. 35 I2
Synya Rus. Fed. 11 R2
Syowa *research stn* Antarctica 76 D2
Syracusae *Sicilia* Italy *see* **Syracuse**
Syracuse *Sicilia* Italy 26 F6
Syracuse *KS* U.S.A. 62 G4
Syracuse *NY* U.S.A. 64 C1
Syrdar'ya *r.* Asia 30 F2
Syrdaryinskiy Uzbek. *see* **Sirdaryo**
Syria *country* Asia 34 E4
Syrian Desert Asia 34 E4
Syrna *i.* Greece 27 L6
Syros *i.* Greece 27 K6
Syrskiy Rus. Fed. 13 H5
Sysmä Fin. 15 N6
Sysola *r.* Rus. Fed. 12 K3
Syumsi Rus. Fed. 12 K4
Syurkum Rus. Fed. 44 F2
Syurkum, Mys *pt* Rus. Fed. 44 F2
Syzran' Rus. Fed. 13 K5
Szabadka Serbia *see* **Subotica**
Szczecin Poland 17 O4
Szczecinek Poland 17 P4
Szczytno Poland 17 R4
Szechwan *prov.* China *see* **Sichuan**
Szeged Hungary 27 I1
Székesfehérvár Hungary 26 H1
Szekszárd Hungary 26 H1
Szentes Hungary 27 I1
Szentgotthárd Hungary 26 G1
Szigetvár Hungary 26 G1
Szolnok Hungary 27 I1
Szombathely Hungary 26 G1
Sztálinváros Hungary *see* **Dunaújváros**

T

Taagga Duudka *reg.* Somalia 48 E3
Tābah Saudi Arabia 32 F4
Tabajara Brazil 68 F5
Tabakhmela Georgia *see* **Kazret'i**
Tabanan Indon. 54 A2
Tabankulu S. Africa 51 I6
Ţabaqah *Ar Raqqah* Syria 39 D2
Ţabaqah *Ar Raqqah* Syria *see* **Madīnat ath Thawrah**
Tabar Islands P.N.G. 52 F2
Tabarka Tunisia 26 C6
Ţabāsīn Iran 33 I3
Ţabask, Kūh-e *mt.* Iran 35 H5
Tabatinga *Amazonas* Brazil 68 E4
Tabatinga *São Paulo* Brazil 71 A3
Tabatinga, Serra da *hills* Brazil 69 J6
Tabatsquri, Tba *l.* Georgia 35 F2
Tabayin Myanmar 37 H5
Tabbita Australia 58 B5
Tabelbala Alg. 22 D6
Tabia Tsaka *salt l.* China 37 F3
Tabiteuea *atoll* Kiribati 53 H2
Tabivere Estonia 15 O7
Table Cape N.Z. 59 F4
Table Mountain Nature Reserve S. Africa 50 D8
Tabligbo Togo 46 D4
Tábor Czech Rep. 17 O6
Tabora Tanz. 49 D4
Tabou Côte d'Ivoire 46 C4
Tabrīz Iran 35 G3
Tabuaeran *atoll* Kiribati 75 J5
Tabūk Saudi Arabia 34 E5
Tabulam Australia 58 F2
Tabwémasana, Mount Vanuatu 53 G3
Täby Sweden 15 K7
Tacalé Brazil 69 H3
Tacheng China 42 E3
Tachov Czech Rep. 17 N6
Tacloban Phil. 41 E6
Tacna Peru 68 D7
Tacoma U.S.A. 62 C2
Taco Pozo Arg. 70 D3
Tacuarembó Uruguay 70 E4
Tadcaster U.K. 18 F5
Tademaït, Plateau du *plat.* Alg. 22 E6
Tadin New Caledonia 53 G4
Tadjikistan *country* Asia *see* **Tajikistan**
Tadjourah Djibouti 32 F7
Tadmur Syria 39 D2
Tadohae Haesang National Park S. Korea 45 B6
Tadoule Lake Canada 61 I4
Tadpatri India 38 C3
Tadwale India 38 C2
Tadzhikskaya S.S.R. *country* Asia *see* **Tajikistan**
T'aean Haean National Park S. Korea 45 B5
Taech'ŏng-do *i.* S. Korea 45 B5
Taedasa-do N. Korea 45 B5
Taedong-man *b.* N. Korea 45 B5
Taegu S. Korea 45 C6
Taehan-min'guk *country* Asia *see* **South Korea**
Taehŭksan-kundo *is* S. Korea 45 B6
Taejŏn S. Korea 45 B5
Taejŏng S. Korea 45 B6
T'aepaek S. Korea 45 C5
Ta'erqi China 43 M3
Taf *r.* U.K. 19 C7
Tafahi *i.* Tonga 53 I3
Tafalla Spain 25 F2
Tafila Jordan *see* **Aţ Ţafilah**
Tafi Viejo Arg. 70 C3
Tafresh Iran 35 H4
Taft Iran 35 I5
Taft *CA* U.S.A. 65 C3
Taftān, Kūh-e *mt.* Iran 33 J4
Taftanāz Syria 39 C2
Taganrog Rus. Fed. 13 H7
Taganrog, Gulf of Rus. Fed./Ukr. 13 H7
Taganrogskiy Zaliv *b.* Rus. Fed./Ukr. *see* **Taganrog, Gulf of**
Tagaung Myanmar 37 I5
Tagchagpu Ri *mt.* China 37 E2
Tagdempt Alg. *see* **Tiaret**
Taghmon Ireland 21 F5
Tagtabazar Turkm. 33 J2
Tagula P.N.G. 56 F1
Tagula Island P.N.G. 56 F1
Tagus *r.* Port. 25 B4
Tagus *r.* Spain 22 C4
Taha China 44 B3
Tahanroz'ka Zatoka *b.* Rus. Fed./Ukr. *see* **Taganrog, Gulf of**
Tahat, Mont *mt.* Alg. 46 D2
Tahe China 44 B1
Taheke N.Z. 59 D2
Tahiti *i.* Fr. Polynesia 75 K7
Tahlequah U.S.A. 63 I4
Tahoe, Lake *CA* U.S.A. 65 B1
Tahoe Lake Canada 61 H3
Tahoe Vista *CA* U.S.A. 65 B1
Tahoua Niger 46 D3
Tahrūd Iran 33 I4
Taï, Parc National de *nat. park* Côte d'Ivoire 46 C4
Tai'an China 43 L5
Taibei Taiwan *see* **T'aipei**
Taibus Qi China *see* **Baochang**
Taidong Taiwan *see* **T'aitung**

The Gambia country Africa 46 B3
The Grampians mts Australia 57 C8
The Great Oasis oasis Egypt see Khārijah, Wāḥāt al
The Grenadines is St Vincent 67 L6
The Gulf Asia 32 H4
The Hague Neth. 16 J4
The Hunters Hills N.Z. 59 C7
The Lakes National Park Australia 58 C6
Thelon r. Canada 61 I3
The Lynd Junction Australia 56 D3
Thembalihle S. Africa 51 I4
The Minch sea chan. U.K. 20 C2
The Naze c. Norway see Lindesnes
The Needles stack U.K. 19 F8
Theni India 38 C4
Thenia Alg. 25 H5
Theniet El Had Alg. 25 H6
The North Sound sea chan. U.K. 20 G1
Theodore Australia 56 E5
Theodosia Ukr. see Feodosiya
The Old Man of Coniston h. U.K. 18 D4
The Paps h. Ireland 21 C5
The Pas Canada 62 G1
The Pilot mt. Australia 58 D6
Thera i. Greece see Santorini
Thermaïkos Kolpos g. Greece 27 J4
Thermopolis U.S.A. 62 F3
The Rock Australia 58 C5
The Salt Lake salt l. Australia 57 C6
The Settlement Christmas I. 74 D4
The Skaw spit Denmark see Grenen
The Skelligs is Ireland 21 B6
The Slot sea chan. Solomon Is see New Georgia Sound
The Solent str. U.K. 19 F8
Thessalon Canada 63 K2
Thessalonica Greece see Thessaloniki
Thessaloniki Greece 27 J4
The Storr h. U.K. 20 C3
Thet r. U.K. 19 H6
The Terraces hills Australia 55 C7
Thetford U.K. 19 H6
Thetford Mines Canada 63 M2
The Triangle mts Myanmar 42 H7
The Trossachs hills U.K. 20 E4
The Twins Australia 57 A6
Theva-i-Ra rf Fiji see Ceva-i-Ra
The Valley Anguilla 67 L5
Thevenard Island Australia 54 A5
Thévenet, Lac l. Canada 61 L4
Theveste Alg. see Tébessa
The Wash b. U.K. 19 H6
The Weald reg. U.K. 19 H7
The Woodlands U.S.A. 63 H5
Thibodaux U.S.A. 63 I6
Thief River Falls U.S.A. 63 H2
Thiel Mountains Antarctica 76 K1
Thiers France 24 F4
Thiès Senegal 46 B3
Thika Kenya 48 D4
Thiladhunmathi Atoll Maldives 38 B5
Thiladunmathi Atoll Maldives see Thiladhunmathi Atoll
Thimbu Bhutan see Thimphu
Thimphu Bhutan 37 G4
Thionville France 24 H2
Thira i. Greece see Santorini
Thirsk U.K. 18 F4
Thiruvananthapuram India see Trivandrum
Thiruvannamalai India see Tiruvannamalai
Thiruvarur India 38 C4
Thiruvattiyur India see Tiruvottiyur
Thisted Denmark 15 F8
Thityabin Myanmar 37 H5
Thiva Greece 27 J5
Thívai Greece see Thiva
Thoen Thai. 42 H9
Thoeng Thai. 42 I9
Thohoyandou S. Africa 51 J2
Thomas Hubbard, Cape Canada 61 I1
Thomaston CT U.S.A. 64 E2
Thomastown Ireland 21 E5
Thomasville GA U.S.A. 63 K5
Thompson Canada 61 I4
Thompson r. U.S.A. 62 I4
Thompson Falls U.S.A. 62 D2
Thompson's Falls Kenya see Nyahururu
Thompson Sound Canada 62 B1
Thoothukudi India see Tuticorin
Thorn Poland see Toruń
Thornaby-on-Tees U.K. 18 F4
Thornbury U.K. 19 E7
Thorne U.K. 18 G5
Thorne NV U.S.A. 65 C1
Thornton r. Australia 56 B3
Thorshavnfjella reg. Antarctica see Thorshavnheiane
Thorshavnheiane reg. Antarctica 76 C2
Thota-ea-Moli Lesotho 51 H5
Thouars France 24 D3
Thoubal India 37 H4
Thousand Oaks CA U.S.A. 65 C3
Thrace reg. Europe 27 L4
Thraki reg. Europe see Thrace
Thrakiko Pelagos sea Greece 27 K4
Three Gorges Reservoir resr China 43 J6
Three Hummock Island Australia 57 [inset]
Three Kings Islands N.Z. 59 D2
Three Points, Cape Ghana 46 C4
Three Springs Australia 55 A7
Thrissur India see Trichur
Throssell, Lake imp. l. Australia 55 D6
Throssel Range hills Australia 54 C5
Thrushton National Park Australia 58 C1
Thuddungra Australia 58 D5
Thul Pak. 36 B3
Thulaythawāt Gharbī, Jabal h. Syria 39 D2
Thule Greenland 61 L2
Thun Switz. 24 H3
Thunder Bay Canada 61 J5
Thurles Ireland 21 E5
Thurn, Pass Austria 17 N7
Thursday Island Australia 56 C1
Thurso U.K. 20 F2
Thurso r. U.K. 20 F2
Thurston Island Antarctica 76 K2
Thurston Peninsula i. Antarctica see Thurston Island
Thuthukudi India see Tuticorin
Thwaite U.K. 18 E4
Thwaites Glacier Tongue Antarctica 76 K1
Thyatira Turkey see Akhisar
Thyborøn Denmark 15 F8
T'ianet'i Georgia 35 G2
Tianjin China 43 L5
Tianjin mun. China 43 L5
Tianjun China 42 H5
Tianqiaoling China 44 C4
Tianshan China 43 M4
Tian Shan mts China/Kyrg. see Tien Shan
Tianshui China 42 J6
Tianshuihai Aksai Chin 36 D2
Tiantang China see Yuexi
Tianzhu Gansu China 42 I5
Tiaret Alg. 25 G6
Tiassalé Côte d'Ivoire 46 C4
Tibagi Brazil 71 A4
Tibal, Wādī watercourse Iraq 35 F4
Tibati Cameroon 46 E4
Tibba Pak. 36 B3
Tibé, Pic de mt. Guinea 46 C4
Tiber r. Italy 26 E4
Tiberias Israel 39 B3
Tiberias, Lake Israel see Galilee, Sea of
Tibesti mts Chad 47 E2
Tibet aut. reg. China see Xizang Zizhiqu
Tibet, Plateau of China 37 F2
Tibooburra Australia 57 C6
Tibrikot Nepal 37 E3
Tibro Sweden 15 I7
Tibur Italy see Tivoli
Tiburón, Isla i. Mex. 66 B3
Ticehurst U.K. 19 H7
Tîchît Mauritania 46 C3
Tichla W. Sahara 46 B2
Ticinum Italy see Pavia
Ticul Mex. 66 G4
Tidaholm Sweden 15 H7
Tiddim Myanmar 37 H5
Tidjikja Mauritania 46 B3
Tieli China 44 B3
Tieling China 44 A4
Tielongtan Aksai Chin 36 D2
Tien Shan mts China/Kyrg. 42 D4
Tientsin mun. China see Tianjin
Tierp Sweden 15 J6
Tierra del Fuego, Isla Grande de i. Arg./Chile 70 C8
Tierra del Fuego, Parque Nacional nat. park Arg. 70 C8
Tiétar r. Spain 25 D4
Tiétar, Valle de val. Spain 25 D3
Tietê r. Brazil 71 A3
Tieyon Australia 55 F6
Tiflis Georgia see T'bilisi
Tifton U.S.A. 63 K5
Tiga Reservoir Nigeria 46 D3
Tigen Kazakh. 35 H1
Tigheciului, Dealurile hills Moldova 27 M2
Tighina Moldova 27 M1
Tigiria India 38 E1
Tignère Cameroon 46 E4
Tignish Canada 63 O2
Tigranocerta Turkey see Siirt
Tigre r. Venez. 68 F2
Tigris r. Asia 32 F2
Tigris r. Asia 35 G5
Tigrovaya Balka Zapovednik nature res. Tajik. 36 B1
Tiguidit, Falaise de esc. Niger 46 D3
Tīh, Gebel el plat. Egypt see Tīh, Jabal at
Tīh, Jabal at plat. Egypt 39 A5
Tijuana Mex. 66 A2
Tikamgarh India 36 D4
Tikanlik China 42 F4
Tikhoretsk Rus. Fed. 13 I7
Tikhvin Rus. Fed. 12 G4
Tikhvinskaya Gryada ridge Rus. Fed. 12 G4
Tiki Basin sea feature S. Pacific Ocean 75 L7
Tikokino N.Z. 59 F4
Tikopia i. Solomon Is 53 G3
Tikrīt Iraq 35 F4
Tikse India 36 D2
Tikshozero, Ozero l. Rus. Fed. 14 R3
Tiksi Rus. Fed. 29 N2
Tiladummati Atoll Maldives see Thiladhunmathi Atoll
Tilaiya Reservoir India 37 F4
Tilbeşar Ovasi plain Turkey 39 C1
Tilbooroo Australia 58 B1
Tilburg Neth. 16 J5
Tilbury U.K. 19 H7
Tilcara Arg. 70 C2
Tilcha Creek watercourse Australia 57 C6
Tilemsès Niger 46 D3
Tilemsi, Vallée du watercourse Mali 46 D3
Tilhar India 36 D4
Tilimsen Alg. see Tlemcen
Tilin Myanmar 37 H5
Tillabéri Niger 46 D3
Tillia Niger 46 D3
Tillicoultry U.K. 20 F4
Tillsonburg Ont. Canada 64 A1
Tillyfourie U.K. 20 G3
Tilos i. Greece 27 L6
Tilothu India 37 F4
Tilpa Australia 58 B3
Tilsit Rus. Fed. see Sovetsk
Tilt r. U.K. 20 F4
Tilton NH U.S.A. 64 F1
Tim Rus. Fed. 13 H6
Ṭīmā Egypt 32 D4
Timakara i. India 38 B4
Timanskiy Kryazh ridge Rus. Fed. 12 K2
Timar Turkey 35 F3
Timaru N.Z. 59 C7
Timashevsk Rus. Fed. 13 H7
Timashevskaya Rus. Fed. see Timashevsk
Timbedgha Mauritania 46 C3
Timber Creek Australia 52 D3
Timber Mountain NV U.S.A. 65 D2
Timberville VA U.S.A. 64 B3
Timbuktu Mali 46 C3
Timétrine reg. Mali 46 C3
Timiaouine Alg. 46 D2
Timimoun Alg. 22 E6
Timirist, Râs pt Mauritania 46 B3
Timişoara Romania 27 I2
Timmins Canada 61 J5
Timon Brazil 69 J5
Timor i. Indon. 54 D2
Timor-Leste country Asia see East Timor
Timor Loro Sae country Asia see East Timor
Timor Sea Australia/Indon. 52 C3
Timor Timur country Asia see East Timor
Timperley Range hills Australia 55 C6
Timrå Sweden 14 J5
Tīn, Ra's at pt Libya 34 A4
Tîna, Khalîg el b. Egypt see Ţīnah, Khalīj aţ
Tinah Syria 39 D1
Ţīnah, Khalīj aţ b. Egypt 39 A4
Tin Can Bay Australia 57 F5
Tindivanam India 38 C3
Tindouf Alg. 22 C6
Ti-n-Essako Mali 46 D3
Tingha Australia 58 E2
Tingis Morocco see Tangier
Tingo María Peru 68 C5
Tingréla Côte d'Ivoire see Tengréla
Tingsryd Sweden 15 I8
Tingvoll Norway 14 F5
Tingwall U.K. 20 F1
Tinharé, Ilha de i. Brazil 71 D1
Tinian i. N. Mariana Is 41 G6
Tini Heke is N.Z. see Snares Islands
Tinnelvelly India see Tirunelveli
Tinogasta Arg. 70 C3
Tinos Greece 27 K6
Tinos i. Greece 27 K6
Tinrhert, Hamada de Alg. 46 D2
Tinsukia India 37 H4
Tintagel U.K. 19 C8
Tîntâne Mauritania 46 B3
Tintina Arg. 70 D3
Tintinara Australia 57 C7
Tionesta PA U.S.A. 64 B2
Tionesta Lake PA U.S.A. 64 B2
Tipasa Alg. 25 H5
Tiphsah Syria see Dibsī
Tipperary Ireland 21 D5
Tipton CA U.S.A. 65 C2
Tipton, Mount AZ U.S.A. 65 E3
Tiptree U.K. 19 H7
Tiptur India 38 C3
Tipturi India see Tiptur
Tiracambu, Serra do hills Brazil 69 I4
Tirana Albania 27 H4
Tiranë Albania see Tirana
Tirano Italy 26 D1
Tirari Desert Australia 57 B5
Tiraspol Moldova 27 M1
Tiraz Mountains Namibia 50 C4
Tire Turkey 27 L5
Tirebolu Turkey 35 E2
Tiree i. U.K. 20 C4
Tîrgovişte Romania see Târgovişte
Tîrgu Jiu Romania see Târgu Jiu
Tîrgu Mureş Romania see Târgu Mureş
Tîrgu Neamţ Romania see Târgu Neamţ
Tîrgu Secuiesc Romania see Târgu Secuiesc
Tiri Pak. 36 A3
Tirich Mir mt. Pak. 33 L2
Tirna r. India 38 C2
Tîrnăveni Romania see Târnăveni
Tírnavos Greece see Tyrnavos
Tiros Brazil 71 B2
Tirourda, Col de pass Alg. 25 I5
Tirreno, Mare sea France/Italy see Tyrrhenian Sea
Tirso r. Sardegna Italy 26 C5
Tirthahalli India 38 B3
Tiruchchendur India 38 C4
Tiruchchirappalli India 38 C4
Tiruchengodu India 38 C4
Tirunelveli India 38 C4
Tirupati India 38 C3
Tiruppattur Tamil Nadu India 38 C3
Tiruppattur Tamil Nadu India 38 C4
Tiruppur India 38 C4
Tiruttani India 38 C3
Tirutturaippundi India 38 C4
Tiruvallur India 38 C3
Tiruvannamalai India 38 C3
Tiruvottiyur India 38 D3
Tiru Well Australia 54 D5
Tisa r. Serbia 27 I2
Tisdale Canada 62 G1
Tisīyah Syria 39 C3
Tissemsilt Alg. 25 G6
Tisza r. Serbia see Tisa
Titalya Bangl. see Tetulia
Titan Dome Antarctica 76 H1
Titao Burkina 46 C3
Tit-Ary Rus. Fed. 29 N2
Titawin Morocco see Tétouan
Titicaca, Lago Bol./Peru see Titicaca, Lake
Titicaca, Lake Bol./Peru 68 E7
Titi Islands N.Z. 59 A8
Tititea mt. N.Z. see Aspiring, Mount
Titlagarh India 38 D1
Titograd Montenegro see Podgorica
Titova Mitrovica Kosovo see Mitrovicë
Titovo Užice Serbia see Užice
Titovo Velenje Slovenia see Velenje
Titov Veles Macedonia see Veles
Titov Vrbas Serbia see Vrbas
Ti Tree Australia 54 F5
Titu Romania 27 K2
Titusville FL U.S.A. 63 K6
Titusville PA U.S.A. 64 B2
Tiumpain, Rubha an hd U.K. see Tiumpan Head
Tiumpan Head hd U.K. 20 C2
Tiva watercourse Kenya 48 D4
Tivari India 36 C4
Tiverton U.K. 19 D8
Tivoli Italy 26 E4
Ţīwī Oman 33 I5
Tizi El Arba h. Alg. 25 H5
Tizimín Mex. 66 G4
Tizi N'Kouilal pass Alg. 25 I5
Tizi Ouzou Alg. 25 I5
Tiznap He r. China 36 D1
Tiznit Morocco 46 C2
Tiztoutine Morocco 25 E6
Tjaneni Swaziland 51 J3
Tjappsåive Sweden 14 K4
Tjirebon Indon. see Cirebon
Tjolotjo Zimbabwe see Tsholotsho
Tjorhom Norway 15 E7
Tkibuli Georgia see Tqibuli
Tlahualilo Mex. 62 G6
Tlaxcala Mex. 66 E5
Tlemcen Alg. 25 F6
Tlhakalatlou S. Africa 50 F5
Tlholong S. Africa 51 I5
Tlokweng Botswana 51 G3
Tlyarata Rus. Fed. 35 G2
Toamasina Madag. 49 E5
Toano VA U.S.A. 64 C4
Toba China 37 I3
Toba and Kakar Ranges mts Pak. 33 K3
Tobago i. Trin. and Tob. 67 L6
Tobelo Indon. 41 E7
Tobercurry Ireland 21 D3
Tobermorey Australia 56 B4
Tobermory Australia 58 A1
Tobermory Canada 63 K2
Tobermory U.K. 20 C4
Tobin, Lake imp. l. Australia 54 D5
Tobin Lake Canada 62 G1
Tobi-shima i. Japan 45 E5
Tobol r. Kazakh./Rus. Fed. 30 F1
Tobol'sk Rus. Fed. 28 H4
Tobruk Libya see Tubruq
Tobseda Rus. Fed. 12 L1
Tobyl r. Kazakh./Rus. Fed. see Tobol
Tobysh r. Rus. Fed. 12 K2
Tocache Nuevo Peru 68 C5
Tocantinópolis Brazil 69 I5
Tocantins r. Brazil 71 A1
Tocantins state Brazil 71 A1
Tocantinzinha r. Brazil 71 A1
Toccoa U.S.A. 63 K5
Tochi r. Pak. 36 B2
Töcksfors Sweden 15 G7
Tocopilla Chile 70 B2
Tocumwal Australia 58 B5
Todd watercourse Australia 56 A5
Todi Italy 26 E3
Todoga-saki pt Japan 45 F5
Todos Santos Mex. 66 B4
Toe Head hd U.K. 20 B3
Tofino Canada 62 B2
Toft U.K. 20 [inset]
Tofua i. Tonga 53 I3
Togatax China 36 E2
Togian, Kepulauan is Indon. 41 E8
Togliatti Rus. Fed. see Tol'yatti
Togo country Africa 46 D4
Togtoh China 43 K4
Togton He r. China 37 H2
Togton Heyan China see Tanggulashan
Toholampi Fin. 14 N5
Toiba China 37 G3
Toijala Fin. 15 M6
Toi-misaki pt Japan 45 C7
Toivakka Fin. 14 O5
Toiyabe Range mts NV U.S.A. 65 D1
Tojikiston country Asia see Tajikistan
Tok U.S.A. 60 D3
Tokar Sudan 32 E6
Tokara-rettō is Japan 45 C7
Tokarevka Rus. Fed. 13 I6
Tokat Turkey 34 E2
Tŏkchŏk-to i. S. Korea 45 B5
Tokdo i. N. Pacific Ocean see Liancourt Rocks
Tokelau terr. S. Pacific Ocean 53 I2
Tokmak Kyrg. see Tokmok
Tokmak Ukr. 13 G7
Tokmok Kyrg. 42 D4
Tokomaru Bay N.Z. 59 G4
Tokoroa N.Z. 59 E4
Tokoza S. Africa 51 I4
Toksun China 42 F4
Tok-to i. N. Pacific Ocean see Liancourt Rocks
Toktogul Kyrg. 42 C4
Tokto-ri i. N. Pacific Ocean see Liancourt Rocks
Tokur Rus. Fed. 44 D1
Tokushima Japan 45 D6
Tokuyama Japan 45 C6
Tōkyō Japan 45 E6
Tokzār Afgh. 36 A2
Tolaga Bay N.Z. 59 G4
Tôlañaro Madag. 49 E6
Tolbo Mongolia 42 G3
Tolbukhin Bulg. see Dobrich
Tolbuzino Rus. Fed. 44 B1
Toledo Brazil 70 F2
Toledo Spain 25 D4
Toledo OH U.S.A. 63 K3
Toledo, Montes de mts Spain 25 D4
Toletum Spain see Toledo
Toliara Madag. 49 E6
Tolitoli Indon. 41 E7
Tol'ka Rus. Fed. 28 J3
Tolmachevo Rus. Fed. 15 P7
Tolo Dem. Rep. Congo 48 B4
Tolochin Belarus see Talachyn
Tolosa France see Toulouse
Tolosa Spain 25 E2
Toluca Mex. 66 E5
Toluca de Lerdo Mex. see Toluca
To-lun Nei Mongol China see Dolonnur
Tol'yatti Rus. Fed. 13 K5
Tom' r. Rus. Fed. 44 B2
Tomah U.S.A. 63 I3
Tomakomai Japan 44 F4
Tomales CA U.S.A. 65 A1
Tomamae Japan 44 F3
Tomanivi mt. Fiji 53 H3
Tomar Brazil 68 F4
Tomar Port. 25 B4
Tomari Rus. Fed. 44 F3
Tomarza Turkey 34 D3
Tomaszów Lubelski Poland 13 D6
Tomaszów Mazowiecki Poland 17 R5
Tomatin U.K. 20 F3
Tomatlán Mex. 66 C5
Tomazina Brazil 71 A3
Tombador, Serra do hills Brazil 69 G6
Tombigbee r. U.S.A. 63 J5
Tomboco Angola 49 B4
Tombouctou Mali see Timbuktu
Tombua Angola 49 B5
Tom Burke S. Africa 51 H2
Tomdibuloq Uzbek. 33 J1
Tome Moz. 51 L2
Tomelilla Sweden 15 H9
Tomelloso Spain 25 E4
Tomi Romania see Constanţa
Tomingley Australia 58 D4
Tomini, Teluk g. Indon. 41 E8
Tominian Mali 46 C3
Tomintoul U.K. 20 F3
Tomislavgrad Bos.-Herz. 26 G3
Tomkinson Ranges mts Australia 55 E6
Tømmerneset Norway 14 I3
Tommot Rus. Fed. 29 N4
Tomo r. Col. 68 E2
Tomortei China 43 K4
Tom Price Australia 54 B5
Tomra China 37 F3
Tomsk Rus. Fed. 28 J4
Toms River NJ U.S.A. 64 D3
Tomtabacken h. Sweden 15 I8
Tomtor Rus. Fed. 29 P3
Tomur Feng mt. China/Kyrg. see Pobeda Peak
Tomuzlovka r. Rus. Fed. 13 J7
Tom White, Mount U.S.A. 60 D3
Tonalá Mex. 66 F5
Tonantins Brazil 68 E4
Tonbridge U.K. 19 H7
Tønder Denmark 15 F9
Tondi India 38 C4
Tone r. U.K. 19 E7
Toney Mountain Antarctica 76 K1
Tonga country S. Pacific Ocean 53 I4
Tongaat S. Africa 51 J5
Tongariro National Park N.Z. 59 E4
Tongatapu Group is Tonga 53 I4
Tonga Trench sea feature S. Pacific Ocean 74 I7
T'ongch'ŏn N. Korea 45 B5
Tongchuan Shaanxi China 43 J5
Tongduch'ŏn S. Korea 45 B5
Tonghae S. Korea 45 C5
Tonghe China 44 C3
Tonghua Jilin China 44 B4
Tonghua Jilin China 44 B4
Tongi Bangl. see Tungi
Tongjiang Heilong. China 44 D3
Tongking, Gulf of China/Vietnam 31 J4
Tongliao China 43 M4
Tongling China 43 L6
Tonglu China 43 L7
Tongo Australia 58 A3
Tongo Lake imp. l. Australia 58 A3
Tongren Guizhou China 43 J7
Tongren Qinghai China 42 I5
Tongsa Bhutan 37 G4
Tongtian He r. Qinghai China 37 H2
Tongtian He r. Qinghai China see Yangtze
Tongue U.K. 20 E2
Tongxin China 42 J5
T'ongyŏng S. Korea 45 C6
Tonk India 36 C4
Tonkābon Iran 35 H3
Tônlé Sab l. Cambodia see Tonle Sap
Tonle Sap l. Cambodia 31 J5
Tonopah AZ U.S.A. 65 F4
Tonopah NV U.S.A. 65 D1
Tønsberg Norway 15 G7
Tonstad Norway 15 E7
Tonzang Myanmar 37 H5
Toobeah Australia 58 D2
Toobli Liberia 46 C4
Tooele U.S.A. 62 E3
Toogoolawah Australia 58 F1
Tooma r. Australia 58 D6
Toompine Australia 58 B1
Toora Australia 58 C7
Tooraweenah Australia 58 D3
Toorberg mt. S. Africa 50 G7
Toowoomba Australia 58 E1
Tooxin Somalia 48 F2
Top Afgh. 36 B2
Top Boğazı Geçidi pass Turkey 39 C1
Topeka U.S.A. 63 H4
Topia Mex. 66 C3
Topoľčany Slovakia 17 Q6
Topolovgrad Bulg. 27 L3
Topozero, Ozero l. Rus. Fed. 12 G2
Tor Eth. 47 G4
Tor Baldak mt. Afgh. 36 A3
Torbalı Turkey 27 L5
Torbat-e Heydarīyeh Iran 33 I2
Torbat-e Jām Iran 33 J2
Torbay Bay Australia 55 B8
Torbert, Mount U.S.A. 60 C3
Torbeyevo Rus. Fed. 13 I5
Tordesillas Spain 25 D3
Tordesilos Spain 25 F3
Töre Sweden 14 M4
Torelló Spain 25 H2
Toretam Kazakh. see Baykonyr
Torgau Germany 17 N5
Torghay Kazakh. see Turgay
Torgun r. Rus. Fed. 13 J6
Torino Italy see Turin
Tori-shima i. Japan 45 F7
Torit Sudan 47 G4
Torkamān Iran 35 G3
Torkovichi Rus. Fed. 12 F4
Torneå Fin. see Tornio
Torneälven r. Sweden 14 N4
Torneträsk l. Sweden 14 K2
Torngat, Monts mts Canada see Torngat Mountains
Torngat Mountains Canada 61 L4
Tornio Fin. 14 N4
Toro Spain 25 D3
Torom Rus. Fed. 44 D1
Toronto Canada 61 K5
Toro Peak CA U.S.A. 65 D4
Toropets Rus. Fed. 12 F4
Tororo Uganda 48 D3
Toros Dağları mts Turkey see Taurus Mountains
Torphins U.K. 20 G3
Torquay Australia 58 B7
Torquay U.K. 19 D8
Torrance CA U.S.A. 65 C4
Torrão Port. 25 B4
Torre mt. Port. 25 C3
Torreblanca Spain 25 G3
Torrecerredo mt. Spain 25 D2
Torre del Greco Italy 26 F4
Torre de Moncorvo Port. 25 C3
Torrelavega Spain 25 D2
Torremolinos Spain 25 D5
Torrens, Lake imp. l. Australia 57 B6
Torrens Creek Australia 56 D4
Torrent Spain 25 F4
Torrente Spain see Torrent
Torreón Mex. 66 D3
Torres Brazil 71 A5
Torres del Paine, Parque Nacional nat. park Chile 70 B8
Torres Islands Vanuatu 53 G3
Torres Novas Port. 25 B4
Torres Strait Australia 52 E2
Torres Vedras Port. 25 B4
Torrevieja Spain 25 F5
Torridge r. U.K. 19 C8
Torridon, Loch b. U.K. 20 D3
Torrijos Spain 25 D4
Torrington Australia 58 E2
Torsby Sweden 15 H6
Tórshavn Faroe Is 14 [inset]
To'rtko'l Uzbek. 33 J1
Tŏrtkŭl Uzbek. see To'rtko'l
Tortoli Sardegna Italy 26 C5
Tortona Italy 26 C2
Tortosa Spain 25 G3
Tortum Turkey 35 F2
Ţorūd Iran 35 I4
Torugart, Pereval pass China/Kyrg. see Turugart Pass
Torul Turkey 35 E2
Toruń Poland 17 Q4
Tory Island Ireland 21 D2
Tory Sound sea chan. Ireland 21 D2
Torzhok Rus. Fed. 12 G4
Tosa Japan 45 D6
Tosbotn Norway 14 H4
Tosca S. Africa 50 F3
Toscano, Arcipelago is Italy 26 C3
Tosham India 36 C3
Tōshima-yama mt. Japan 45 F4
Toshkent Uzbek. 33 K1
Tosno Rus. Fed. 12 F4
Toson Hu l. China 37 I1
Tostado Arg. 70 D3
Tosya Turkey 34 D2
Totapola mt. Sri Lanka 38 D5
Tôtes France 19 I9
Tot'ma Rus. Fed. 12 I4
Totness Suriname 69 G2
Tottenham Australia 58 C4
Totton U.K. 19 F8
Tottori Japan 45 D6
Touba Côte d'Ivoire 46 C4
Touba Senegal 46 B3
Toubkal, Jbel mt. Morocco 22 C5
Toubkal, Parc National du nat. park Morocco 22 C5
Touboro Cameroon 47 E4
Tougan Burkina 46 C3
Touggourt Alg. 22 F5
Tougué Guinea 46 B3
Touil Mauritania 46 B3
Toul France 24 G2
Toulon France 24 G5
Toulouse France 24 E5
Toumodi Côte d'Ivoire 46 C4
Tourane Vietnam see Đa Nâng
Tourlaville France 19 F9
Tournai Belgium 16 I5
Tournon-sur-Rhône France 24 G4
Tournus France 26 A1
Touros Brazil 69 K5
Tours France 24 E3
Toussidé, Pic mt. Chad 47 E2
Toussoro, Mont mt. Cent. Afr. Rep. 48 C3
Toutai China 44 B3
Touwsrivier S. Africa 50 E7
Tovarkovo Rus. Fed. 13 G5
Tovuz Azer. 35 G2
Towada Japan 44 F4
Towak Mountain h. U.S.A. 60 B3
Towanda PA U.S.A. 64 C2
Towcester U.K. 19 G6
Tower Ireland 21 D6
Townes Pass CA U.S.A. 65 D2
Townsend U.S.A. 62 E2
Townsend, Mount Australia 58 D6
Townshend Island Australia 56 E4
Townsville Australia 56 D3
Towot Sudan 47 G4
Towr Kham Afgh. 36 B2
Towson MD U.S.A. 64 C3
Towyn U.K. see Tywyn
Toyama Japan 45 E5
Toyama-wan b. Japan 45 E5
Toyohashi Japan 45 E6
Toyokawa Japan 45 E6
Toyonaka Japan 45 D6
Toyooka Japan 45 D6
Toyota Japan 45 E6
Tozanlı Turkey see Almus
Tozê Kangri mt. China 37 E2
Tozeur Tunisia 22 F5
Tozi, Mount U.S.A. 60 C3
Tqibuli Georgia 35 F2
Trâblous Lebanon see Tripoli
Trabotivište Macedonia 27 J4
Trabzon Turkey 35 E2
Tracy CA U.S.A. 65 B2
Trafalgar, Cabo c. Spain 25 C5
Tràille, Rubha na pt U.K. 20 D5
Traill Island Greenland see Traill Ø
Traill Ø i. Greenland 61 P2
Trajectum Neth. see Utrecht
Trakai Lith. 15 N9
Trakiya reg. Europe see Thrace
Trakt Rus. Fed. 12 K3
Trakya reg. Europe see Thrace
Tralee Ireland 21 C5
Tralee Bay Ireland 21 C5
Trá Li Ireland see Tralee
Tramandaí Brazil 71 A5
Tramán Tepuí mt. Venez. 68 F2
Trá Mhór Ireland see Tramore
Tramore Ireland 21 E5
Tranås Sweden 15 I7
Trancas Arg. 70 C3
Trancoso Brazil 71 D2
Tranemo Sweden 15 H8
Tranent U.K. 20 G5
Trangan i. Indon. 41 F8
Trangie Australia 58 C4
Transantarctic Mountains Antarctica 76 H2
Transylvanian Alps mts Romania 27 J2
Transylvanian Basin plat. Romania 27 K1
Trapani Sicilia Italy 26 E5
Trapezus Turkey see Trabzon
Traralgon Australia 58 C7
Trashigang Bhutan see Tashigang
Trasimeno, Lago l. Italy 26 E3
Trasvase, Canal de Spain 25 E4
Traunsee l. Austria 17 N7
Traunstein Germany 17 N7
Travellers Lake imp. l. Australia 57 C7
Travers, Mount N.Z. 59 D6
Traverse City U.S.A. 63 J3
Travnik Bos.-Herz. 26 G2
Trbovlje Slovenia 26 F1
Treasury Islands Solomon Is 52 F2
Trebević nat. park Bos.-Herz. 26 H3
Třebíč Czech Rep. 17 O6
Trebinje Bos.-Herz. 26 H3
Trebišov Slovakia 13 D6
Trebizond Turkey see Trabzon
Trebnje Slovenia 26 F2
Tree Island India 38 B4
Trefaldwyn U.K. see Montgomery
Treffynnon U.K. see Holywell
Trefyclawdd U.K. see Knighton
Trefynwy U.K. see Monmouth
Tregosse Islets and Reefs Australia 56 E3
Treinta y Tres Uruguay 70 F4
Trelew Arg. 70 C6
Trelleborg Sweden 15 H9
Tremblant, Mont h. Canada 63 M2
Tremiti, Isole is Italy 26 F3
Tremont PA U.S.A. 64 C2
Tremonton U.S.A. 62 E3
Tremp Spain 25 G2
Trenance U.K. 19 B8
Trenčín Slovakia 17 Q6
Trenque Lauquén Arg. 70 D5
Trent Italy see Trento
Trent r. U.K. 19 G5
Trento Italy 26 D1
Trenton Canada 63 L3
Trenton MO U.S.A. 63 I3
Trenton NJ U.S.A. 64 D2
Treorchy U.K. 19 D7
Trepassey Canada 61 M5
Tres Arroyos Arg. 70 D5
Tresco i. U.K. 19 A9
Três Corações Brazil 71 B3
Tres Esquinas Col. 68 C3
Tres Forcas, Cabo c. Morocco see Trois Fourches, Cap des
Três Lagoas Brazil 71 A3
Três Marias, Represa resr Brazil 71 B2
Tres Picos, Cerro mt. Arg. 70 D5
Três Pontas Brazil 71 B3
Tres Puntas, Cabo c. Arg. 70 C7
Três Rios Brazil 71 C3
Tretten Norway 15 G6
Tretyy Severnyy Rus. Fed. see 3-y Severnyy
Treungen Norway 15 F7
Treves Germany see Trier
Treviglio Italy 26 C2
Treviso Italy 26 E2
Trevose Head hd U.K. 19 B8
Triánda Greece see Trianta
Triangle VA U.S.A. 64 C3
Trianta Greece 27 M6
Tribal Areas admin. div. Pak. 36 B2
Tri Brata, Gora h. Rus. Fed. 44 F1
Tricase Italy 26 H5
Trichinopoly India see Tiruchchirappalli
Trichur India 38 C4
Trida Australia 58 B4
Tridentum Italy see Trento
Trier Germany 17 K6
Trieste Italy 26 E2
Trieste, Golfo di g. Europe see Trieste, Gulf of
Trieste, Gulf of Europe 26 E2
Triglav mt. Slovenia 26 E1
Triglavski narodni park nat. park Slovenia 26 E1
Trikala Greece 27 I5
Tríkkala Greece see Trikala
Trikora, Puncak mt. Indon. 41 F8
Trim Ireland 21 F4
Trincomalee Sri Lanka 38 D4
Trindade Brazil 71 A2
Trindade, Ilha da i. S. Atlantic Ocean 72 G7
Trinidad Bol. 68 F6
Trinidad Cuba 67 I4
Trinidad i. Trin. and Tob. 67 L6
Trinidad Uruguay 70 E4
Trinidad U.S.A. 62 G4
Trinidad country West Indies see Trinidad and Tobago
Trinidad and Tobago country West Indies 67 L6
Trinity Bay Canada 61 M5
Trinity Islands U.S.A. 60 C4
Trionto, Capo c. Italy 26 G5
Tripoli Greece 27 J6
Tripoli Lebanon 39 B2
Tripoli Libya 47 E1
Trípolis Greece see Tripoli
Tripolis Lebanon see Tripoli
Tripunittura India 38 C4
Tripura state India 37 G5
Tristan da Cunha i. S. Atlantic Ocean 72 H8
Trisul mt. India 36 D3
Trivandrum India 38 C4
Trivento Italy 26 F4

...hava Slovakia 17 P6
...obriand Islands P.N.G. 52 F2
...ofors Norway 14 H4
...ogir Croatia 26 G3
...isdorf Germany 17 K5
...ia Italy 26 H4
...ois Fourches, Cap des i. Morocco 25 E6
...ois-Rivières Canada 63 M2
...oitsko-Pechorsk Rus. Fed. 11 R3
...oitskoye Altayskiy Kray Rus. Fed. 42 E2
...oitskoye Khabarovskiy Kray Rus. Fed.
   44 E2
...oitskoye Respublika Kalmykiya-Khalm'g-
   Tangch Rus. Fed. 13 J7
...oll research trn 76 B2
...ollhättan Sweden 15 H7
...ombetas r. Brazil 69 G4
...omelin, Île i. Indian Ocean 73 L7
...omen, Volcán vol. Arg. 70 B5
...omie r. U.K. 20 E5
...omsø Norway 14 K2
...ona CA U.S.A. 65 D3
...ondador, Monte mt. Arg. 70 B6
...ondheim Norway 14 G4
...ondheimsfjorden sea chan. Norway 14 F5
...ongsa Bhutan see Tongsa
...ōdos, Mount Cyprus 39 A2
...on U.K. 20 E5
...opeiros, Serra dos hills Brazil 71 B1
...osh Iran, Fed. 11
...ostan h. U.K. 21 F2
...out Lake Alta Canada 60 G4
...out Lake N.W.T. Canada 60 F3
...out Lake Ont. Canada 63 I1
...out Run U.S.A. 64 C2
...ouville-sur-Mer France 19 H9
...owbridge U.K. 19 E7
...oy tourist site Turkey 27 L5
...oy AL U.S.A. 63 J5
...oy NH U.S.A. 64 E1
...oy NY U.S.A. 64 E1
...oy PA U.S.A. 64 D2
...oyan Bulg. 27 K3
...oyes France 24 G2
...oy Lake CA U.S.A. 65 D3
...oy Peak NV U.S.A. 65 F2
...stenik Serbia 27 I3
...ucial Coast country Asia see
   United Arab Emirates
...ucial States country Asia see
   United Arab Emirates
...ujal r. Fed. 12 G4
...ufanovo Rus. Fed. 12 J2
...ujillo Hond. 67 G5
...ujillo Peru 68 C5
...ujillo Spain 25 D4
...ujillo Venez. 68 D2
...ujillo, Monte mt. Dom. Rep. see
   Duarte, Pico
...uk is Micronesia see Chuuk
...umbull, Mount AZ U.S.A. 65 F2
...undle Australia 55 F2
...uong Sa is S. China Sea see
   Spratly Islands
...uro Canada 63 O2
...uro U.K. 19 B8
...uskmore h. Ireland 21 D3
...uth or Consequences NM U.S.A. 62 F5
...uli Peak U.S.A. 62 F4
...uva tourist site Turkey see Troy
...ypiti, Akrotirio pt Greece 27 K7
...ysil Norway 15 H6
...zebiatów Poland 17 O3
...agaan-Uul Mongolia 42 H3
...agaan-Uul Mongolia see Tsagaan-Uul
...agan Aman Rus. Fed. 13 J7
...agan-Nur Rus. Fed. 13 J7
...aidam Basin China see Qaidam Pendi
...aka La pass China/India 36 D2
...alenjikha Georgia 35 F2
...angbo r. China see Brahmaputra
...angpo r. China see Brahmaputra
...aratanana, Massif du mts Madag. 49 E5
...arevo Bulg. 27 L4
...aris Mountains Namibia 50 C3
...aritsyn Rus. Fed. see Volgograd
...aukaib Namibia 50 B4
...avo East National Park Kenya 48 D4
...avo West National Park Africa 48 D3
...efat Israel see Zefat
...selinograd Kazakh. see Astana
...senhermandal Mongolia 43 J3
...senogora Rus. Fed. 12 J2
...ses Namibia 50 D3
...setseng Mongolia 42 G3
...setseng Botswana 50 E2
...setserleg Arhangay Mongolia 42 I3
...setserleg Mongolia 42 H3
...setserleg Hövsgöl Mongolia see Tsetserleg
...shabong Botswana 50 E3
...shad country China see Chad
...shane Botswana 50 E3
...shela Dem. Rep. Congo 49 B4
...shikapa Dem. Rep. Congo 49 C4
...shing S. Africa 51 H4
...shipise S. Africa 51 J3
...shitanzu Dem. Rep. Congo 49 C4
...shofa Dem. Rep. Congo 49 C4
...shokwane S. Africa 51 J3
...sholotsho Zimbabwe 49 C5
...shootsha Botswana 50 E2
...shuapa r. Dem. Rep. Congo 47 C4
...shwane S. Africa see Pretoria
...sil'ma r. Rus. Fed. 12 J2
...simlyansk Rus. Fed. 13 I7
...simlyanskoye Vodokhranilishche resr
   Rus. Fed. 13 I7
...simmermanovka Rus. Fed. 44 E2
...sinan China see Jinan
...sineng S. Africa 51 H4
...singhai prov. China see Qinghai
...singtao China see Qingdao
...sining China see Jining
...siombe Madag. 49 E6
...siroanomandidy Madag. 49 E5
...sitsikamma Forest and Coastal National
   Park S. Africa 51 H7
...sivil'sk Rus. Fed. 12 J5
...skhaltubo Georgia see Tsqaltubo
...s'khinvali Georgia 35 F2
...snori Georgia 35 G2
...sokar Chumo l. India 36 D2
...solo S. Africa 51 H7
...somo S. Africa 51 I6
...sqaltubo Georgia 35 F2
...su Japan 45 E6
...suchiura Japan 45 F5
...sugarū-kaikyō str. Japan 44 F4
...sugarū Strait Japan see Tsugarū-kaikyō
...sumeb Namibia 49 B5
...sumis Park Namibia 50 C2
...sumkwe Namibia 49 C5
...suruga Japan 45 E6

Tsurugi-san mt. Japan 45 D6
Tsurukhaytuy Rus. Fed. see Priargunsk
Tsuruoka Japan 45 E5
Tsushima is Japan 45 C6
Tsushima-kaikyō str. Japan/S. Korea see
   Korea Strait
Tsuyama Japan 45 D6
Tswaane Botswana 50 E2
Tswaraganang S. Africa 51 G5
Tswelelang S. Africa 51 G4
Tsyelyakhany Belarus 15 N10
Tsyp-Navolok Rus. Fed. 14 R2
Tua Dem. Rep. Congo 48 B4
Tuam Ireland 21 D4
Tuamotu, Archipel des is Fr. Polynesia see
   Tuamotu Islands
Tuamotu Islands Fr. Polynesia 75 K6
Tuapse Rus. Fed. 13 H7
Tuath, Loch a' b. U.K. 20 C2
Tuba City U.S.A. 62 E4
Tubarão Brazil 71 A5
Tubarjal Saudi Arabia 39 D4
Tübingen Germany 17 L6
Tubmanburg Liberia 46 B4
Tubruq Libya 34 A4
Tubuai i. Fr. Polynesia 75 K7
Tubuai Islands Fr. Polynesia 75 J7
Tucano Brazil 69 K6
Tucavaca Bol. 69 G7
Tuchitua Canada 60 D2
Tucopia i. Solomon Is see Tikopia
Tucson U.S.A. 62 E5
Tucumán Arg. see San Miguel de Tucumán
Tucumcari U.S.A. 62 G4
Tucupita Venez. 68 F2
Tucuruí Brazil 69 I4
Tucuruí, Represa resr Brazil 69 I4
Tudela Spain 25 F2
Tuder Italy see Todi
Tüdevtey Mongolia 42 H3
Tuela r. Port. 25 C3
Tuensang India 37 H4
Tufts Abyssal Plain sea feature
   N. Pacific Ocean 75 K3
Tugela r. S. Africa 51 J5
Tuglung China 37 H3
Tuguegarao Phil. 41 E6
Tugur Rus. Fed. 44 E1
Tujiabu China see Yongxiu
Tukangbesi, Kepulauan is Indon. 41 E8
Tukituki r. N.Z. 59 F4
Tuktoyaktuk Canada 60 E3
Tuktut Nogait National Park Canada 60 F3
Tukums Latvia 15 M8
Tukuringra, Khrebet mts Rus. Fed. 44 B1
Tukuyu Tanz. 49 D4
Tula Rus. Fed. 13 H5
Tulach Mhór Ireland see Tullamore
Tulagt Ar Gol r. China 37 H1
Tula Mountains Antarctica 76 D2
Tulancingo Mex. 66 E4
Tulare CA U.S.A. 65 C3
Tulare Lake Bed U.S.A. 65 C3
Tulasi mt. India 38 D2
Tulbagh S. Africa 50 D7
Tulcán Ecuador 68 C3
Tulcea Romania 27 M2
Tuléar Madag. see Toliara
Tulemalu Lake Canada 61 I3
Tulia U.S.A. 62 G5
Tulihe China 44 A2
Tulkarem West Bank see Tülkarm
Tülkarm West Bank 39 B3
Tulla Ireland 21 D5
Tullamore Australia 58 C4
Tullamore Ireland 21 E4
Tulle France 24 E4
Tulleråsen Sweden 14 I5
Tullibigeal Australia 58 C4
Tullow Ireland 21 F5
Tully r. Australia 56 D3
Tully U.K. 21 E3
Tulos Rus. Fed. 14 Q5
Tulqarem West Bank see Tülkarm
Tulsa U.S.A. 63 H4
Tulsipur Nepal 37 E3
Tuluá Col. 68 C3
Tulukak U.S.A. 77 B2
Tulun Rus. Fed. 42 I2
Tulu-Tuloi, Serra hills Brazil 68 F3
Tulu Welel mt. Eth. 48 D3
Tuma r. Rus. Fed. 13 I5
Tumaco Col. 68 C3
Tumahole S. Africa 51 H4
Tumannyy Rus. Fed. 14 S2
Tumasik Sing. see Singapore
Tumba Dem. Rep. Congo 49 B4
Tumba Sweden 15 J7
Tumba, Lac l. Dem. Rep. Congo 48 B4
Tumbarumba Australia 58 D5
Tumbes Peru 68 B4
Tumby Bay Australia 57 B7
Tumcha r. Fin./Rus. Fed. 14 Q3
Tumen Jilin China 44 C4
Tumereng Guyana 68 F2
Tumiritinga Brazil 71 C2
Tumkur India 38 C3
Tummel r. U.K. 20 F4
Tummel, Loch l. U.K. 20 F4
Tumnin r. Rus. Fed. 44 F2
Tump Pak. 33 J4
Tumu Ghana 46 C3
Tumucumaque, Serra hills Brazil 69 G3
Tumudibandh India 38 D2
Tumut Australia 58 D5
Tuna India 36 B5
Tunbridge Wells, Royal U.K. 19 H7
Tunceli Turkey 35 E3
Tuncurry Australia 58 F4
Tundun-Wada Nigeria 46 D3
Tunduru Tanz. 49 D5
Tunes Tunisia see Tunis
Tunga Nigeria 46 D4
Tungabhadra Reservoir India 38 C3
Tungi Bangl. 37 G5
Tungnaá r. Iceland 14 [inset]
Tungor Rus. Fed. 44 F1
Tungsten (abandoned) Canada 60 E3
Tuni India 38 D2
Tūnis country Africa see Tunisia
Tunis Tunisia 26 D6
Tunis, Golfe de g. Tunisia 26 D6
Tunja Col. 68 D2
Tunkhannock PA U.S.A. 64 D2
Tunnsjøen l. Norway 14 H4
Tunstall U.K. 19 I6
Tuntsa Fin. 14 P3
Tuntsajoki r. Fin./Rus. Fed. see Tumcha
Tununak U.S.A. 77 B3
Tunxi China see Huangshan
Tuotuo He r. China see Togton He
Tuotuoheyan China see Tanggulashan
Tüp Kyrg. 42 D4

Tupã Brazil 71 A3
Tupelo U.S.A. 63 J5
Tupik Rus. Fed. 43 L2
Tupinambarama, Ilha i. Brazil 69 G4
Tupiraçaba Brazil 71 A1
Tupiza Bol. 68 E8
Tüpqaraghan Tübegi pen. Kazakh. see
   Mangyshlak, Poluostrov
Tupungato, Cerro mt. Arg./Chile 70 C4
Tuquan China 44 M3
Tura China 33 I3
Tura Rus. Fed. 37 F1
Tura India 37 G4
Tura Rus. Fed. 29 L3
Turabah Saudi Arabia 32 F5
Turakina N.Z. 59 E5
Turan Rus. Fed. 42 G2
Turana, Khrebet mts Rus. Fed. 44 C2
Turan Lowland Asia 33 I2
Turan Oypaty lowland Asia see
   Turan Lowland
Turan Pasttekisligi lowland Asia see
   Turan Lowland
Turan Pesligi lowland Asia see
   Turan Lowland
Turanskaya Nizmennost' lowland Asia see
   Turan Lowland
Turāq al 'Ilab hills Syria 39 D3
Turar Ryskulov Kazakh. 33 L1
Tura-Ryskulova Kazakh. see Turar Ryskulov
Turayf Saudi Arabia 39 D4
Turba Estonia 15 N7
Turbat Pak. 33 J4
Turbo Col. 68 C2
Turda Romania 27 J1
Türeh Iran 35 H4
Turfan China see Turpan
Turfan Basin depr. China see Turpan Pendi
Turfan Depression China see Turpan Pendi
Turgay Kazakh. 42 A3
Türgovishte Bulg. 27 L3
Turgutlu Turkey 27 L5
Turhal Turkey 34 E2
Türi Estonia 15 N7
Turia r. Spain 25 F4
Turin Italy 26 B2
Turiy Rog Rus. Fed. 44 C3
Turkana, Lake salt l. Eth./Kenya 48 D3
Turkestan Kazakh. 42 B4
Turkey country Asia/Europe 34 D3
Turki Rus. Fed. 13 I6
Türkistan Kazakh. see Turkestan
Türkiye country Asia/Europe see Turkey
Türkmenabat Turkm. 30 F3
Türkmen Adasy i. Turkm. see
   Ogurjaly Adasy
Türkmen Aýlagy b. Turkm. see
   Türkmenbaşy Aýlagy
Türkmenbaşy Turkm. 35 I2
Türkmenbaşy Turkm. see Türkmenbaşy
Türkmenbaşy Aýlagy b. Turkm. 35 I3
Türkmenbaşy Aýlagy b. Turkm. see
   Türkmenbaşy Aýlagy
Türkmenbaşy Döwlet Gorugy nature res.
   Turkm. 35 I3
Turkmenistan country Asia 33 I2
Turkmeniya country Asia see Turkmenistan
Türkmenostan country Asia see
   Turkmenistan
Turkmenskaya S.S.R. country Asia see
   Turkmenistan
Türkoğlu Turkey 34 E3
Turks and Caicos Islands terr. West Indies
   67 J4
Turks Islands Turks and Caicos Is 67 J4
Turku Fin. 15 M6
Turkwel watercourse Kenya 48 D3
Turlock CA U.S.A. 65 B1
Turlock Lake CA U.S.A. 65 B2
Turmalina Brazil 71 C2
Turnagain, Cape N.Z. 59 F5
Turnberry U.K. 20 E5
Turneffe Islands atoll Belize 66 G5
Turnor Lake Canada 60 H4
Turnovo Bulg. see Veliko Tŭrnovo
Turnu Măgurele Romania 27 K3
Turnu Severin Romania see
   Drobeta-Turnu Severin
Turon r. Australia 58 D4
Turones France see Tours
Turovets Rus. Fed. 12 I4
Turpan China 42 F3
Turpan Pendi depr. China 42 F4
Turquino, Pico mt. Cuba 67 I4
Turriff U.K. 20 G3
Turris Libisonis Sardegna Italy see
   Porto Torres
Tursãq Iraq 35 G4
Turtle Island Fiji see Vatoa
Turugart Pass China/Kyrg. 31 G2
Turugart Shankou pass China/Kyrg. see
   Turugart Pass
Turuvanur India 38 C3
Turvo r. Brazil 71 A3
Turvo r. Brazil 71 A2
Tuscaloosa U.S.A. 63 J5
Tuscarawas r. OH U.S.A. 64 A2
Tuscarora Mountains hills PA U.S.A. 64 C2
Tuskegee U.S.A. 63 J5
Tussey Mountains hills PA U.S.A. 64 B2
Tutak Turkey 35 F3
Tutayev Rus. Fed. 12 H4
Tutera Spain see Tudela
Tuticorin India 38 C4
Tuttut Nunaat reg. Greenland 61 P2
Tutuala East Timor 54 E2
Tutubu Tanz. 49 D4
Tutuila i. American Samoa 53 J3
Tutume Botswana 49 C6
Tuun-bong mt. N. Korea 44 B4
Tutlingen Germany 17 L7
Tuvalu country S. Pacific Ocean 53 H2
Tuwayq, Jabal mts Saudi Arabia 32 G5
Tuwayyil ash Shihaq mt. Jordan 39 C4
Tuwwal Saudi Arabia 32 E5
Tuxpan Mex. 66 E4
Tuxtla Gutiérrez Mex. 66 F5
Tuy Hoa Vietnam 31 E5
Tuz, Lake salt l. Turkey see Tuz, Lake
Tuz Gölü salt l. Turkey 34 D3
Tuzha Rus. Fed. 12 J4
Tuz Khurmātū Iraq 35 G4
Tuzla Bos.-Herz. 26 H2
Tuzla Gölü lag. Turkey 27 L4
Tuzlov r. Rus. Fed. 13 I7
Tuzu r. Myanmar 37 H4
Tvedestrand Norway 15 F7
Tver' Rus. Fed. 12 G4
Twain Harte CA U.S.A. 65 B1
Tweed r. U.K. 20 G5
Tweed Heads Australia 58 F2
Tweefontein S. Africa 50 D7
Twee Rivier Namibia 50 D3
Twentynine Palms CA U.S.A. 65 D3
Twin Bridges CA U.S.A. 65 B1

Twin Falls U.S.A. 62 E3
Twin Heads h. Australia 54 D5
Twin Peak CA U.S.A. 65 B1
Twitchen Reservoir CA U.S.A. 65 B3
Twofold Bay Australia 58 D6
Two Harbors U.S.A. 63 I2
Tyan' Shan' mts China/Kyrg. see Tien Shan
Tyatya, Vulkan vol. Rus. Fed. 44 G3
Tydal Norway 14 G5
Tygart Valley val. WV U.S.A. 64 B3
Tygda Rus. Fed. 44 B1
Tygda r. Rus. Fed. 44 B1
Tyler U.S.A. 63 H5
Tym' r. Rus. Fed. 44 F2
Tymovskoye Rus. Fed. 44 F2
Tynda Rus. Fed. 43 M1
Tyndinskiy Rus. Fed. see Tynda
Tyne r. U.K. 20 G4
Tynemouth U.K. 18 F3
Tynset Norway 14 G5
Tyoploozyorsk Rus. Fed. see Teploozersk
Tyoploye Ozero Rus. Fed. see Teploozersk
Tyr Lebanon 39 B3
Tyras Ukr. see Bilhorod-Dnistrovs'kyy
Tyre Lebanon see Tyr
Tyrma Rus. Fed. 13 15
Tyrma r. Rus. Fed. 44 C2
Tyrnävä Fin. 14 N4
Tyrnavos Greece 27 J5
Tyrnyauz Rus. Fed. 35 F2
Tyrone PA U.S.A. 64 B2
Tyrrell r. Australia 58 A5
Tyrrell, Lake dry lake Australia 57 C7
Tyrrhenian Sea France/Italy 26 D4
Tyrus Lebanon see Tyr
Tysa r. Serbia see Tisa
Tyukalinsk Rus. Fed. 28 I4
Tyulen'i Ostrova is Kazakh. 35 H1
Tyumen' Rus. Fed. 28 H4
Tyup Kyrg. see Tüp
Tyuratam Kazakh. see Baykonyr
Tywi r. U.K. 19 C7
Tywyn U.K. 19 C6
Tzaneen S. Africa 51 J2
Tzia i. Greece 27 K6

Uaco Congo Angola see Waku-Kungo
Ualan atoll Micronesia see Kosrae
Uamanda Angola 49 C5
Uarc, Ras c. Morocco see
   Trois Fourches, Cap des
Uaroo Australia 55 A5
Uatumã r. Brazil 69 G4
Uaué r. Brazil 69 K5
Uaupés r. Brazil 68 E4
U'aylī, Wādī al watercourse Saudi Arabia
   39 D4
U'aywij well Saudi Arabia 35 G5
U'aywij, Wādī al watercourse Saudi Arabia
   35 F5
Ubá Brazil 71 C3
Ubaí Brazil 71 B2
Ubaitaba Brazil 71 D1
Ubangi r. Cent. Afr. Rep./Dem. Rep. Congo
   48 B4
Ubangi-Shari country Africa see
   Central African Republic
Ubauro Pak. 36 B3
Ubayyid, Wādī al watercourse
   Iraq/Saudi Arabia 35 F4
Ube Japan 45 C6
Úbeda Spain 25 E4
Uberaba Brazil 71 B2
Uberlândia Brazil 71 A2
Ubombo S. Africa 51 K4
Ubon Ratchathani Thai. 31 J5
Ubundu Dem. Rep. Congo 47 C4
Üçajy Turkm. 33 J2
Ucar Azer. 35 G2
Uçan Turkey 39 A1
Ucayali r. Peru 68 D4
Uch Pak. 36 B3
Üçhan Iran 35 H3
Ucharal Kazakh. 42 E3
Uchiura-wan b. Japan 44 F4
Uchkeken Rus. Fed. 35 F2
Uchkuduk Uzbek. see Uchquduq
Uchquduq Uzbek. 33 J1
Uchto r. Pak. 36 A4
Uchur r. Rus. Fed. 29 O4
Uckfield U.K. 19 H8
Uda r. Rus. Fed. 43 J2
Uda r. Rus. Fed. 44 D1
Udachnoye Rus. Fed. 13 J7
Udachnyy Rus. Fed. 77 C2
Udagamandalam India 38 C4
Udaipur Rajasthan India 36 C4
Udaipur Tripura India 37 G5
Udanti r. India/Myanmar 37 E5
Uday r. Ukr. 13 G6
Uddevalla Sweden 15 G7
Uddingston U.K. 20 E5
Uddjaure l. Sweden 14 J4
Udgir India 38 C2
Udhagamandalam India see
   Udagamandalam
Udhampur India 36 C2
Udia-Milai atoll Marshall Is see Bikini
Udimskiy Rus. Fed. 12 J3
Udine Italy 26 E1
Udmalaippettai India see Udumalaippettai
Udomlya Rus. Fed. 12 G4
Udon Thani Thai. 31 J5
Udskaya Guba b. Rus. Fed. 29 O4
Udskoye Rus. Fed. 44 D1
Udumalaippettai India 38 C4
Udupi India 38 B3
Udyl', Ozero l. Rus. Fed. 44 E1
Udzhary Azer. see Ucar
Udzungwa Mountains National Park Tanz.
   49 D4
Uéa atoll New Caledonia see Ouvéa
Ueckermünde Germany 17 O4
Ueda Japan 45 E5
Uele r. Dem. Rep. Congo 48 C3
Uelen Rus. Fed. 77 U3
Uelzen Germany 17 M4
Ufa Rus. Fed. 11 R5
Ufa r. Rus. Fed. 11 R5
Uftyuga r. Rus. Fed. 12 I3
Ugab watercourse Namibia 49 B6
Ugalla r. Tanz. 49 D4
Uganda country Africa 48 D3
Ugie S. Africa 51 I6
Uglegorsk Rus. Fed. 44 F2
Uglich Rus. Fed. 12 H4
Ugljan i. Croatia 26 F2
Uglovoye Rus. Fed. 44 C2
Ugol'noye Rus. Fed. 29 P3
Ugolnyye Kopi Rus. Fed. 29 S3
Ugra Rus. Fed. 13 G5
Uherské Hradiště Czech Rep. 17 P6
Uhrichsville OH U.S.A. 64 A2

Uibhist a' Deas i. U.K. see South Uist
Uibhist a' Tuath i. U.K. see North Uist
Uig U.K. 20 C2
Uíge Angola 49 B4
Uijeongbu S. Korea 45 B5
Üiju N. Korea 45 B4
Uimaharju Fin. 14 Q5
Uinta Mountains U.S.A. 62 E3
Uis Mine Namibia 49 B6
Uitenhage S. Africa 51 G7
Ujhani India 36 D4
Uji Japan 45 D6
Uji-guntō is Japan 45 C7
Ujiyamada Japan see Ise
Ujjain India 36 D5
Ujung Pandang Indon. see Makassar
Újvidék Serbia see Novi Sad
Ukal Sagar l. India 36 C5
Ukata Nigeria 46 D3
'Ukayrishah well Saudi Arabia 35 G6
uKhahlamba-Drakensberg Park nat. park
   S. Africa 51 I5
Ukholovo Rus. Fed. 13 I5
Ukhrul India 37 H4
Ukhta Respublika Kareliya Rus. Fed. see
   Kalevala
Ukhta Respublika Komi Rus. Fed. 12 L3
Ukiah CA U.S.A. 65 A1
Ukkusissat Greenland 61 M2
Ukmergė Lith. 15 N9
Ukraine country Europe 13 F6
Ukrainskaya S.S.R. country Europe see
   Ukraine
Ukrayina country Europe see Ukraine
Uku-jima i. Japan 45 C6
Ukwi Botswana 50 E2
Ukwi Pan salt pan Botswana 50 E2
Ulaanbaatar Mongolia see Ulan Bator
Ulaangom Mongolia 42 G3
Ulan Australia 58 D4
Ulan Bator Mongolia 42 J3
Ulanbel' Kazakh. 42 C4
Ulan Erge Rus. Fed. 13 J7
Ulanhad China see Chifeng
Ulanhot China 44 A4
Ulan Hua China 43 K4
Ulan-Khol Rus. Fed. 13 J7
Ulan-Ude Rus. Fed. 43 J2
Ulan Ul Hu l. China 37 G2
Ulaş Turkey 34 E3
Ulawa Island Solomon Is 53 G2
Ul'banskiy Zaliv b. Rus. Fed. 44 E1
Ulchin S. Korea 45 C5
Uldz r. Mongolia 43 L3
Uleåborg Fin. see Oulu
Ulefoss Norway 15 F7
Ülenurme Estonia 15 O7
Ulety Rus. Fed. 43 L2
Ulhasnagar India 38 B2
Uliastai China 43 J3
Uliastay Mongolia 42 H3
Uliatea i. Fr. Polynesia see Raiatea
Ulita r. Rus. Fed. 14 R2
Ulithi atoll Micronesia 41 F6
Ulladulla Australia 58 E5
Ullapool U.K. 20 D3
Ulla Ulla, Parque Nacional nat. park Bol.
   68 E6
Ullava Fin. 14 M5
Ullersuaq c. Greenland 61 K2
Ullswater l. U.K. 18 E4
Üllüng-do i. S. Korea 45 C5
Ulm Germany 17 L6
Ulmarra Australia 58 F2
Ulsan S. Korea 45 C6
Ulsberg Norway 14 F5
Ulster reg. Ireland/U.K. 21 E3
Ulster PA U.S.A. 64 C2
Ulster Canal Ireland/U.K. 21 E3
Ultima Australia 58 A5
Ulubat Gölü l. Turkey 27 M4
Ulubey Turkey 27 M5
Uluborlu Turkey 27 N5
Uludağ mt. Turkey 27 M4
Uludağ Milli Parkı nat. park Turkey 27 M4
Uluguat China see Wuqia
Ulukhaktok Canada 60 G2
Ulukışla Turkey 34 D3
Ulundi S. Africa 51 J5
Ulungur Hu l. China 42 G2
Ulunkhan Rus. Fed. 43 K2
Uluqsaqtuuq Canada see Ulukhaktok
Uluru h. Australia 55 E6
Uluru-Kata Tjuta National Park Australia
   55 E6
Uluru National Park Australia see
   Uluru-Kata Tjuta National Park
Ulutau Kazakh. see Ulytau
Ulutau, Gory mts Kazakh. see Ulytau, Gory
Uluyatır Turkey 39 C1
Ulva i. U.K. 20 C4
Ul'yanovsk Kazakh. see Ul'yanovskiy
Ul'yanovsk Rus. Fed. 13 K5
Ul'yanovskiy Kazakh. 42 C2
Ul'yanovskoye Kazakh. see Ul'yanovskiy
Ulysses KS U.S.A. 62 G4
Ulytau Kazakh. 42 B3
Ulytau, Gory mts Kazakh. 42 B3
Uma Rus. Fed. 44 A1
Umalthinskiy Rus. Fed. 44 D2
'Umān country Asia see Oman
Uman' Ukr. 13 F6
'Umari, Qā' al salt pan Jordan 39 C4
Umaria India 36 E5
Umarkhed India 38 C2
Umarkot India 38 D2
Umarkot Pak. 36 B3
Umarkot Rus. Fed. 33 K4
Umaroona, Lake imp. l. Australia 57 B5
Umarpada India 36 C5
Umba r. Rus. Fed. 12 G2
Umbeara Australia 55 F6
Umboi i. P.N.G. 52 E2
Umeå Sweden 14 L5
Umeälven r. Sweden 14 L5
Umfolozi r. S. Africa 51 J5
Umhlanga Rocks S. Africa 51 J5
Umiiviip Kangertiva inlet Greenland 61 N3
Umingmaktok (abandoned) Canada 77 L2
Umirzak Kazakh. 35 H2
Umkomaas S. Africa 51 J6
Umlazi S. Africa 51 J5
Umm ad Daraj, Jabal mt. Jordan 39 B3
Umm al 'Amad Syria 39 C3
Umm ar Raqabah, Khabrat salt pan
   Saudi Arabia 39 C5
Umm at Qalbān Saudi Arabia 35 F6
Umm Bel Sudan 32 C7
Umm Keddada Sudan 32 C7
Umm Lajj Saudi Arabia 32 E5
Umm Nukhaylah h. Saudi Arabia 39 D5
Umm Qaşr Iraq 35 H5
Umm Quşūr i. Saudi Arabia 34 D6
Umm Ruwaba Sudan 32 D7
Umm Sa'ad Libya 34 B4
Umm Shugeira Sudan 32 C7

Umm Wa'al h. Saudi Arabia 39 D4
Umnak Island U.S.A. 60 B4
Umpulo Angola 49 B5
Umraniye Turkey 27 N5
Umred India 38 C1
Umri India 36 C4
Umtali Zimbabwe see Mutare
Umtata S. Africa 51 I6
Umtentweni S. Africa 51 J6
Umuahia Nigeria 46 D4
Umuarama Brazil 70 F2
Umvuma Zimbabwe see Mvuma
Umzimkulu S. Africa 51 I6
Una r. Bos.-Herz./Croatia 26 G2
Una Brazil 71 D1
Una India 36 D3
'Unāb, Jabal al h. Jordan 39 C5
'Unāb, Wādī al watercourse Jordan 39 C4
Unaí Brazil 71 B2
Unalakleet U.S.A. 60 B3
Unalaska Island U.S.A. 60 B4
Unapool U.K. 20 D2
'Unayzah Saudi Arabia 32 F4
'Unayzah, Jabal h. Iraq 35 F4
Uncia Bol. 68 E7
Undara National Park Australia 56 D3
Underberg S. Africa 51 I5
Underbool Australia 57 C7
Unecha Rus. Fed. 13 G5
Ungama Bay Kenya see Ungwana Bay
Ungarie Australia 58 C4
Ungava, Baie d' b. Canada see Ungava Bay
Ungava, Péninsule d' pen. Canada 61 K3
Ungava Bay Canada 61 L4
Ungava Peninsula Canada see
   Ungava, Péninsule d'
Ungeny Moldova see Ungheni
Ungheni Moldova 27 L1
Unguana Moz. 51 L2
Unguja i. Tanz. see Zanzibar Island
Unguz, Solonchakovyye Vpadiny salt flat
   Turkm. 33 I2
Üngüz Angyrsyndaky Garagum des. Turkm.
   33 I1
Ungvár Ukr. see Uzhhorod
Ungwana Bay Kenya 48 E4
Uni Rus. Fed. 12 K4
União Brazil 69 J4
União da Vitória Brazil 71 A4
União dos Palmares Brazil 69 K5
Unimak Island U.S.A. 60 B4
Unini r. Brazil 68 F4
Union WV U.S.A. 64 A4
Union City PA U.S.A. 64 B1
Union City TN U.S.A. 63 J4
Uniondale S. Africa 50 F7
Uniontown PA U.S.A. 64 B3
Unionville PA U.S.A. 64 C2
United Arab Emirates country Asia 33 H5
United Arab Republic country Africa see
   Egypt
United Kingdom country Europe 16 G3
United Provinces state India see
   Uttar Pradesh
United States of America country
   N. America 62 F3
United States Range mts Canada 61 L1
Unity Canada 62 F1
Unjha India 36 C5
Unnao India 36 E4
Ünp'a N. Korea 45 B5
Unsan N. Korea 45 B4
Ŭnsan N. Korea 45 B5
Unst i. U.K. 20 [inset]
Untor, Ozero l. Rus. Fed. 11 T3
Unuli Horog China 37 G2
Unzen-dake vol. Japan 45 C6
Unzha Rus. Fed. 12 J4
Upar Ghat reg. India 37 E5
Upemba, Lac l. Dem. Rep. Congo 49 C4
Uperbada India 37 F5
Upernavik Greenland 61 M2
Upington S. Africa 50 E5
Upland CA U.S.A. 65 D4
Upleta India 36 B5
Upoloksha Rus. Fed. 14 Q3
'Upolu i. Samoa 53 I3
Upper Chindwin Myanmar see Mawlaik
Upper Hutt N.Z. 59 E5
Upper Klamath Lake U.S.A. 62 C3
Upper Lough Erne l. U.K. 21 E3
Upper Marlboro MD U.S.A. 64 C3
Upper Tunguska r. Rus. Fed. see Angara
Upper Volta country Africa see Burkina
Upper Yarra Reservoir Australia 58 B6
Uppingham India 38 B3
Uppsala Sweden 15 J7
Upshi India 36 D2
Upton MA U.S.A. 64 F1
'Uqayqah, Wādī watercourse Jordan 39 B4
'Uqlat al 'Udhaybah well Iraq 35 G5
Urad Houqi China see Sain Us
Urakawa Japan 44 F4
Ural r. Kazakh./Rus. Fed. 30 C2
Ural h. Rus. Fed. 12 J4
Uralla Australia 58 E3
Ural'sk Kazakh. 30 E1
Ural Mountains Rus. Fed. 11 S2
Ural'skaya Oblast' admin. div. Kazakh. see
   Zapadnyy Kazakhstan
Ural'skiye Gory mts Rus. Fed. see
   Ural Mountains
Ural'skiy Khrebet mts Rus. Fed. see
   Ural Mountains
Urambo Tanz. 49 D4
Uran India 38 B2
Urana Australia 58 C5
Urana, Lake Australia 58 C5
Urandangi Australia 56 B4
Urandi Brazil 71 C1
Uranium City Canada 60 H4
Uranquinty Australia 58 C5
Uraricoera r. Brazil 68 F3
Urartu country Asia see Armenia
Uravakonda India 38 C3
Urawa Japan 45 E6
'Urayf an Nāqah, Jabal h. Egypt 39 B4
Urbino Italy 26 E3
Urbinum Italy see Urbino
Urbs Vetus Italy see Orvieto
Urdoma Rus. Fed. 12 K3
Urdyuzhskoye, Ozero l. Rus. Fed. 12 K2
Ure r. U.K. 18 F4
Ureki Georgia 35 F2
Uren' Rus. Fed. 12 J4
Urengoy Rus. Fed. 28 I3
Uréparapara i. Vanuatu 53 G3
Urewera National Park N.Z. 59 F4
Urfa Turkey see Şanlıurfa
Urfa, Turkey see Şanlıurfa
Urga Mongolia see Ulan Bator
Urgal r. Rus. Fed. 44 D2
Urganch Uzbek. 33 J1
Urgench Uzbek. see Urganch
Ürgüp Turkey 34 D3
Urho China 42 F3
Urho Kekkosen kansallispuisto nat. park
   Fin. 14 O2
Urie r. U.K. 20 G3
Uril Rus. Fed. 44 C2
Urisino Australia 58 A4

Urjala Fin. 15 M6
Urkan Rus. Fed. 44 B1
Urkan r. Rus. Fed. 44 B1
Urlingford Ireland 21 E5
Urluk Rus. Fed. 43 J2
Urmä aş Şughrá Syria 39 C1
Urmai China 37 F3
Urmia Iran 35 G3
Urmia, Lake salt l. Iran 35 G3
Uromi Nigeria 46 D4
Uroševac Kosovo see Ferijaz
Urosozero Rus. Fed. 12 G3
Urru Co salt l. China 37 F3
Urt Moron China 42 G5
Uruaçu Brazil 71 A1
Uruana Brazil 71 A1
Uruapan Michoacán Mex. 66 D5
Urubamba r. Peru 68 D6
Urucara Brazil 69 G4
Urucu r. Brazil 68 F4
Uruçuca Brazil 71 D1
Uruçuí Brazil 69 J5
Uruçuí, Serra do hills Brazil 69 I5
Urucuia Brazil 71 B2
Urucurituba Brazil 69 G4
Uruguai r. Brazil 70 E3
Uruguaiana Brazil 70 E3
Uruguay r. Arg./Uruguay see Uruguay
Uruguay r. Arg./Uruguay 70 E4
Uruguay country S. America 70 E4
Uruhe China 44 B3
Urumchi China see Ürümqi
Ürümqi China 42 F4
Urundi country Africa see Burundi
Urup, Ostrov i. Rus. Fed. 43 S3
Urusha Rus. Fed. 44 A1
Urutaí Brazil 71 A2
Uryupino Rus. Fed. 43 M2
Uryupinsk Rus. Fed. 13 I6
Urzhum Rus. Fed. 12 J4
Urziceni Romania 27 L2
Usa r. Rus. Fed. 12 M2
Usa Turkey 27 M5
Usakos Namibia 50 B4
Usarp Mountains Antarctica 76 H2
Usborne, Mount h. Falkland Is 70 E8
Ushakova, Ostrov i. Rus. Fed. 28 I1
Ushant i. France see Ouessant, Île d'
Üsharal Kazakh. see Ucharal
Ush-Bel'dyr Rus. Fed. 42 H2
Ushtobe Kazakh. 42 I2
Ush-Tyube Kazakh. see Ushtobe
Ushuaia Arg. 70 C8
Ushumun Rus. Fed. 44 B1
Usinsk Rus. Fed. 11 R2
Usk U.K. 19 E7
Usk r. U.K. 19 E7
Uskhodni Belarus 15 O10
Uskoplje Bos.-Herz. see Gornji Vakuf
Üsman' Rus. Fed. 13 H5
Usogorsk Rus. Fed. 12 K3
Usol'ye-Sibirskoye Rus. Fed. 42 I2
Ussel France 24 F4
Ussuri r. China/Rus. Fed. 44 D2
Ussuriysk Rus. Fed. 44 C3
Ust'-Abakanskoye Rus. Fed. see Abakan
Usta Muhammad Pak. 36 B3
Ust'-Balyk Rus. Fed. see Nefteyugansk
Ust'-Donetskiy Rus. Fed. 13 I7
Ust'-Dzheguta Rus. Fed. 35 F1
Ust'-Dzhegutinskaya Rus. Fed. see
Ust'-Dzheguta
Ustica, Isola di i. Sicilia Italy 26 E5
Ust'-Ilimsk Rus. Fed. 29 L4
Ust'-Ilimskiy Vodokhranilishche resr
Rus. Fed. 29 L4
Ust'-Ilych Rus. Fed. 11 R3
Ústí nad Labem Czech Rep. 17 O5
Ustinov Rus. Fed. see Izhevsk
Üstirt plat. Kazakh./Uzbek. see
Ustyurt Plateau
Ustka Poland 17 P3
Ust'-Kamchatsk Rus. Fed. 29 R4
Ust'-Kamenogorsk Kazakh. 42 E3
Ust'-Kan Rus. Fed. 42 F2
Ust'-Koksa Rus. Fed. 42 F2
Ust'-Kulom Rus. Fed. 12 L3
Ust'-Kut Rus. Fed. 29 L4
Ust'-Kuyga Rus. Fed. 29 O2
Ust'-Labinsk Rus. Fed. 35 E1
Ust'-Labinskaya Rus. Fed. see Ust'-Labinsk
Ust'-Lyzha Rus. Fed. 12 L2
Ust'-Maya Rus. Fed. 29 O3
Ust'-Nera Rus. Fed. 29 P3
Ust'-Ocheya Rus. Fed. 12 K3
Ust'-Olenek Rus. Fed. 29 M2
Ust'-Omchug Rus. Fed. 29 P3
Ust'-Ordynskiy Rus. Fed. 42 I2
Ust'-Penzhino Rus. Fed. see Kamenskoye
Ust'-Port Rus. Fed. 28 J3
Ustrem Rus. Fed. 11 T3
Ust'-Tsil'ma Rus. Fed. 12 L2
Ust'-Uda Rus. Fed. 42 I2
Ust'-Umalta Rus. Fed. 44 D2
Ust'-Undurga Rus. Fed. 43 L2
Ust'-Ura Rus. Fed. 12 J3
Ust'-Urgal Rus. Fed. 44 D2
Ust'-Usa Rus. Fed. 12 M2
Ust'-Vayen'ga Rus. Fed. 12 I3
Ust'-Voya Rus. Fed. 11 R3
Ust'-Vyyskaya Rus. Fed. 12 J3
Ust'ya r. Rus. Fed. 12 I3
Ust'ye Rus. Fed. 12 H4
Ustyurt, Plato plat. Kazakh./Uzbek. see
Ustyurt Plateau
Ustyurt Plateau Kazakh./Uzbek. 30 E2
Ustyurt Platosi plat. Kazakh./Uzbek. see
Ustyurt Plateau
Ustyuzhna Rus. Fed. 12 H4
Usuki Japan 45 C6
Usulután El Salvador 66 G6
Usumbura Burundi see Bujumbura
Usvyaty Rus. Fed. 12 F5
Utah state U.S.A. 62 E4
Utah Lake U.S.A. 62 E4
Utajärvi Fin. 14 O4
Utashinai Rus. Fed. see Yuzhno-Kuril'sk
'Utaybah, Buḩayrat al imp. l. Syria 39 C3
Utena Lith. 15 N9
Uterlai India 36 B4
Uthal Pak. 36 A4
'Uthmānīyah Syria 39 C2
Utiariti Brazil 69 G6
Utica NY U.S.A. 64 D1
Utiel Spain 25 F4
Utlwanang S. Africa 51 G4
Utrecht Neth. 16 J3
Utrecht S. Africa 51 J4
Utrera Spain 25 D5
Utsjoki Fin. 14 O2
Utta Rus. Fed. 13 J7
Uttaradit Thai. 31 J5
Utsunomiya Japan 45 E5
Uttarakhand state India see Uttaranchal
Uttaranchal state India 36 D3
Uttarkashi India 36 D3

Uttar Kashi India see Uttarkashi
Uttar Pradesh state India 36 D4
Uttoxeter U.K. 19 F6
Utubulak China 42 G2
Utupua i. Solomon Is 53 G3
Uummannaq Greenland see Dundas
Uummannaq Greenland 77 J2
Uummannaq Fjord inlet Greenland 77 J2
Uummannarsuaq c. Greenland see
Farewell, Cape
Uurainen Fin. 14 N5
Uusikaarlepyy Fin. see Nykarleby
Uusikaupunki Fin. 15 L6
Uutapi Namibia 49 B5
Uva Rus. Fed. 12 L4
Uvalde salt l. Turkey 35 F3
Uvarovo Rus. Fed. 13 I6
Uvéa atoll New Caledonia see Ouvéa
Uvinza Tanz. 49 D4
Uvs Nuur salt l. Mongolia 42 G2
Uwajima Japan 45 D6
'Uwayriḍ, Ḩarrat al lava field Saudi Arabia
32 E4
Uwaysiṭ well Saudi Arabia 39 D4
Uweinat, Jebel mt. Sudan 32 C5
Uxbridge U.K. 19 G7
Uxin Qi China see Dabqig
Uyar Rus. Fed. 42 G1
Uyo Nigeria 46 D4
Uyu Chaung r. Myanmar 37 H4
Uyuni Bol. 68 E8
Uyuni, Salar de salt flat Bol. 68 E8
Uza r. Rus. Fed. 12 C2
Uzbekistan country Asia 30 F2
Uzbekiston country Asia see Uzbekistan
Uzbekskaya S.S.R. country Asia see
Uzbekistan
Uzbek S.S.R. country Asia see Uzbekistan
Uzboy Azer. 35 I1
Uzboý Turkm. 35 I3
Uzen' Kazakh. see Kyzylsay
Uzhhorod Ukr. 13 D6
Uzhnorod Ukr. 13 D6
Užhorod Ukr. see Uzhhorod
Užice Serbia 27 H3
Uzlovaya Rus. Fed. 13 H5
Üzümlü Turkey 27 M6
Uzunköprü Turkey 27 L4

Vaajakoski Fin. 14 N5
Vaal r. S. Africa 51 F5
Vaala Fin. 14 O4
Vaalbos National Park S. Africa 50 G5
Vaal Dam S. Africa 51 I4
Vaalwater S. Africa 51 I3
Vaasa Fin. 14 L5
Vác Hungary 17 Q7
Vacaria Brazil 71 A5
Vacaria, Campo da plain Brazil 71 A5
Vacaville CA U.S.A. 65 B1
Vad Rus. Fed. 12 J5
Vada India 38 B2
Vadla Norway 15 E7
Vadodara India 36 C5
Vadsø Norway 14 P1
Vaduz Liechtenstein 24 I3
Værøy i. Norway 14 H3
Vaga r. Rus. Fed. 12 I3
Vågåmo Norway 15 F6
Vaganski Vrh mt. Croatia 26 F2
Vágar i. Faroe Is 14 [inset]
Vågsele Sweden 14 K4
Vågur Faroe Is 14 [inset]
Váh r. Slovakia 17 Q7
Vähäkyrö Fin. 14 M5
Vaiaku Tuvalu 53 H2
Vaida Estonia 15 N7
Vail U.S.A. 62 F4
Vaitupu i. Tuvalu 53 H2
Vajrakarur India see Kanur
Vakfıkebir India J333 I4
Valbo Sweden 15 J6
Valcheta Arg. 70 C6
Valdai Hills Rus. Fed. see
Valdayskaya Vozvyshennost'
Valday Rus. Fed. 12 G4
Valdayskaya Vozvyshennost' hills Rus. Fed.
12 G4
Valdecañas, Embalse de resr Spain 25 D4
Valdemārpils Latvia 15 M8
Valdemarsvik Sweden 15 J7
Valdepeñas Spain 25 E4
Val-de-Reuil France 24 E2
Valdés, Península pen. Arg. 70 D6
Valdez U.S.A. 60 D3
Valdivia Chile 70 B5
Val-d'Or Canada 63 F2
Valdosta U.S.A. 63 I5
Valdres val. Norway 15 F6
Vale Georgia 35 F2
Valemount Canada 62 D1
Valença Brazil 71 D1
Valença do Piauí Brazil 69 J5
Valence France 24 G4
Valencia Spain 25 F4
València Spain see Valencia
Valencia reg. Spain 25 F4
Valencia Venez. 68 E1
Valencia, Golfo de g. Spain 25 G4
Valencia de Don Juan Spain 25 D2
Valencia Island Ireland 21 B6
Valenciennes France 24 F1
Valentia Spain see Valencia
Valentin Rus. Fed. 44 D4
Valentine U.S.A. 62 G3
Valenzuela Spain 25 D4
Valentín Rus. Fed. see Valentin
Våler Norway 15 G6
Valera Venez. 68 D2
Valga Estonia 15 O7
Valjevo Serbia 27 H2
Valka Latvia 15 O8
Valkeakoski Fin. 15 N6
Valky Ukr. 13 G6
Valladolid Mex. 66 G4
Valladolid Spain 25 D3
Valle Norway 15 E7
Valle de la Pascua Venez. 68 E2
Valledupar Col. 68 D1
Vallée Fértil, Sierra de mts Arg. 70 C4
Valle Grande Bol. 68 F7
Vallejo CA U.S.A. 65 A1
Vallenar Chile 70 B3
Valletta Malta 26 F7
Valley U.K. 18 C5
Valley City U.S.A. 62 H2
Valls Spain 25 G3
Val Marie Canada 62 F2
Valmiera Latvia 15 N8
Valnera mt. Spain 25 E2
Valognes France 19 F9
Valona Albania see Vlorë

Valozhyn Belarus 15 O9
Valparai India 38 C4
Valparaíso Chile 70 B4
Valpoi India 38 B3
Valréas France 24 G4
Valsad India 38 B2
Valspan S. Africa 50 G4
Val'tevo Rus. Fed. 12 J3
Valtimo Fin. 14 P5
Valuyevka Rus. Fed. 13 I7
Valuyki Rus. Fed. 13 H6
Vammala Fin. 15 M6
Van Turkey 35 F3
Van, Lake salt l. Turkey 35 F3
Vanadzor Armenia 35 G2
Vancouver Canada 62 C2
Vancouver U.S.A. 62 C2
Vancouver Island Canada 62 B2
Vanda Fin. see Vantaa
Vanderbijlpark S. Africa 51 H4
Vandergrift PA U.S.A. 64 F3
Vanderkloof Dam dam S. Africa 50 G6
Vanderlin Island Australia 56 B2
Van Diemen, Cape N.T. Australia 54 E2
Van Diemen, Cape Qld Australia 56 B3
Van Diemen Gulf Australia 54 E2
Van Diemen's Land state Australia see
Tasmania
Vändra Estonia 15 N7
Väner, Lake Sweden see Vänern
Vänern l. Sweden 15 H7
Vänersborg Sweden 15 H7
Vangaindrano Madag. 49 E6
Van Gölü salt l. Turkey see Van, Lake
Van Horn U.S.A. 62 G5
Vanikoro Islands Solomon Is 53 G3
Vanimo P.N.G. 52 E2
Vanino Rus. Fed. 44 F2
Vanivilasa Sagara resr India 38 C3
Vaniyambadi India 38 C3
Vännäs Sweden 14 K5
Vannes France 24 C3
Vannovka Kazakh. see Turar Ryskulov
Vannøya i. Norway 14 K1
Van Rees, Pegunungan mts Indon. 41 F8
Vanrhynsdorp S. Africa 50 D6
Vansbro Sweden 15 I6
Vansittart Island Canada 61 J3
Vantaa Fin. 15 N6
Vanua Lava i. Vanuatu 53 G3
Vanua Levu i. Fiji 53 H3
Vanuatu country S. Pacific Ocean 53 G3
Vanwyksvlei S. Africa 50 E6
Vanwyksvlei l. S. Africa 50 E6
Van Zylsrus S. Africa 50 F4
Varahi India 36 B5
Varakļāni Latvia 15 O8
Varalé Côte d'Ivoire 46 C4
Varāmīn Iran 35 H4
Varanasi India 37 E4
Varandey Rus. Fed. 12 M1
Varangerfjorden sea chan. Norway 14 P1
Varangerhalvøya pen. Norway 14 P1
Varangerhalvøya Norway 14 P1
Varaždin Croatia 26 G1
Varberg Sweden 15 H8
Vardar r. Macedonia 27 J4
Varde Denmark 15 F9
Vardenis Armenia 35 G2
Vardø Norway 14 Q1
Varėna Lith. 15 N9
Varese Italy 26 C2
Varfolomeyevka Rus. Fed. 44 D3
Vårgårda Sweden 15 H7
Varginha Brazil 71 B3
Varillas Chile 70 B2
Varkana Iran see Gorgän
Varkaus Fin. 14 O5
Varna Bulg. 27 L3
Värnamo Sweden 15 I8
Värnäs Sweden 15 H6
Varnavino Rus. Fed. 12 J4
Várnjárg pen. Norway see
Varangerhalvøya
Varpaisjärvi Fin. 14 O5
Várpalota Hungary 26 H1
Varsaj Afgh. 36 B1
Varsh, Ozero l. Rus. Fed. 12 J2
Varto Turkey 35 F3
Várzea da Palma Brazil 71 B2
Vasa Fin. see Vaasa
Vasai India 38 B2
Vashka r. Rus. Fed. 12 J2
Vasht Iran see Khäsh
Vasilkov Ukr. see Vasyl'kiv
Vasknarva Estonia 15 O7
Vaslui Romania 27 L1
Vass-Soproni-síkság hills Hungary 26 G1
Vastan Turkey see Gevaş
Västerås Sweden 15 J7
Västerdalälven r. Sweden 15 I6
Västerfjäll Sweden 14 J3
Västerhaninge Sweden 15 K7
Västervik Sweden 15 J8
Vasto Italy 26 F3
Vasyl'kiv Ukr. 13 F6
Vatan France 24 E3
Vaté i. Vanuatu see Éfaté
Vatersay i. U.K. 20 B4
Vathar India 38 B2
Vathí Greece see Vathy
Vathy Greece 27 L6
Vatican City Europe 26 E4
Vaticano, Città del Europe see Vatican City
Vatnajökull Iceland 14 [inset]
Vatnajökull nat. park Iceland 14 [inset]
Vatoa i. Fiji 53 I3
Vatra Dornei Romania 27 K1
Vättern, Lake Sweden see Vättern
Vättern l. Sweden 15 I7
Vaughn U.S.A. 62 F5
Vaupés r. Col. 68 E3
Vauvert France 24 G5
Vavatenina Madag. 49 E5
Vava'u Group is Tonga 53 I3
Vavitao i. Fr. Polynesia see Raivavae
Vavoua Côte d'Ivoire 46 C4
Vavozh Rus. Fed. 12 L4
Vavuniya Sri Lanka 38 D4
Vawkavysk Belarus 15 N10
Växjö Sweden 15 I8
Vayenga Rus. Fed. see Severomorsk
Vazante Brazil 71 B2
Vazáš Sweden see Vittangi
Veaikevárri Sweden see Svappavaara
Vedaranniyam India 38 C4
Vedasandur India 38 C4
Veddige Sweden 15 H8
Vedea r. Romania 27 K3
Veendam Neth. 17 K4
Vega i. Norway 14 H4
Vehari Pak. 36 C3
Vehkalahti Fin. 15 O6
Vehoa Bol. 68 F6
Veinticinco de Mayo Buenos Aires Arg. see
25 de Mayo
Veinticinco de Mayo La Pampa Arg. see
25 de Mayo

Veirwaro Pak. 36 B4
Vejle Denmark 15 F9
Velbüzhdki Prokhod pass Bulg./Macedonia
27 J3
Velddrif S. Africa 50 D7
Velebit mts Croatia 26 F2
Velenje Slovenia 26 F1
Veles Macedonia 27 I4
Vélez-Málaga Spain 25 D5
Vélez-Rubio Spain 25 E5
Velhas r. Brazil 71 B2
Velibaba Turkey see Aras
Velika Gorica Croatia 26 G2
Velika Plana Serbia 27 I2
Velikaya r. Rus. Fed. 15 K4
Velikaya r. Rus. Fed. 15 P8
Velikaya r. Rus. Fed. 29 T3
Velikaya Kema Rus. Fed. 44 E3
Veliki Preslav Bulg. 27 L3
Velikiye Luki Rus. Fed. 12 F4
Velikiy Novgorod Rus. Fed. 12 F4
Velikiy Ustyug Rus. Fed. 12 J3
Velikonda Range hills India 38 C3
Velikoye Rus. Fed. 12 H4
Velikoye, Ozero l. Rus. Fed. 13 I5
Veli Lošinj Croatia 26 F2
Velizh Rus. Fed. 12 F5
Vella Lavella i. Solomon Is 53 F2
Vellore India 38 C3
Vel'sk Rus. Fed. 12 I3
Velsuna Italy see Orvieto
Velten Germany 17 N4
Velykyy Tokmak Ukr. see Tokmak
Vel'yu r. Rus. Fed. 12 L3
Vemalwada India 38 C2
Vema Seamount sea feature
S. Atlantic Ocean 72 I8
Vema Trench sea feature Indian Ocean
73 M6
Vempalle India 38 C3
Venado Tuerto Arg. 70 D4
Venafro Italy 26 F4
Venceslau Bráz Brazil 71 A3
Vendinga Rus. Fed. 12 J3
Vendôme France 24 E3
Venetia Italy see Venice
Venetie Landing U.S.A. 60 D3
Venev Rus. Fed. 13 H5
Venezia Italy see Venice
Venezia, Golfo di g. Europe see
Venice, Gulf of
Venezuela country S. America 68 E2
Venezuela, Golfo de g. Venez. 68 D1
Venezuelan Basin sea feature
S. Atlantic Ocean 72 D4
Vengurla India 38 B3
Veniaminof Volcano U.S.A. 60 C4
Venice Italy 26 E2
Venice, Gulf of Europe 26 E2
Venice U.S.A. 63 K6
Venissieux France 24 G4
Venkatapalem India 38 D2
Venkatapuram India 38 D2
Vennesla Norway 15 E7
Venta r. Latvia/Lith. 15 M8
Venta Lith. 15 M8
Ventersburg S. Africa 51 H5
Ventersdorp S. Africa 51 H4
Venterstad S. Africa 51 G6
Ventnor U.K. 19 F8
Ventotene, Isola i. Italy 26 E4
Ventoux, Mont mt. France 24 G4
Ventspils Latvia 15 L8
Ventura CA U.S.A. 65 C3
Venus Bay Australia 58 B7
Vera Arg. 70 D3
Vera, Point CA U.S.A. 65 F2
Vera Cruz Brazil 71 A3
Veracruz Mex. 66 E5
Vera Cruz Mex. see Veracruz
Veraval India 36 B5
Verbania Italy 26 C2
Vercelli Italy 26 C2
Vercors reg. France 24 G4
Verdalsøra Norway 14 G5
Verde r. Goiás Brazil 71 A2
Verde r. Goiás/Minas Gerais Brazil 71 B2
Verde r. Minas Gerais Brazil 71 A2
Verde r. Mex. 66 C4
Verde r. Mex. 66 C4
Verden (Aller) Germany 17 L4
Verde Pequeno r. Brazil 71 C1
Verdon r. France 24 G5
Verdun France 24 G5
Vereeniging S. Africa 51 H4
Vereshchagino Rus. Fed. 11 Q4
Véria Greece see Veroia
Verín Spain 25 C3
Veríssimo Brazil 71 A2
Vietnam country Asia 31 J5
Viêt Nam country Asia see Vietnam
Viêt Tri Vietnam 42 J8
Vigan Phil. 41 N3
Vigevano Italy 26 C2
Vigia Brazil 69 I4
Vignemale mt. France 22 D3
Vignola Italy 26 D2
Vigo Spain 25 B2
Vihanti Fin. 14 N4
Vihti Fin. 15 N6
Viipuri Rus. Fed. see Vyborg
Viitasaari Fin. 14 N5
Vijayadurg India 38 B2
Vijayanagaram India see Vizianagaram
Vijayapati India 38 C4
Vijayawada India 38 D2
Vík Iceland 14 [inset]
Vikajärvi Fin. 14 O3
Vikeke East Timor see Viqueque
Vikna i. Norway 14 G4
Vikøyri Norway 15 E6
Vila Vanuatu see Port Vila
Vila Alferes Chamusca Moz. see Guija
Vila Bittencourt Brazil 68 E4
Vila Bugaço Angola see Camanongue
Vila Cabral Moz. see Lichinga
Vila da Ponte Angola see Kuvango
Vila de Aljustrel Angola see Cangamba
Vila de Almoster Angola see Chiange
Vila de João Belo Moz. see Xai-Xai
Vila de María Arg. 70 D3
Vila de Trego Morais Moz. see Chókwè
Vila do Tarrafal Cape Verde see Tarrafal
Vila Fontes Moz. see Caia
Vila Franca de Xira Port. 25 B4
Vilagarcia de Arousa Spain 25 B2
Vila Gomes da Costa Moz. 51 K3
Vila Luísa Moz. see Marracuene
Vila Marechal Carmona Angola see Uíge
Vila Miranda Moz. see Macaloge
Vilanandro, Tanjona c. Madag. 49 E5
Vilanculos Moz. 51 L1
Vila Nova de Gaia Port. 25 B3
Vila Pery Moz. see Chimoio
Vila Real Port. 25 C3
Vilar Formoso Port. 25 C3
Vila Salazar Angola see N'dalatando
Vila Salazar Zimbabwe see Sango

Vesoul France 24 H3
Vesterålen is Norway 14 H2
Vesterålsfjorden sea chan. Norway 14 H2
Vestertana Norway 14 O1
Vestfjorddalen Norway 15 F7
Vestfjorden sea chan. Norway 14 H3
Véstia Brazil 71 A3
Vestmanna Faroe Is 14 [inset]
Vestmannaeyjar Iceland 14 [inset]
Vestmannaeyjar is Iceland 14 [inset]
Vestnes Norway 14 E5
Vesturhorn hd Iceland 14 [inset]
Vesuvio vol. Italy see Vesuvius
Vesuvius vol. Italy 26 F4
Ves'yegonsk Rus. Fed. 12 H4
Veszprém Hungary 26 G1
Veteli Fin. 14 M5
Vetlanda Sweden 15 I8
Vetluga Rus. Fed. 12 J4
Vetluga r. Rus. Fed. 12 J4
Vetluzhskiy Kostromskaya Oblast' Rus. Fed.
12 J4
Vetluzhskiy Nizhegorodskaya Oblast'
Rus. Fed. 12 J4
Vettore, Monte mt. Italy 26 E3
Vevey Switz. 24 H3
Veyo UT U.S.A. 65 F2
Vézère r. France 24 E4
Vezirköprü Turkey 34 D2
Viamao Brazil 71 A5
Viana Espírito Santo Brazil 71 C3
Viana Maranhão Brazil 69 J4
Viana do Castelo Port. 25 B3
Viangchan Laos see Vientiane
Viannos Greece 27 K7
Viánopolis Brazil 71 A2
Viareggio Italy 26 D3
Viborg Denmark 15 F8
Viborg Rus. Fed. see Vyborg
Vic Spain 25 H3
Vicecomodoro Marambio research stn
Antarctica see Marambio
Vicente, Point CA U.S.A. 65 C4
Vicente Guerrero Mex. 66 A2
Vicenza Italy 26 D2
Vich Spain see Vic
Vichada r. Col. 68 E3
Vichy France 24 F3
Vicksburg AZ U.S.A. 65 F4
Vicksburg MS U.S.A. 63 I5
Viçosa Brazil 71 C3
Victor, Mount Antarctica 76 D2
Victor Harbor Australia 57 B7
Victoria r. Australia 54 E3
Victoria state Australia 58 B6
Victoria Canada 62 C2
Victoria Chile 70 B5
Victoria Malta 26 F6
Victoria Seychelles 73 L6
Victoria TX U.S.A. 63 H6
Victoria VA U.S.A. 64 F4
Victoria prov. Zimbabwe see Masvingo
Victoria, Lake Africa 48 D4
Victoria, Lake Australia 57 C7
Victoria, Mount Fiji see Tomanivi
Victoria, Mount Myanmar 37 H5
Victoria, Mount P.N.G. 52 E2
Victoria and Albert Mountains Canada
61 K2
Victoria Falls Zambia/Zimbabwe 49 C5
Victoria Island Canada 60 H2
Victoria Land coastal area Antarctica 76 H2
Victoria Peak Belize 66 G5
Victoria Range mts N.Z. 59 D6
Victoria River Downs Australia 54 E4
Victoria West S. Africa 50 F6
Victorica Arg. 70 D5
Victorville CA U.S.A. 65 D3
Victory Downs Australia 55 F6
Vidal Junction CA U.S.A. 65 E3
Videle Romania 27 K2
Vidisha India 36 D5
Vidin Bulg. 27 J3
Vidlin U.K. 20 [inset]
Vidlitsa Rus. Fed. 12 G3
Viedma Arg. 70 D6
Viedma, Lago l. Arg. 70 B7
Vienna Austria 17 P6
Vienna France 24 G4
Vienne r. France 24 E3
Vientiane Laos 41 C6
Vieques i. Puerto Rico 67 K5
Vieremä Fin. 14 O5
Vierzon France 24 F3
Viesīte Latvia 15 N8
Vieste Italy 26 G4
Vietas Sweden 14 K3
Vimmerby Sweden 15 I8
Vina r. Cameroon 47 D4
Viña del Mar Chile 70 B4
Vinaròs Spain 25 G3
Vinaroz Spain see Vinaròs
Vincennes U.S.A. 63 J4
Vincennes Bay Antarctica 76 F2
Vinchina Arg. 70 C3
Vindelälven r. Sweden 14 K5
Vindeln Sweden 14 K4
Vindhya Range hills India 36 C5
Vindobona Austria see Vienna
Vineland NJ U.S.A. 64 D3
Vinh Vietnam 42 J8
Vinita U.S.A. 63 H4
Vinjhan India 36 B5
Vinland i. Canada see Newfoundland
Vinnitsa Ukr. see Vinnytsya
Vinnytsya Ukr. 13 F6
Vinogradov Ukr. see Vynohradiv
Vinson Massif mt. Antarctica 76 L1
Vinstra Norway 15 F6
Vinukonda India 38 C2
Viqueque East Timor 54 D2
Viramgam India 36 C5
Viranşehir Turkey 35 E3
Virawah Pak. 36 B4
Virchow, Mount h. Australia 54 B5
Virdel India 36 C5
Virden Canada 62 G2
Vire France 24 D2
Virei Angola 49 B5
Virgem da Lapa Brazil 71 C2
Virgin r. AZ U.S.A. 65 E2
Virginia Ireland 21 E4
Virginia S. Africa 51 H5
Virginia state U.S.A. 64 E4
Virginia Beach VA U.S.A. 64 D4
Virginia City NV U.S.A. 65 C1
Virgin Islands (U.K.) terr. West Indies 67 L5
Virgin Islands (U.S.A.) terr. West Indies
67 L5
Virgin Mountains AZ U.S.A. 65 E2
Virginópolis Brazil 71 C2
Virkkala Fin. 15 N6
Virovitica Croatia 26 G2
Virrat Fin. 14 M5
Virtsu Estonia 15 M7
Virudhunagar India 38 C4
Virudunagar India see Virudhunagar
Virunga, Parc National des nat. park
Dem. Rep. Congo 48 C4
Vis i. Croatia 26 G3
Visaginas Lith. 15 O9
Visakhapatnam India see Vishakhapatnam
Visalia CA U.S.A. 65 C2
Visapur India 38 B2
Visby Sweden 15 K8
Viscount Melville Sound sea chan. Canada
61 G2
Viseu Brazil 69 I4
Viseu Port. 25 C3
Vishakhapatnam India 38 D2
Vishera r. Rus. Fed. 11 R4
Vishera r. Rus. Fed. 12 L3
Viški Latvia 15 O8
Visnagar India 36 C5

(125)

Wien Austria see Vienna
Wiener Neustadt Austria 17 P7
Wiesbaden Germany 17 L5
Wieżyca h. Poland 17 Q3
Wigan U.K. 18 E5
Wight, Isle of i. England U.K. 19 F8
Wigierski Park Narodowy nat. park Poland 15 M9
Wigston U.K. 19 F6
Wigton U.K. 18 D4
Wigtown U.K. 20 E6
Wigtown Bay U.K. 20 E6
Wilberforce, Cape Australia 56 B1
Wilcannia Australia 58 A3
Wilcox PA U.S.A. 64 F4
Wilczek Land i. Rus. Fed. see Vil'cheka, Zemlya
Wildcat Peak NV U.S.A. 65 D1
Wild Coast S. Africa 51 I6
Wilderness National Park S. Africa 50 F8
Wildspitze mt. Austria 17 M7
Wildwood NJ U.S.A. 64 D3
Wilge r. S. Africa 51 I4
Wilge r. S. Africa 51 I3
Wilgena Australia 55 F7
Wilhelm, Mount P.N.G. 52 E2
Wilhelm II Land reg. Antarctica see Kaiser Wilhelm II Land
Wilhelmina Gebergte mts Suriname 69 G3
Wilhelmshaven Germany 17 L4
Wilhelmstal Namibia 50 C1
Wilkes-Barre PA U.S.A. 64 D2
Wilkes Coast Antarctica 76 G2
Wilkes Land reg. Antarctica 76 G2
Wilkie Canada 62 F1
Wilkins Coast Antarctica 76 L2
Wilkins Ice Shelf Antarctica 76 L2
Wilkinson Lakes imp. l. Australia 55 F7
Willand U.K. 19 D8
Willandra Billabong watercourse Australia 58 B4
Willandra National Park Australia 58 B4
Willcox AZ U.S.A. 62 F5
Willemstad Neth. Antilles 67 K6
Willeroo Australia 54 E3
William, Mount U.S.A. see Jalapa
William Creek Australia 57 B6
Williams AZ U.S.A. 62 E4
Williams CA U.S.A. 65 A1
Williamsburg VA U.S.A. 64 C4
Williams Lake Canada 62 C1
Williamson NY U.S.A. 64 C1
Williamson WV U.S.A. 63 K4
Williamsport PA U.S.A. 64 C2
Williamstown NJ U.S.A. 64 D3
Williamstown NY U.S.A. 64 D1
Willimantic CT U.S.A. 64 E2
Willis Group atolls Australia 56 E3
Williston S. Africa 50 E6
Williston ND U.S.A. 62 G2
Williston Lake Canada 60 F4
Williton U.K. 19 D7
Willmar U.S.A. 63 H2
Willow Beach AZ U.S.A. 65 E3
Willow Hill PA U.S.A. 64 C2
Willowmore S. Africa 50 F7
Willowra Australia 54 F5
Willowvale S. Africa 51 I7
Wills, Lake imp. l. Australia 54 E5
Wilmington DE U.S.A. 64 D3
Wilmington NC U.S.A. 63 L5
Wilmslow U.K. 18 E5
Wilno Lith. see Vilnius
Wilpattu National Park Sri Lanka 38 D4
Wilson watercourse Australia 57 C5
Wilson NC U.S.A. 63 L4
Wilson NY U.S.A. 64 B1
Wilson, Mount NV U.S.A. 65 E1
Wilsonia CA U.S.A. 65 C2
Wilson's Promontory pen. Australia 58 C7
Wilson's Promontory National Park Australia 58 C7
Wilton r. Australia 54 F3
Wiluna Australia 55 C6
Wimereux France 19 I8
Wina r. Cameroon see Vina
Winbin watercourse Australia 57 D5
Winburg S. Africa 51 H5
Wincanton U.K. 19 E7
Winchester U.K. 19 F7
Winchester KY U.S.A. 63 K4
Winchester NH U.S.A. 64 E1
Winchester VA U.S.A. 64 B3
Windau Latvia see Ventspils
Windber PA U.S.A. 64 B2
Windermere U.K. 18 E4
Windermere l. U.K. 18 E4
Windhoek Namibia 50 C1
Windlestraw Law h. U.K. 20 G5
Windom U.S.A. 63 H3
Windorah Australia 56 C5
Wind River Range mts U.S.A. 62 F3
Windrush r. U.K. 19 F7
Windsor Australia 58 E4
Windsor Ont. Canada 63 K3
Windsor U.K. 19 G7
Windsor NY U.S.A. 64 D1
Windsor VT U.S.A. 64 E1
Windsor Locks CT U.S.A. 64 E2
Windward Islands Caribbean Sea 67 L5
Windward Passage Cuba/Haiti 67 J5
Windy U.S.A. 60 D3
Winfield KS U.S.A. 63 H4
Winfield U.S.A. 63 J5
Wingate U.K. 18 F4
Wingen Australia 58 E3
Wingham Australia 58 F3
Winisk r. Canada 61 J4
Winisk (abandoned) Canada 61 J4
Winisk Lake Canada 63 J1
Winneba Ghana 46 C4
Winnecke Creek watercourse Australia 54 E4
Winnemucca U.S.A. 62 D3
Winner U.S.A. 62 G3
Winnfield U.S.A. 63 I5
Winning Australia 55 A5
Winnipeg Canada 61 I5
Winnipeg, Lake Canada 61 I4
Winnipegosis, Lake Canada 61 H4
Winnipesaukee, Lake NH U.S.A. 64 F1
Winona MN U.S.A. 63 I3
Winona MS U.S.A. 63 J5
Winsford U.K. 18 E5
Winslow AZ U.S.A. 62 E4
Winsted CT U.S.A. 64 E2
Winston-Salem U.S.A. 63 K4
Winters CA U.S.A. 65 B1
Winterthur Switz. 24 I3
Winterton S. Africa 51 I5
Winton Australia 56 C4
Winton N.Z. 59 B8
Winwick U.K. 19 G6
Wirral pen. U.K. 18 D5
Wirrulla Australia 57 A7
Wisbech U.K. 19 H6
Wisconsin state U.S.A. 63 J3
Wisconsin r. U.S.A. 63 J3
Wisconsin Rapids U.S.A. 63 J3
Wiseman U.S.A. 60 C3
Wishaw U.K. 20 F5
Wisil Dabarow Somalia 48 E3
Wisła r. Poland see Vistula

Wismar Germany 17 M4
Witbank S. Africa 51 I3
Witbooisvlei Namibia 50 D3
Witham U.K. 19 H7
Witham r. U.K. 19 H6
Withernsea U.K. 18 H5
Witjira National Park Australia 57 A5
Witney U.K. 19 F7
Witrivier S. Africa 51 J3
Wittenberg Germany see Lutherstadt Wittenberg
Wittenberge Germany 17 M4
Wittenburg Germany 17 M4
Wittlich Germany 17 K6
Wittstock Germany 17 N4
Witu Islands P.N.G. 52 E2
Witvlei Namibia 50 D2
Wivenhoe, Lake Australia 58 F1
Władysławowo Poland 17 Q3
Włocławek Poland 17 Q4
Włodawa Poland 17 R5
Woburn Canada 62 G2
Wodonga Australia 58 C6
Wohlthat Mountains Antarctica 76 C2
Wöjjä atoll Marshall Is see Wotje
Wokam i. Indon. 41 I8
Woken He r. China 44 C3
Wokha India 37 H4
Woking U.K. 19 G7
Wokingham watercourse Australia 56 C4
Wokingham U.K. 19 G7
Woko National Park Australia 58 E3
Wolcott NY U.S.A. 64 C1
Wolfenbüttel Germany 17 M4
Wolf Point U.S.A. 62 F2
Wolfsberg Austria 17 O7
Wolfsburg Germany 17 M4
Wolfville Canada 63 O2
Wolgast Germany 17 N3
Wolin Poland 17 O4
Wollaston Lake Canada 60 H4
Wollaston Lake l. Canada 60 H4
Wollaston Peninsula Canada 60 G3
Wollemi National Park Australia 58 E4
Wollongong Australia 58 E5
Wolmaransstad S. Africa 51 G4
Wolseley Australia 57 C8
Wolseley S. Africa 50 D7
Wolsingham U.K. 18 F4
Wolverhampton U.K. 19 E6
Wonarah Australia 56 B3
Wonay, Kowtal-e Afgh. 36 B2
Wondai Australia 57 E5
Wongalarroo Lake salt l. Australia 58 B3
Wongarbon Australia 58 D4
Wŏnju S. Korea 45 B5
Wonowon Canada 60 F4
Wŏnsan N. Korea 45 B5
Wonthaggi Australia 58 B7
Wonyulgunna, Mount h. Australia 55 B6
Woocalla Australia 57 B6
Woodbine NJ U.S.A. 64 D3
Woodbridge U.K. 19 I6
Woodbridge VA U.S.A. 64 C3
Woodbury NJ U.S.A. 64 D3
Wooded Bluff hd Australia 58 F2
Woodlake CA U.S.A. 65 C2
Woodland CA U.S.A. 65 B1
Woodland PA U.S.A. 64 B2
Woodlark Island P.N.G. 52 F2
Woodroffe watercourse Australia 56 B4
Woodroffe, Mount Australia 55 E6
Woods, Lake imp. l. Australia 54 F4
Woods, Lake of the Canada/U.S.A. 63 I2
Woodside Australia 58 C7
Woodsfield OH U.S.A. 64 A3
Woodstock Ont. Canada 64 A1
Woodstock U.K. 19 F7
Woodstock VT U.S.A. 64 E1
Woodward U.S.A. 62 H4
Woody CA U.S.A. 65 C3
Wooler U.K. 18 E3
Woolgoolga Australia 58 F3
Wooli Australia 58 F3
Woollard, Mount Antarctica 76 K1
Woolyeenyer Hill h. Australia 55 C8
Woomera Australia 57 B6
Woomera Prohibited Area Australia 55 F7
Woonsocket RI U.S.A. 64 F1
Woorabinda Australia 56 E5
Wooramel r. Australia 55 A6
Wooster U.S.A. 63 K3
Worbody Point Australia 56 C2
Worcester S. Africa 50 D7
Worcester U.K. 19 E6
Worcester MA U.S.A. 64 F1
Worcester NY U.S.A. 64 D1
Wörgl Austria 17 N7
Workington U.K. 18 D4
Worksop U.K. 18 F5
Worland U.S.A. 62 F3
Worms Head hd U.K. 19 C7
Wortel Namibia 50 C2
Worthing U.K. 19 G8
Wotje atoll Marshall Is 74 H5
Wotu Indon. 52 C2
Wowoni i. Indon. 41 E8
Wrangel Island Rus. Fed. 29 T2
Wrangell U.S.A. 60 D4
Wrangell Mountains U.S.A. 77 B3
Wrangell-St Elias National Park and Preserve U.S.A. 60 D3
Wrath, Cape U.K. 20 D2
Wray U.S.A. 62 G3
Wreake r. U.K. 19 F6
Wreck Point S. Africa 50 C5
Wreck Reef Australia 56 F4
Wrecsam U.K. see Wrexham
Wrexham U.K. 19 E5
Wrightwood CA U.S.A. 65 D3
Wrigley Canada 60 F3
Wrigley Gulf Antarctica 76 J2
Wrocław Poland 17 P5
Września Poland 17 P4
Wubin Australia 55 B7
Wuchang Heilong. China 44 B3
Wuchow China see Wuzhou
Wudalianchi China 44 B2
Wudinna Australia 55 F8
Wuhai China 42 J5
Wuhan China 43 L6
Wuhu China 43 L6
Wüjang China 36 D2
Wujin Jiangsu China see Changzhou
Wukari Nigeria 46 D4
Wuli China 42 G6
Wuliang Shan mts China 42 I8
Wuliaru i. Indon. 54 E1
Wulur Indon. 54 E1
Wundwin Myanmar 37 I5
Wunnummin Lake Canada 61 J4
Wuppertal Germany 17 K5
Wuppertal S. Africa 50 D7
Wuqi China 43 J5
Wuqia China 42 G4
Wuranga Australia 55 B7
Wurno Nigeria 46 D3
Würzburg Germany 17 L6
Wushi China 42 I5
Wusuli Jiang r. China/Rus. Fed. see Ussuri
Wuvulu Island P.N.G. 52 E2
Wuwei China 42 I5
Wuxi Jiangsu China 43 M6

Wuxian China see Suzhou
Wuxing China see Huzhou
Wuyang Guizhou China see Zhenyuan
Wuyiling China 44 B2
Wuyi Shan mts China 43 L7
Wuyuan Nei Mongol China 43 J4
Wuzhong China 42 J5
Wuzhou China 43 K8
Wyalkatchem Australia 55 B7
Wyalong Australia 58 C4
Wyandra Australia 58 B1
Wyangala Reservoir Australia 58 D4
Wyara, Lake imp. l. Australia 58 B2
Wycheproof Australia 58 A6
Wylliesburg VA U.S.A. 64 B4
Wyloo Australia 54 B5
Wylye r. U.K. 19 F7
Wymondham U.K. 19 I6
Wynbring Australia 55 F7
Wyndham Australia 58 F1
Wyndham-Werribee Australia 58 B6
Wynyard Canada 62 G1
Wyola Lake imp. l. Australia 55 E7
Wyoming state U.S.A. 62 F3
Wyong Australia 58 E4
Wyperfeld National Park Australia 57 C7
Wysox PA U.S.A. 64 C2
Wyszków Poland 17 R4
Wythall U.K. 19 F6
Wytheville VA U.S.A. 64 A4

X

Xaafuun Somalia 48 F2
Xaafuun, Raas pt Somalia 32 H7
Xabyaisamba China 37 I3
Xaçmaz Azer. 35 H2
Xago China 37 G3
Xagquka China 37 H3
Xaidulla China 36 D1
Xaignabouli Laos 42 I9
Xaignabouri Laos see Xaignabouli
Xainza China 37 G3
Xai-Xai Moz. 51 K3
Xalapa Mex. see Jalapa
Xambioá Brazil 69 I5
Xam Nua Laos 40 C5
Xá-Muteba Angola 49 B4
Xanagas Botswana 50 E2
Xangda China see Nangqên
Xangdin Hural China 43 K4
Xangdoring China 37 E2
Xangongo Angola 49 B5
Xankändi Azer. 35 G3
Xanlar Azer. 35 G2
Xanthi Greece 27 K4
Xarag China 37 I1
Xarardheere Somalia 48 E3
Xàtiva Spain 25 F4
Xavantes, Serra dos hills Brazil 69 I6
Xaxa China 37 E2
Xayar China 42 E4
Xela Guat. see Quetzaltenango
Xelva Spain see Chelva
Xero Potamos r. Cyprus see Xeros
Xeros r. Cyprus 39 A2
Xhora S. Africa see Elliotdale
Xiabole Shan mt. China 44 B2
Xiaguan China see Dali
Xiamen China 43 L8
Xi'an China 43 J5
Xianfeng China 43 J7
Xiangfan China 43 K6
Xianggang H.K. China see Hong Kong
Xianggang Tebie Xingzhengqu aut. reg. China see Hong Kong
Xianggelila China 42 H7
Xiangning China 43 K5
Xiangquan He r. China see Langqên Zangbo
Xiangride China 37 I2
Xiangtan China 43 K7
Xiangyang China see Xiangfan
Xiangyang Hu l. China 37 G2
Xianning China 43 K7
Xiantao China 43 K6
Xianxia Ling mts China 43 L7
Xianyang China 43 J6
Xiaocaohu China 42 F4
Xiao'ergou China 44 A2
Xiaogan China 43 K6
Xiao Hinggan Ling mts China 44 B2
Xiaonanchuan China 37 H2
Xiaoshi China see Benxi
Xiao Surmang China 37 H2
Xiashan China see Zhanjiang
Xiayingpan Guizhou China see Lupanshui
Xichang China 42 I7
Xieng Khouang Laos see Phônsavan
Xifeng Liaoning China 44 B4
Xigazê China 37 G3
Xi Jiang r. China 43 K8
Xijir China 37 G2
Xijir Ulan Hu salt l. China 37 G2
Xiliao He r. China 44 A4
Xilinhot China 43 L4
Ximiao China 42 I4
Xinavane Moz. 51 K3
Xin Barag Zuoqi China see Amgalang
Xincun China see Dongchuan
Xindian China 44 B3
Xindu Sichuan China see Luhuo
Xing'an Shaanxi China see Ankang
Xingba China 42 G7
Xingguo Jiangxi China 43 L7
Xinghai China 42 H5
Xingkai China 44 D3
Xingkai Hu l. China/Rus. Fed. see Khanka, Lake
Xinglong China 44 B2
Xinglongzhen Heilong. China 44 B3
Xingning Guangdong China 43 L8
Xingtai China 43 K5
Xingu r. Brazil 69 H4
Xingu, Parque Indígena do res. Brazil 69 H6
Xinguara Brazil 69 H5
Xingyi China 42 I7
Xinhua Yunnan China see Funing
Xinhuang China 43 J7
Xining China 42 I5
Xinjiang aut. reg. China see Xinjiang Uygur Zizhiqu
Xinjiang Uygur Zizhiqu aut. reg. China 36 E1
Xinkai He r. China 44 A4
Xinlitun China 44 B2
Xinmin China 44 B2
Xinning Gansu China see Ningxian
Xinqing China 44 C2
Xintai China 43 L5
Xinxiang China 43 K5
Xinyang Henan China 43 K6
Xinyi Jiangsu China 43 L6
Xinyu China 43 K7
Xinyuan Qinghai China see Tianjun
Xinyuan Xinjiang China 42 E4
Xinzhangfang China 44 A2

Xinzhou Shanxi China 43 K5
Xinzhu Taiwan see Hsinchu
Xinzo de Limia Spain 25 C2
Xiongzhou China see Nanxiong
Xiqing Shan mts China 42 I6
Xisha Qundao is S. China Sea see Paracel Islands
Xiugu China see Jinxi
Xi Ujimqin Qi China see Bayan Ul Hot
Xiwu China 37 I2
Xixabangma Feng mt. China 37 F3
Xixiang China 43 J6
Xixiu China see Anshun
Xizang aut. reg. China see Xizang Zizhiqu
Xizang Gaoyuan plat. China see Tibet, Plateau of
Xizang Zizhiqu aut. reg. China 37 G3
Xo'jayli Uzbek. 33 I1
Xorkol China 42 G5
Xuanhua China 43 L4
Xuanwei China 42 I7
Xucheng China see Xuwen
Xugui China 43 I4
Xuguit Qi China see Yakeshi
Xümatang China 37 I2
Xungba China see Xangdoring
Xungmai China 37 G3
Xunhe China 44 B2
Xun He r. China 44 C2
Xun Jiang r. China 40 D5
Xúquer, Riu r. Spain 25 F4
Xuru Co l. China 37 G3
Xuwen China 31 K4
Xuyong China 42 J7
Xuzhou China 43 L6

Y

Ya'an China 42 I6
Yabanabat Turkey see Kızılcahamam
Yabēlo Eth. 48 D3
Yablonovyy Khrebet mts Rus. Fed. 43 J2
Yabuli China 44 C3
Yacuma r. Bol. 68 E6
Yadgir India 38 C2
Yadrin Rus. Fed. 12 J5
Yaeyama-rettō is Japan 43 M8
Yafa Israel see Tel Aviv-Yafo
Yagaba Ghana 46 C4
Yagan China 42 I4
Yagan r. Asia 39 B3
Yağda Turkey see Erdemli
Yaghan Basin sea feature S. Atlantic Ocean 72 D9
Yagman Turkm. 35 I3
Yagodnoye Rus. Fed. 29 P3
Yagodnyy Rus. Fed. 44 E2
Yagoua Cameroon 47 E3
Yagra China 37 E2
Yagradagzê Shan mt. China 37 H2
Yahualica Mex. 66 D4
Yahyalı Turkey 23 L4
Yaizu Japan 45 E6
Yakacık Turkey 39 C1
Yakeshi China 43 M3
Yakima U.S.A. 62 C2
Yako Burkina 46 C3
Yakovlevka Rus. Fed. 44 D3
Yaku-shima i. Japan 45 C7
Yakutat U.S.A. 60 D4
Yakutat Bay U.S.A. 60 D4
Yakutsk Rus. Fed. 29 N3
Yakymivka Ukr. 13 G7
Yala Thai. 31 J6
Yalai China 37 F3
Yala National Park Sri Lanka see Ruhuna National Park
Yalan Dünya Mağarası tourist site Turkey 39 A1
Yalgoo Australia 55 B7
Yalleroi Australia 56 D4
Yaloké Cent. Afr. Rep. 48 B3
Yalova Turkey 27 M4
Yalta Ukr. 34 D1
Yalu r. China/N. Korea 44 B4
Yalujiang Kou r. mouth China/N. Korea 45 B5
Yalvaç Turkey 27 N5
Yamagata Japan 45 F5
Yamaguchi Japan 45 C6
Yamal, Poluostrov pen. Rus. Fed. see Yamal Peninsula
Yam-Alin', Khrebet mts Rus. Fed. 44 D1
Yamal Peninsula Rus. Fed. 28 H2
Yamanie Falls National Park Australia 56 D3
Yamba Australia 58 F2
Yambarran Range hills Australia 54 E3
Yambi, Mesa de hills Col. 68 D3
Yambio Sudan 47 F4
Yambol Bulg. 27 L3
Yamdena i. Indon. 54 E1
Yamethin Myanmar 37 I5
Yamkanmardi India 38 B2
Yamkhad Syria see Aleppo
Yamm Rus. Fed. 15 P7
Yamma Yamma, Lake imp. l. Australia 57 C5
Yamoussoukro Côte d'Ivoire 46 C4
Yampil' Ukr. 13 G6
Yampol' Ukr. see Yampil'
Yamuna r. India 36 D4
Yamunanagar India 36 D3
Yamzho Yumco l. China 37 G3
Yana r. Rus. Fed. 29 O2
Yan'an China 43 J5
Yanaoca Peru 68 D6
Yanaon India see Yanam
Yanaul Rus. Fed. 11 Q4
Yanbu' al Baḥr Saudi Arabia 32 E5
Yancheng Jiangsu China 43 M6
Yanchep Australia 55 A7
Yanco Australia 58 C5
Yanco Glen Australia 57 C6
Yandama Creek watercourse Australia 57 C6
Yandun China 42 G4
Yanfolila Mali 46 C3
Ya'ngamdo China 37 H3
Yang Hu l. China 37 F2
Yangi Qal'ah Afgh. 36 B1
Yangiqishloq Uzbek. 33 K1
Yangirabot Uzbek. 33 K1
Yangiyo'l Uzbek. 42 B4
Yangôn Myanmar see Rangoon
Yangquan China 43 K5
Yangtze r. Qinghai China 42 H6
Yangtze r. China 43 M6
Yangtze Kiang r. Qinghai China see Yangtze

Yangtze Kiang r. China see Yangtze
Yangudi Rassa National Park Eth. 48 E2
Yangyang S. Korea 45 C5
Yangzhou Jiangsu China 43 L6
Yanhuqu China 37 E2
Yanishpole Rus. Fed. 12 G3
Yanji China 44 C4
Yanjiang China see Ziyang
Yanjing Sichuan China see Yanyuan
Yankara National Park Nigeria 46 E4
Yankton U.S.A. 62 H3
Yannina Greece see Ioannina
Yano-Indigirskaya Nizmennost' lowland Rus. Fed. 29 P2
Yanrey r. Australia 55 A5
Yanshan Yunnan China 42 I8
Yanshiping China 37 H2
Yanskiy Zaliv g. Rus. Fed. 29 O2
Yantabulla Australia 58 B2
Yantai China 43 M5
Yantongshan China 44 B4
Yany-Kurgan Kazakh. see Zhanakorgan
Yanyuan China 42 I7
Yao Chad 47 E3
Yaoundé Cameroon 46 E4
Yaoxiaoling China 44 B2
Yap i. Micronesia 41 F7
Yapen i. Indon. 41 F8
Yappar r. Australia 56 C3
Yap Trench sea feature N. Pacific Ocean 74 F5
Yaqui r. Mex. 66 B3
Yar Rus. Fed. 12 L4
Yaraka Australia 56 D5
Yarangüme Turkey see Tavas
Yaransk Rus. Fed. 12 K4
Yardea Australia 57 A7
Yardımcı Burnu pt Turkey 27 N6
Yardımlı Azer. 35 H3
Yardymly Azer. see Yardımlı
Yare r. U.K. 19 I6
Yarega Rus. Fed. 12 L3
Yaren Nauru 53 G2
Yarensk Rus. Fed. 12 K3
Yariga-take mt. Japan 45 E5
Yarkand China see Shache
Yarkant China see Shache
Yarkant He r. China 36 D1
Yarkhun r. Pak. 36 C1
Yarlung Zangbo r. China see Brahmaputra
Yarmouth Canada 63 N3
Yarmouth England U.K. 19 F8
Yarmouth England U.K. see Great Yarmouth
Yarmuk r. Asia 39 B3
Yarnell AZ U.S.A. 65 F3
Yaroslavl' Rus. Fed. 12 H4
Yaroslavskiy Rus. Fed. 44 D3
Yarra r. Australia 58 B6
Yarra Junction Australia 58 B6
Yarram Australia 58 C7
Yarraman Australia 58 C1
Yarrawonga Australia 58 B6
Yarra Yarra Lakes imp. l. Australia 55 A7
Yarronvale Australia 58 B1
Yarrowmere Australia 56 D4
Yartö Tra La pass China 37 H3
Yartsevo Krasnoyarskiy Kray Rus. Fed. 28 J3
Yartsevo Smolenskaya Oblast' Rus. Fed. 13 G5
Yarumal Col. 68 C2
Yaş Romania see Iaşi
Yasawa Group is Fiji 53 H3
Yashkul' Rus. Fed. 13 J7
Yasin Pak. 36 C1
Yasnogorsk Rus. Fed. 13 H5
Yasnyy Rus. Fed. 44 C1
Yass Australia 58 D5
Yass r. Australia 58 D5
Yassı Burnu c. Cyprus see Plakoti, Cape
Yāsūj Iran 35 H4
Yasuní, Parque Nacional nat. park Ecuador 68 C4
Yatağan Turkey 27 M6
Yaté New Caledonia 53 G4
Yathkyed Lake Canada 61 I3
Yatsushiro Japan 45 C6
Yatta West Bank 39 B4
Yatton U.K. 19 E7
Yauca Peru 68 D7
Yavari r. Brazil/Peru 68 E4
Yavatmal India 38 C1
Yavi Turkey 35 F3
Yaví, Cerro mt. Venez. 68 E2
Yavoriv Ukr. 13 D6
Yavuzlu Turkey 39 C1
Yawatongguzlangar China 37 G1
Yaw Chaung r. Myanmar 37 H5
Yaxian China see Sanya
Yayladağı Turkey 39 C2
Yazd Iran 35 I3
Yazd-e Khvāst Iran 35 I5
Yazıhan Turkey 34 E2
Yazoo City U.S.A. 63 I5
Y Bala U.K. see Bala
Yding Skovhøj h. Denmark 17 L3
Ydra i. Greece 27 J6
Y Drenewydd U.K. see Newtown
Yea Australia 58 B6
Yealmpton U.K. 19 D8
Yebawmi Myanmar 37 H4
Yebbi-Bou Chad 47 E2
Yecheng China 42 D5
Yécora Mex. 62 F6
Yedatore India 38 C4
Yedi Burun Başı pt Turkey 27 M6
Yeeda River Australia 54 C4
Yefremov Rus. Fed. 13 H5
Yeghegnadzor Armenia 35 G3
Yegorlykskaya Rus. Fed. 13 I7
Yegorova, Mys pt Rus. Fed. 44 E3
Yegor'yevsk Rus. Fed. 13 H5
Yei Sudan 47 G4
Yei r. Sudan 47 G4
Yeji China 43 L6
Yejiaji China see Yeji
Yekaterinburg Rus. Fed. 28 H4
Yekaterinodar Rus. Fed. see Krasnodar
Yekaterinoslav Ukr. see Dnipropetrovs'k
Yekaterinoslavka Rus. Fed. 44 C2
Yekhegnadzor Armenia see Yeghegnadzor
Yelabuga Khabarovskiy Kray Rus. Fed. 44 D2
Yelabuga Respublika Tatarstan Rus. Fed. 12 K5
Yelan' Rus. Fed. 13 I6
Yelan' r. Rus. Fed. 13 I6
Yelandur India 38 C3
Yelantsy Rus. Fed. 42 J2
Yelarbon Australia 58 E2
Yelenovskiye Kar'yery Ukr. see Dokuchayevs'k
Yelets Rus. Fed. 13 H5
Yélimané Mali 46 B3
Yelizavetgrad Ukr. see Kirovohrad
Yelkhovka Rus. Fed. 13 K5
Yell i. U.K. 20 [inset]
Yellabina Regional Reserve nature res. Australia 55 F7

Yellandu India 38 D2
Yellapur India 38 B3
Yellow r. China 43 L5
Yellowknife Canada 60 G3
Yellow Mountain h. Australia 58 C4
Yellow Sea N. Pacific Ocean 43 N5
Yellowstone r. U.S.A. 62 G2
Yellowstone Lake U.S.A. 62 E3
Yell Sound str. U.K. 20 [inset]
Yelovo Rus. Fed. 11 Q4
Yel'sk Belarus 13 F6
Yelva r. Rus. Fed. 12 K3
Yematan China 37 I2
Yemen country Asia 32 G6
Yemetsk Rus. Fed. 12 I3
Yemişenbükü Turkey see Taşova
Yemmiganur India see Emmiganuru
Yemtsa Rus. Fed. 12 I3
Yemva Rus. Fed. 12 K3
Yena Rus. Fed. 14 Q3
Yenagoa Nigeria 46 D4
Yenakiyeve Ukr. 13 H6
Yenakiyevo Ukr. see Yenakiyeve
Yenangyat Myanmar 37 H5
Yenanma Myanmar 37 H6
Yenda Australia 58 C5
Yengisar China 33 M2
Yengo National Park Australia 58 E4
Yenice Turkey 27 L5
Yenidamlar Turkey see Demirtaş
Yenihan Turkey see Yıldızeli
Yenije-i-Vardar Greece see Giannitsa
Yenişehir Greece see Larisa
Yenişehir Turkey 27 M4
Yenisey r. Rus. Fed. 28 J2
Yenisey-Angara-Selenga r. Rus. Fed. 28 J2
Yeniseysk Rus. Fed. 28 K4
Yeniseyskiy Kryazh ridge Rus. Fed. 28 K3
Yeniseyskiy Zaliv inlet Rus. Fed. 77 F2
Yeniyol Turkey see Borçka
Yenotayevka Rus. Fed. 13 J7
Yeola India 38 B1
Yeotmal India see Yavatmal
Yeoval Australia 58 D4
Yeovil U.K. 19 E8
Yeo Yeo r. Australia see Bland
Yeppoon Australia 56 E4
Yeraliyev Kazakh. see Kuryk
Yerbogachen Rus. Fed. 29 L3
Yercaud India 38 C4
Yerevan Armenia 35 G2
Yereymentau Kazakh. 42 D2
Yergara India 38 C2
Yergeni hills Rus. Fed. 13 J7
Yergoğu Romania see Giurgiu
Yeriho West Bank see Jericho
Yerilla Australia 55 C7
Yerington NV U.S.A. 65 C1
Yerköy Turkey 34 D3
Yerla r. India 38 B2
Yermak Kazakh. see Aksu
Yermakovo Rus. Fed. 44 B1
Yermak Plateau sea feature Arctic Ocean 77 H1
Yermentau Kazakh. see Yereymentau
Yermo CA U.S.A. 65 D3
Yerofey Pavlovich Rus. Fed. 44 A1
Yersa r. Rus. Fed. 12 L2
Yershov Rus. Fed. 13 K6
Yertsevo Rus. Fed. 12 I3
Yeruham Israel 39 B4
Yerupaja mt. Peru 68 C6
Yerushalayim Israel/West Bank see Jerusalem
Yeruslan r. Rus. Fed. 13 J6
Yesagyo Myanmar 37 H5
Yesan S. Korea 45 B5
Yesil' Kazakh. 30 F1
Yeşilhisar Turkey 34 D3
Yeşilırmak r. Turkey 34 E2
Yeşilova Burdur Turkey 27 M6
Yeşilova Yozgat Turkey see Sorgun
Yessentuki Rus. Fed. 35 F1
Yessey Rus. Fed. 29 L3
Yes Tor h. U.K. 19 C8
Yêtatang China see Baqên
Yetman Australia 58 E2
Ye-U Myanmar 37 H5
Yeu, Île d' i. France 24 C3
Yevdokimovskoye Rus. Fed. see Krasnogvardeyskoye
Yevlakh Azer. see Yevlax
Yevlax Azer. 35 G2
Yevpatoriya Ukr. 34 D1
Yevreyskaya Avtonomnaya Oblast' admin. div. Rus. Fed. 44 D2
Yexian China see Laizhou
Yeyik China 37 E1
Yeysk Rus. Fed. 13 H7
Yeyungou China 42 F4
Yezhuga r. Rus. Fed. 12 J2
Yezo i. Japan see Hokkaidō
Yezyaryshcha Belarus 12 F5
Y Fenni U.K. see Abergavenny
Y Fflint U.K. see Flint
Y Gelli Gandryll U.K. see Hay-on-Wye
Yialí i. Greece see Gyali
Yi'allaq, Gebel mt. Egypt see Yu'alliq, Jabal
Yialousa Cyprus see Aigialousa
Yi'an China 44 B3
Yianisádha i. Greece see Gianisada
Yiannitsá Greece see Giannitsa
Yibin Sichuan China 42 I7
Yibug Caka salt l. China 37 F2
Yichang Hubei China 43 K6
Yicheng Henan China see Zhumadian
Yichun Heilong. China 44 C3
Yichun Jiangxi China 43 K7
Yilaha China 44 A2
Yilan China 44 C3
Yilan China see Ilan
Yıldız Dağları mts Turkey 27 L4
Yıldızeli Turkey 34 E3
Yilehuli Shan mts China 44 A2
Yilong Heilong. China 44 B3
Yimianpo China 44 C3
Yinchuan China 42 J5
Yindarlgooda, Lake imp. l. Australia 55 C7
Yinggehai China 42 J5
Yingkou China 43 M4
Yingtan China 43 L7
Yining Xinjiang China 42 E4
Yinmabin Myanmar 37 H5
Yin Shan mts China 43 J4
Yinxian China see Ningbo
Yirga Alem Eth. 48 D3
Yirol Sudan 47 G4
Yishan Guangxi China see Yizhou
Yishui China 43 L5
Yithion Greece see Gytheio
Yitiaoshan China see Jingtai
Yitong He r. China 44 B3
Yitulihe China 44 A2
Yixing China 43 L6
Yiyang China 43 K7
Yizhou China 43 J8
Yizra'el country Asia see Israel
Yläne Fin. 15 M6

ihärmä Fin. 14 M5
i-li Fin. 14 N4
i-Kärppä Fin. 14 N4
ikiiminki Fin. 14 O4
i-Kitka l. Fin. 14 P3
istaro Fin. 14 M5
itornio Fin. 14 M3
ivieska Fin. 14 N4
öjärvi Fin. 15 M6
mer Ø i. Greenland 61 P2
nys Enlli i. U.K. see Bardsey Island
nys Môn i. U.K. see Anglesey
ogan, Cerro mt. Chile 70 B8
ogyakarta Indon. 41 D8
okadouma Cameroon 47 E4
okkaichi Japan 45 E6
oko Cameroon 46 E4
okohama Japan 45 E6
okosuka Japan 45 E6
okote Japan 45 F5
ola Nigeria 46 E4
olo CA U.S.A. 65 B1
olombo Dem. Rep. Congo 48 C4
olöten Turkm. 33 J2
omou Guinea 46 C4
ŏnan N. Korea 45 B5
onezawa Japan 45 F5
ong'an Fujian China 43 L7
ŏnghŭng N. Korea 45 B5
ŏnghŭng-man b. N. Korea 45 B5
ŏngil-man b. S. Korea 45 C6
ongjing Liaoning China see Xifeng
ŏngju S. Korea 45 C5
ongkang Yunnan China 42 H8
ongning Sichuan China see Xuyong
ongxiu China 43 L7
ongzhou China 43 K7
onkers NY U.S.A. 64 E2
opal Col. 68 D2
opurga China 42 D5
ordu India 36 C2
ork Australia 55 B7
ork Ont. Canada 64 B1
ork U.K. 18 F5
ork PA U.S.A. 64 C3
ork, Cape Australia 56 C1
ork, Kap c. Greenland see Innaanganeq
ork, Vale of val. U.K. 18 F4
orke Peninsula Australia 57 B7
orkshire Dales National Park U.K. 18 E4
orkshire Wolds hills U.K. 18 G5
orkton Canada 62 G1
orktown VA U.S.A. 64 C4
orosso Mali 46 C3
osemite National Park CA U.S.A. 65 C2
oshkar-Ola Rus. Fed. 12 J4
os Sudarso i. Indon. see Dolok, Pulau
ŏsu S. Korea 45 B6
otvata Israel 39 B5
oughal Ireland 21 E6
oung Australia 58 D5
ounghusband, Lake imp. l. Australia 57 B6
ounghusband Peninsula Australia 57 B7
oung Island Antarctica 76 H2
oungstown OH U.S.A. 64 A2
oussoufia Morocco 22 C5
ouvarou Mali 46 C3
ouyang China 43 J7
ouyi China 44 C3
ouyi Feng mt. China/Rus. Fed. 42 F3
owah watercourse Australia 58 B2
ozgat Turkey 34 D3
eka U.S.A. 62 C3
ghyz Kazakh. see Irgiz
Wyddfa mt. U.K. see Snowdon
stad Sweden 15 H9
stwyth r. U.K. 19 C6
syk-Köl Kyrg. see Balykchy
syk-Köl salt l. Kyrg. 42 D4
han r. U.K. 20 G3
Trallwng U.K. see Welshpool
yk-Kyuyel' Rus. Fed. 29 O3
'alliq, Jabal mt. Egypt 39 A4
anlin China 44 A2
anquan China see Anxi
ab'ā i. Saudi Arabia 34 D6
ba City CA U.S.A. 65 B1
ucatán pen. Mex. 66 F5
ucatan Channel Cuba/Mex. 67 G4
ucca AZ U.S.A. 65 E3
ucca Lake NV U.S.A. 65 D2
ucca Valley CA U.S.A. 65 D3
ucheng Sichuan China see Ya'an
uci China see Jinzhong
udi Shan mt. China 44 A1
uelai China see Huachuan
ueliang Pao l. China 44 A3
uendumu Australia 54 E5
uexi China 43 L6
ueyang Hunan China 43 K7
ug r. Rus. Fed. 12 J3
ugorsk Rus. Fed. 11 S3
ugoslavia
uhu China see Eryuan
uin Australia 55 B6
ukagirskoye Ploskogor'ye plat. Rus. Fed.
29 Q3
ukamenskoye Rus. Fed. 12 L4
ukarı Sakarya Ovaları plain Turkey 27 N5
ukarısarıkaya Turkey 34 D3

Yukon r. Canada/U.S.A. 60 B3
Yukon Territory admin. div. Canada 60 E3
Yüksekova Turkey 35 G3
Yulara Australia 55 E6
Yule r. Australia 54 B5
Yuleba Australia 58 D1
Yulin Guangxi China 43 K8
Yulin Shaanxi China 43 J5
Yulong Xueshan mt. China 42 I7
Yuma AZ U.S.A. 65 E4
Yumen China 42 H5
Yumenguan China 42 G4
Yumurtalık Turkey 39 B1
Yuna Australia 55 A7
Yunak Turkey 34 C3
Yunaska Island U.S.A. 60 A4
Yuncheng China 43 K6
Yundamindera Australia 55 C7
Yungas reg. Bol. 68 E7
Yungui Gaoyuan plat. China 42 I7
Yunjinghong China see Jinghong
Yunkai Dashan mts China 43 K8
Yunling China see Yunxiao
Yunnan prov. China 42 I8
Yunta Australia 57 B7
Yunt Dağı mt. Turkey 39 A1
Yunxiao China 43 L8
Yuraygir National Park Australia 58 F2
Yurba Co l. China 37 F2
Yürekli Turkey 39 B1
Yurga Rus. Fed. 28 J4
Yuriria Mex. 66 D4
Yurungkax He r. China 36 E1
Yur'ya Rus. Fed. 12 K4
Yur'yakha r. Rus. Fed. 12 L2
Yuryev Estonia see Tartu
Yur'yevets Rus. Fed. 12 I4
Yur'yev-Pol'skiy Rus. Fed. 12 H4
Yü Shan mt. Taiwan 43 M8
Yushino Rus. Fed. 12 L1
Yushkozero Rus. Fed. 12 G2
Yushu Jilin China 44 B3
Yushu Qinghai China 42 H6
Yushuwan China see Huaihua
Yusufeli Turkey 35 F2
Yus'va Rus. Fed. 11 Q4
Yuta West Bank see Yatta
Yuxi Yunnan China 42 I8
Yuzawa Japan 45 F5
Yuzha Rus. Fed. 12 I4
Yuzhno-Kamyshovyy Khrebet ridge Rus. Fed. 44 F3
Yuzhno-Kuril'sk Rus. Fed. 44 G3
Yuzhno-Muyskiy Khrebet mts Rus. Fed. 43 K1
Yuzhno-Sakhalinsk Rus. Fed. 44 F3
Yuzhno-Sukhokumsk Rus. Fed. 13 J7
Yuzhnoukrayinsk Ukr. 13 F7
Yuzhnyy Rus. Fed. see Adyk
Yuzhou Chongqing China see Chongqing
Yuzhou Henan China 43 K6
Yuzovka Ukr. see Donets'k
Yverdon Switz. 24 H3
Yvetot France 24 E2
Ywamun Myanmar 37 H5

Z

Zaandam Neth. 16 J4
Zab, Monts du mts Alg. 25 I6
Zabaykal'sk Rus. Fed. 43 L3
Zabīd Yemen 32 F7
Zābol Iran 33 J3
Zacapa Guat. 66 G5
Zacatecas Mex. 66 D4
Zacharo Greece 27 I6
Zacoalco Mex. 66 D4
Zacynthus i. Greece see Zakynthos
Zadar Croatia 26 F2
Zadoi China 42 H6
Zadonsk Rus. Fed. 13 H5
Za'farâna Egypt see Za'farānah
Za'farānah Egypt 34 D5
Zafer Adaları is Cyprus see Kleides Islands
Zafer Burnu c. Cyprus see Apostolos Andreas, Cape
Zafra Spain 25 C4
Zagazig Egypt see Az Zaqāzīq
Zaghouan Tunisia 26 D6
Zagorsk Rus. Fed. see Sergiyev Posad
Zagreb Croatia 26 F2
Zagros Mountains Iran 35 G4
Za'gya Zangbo r. China 37 G3
Zāhedān Iran 33 J4
Zahir Pir Pak. 36 B3
Zaḩlah Lebanon see Zahlé
Zahlé Lebanon 39 B3
Ẓahrān Saudi Arabia 32 F6
Zahrez Chergui salt pan Alg. 25 H6
Zahrez Rharbi salt pan Alg. 25 H6
Zainsk Rus. Fed. see Novyy Zay
Zaire country Africa see Congo, Democratic Republic of the
Zaïre r. Congo/Dem. Rep. Congo see Congo
Zaječar Serbia 27 J3
Zaka Zimbabwe 49 D6
Zakamensk Rus. Fed. 42 I2
Zakataly Azer. see Zaqatala
Zakháro Greece see Zacharo
Zākhō Iraq 35 F3
Zakhodnyaya Dzvina r. Europe see Zapadnaya Dvina
Zákinthos i. Greece see Zakynthos
Zakopane Poland 17 Q6
Zakouma, Parc National de nat. park Chad 47 E3
Zakynthos Greece 27 I6
Zakynthos i. Greece 27 I6
Zalaegerszeg Hungary 26 G1
Zalai-domsag hills Hungary 26 G1
Zalamea de la Serena Spain 25 D4
Zalantun China 44 A3
Zalari Rus. Fed. 42 I2
Zalău Romania 27 J1
Ẓalim Saudi Arabia 32 F5
Zalingei Sudan 47 F3
Ẓalmā, Jabal aẓ mt. Saudi Arabia 32 E4
Zambeze r. Africa 49 C5 see Zambezi
Zambezi r. Africa 49 C5
Zambezi Zambia 49 C5
Zambia country Africa 49 C5
Zamboanga Phil. 41 E7
Zamfara watercourse Nigeria 46 D3
Zamkog China see Zamtang
Zamora Ecuador 68 C4
Zamora Spain 25 D3
Zamora de Hidalgo Mex. 66 D5
Zamość Poland 13 D6
Zamost'ye Poland see Zamość
Zamtang China 42 I6
Zamuro, Sierra del mts Venez. 68 F3
Zanaga Congo 48 B4
Zancle Sicilia Italy see Messina
Zandamela Moz. 51 L3
Zanesville U.S.A. 63 K4
Zangguy China 36 D1
Zangsêr Kangri mt. China 37 F2
Zangskar reg. India see Zanskar
Zangskar Mountains India see Zanskar Mountains
Zanjān Iran 35 H3
Zanjān Rūd r. Iran 35 G3
Zanskar reg. India 36 D2
Zanskar Mountains India 36 D2
Zante i. Greece see Zakynthos
Zanthus Australia 55 C7
Zanzibar Tanz. 49 D4
Zanzibar Island Tanz. 49 D4
Zaouatallaz Alg. 46 D2
Zaouet el Kahla Alg. see Bordj Omer Driss
Zaozernyy Rus. Fed. 29 K4
Zaozhuang China 43 L6
Zapadnaya Dvina r. Europe 12 F5
Zapadnaya Dvina Rus. Fed. 12 G4
Zapadni Rodopi mts Bulg. 27 J4
Zapadno-Kazakhstanskaya Oblast' admin. div. Kazakh. see Zapadnyy Kazakhstan
Zapadno-Sakhalinskiy Khrebet mts Rus. Fed. 44 F2
Zapadno-Sibirskaya Nizmennost' plain Rus. Fed. see West Siberian Plain
Zapadno-Sibirskaya Ravnina plain Rus. Fed. see West Siberian Plain
Zapadnyy Chink Ustyurta esc. Kazakh. 35 I2
Zapadnyy Chink Ustyurta esc. Kazakh. 35 I2
Zapadnyy Kazakhstan admin. div. Kazakh. 11 Q6
Zapadnyy Kil'din Rus. Fed. 14 S2
Zapadnyy Sayan reg. Rus. Fed. 42 F2
Zapata U.S.A. 62 H6
Zapiga Chile 68 E7
Zapolyarnyy Rus. Fed. 12 F1
Zapol'ye Rus. Fed. 12 H4
Zaporizhzhya Ukr. 13 G7
Zaporozh'ye Ukr. see Zaporizhzhya
Zapug China 36 E2
Zaqatala Azer. 35 G2
Zaqên China 37 H2
Za Qu r. China 42 H6
Zaqāzīq Egypt see Az Zaqāzīq
Zaqungngomar mt. China 37 G2
Zara China see Moinda
Zara Croatia see Zadar
Zara Turkey 34 E3
Zarafshan Uzbek. see Zarafshon
Zarafshon Uzbek. 33 J1
Zaragoza Spain 25 F3
Zarand Iran 33 I3
Zarang China 36 D3
Zaranikh Reserve nature res. Egypt 39 B4
Zaranj Afgh. 33 J3
Zarasai Lith. 15 O9
Zárate Arg. 70 E4
Zaraysk Rus. Fed. 13 H5
Zaraza Venez. 68 E2
Zärdab Azer. 13 J8
Zarechensk Rus. Fed. 14 Q3
Zāreh Iran 35 H4
Zargun mt. Pak. 36 A3
Zari Afgh. 36 A2
Zaria Nigeria 46 D3
Zarichne Ukr. 13 E6
Zarifète, Col des pass Alg. 25 F6
Zaring China see Liangdaohe
Zarinsk Rus. Fed. 42 E2
Zarneh Iran 35 G4
Zărneşti Romania 27 K2
Zarqā' Jordan see Az Zarqā'
Zarqā', Nahr az r. Jordan 39 B3
Ẓarubino Rus. Fed. 44 C4
Żary Poland 17 O5
Zarzis Tunisia 22 G5
Zasheyek Rus. Fed. 14 Q3
Zaskar reg. India see Zanskar
Zaskar Range mts India see Zanskar Mountains
Zaslawye Belarus 15 O9
Zastron S. Africa 51 H6
Za'tarī, Wādī az watercourse Jordan 39 C3
Zaterechnyy Rus. Fed. 13 J7
Zavetnoye Rus. Fed. 13 I7
Zavety Il'icha Rus. Fed. 44 F2
Zavidoviči Bos.-Herz. 26 H2
Zavitaya Rus. Fed. see Zavitinsk
Zavitinsk Rus. Fed. 44 C2
Zavolzhsk Rus. Fed. 12 I4
Zavolzh'ye Rus. Fed. see Zavolzhsk
Závora, Ponta pt Moz. 51 L3
Zawiercie Poland 17 Q5
Zawīlah Libya 47 E2
Zāwīyah, Jabal az hills Syria 39 C2
Zaydī, Wādī az watercourse Syria 39 C3
Zaysan Kazakh. 42 E3
Zaysan, Lake Kazakh. 42 E3
Zaysan, Ozero l. Kazakh. see Zaysan, Lake
Zayü China see Gyigang
Zayü Qu r. China/India 37 I3
Žďár nad Sázavou Czech Rep. 17 O6
Zdolbuniv Ukr. 13 E6
Zdolbunov Ukr. see Zdolbuniv
Zealand i. Denmark 15 G9
Zēbāk Afgh. 36 B1
Zeerust S. Africa 51 H3
Ẕefat Israel 39 B3
Zeil, Mount Australia 55 F5
Zela Turkey see Zile
Zelennik Rus. Fed. 12 J3
Zelenoborsk Rus. Fed. 11 S3
Zelenoborskiy Rus. Fed. 14 R3
Zelenodol'sk Rus. Fed. 12 K5
Zelenogorsk Rus. Fed. 12 F3
Zelenograd Rus. Fed. 12 H4
Zelenogradsk Rus. Fed. 15 L9
Zelenokumsk Rus. Fed. 35 F1
Zelentsovo Rus. Fed. 12 J4
Zelenyy, Ostrov i. Rus. Fed. 44 G4
Zell am See Austria 17 N7
Žemaitijos nacionalinis parkas nat. park Lith. 15 L8
Zemetchino Rus. Fed. 13 I5
Zémio Cent. Afr. Rep. 48 C3
Zemmora Alg. 25 G6
Zempoaltépetl, Nudo de mt. Mex. 66 E5
Zenica Bos.-Herz. 26 G2
Ẕenifim watercourse Israel 39 B4
Zennor U.K. 19 B8
Zenta Serbia see Senta
Zenzach Alg. 25 H6
Zerenike Reserve nature res. Egypt see Zaranikh Reserve
Zernograd Rus. Fed. 13 I7
Zernovoy Rus. Fed. see Zernograd
Zêtang China 37 G3
Zeven Germany 17 L4
Zevgari, Cape Cyprus 39 A2
Zeya Rus. Fed. 44 B1
Zeya r. Rus. Fed. 44 B2
Zeyskiy Zapovednik nature res. Rus. Fed. 44 B1
Zeysko-Bureinskaya Vpadina depr. Rus. Fed. 44 C2
Zeyskoye Vodokhranilishche resr Rus. Fed. 44 B1
Zeytin Burnu c. Cyprus see Elaia, Cape
Zêzere r. Port. 25 B4
Zgharta Lebanon 39 B2
Zghorta Lebanon see Zgharta
Zgierz Poland 17 Q5
Zhabdün China see Zhongba
Zhabinka Belarus 15 N10
Zhaggo China see Luhuo
Zhaksy Sarysu watercourse Kazakh. see Sarysu
Zhalpaktal Kazakh. 11 P6
Zhalpaqtal Kazakh. see Zhalpaktal
Zhaltyr Kazakh. 28 H4
Zhambyl Karagandinskaya Oblast' Kazakh. 42 C3
Zhambyl Zhambylskaya Oblast' Kazakh. see Taraz
Zhamo China see Bomi
Zhanakorgan Kazakh. 42 B4
Zhanaozen Kazakh. 30 E2
Zhanatas Kazakh. 42 B4
Zhanbei China 44 B2
Zhangaözen Kazakh. see Zhanaozen
Zhanga Qazan Kazakh. see Novaya Kazanka
Zhangaqorghan Kazakh. see Zhanakorgan
Zhangatas Kazakh. see Zhanatas
Zhangbei China 43 K4
Zhangde China see Anyang
Zhangdian China see Zibo
Zhangguangcai Ling mts China 44 C3
Zhanghua Taiwan see Changhua
Zhangjiajie China 43 K7
Zhangjiakou China 43 K4
Zhangjiapan China see Jingbian
Zhangling China 44 A1
Zhangqiangzhen China 44 A4
Zhangshu China 43 L7
Zhangye China 42 I5
Zhangzhou China 43 L8
Zhanhe China see Zhanbei
Zhanibek Kazakh. 11 P6
Zhanjiang China 43 K8
Zhaodong China 44 B3
Zhaoqing China 43 K8
Zhaotong China 42 I7
Zhaoyuan China 44 B3
Zhaozhou China 44 B3
Zhari Namco salt l. China 37 F3
Zharkent Kazakh. 42 E4
Zharkovskiy Rus. Fed. 12 G5
Zharma Kazakh. 42 E3
Zhashkiv Ukr. 13 F6
Zhashkov Ukr. see Zhashkiv
Zhaslyk Uzbek. see Jasliq
Zhaxi Co salt l. China 37 F2
Zhaxigang China 36 D2
Zhaxizê China 37 I3
Zhaxizong China 37 F3
Zhayyq r. Kazakh./Rus. Fed. see Ural
Zhdanov Ukr. see Mariupol'
Zhdanovsk Azer. see Beyläqan
Zhejiang prov. China 43 M7
Zhelaniya, Mys c. Rus. Fed. 28 H2
Zheleznodorozhnyy Rus. Fed. see Yemva
Zheleznodorozhnyy Uzbek. see Qo'ng'irot
Zheleznogorsk Rus. Fed. 13 G5
Zheltyye Vody Ukr. see Zhovti Vody
Zhem Kazakh. see Emba
Zhengjiatun China see Shuangliao
Zhengzhou China 43 K6
Zhenlai China 44 A3
Zhenxi China 44 A3
Zhenyuan China 43 J7
Zherdevka Rus. Fed. 13 I6
Zheshart Rus. Fed. 12 K3
Zhetikara Kazakh. see Zhitikara
Zhêxam China 37 F3
Zhezkazgan Kazakh. 42 B3
Zhezqazghan Kazakh. see Zhezkazgan
Zhidoi China 42 H6
Zhigalovo Rus. Fed. 42 J2
Zhigansk Rus. Fed. 29 N3
Zhigung China 37 G3
Zhi Qu r. China see Yangtze
Zhitikara Kazakh. 30 F1
Zhitkovichi Belarus see Zhytkavichy
Zhitkur Rus. Fed. 13 J6
Zhitomir Ukr. see Zhytomyr
Zhīvār Iran 35 G4
Zhlobin Belarus 13 F5
Zhmerinka Ukr. see Zhmerynka
Zhmerynka Ukr. 13 F6
Zhob Pak. 33 K3
Zhob r. Pak. 36 B2
Zhongba Xizang China 37 F3
Zhongduo China see Youyang
Zhongguo country Asia see China
Zhongguo Renmin Gongheguo country Asia see China
Zhongping China see Huize
Zhongshan research stn Antarctica 76 E2
Zhongshan Guizhou China see Lupanshui
Zhongwei China 42 J5
Zhongxin Yunnan China see Xianggelila
Zhongyaozhan China 44 B2
Zhosaly Kazakh. see Dzhusaly
Zhoujiajing China 42 I5
Zhoukou Henan China 43 K6
Zhoushan Dao i. China 43 M6
Zhovti Vody Ukr. 13 G6
Zhuanghe China 45 A5
Zhubgyügoin China 37 I2
Zhukovka Rus. Fed. 13 G5
Zhukovskiy Rus. Fed. 13 H5
Zhumadian China 43 K6
Zhuxi China 43 J6
Zhuzhou Hunan China 43 K7
Zhydachiv Ukr. 13 E6
Zhympity Kazakh. 11 Q5
Zhytkavichy Belarus 15 O10
Zhytomyr Ukr. 13 F6
Zīā'ābād Iran 35 H4
Žiar nad Hronom Slovakia 17 Q6
Zibā salt pan Saudi Arabia 39 D4
Zibo China 43 L5
Zicheng China see Zijin
Zidi Pak. 36 A4
Ziel, Mount Australia see Zeil, Mount
Zielona Góra Poland 17 O5
Ziemelkursas augstiene hills Latvia 15 M8
Ziftá Egypt 34 C5
Zīghan Libya 47 F2
Zigong China 42 I7
Ziguey Chad 47 E3
Ziguinchor Senegal 46 B3
Žīguri Latvia 15 O8
Zihuatanejo Mex. 66 D5
Zijin China 43 L8
Ziketan China see Xinghai
Zile Turkey 34 D2
Žilina Slovakia 17 Q6
Zillah Libya 47 E2
Zima Rus. Fed. 42 I2
Zimba Zambia 49 C5
Zimbabwe country Africa 49 C5
Zimi Sierra Leone see Zimmi
Zimmerbude Rus. Fed. see Svetlyy
Zimmi Sierra Leone 46 B4
Zimnicea Romania 27 K3
Zimniy Bereg coastal area Rus. Fed. 12 H2
Zimovniki Rus. Fed. 13 I7
Zimrīn Syria 39 B2
Ẕin watercourse Israel 39 B4
Zinave, Parque Nacional de nat. park Moz. 49 D6
Zinder Niger 46 D3
Ziniaré Burkina 46 C3
Zinjibār Yemen 32 G7
Zinoyevsk Ukr. see Kirovohrad
Zion National Park UT U.S.A. 65 F2
Zippori Israel 39 B3
Ziqudukou China 37 H2
Zirc Hungary 26 G1
Ziro India 37 H4
Zīr Rūd Iran 32 H4
Zi Shui r. China 43 K7
Zistersdorf Austria 17 P6
Zitácuaro Mex. 66 D5
Zito China see Lhorong
Zittau Germany 17 O5
Ziyang Sichuan China 42 I6
Ziyaret Dağı h. Turkey 39 B1
Ziz, Oued watercourse Morocco 22 D5
Zlatoustovsk Rus. Fed. 44 D1
Zlín Czech Rep. 17 P6
Zmeinogorsk Rus. Fed. 42 E2
Zmiyevka Rus. Fed. 13 H5
Znamenka Rus. Fed. 13 I5
Znamenka Ukr. see Znam"yanka
Znam"yanka Ukr. 13 G6
Znojmo Czech Rep. 17 P6
Zoar S. Africa 50 E7
Zogang China 42 H7
Zoigê China 42 I6
Zoji La pass India 36 C2
Zola S. Africa 51 H7
Zolochev Kharkivs'ka Oblast' Ukr. see Zolochiv
Zolochev L'vivs'ka Oblast' Ukr. see Zolochiv
Zolochiv Kharkivs'ka Oblast' Ukr. 13 G6
Zolochiv L'vivs'ka Oblast' Ukr. 13 E6
Zolotonosha Ukr. 13 G6
Zolotoye Rus. Fed. 13 J6
Zolotukhino Rus. Fed. 13 H5
Zomba Malawi 49 D5
Zombor Serbia see Sombor
Zongga China see Gyirong
Zonguldak Turkey 27 N4
Zongxoi China 37 G3
Zorgho Burkina 46 C3
Ẓorgo Burkina see Zorgho
Żory Poland 17 Q5
Zouar Chad 47 E2
Zouérat Mauritania 46 B2
Zousfana, Oued watercourse Alg. 22 D5
Zrenjanin Serbia 27 I2
Zubālah, Birkat waterhole Saudi Arabia 35 F5
Zubillaga Arg. 70 D5
Zubova Polyana Rus. Fed. 13 I5
Zubtsov Rus. Fed. 12 G4
Zuénoula Côte d'Ivoire 46 C4
Zug Switz. 24 I3
Zugdidi Georgia 35 F2
Zugspitze mt. Austria/Germany 17 M7
Zugu Nigeria 46 D3
Zuider Zee l. Neth. see IJsselmeer
Zújar r. Spain 25 D4
Zumba Ecuador 68 C4
Zunheboto India 37 H4
Zuni Mountains U.S.A. 62 F4
Zunyi Guizhou China 42 J7
Županja Croatia 26 H2
Zūrābād Āzarbāyjān-e Gharbī Iran 35 G3
Zurhen Ul Shan mts China 37 G2
Zürich Switz. 24 I3
Zuru Nigeria 46 D3
Zurzuna Turkey see Çıldır
Zuwārah Libya 46 E1
Zuyevka Rus. Fed. 12 K4
Zvishavane Zimbabwe 49 D6
Zvolen Slovakia 17 Q6
Zvornik Bos.-Herz. 27 H2
Zwedru Liberia 46 C4
Zweletemba S. Africa 50 D7
Zwelitsha S. Africa 51 H7
Zwettl Austria 17 O6
Zwickau Germany 17 N5
Zwolle Neth. 17 K4
Zyablovo Rus. Fed. 12 L4
Zygi Cyprus 39 A2
Zyryan Kazakh. see Zyryanovsk
Zyryanka Rus. Fed. 29 Q3
Zyryanovsk Kazakh. 42 E3
Zyyi Cyprus see Zygi